DECISION TECHNOLOGIES FOR

Advances in Computational Management Science

VOLUME 2

The titles published in this series are listed at the end of this volume.

Decision Technologies for Computational Finance

Proceedings of the fifth International Conference
Computational Finance

Edited by

Apostolos-Paul N. Refenes

London Business School, U.K.

Andrew N. Burgess

London Business School, U.K.

and

John E. Moody

*Oregon Graduate Institute,
Portland, U.S.A.*

KLUWER ACADEMIC PUBLISHERS

DORDRECHT / BOSTON / LONDON

A C.I.P. Catalogue record for this book is available from the Library of Congress.

ISBN 0-7923-8308-7 (HB)
ISBN 0-7923-8309-5 (PB)

Published by Kluwer Academic Publishers,
P.O. Box 17, 3300 AA Dordrecht, The Netherlands.

Sold and distributed in the North, Central and South America
by Kluwer Academic Publishers,
101 Philip Drive, Norwell, MA 02061, U.S.A.

In all other countries, sold and distributed
by Kluwer Academic Publishers,
P.O. Box 322, 3300 AH Dordrecht, The Netherlands.

Printed on acid-free paper

COMPUTATIONAL FINANCE 1997
Programme Committee

FOREWORD

This volume contains selected papers that were presented at the International Conference COMPUTATIONAL FINANCE 1997 held at London Business School on December 15-17 1997. Formerly known as Neural Networks in the Capital Markets (NNCM), this series of meetings has emerged as a truly multi-disciplinary international conference and provided an international focus for innovative research on the application of a multiplicity of advanced decision technologies to many areas of financial engineering. It has drawn upon theoretical advances in financial economics and robust methodological developments in the statistical, econometric and computer sciences. To reflect its multi-disciplinary nature, the NNCM conference has adopted the new title COMPUTATIONAL FINANCE.

The papers in this volume are organised in six parts. Market Dynamics and Risk, Trading and Arbitrage strategies, Volatility and Options, Term-Structure and Factor models, Corporate Distress Models and Advances on Methodology. This years' acceptance rate (38%) reflects both the increasing interest in the conference and the Programme Committee's efforts to improve the quality of the meeting year-on-year.

I would like to thank the members of the programme committee for their efforts in refereeing the papers. I also would like to thank the members of the computational finance group at London Business School and particularly Neil Burgess, Peter Bolland, Yves Bentz, and Nevil Towers for organising the meeting.

Apostolos-Paul N. Refenes

Chair, COMPUTATIONAL FINANCE 1997

CONTENTS

x

PART 6: ADVANCES ON METHODOLOGY - SHORT NOTES

PART 1

MARKET DYNAMICS AND RISK

PITFALLS AND OPPORTUNITIES IN THE USE OF EXTREME VALUE THEORY IN RISK MANAGEMENT

FRANCIS X. DIEBOLD
University of Pennsylvania
and Oliver Wyman Institute
3718 Locust Walk, Philadelphia, PA 19104-6297, USA
E-mail: fdiebold@mail.sas.upenn.edu

TIL SCHUERMANN, JOHN D. STROUGHAIR
Oliver, Wyman and Company
666 Fifth Avenue
New York, NY 10103, USA
E-mail: tschuermann@owc.com, jstroughair@owc.com

Recent literature has trumpeted the claim that extreme value theory (EVT) holds promise for accurate estimation of extreme quantiles and tail probabilities of financial asset returns, and hence holds promise for advances in the management of extreme financial risks. Our view, based on a disinterested assessment of EVT from the vantage point of financial risk management, is that the recent optimism is partly appropriate but also partly exaggerated, and that at any rate much of the potential of EVT remains latent. We substantiate this claim by sketching a number of pitfalls associated with use of EVT techniques. More constructively, we show how certain of the pitfalls can be avoided, and we sketch a number of explicit research directions that will help the potential of EVT to be realized.

1   Introduction

Financial risk management is intimately concerned with tail quantiles (e.g., the value of x such that $P(X>x)=.05$) and tail probabilities (e.g., $P(X>x)$, for a large value x). *Extreme* quantiles and probabilities are of particular interest because ability to assess them accurately translates into ability to manage extreme financial risks effectively, such as those associated with currency crises, stock market crashes, and large bond defaults.

Unfortunately, traditional parametric statistical and econometric methods, typically based on estimation of entire densities, are ill-suited to the assessment of extreme quantiles and event probabilities. These parametric methods implicitly strive to produce a good fit in regions where most of the data fall, potentially at the expense of good fit in the tails, where, by definition, few observations fall.[1]

---

[1]   This includes, for example, the fitting of stable distributions, as in McCulloch (1996).

A.-P.N. Refenes et al. (eds.), Decision Technologies for Computational Finance, 3–12.
© 1998 *Kluwer Academic Publishers. Printed in the Netherlands..*

4

Seemingly-sophisticated nonparametric methods of density estimation, such as kernel smoothing, are also well-known to perform poorly in the tails.[2]

It is common, moreover, to require estimates of quantiles and probabilities not only *near* the boundary of the range of observed data, but also *beyond* the boundary. The task of estimating such quantiles and probabilities would seem to be hopeless. A key idea, however, emerges from an area of probability and statistics known as "extreme value theory" (EVT): one can estimate extreme quantiles and probabilities by fitting a "model" to the empirical survival function of a set of data using only the extreme event data rather than all the data, thereby fitting the tail, and only the tail.[3] The approach has a number of attractive features, including:

(a) the estimation method is tailored to the object of interest, the tail of the distribution, rather than the center of the distribution

(b) an arguably-reasonable functional form for the tail can be formulated from a priori considerations.

The upshot is that the methods of EVT offer hope for progress toward the elusive goal of reliable estimates of extreme quantiles and probabilities.

The concerns of EVT are in fact wide-ranging and include fat-tailed distributions, time series processes with heavy-tailed innovations, general asymptotic theory, point process theory, long memory and self-similarity, and much else. Our concerns in this paper, already alluded to above, are much more narrow: we focus primarily on estimation of extreme quantiles and probabilities, with applications to financial risk management. Specifically, we provide a reaction, from the perspective of financial risk management, to recent developments in the EVT literature, the maturation of which has resulted in optimism regarding the prospects for practical applications of the ideas to financial risk management.[4] In our view, as we hope to make clear, the optimism is partly appropriate but also partly exaggerated, and at any rate much of the potential of EVT remains latent; hence what follows is partly praise, partly criticism, and partly a wish-list.

2   Pitfalls and Opportunities

Much of our discussion is related directly or indirectly to the idea of tail estimation under a power law assumption, so we begin by introducing the basic framework. We assume that returns are in the maximum domain of attraction of a

---

[2] See Silverman (1986).

[3] The survival function is simply one minus the cumulative density function, 1-F(x). Note, in particular, that because F(x) approaches 1 as x grows, the survival function approaches 0.

[4] Embrechts, Klüppelberg and Mikosch (1997), for example, provide both a masterful summary of the literature and an optimistic assessment of its potential. See also the papers introduced by Paul-Choudhury (1998).

$$P(X > x) = k(x)x^{-\alpha} \tag{1}$$

That family includes, for example, α-stable laws with $\alpha < 2$ (but not the Gaussian case, $\alpha = 2$). Often it is assumed that $k(x)$ is in fact constant, in which case attention is restricted to densities with tails of the form

$$P(X>x) = kx^{-\alpha} \tag{2}$$

with the parameters k and α to be estimated.

A number of estimation methods can be used. The most popular, by far, is Hill's (1975) estimator, which is based directly on the extreme values and proceeds as follows. Order the observations with $x_{(1)}$ the largest, $x_{(2)}$ the second largest, and so on, and form an estimator based on the difference between the m-th largest observation and the average of the m largest observations:

$$\hat{\alpha} = \left[\left(\frac{1}{m} \sum_{i=1}^{m} \ln(x_{(i)}) \right) - \ln(x_{(m)}) \right]^{-1} \tag{3}$$

It is a simple matter to convert an estimate of α to estimates of the desired quantiles and probabilities. The Hill estimator has been used in empirical financial settings; see, for example, the impressive early work of Koedijk, Schafgans and deVries (1990). It also has good theoretical properties: it can be shown that it is consistent and asymptotically normal, assuming the data are *iid* and that m grows at a suitable rate with sample size.[5]

2.1 Selecting the Cutoff for Hill Estimation

We shall have more to say about the *iid* assumption subsequently; here we focus on choice of m. Roughly speaking, consistency and asymptotic normality of the Hill estimator require that m approach infinity with sample size, but at a slower rate. Unfortunately, however, this asymptotic condition gives no guidance regarding choice of m for any asset return series of fixed length, and the finite-sample properties of the estimator depend crucially on the choice of m. In particular, there is an important bias-variance tradeoff when varying m for fixed sample size: increasing m, and therefore using progressively more data (moving toward the center of the distribution), reduces variance but increases bias. Increasing m reduces variance because more date are used, but it increases bias because the power law is assumed to hold only in the extreme tail.

The bias-variance tradeoff regarding choice of m is precisely analogous to the bias-variance tradeoff in regarding choice of bandwidth in nonparametric density estimation. Unfortunately, although much of the recent nonparametric density estimation literature is devoted to "automatic" bandwidth selection rules that

---

[5] Other estimators are available, but none are demonstrably superior, and certainly none are as popular. Hence we focus on the Hill estimator throughout this paper.

The bias-variance tradeoff regarding choice of m is precisely analogous to the bias-variance tradeoff in regarding choice of bandwidth in nonparametric density estimation. Unfortunately, although much of the recent nonparametric density estimation literature is devoted to "automatic" bandwidth selection rules that optimizes an objective function depending on both variance and bias, until very recently no such rules had been developed for choice of m in tail estimation. Instead, m is typically chosen via ad hoc rules of thumb, sometimes supplemented with plots of the empirical survival function with the estimated tail superimposed. In our view, such plots are invaluable -- and although they are used sometimes, they are not used often enough -- but they need to be supplemented with complementary and rigorous rules for suggesting a choice of m. Recent unpublished work by Danielsson and deVries (1997a) offers hope in that regard; they develop a bootstrap method for selecting m and establish optimality properties. We very much look forward to continued exploration of bootstrap and other methods for optimal selection of m, and to the accumulation of practical experience with the methods in financial settings.

2.2   Convenient Variations on the Hill Estimator I: Estimation by Linear Regression

Although the Hill estimator was not originally motivated by a regression framework, the basic idea -- assume a power law for the tail and then base an estimator directly on the extreme observations -- has an immediate regression interpretation, an idea that traces at least to Kearns and Pagan (1997). Simply note that $P(X > x) = k x^{-\alpha}$ implies

$$\ln P(X > x) = \ln(k) - \alpha \ln(x) \qquad (4)$$

so that α is the slope coefficient in a simple linear relationship between the log tail of the empirical survival function and the log extreme values. One should therefore be able to estimate α by a linear regression of the log tail of the empirical survival function on an intercept and the logs of the m most extreme values.

We hasten to add that nothing is presently known about the properties of standard estimators (e.g., least squares) in this context; more research is needed. The basic insight nevertheless strikes us as important. First, it highlights the conceptual fact that the essence of the tail estimation problem is fitting a log-linear function to a set of data. Second, it may have great practical value, because it means that the extensive kit of powerful tools developed for regression can potentially be brought to bear on the tail estimation problem. Huge literatures exist, for example, on robust estimation of regression models (which could be used to guide strategies for model fitting), recursive methods for diagnosing structural change in regression models (which could be used to guide selection of m), and bootstrapping regression models (which could be used to improve finite-sample inference).

2.3 Convenient Variations on the Hill Estimator II: Estimation by Nonlinear Regression

A more accurate tail expansion, used for example in Danielsson and deVries (1997b) and asymptotically equivalent to the one given above, but which may have better properties in small samples, is

$$P(X > x) = k x^{-\alpha} (1 + c x^{-d}) \qquad (5)$$

where k, α, c and d are parameters to be estimated. Again, the relevant parameters could be estimated very simply by nonlinear regression methods, with choice of m and much else guided by powerful regression diagnostics.

2.4 Convenient Variations on the Hill Estimator III: Imposing Symmetry

In many (although not all) financial applications we may want to impose symmetry on the distribution, which is to say, we may want to impose that the parameters governing the left and right tail behavior be identical. The regression technology again comes to the rescue. Using standard methods, one may estimate a system of two equations, one for each tail, imposing parameter equality across equations.

2.5 Finite-Sample Estimation and Inference

A reading of the EVT literature reveals a sharp and unfortunate contrast between the probability theory and the statistical theory. The probability theory is elegant and rigorous and voluminous, whereas the statistical theory remains primitive and skeletal in many respects. The reader who has reached this point will appreciate already certain aspects of this anticlimax, such as the difficulty of choosing the cutoff in Hill estimation. But the situation is in fact worse.

First, notoriously little is known about the finite-sample properties of the tail index estimator under various rules for cutoff selection, even under the standard heroic maintained assumptions, most importantly that the data are *iid*. In our view, a serious and thorough Monte Carlo study is needed, standardizing on choice of m by a defensible automatic selection rule such as the Danielsson-deVries bootstrap, and characterizing the sampling distribution of the tail index estimator as a function of sample size for various data-generating processes satisfying the power law assumption. Such a Monte Carlo analysis would be facilitated by the simplicity of the estimator and the speed with which it can be computed, but hindered by the tedious calculations required for bootstrap cutoff selection.

Second, the problem is not simply that the properties of the existing approach to estimation of the tail index have been inadequately explored; rather, it is

8

augmented by the fact that crucial variations on the theme have been left untouched. For example, in financial risk management, interest centers not on the tail index per se, but rather on the extreme quantiles and probabilities. The ability to withstand big hits, quantified by specific probabilities, translates directly into credit ratings, regulatory capital requirements, and so on. The extreme quantile and probability estimators are highly nonlinear functions of the tail index; hence, poor sampling properties of the tail index estimator will likely translate into even worse properties of the quantile and probability estimators, and the standard approximation based on a Taylor series expansion ("the delta method") is likely to be poor. Moreover, often one would like an *interval* estimate of, say, an extreme event probability. One rarely sees such intervals computed in practice, and we know of no Monte Carlo work that bears on their coverage accuracy or width.

Third, various maintained assumptions may of course be violated and may worsen the (potentially already poor) performance of the estimator. Again, a systematic Monte Carlo analysis would help us to assess the severity of the induced complications. To take one example, the scant evidence available suggests the estimator is likely to perform poorly if the assumed slowly-varying function $k(x)$ is far from constant, even if the tail behavior satisfies the power law assumption (e.g., Embrechts, Klüppelberg and Mikosch, 1997, Chapter 6). This is unfortunate insofar as, although power-law tail behavior can perhaps be justified as reasonable on a priori grounds, no such justification can be given for the assumption that $k(x)$ is constant.

Other maintained assumptions can also fail and may further degrade the performance of the estimator. We now consider two such crucial assumptions, *iid* data and power law tail behavior, in greater detail.

2.6   Violations of Maintained Assumptions I: Dependent Data

It is widely agreed that high-frequency financial asset returns are conditionally heteroskedastic, and hence not *iid*.[6] Unfortunately, the EVT literature routinely assumes *iid* data. Generalizations to dependent data have been attempted (e.g., Leadbetter, Lindgren and Rootzen, 1983), but they typically require "anti-clustering" conditions on the extremes, which rule out precisely the sort of volatility clustering routinely found in financial asset returns. It seems clear that Monte Carlo analyses need to be done on the performance of the tail estimator under realistic data-generating processes corresponding to routine real-world complications, such as the dependence associated with volatility dynamics. The small amount of Monte Carlo that has been done (e.g., Kearns and Pagan, 1997) indicates that the performance can be very poor.

We see at least two routes to improving the performance of the tail index estimator in the presence of dependent data. First, one can fit generalized extreme-

---

[6] See, for example, the surveys by Bollerslev, Chou and Kroner (1992) and Diebold and Lopez (1995).

value distributions directly to series of per-period maxima. This idea is not new, but it is curiously underutilized in our view, and it has a number of advantages. Use of per-period maxima naturally reduces dependence, use of an exact generalized extreme value distribution is justified if the periods are taken to be long enough, and maximum likelihood estimation is easily implemented. Moreover, the question addressed -- the distribution of the maximum -- is of intrinsic interest in risk management. On the downside, however, the aggregation reduces efficiency, and a new "bandwidth" selection problem of sorts is introduced -- selection of the appropriate amount of aggregation. That is, should one use weekly, monthly, quarterly or annual maxima?

Second, one can estimate the tail of the conditional, rather than the unconditional, distribution. In the *iid* case the two of course coincide, but they diverge under dependence, in which case the conditional distribution is of greater interest. One can fit the tail of the conditional distribution by first fitting a conditional volatility model, standardizing the data by the estimated conditional standard deviation, and then estimating the tail index of the standardized data. Such a procedure is similar to Engle and González-Rivera (1991), except that we fit only the tail rather than the entire density of the standardized data. The key is recognition of the fact that, if the adopted volatility model is a good approximation to the true volatility dynamics, then the standardized residuals will be approximately *iid*, which takes us into the world for which EVT was designed.

2.7 Violations of Maintained Assumptions II: Assessing the Power Law Assumption

As we have seen, most of the tail estimation literature assumes that returns are in the maximum domain of attraction of a Frechet distribution, so that the tail of the survival function follows a power law. But how do we check that assumption, and what is the evidence? Inoue (1998) provides some key results that will help us to answer such questions; he develops a general framework for consistent testing of hypotheses involving conditional distributions of time series, which include conditional tail behavior restrictions of the form

$$P(X_t > x | \Omega_{t-1}) = k\, x^{-\alpha} \tag{6}$$

for sufficiently large x.[7] The hypothesized conditional tail behavior restriction means that k and α are independent of the information set, which simplifies the assessment of the conditional probabilities.

---

[7] Here X_t is centered around its conditional mean and scaled by its conditional standard deviation.

3   Concluding Remarks

EVT is not needed for estimating routine quantities in financial risk management, such as ten percent, five percent, and perhaps even one percent value at risk. Rather, EVT is concerned with *extreme* (e.g., one tenth of one percent) tail behavior. So EVT has its place, but it's important that it be kept in its place, and that tools be matched to tasks.[8] EVT promises exciting opportunities for certain sub-areas of risk management, and for helping to fill some serious gaps in our current capabilities, but it will not revolutionize the discipline.

Even in those situations in which EVT is appropriate, we have argued that caution is needed, because estimation of aspects of very low-frequency events from short historical samples is fraught with pitfalls. This has been recognized in other fields, albeit often after long lags, including the empirical macroeconomics literature on long-run mean reversion in real output growth rates (e.g., Diebold and Senhadji, 1996) and the empirical finance literature on long-run mean reversion in asset returns (e.g., Campbell, Lo and MacKinlay, 1997). The problem as relevant for the present context -- applications of EVT in financial risk management -- is that for estimating objects such as a "once every hundred years" quantile, the relevant measure of sample size is likely much better approximated by the number of non-overlapping hundred-year intervals than by the number of data points. From that perspective, our data samples are terribly small relative to the demands we place on them.

We emphasize, however, that the situation is *not* hopeless. EVT is here to stay, but we believe that best-practice applications of EVT to financial risk management will benefit from awareness of the limitations -- as well as the strengths -- of EVT. When the smoke clears, the contribution of EVT remains basic and useful: it helps us to draw smooth curves through the extreme tails of empirical survival functions in a way that is guided by powerful theory and hence provides a rigorous complement to alternatives such as graphical analysis of empirical survival functions.[9] Our point is simply that we shouldn't ask more of the theory than it can deliver.

Finally, we have also tried to highlight a number of areas in which additional research will lead to stronger theory and more compelling applications, including strategies for automatic cutoff selection, linear and nonlinear regression implementations, thorough Monte Carlo analysis of estimator performance under

---

[8] Einmahl (1990), for example, stresses the success of the empirical survival function for analyzing all but the most extreme risks.

[9] See Danielsson and deVries (1997c) for just such a blend of rigorous EVT and intuitive graphics. Note that the conditional heteroskedasticity diminishes as the periodicity increases from daily to weekly and higher periodicity (lower frequency). Therefore many of the EVT tools may in fact be applicable to lower frequency financial data.

ideal and non-ideal conditions, focus on interval as well as point estimation, strategies for handling dependent data, and tests of the power law assumption.

We look forward to vigorous exploration of the role of EVT in risk management. In particular we await progress on the multivariate front since the risk manager almost always has not an individual asset but a portfolio of assets or securities to worry about and to date the EVT literature describes a *uni*variate theory. While we could simply treat the extreme value problem directly at the portfolio level, the top-down approach, it is much more useful to take the bottom-up view where we explicitly model the joint stochastic structure of the portfolio elements.

Current risk management is based on confidence intervals rather than tail probabilities. Clearly, the two are dual, but the former is easier to estimate than the latter. Perhaps unsurprisingly, risk managers at the leading financial institutions are often concerned about tail probabilities, in particular the severity and frequency of really big hits. Meanwhile it is important to note that the regulatory agencies, the Fed and the BIS, for instance, assign capital, the currency in which punishment and reward are denominated, on the basis of confidence interval performance. Successful characterization of the tail would therefore enliven considerably the current regulatory discussion.

Acknowledgments

We thank Casper de Vries for his thoughtful comments. The first author would like to thank the Oliver Wyman Institute for its hospitality and inspiration. All errors, however, are ours alone. We gratefully acknowledge support from the National Science Foundation and the University of Pennsylvania Research Foundation.

References

Bollerslev, T., Chou, R.Y. and Kroner, K.F. (1992), "ARCH Modeling in Finance: A Selective Review of the Theory and Empirical Evidence," Journal of Econometrics, 52, 5-59.

Campbell, J.Y., Lo., A.W. and MacKinlay, A.C. (1997), The Economics of Financial Markets. Princeton: Princeton University Press.

Danielsson, J. and deVries, C.G. (1997a), "Beyond the Sample: Extreme Quantile and Probability Estimation," Manuscript, Tinbergen Institute Rotterdam.

Danielsson, J. and deVries, C.G. (1997b), "Tail Index and Quantile Estimation with Very High Frequency Data," Journal of Empirical Finance, 4, 241-257.

Danielsson, J. and deVries, C.G. (1997c), "Extreme Returns, Tail Estimation, and Value-at-Risk," Manuscript, Tinbergen Institute Rotterdam.

Diebold, F.X. and Lopez, J. (1995), "Modeling Volatility Dynamics," in Kevin Hoover (ed.), Macroeconometrics: Developments, Tensions and Prospects. Boston: Kluwer Academic Press, 427-472.

Diebold, F.X. and Senhadji, A. (1996), "The Uncertain Unit Root in U.S. GNP: Comment," American Economic Review, 86, 1291-1298.

Einmahl, J.H.J. (1990), "The Empirical Distribution Function as a Tail Estimator," Statistica Neerlandica, 44, 79-82.

Embrechts, P., Klüppelberg, C. and Mikosch, T. (1997), Modelling Extremal Events. New York: Springer-Verlag.

Engle, R.F. and González-Rivera, G. (1991), "Semiparametric ARCH Models," Journal of Business and Economic Statistics, 9, 345-359.

Hill, B.M. (1975), "A Simple General Approach to Inference About the Tail of a Distribution," Annals of Statistics, 3, 1163-1174.

Inoue, A. (1998), "A Conditional Goodness-of-Fit Test for Time Series," Manuscript, Department of Economics, University of Pennsylvania.

Kearns, P. and Pagan, A.R. (1997), "Estimating the Tail Density Index for Financial Time Series," Review of Economics and Statistics, 79, 171-175.

Koedijk, K.G., Schafgans, M.A. and deVries, C.G. (1990), "The Tail Index of Exchange Rate Returns," Journal of International Economics, 29, 93-108.

Leadbetter, M.R., Lindgren, G. and Rootzen, H. (1983), Extremes and Related Properties of Random Sequences and Processes. New York: Springer-Verlag.

McCulloch, J.H. (1996), "Financial Applications of Stable Distributions," Handbook of Statistics, Vol. 14, 393-425.

Paul-Choudhury, S. (1998), "Beyond Basle," Risk, 11, 89. (Introduction to a symposium on new methods of assessing capital adequacy, Risk, 11, 90-107).

Silverman, B.W. (1986), Density Estimation for Statistics and Data Analysis. New York: Chapman and Hall.

STABILITY ANALYSIS AND FORECASTING IMPLICATIONS

J. del Hoyo
J. Guillermo Llorente
Departamento de Economía Cuantitativa
Universidad Autónoma de Madrid
28049 Madrid, SPAIN
E-mail: juan.hoyo@uam.es or guiller@uam.es

Forecasting with unstable relationships under the assumption that they are constant, might cause inefficient forecasts. Thus, before embarking upon any forecast exercise, it is convenient to first verify the sequential significance of the relationship, and then its stability. This paper studies recursive and rolling estimators, and related sequential tests to test for significant and constant coefficients. If constancy is rejected, the estimations may suggest dynamic models, that jointly with the considered model, could improve the results of the forecasting exercise. These procedures are applied to the price volume relationship in the stock market as postulated in Campbell, Grossman and Wang (1993). The significance but non stability of the relationship is shown. There are gains in the forecast performance when considering the empirical model for the rolling estimators, jointly with the initial structural model.
Key Words: Recursive Estimators, Rolling Estimators, Recursive Sequential Test, Monte Carlo Methods, Campbell-Grossman-Wang model.

1 Introduction

There are some issues in the development of theoretical models that receive little or no attention in their empirical implementation. We refer, for example, to transformations made to achieve linear approximations, hypotheses about the permanence through time of the derived structures, constancy of the coefficients, etc. For example, most models of asset pricing in financial economics have non linear solutions, linearization implies linear around some point, that is "local linearity". But the local property can change over time. Avoiding high order terms in the Taylor's expansion is not supposed to be a great problem. Local linearity can also be a characteristic of any time series model.

Asymptotic results are usually claimed when using huge data bases, leading to minimize the information any observation or group of observations can add to the estimation results, even if they have important insights. There is also increasing evidence about the time evolving nature of some relationships.

The econometric literature associates time varying parameters with mis-specification errors (*i.e.* omitted variables, structural changes, local validity,...). This paper starts with the presumption that if there is an specification error, it will induce at least one break when testing the model, the break date is not known a priori but is gleaned from the data. Thus, testing for insample stability

A.-P.N. Refenes et al. (eds.), Decision Technologies for Computational Finance, 13–24.
© 1998 *Kluwer Academic Publishers. Printed in the Netherlands..*

of the model is one of the best ways to evaluate its appropriateness and to detect specification errors.

All these considerations lead one to think about the necessity of knowing whether the studied relation is statistically significant along the sample, and if the coefficients of the model change as new information is added. The common answer in the traditional econometric literature is recursive estimation, adding one observation at a time. Constancy of the coefficients or structural changes can be tested under several assumptions. The recursive method has the disadvantage that the information added by new observations gets smoothed as the sample size increases. Nevertheless, compared to other procedures, this technique is very easy to implement.

The answer to the above problem is to estimate the model with a constant sample size, or rolling estimators, by means of a rectangular window with constant length. This algorithm gives any single sample the same chance to influence on the estimations. The result is a series of parameters to be studied. Keeping the length of the window constant allows one to think in terms of the local adequacy of the model, either motivated by a local linear structure or by linearization. The series of parameters should not have significant time changes if the null hypothesis of correct specification is true. Thus, if the null is rejected it will be a signal of some specification error. In general, it is not possible to identify its source, because of the joint nature of the null hypothesis.

If the relationship among the variables along the sample is significant, but stability is rejected, the optimal way to use these results for forecasting is to consider the information given by the rolling estimates jointly with the equation model.

The window width, or optimal size of the local sample, presents a trade off between smoothness of the estimated series of parameters and their variability. Research on its optimal size is out of the scope of this paper.

This paper presents Wald type sequential statistical tests based on recursive and rolling estimators to test for significative relation and stability under several null hypotheses. Their asymptotic distributions are presented. Monte Carlo Methods are used to tabulate the derived distributions and to analyze the size and nominal power of the performed tests.

Other related work are Stock(1994), Banerjee et al. (1992), Chu et al. (1995), Chu et al. (1996), and Bai and Perron (1997), to cite a few. Stock (1994) reviews the literature on structural breaks at unknown change point mainly related to recursive estimators. Banerjee et al. (1992) study sequential tests based on recursive and rolling estimators to test for unit-root hypothesis. Chu et al. (1995) study what they call moving-estimates, the analogy to what is called in this paper rolling estimators, and apply them to the Fluctuation test of Ploberger et al. (1989). Chu et al. (1996) concentrate on testing whether new incoming observations belong to an already accepted model. Bai and Perron (1997) develop statistics to test for multiple breaks.

The new feature of this paper is to particularize the Wald type statistics using the rolling estimators to test for significant relation among variables and for stability in linear models.

The relationships between price and trading volume as developed in Campbell, Grossman and Wang (1993) (hereafter CGW) is analyzed as an application. The concern is on persistence of the relationship and possible shifts along time. We are persuaded by recent empirical studies in the financial field, about the possible instability of the relation when considering several years of highly frequency data. Changes are due either to specification errors or to the intrinsic nature of the relationship to change over time.

These techniques are applied to data on the USA and Spanish stock market following the specification on CGW. In both cases the existence of a significative relationship among variables is accepted, but the stability hypothesis is rejected. The improvement in forecasting expected returns is studied when the information given by the estimated rolling parameters is added to the initial proposed relationship.

The rest of the paper is organized as follows. Section 2 explains the econometric techniques used to test the null hypothesis of stability. Section 3 presents the empirical application. Finally, Section 4 concludes the paper.

2 Sequential Tests

This section provides asymptotic distribution theory for the sequential statistics (recursive and rolling) that consider the possibility of at least one change with unknown a priori date. Recursive statistics are computed using subsamples of increasing size $t = [\lambda_{min}T], [\lambda_{min}T] + 1, \ldots, T$, that is equivalent to $t = t_{min}, \ldots, T$, where $\lambda = \frac{t}{T}$, λ_{min} is a startup value, T is the full sample size, $[T\lambda] = t$, and $[\bullet]$ represents the integer part of the value inside brackets. The algorithm for the rolling estimators with window width s can be derived from the recursive one in two steps: (1) adding a new observation and (2) removing the oldest observation, keeping s observations in the estimation process[1]. The observations on y_t are assumed to be generated by a model of the following type[2].

$$y_t = \boldsymbol{X}_{t-1}\boldsymbol{\beta}_t + \epsilon_t , \quad t = 2, 3, \ldots \tag{1}$$

Under the null hypothesis $\boldsymbol{\beta}_t = \boldsymbol{\beta}$ is a $(k \times 1)$ vector of constant parameters, the errors (ϵ_t) are assumed to be a martingale difference sequence with respect to the σ-fields generated by $\{\epsilon_{t-1}, \boldsymbol{X}_{t-1}, \epsilon_{t-2}, \boldsymbol{X}_{t-2}, \ldots\}$, where $\boldsymbol{X}_t$ is a $(k \times 1)$ vector of regressors. The regressors are assumed to be constant and/or $I(0)$ with $E(\boldsymbol{X}_t'\boldsymbol{X}_t) = \boldsymbol{\Sigma}_X$. It is also assumed that $T^{-1} \sum_{i=1}^{[T\lambda]} \boldsymbol{X}_i'\boldsymbol{X}_i \xrightarrow{P} \lambda\boldsymbol{\Sigma}_X$ uniformly in λ for $\lambda \in [0, 1]$; $E(\epsilon_t^2) = \sigma^2 \ \forall \ t$, and $T^{-1} \sum_{i=2}^{[T\lambda]} \boldsymbol{X}_i'\epsilon_i \Rightarrow \sigma\boldsymbol{\Sigma}^{1/2}{}_X \boldsymbol{W}_k(\lambda)$, with

---

[1]See Young (1984) for a description of these algorithms. Both algorithms can be reformulated to actualize the estimations by groups of observations.

[2]The hypotheses about this model are made according to the characteristics of the empirical application.

$\Sigma_X = \Sigma^{1/2}{}_X \Sigma^{1/2}{}_X$, $W_k(\lambda)$ is a k-dimensional vector of independent Wiener or Brownian motion process [3], and $\Rightarrow$ denotes weak convergence on $D[0,1]$. X_{t-1} can include lagged dependent variables as long as they are $I(0)$ under the null (see Stock (1994)).

The recursive OLS coefficient can be written as random elements of $D[0,1]$:

$$\hat{\beta}(\lambda) = \left(\sum_{t=2}^{[T\lambda]} X'_{t-1} X_{t-1} \right)^{-1} \left(\sum_{t=2}^{[T\lambda]} X'_{t-1} y_t \right) \qquad 0 \le \lambda_{min} \le \lambda \le 1 \qquad (2)$$

The expression for rolling estimator as random elements of $D[0,1]$ is:

$$\tilde{\beta}(\lambda; \lambda_0) = \left(\sum_{t=[T(\lambda-\lambda_0)]+1}^{[T\lambda]} X'_{t-1} X_{t-1} \right)^{-1} \left(\sum_{t=[T(\lambda-\lambda_0)]+1}^{[T\lambda]} X'_{t-1} y_t \right) \qquad (3)$$

for $0 \le \lambda_0 \le \lambda \le 1$ and with $\lambda_0 = \frac{s}{T}$ the window width.

The Wald type statistics used in this paper to test the m null hypotheses $R\beta = r$ ($H_0 : R\hat{\beta}(*) = r$, where $\hat{\beta}(*)$ is either $\hat{\beta}(\lambda)$ or $\tilde{\beta}(\lambda; \lambda_0)$) have as general form

$$\hat{F}_T(*) = \frac{\left(R\hat{\beta}(*) - r \right)' \left[R \left(\sum_{t_*}^{[T\lambda]} X'_{t-1} X_{t-1} \right)^{-1} R' \right]^{-1} \left(R\hat{\beta}(*) - r \right)}{m\hat{\sigma}^2(*)} \qquad (4)$$

where $\hat{\sigma}^2(*)$ is either the recursive or the rolling estimation of the variance, and t_* is the beginning of the corresponding sample.

The asymptotic behavior of this statistic is derived by applying the Functional Central Limit Theorem (FCLT) and the Continuous Mapping Theorem (CMT). The form of the final distributions depends on the particular values of R and r determined by the null hypothesis.

In what follows, the subscripts refer to the null hypothesis to be tested, and the superscripts to the number of parameters involved. For example, $\hat{F}(\lambda)_0^k$ represents the particularization of the $\hat{F}_T(*)$ statistics to test the null hypothesis that all the recursive parameters of the model are equal to zero.

Following Stock (1994), define $V_T(\cdot) = T^{-1} \sum_{t_*}^{[T\lambda]} X'_{t-1} X_{t-1}$ and $v_T(\cdot) = T^{-1/2} \sum_{t_*}^{[T\lambda]} X'_{t-1} \epsilon_t$; then, under the general hypotheses of model (1), $V_T(\cdot) \xrightarrow{P} V(\cdot)$, $v_T \Rightarrow v(\cdot)$, and $\sqrt{T}(\hat{\beta}(\cdot) - \beta) \Rightarrow \hat{\delta}(\cdot)^*$, with $\hat{\delta}(\lambda)^* \equiv V(\cdot)^{-1} v(\cdot)$. Thus, for the recursive estimators under $H_0 : R\beta = r$

$$\hat{F}_T(\lambda) \Rightarrow \left[R\hat{\delta}(\lambda)^* \right]' \left[RV(\lambda)^{-1} R' \right]^{-1} \left[R\hat{\delta}(\lambda)^* \right] / q\sigma^2 \equiv \hat{F}(\lambda) \qquad (5)$$

---

[3] ϵ_t can be conditionally (on lagged ϵ_t and X_t) homoskedastic and the results do not change.

with $V(\lambda) = \lambda\Sigma_X$, R is the restriction matrix, $v_T(\cdot) \Rightarrow \sigma_\epsilon\Sigma_X^{1/2}W_k(\cdot)$, and $\hat{\delta}(\lambda)^* = \frac{\sigma_\epsilon\Sigma_X^{-1/2}W_k(\lambda)}{\lambda}$. The final expression of the statistics depends on R and r.

The paper tests first for the significance of the relationship along the sample (firstly for all the coefficients, and secondly for all the coefficientes except the constant). $H_0 : R\hat{\beta}(\cdot) = 0 \ \forall \ \lambda$ with $R_{(m\times k)}$ matrix, $r = 0$, and $m \leq k$. The Wald test for the recursive estimators under this null hypothesis has the following expression:

$$\hat{F}(\lambda)_0^m \equiv \max_{\lambda_{min} \leq \lambda \leq 1} \left[\lambda m * \hat{F}(\lambda)\right] \Rightarrow \sup_{\lambda_{min} \leq \lambda \leq 1} W_m(\lambda)'W_m(\lambda) \tag{6}$$

The sequential statistic based on the rolling estimates for similar null hypotheses $H_0 : R\tilde{\beta}(\lambda; \lambda_0) = 0 \ \forall \ \lambda$ with $R_{(m\times k)}$, $r = 0$, and $m \leq k$, has the following final expression, where $H_m(-) = W_m(\lambda) - W_m(\lambda - \lambda_0)$:

$$\tilde{F}(\lambda; \lambda_0)_0^m \equiv \max_{\lambda_0 \leq \lambda \leq 1} \left[\lambda_0 m * \tilde{F}(\lambda; \lambda_0)\right] \Rightarrow \sup_{\lambda_0 \leq \lambda \leq 1} \{H_m(-)'H_m(-)\} \tag{7}$$

Once the significance of relationship is tested and if it is accepted, the next hypothesis to test is its stability, comparing the sequential estimations with the estimations from the full sample $(R = I, \ r = \hat{\beta}(*))$. The final expression for the recursive statistic $(H_0 : \hat{\beta}(\lambda) = \hat{\beta}(1) \ \forall \ \lambda)$ is

$$\hat{F}(\lambda)_{\hat{\beta}(1)}^k \equiv \max_{\lambda_{min} \leq \lambda \leq 1} \left[\frac{\lambda k}{\lambda(1-\lambda)}\hat{F}(\lambda)\right] \Rightarrow \sup_{\lambda_{min} \leq \lambda \leq 1} \left\{\frac{B_k(\lambda)'B_k(\lambda)}{\lambda(1-\lambda)}\right\} \tag{8}$$

where $B_k(\lambda) = W_k(\lambda) - \lambda W_k(1)$ is a k dimensional Brownian Bridge. This expression is the same as the $supW$ in Andrews (1993).

The rolling statistics for the same null hypothesis $(H_0 : \tilde{\beta}(\lambda; \lambda_0) = \tilde{\beta}(1; 1) = \hat{\beta}(1) \ \forall \ \lambda)$ calling $G_k(-) = W_k(\lambda) - W_k(\lambda - \lambda_0) - \lambda_0 W_k(1)$, is:

$$\tilde{F}(\lambda; \lambda_0)_{\tilde{\beta}(1;1)}^k \equiv \max_{\lambda_0 \leq \lambda \leq 1} \left[\lambda_0 k * \tilde{F}(\lambda; \lambda_0)\right] \Rightarrow \sup_{\lambda_0 \leq \lambda \leq 1} \{G_k(-)'G_k(-)\} \tag{9}$$

2.1 Monte Carlo Results

Critical values for all entertained statistics are reported in this section, size and power are also presented. The basic model is of the type presented in Eq. (1) with either $k = 7$ or $k = 9$ parameters (explanatory variables) corresponding to the empirical example.

Three recursive and three rolling sequential statistics are examined. Following the convention established above, they will be denoted by $\hat{F}(\lambda)_0^k$, $\hat{F}(\lambda)_0^{k-1}$,

Table 1: Recursive and Rolling Tests Statistics: Critical Values

| Panel A: Recursive Test Statistics: Critical Values | | | | | |
| $\hat{F}(\lambda)_0^k$ | | $\hat{F}(\lambda)_0^{k-1}$ | | $\hat{F}(\lambda)_{\hat{\beta}(1)}^k$ | |
Percentile	$k = 7$	$k = 9$	$k = 7$	$k = 9$	$k = 7$	$k = 9$
0.100	2.62	2.40	2.73	2.48	1.88	1.77
0.050	2.94	2.67	3.12	2.77	2.13	1.97
0.010	3.59	3.23	3.91	3.32	2.64	2.42

| Panel B: Rolling Tests Statistics: Critical Values | | | | | |
| $\tilde{F}(\lambda; \lambda_0)_0^k$ | | $\tilde{F}(\lambda; \lambda_0)_0^{k-1}$ | | $\tilde{F}(\lambda; \lambda_0)_{\hat{\beta}(1;1)}^k$ | |
Percentile	$k = 7$	$k = 9$	$k = 7$	$k = 9$	$k = 7$	$k = 9$
		Window width 100 observations				
0.100	4.09	2.99	4.42	3.16	4.05	2.72
0.050	4.36	3.23	4.71	3.40	4.30	2.94
0.010	4.85	3.74	5.32	3.95	4.78	3.44
		Window width 150 observations				
0.100	3.95	2.86	4.30	2.99	3.88	2.44
0.050	4.23	3.11	4.58	3.23	4.14	2.65
0.010	4.78	3.72	5.13	3.79	4.71	3.05

and $\hat{F}(\lambda)_{\hat{\beta}(1)}^k$, to test the significance of the relationship along the sample, the significance of all parameters except the constant, and the deviation of the recursive estimations from the full sample estimates, respectively. The analogy statistics using rolling estimators are $\tilde{F}(\lambda; \lambda_0)_0^k$, $\tilde{F}(\lambda; \lambda_0)_0^{k-1}$, and $\tilde{F}(\lambda; \lambda_0)_{\hat{\beta}(1;1)}^k$.

The statistics were tabulated using a symmetric 15 percent trimming, as is usual in this kind of work. The window width for the rolling statistics are 100 and 150 observations. This could have been chosen as a percentage of the sample size, nevertheless, the selection made is reasonable in the context of the empirical work to be done. It reflects the a priori of the researcher about the "reasonable memory" of the considered problem. Size and Power of the statistics were not examined as a function of the window width. Power is presented only for the 100 observation window. Further investigation into the choice of the optimal window is left for future research. The study of the power does not tend to be exhaustive, it just investigates the main characteristics of the statistics in Eq. (6), (7), (8), and (9).

Approximate critical values for these sequential statistics are reported in Table 1. Entries are the *sup* values of the functionals of Brownian motions. The critical values were computed performing Monte Carlo simulations of the limiting functionals of Brownian Motion processes involved in the statistics. All critical values were computed using 10,000 replications and $T = 3,600$ in each replication.

Table 2: Size and Power of Recursive and Rolling Tests: Monte Carlo Results

	Test	Size		Power	
		$k = 7$	$k = 9$	$k = 7$	$k = 9$
Recursive Statistics	$\hat{F}(\lambda)_0^k$	10.40	15.20	100	100
	$\hat{F}(\lambda)_0^{k-1}$	11.00	12.80	100	100
	$\hat{F}(\lambda)_{\hat{\beta}(1)}^k$	11.00	8.50	100	100
Rolling Statistics (100 obs)	$\tilde{F}(\lambda; \lambda_0)_0^k$	36.80	17.00	100	100
	$\tilde{F}(\lambda; \lambda_0)_0^{k-1}$	29.80	21.40	100	100
	$\tilde{F}(\lambda; \lambda_0)_{\hat{\beta}(1;1)}^k$	39.80	24.80	100	100

Size and nominal power (not adjusted by size) of the statistics are summarized in Table 2 for a number of observations similar to the ones used in the empirical part ($T = 1000$ for $k = 9$, and $T = 8000$ for $k = 7$). Entries are percent rejections at 10% critical values from Table 1. Power was simulated under the hypothesis that the coefficients follow a random walk. All pseudodata, based on 500 replications, were generated including T startup values (initial observations not used in computing the statistics)[4] [5].

The first two columns in Table 2 report size for the null hypotheses. Recursive tests have size near their levels. The empirical size of the rolling tests depends on the number of parameters, and though not presented here, on the percentage of the window width to the total number of observations; which is reflected in Table 2. In this sense, the rolling tests are conservative, they are likely to produce false rejections of the null hypothesis.

The last two columns in Table 2 present nominal power (not size adjusted) against the alternative that the coefficients follow a random walk with perturbations white noise $N(0, 1)$. Some other power experiments not reported, and using as alternative hypothesis one break in the middle of the sample, indicate that the power depends on the magnitude of the change when testing against the estimation with the full sample. The power with one break has the same features as those presented in Table 2 when the null hypothesis is that the parameters are zero.

---

[4] The coefficients were drawn from a $N(0, 1)$ distribution, when needed in the simulations.

[5] According to the hypothesis of the theoretical model conditional heteroskedasticity was not considered in the simulations, though the studied series could have some ARCH type scheme.

3 Empirical Results

The sequential tests presented in Section 2 are used here to examine the stability of the relationship between price and volume as postulated by Campbell, Grossman and Wang (1993). The application is done for the USA and Spanish stock markets. Full sample estimations are computed first, and the sequential tests are applied afterwards.

The model used for the estimations is the same as the one used in CGW. The working expression is achieved after two quadratic approximations of the general solution in the theoretical model. The estimated equation is[6]

$$R_{t+1} = \beta_0 + (\sum_{i=1}^{5} \beta_i D_i + \gamma V_t) R_t + \epsilon_t \tag{10}$$

where R_t is the return of the market on day t, V_t is the volume traded on the market on day t, and D_i is a dummy variable corresponding to day i of the week. The consideration of dummy variables, one for each day of the week, tries to account for the accepted different behavior of the relationship between returns depending on the day of the week. For the Spanish market two additional variables were added, as mentioned below.

The data used comes from the Center for Research in Security Prices (CRSP) for the USA stock market, and from the Sociedad de Bolsas for the Spanish market. The data on the USA market is daily data of return on the value-weighted index of stocks traded on the New York Stock Exchange and American Stock Exchange, reported by CRSP over the period 7/3/62 through 12/31/93. Results over this period are likely to be dominated by a few observations around the market crash of October 1997. For this reason the sample has been divided and studied in two parts, before and after that date. The full sample has also been studied. The main results are independent of the period considered, therefore the comments only refer to the full sample.

The daily return for the Spanish market is calculated from a value-weighted index of the 35 most liquid stocks of the Stock Exchange, this index is called Ibex-35. The period considered is 1/4/92 through 12/31/95.

Stock market trading volume data is measured as the daily series of market turnover from all the stocks traded during this period in the cited exchanges. Market turnover is defined as the ratio of the dollar value of all valid transactions to the dollar value of all shares outstanding in the market. Turnover is a common measure of volume in these kind of studies.

According to the theoretical model, trading volume should be measured relative to the capacity of the market to absorb volume. The volume series should also be stationary. For both of these reasons the original series is transformed taking logarithms and detrending it[7].

---

[6]The hypotheses of the model are similar to those used in the derivation of the sequential tests.

[7]Two methods were used for detrending. The first subtracts a two hundred day moving

Table 3: Empirical Results: Estimations with the Full Sample

	β_0	β_1	β_2	β_3	β_4	β_5	γ	$dowov$	$dowin$
	(s.e)	(s.e)	(s.e)	(s.e)	(s.e)	(s.e)	(s.e)	(s.e)	(s.e)
USA	0.0003	0.07	0.22	0.18	0.31	0.42	-0.25		
	(0.0001)	(0.03)	(0.04)	(0.04)	(0.04)	(0.09)	(0.09)		
Spain	0.0001	-0.02	0.23	0.19	0.15	0.25	-0.10	1.05	0.31
	(0.0003)	(0.07)	(0.07)	(0.09)	(0.09)	(0.07)	(0.10)	(0.13)	(0.05)

The small market characteristics, and the heavy external influence on the Spanish market, requires consideration of the foreign influence in the form of two variables representing the USA stock market behavior. The first one is called *dowov* and represents the overnight return of the Dow Jones Index; the second, called *dowin*, reports the intraday return on the Dow Jones Index. Both variables are included in the equation corresponding to the Spanish market.

Table (3) presents the estimation of the model for the whole sample period for both markets[8]. The estimated R^2 is approximately 5.5% for USA and 17% for Spain respectively. The external influence in the Spanish market accounts for approximately 13% of the explanatory power in terms of R^2 [9].

Recursive and rolling estimations were calculated to test the hypotheses[10]. The first hypothesis studies the significance of the relationship through time (all the parameters equal to zero, and all but the constant equal to zero). The second its stability compared to the estimations with the full sample. The results are summarized in Table 4. Entries are test statistics. Test are significant at the * 10 percent, ** 5 percent and *** 1 percent level.

Recursive and rolling statistics, reported in Table 4 provide clear evidence of the validity of the model through time, the relation is significative at the 1% level for both countries ($\hat{F}(\lambda)_0^k$ and $\hat{F}(\lambda; \lambda_0)_0^k$). The non consideration of the intercept does not change the results ($\hat{F}(\lambda)_0^{k-1}$ and $\hat{F}(\lambda; \lambda_0)_0^{k-1}$). Statistics, $\hat{F}(\lambda)_{\hat{\beta}(1)}^k$, and $\hat{F}(\lambda; \lambda_0)_{\hat{\beta}(1;1)}^k$ reject the null hypothesis that all of the coefficients are constant and equal to the full sample estimation at the 1% level for USA ($k = 7$) and at the 5% percent level for Spain ($k = 9$).

Once the null hypothesis of constant coefficients has been rejected, the next

average of the logarithm of the original series (This method is used in CGW and in LeBaron (1991)); the second is to use a non observable components model with time varying parameters to estimate the trend (Young *et al.* (1991). The differences between both alternative methods are negligible.

[8] The standard errors corrected for heteroscedasticity are reported into braces. CGW study a different sample period for the USA market, their main conclusions still apply in the sample we used.

[9] The temporal reference for the *dow* variables in the Spanish market with respect to R_{t+1} is $dowov_{t+1}$, and $dowin_t$, to represent their different influence over future returns. There is no strict simultaneity between $dowov_{t+1}$ and R_{t+1}, they have different time period in their determination.

[10] The graphs of the recursive and rolling estimations, not presented for space reasons, show evolving patterns in both markets, a characteristic that could be a first sign of instability.

Table 4: Empirical Results: Evidence on Recursive and Rolling Statistics

Panel A: Evidence on Recursive Statistics					
$\hat{F}(\lambda)_0^k$		$\hat{F}(\lambda)_0^{k-1}$		$\hat{F}(\lambda)_{\hat{\beta}(1)}^k$	
$k = 7$	$k = 9$	$k = 7$	$k = 9$	$k = 7$	$k = 9$
75.37***	24.31***	84.92***	27.09***	8.39***	2.26**
Panel B: Evidence on Rolling Statistics					
$\tilde{F}(\lambda; \lambda_0)_0^k$		$\tilde{F}(\lambda; \lambda_0)_0^{k-1}$		$\tilde{F}(\lambda; \lambda_0)_{\tilde{\beta}(1;1)}^k$	
$k = 7$	$k = 9$	$k = 7$	$k = 9$	$k = 7$	$k = 9$
window width 100 observations					
52.44***	9.42***	60.50***	10.23***	43.48***	2.82*
window width 150 observations					
30.17***	11.26***	34.87***	12.50***	23.78***	2.86**

step is to model the series of rolling estimations and to incorporate their information into the prediction exercise. Following the normal steps in the simple Box-Jenkins framework it is possible to identify and estimate the most suitable models for the series of estimated parameters. These empirical models are mainly random walks with weak MA(1) and MA(5) components, depending on the parameter and the considered sample period. Some series also have an ARCH structure.

Table 5 compares the forecasting performance for several alternatives in the USA and Spanish market. Entries are in percent values. The first alternative is fitting a time series model to the rolling volume parameter and to make several one-step-ahead forecasts. The dummy variables are considered to be random walks. The second alternative is similar to the previous one but now the forecast of the dummy variables is an average of the previous rolling estimations, the length of the average is the same as the window width used in their estimation. The third model used in the forecast evaluation is to use the estimates from the last rolling window and forecast, maintaining these values constant over the whole evaluation period. The fourth is to consider the estimates from the full sample. Finally the fifth method is a random walk for the return variable.

The forecasting analysis is performed for two periods in which the recursive estimation was relatively stable, trying to avoid biasing the results towards any alternative as could happen if they were done over periods with sudden changes[11]. The periods are labeled as "beginning", and "end" of the sample, respectively. The forecast are evaluated for several horizons: ten, fifteen, twenty and, thirty days[12].

Two criteria were used to compare the goodness of each alternative, the

---

[11]The origins of the forecast are 8/23/77 and 11/17/93 for USA, and 5/12/93 and 7/6/95 for Spain.

[12]For space reasons only the forecast with twenty days is presented, the rest is available upon request.

Table 5: Forecasting 20 days ahead, USA and Spain

Criterion	Model	USA Window Width		Spain Window Width	
		100obs.	150 obs	100obs.	150 obs.
	Beginning the sample				
	Chang. param.	0.49	0.48	1.43	1.42
	Chang par mean dum	0.48	0.48	1.41	1.49
RMSE	Last. estim.	0.48	0.48	1.44	1.43
	Full sample	0.52	0.52	1.45	1.45
	Random Walk	0.62	0.62	1.93	1.93
	Chang. param.	0.41	0.40	0.91	0.94
	Chang par mean dum	0.40	0.40	0.97	1.05
MAE	Last. estim.	0.41	0.40	0.94	0.97
	Full sample	0.42	0.42	1.01	1.01
	Random Walk	0.53	0.53	1.45	1.45
	End of the sample				
	Chang. param.	0.34	0.34	1.01	0.95
	Chang par mean dum	0.35	0.36	0.96	0.96
RMSE	Last. estim.	0.34	0.34	1.00	0.95
	Full sample	0.36	0.36	0.94	0.94
	Random Walk	0.44	0.44	1.29	1.29
	Chang. param.	0.27	0.27	0.82	0.77
	Chang par mean dum	0.27	0.28	0.78	0.76
MAE	Last. estim.	0.26	0.27	0.83	0.76
	Full sample	0.28	0.28	0.76	0.76
	Random Walk	0.30	0.30	1.02	1.02

Root Mean Squared Error (RMSE) and the Mean Absolute Error (MAE)[13]. In general, for both criteria and for the two window sizes, independently of the number of periods forecast and of the period of the sample, the best alternative is to model the rolling estimations with either of the first two alternatives, the second best method is to use the last estimations of the rolling algorithm. The worst methods are the random walk and the model with the full sample.

4 Conclusions

The motivation of the paper is to verify the likely improvement in forecasting when considering the possible instability of the entertained model. Thus, before doing any prediction it should pay to test for insample significance and stability of the studied relationship.

Section 2 provides sequential statistics to test for significant and stable relationships using recursive and rolling estimators. Their good size and power properties are shown.

As an empirical application the stability of the price and volume relationships in the USA and Spanish stock market have been studied. The null hypothesis

---

[13] The Root Mean Squared Error is defined as $RMSE = \sqrt{\frac{1}{n}\sum_{t=1}^{n}(y_t - y_{f,t})^2}$, with n as the number of forecasting periods, y_t is the real value, and $y_{f,t}$ is the forecasted value. The Mean Absolute Error is defined as $MAE = \frac{1}{n}\sum_{t=1}^{n}|y_t - y_{f,t}|$.

about the significance of the relation along the sample is accepted, though the constant coefficients hypothesis is rejected. These results imply an improvement in forecasting when the time varying parameters are taken into consideration.

5   Acknowledgements

We are grateful to Halbert White, Paul Refenes, Blake LeBaron, and two anonymous referees, whose comments have improved this paper significantly. An early version of this paper, entitled "Testing and Forecasting Volume and Return Relationships in the Stock Market", was presented in the ISF'96 held in Istanbul, and in the QMF'97 held in Sydney. Financial support from the DGICYT under Grant PB94-018 is acknowledged.

6   References

Andrews, D. W. K. "Tests for Parameter Instability and Structural Change with Unknown Change Point", *Econometrica*, 1993, 61, 821-856.

Bai, J., Perron P. "Estimating and Testing Linear Models with Multiple Structural Changes", mimeo MIT, 1997

Banerjee, A., Lumsdaine R. L., Stock J. "Recursive and Sequential Tests of the Unit-Root and Trend-Break Hypotheses: Theory and International Evidence", *Journal of Business and Economic Statistics*, July 1992, 10, 3, 271-287.

Campbell, J., Grossman S., Wang J. "Trading Volume and Serial Correlation in Stock Returns", *Quarterly Journal of Economics*, November 1993, 905-940.

Chu, C.-S. J., Hornik K., Kuan C.-M. "The Moving-Estimates Test for Parameter Stability", *Econometric Theory*, 1995, 11, 699-720.

Chu, C.-S. J., Stinchcombe M., White H. "Monitoring Structural Change", *Econometrica*, September 1996, 64, 5, 1045-1065.

LeBaron, B. "Persistence of the Dow Jones Index on Rising Volume", *Working paper University of Wisconsin*, September 1991.

Ploberger, W., Kramer K., Contrus K. "A New Test for Structural Stability in Linear Regression Model", *Journal of Econometrics*, 1989, 40, 307-318.

Stock, J. H. "Unit Roots Structural Breaks and Trends", in: *Handbook of Econometrics*, Vol. IV, Chapter 46, 2739-2839, Engle R. F. and McFadden D. L., ed., Elsevier Science 1994.

Young, P.C. *Recursive Estimation and Time Series Analysis*, Berlin: Springer-Verlag, 1984.

Young, P. C., Ng, C. N., Lane, K., Parker, D. "Recursive Forecasting, Smoothing and Seasonal Adjustment of Non-Stationary Environmental Data", *Journal of Forecasting*, 1991,10, 57-89.

TIME VARYING RISK PREMIA

M. STEINER, S. SCHNEIDER

Department of Finance and Banking
Universitaet Augsburg
Universitaetsstrasse 16, Augsburg, 86159, Germany
E-mail: Sebastian.Schneider@wiso.uni-augsburg.de

Since the moments of asset returns may contain information about the stochastic discount factor that correspond to a present value model with time-variable discount rates and expected returns, this paper uses Hansen-Jagannathan bounds to estimate valid stochastic discount factors under certain conditions. Thus we differentiate stochastic discount factors estimated on individual asset returns and stochastic discount factors using portfolio returns. The bounds were created using data sets on stock and bond returns for the 1965 - 1995 period. We find that different classes of returns impose different restrictions on the bounds and also on the mean-variance frontier. In order to test if the mean-variance frontier is expanded by the portfolio returns, we create a simple trading system by buying portfolios that lift the Hansen-Jagannathan bound upward. By proceeding we find significant excess returns on this trading strategy implying that these portfolio returns do expand the mean-variance frontier. Thus the underlying present value model leaves residuals since discounted returns are forecastable. A multifactor asset pricing model relates the variation of expected returns to a proxy for future business conditions. Thus we suggest that variations in real investment opportunities cause the variation in expected returns. Since we cannot measure real investment opportunities or related variables without error, multifactor models might better approximate consumption influence on asset pricing. For the parallel time-series and cross-sectional analysis we exploit the properties of Ivakhnenko's 'Group Method of Data Handling'.

1   Introduction

There is no lack of evidence in the capital markets literature that either short and long-horizon returns are predictable, caused by the variation of expected returns through time. The early studies focused on the forecasting power of past returns. Fama (1965) finds significant positive first-order autocorrelations of daily returns for 11 of 30 Dow Jones Industrial stocks. Fisher (1966) suggests that the autocorrelations of monthly returns on diversified portfolios are larger than for individual stocks. Lo and MacKinlay (1988) report that the autocorrelations of weekly returns are stronger for portfolios of smaller stocks.

This contradicts the early efficient market hypothesis, which states that expected returns are constant through time and therefore unpredictable from past returns. Shiller (1984) and Summer (1986) first challenged the view that autocorrelations are, even when they deviate reliably from zero, close to zero and thus economically insignificant. Shiller and Summer present models where stock prices have little short-horizon autocorrelation and take long swings in decaying cycles away from the fundamental value. This phenomenon is usually called irrational bubbles or fads. Stambaugh (1986) points out that those long-horizon swings imply strong negative autocorrelation for long-horizon returns.

A.-P.N. Refenes et al. (eds.), Decision Technologies for Computational Finance, 25–48.
© 1998 *Kluwer Academic Publishers. Printed in the Netherlands..*

Fama and French (1988b) find that the autocorrelations on diversified NYSE portfolios for the 1926 - 1985 period follow the pattern described by the Shiller-Summers-Stambaugh model. The negative long-horizon autocorrelation also implies that the variance of returns should grow less fast than the return horizon. This was first verified by Poterba and Summers (1988) for two to eight-year return horizons. Since variation in expected returns through time is only a part of the variation in returns (Cochrane (1992)) test statistics based on autocorrelations lack power because past returns are insufficient measures of expected returns (Fama (1991)). Therefore it is necessary to identify other forecasting variables that are better proxies for expected returns to enhance the power of the tests.

The early studies find that short-horizon returns are negatively related to and therefore predictable from expected inflation (Bodie (1976), Nelson (1976), Fama (1981)). Also short-term interests (Fama and Schwert (1977)) and dividend yields (Shiller (1984)) forecast short horizon returns. Fama and French (1988a) use dividend yields to forecast returns on either value-weighted and equally weighted portfolios of NYSE stocks. However, expected inflation, short-term interests and dividend yields only explain small fractions of the return variances. Campbell and Shiller (1988a) find similar results for E/P-Ratios. Especially when past earnings are averaged, the forecasting power increases with the return horizon. The underlying statistical circumstances were first challenged by Kirby (1988), since small population R^2s can produce t-ratios that might be misinterpreted as evidence of strong predictability. Finally, we argue that dividend yields and E/P-ratios are general proxies for risk. If two stocks have the same dividends or earnings, the riskier stock necessarily has a higher expected return.

Cochrane (1991) suggested that return-forecasting regressions are simple tests of specific discount-rate models. This resolves the conflicting views that asset prices were governed exclusively by their future payoffs or that present value models are naive academic asset pricing models. Also, tests of return-forecasting regressions always "run head-on into the joint hypothesis problem: Does return predictability reflect rational variation through time in expected returns, irrational deviations of price from fundamental value, or some combination of the two?" (Fama (1981), p. 1579). Samuelson (1965) points out that rejections of the present value model necessarily implies the existence of profitable trading strategies.

However, return-forecasting regressions are not tests of market efficiency. First they are not pure tests of rational pricing, but tests of a joint hypothesis that includes constant investment opportunities. Second it is always possible to construct discount rates that price assets exactly. Finally they „seemed to miss the point" (Cochrane (1991), p. 468), since we do not have all the information agents use to forecast returns (Grossman (1976)), Hellwig (1980)). In their excellent review of information aggregation in financial markets Habib and Naik (1996) highlight these implicit problems.

The early present-value model volatility tests pioneered by LeRoy and Parker (1981), Shiller (1979) and Grosman and Shiller (1981) find that stock prices vary too strongly to be explained by present value models. This even holds for stationary variables (Shiller (1981), Campbell and Shiller (1988b)). One reason might be, that corporate managers smooth dividend streams to mirror the long-horizon earnings stream (Mash and Merton (1986)). Other excellent reviews of volatility tests and return-forecasting regressions are available (Cochrane (1991), Fama (1991), LeRoy (1996)), so here we well only briefly comment that variations in real investment opportunities might also explain the excess volatility of prices.

Since variations of real investment opportunities are due to variations in the intertemporal marginal rates of substitution or transformation and thus only tractable with modern intertemporal asset pricing models introduced by Lucas (1978) and Breeden (1978), these shifts should signal variation in tastes for current against future consumption or production. Then some 'common factors' should forecast the expected returns of different assets. Therefore expected returns should be predictable both in time-series and cross-section. Keim and Stambaugh (1986) and Campbell (1987) find that some common stock market and term-structure variables indeed forecast the returns on bonds and stocks. Fama and French (1989) show that the dividend yield on NYSE value-weighted portfolio forecasts the returns on common stocks and corporate bonds. Even the returns on value- and equally-weighted portfolios of NYSE stocks and bonds are predictable from the default and the term spreads.

Finally the key questions is, whether variation in expected returns is caused by variations in real investment opportunities not captured by standard discount rate models. The answer to this question is never clear-cut, since it is always possible to construct some discount rates that satisfy the present value model, „given enough flexibility in the discount rate" (Cochrane (1991), p. 473). Hansen and Richard (1987), Hansen and Jagannathan (1991, 1997) and Balduzzi and Kallal (1998) among others show how to construct a single discount rate that prices an unlimited number of assets simultaneously. Also volatility tests and return regressions are equivalent to forecasts of discounted sums of returns (Cochrane (1992)) and therefore identical to Euler Equations. The empirical work on Euler Equations often jointly tests the consumption-based model, since only this reflects variations in real investment opportunities. Using the pathbreaking approach in Hansen and Singleton (1982) together with Hansen's (1982) 'generalized method of moments' we also jointly test a model's time-series and cross-section predictions.

We argue that consumption-based asset pricing models describe the variations in expected returns due to variations in real investment opportunities. Since consumption data on non-durables and service goods are always noisy measures, the estimated βs of a multifactor model may be better proxies for consumption βs than poorly estimated consumption βs themselves. In this context we treat a multifactor model as an extension of the consumption model (Constantinides (1989)). We find that returns on German equally weighted stock portfolios and bond portfolios are predictable from the default spread (the difference between the yields on AAA long-term Bundesanleihen (Bunds) and bonds issued by private held German companies). Similar to Mankiw and Sharpio (1986), however, whose results are clouded by a survivorship bias (Fama (1991)), we find that the market β also has marginal explanatory power.

Finally we introduce Ivakhnenko's (1968) 'group method of data handling' (GMDH) to jointly test time-series and cross-section predictions of our multifactor model. Instead of standard statistical tools and neural networks the GMDH need less a-priori information. Also, the GMDH always finds a model of optimal complexity and minimum bias. Using the GMDH we estimate Hansen-Jagannathan bounds. Because these bounds correspond to the Sharpe-ratio by adding an asset return we test whether the bound goes up and expands the mean-variance frontier. Snow (1991) uses this idea to test the "small firm effect". Therefore our trading system is based on the multifactor forecast of expected returns and tests whether the Hansen-Jagannathan bound goes up, since that variation might expand the mean-variance frontier.

2   Conditional asset pricing models and unconditional returns

2.1   The discount factor

A discount rate m_t is a variable such that the Euler equation holds for multiple assets:

$$1 = E_t\left(m_{t+1}\mathbf{r}_{t+1}\right),\tag{1}$$

where $\mathbf{r}_t$ is the vector of asset's gross returns and E_t is conditional expectation. Hence, if the discount rate is not constant and varies over business cycles, discounted returns should not be forecastable. Hansen and Richard (1987), Hansen and Jagannathan (1991, 1997), Bekaert and Hodrick (1992) and Balduzzi and Kallal (1998) show how to construct a single discount rate that prices various assets simultaneously. Therefore interest-rate-based tests of discount rates (Campbell and Shiller (1988a)) can always be generalized until the test fails to reject. Thus interest-rate-based discount rates show that expected returns vary in cross-section, because expected returns on some other asset change over time. The capital markets literature confirms that excess returns are forecastable, due to time variation in risk premia induced by the time variation in real investment opportunities.

Since (1) can be iterated forward, we obtain a simple present value model that generalizes the Euler equation with time-varying discount rates. Implicitly the generalization imposes a transversality condition that the second term in (2) is zero:

$$p_t = E_t\left[\sum_{j=1}^{\infty}\left(\prod_{k=1}^{j} m_{t-k}\right)d_{t+j}\right] + \lim_{T\to\infty}\left(\prod_{k=1}^{T} m_T\right)p_{t+T}, \tag{2}$$

where p_t is the assets price and d_t its dividend or arbitrary payoff. Since we do not have all the information agents use to forecast expected returns, we cannot test whether a given price change is consistent with the present value model. Instead we might check whether returns are consistent with the present value model on average, in two ways pioneered by LeRoy and Parke (1991). The variance-bounds tests exploit the fact that the variance of stock price movements must be lower than the variance of its conditional expectation, the present values:

$$\text{var}(p_t) \le \text{var}\left[\sum_{j=1}^{\infty}\left(\prod_{k=1}^{j} m_{t-k}\right)d_{t+j}\right]. \tag{3}$$

Orthogonality tests can also be used to examine volatility:

$$E_t(z_t p_t) = E_t\left[z_t\left(\sum_{j=1}^{\infty}\left(\prod_{k=1}^{j} m_{t-k}\right)d_{t+j}\right)\right], \tag{4}$$

where z_t is an instrumental variable. With $z_t = (p_t - E(p_t))$, equation (4) implies that prices should only vary in response to changes in future dividends:

$$\text{var}(p_t) = \text{cov}\left[p_t, \sum_{j=1}^{\infty}\left(\prod_{k=1}^{j} m_{t-k}\right)d_{t+j}\right]. \tag{5}$$

However, prices and dividends are not stationary. In nonstationary populations there is essentially no relation between the population and the corresponding sample moments, since finite sample moments cannot be expected to satisfy time-varying or infinite population moments (Mash and Merton (1986)). Thus violations of sample based variance bounds are no evidence against present value models, because the population counterpart might be satisfied at every date. This point caused many researchers to examine ways of writing (2) in terms of stationary variables. Most authors obtain stationary variables by dividing (2) by dividends to receive a present value relation between inverse dividend yields and dividend-growth rates η_t:

$$\frac{p_t}{d_t} = E_t\left[\sum_{j=1}^{\infty}\left(\prod_{k=1}^{j} r_{t+k}^{-1}\eta_{t+k}\right)\right]. \tag{6}$$

Shiller's (1981) assumption of trend-stationarity has been controversial, since many papers suggest that major macroeconomic time series have a unit root. Kleidon (1986) argued that excess volatility reflects nothing else than nonstationarity of dividends since dividend shocks have a permanent component if dividends have a unit root. This view was challenged by West (1988). West showed that an unit root in dividends implies cointegration of dividends and stock prices.

Thus the present value relation (2) is derived from iterated Euler equations and a transversality condition. Therefore volatility tests only test the Euler equation, i. e. whether discounted returns are forecastable or not. The following example is adapted from Cochrane (1991). Linearizing (6) by taking Taylor expansions around the unconditional means on the term inside the expectation with respect to $\hat{r}_t$ and $\hat{\eta}_t$, we have:

$$\text{var}\left(\frac{p}{d}\right) \cong \frac{1}{1-\Omega}\sum_{j=1}^{\infty}\Omega^j \text{cov}\left(\frac{p_t}{d_t},\hat{\eta}_{t+j}\right) - \frac{1}{1-\Omega}\sum_{j=1}^{\infty}\Omega^j \text{cov}\left(\frac{p_t}{d_t},\hat{r}_{t+j}\right), \tag{7}$$

where Ω is a constant slightly less than one, $\hat{\eta}_t = \ln(d_t/d_{t-1})$, $\hat{r}_t = \ln(r_t)$ and $\Omega^j = \exp[E(\hat{\eta}_t) - E(\hat{r}_t)]$. The volatility test rejection documents that if dividend-price-ratio forecasts of dividend growth are not sufficient to explain the variance of dividend-price-ratios, then dividend-price-ratio forecasts of returns have to fill in the gap. Since the covariance between the dividend-price-ratio and the returns is the numerator of the slope coefficient in return-forecasting regressions, volatility tests and return-forecasting regressions provide the same evidence and are only tests of discount-rate processes and thus of Euler equations.

2.2 The stochastic discount factor

Ross (1978), Harrison and Kreps (1979), Chamberlain and Rothschild (1983), Hansen and Richard (1987), Duffie (1992) and Clark (1993), among others, have shown that under certain arbitrage-free conditions, the valuation functional, mapping uncertain payoffs into prices, can be presented as a linear functional on a space of random payoffs. This payoff space has to have an arbitrary topological vector lattice (Mas-Colell (1986), Zame (1987)) for evaluating contingent claims (Clark (1993)), but Hilbert Space is especially common in financial research. The payoff space X is a subset of the contingent claim space R^s, spanned by s states. In complete markets we have $X = R^s$, otherwise $X \subset R^s$. We assume that there are no short sales restrictions, market frictions, transaction costs and no trivial payoffs in X. That means investors can form any portfolio of traded assets: a, b $\in X \Rightarrow w_a a + w_b b \in X$, where a, b are portfolios and w_i's are weights in the linear combination. Thus the payoff space is spanned by all traded contingent claim payoffs $X = \{c^T x\}$, where c is an arbitrary portfolio. The law of one price implies that each payoff in X has a unique price. This does not mean that the discount factor must be unique, since all $m_t + \varepsilon_t$ with $E(m_t\varepsilon_t) = 0$ satisfy (1).

Given the above assumptions there must exist a unique payoff $x^* \in X$ such that:

$$p(x) = E_t(x^*x).$$ (8)

Then the payoff x^* is the projection of the stochastic discount factor on the payoff space. Therefore any discount factor satisfying (1) might be expressed as a portfolio b or even as a linear functional on a space of random payoffs since X is linear by construction. Thus we have (8) with: $p = E_t(xx^Tb)$ and $b = E(xx^T)^{-1}p$. Hansen, Heaton and Luttmer (1995) suggest that b is unique if $E_t(xx^T)$ is nonsingular. Thus the projection of the stochastic discount factor on X is: $x^* = p^TE_t(xx)^{-1}x$. From the law of iterated expectations (Burnside (1994)) we have: $x^* = p^TE(xx)^{-1}x$ satisfying $p(x) = E(x^*x)$.

The arbitrage-free condition implies further that prices must be linear and the stochastic discount factor must be positive, where the latter comes from the separating hyperplane theorem (Duffie (1992)). Let $L^- = \{-pa, ax; a \in X\}$ be a linear subspace of $L = \{-pa, ax; a \in R^s\}$. It is straightfortward that $L^+ = \{pa, ax; a \in R^s, a,p,x \geq 0\}$ and L^- are convex sets that intersect at point zero. Then there must exist a linear function $F: L^+ \to R$ such that $F(l) < F(x)$ for all l in L^- and x in L^+. Because L^- is by definition a linear space $F(l)$ must be zero for all $l \in L^-$ and $F(x)$ is strictly positive for all $x \in L^+$ except the origin. Using the Rietz representation theorem we can decompose F as an inner product with some vector m: $F(-p,x) = -p + E(mx)$. Hence, $F(-p,x)$ must be positive for $-p,x > 0$ and the stochastic discount factor m must be positive (original proof: Ross (1978)). Since the separating hyperplane theorem also confirms that the pricing functional is defined over R^s, we can extend the pricing function defined over X to all possible payoffs in R^s without inducing any arbitrage opportunities on this larger space of payoffs (also Clark (1993)).

2.3   Hansen-Jagannathan bounds

From the above analysis it is clear that a stochastic discount factor always exist that prices a number of assets simultaneously. Thus the present value model always corresponds to a stochastic discount factor. Therefore discounted returns should not be forecastable, unless we do not catch all the variation of real investment opportunities. Hence, returns are payoffs with price one, such that the above derived results also holds for returns. Since the stochastic discount factor can be projected on the payoff space and thus be expressed as a portfolio, the pricing implications of that portfolio are then the same as those of any model of the stochastic discount factor for the same set of payoffs. One further important point is, that under this assumption all mimicking portfolios for approximating risk factors in multifactor models also have to lie in the same payoff space. This will be considered later in our analysis.

If the set of stochastic discount factors is not empty, which is emphasized by the Rietz representation theorem, then we might be able to distinguish different stochastic discount factors by their first and second unconditional moments. Since all $m + \varepsilon$ with $E(m\varepsilon) = 0$ and $E(\varepsilon) = 0$ satisfy (1), the variance of all possible stochastic discount factors (given the same mean) is the sum of the variance of the stochastic discount factor without added orthogonal random variables and the variance of the orthogonal random variables. Thus a lower bound on the variance of the stochastic discount factors must necessarily exist for arbitrary means.

In this context Hansen and Jagannathan (1991) run a regression of the stochastic discount factor on the asset returns in question:

$$m^{*}_{t+j}(\overline{m}) = \overline{m} + \left[\mathbf{r}_{t+j} - E(\mathbf{r}_{t+j}) \right]^{T} \beta_{\overline{m}} + \varepsilon ,$$ (9)

where $\overline{m}$ is the unconditional mean of the stochastic discount factor and β is the vector of portfolio weights. From (9) it follows that:

$$1 = \overline{m} E_{t}\left(1 + \mathbf{r}_{i,t+j}\right) + \Omega \beta_{\overline{m}} ,$$ (10)

where Ω is the nonsingular variance-covariance-matrix of asset returns. Solving (10) we have:

$$\beta_{\overline{m}} = \Omega^{-1}\left[1 - \overline{m} E_{t}\left(1 + \mathbf{r}_{i,t+j}\right) \right] .$$ (11)

Hence, regression residuals are uncorrelated with the other terms in (9), such that by construction:

$$\mathrm{var}(m) = \mathrm{var}\left[\left(\mathbf{r}_{t+j} - E(\mathbf{r}_{t+j}) \right)^{T} \beta_{\overline{m}} \right] + \mathrm{var}(\varepsilon) .^{1}$$ (12)

Since the added random variables are orthogonal to the stochastic discount factors we have also by construction for arbitrary discount factors $m_{t+j}(\overline{m}) = m^{*}_{t+j}(\overline{m}) + \varepsilon$ satisfying (1):

---

[1] Indeed from (14) it is follows already that: $\mathrm{var}\left[m_{t,j}(\overline{m}) \right] > \left[1 - \left(\mathbf{r}_{t,j} - E(\mathbf{r}_{t,j}) \right) \right] \Omega^{-1}\left[1 - \left(\mathbf{r}_{t,j} - E(\mathbf{r}_{t,j}) \right) \right] .$

$$0 = E_t\left[\mathbf{r}_{i,t+j}\left(m_{t+j}(\overline{m}) - m^*_{t+j}(\overline{m})\right)\right] = \mathrm{cov}\left[\mathbf{r}_{i,t+j}, m_{t+j}(\overline{m}) - m^*_{t+j}(\overline{m})\right]. \tag{13}$$

Finally we have by construction:

$$0 = \mathrm{cov}\left[m^*_{t+j}(\overline{m}), m_{t+j}(\overline{m}) - m^*_{t+j}(\overline{m})\right]$$

$$0 = \mathrm{var}\left[m^*_{t+j}(\overline{m})\right] + Var\left[m_{t+j}(\overline{m}) - m^*_{t+j}(\overline{m})\right] - Var\left[m_{t+j}(\overline{m})\right]$$

and the variance for an arbitrary stochastic discount factor that prices all asset in question simultaneously must equal:

$$Var\left[m_{t+j}(\overline{m})\right] = Var\left[m^*_{t+j}(\overline{m})\right] + Var\left[m_{t+j}(\overline{m}) - m^*_{t+j}(\overline{m})\right]. \tag{14}$$

Since arbitrarily stochastic discount factors given the same unconditional mean might only be distinguished by the variance of the orthogonal random variables ε we can infer the variance bounds by neglecting the ε's variance:

$$Var\left[m_{t+j}(\overline{m})\right] \geq Var\left[m^*_{t+j}(\overline{m})\right].$$

Campbell, Lo and MacKinlay give a nice overview over Hansen-Jagannathan bounds. The major argument against these variance bounds is also clear. Even if we reject an arbitrary asset pricing model we might add some orthogonal noise and the model fails to reject. Since this is not the objective of this paper we do not discuss this issue here. Hansen and Jagannathan (1997) modify their variance bounds and Balduzzi and Kallal (1998) suggest even sharper variance bounds.

2.4   Duality between Hansen-Jagannathan bounds and the Sharpe-ratio

From the above analysis it is obvious that the variance bounds are determined by its unconditional means and the unconditional mean and volatility of an asset's returns. At this point it is clear that some connection must exist between the efficient set and the Hansen-Jagannathan bounds. We can restate these results in a more familiar way by decomposing (1):

$$1 = E(m_{t+j})E(r_{t+j}) + \sigma_m \sigma_r \rho_{m,r}, \tag{15}$$

where ρ represents the correlation coefficient. Thus expected returns are determined by discounting the uncertain future payoffs and correcting for risk with the right-hand side covariance term:

$$E\big(r_{t+j}\big) = \big(1 - \sigma_r \sigma_m \rho_{m,r}\big) E\big(m_{t+j}\big)^{-1}. \tag{16}$$

Because of the arbitrage-free condition the first right-hand side term in (16) divided by the $E(m_{t+j})$ must equal the riskless rate of return. If we have only one single return, then this condition resembles the Sharpe-ratio:

$$\frac{E\big(r_{t+j}\big) - r_f}{\sigma_r} = \left| \frac{\sigma_m}{E(m)} \rho_{r,m} \right|, \tag{17}$$

where r_f is the riskless rate of return.[2] Correlation coefficients cannot be greater than one in magnitude and because of the arbitrage-free assumption discount factors must be positive, so all assets must obey:

$$\frac{E\big(r_{t+j}\big) - r_f}{\sigma_r} \le \frac{\sigma_m}{E(m)}. \tag{18}$$

This suggests an easy way to find a Hansen-Jagannathan bound with a number of assets for an arbitrary riskless rate of return: simply calculate the highest Sharpe-ratio. By definition this is the tangency portfolio, given the efficient set. This highlights the equivalence between the Hansen-Jagannathan bounds and the Sharpe-ratio or the duality between the bounds and the mean-variance frontiers. Breeden, Gibbons and Litzenberger (1989) exploit this fact by building a maximum correlation portfolio, that by definition has greater correlation to the stochastic discount factor than any other portfolio and thus necessarily must be mean-variance efficient.

By varying the unconditional mean of the stochastic discount factor we trace out the feasible region for discount factors satisfying the present value model. The challenge for asset pricing models is that high Sharpe-ratios require the stochastic discount factor to be highly variable. Therefore consumption based asset pricing models are usually rejected for acceptable levels of risk aversion, e. g. the equity risk premium puzzle by Mehra and Prescott (1985), which was also confirmed for the German equity market (Meier (1997)).

2.5 Real investment opportunities and Hansen-Jagannathan bounds

If moments of asset returns other than the variance are bounded, restrictions on the stochastic discount factor can be generated as a function of asset's returns in question. Snow's (1992) suggestion that a "measure of m which lies in the mean-

---

[2] The analysis can easy be generalized without a riskless asset.

variance frontier may not lie in the mean-σ-norm frontier" could help to differentiate asset pricing models. Thus, if an asset contains information about the Hansen-
Jagannathan bound which is not embedded in other assets, its inclusion will increase the bound and hence the mean-variance frontier.

Hansen-Jagannathan bounds are by definition perfectly correlated with some
portfolio of asset returns. Most general equilibrium models also feature stock returns that are highly correlated with consumption growth. In the real economy
consumption growth is not highly correlated with returns. This might cause the
equity puzzle. However, consumption is measured with an error and consumption
flows from durable goods are difficult to impute. Therefore most empirical studies
neglect durables. Since the estimation of consumption βs, which by definition
should exactly describe real investment opportunities, poses serious problems, it is
possible that estimates of market βs or even other proxies for risk might be better
proxies for consumption βs than poorly estimated consumption βs (Fama (1991)).
Also Reisman (1992) and Nawalkha (1997) point out that in an arbitrage-free economy the use of arbitrary reference variables that are not the true factors but correlated with them also applies to asset pricing.

Thus our objective is to extend consumption based models to multifactor
models as supposed by Constantinides (1989). By using the default spread and per
head capita income growth as proxies for real investment opportunities we estimate
expected returns on some pre-built portfolios. To account for risk effects we use
market βs for portfolio formation. Once the positive excess returns are estimated we
add the portfolio returns to the data to recalculate the Hansen-Jagannathan bounds
and check whether the bounds or the mean-variance frontier expands. To ascertain
whether these factors are 'common' we add also the returns of some bond portfolios.
We use the 'Group Method of Data Handling' to calculate the bounds.

3.   Group Method of Data Handling (GMDH)

3.1   Why GMDH?

Conventional mathematical-statistical analysis usually prespecifies the structure of the decision space or the instruments of analysis. The definition of optimality criteria requires a knowledge of a priori probabilities. Density functions are also
described by a number of parameters. Implicitly the assumption is made that these
parameters remain untouched by the determinants of the estimation (Malone
(1984)). In empirical analyses researchers are often confronted with complex problems of unknown structure like the Hansen-Jagannathan bounds. Applying traditional statistical methods means possibly incompletely describing the decision space
and thus misspecifying the procedures. The results can then only be interpreted
conditionally. Several techniques have been developed to solve such problems. We

present one relevant GMDH algorithm in more detail here. GMDH algorithms currently present the most powerful self-organizing process available. They extract information from existing data using fairly complex but also flexible mathematical models.

Neural networks are common for financial research. Bansal and Viswannathan (1993) estimate nonlinear arbitrage pricing functionals with standard feed-forward networks. Steiner and Wittkemper (1993) estimate fundamental market βs using more sophisticated general regression neural networks. Steiner and Wittkemper (1996) also test the Coherent Market Hypothesis for the German stock market using probabilistic and general regression neural networks. Refenes (1996) highlights the advantage of neural networks for asset allocation purposes.

However, the self-organizing characteristics of GMDH sets its algorithms apart from neural networks. Both neural networks and GMDH do not need any functional relationship to be provided, but neural networks have to have the typology and the structure of the network predetermined before they can be applied. GMDH do not need any of this prespecified, as they determine even the optimal structure and the optimal model that best fits the data. They do need a predetermination of some optimality criteria they use to choose which models will be retained from one generation to the next. Another major advantage is that the GMDH algorithms we use always converge to a minimum bias model of optimal complexity. This is evident from proofs by Stepashko (1989a, 1989b) and Kocherga (1989). Since we look for an optimal discount factor that captures almost all the variation in expected returns, GMDH algorithms seem to be the optimal econometric method to calculate variance bounds. Finally, GMDH algorithms break with the 'black box' characteristics of neural networks since it is possible to print out the ultimate functional relationship a GMDH algorithm settles on.

3.2 Basic GMDH Properties

The GMDH algorithms, almost all developed by Ivakhnenko from 1968 on, allow a successive development of a system description. The basic idea originating from cybernetics is that simple mathematics can describe arbitrary systems. Excellent reviews of GMDH are available (Ivakhnenko and Ivakhnenko (1995), Müller (1995) and Müller and Ivakhnenko (1997)), so here we only briefly comment that of a great number of algorithms, for this analysis "Iterative Multilayered GMDH Algorithms" proved most useful.

Optimization is a three-step process (Farlow (1984)). In the first step all independent variables $(x_1, ..., x_n)$ are grouped pairwise $\{(x_1, x_2), (x_1, x_3), ..., (x_1, x_n), ..., (x_{n-1}, x_n)\}$. Using these variables $n(n-1)/2$ regression equations $y = A + Bx_i + Cx_j + Dx_ix_j$ are created. Then each regression term is verified out of sample $\{(x_{1i}, x_{1j}), (x_{2i}, x_{2j}), ..., (x_{mi}, x_{mj})\}$. The regressions that perform best are selected for further optimization using an optimality criterion. Then a second goodness criterion is applied to decide which of the best models are retained from one generation to the next. These tests are also out-of-sample. Except for the first generation, the second criterion is also used to decide whether to continue or to abort the optimization process. Once the best criterion of a successive generation is not better than the previous, the optimization process is aborted. Thus only the best new variables as determined using the out-of-sample tests are retained ('survival of the fittest').

Variables	parametric GMDH algorithms	non-parametric GMDH algorithms
continuous	<ul><li>Combinatory</li><li>Multilayered Iterative</li><li>Objective System Analysis</li><li>Harmonious</li><li>Two-Level</li><li>Multiplicative-Additive</li></ul>	<ul><li>Objective Computer Clusterization</li><li>Analogues Complexing</li></ul>
discrete	<ul><li>Harmonious Rediscretion</li></ul>	<ul><li>Algorithm based on Multilayered Theory of Statistical Decisions</li></ul>

Figure 1: Overview over the most popular GMDH algorithms (Ivakhnenko and Ivakhnenko (1995))

Each generation of models follows the three optimization steps. All surviving models from the previous generation are again grouped pairwise and applied to the same regression model as before to obtain a new set of models. From this set we choose again those models that best fits the data and finally decide whether to continue the optimization or not using again the two statistical optimality criteria. This is shown in Figure 3.

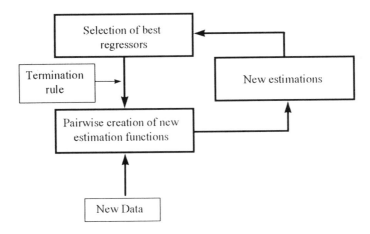

Figure 2: Iterative multilayered GMDH algorithm structure

38

The statistical criteria used to evaluate the regression models can be arbitrary statistical criteria. Among them information criteria like the Akaike-criterion are effective. We use the information based PSE-criterion (Barron (1984)) as the second criterion. For the preselection we use a standard MSE-criterion.

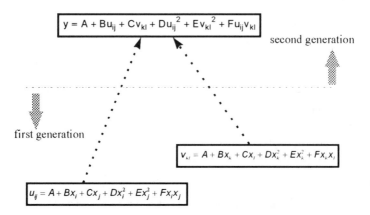

Figure 3: Variable generation with iterative multilayered GMDH algorithms

The final regression term consists of regressors that were created as a synthesis of various variables from earlier generations. These variables can be recursively expressed in terms of the original variables. The resulting term is called an Ivakhnenko polynomial (or Kolmogorov-Gabor polynomial).

$$ y = a + \sum_{i=1}^{n} b_i x_i + \sum_{i=1}^{n} \sum_{j=1}^{n} c_{ij} x_i x_j + \sum_{i=1}^{n} \sum_{j=1}^{n} \sum_{k=1}^{n} d_{ijk} x_i x_j x_k + \ldots . \tag{19} $$

4.   Empirical Results

4.1   Data

The data set used in estimation consisted of monthly observations over the time period 1965:1 to 1995:3. It was select in order to match recent studies on the German stock market, such as Wallmeier (1997). The assets used in our investigations were the returns on 239 German stocks from the "Karlsruher Kapitalmarktdatenbank". The calculation of the Hansen-Jagannathan bounds was based solely on these returns using the GMDH. For the investigation whether risk premia vary over time or not portfolios were formed based on size and beta. Annual statements were provided by the annual report database of the „Rheinisch-Westfälische Technische Hochschule in Aachen". Therefore the database is identical to that used in Steiner, Schneider and Wolf (1998). In addition bond returns, aggregate income figures and the default spread were taken from the "Monatsberichte" of the Bundesbank.

4.2   Time-varying risk premia?

From the above analysis it is clear that only consumption based asset pricing models might describe the real investment opportunities. Variations in real investment opportunities are by construction covered by the intertemporal marginal rate of substitution for a representative investor. However, as already pointed out, consumption is measured with an error and Mankiw and Zeldes (1991) suggest that the representative investor doesn't exist, since consumption of stockholders and nonstockholders differ. Thus we use an arbitrarily chosen multifactor model of asset returns.

Our basic objective here is to ask whether asset prices vary over business cycles. Nowak (1995) suggests that interest rate variables are most useful to predict future business conditions. Therefore we use the default spread between AAA German government 'Bunds' and bonds issued by private held companies as a proxy for variation in real investment opportunities. As a second variable we simply use the market beta. If the market βs are correlated with consumption βs they might be better proxies for consumption risk than poorly estimated consumption βs. Diaz-Gimenez, Prescott, Fitzgerald and Alvarez (1992) report for the US equity market that stock returns account for less than three percent of total monthly income from all sources. Historically the German equity market is much less important than US equity market. Thus we add the variation in total personal income as a third proxy for risk. Finally we obtain a three factor model of ex-post asset returns:

$$r_{portfolio} - r_f = a_0 + a_1 f_1 + a_2 f_2 + a_3 f_3, \tag{20}$$

where a_0 is a constant, f_1 is the return on a diversified stock market index, (we use the DAFOX index), f_2 is the default spread and f_3 the variation in total income. We form 36 equally-weighted stock portfolios sorted by market beta and size. Since our objective is to test whether these factors are common we add the returns from six bond portfolios grouped by maturity ($N = 2$ to 7 years). Using Hansen's generalized method of moments we find significant coefficients for the market β and the default spread, indicating that there is some variation in expected returns due to variation in real investment opportunities. There is also some evidence against our model. Since we use excess returns over the riskless rate of return, the absolute coefficient in our regression should be zero. Indeed it is significantly not. However all the three coefficients are significant at a 10% level. Only our fourth variable, total income variation, has no marginal explanatory power. This might be due to the measurement with error and even to the historically small role of stock-holders relative to consumers in Germany. However, the results indicate that the default spread is a common factor to both bonds and stocks indicating variations in real investment opportunities.

Variable	coefficient	standard error	t-value	p-value
a0	-0.230550	0.105538	-2.184525	0.030
a1	9.638844	2.855087	3.376025	0.001
a2	103.883485	54.040339	1.922332	0.056
a3	-1.843120	5.521569	-0.333804	0.739
Minimum Distance	0.3904			
Standard error of the test	0.1821			
Mean of LHS. Var.	-0.0007			
Std. dev. of LHS Var.	0.0629			

Figure 4: Regression of asset returns against the three factor model using GMM

4.3 Hansen-Jagannathan bounds

Since we have found some evidence for time varying expected returns due to fundamental economic variables we test whether we can use the variation in expected returns to built a successful trading system. This is equivalent to the question if our multiple-asset, return-based stochastic discount factor prices the returns on some, here equally-weighted, portfolios. If the discount factor does not our present value model leaves residuals and the trading system has to forecast returns by construction (Samuelson (1965)).

In order to examine whether the restrictions on the stochastic discount factor implied by some equally weighted portfolios differ significantly from the restrictions imposed by individual stock returns, the Hansen-Jagannathan bounds are calculated for different data sets. Thus the generation of the different bounds permits us to determine whether an estimate of the stochastic discount factor lies within the region generated by either one or another bound. If one candidate for the stochastic discount factor does not lie within both calculated bounds, then the possibility exists that a particular present value model might correctly price some assets and not others. Similar to Snow (1992), in order to take sample errors into account, tests were conducted to determine whether equally weighted portfolio returns imply restrictions on the stochastic discount factor beyond the restrictions implied by individual stock returns.

Since we want to extend the Hansen-Jagannathan bound tests to check whether we can forecast returns, we exploit the duality between the bounds and the Sharpe-ratio. If the equally weighted portfolio returns impose sharper restrictions on the bounds, then an expansion of the mean-variance frontier is possible. That is expressed either by stating how much the addition of portfolio returns raises the

Hansen-Jagannathan bound or by calculating how those assets expand the mean-variance frontier (see also: Knez and Chen (1996)).

Since such a variety of portfolios like in the previous chapter would not be suitable for asset allocation purposes in the real world, we use only eight pre-built beta and the bond portfolios for trading decisions. Since all the assets contained in the beta portfolios are also contained in the individual stock data set, a rejection of the stochastic discount factor using additional beta portfolios for the Hansen-Jagannathan bound calculation also implies the misspecification of the payoff space. Indeed if the portfolio formation properties are violated, the payoff space must be nonlinear compared to theoretical suggestions of a linear payoff space.

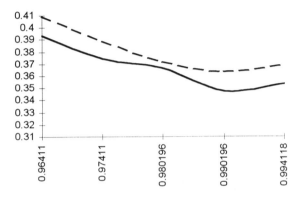

Figure 5: Approximate Hansen-Jagannathan bounds (x axis: mean of the stochastic discount factor; y axis: standard deviation of the stochastic discount factor, solid line: bounds estimated without portfolio returns, not drawed through graph: bounds estimated with additional portfolio returns)

Figure 5 shows the calculated Hansen-Jagannathan bounds. Since we use a large number of assets, the bound is an approximate bound.[3] Thus we do not find the typical parabola form. If we add the portfolio returns, the bound shifts upwards. This implies that the additional beta portfolios impose sharper restrictions on the Hansen-Jagannathan bounds than individual stock returns and a nonlinear payoff space. Thus the estimation for the stochastic discount factor does not lie inside both bounds. Therefore expansions of the mean-variance frontier by adding the portfolio returns seem to be plausible. Our simple trading system always invests in portfolios that, by Hansen-Jagannathan bound calculations, expand the mean-variance frontier, if we also forecast some positive excess returns. Encouraged by the evidence for time varying risk premia we use the above multifactor model to forecast returns on the beta and bond portfolios. The portfolio weights in the selected portfolios. i. e.

---

[3] Indeed the GMDH is adaptable to finding bounds on fancier moments or even with market frictions. It also shows how to construct a stochastic process for the discount factor. Thus we pick an arbitrary variable m and since the mean is held fixed, we minimize the variance or any other second moment.

42

the portfolios where positive excess returns were forecasted, are set to maximize the correlation between the active managed portfolio and the projected stochastic discount factor portfolio to obtain a maximum correlation portfolio that corresponds to the new Sharpe-ratio. Since we then expect to be on a lifted mean-variance frontier, we expect to beat the passive buy-hold-portfolio by construction.

Indeed our trading system leads to significant excess returns over the passive DAFOX-portfolio implying that these portfolio returns expand the mean-variance frontier. Since the portfolios are diversified there is no unsystematic risk effect.

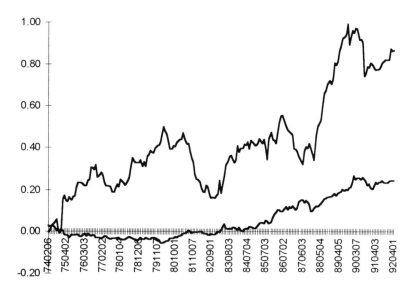

Figure 6: Excess returns over the DAFOX (the dark line represents the aggregated excess returns where the thin line represents the accumulated returns of the buy-and-hold portfolio)

The accumulated excess returns from 1974:2 to 1992:03 were 86.79 percent.[4] Since the variances of the returns differ significantly, we also confirm that the means of the active and buy-hold returns differ significantly on a monthly basis. These results obviously correspond to the above hypothesis. Since the estimated stochastic discount factor that prices individual assets fails to price some equally weighted portfolios, the present value model leaves some residuals. These residuals can be explained by the default spread using a multifactor asset pricing model, so the residuals might be induced by variations in real investment opportunities and thus in risk premia. Therefore we argue that the variation in expected returns is not caused by irrational bubbles but by fundamental macroeconomic variables. Since we are not able to measure consumption data without error this indicates that multi-

---

[4] One might also introduce some filter variables to avoid high transaction costs. With this filter, optimized by the GMDH, we get an accumulated excess return on 127% for the same time period.

factor asset pricing models as extensions of consumption based models are better models of consumption-investment behavior than poorly estimated consumption models. Also other variables related to business conditions seem to be better proxies for the intertemporal marginal rate of consumption than the latter poorly estimated.

	active returns	passive returns
mean	0.00413269	0.0011636
variance	0.00106233	0.000079055
degrees of freedom	240	240
test for identical variances (2 sided F)		
F	13.4378158	
P(F≤f)	9.8666E-64	
critical F value	1.2561765	
test for identical means with different variances (2 sided t)		
t	1.27355465	
P(T≤t)	0.10202667	
critical t value	1.65122856	
P(T≤t) (two side)	0.20405334	
critical t value (two side)	1.96989731	
test for a hypothetical difference of 0.03 in means (2 sided t)		
t	11.594549	
P(T≤t)	2.8185E-25	
critical t value	1.65122856	
P(T≤t) (two side)	5.637E-25	
critical t value (two side)	1.96989731	

Figure 7: Test statistics for differences in means of trading strategy returns

5.   Summary

Since the moments of asset returns may contain information about the sto-chastic discount factor that correspond to a present value model with time-variable discount rate and expected returns, this paper uses Hansen-Jagannathan bounds to estimate valid stochastic discount factors under certain conditions. Thus we differ-entiate stochastic discount factors estimated on individual asset returns and sto-chastic discount factors using portfolio returns.

The bounds were created using data sets on stock and bond returns for the 1965 - 1995 period. We find that different classes of returns impose different re-strictions on the bounds and also on the mean-variance frontier. In order to test if the mean-variance frontier is expanded by the portfolio returns, we create a simple trading system by buying portfolios that lift the Hansen-Jagannathan bound upward. By proceeding in this fashion we find significant excess returns on this trading strategy implying that these portfolio returns do expand the mean-variance frontier.

Thus the underlying present value model leaves residuals, since discounted returns are forecastable. A multifactor asset pricing model relates the variation of expected returns to a proxy for future business conditions. We suggest that variations in real investment opportunities cause the variation in expected returns. Since we cannot measure real investment opportunities or related variables without error, multifactor models might better approximate consumption influence on asset pricing.

For the parallel time-series and cross-sectional analysis we exploit the properties of Ivakhnenko's 'Group Method of Data Handling'. This econometric method with excellent small sample and minimum bias properties performs well in our analysis.

6   Acknowledgements

This study was presented at the "Computational Finance 1997" conference at London under the title 'Time Varying Risk Premia under an Asset Allocation Perspective - A GMDH Analysis'. We thank J. Benedict Wolf, an anonymous referee and the participants in the "Computational Finance 1997" conference for useful comments on the paper.

The original presentation was based on the conditional CAPM instead of generalized multifactor models. Since multifactor models can be interpreted as extensions of consumption based asset pricing models we use a multifactor model instead of the more restrictive conditional CAPM.

7   References

Balduzzi P., Kallal H., Risk premia and variance bounds. Journal of Finance 1998; 54: forthcoming.

Bansal R., Viswanathan S., No arbitrage and arbitrage pricing: A new approach. Journal of Finance 1993; 48: 1231-62.

Barron, A. R. „Predicted squared error: A criterion for automatic model selection. In *Self-Organizing Methods in Modeling - GMDH Type Algorithms*. Farlow J., ed. New York: Marcel Dekker, 1984.

Bekaert G., Hodrick R. J., Characterizing predictable components in excess returns on equity and foreign exchange markets. Journal of Finance 1992; 47: 467 - 510.

Bodie Z., Common stocks as a hedge against inflation. Journal of Finance 1976; 31: 459-70.

Breeden D. T., An intertemporal asset pricing model with stochastic consumption and investment opportunities. Journal of Financial Economics 1979; 7: 265-96.

Breeden D., Gibbons M., Litzenberger R., Empirical tests of the consumption-oriented CAPM. Journal of Finance 1989, 44: 231-62.

Burnside, C., Hansen-Jagannathan bounds as classical tests of asset pricing models.

Journal of Business and Economic Statistics 1994, 12: 57-79.

Campbell J. Y., Shiller R. J., Stock prices, earnings, and expected dividends. Journal of Finance 1988b; 43: 661-75.

Campbell J. Y., Shiller R. J., The dividend-price ratio and expectations of future dividends and discount factors. Review of Financial Studies 1988a; 1: 195-228.

Campbell J. Y., Stock returns and the term structure. Journal of Financial Economics 1987; 18: 373-99.

Campbell, J. Y., Lo, A. W., MacKinlay, A. C. *The Econometrics of Financial Markets*, Princeton: Princeton University Press, 1997.

Chamberlain G., Rothschild M., Arbitrage, factor structure, and mean-variance-analysis of large asset markets. Econometrica 1983; 51: 1281-1304.

Clark A., The valuation problem in arbitrage pricing theory. Journal of Mathematical Economics 1993; 22: 463-78.

Cochrane J. H., Explaining the variance of price-dividend ratios. Review of Financial Studies 1992; 5: 243-80.

Cochrane J. H., Volatility tests and efficient markets. Journal of Monetary Economics 1991; 21: 463-85.

Constantinides G. M. „Theory of Valuation: Overview and Recent Developments", In: *Theory of Valuation*, Bhattacharya S., Constantinides G. M., ed. Totowa, NJ: Rowman & Littlefield Publishers, 1989.

Diaz-Gimenez J., Prescott E. C., Fitzgerald T., Alvarez F., Banking in computable general equilibrium models. Journal of Economic Dynamics and Control 1992; 16: 533-59.

Duffie, D. *Dynamic Asset Pricing Theory*, Princeton: Princeton University Press, 1992.

Fama E. F., Efficient capital markets: II. Journal of Finance 1991, 46: 1575-1617.

Fama E. F., French K. R., Business conditions and expected returns on stocks and bonds. Journal of Financial Economics 1989; 25: 23-49.

Fama E. F., French K. R., Dividend yields and expected stock returns. Journal of Financial Economics 1988a; 19: 3-29.

Fama E. F., French K. R., Permanent and temporary components of stock prices. Journal of Political Economy 1988b; 96: 246-73.

Fama E. F., Schwert G. W., Asset returns and inflation. Journal of Financial Economics 1977; 5: 115-46.

Fama E. F., Stock returns, real activity, inflation and money. American Economic Review 1981; 71: 545-65.

Fama E. F., The behavior of stock market prices. Journal of Business 1965; 38: 34-105.

Farlow, J. „The GMDH Algorithm", In *Self-Organizing Methods in Modeling - GMDH Type Algorithms*, Farlow J., ed. New York: Marcel Dekker, 1984.

Fisher, I. *The Theory of Interest*, New York, 1965.

Grossman J., On the efficiency of the stock market when traders have diverse information. Journal of Finance 1976; 31: 573-85.

Grossman J., Shiller R. J., The determinants of the variability of stock market prices. American Economic Review - Papers & Proceedings 1981; 71: 222-27.

Habib M., Naik N., Models of information aggregation in financial markets. Applied Mathematical Finance 1996; 3: 159-66.

Hansen L. P., Jagannathan R., Asessing specification errors in stochastic discount factor models. Journal of Finance 1997; 52: 557-90.

Hansen L. P., Jagannathan R., Implications of security market data for models of dynamic economics. Journal of Political Economy 1991; 99: 225-62.

Hansen L. P., Large sample properties of generalized method of moments estimators. Econometrica 1982; 50: 1029-54.

Hansen L. P., Richard F., The role of conditioning information in deducing testable restrictions implied by dynamic asset pricing models. Econometrica 1987; 55: 587-613.

Hansen L. P., Singleton K. J., Generalized instrumental variables estimation of nonlinear expectations models. Econometrica 1982; 50: 1269-86.

Harrison J. M., Kreps D. M., Martingales and arbitrage in multiperiod securities markets. Journal of Economic Theory 1979; 20: 381-408

Hellwig M., On the aggregation of information in competitive markets. Journal of Economic Theory 1980; 26: 279-312.

Ivakhnenko A. G., Ivakhnenko G. A., The review of problems solvable by algorithms of the Group Method of Data Handling (GMDH). Pattern Recognition and Image Analysis 1995; 5: 527-35.

Ivakhnenko A. G., The Group Method of Data Handling - A rival of the method of stochastic approximation. Avtomatika 1968; 3: 57-73.

Keim D. B., Stambaugh R. F., Predicting returns in the stock and bond markets. Journal of Financial Economics 1986; 17: 357-90.

Kirby C., Measuring the predictable variation in stock and bond returns. Review of Financial Studies 1997; 10: 579-630.

Kleidon A. W., Variance bounds tests and stock price valuation models. Journal of Political Economy 1986; 94: 953-1001.

Knez P. J., Chen Z., Portfolio performance measurement: Theory and applications. Review of Financial Studies 1996; 9: 511-55.

Kocherga Y. L., J-optimal reduction of a model structure in a Gauss-Markov schema. Soviet Journal of Automation and Information Sciences 1989; 21: 31-35.

LeRoy F. „Stock price volatility", In: Handbook of Statistics 14, Statistical Methods in Finance, Maddala G., Rao C. R., ed, Amsterdam: North Holland, 1996.

LeRoy F., Parke W. R., Stock price volatility: Tests based on the geometric random qalk. American Economic Review 1992; 82: 981-92.

Lo A. W., MacKinlay A. C., Stock market prices do not follow random walks: Evidence from a simple specification test. Review of Financial Studies 1988; 1: 41-66

Lucas R. E. Jr., Asset prices in an exchange economy. Econometrica 1978; 46: 1429-45.

Malone II J. M. „Regression without models: Directions in the search for structure",

In *Self-Organizing Methods in Modeling - GMDH Type Algorithms*, Farlow J., ed. New York: Marcel Dekker, 1984.

Mankiw N. G., Sharpio M., Risk and return: Consumption beta versus market beta. Review of Economics and Statistics 1986; 48: 452-9.

Mankiw N. G., Zeldes P., The consumption of stockholders and non-stockholders. Journal of Financial Economics 1991; 29: 97-112.

Mas-Collel A., The price equilibrium existence problem in topological vector lattices. Econometrica 1986; 54: 1039-53.

Mash T. A., Merton R. C., Dividend variability and variance bounds tests for the rationality of stock market prices. American Economic Review 1986; 76: 483-98.

Mehra R., Prescott E., The equity risk premium: A puzzle. Journal of Monetary Economics 1985; 10: 335-59.

Meyer B: Variance bounds for pricing kernels in intertemporal asset pricing models: The German case. Geld, Banken, Versicherungen 1997.

Müller J.-A., „Self-organization of models - Present state", In *Proceedings of EUROSIM'95 Conference Vienna*, 1995.

Müller J.-A., Ivakhnenko G. A., Recent developments of self-organizing modeling in prediction and analysis of stock market. Working Paper, HTW Dresden, 1997.

Nawalkha K., A multibeta representation theorem for linear asset pricing theories. Journal of Financial Economics 1997; 46: 357-81.

Nelson C. R., Inflation and rates of returns on common stocks. Journal of Finance 1976; 31: 471-83.

Nowak, T. *Faktormodelle in der Kapitalmarkttheorie*, Cologne: Bottermann 1994.

Poterba J., Summers L., Mean reversion in stock prices: Evidence and implications. Journal of Financial Economics 1988; 22: 27-59.

Refenes, A. N., Neural model identification, variable selection and model adequacy. In *Proceedings of the 6th Karslruhe Econometrics Workshop*, Heidelberg: Physica 1998.

Reisman H., Reference variables, factor structure, and the approximate multibeta representation. Journal of Finance 1992; 47: 1303-14.

Ross A., A simple approach to the valuation of risky streams. Journal of Business 1978; 51: 453-75.

Samuelson P. A., Proof that properly anticipated prices fluctuate randomly. Industrial Management Review 1965; 6: 41-9.

Shiller R. J., Do stock prices move too much to be justified by subsequent changes in dividends?. American Economic Review 1981; 71: 421-36.

Shiller R. J., Stock prices and social dynamics. Brookings Papers on Economic Activity 1984; 2: 457-510.

Shiller R. J., The volatility of long-term interest rates and expectations models of the term structure. Journal of Political Economy 1979; 87: 1190-219.

Snow K. N., Diagnosing asset pricing models using the distribution of asset returns. Journal of Finance 1991; 46: 955-83.

Stambaugh R. F., Discussion. Journal of Finance 1986; 41: 601-2.

48

Steiner M., Wittkemper H.-G., Aktienrendite-Schätzungen mit Hilfe künstlicher neuronaler Netze. Finanzmarkt und Portfolio-Management 1993; 7: 443-458.

Steiner M., Wittkemper H.-G., Portfolio optimization with a neural network implementation of the Coherent Market Hypothesis. European Journal of Operational Research 1997; 27-40.

Steiner, M., Schneider, S., Wolf, J. B. „An analysis of the financing behavior of German stock corporations using artificial neural networks". In *Proceedings of the 6th Karslruhe Econometrics Workshop*, Heidelberg: Physica, 1998.

Stepashko V., Asymptotic properties of external criteria for model selection. Soviet Journal of Automation and Information Sciences 1989b; 21: 84-92.

Stepashko V., GMDH algorithms as basis of modeling process automation after experimental data. Soviet Journal of Automation and Information Sciences 1989a; 21: 43-53.

Summers L. H., Does the stock market rationally reflect fundamental values?. Journal of Finance 1986; 41: 591-601.

Wallmeier, M. *Prognose von Aktienrenditen und -risiken mit Mehrfaktorenmodellen*, Bad Soden: Uhlenbruch, 1997.

West K., Bubbles, fads and stock price volatility: A partial evaluation. Journal of Finance 1988; 43: 636-56.

Zame W. R., Competitive equilibria in production economics with an infinite dimensional commodity space. Econometrica 1987; 55: 1075-1108.

A DATA MATRIX TO INVESTIGATE INDEPENDENCE, OVERREACTION AND/OR SHOCK PERSISTENCE IN FINANCIAL DATA.

R. DACCO'

Department of Applied Economics
University of Cambridge

S.E. SATCHELL

Trinity College
University of Cambridge

The question of dependence of returns has been investigated in many ways. This paper proposes a matrix that sheds some light on many of these dependencies. In particular, overreaction and shock persistence and delayed reaction seem to play important roles and could well explain the presence of nonlinearities in the return series.
Keywords: Market Over Reaction, Delayed Reaction, Henriksson-Merton Nonparametric Test, Pesaran-Timmermann Test.

1   Introduction

There are many theories as to how returns change from period to period and the question of dependence in returns has been investigated in a number of ways. These include the random walk model (Fama (1991), Fama and French (1989)) and the contrarian and the overreaction literature, (Summers and Summers (1989), Lo and MacKinlay (1990), Jegadeesh (1990) and Jegadeesh and Titman (1996)). An alternative literature suggests that correlations vary depending upon whether the market is volatile or not (Merton (1980), Pagan and Hong (1991), Glosten et al. (1993), Chou et al. (1992), Engle et al. (1982,1991), Bollerslev et al. (1992), Solnik et al. (1996)).

The aim of this paper is to present a robust data summary for daily data which can shed light on all these issues. We see this analysis as a useful preliminary exercise prior to the specification of a nonlinear model. It is similar in style to the ``compass rose'' analysis by Crach and Ledoit (1996). In the next section, a general hypothesis of independence can be tested. This is a generalization of tests proposed by Henriksson and Merton (1981) (H-M) and Pesaran and Timmermann (1992,1994) (P-T). Results and empirical investigations are carried out in section 3, where we shall analyze both index and security returns. Finally section 4 presents conclusions and directions for future research.

A.-P.N. Refenes et al. (eds.), Decision Technologies for Computational Finance, 49–60.
© 1998 *Kluwer Academic Publishers. Printed in the Netherlands..*

2   The H-M and P-T Tests

We first discuss techniques that are related to our procedure.

Henriksson and Merton (1981) developed a nonparametric statistical procedure to test for superior forecasting skills. They developed a framework for analyzing the statistical significance of the correlation between forecasts and actual values. Let y_t be the realized value and denote its forecast by x_t, then we can define the probabilities

$$p_{11} = \text{prob}(x_t < r , y_t < r) \qquad\qquad (1)$$
$$p_{12} = \text{prob}(x_t \geq r , y_t < r)$$
$$p_{21} = \text{prob}(x_t < r , y_t \geq r)$$
$$p_{22} = \text{prob}(x_t \geq r , y_t \geq r)$$

Henriksson and Merton (1981) proposed a nonparametric test of independence between two attributes assuming that the margins $n_{01} = \Sigma_{t=1}^{n} I(x_t < r)$, $n_{10} = \Sigma_{t=1}^{n} I(x_t < r)$ and $n_{20} = \Sigma_{t=1}^{n} I(y_t \geq r)$ are fixed, where I is an indicator variable that takes value 0 and 1. The nonparametric test of H-M is based on the conditional probabilities p_1, p_2 which in above notation are given by $p_1 = p_{11}/p_{10}$ where $p_{10} = p_{11} + p_{12}$ and $p_2 = p_{22}/p_{20}$ where $p_{20} = p_{22} + p_{21}$. The null hypothesis of independence between two attributes assuming that both margins are fixed is given by

H_0: $p_{11} / p_{10} = p_{21} / p_{20}$

which states that the probability distribution according to the first attribute is independent of the probability distribution according to the second attribute. Using the result that $p_{21}/p_{20} + p_{22}/p_{20} = 1$, the null hypothesis H_0 can also be rewritten as

H_0: $p_{11} / p_{10} + p_{22} / p_{20} = 1$

On the basis of the null H_0 H-M develop a nonparametric test for market timing. Analogously to the probabilities in (1), they consider sample data $n_{i,j}$ where n_{11}, for example, is the number of times, out of n periods, that $x_t < r$ and $y_t < r$. They show that under H_0, i.e. $p_1 + p_2 = 1$ a test can be based on an exact test whose large sample equivalent is

$$U = (n_{11} - n_{10}n_{01}/n) / \sqrt{ (\{n_{10}n_{01}n_{20}n_{02}\} / \{n^2(n-1)\}) } \sim N(0,1)$$

However, Pesaran and Timmermann (1992,1994) claim that the H-M test is difficult to interpret from an economic point of view. They note the fundamental equivalence between the H-M test and a 2×2 contingency table. They address the following point. If we are interested in the correlation between n forecasts and actual values of n excess returns on stocks, the above test is conditional on a fixed number of predicted negative excess returns n_{01}, a fixed number of realised negative excess returns n_{10} and a fixed number of realised positive excess returns n_{20}. For fixed n there are 3 degrees of freedom, 2 degrees of freedom if we fix row or column sums, and 1 degree of freedom if we fix row and column sums .

Pesaran and Timmermann (1992) refer to a result of Tocher (1950) that, for k=2 under the null of independence, an exact test has the same distribution whether we have 1, 2 or 3 degrees of freedom and it is a uniformly most powerful against a discrete alternative. However the equivalence breaks down when the number of states is greater than 2. See Kendall and Stuart (1979).

In constructing their generalisation of the M-H test, Pesaran and Timmermann (1992,1994) concentrate only on the diagonal elements of the p matrix and not on the off-diagonal values and extend the H-M test to k>2 states. Hence they concentrate on a k state test based on an asymptotic N(0,1). Consider the following null hypothesis

$$H_0: \sum_{i=1}^{k} (p_{ii} - p_{i0} p_{0i}) = 0 \tag{2}$$

It is standard result for the maximum likelihood estimator of p_{ij} , ($\hat{p}_{ij}$), that

$$\sqrt{n} \, (\hat{p} - p_0) \sim N(0, \, \psi_0 - p_0 \, p_0')$$

where p_0 is the ($k^2 \times 1$) vector of the true values of p and ψ_0 is an ($k^2 \times k^2$) diagonal matrix which has p_0 as its diagonal matrix. The test of H_0 can be based on the following statistic

$$S_n = \sum_{i=1}^{n} (\hat{p}_{ii} - \hat{p}_{i0} \, \hat{p}_{0i})$$

where $\hat{p}_{ii} = n_{ii}/n$, $\hat{p}_{i0} = n_{i0}/n$ and $\hat{p}_{0i} = n_{0i}/n$. Using the result that, under H_0

$$\sqrt{n} S_n \sim N(0, V)$$

where

$$V = (\partial \, f(p_0) \, / \, \partial p)' \, (\psi_0 - p_0 \, p_0') (\, \partial f(p_0) \, / \, \partial p)$$

and

$$\partial f(p_0) \, / \, \partial p = 1 - p_{0i} - p_{i0} \quad \text{for } j=i$$
$$= -p_{0i} - p_{i0} \quad \text{otherwise.}$$

Thus, we have a well-defined test statistic with a known asymptotic distribution. We have several points to discuss about this test. In a bond equity switching situation (k=2) the P-T test may be useful if we want to compare the excess returns of equity over bonds and we are concerned only with which asset pays the highest return. In this case the M-H exact test is perfectly adequate anyway. In a more general framework we would be interested in the off-diagonal matrix arguments. Let us consider the following (3 × 3) example,

$$
\begin{array}{lll}
p_{11} & p_{12}+\varepsilon & p_{13}-\varepsilon \\
p_{21}-\varepsilon & p_{22} & p_{23}+\varepsilon \\
p_{31}+\varepsilon & p_{32}-\varepsilon & p_{33}
\end{array}
$$

where $p_{ii}=p_{0i}p_{i0}$ and p_{i0}, p_{0i} refer to row and column proportions. Under these circumstances the P-T test, for large n, will not reject the null hypothesis irrespective of the value of ε. A positive ε would be interpreted as follows. If forecasts and realisations can be low, medium, or high then $(p_{11},p_{12}+\varepsilon,p_{13}-\varepsilon)$ means that for low realisations and low forecast the joint event is proportional to the marginals $(p_{11}=p_{10}p_{01})$. The events $(p_{12}+\varepsilon > p_{10}p_{02})$ and $(p_{13}-\varepsilon < p_{10}p_{03})$ imply that low realisations and medium forecasts are over-represented whilst low realisations and high forecasts are underrepresented. In particular, the important cases of underreaction and overreaction may not be able to be addressed by the P-T test.

One motivation given by P-T for building their test statistic is that it should be robust to randomness in row and column totals. Whilst this seems worthwhile, the large sample sizes used in finance remove the need for finite sample concerns. A second motivation given is that it is a test of market-timing and is motivated by the parable of a risk-neutral investor selecting the market with maximum forecasted return, this is the y_t value. The x_t is the actual maximum return across the set of markets. Whilst such an analysis could be interesting the null given by (2) does not include the case of market timing specialists - i.e. an investor above average at equity return forecasting but below par in bonds. In this case we would have positive and negative perturbations to p_{11} and p_{22} respectively but the left hand side of the (3 ×3) example could stay the same. The test, therefore, leads to a test of *global* market timing. Incidentally, a large number of market-timers are specialists. In any case their use of the asymptotic distribution rather weakens their argument as the standard χ^2 test will be asymptotically distributed independently of the nuisance parameter in row or column totals and will outperform their test statistic in virtually all circumstances. There may, however, be a role for the use of the P-T test when n is small and k is large such as in the analysis of managed fund performance with quaterly or annual data.

In the following section we thus present a further generalisation of the M-H test, where we fixed the number of entries in each cell by reordering the observations and considering the implied percentiles. In this way our test shares certain similarities with the test considered by Tsay (1989), although his procedure relies more on actual magnitudes.

3 A Simple Data Matrix

Let us consider the general case where we have k different classes and we define $n_{i,j}$ as follows

$n_{i,j,t}$ = 1 if $r_{i-1} \leq x_t \leq r_i$ and $r_{i-1} \leq y_t \leq r_j$
 = 0 otherwise

$n_{i,j,t}$ is thus a binary variable that takes the value in the rectangle in (x_t, y_t) space and is zero otherwise. Summing $n_{i,j,t}$ over t for i,j=1,...k and t=1,...n we form an (k ×k) matrix. From these we can easily get

$B_{i,j}$ = the number of times $r_{i-1} \leq x_t < r_i$ and $r_{j-1} \leq y_t < r_j$ (3)

where $B_{i,j} = \sum_{t=1}^{n} n_{i,j,t}$, i=1,...k and j=1,...k.

Then rearranging the observations of both x_t and y_t from the minimum to the maximum value, we note that the expected number of entries in each cell is determined under the null hypothesis of independence by

$m_{i,j} = n \times pr_i \times pr_j$ (4)

where n is the sample size and pr_i is the *ith* percentiles determined from the empirical steady state distribution function of x_t, y_t. For example if we have n=1500 and we would like to consider ten *0.10* percentiles (k=10), we would expect under the null to have 15 observations in each of the $k^2 = 100$ cells. Under the null hypothesis of independence between x_t and y_t, the following statistic

$S = \{ \sum_i \sum_j ([B_{i,j} - m_{i,j}]^2) \} / m_{i,j}$ (5)

follows asymptotically a χ^2 with $(k-1)^2$ degrees of freedom. This is a variant for the standard test of independence in a (k×k) contingency table, see Kendall and Stuart (1979). A derivation of its asymptotic distributions is presented in Appendix 1 of Dacco' and Satchell (1997).
This can be considered a minor extension of the test suggested by Henriksson and Merton (1981) where the number of entries of each row and column is fixed a priori by the investigators. The contribution of our statistical procedure is not

theoretical, but empirical, it allows us to shed light on a set of different issues in empirical finance.

We shall now concentrate on the univariate case where $y_t=x_{t-1}$, i.e. our best forecast is the past value of the dependent variable. We have

$\{ B_{i,j} \} = \{$ the number of times $r_{i-1} < x_t < r_i$ and $r_{j-1} < x_{t-1} < r_j \}$

that forms a (k×k) matrix. Again as before the iid hypothesis suggests the following entries

$m_{i,j}= n \times \alpha_i \times \alpha_j$

where n is the sample size and $\alpha_i=F(r_i)-F(r_{i-1})$ is the *ith* percentile and *F* the appropriate distribution function. All this information can be grouped in a single matrix $B(k,\alpha_1,\alpha_2...\alpha_k)$, called a B matrix after Peter Bernstein who suggested the topic to us. For example B(3,0.05,0.9,0.05) would be a (3 × 3) matrix with a 5% probability in the left tail, 90% probability in the middle group and 5% in the upper tail. Such a specification will fix the row and column sums since if we have, for example, n=1000 observations, the row or columns sums will be 50, 900 and 50 respectively. Minor adjustments may be needed if these totals were not integers, we ignore this effect since in all cases our samples sizes are large.

If we follow the general principle of contingency tables that m_{ij}, the expected number in a cell should be greater than 5, then for a lower 5% cell we require (0.05) × (0.05) n* > 5 or n*>2000 observations, which, for weekly data, requires 40 years and for daily data requires 8 years, for a lower 2.5% point n* becomes 8000, approximately 32 years of daily data. These are the samples sizes currently available in some mature markets. Although our above results are only appropriate for one-period dependency it could be generalised to τ periods. Then we would have $p\{i_1,i_2,...,i_\tau\}$ and $m\{i_1,i_2,...,i_\tau\}$ defined analogously to (3) and (4). A general test of the form (5) could be constructed, we would run out of data if we use daily observations for a lower 2.5% point and τ=3 we need 1200 years of data, if $m\{i_1,i_2, i_3\}$ is to be greater than 5.

If we observe p_{ii} greater than m_{ii} along the diagonal, then this indicates the presence of positive autocorrelation in the x_t. The χ^2 statistics allows us to test different hypotheses such as over reaction and / or shock persistence. In this way the above matrix is able to suggest where and when we would expect the hypothesis of independence not to hold.

4   Results and Empirical Questions

We now proceed with empirical analysis. For reasons of brevity we consider the US Datastream total market index (``TOTMKUS").

We consider daily returns from 1/1/1980 to 30/8/96, we have 4329 observations ignoring weekends and holidays.

The matrix we consider is B=B(8,0.05,0.05,0.1,0.3,0.3,0.1,0.05,0.05). For n=4329, the expected B matrix, under H_0 is given by Table 1.

Table 1: US Stock Market

DataStream Daily Returns (sample 4329) 1/1/80-30/8/96

The iid case ....

Percentiles	0-5,	5-10,	10-20,	20-50,	50-80,	80-90,	90-95,	95-100
0-5,	11	11	22	65	65	22	11	11
5-10,	11	11	22	65	65	22	11	11
10-20,	22	22	43	130	130	43	22	22
20-50,	65	65	130	391	391	130	65	65
50-80,	65	65	130	391	391	130	65	65
80-90,	22	22	43	130	130	43	22	22
90-95,	11	11	22	65	65	22	11	11
95-100	11	11	22	65	65	22	11	11

Any deviation from randomness can be seen against this matrix. In table 2 we report the matrix B and the contribution of each cell to the χ^2 statistic, this second table stresses the departure of the iid hypothesis and gives a scaled magnitude of departure so that comparisons of one region against the others are appropriate. Examining table 2, we note strong shock persistence in extreme values, very high returns and very low returns are more likely to be followed by very high returns and very low returns relative to average returns, i.e. big values for b_{11} and b_{88}.

Table 2: US Stock Market

DataStream Daily Returns (sample 4329) 1/1/80-30/8/96

the chi - square test

Percentiles	0-5,	5-10,	10-20,	20-50,	50-80,	80-90,	90-95,	95-100
0-5,	37	0	0	2	1	2	0	2
5-10,	0	2	1	1	0	1	0	1
10-20,	0	0	1	0	0	1	1	0
20-50,	1	1	1	0	1	1	2	1
50-80,	4	0	2	0	0	3	4	3
80-90,	5	1	0	2	0	1	0	1
90-95,	1	1	0	0	0	0	0	2
95-100	1	1	5	1	1	0	1	11

Chi Square Test = 114

Number of observations: 4329

Degree of freedoms: (p-1)^2 = 63

95% critical value: 82.53

The significance levels of χ^2_{63} is 82.53 for the 95% percentiles. Together with the test statistic for the whole matrix, i.e. χ^2_{63}, we can also run a test on a single cell, i.e. b_{11} cell. In this case we have χ^2_1 where

$$S_{ij} = ([B_{i,j} - m_{i,j}]^2) / (m_{i,j}(1-pr_i)(1-pr_j))$$

for each i,j=1,2...k follows asymptotically a χ^2_1. This has the same relationship to the whole matrix chi-square test as a t-test has to a conventional F-test.

Since it is well known that nonsynchronous trading can cause spurious positive autocorrelation in the series making up an index, we compare our index results with results obtained for some highly liquid US equities. Due to data availability, we shall consider daily observations from 1/7/1962 to 31/12/1993 for General Electrics and IBM. This consists of time series with 7927 observations, see tables 3-4.

Table 3: IBM

CRSP Dataset Daily Returns (sample 7927) 1/7/62-31/12/93

the chi - square test

Percentiles	0-5,	5-10,	10-20,	20-50,	50-80,	80-90,	90-95,	95-100
0-5,	37	1	0	27	11	11	1	41
5-10,	6	0	0	10	1	12	0	2
10-20,	0	3	2	8	16	3	0	0
20-50,	5	1	0	2	0	10	5	16
50-80,	10	7	1	3	39	1	2	1
80-90,	3	2	0	5	1	6	1	6
90-95,	2	0	0	0	0	3	1	0
95-100	19	10	0	5	1	1	0	10

Chi Square Test = 376
Number of observations: 7927
Degree of freedoms: (p-1)^2 = 63
95% critical value: 82.53

Table 4: General Electric

CRSP Dataset Daily Returns (sample 7927) 1/7/62-31/12/93

the chi - square test

Percentiles	0-5,	5-10,	10-20,	20-50,	50-80,	80-90,	90-95,	95-100
0-5,	21	2	1	35	4	8	19	12
5-10,	14	8	0	17	2	2	0	5
10-20,	2	2	0	24	23	1	10	1
20-50,	2	2	5	70	2	38	18	57
50-80,	8	2	5	2	190	19	2	0
80-90,	7	1	2	3	6	0	0	11
90-95,	0	0	1	10	0	2	19	19
95-100	6	2	1	10	10	0	8	41

Chi Square Test = 791
Number of observations: 7927
Degree of freedoms: $(p-1)^2 = 63$
95% critical value: 82.53

The results are striking: our chi-squared statistics are now much larger suggesting large amounts of first order correlation at certain levels of returns. We confirm the presence of positive and negative shock persistence: in all cases b_{11} and b_{88} are well above the IID case. Furthermore we note in most cases the effect of overreactions, i.e. cells b_{81} and b_{18}. Interestingly, for General Electrics, a small above average return (50%-80%) is usually more likely to be followed by a small above average return (50%-80%). This effect could be explained by the presence of zero returns due to nontrading days especially at the beginning of the sample or it could be similar to the result of Solnik et al. (1996) and LeBaron (1992), with daily exchange rate data; when volatility is low, correlation is high. In all cases the results for the indices are actually strengthened by comparison with the single stocks. This suggests that what we have discussed for the indices cannot be attributed to spurious effects.

The elegance of our procedure is that all calculations are relative to the steady state distribution of (daily) log returns, skewness or kurtosis are automatically taken into account, and as mentioned in the introduction, the procedure is robust to regime shifts and other nonlinearities.

5   Conclusions

We have presented a general summary matrix for return data that is capable of shedding light on a large range of different hypothesis about asset returns.

58

Noting that the H-M test is simply an exact version of a chi-squared test of independence for a (2 ×2) contingency table, we argue that the testing procedure we associate with our matrix is the correct generalisation of the H-M test, the generalisation by P-T is a specialisation which will lack power against some commonly occurring alternatives.

Applying the usual χ^2 test to our contingency tables, we find strong evidence of non-independence at different levels of daily returns. In particular very high, very low and slightly above average returns seem to be more likely to be followed by returns of the same size at both index and stock levels. The use of the chi-square ``map" is very helpful in isolating deviations from independence. Referees have mentioned that the patterns of significance that we find in the four corners of the matrix could be a signature of stochastic volatility models, we hope to report on this question in future work.

These results differ from the ``compass rose" pattern of Crach and Ledoit (1996). They find lines emerging from the origin on a grid where the horizontal axis shows today return and the vertical axis shows tomorrow return. It may be that this effect, due to the impact of tick size, has contaminated our individual stock analysis. Crach and Ledoit (1996) do not find strong ``compass rose" pattern in indices, whilst we continue to find correlation patterns in all classes of daily data.

Further research by the authors hopes to use the extensive χ^2 testing literature to develop more precise testing procedures against specific alternative hypothesis and try and relate more precisely the patterns in the matrix to specific financial anomalies.

6   Acknowledgments

Roberto Dacco' is funded by Kleinwort Benson Investment Management and the Newton Trust, Steve Satchell would like to thank INQUIRE for research support. We would like to thank Peter Bernstein for suggesting this topic to one of the authors and Babak Eftekhari for helpful comments.

7   References

Bollerslev, T., Chou, R.Y. and Kroner, K.F. (1992) ``ARCH Model in Finance: A Review of the Theory and Empirical Evidence". *Journal of Econometrics*, 52: 5-59.
Chou, R., Engle, R.F. and A. Kane (1992) ``Measuring Risk Aversion from Excess Returns on a Stock Index," *Journal of Econometrics*, 52: 201-224.
Crach, T. and O. Ledoit (1996) ``Robust Structure Without Predictability: The ``Compass Rose" Pattern of the Stock Market", *Journal of Finance*, 2: 251-261.

Dacco',R. and S.E. Satchell (1997) `` A Data Matrix to Investigate Independence, Overreaction and/or Shock Persistence in Financial Data". Discussion Paper in Financial Economics FE39, Birkbeck College, University of London.

Engle, R.F. (1982) ``Autoregressive Conditional Heteroskedasticity with Estimates of the Variance of UK Inflation". *Econometrica*, 50: 987-1007.

Engle, R.F. and Gonzalez-Rivera, G. (1991) ``Semiparametric ARCH Models". *Journal of Business and Economic Statistics*, 9: 345-359.

Fama, E. (1991) ``Efficient Capital Markets: II," *Journal of Finance*, 46: 1575-1617.

Fama, E. and K.R. French (1989) ``Business Conditions and Expected Returns on Stocks and Bonds". *Journal of Financial Economics*, 25: 23-49.

Glosten, L.R., Jagannathan, R. and D.E. Runkle (1993) ``On the Expected Value and the Volatility of the Nominal Excess Return on Stocks," *Journal of Finance*, 5: 1779-1801.

Granger, C.W.J., and T. Terasvirta (1993) ``Modelling Nonlinear Economic Relationships," Oxford University Press.

Henriksson, R.D. and R.C. Merton (1991) ``On Market Timing and Investment Performance". *Journal of Business*, 54:513-533.

Jegadeesh, N. (1990) ``Evidence of Predictable Behaviour of Security Returns". *Journal of Finance*, 45:881-898.

Jegadeesh, N. and S. Titman (1995) ``Short Horizon Return Reversals and the Bid-Ask Spread". *Journal of Financial Intermediation*, 4: 116-132.

Jegadeesh, N. and S. Titman (1995) ``Overreaction, Delayed Reaction, and Contrarian Profits". *The Review of Financial Studies*, 8: 973-993.

Kendall, M. and A. Stuart (1979) ``The Advanced Theory of Statistics". vol 2, Charles Griffin and Company ltd.

LeBaron, B. (1992) ``Forecasting Improvements Using a Volatility Index". *Journal of Applied Econometrics*, 7: 137-150.

Lo, A. W. and A.C. MacKinlay, (1990) ``When Are Contrarian Profits due to Market Overreaction ?" *The Review of Financial Studies*, 3: 175-205.

Merton, R.C. (1980) ``On Estimating the Expected Return on the Market," *Journal of Financial Economics*, 8: 323-361.

Merton, R.C. (1990) ``Continuous-Time Finance," Blackwell.

Pagan, A.R., and Y.S. Hong (1991) ``Non-parametric Estimation and the Risk Premium," in Barnett, W. et al. Semiparametric and Nonparametric Methods In Econometrics and Statistics , Cambridge University Press.

Pesaran, H.M., and A. Timmermann (1992) ``A Simple Non Parametric Test of Predictive Performance," *Journal of Business and Economic Statistics*, 10: 461-465.

Pesaran, H.M., and A. Timmermann (1994) ``A Generalisation of the Nonparametric Henriksson-Merton Test of Market Timing". *Economics Letters*, 44: 1-7.

Petrucelli, J.D. and Davies. N. (1986) ``A Portmanteau Test for Self Exiting Threshold Autoregressive Type Nonlinearity in Time Series''. *Biometrika*, 73: 687-694.

Solnik, B., Boucrelle, C. and LeFur, Y. (1996) ``International Market Correlation and Volatility''. Groupe MEC Discussion Paper CR 571.

Summers, L.H. and V.P. Summers (1989) ``When Financial Markets Work too Well: A Cautious Case for Security Transactions Tax''. *Journal of Financial Services*, 3:261-286.

Tocher, K.F (1950) ``Extension of the Neyman-Pearson Theory of Test to Discontinuous Variables''. *Biometrika*, 37:130-144.

Tsay, R.S. (1989) ``Testing and Modeling Threshold Autoregressive Processes,'' *Journal of the American Statistical Association*, 84: 461-489.

FORECASTING HIGH FREQUENCY
EXCHANGE RATES USING CROSS-BICORRELATIONS

CHRIS BROOKS
ISMA Centre, P.O. Box 242
The University of Reading
Whiteknights, Reading RG6 6BA, England
E-mail: C.Brooks@rdg.ac.uk

MELVIN J. HINICH
Department of Government , University of Texas at Austin
Austin, Texas, USA

The central motivation for this paper is to combine a multivariate nonlinearity test with a nonlinear time series forecasting model of the VAR-type which incorporates lags of the cross-products with the other exchange rate in the system using high frequency data. The paper draws together two sets of literature which have previously been considered entirely separately: namely time series tests for nonlinearity and multivariate exchange rate forecasting. The out-of-sample forecasting performance of the new technique using cross-bicorrelations is inferior to that of univariate time series models, in spite of significant in-sample cross-bicorrelation statistics, although it does seem to be able to predict the signs of the returns well in certain cases. A number of explanations for this apparent paradox are proposed.

1. Introduction

Following a seminal article by Meese and Rogoff (1983), there has been much debate surrounding the usefulness of structural models such as the Dornbusch (1976) sticky price model and the Hooper-Morton (1982) model for out-of-sample exchange rate prediction. Although there still appears to be little consensus over whether structural models can consistently beat the random walk, researchers are in broad agreement that structural models can provide at best only fairly modest improvements in forecasting power over simple time series models for prediction of monthly or quarterly exchange rates.

Results on the usefulness of time series models in this context are, again, mixed. Linear time series models (such as ARIMA or exponential smoothing models) have not proved particularly useful for forecasting financial asset returns either (see, for example, Kuan and Lim, 1994). A natural question which follows, therefore, is whether (more complex) nonlinear models can do better. All of the entries in a recent forecasting competition, which included financial and other types of data, were all essentially nonlinear in nature (see Weigend, 1994).

A.-P.N. Refenes et al. (eds.), Decision Technologies for Computational Finance, 61–72.
© 1998 *Kluwer Academic Publishers. Printed in the Netherlands..*

Brooks and Hinich (1997) have recently proposed a third order cross-bicorrelation test for multivariate nonlinear relationships between series. The test can be viewed as a multivariate generalisation of the bicorrelation test for nonlinearity in mean in the same way that Baek and Brock (1992) or Hiemstra and Jones (1994) extended the BDS test to the multivariate case. One advantage of the bicorrelation testing approach over more general portmanteau tests is that it is applicable to small samples (the mini-Monte Carlo study of Brooks and Hinich, 1997, shows that the test is well sized with as few as 200 observations) and so we split the data into smaller sub-samples for analysis. This point is pertinent for rapidly evolving financial markets where the implicit assumption of strict stationarity is less likely to hold[1]. Wu & Rehfuss (1997) argue that information in financial markets decays rapidly over time so that "adaptation to nonstationarity seems critical" (p218). A further bonus of the cross-bicorrelation approach is that it suggests a model class for forecasting the future path of the data. This is an important point given the discussion above, and it will be developed further below.

The remainder of this paper develops as follows. Section 2 outlines the testing and forecasting methodology employed in this study, while section 3 gives a description of the data. Section 4 presents our results while section 5 concludes and offers a number of suggestions for further research.

2. Methodology
2.1 Testing for Significant Cross-Bicorrelations
The cross-bicorrelation test statistic, and a simple cross-correlation statistic are calculated as follows. Let the data be a sample of length N, from two jointly stationary time series $\{x(t_k)\}$ and $\{y(t_k)\}$ which have been standardised to have a sample mean of zero and a sample variance of one by subtracting the sample mean and dividing by the sample standard deviation in each case. Since we are working with small sub-samples of the whole series, stationarity is not a stringent assumption. The null hypothesis for the test is that the two series are independent pure white noise processes, against an alternative that some cross-covariances, $C_{xy}(r) = E[x(t_k)y(t_k+r)]$ or cross-bicovariances $C_{xxy}(r,s) = E[x(t_k)x(t_k+r)y(t_k+s)]$ are non-zero. As consequence of the invariance of $E[x(t_1)x(t_2)y(t_3)]$ to permutations of (t_1,t_2), stationarity implies that the expected value is a function of two lags and that $C_{xxy}(-r,s) = C_{xxy}(r,s)$. If the maximum lag used is $L < N$, then the principal domain for the bicovariances is the rectangle $\{1\leq r\leq L, -L\leq s\leq L\}$.

Under the null hypothesis that $\{x(t_k)\}$ and $\{y(t_k)\}$ are pure white noise, then $C_{xy}(r)$ and $C_{xxy}(r,s) = 0 \ \forall \ r,s$ except when $r = s = 0$. This is also true for the less restrictive case that the two processes are merely uncorrelated, but the theorem given in Brooks and Hinich (1997) to show that the test statistic is asymptotically normal requires

---

[1] Although in this study, the data used is of such a high frequency that large samples can be used without the likelihood of incurring large structural breaks.

independence between the series and pure white noise. If there is second or third order lagged dependence between the two series, then $C_{xy}(r)$ or $C_{xxy}(r,s) \neq 0$ for at least one r value or one pair of r and s values respectively. The following statistics give the r sample xy cross-correlation and the r,s sample xxy cross-bicorrelation respectively:

$$C_{xy}(r) = (N-r)^{-1} \sum_{t=1}^{N-r} x(t_k) y(t_k + r), r \neq 0 \tag{2}$$

and

$$C_{xxy}(r,s) = (N-m)^{-1} \sum_{t=1}^{N-m} x(t_k) x(t_k + r) y(t_k + s) \tag{3}$$

where $m = \max(r,s)$.

Note that the summation in the second order case (2) does not include contemporaneous terms, so that contemporaneous correlations will not cause rejections, and for the third order test, we estimate the test on the residuals of a bivariate vector autoregressive model containing a contemporaneous term in one of the equations. The motivation for this pre-whitening step is to remove any traces of linear correlation or cross-correlation so that any remaining dependence between the series must be of a nonlinear form. Let $L=N^c$ where $0 < c < 0.5$ [2]. The test statistics for non-zero cross-correlations and cross-bicorrelations are then given by

$$H_{xy}(N) = \sum_{r=1}^{L} (N-r) \; C_{xy}^{\;2}(r) \tag{4}$$

and

$$H_{xxy}(N) = \sum_{s=-L}^{L} {}^{'} \sum_{r=1}^{L} (N-m) \; C_{xxy}^{\;2}(r,s), \quad ('-s \neq -1,1,0) \tag{5}$$

respectively. Theorem 1 of Brooks and Hinich (1997) shows that H_{xy} and H_{xxy} are asymptotically chi-squared with L and $L(2L-1)$ degrees of freedom respectively. The cross-bicorrelation can be viewed as a correlation between one exchange rate return (x) and the temporal cross-correlation between the two returns (xy) or between the other exchange rate return (y) and the cross-correlation (yx), so that for every pair of exchange rates, there will exist a separate H_{xxy} and an H_{yyx} statistic. In this study, a window length of 960, corresponding to approximately 4 trading weeks, is used for the cross-bicorrelation testing. The tests are conducted on all possible pair-wise combinations of the seven exchange rates (21 pairs).

---

[2] In this application, we use $c=0.25$, although the results and the null distribution of the test are not very sensitive to changes in this parameter.

2.2 Forecasting Using Cross-Bicorrelations

Armed with evidence of when the test leads to rejections of the null hypothesis that the two series are two independent random processes, we consider the forecasting performance of a VAR-type model for the returns, extended to incorporate nonlinear terms suggested by the test. The forecast accuracy of this model is evaluated and compared to that of linear univariate and multivariate models. We also evaluate whether the models have evidence of market timing ability using the generalisation of the Henriksson-Merton test proposed by Pesaran and Timmerman (1992).

2.2a A Linear Vector Autoregressive Model

Changing the notation slightly from that used above for ease of exposition, assume that two time series $\{x_1(t) , x_2(t)\}$ are related by a vector autoregressive model with p lags[3]. A two lag model is of the form

$$x_1(t) = c_{111}x_1(t-1) + c_{121}x_2(t-1) + c_{112}x_1(t-2) + c_{122}x_2(t-2) + e_1(t)$$
$$x_2(t) = c_{211}x_1(t-1) + c_{221}x_2(t-1) + c_{212}x_1(t-2) + c_{222}x_2(t-2) + e_1(t)$$

$$(6)$$

where $\{e_1(t) , e_2(t)\}$ are independently distributed *pure white noise* random processes. This model has the state space or companion form representation

$$\mathbf{x}(t) = \mathbf{A}\mathbf{x}(t-1) + \mathbf{e}(t) \tag{7}$$

and

$$\mathbf{A} = \begin{pmatrix} c_{111} & c_{121} & c_{112} & c_{122} \\ c_{211} & c_{221} & c_{212} & c_{222} \\ 1 & 0 & 0 & 0 \\ 0 & 1 & 0 & 0 \end{pmatrix} \text{ and}$$

$\mathbf{x}(t) = \left(x_1(t), x_2(t), x_1(t-1), x_2(t-1) \right)^T$. The system is initialized by setting $x_1(0) = e_1(0)$, $x_2(0) = e_2(0)$, $x_1(1) = e_1(1)$, $x_2(1) = e_2(1)$.

Any vector autoregressive model can be written in such a form. If the model has p lags then each time series has p lags as state space variates. The system matrix $\mathbf{A}$ for a system with m variates each of whom have p lags is a non-symmetric matrix with dimension $n = mp$. Let λ_k and v_k denote the kth eigenvalue of $\mathbf{A}$ and its associated eigenvector respectively, where $k = 1,...,n$. Then $\mathbf{A} = \mathbf{V}^{-1} \Lambda \mathbf{V}$ where Λ is a diagonal matrix whose diagonal elements are λ_k and $\mathbf{V}$ is an n x n matrix whose kth column is v_k. The linear system can then be transformed into the n uncoupled first order equations $\mathbf{y}(t) = \Lambda\mathbf{y}(t-1) + \varepsilon(t)$ by the following linear transformation of the coordinate system: $\mathbf{y}(t) = \mathbf{T}^{-1}\mathbf{x}(t)$ and $\varepsilon(t) = \mathbf{T}^{-1}\mathbf{e}(t)$.

---

[3] These were previously called x and y.

2.2b Introducing nonlinearity into the VAR Model
To introduce nonlinearity into the system suppose that at time t the kth eigenvalue is slightly perturbed by $y_k(t-1), \ldots, y_k(t-M)$ Formally, let $\lambda_k(t) = \lambda_k + \sum_{m=1}^{M} \beta_{km} y_k(t-m)$ where β_{km} are small parameters for each $k=1,\ldots,n$ and $m=1,M$. Thus

$$y_k(t) = \lambda_k y_k(t-1) + \sum_{m=1}^{M} \beta_{km} y_k(t-1) y_k(t-m) \qquad (8)$$

for each k. To simplify exposition suppose that $p = 1$ rather than $p = 2$ for the two variable model (1/1) and let $M=2$. Since $y_1(t)$ and $y_2(t)$ are linear functions of $(x_1(t), x_2(t))$, the linear system in the observed variates is

$$x_1(t) = c_{111}x_1(t-1) + c_{121}x_2(t-1) + c_{131}x_1^2(t-1) + c_{141}x_1(t-1)x_1(t-2) +$$
$$c_{151}x_2^2(t-1) + c_{161}x_2(t-1) + c_{171}x_1(t-1) + c_{181}x_2(t-1)x_1(t-2) + e_1(t)$$
$$x_2(t) = c_{211}x_1(t-1) + c_{221}x_2(t-1) + c_{231}x_1^2(t-1) + c_{241}x_1(t-1)x_1(t-2) +$$
$$c_{251}x_2^2(t-1) + c_{261}x_2(t-1) + c_{271}x_1(t-1) + c_{281}x_2(t-1)x_1(t-2) + e_2(t)$$
$$(9)$$

The general model for two variates will have four groups of M cross products each lagged by p. In order to keep the size manageable we did not use the $x_1^2(t-m)$ and $x_2^2(t-m)$ in the models we use to fit the data. It would, of course, be possible to generalise the model to incorporate more than two series in the VAR or to allow each dependent variable to be explained by more than two lags of each variable.

In this study, we construct only one step ahead forecasts for the models. The sample is split approximately in half, with the first 6238 observations being used for in-sample model estimation, while the remainder are saved for out-of-sample evaluation. All models are estimated using a moving window of length 6238, working through the sample one observation at a time. This produces a total of 6337 one-step-ahead forecasts for each model to be compared with the actual realised returns.

2.2c Linear Models for Comparison
In order to have an appropriate benchmark for comparison with the one step ahead forecasts generated by the cross-bicorrelation VAR model, forecasts are also produced using a long term historic mean (average of the last 6238 observations), a random walk in the log-levels (i.e. a zero return forecast), autoregressive models of order 1, 3, and 10, and autoregressive models of order selected using information criteria. The generation of forecasts using all but the last of these is described in detail in Brooks (1997).

2.2d The Pesaran-Timmerman Non-parametric Test of Predictive Performance
Pesaran and Timmerman (1992), hereafter PT, have recently suggested a non-parametric test for market timing ability which is generalised from the Henriksson Merton (Henriksson and Merton, 1981; Merton, 1981) test for independence between forecast and realised values. Using a notation which differs slightly from that of PT, let $P_x = Pr(x_{t+n} > 0), P_f = Pr(f_{t,n} > 0)$ and

$$\hat{P} = \frac{1}{T - T_1} \sum_{t=T_1}^{T} z_{t+n},$$ where x_{t+n} denotes the realised value of x at time $t+n$, $f_{t,n}$ is the forecasted value (made at time t for n steps ahead) corresponding to this realised value, $z_{t+n} = x_{t+n} \times f_{t,n}$, T_1 is the first forecasted observation (6239), and T is the final observation (12575). Denoting the *ex ante* probability that the sign will correctly be predicted as P_*, then

$$P_* = Pr(z_{t+n} = 1) = Pr(x_{t+n} f_{t,n} > 0) = P_x P_f + (1 - P_x)(1 - P_f) \tag{10}$$

It can be shown that

$$S_n = \frac{\hat{P} - P_*}{\{\text{vâr}(\hat{P}) - \text{vâr}(\hat{P}_*)\}^{1/2}} \tag{11}$$

is a standardised test statistic for predictive performance which is asymptotically distributed as a standard normal variate under the null hypothesis of independence between corresponding actual and forecast values, where symbols with hats (e.g.

$\hat{P}_*$) denote estimated values, $\text{vâr}(\hat{P}) = \dfrac{1}{T - T_1} \hat{P}_*(1 - \hat{P}_*)$,

and

$$\text{vâr}(\hat{P}_*) = \begin{bmatrix} \dfrac{1}{T - T_1}(2\hat{P}_x - 1)^2 \hat{P}_f(1 - \hat{P}_f) + \dfrac{1}{T - T_1}(2\hat{P}_f - 1)^2 \hat{P}_x(1 - \hat{P}_x) \\ + \dfrac{1}{(T - T_1)^2} \hat{P}_x \hat{P}_f(1 - \hat{P}_x)(1 - \hat{P}_f) \end{bmatrix}.$$

3. Data
The high frequency financial data provided by Olsen and Associates as part of the HFDF-96 package includes 25 exchange rate series sampled half-hourly for the whole of 1996, making a total of 17,568 observations. However, this series contains observations corresponding to weekend periods when all the world's exchanges are closed simultaneously and there is, therefore, no trading. This period is the time from 23:00 GMT on Friday when North American financial centres close until 23:00 GMT on Sunday when Australasian markets open[4]. The incorporation of such prices would lead to spurious zero returns and would potentially render trading

---

[4] We do not account for differences in the dates that different countries switch to daylight saving time, since the effect of this one-hour difference is likely to be negligible.

strategies which recommended a buy or sell at this time to be nonsensical. Removal of these weekend observations leaves 12,576 observations for subsequent analysis and forecasting. The price series are transformed into a set of continuously compounded half-hourly percentage returns in the standard fashion. Of the 25 exchange rate series provided by Olsen, only 7 are used in this study for illustrative purposes, to avoid repetition, and due to space constraints. These are (using the usual Reuters neumonic) DEM_JPY, GBP_DEM[5], GBP_USD, USD_CHF, USD_DEM, USD_ITL, and USD_JPY. Summary statistics for these returns series are calculated, and are available from the authors upon request, but are not shown here due to space constraints.

4. Results

The results of the one step ahead forecasting approach using the linear and cross-bicorrelation models are presented for each exchange rate in tables 1 to 4. Considering first the mean squared error and mean absolute error evaluation criteria, there is little to choose between most of the linear models. Typically, an AR(1) or AR(3) gives the smallest overall error (MSE or MAE give the same model ordering), with exponential smoothing giving the largest. Exponential smoothing is a technique originally formulated for forecasting periodic, seasonal data, so it was not envisaged that it would perform particularly well for forecasting high frequency financial asset returns, which have very different properties to monthly sales data. In particular, single exponential smoothing implies that the returns are generated by an ARIMA (0,1,1) process with moving average parameter equal to one minus the smoothing coefficient. Given that the returns are covariance stationary, this must imply an over-differencing, and hence the smoothing parameter must be close to zero so that the unit root is cancelled out to leave a model very similar to the random walk

However, the inability of traditional forecast evaluation criteria to select models which produce positive risk adjusted trading profits is well documented (see, for example Gerlow *et al.*, 1993). Models which can accurately predict the sign of future asset returns (irrespective of the size) are, however, more likely to produce profitable trading performances than those which do well on MSE grounds. Thus the proportion of times that the one step ahead forecast has the correct sign is given in the last row of each table. For the linear models, the story is very similar to that given above - that is, there is very little to choose between most of the models, which produce almost the same proportion of correct sign predictions, although the long term mean and exponential smoothing are worst and the AR(1) is generally (although now not universally) superior.

---

[5] Other users of this data should be aware that there are two erroneous price entries on 27 May 1996 at 13:30 and 14:00, where values of 3609.13 and 3609.22 appear respectively. These clearly represent incorrectly keyed in quotes, and hence both have been set to the immediately proceeding price.

The results for the cross-bicorrelation models are somewhat mixed. The proportion of correctly predicted signs rises over 60% (for example, the USD_DEM cross-bicorrelation helping to predict the DEM_JPY), although it never falls below 57%. The Pesaran Timmerman market timing ability results also concur with this story. For the linear autoregressive models, there is usually strong evidence of significant (at the 1% level) market timing ability, particularly for the AR(1). As anticipated from the sign prediction results, the long term mean and exponential smoothing models produce negative (and in most cases significantly negative) PT test statistics. The results for the cross-bicorrelation models are, again, very mixed. In most cases there is very strong evidence of negative market timing ability (in other words, our forecasting models perform significantly worse than if the forecasts and the realised values had been completely independent). Another way to put this is that we would have been much better off producing the sign predictions by tossing a coin. But for some combinations of exchange rates, there is very highly significant evidence of positive market timing ability. For example, the PT statistic for predicting the US Dollar / German Mark using the Mark / Yen is 25.98.

So which exchange rates can be used to predict which others? It seems that when the cross-bicorrelation between two exchange rates can be used to predict the next sign of one of them, it can also be used to predict the sign of the other, so that predictability seems to flow in both directions or not at all[6]. It seems that the USD_CHF, USD_DEM and USD_ITL can be used to predict the DEM_JPY; the USD_CHF, USD_DEM, USD_ITL and USD_JPY can be used to predict the GBP_USD; the DEM_JPY and GBP_USD can be used to predict the USD_CHF; the DEM_JPY and GBP_USD can be used to predict the USD_DEM; the DEM_JPY and GBP_USD can be used to predict the USD_ITL, and the GBP_USD can be used to predict the USD_JPY. None of the cross-bicorrrelation combinations investigated here could help to forecast the GBP_DEM.

5. Conclusions
What might explain observed cross-bicorrelations? Epps (1979) undertook a detailed study of the cross-correlations between various stocks traded on the NYSE, and observed positive cross-correlations between hourly stock returns. One possible explanation is that, if some traders specialise in some stocks, and do not transact in all stocks when relevant news is received, and provided that information processing in the market is sufficiently slow, then changes in the value of some stocks will have predictive power for price changes in other, related stocks. Transactions costs and the costs associated with acquiring the relevant information could lead such relationships to exist. Clearly, such an explanaltion can also be applied to exchange rate series. Apparent relationships might simply, however, be due to non-trading effects, where the first stock to trade following a new piece of information will

---

[6] This is partly indicated by the interesting degree of symmetry in the right had side of table 10 about the leading diagonal of dashes starting with CVAR DEM_JPY.

appear to lead the other stocks, since the last traded prices for those other stocks are now stale and no longer indicative of the appropriate market price, as Fisher (1966) suggested. Boudokh *et al.* (1994) suggest that these nontrading and nosynchronous trading effects can explain virtually all of the observed auto- and cross-correlation in stock portfolio returns, although this effect is more likely to be relevant to analyses of high frequency individual stock returns than the exchange rates used here which are all highly liquid.

This paper has developed a new type of model that can be used for testing for mulitvariate nonlinearity between time series and also for forecasting the future conditional means of each of these series. The forecasting performance of these cross-bicorrelation models has been evaluated on a number of different statistical grounds, and the results are somewhat disappointing. The prediction accuracy of this technique was marginally worse than that of standard linear models on conventional statistical measures. It is hoped, however, that by refining the models - that is, by selecting the lag lengths, the window lengths, and the series to use in each VAR "optimally" in some sense, that the forecast accuracies will be improved. The predictive power of the models for suggesting the next sign of the exchange rate return is highly variable according to which series are used in the bicorrelation. It seems that more investigation of these models is warranted to see whether models can be produced that consistently produce accurate sign predictions, and whether the models can generate excess (risk-adjusted) profits when used in a trading strategy[7]. More research on the implications and consequences of significant cross-bicorrelations would also be useful.

It has been argued here that one important reason for the failure of nonlinear models to accurately forecast the conditional mean of asset return series in spite of the presence of nonlinearity is that it is likely that the class of model estimated is not one from that class which caused the rejection of iid in the first place. Once we move from a linear to a nonlinear time series world, then, even in the univariate case, the number of potential families of models for consideration is infinite. Hence it is also, alas, likely that it could take an infinite amount of time to find one that is a good approximation to the DGP.

Acknowledgements
The authors would like to thank participants of the 1997 Computational Finance Conference for useful comments on an earlier version of this paper and Amanda Wright for her assistance with typing. The usual disclaimer applies.

---

[7] We think it unlikely that this would be the case since the transactions costs involved in implementing a half-hourly trading rule with so many trades would be prohibitive.

References

Andersen, T.G. and Bollerslev, T. (1997) Answering the Skeptics: Yes, Standard Volatility Models Do Provide Accurate Forecasts *Presented at Issues In Empirical Finance*, LSE 21-22 November

Baek, E. and Brock, W.A. (1992) A Nonparameteric Test for Independence of a Multivariate Time Series, *Statistica Sinica* 2, 137-156

Brock, W.A., Lakonishok, J. and LeBaron, B. (1992) Simple Technical Trading Rules and the Stochastic Properties of Stock Returns *Journal of Finance* 47, 1731-1764

Brooks, C. (1997) Linear and Nonlinear (Non-) Forecastability of Daily Sterling Exchange Rates *Journal of Forecasting* 16, 125-145

Brooks, C. (1996) Testing for Nonlinearity in Daily Pound Exchange Rates *Applied Financial Economics* 6, 307-317

Brooks, C. and Hinich, M.J. (1997) Cross-Correlations and Cross-Bicorrelations in Sterling Exchange Rates *Mimeo.*, ISMA Centre, University of Reading

Dornbusch, R. (1976) Expectations and Exchange Rate Dynamics *Journal of Political Economy* 84, 1161-1176

Epps, T.W. (1979) Comovements in Stock Prices in the Very Short Run *Journal of the American Statistical Association* 74, 291-298

Fisher, L. (1966) Some New Stock Market Indices *Journal of Business* 39, 191-225

Hiemstra, C. and Jones, J.D. (1994) Testing for Linear and Nonlinear Granger Causality in the Stock Price-Volume Relation, *Journal of Finance* 49(5), 1639-1664

Hooper, P. and Morton, J.E. (1982) Fluctuations in the Dollar: A Model of Nominal and Real Exchange Rate Determination *Journal of International Money and Finance* 1, 39-56

Kuan, C-M. and Lim, T. (1994) Forecasting Exchange Rates Using Feedforward and Recurrent Neural Networks *Journal of Applied Econometrics* 10, 347-364

Meese, R.A. and Rogoff, K (1983) Empirical Exchange Rate Models of the Seventies: Do they Fit Out of Sample? *Journal of International Economics* 14, 3-24

Mizrach, B. (1992) Multivariate Nearest Neighbour Forecasts of EMS Exchange Rates *Journal of Forecasting* 7, S151-S163

Pesaran, M.H. and Timmerman, A. (1992) A Simple Non-Parametric Test of Predictive Performance *Journal of Business and Economic Statistics* 10(4), 461-465

Sarantis, N. and Stewart, C. (1995) Structural VAR and BVAR Models of Exchange Rate Determination: A Comparison of their Forecasting Performance *Journal of Forecasting* 14, 205-215

Tse, Y.K. (1995) Lead-Lag Relationship Between Spot and Index Futures Price of the Nikkei Stock Average *Journal of forecasting* 14, 553-563

Weigend, A.S. (1994) Paradigm Change in Prediction *Philosophical Transactions of the Royal Society of London A* 348, 405-420

Wu, L. and Rehfuss, S. (1997) An Adaptive Committee-based Approach to Trading in Caldwell, R.B. (ed.) *Nonlinear Financial Forecasting: Proceedings of the First INFFC* Finance & Technology Publishing, Haymarket, VA.

Table 1: Forecasting Performance for German Mark / Japanese Yen

| | mean | r.w. | AR of order | | | AR-AIC | AR-SIC | AR-HQ | Exp. Smooth | CVAR GBP_DEM | CVAR GBP_USD | CVAR USD_CHF | CVAR USD_DEM | CVAR USD_ITL | CVAR USD_JPY |
			1	3	10										
MSE	6.06	6.07	5.86	5.84	5.86	5.86	5.85	5.86	6.10	33.01	35.98	34.52	36.41	33.70	42.87
MAE	5.38	5.38	5.31	5.30	5.31	5.31	5.30	5.31	5.40	12.81	13.49	13.12	13.54	12.94	14.62
% sign prediction	53.92	-	60.11	60.23	60.12	60.30	60.42	60.20	53.98	59.92	59.47	59.75	60.10	59.78	60.24

Notes: MSE is true MSE X 1000, MAE is true MAE X 100; mean denotes forecasts are a long term mean of the returns series; r.w. denotes forecasts produced assuming a random walk in the log-levels, AR-AIC are forecasts produced using an AR of order selected by AIC etc.; CVAR GBP_DEM are forecasts produced using cross-bicorrelations between the DEM_JPY and GBP_DEM etc.

Table 2: Forecasting Performance for British Pound / German Mark

| | mean | r.w. | AR of order | | | AR-AIC | AR-SIC | AR-HQ | Exp. Smooth | CVAR DEM_JPY | CVAR GBP_USD | CVAR USD_CHF | CVAR USD_DEM | CVAR USD_ITL | CVAR USD_JPY |
			1	3	10										
MSE	7.09	7.09	7.05	7.06	7.17	7.15	7.15	7.15	7.12	42.90	43.27	45.90	52.12	41.89	46.28
MAE	4.88	4.88	4.89	4.89	4.94	4.94	4.93	4.94	4.90	12.21	12.40	12.41	13.25	11.98	12.75
% sign prediction	54.50	-	57.71	58.13	57.55	57.49	57.53	57.15	53.88	57.49	57.16	58.32	58.99	57.48	58.08

Table 3: Forecasting Performance for British Pound / US Dollar

	mean	r.w.	AR of order 1	AR of order 3	AR of order 10	AR-AIC	AR-SIC	AR-HQ	Exp. Smooth	CVAR DEM_JPY	CVAR GBP_DEM	CVAR USD_CHF	CVAR USD_DEM	CVAR USD_ITL	CVAR USD_JPY
MSE	5.20	5.39	5.03	5.03	5.04	5.04	5.03	5.03	5.22	46.85	46.45	50.39	59.59	46.15	47.74
MAE	4.67	4.69	4.59	4.57	4.58	4.59	4.58	4.58	4.70	14.43	14.48	14.98	16.23	14.28	14.59
% sign prediction	53.32	-	59.65	60.41	59.87	59.87	60.41	60.00	50.93	60.02	59.94	59.66	60.07	59.97	59.80

Table 4: Forecasting Performance for US Dollar / Swiss Franc

	mean	r.w.	AR of order 1	AR of order 3	AR of order 10	AR-AIC	AR-SIC	AR-HQ	Exp. Smooth	CVAR DEM_JPY	CVAR GBP_DEM	CVAR GBP_USD	CVAR USD_DEM	CVAR USD_ITL	CVAR USD_JPY
MSE	10.63	10.63	10.28	10.28	10.28	10.28	10.28	10.28	10.65	47.24	54.09	57.62	119.69	47.33	51.77
MAE	6.25	6.25	6.19	6.18	6.20	6.20	6.19	6.20	6.28	13.93	14.60	15.81	22.06	13.91	14.72
% sign prediction	53.08	-	59.48	58.83	58.32	58.37	58.43	51.96	52.42	59.25	58.95	57.76	58.99	59.26	58.77

STOCHASTIC LOTKA-VOLTERRA SYSTEMS OF COMPETING AUTO-CATALYTIC AGENTS LEAD GENERICALLY TO TRUNCATED PARETO POWER WEALTH DISTRIBUTION, TRUNCATED LEVY-STABLE INTERMITTENT MARKET RETURNS, CLUSTERED VOLATILITY, BOOMS AND CRASHES

SORIN SOLOMON

Racah Institute of Physics
Givat Ram, Hebrew University of Jerusalem
E-mail: sorin@vms.huji.ac.il; http://shum.huji.ac.il/~sorin

We give a microscopic representation of the stock-market in which the microscopic agents are the individual traders and their capital. Their basic dynamics consists in the auto-catalysis of the individual capital and in the global competition/cooperation between the agents mediated by the total wealth/index of the market. We show that such systems lead generically to (truncated) Pareto power-law distribution of the individual wealth. This, in turn, leads to intermittent market returns parametrized by a (truncated) Levy-stable distribution. We relate the truncation in the Levy-stable distribution to the fact that at each moment no trader can own more than the total wealth in the market. In the cases where the system is dominated by the largest traders, the dynamics looks similar to noisy low-dimensional chaos. By introducing traders memory and/or feedback between global and individual wealth fluctuations, one obtains auto-correlations in the time evolution of the "volatility" as well as market booms and crashes.

The financial markets display some puzzling universal features which while identified long ago are still begging for explanation. Recently, following the availability of computer for data acquisition, processing and simulation these features came under more precise, quantitative study [1]. We first describe phenomenologically these effects and then the unified conceptual framework which accounts for all of them.

1   Phenomenological Puzzles

1.1   Pareto Power Distribution of Individual Wealth

Already 100 years ago, it was observed by Vilifredo Pareto [2] that the number of people $P(w)$ possessing the wealth w can be parametrized by a power law:

$$P(w) \sim w^{-1-\alpha} \tag{1}$$

The actual value for α in Eq. (1), was of course only approximately known to Pareto, due to the limited data at his disposal but, modulo improvement in the accuracy of the statistics seems to have been constantly 1.4 throughout most of the

A.-P.N. Refenes et al. (eds.), Decision Technologies for Computational Finance, 73–86.
© 1998 *Kluwer Academic Publishers. Printed in the Netherlands..*

free-economies in the last 100 years. This wealth distribution is quite nontrivial in as far as it implies the existence of many individuals with wealth 3 orders of magnitude larger than the average. To compare, if such a distribution would hold for personal weight, height or life span it would imply the existence of individual humans 1 Km tall, weighting 70 tons and living 70 000 years.

1.2 Intermittent market fluctuations with Levy-stable distribution of returns

It was observed by Benoit Mandelbrot [4] in the 60's that the market returns defined in terms of the time relative variation of the stock index w (t):

$$r\ (t,T)\ =\ (w(t)-\ w(t-T))/w(t-T) \tag{2}$$

are not behaving as a Gaussian (random walk with given size steps) but rather as a so called Levy-stable distribution [3].

In practical terms this meant that the probability $Q\ (\ r\ )$ for large returns r to occur is not proportional to $Q\ (\ r\ )\ \sim\ e^{-kr**2}$ as for usual uncorrelated random Gaussian noise but rather to $Q\ (\ r\ )\ \sim r^{-1-\beta}$. The Levy-stable distribution implies that the actual market fluctuations are very significantly larger than the ones estimated by assuming the usual Gaussian noise. This in turn implies larger risks for the stock market traders and affects the prices of futures, options, insurances and other contracts. The difference between the Gaussian and the Levy-stable distribution is dramatically experienced by traders occasionally, when the gains accumulated over a previous long period of time are lost overnight.

1.3 Deterministic Chaotic Dynamics of the Global Lotka-Volterra Maps

With the arrival of the Chaos theories, it was noticed that the prices in the markets behave in a way as if they would be governed by the deterministic motion of a point moving under nonlinear kinematical rules in a space with a small number of dimensions/parameters [5].

One of the earliest chaotic systems was invented in the late 20's by Lotka and Volterra [6] in order to explain the annual fluctuations in the volume of fish populations in the Adriatic Sea.

If one denotes by $w(t)$ the number of fish in the year t, these "discrete logistic" equations would predict that the fish population at the year t+1 to be:

$$w\ (t+1)\ =\ (1-d+\ b)\ w(t)\ -\ c\ w^2\ (t) \tag{3}$$

The terms in the bracket in Eq. (3) represent respectively :
- The fish population in the year t.
- Minus the proportion (d) of fish which die of natural death (or emigrate from the ecology) from one year (t) to another ($t+1$)
- Plus the proportion (b) of fish born (or immigrated) from year t to year $t+1$.

The quadratic term $-c\,w^2\,(t)$ in Eq. (3) originates in the fact that the probability that 2 fish would meet and compete for the same territory /food /mate is proportional to the product $w(t) \times w(t)$. Obviously, only one will obtain the resource and the other one will die, emigrate (be driven out) or be prevented from procreating.

For certain values of the constants b, d, c, the population $w(t)$ approaches a stationary value: $w(t) = (b-d)/c$ but for an entire range of parameters, the system Eq. (3) leads to chaotic annual changes in $w(t)$. To understand it, consider for instance the case in which in the year t the population $w(t)$ is very small such that the quadratic term $-c\,w(t)^2$ is much smaller than the linear term $(1-d+b)\,w(t)$. If $(1-d+b)$ is large enough, then the number of fish in the following year $w(t+1) \sim (1-d+b)\,w(t)$ might become quite large. In fact $w(t+1)$ may become so large as to make the quadratic term next year $-b\,w^2\,(t+1)$ comparable to $(1-d+b)\,w(t+1)$. The two terms would then cancel and the population $w\,(t+2)$ in the following year would decrease. This may lead to a large $w(t+3)$ and so on up and down. It is clear then, that in certain ranges of the parameters, the population will have a quite chaotic (but deterministic) fluctuating dynamics.

However, when people tried to exploit this kind of deterministic systems to predict the markets, it turned out that in fact the fluctuations have in addition to the deterministic chaotic motion very significant random noisy components as well as a continuos time drift in the parameters of the putative deterministic dynamics.

1.4 Quasi-periodic Market Crashes and Booms

In addition to the phenomena above, the market seemed to have strong positive feed-back mechanisms which in certain conditions would reinforce the trends leading to "volatility" clustering, booms and crashes which we will address later.

2   Theoretical Explanations

It came [7]as a surprise, 70 years after the introduction [6] of systems of the type Eq. (3), 100 years after the discovery [2] of the Pareto law Eq. (1) and about 30 years after noticing [4] the intermittent market fluctuations (1.2) that, in fact the generalized discrete logistic (Lotka-Volterra) systems (Eq. (3) and Eq. (5) below), do lead [7] generically to the effects 1.1.-1.3.

Moreover we have constructed realistic market models [8,20] which represent explicitly the individual investors and their market interactions and showed that these realistic models reduce effectively to generalized Lotka -Volterra dynamics Eq. (5) and that these models lead generically to the intrinsic emergence of occasional crashes and booms (effect 1.4). Let us explain how all this happens.

2.1 Generic Scaling Emergence in Stochastic Systems with Auto-catalytic Elements

Consider the population $w(t)$ of the Lotka-Volterra system Eq. (3) as a sum of N sub-populations (families, tribes, sub-species) indexed by an index i :

$$w(t) = w_1(t) + w_2(t) + \ldots + w_N(t) \tag{4}$$

Obviously, the evolution equations for the $w_i(t+1)$'s have to be such as to reproduce upon summation the discrete logistic Lotka-Volterra system Eq. (3) for $w(t+1)$. We are therefore lead to postulate that the parts $w_i(t)$ fulfill the following dynamics.

At each time interval t one of the i's is chosen randomly to be updated according to the rule:

$$w_i(t+1) = \lambda(t) \, w_i(t) + a(t) \, w(t) - c(t) \, w(t) \, w_i(t) \tag{5}$$

The variability originating in the individual local conditions is reflected in the dependence of the coefficients $\lambda(t)$, a and c on time. In particular, $\lambda(t)$ are random numbers of order 1 extracted each time from a strictly positive distribution $\Pi(\lambda)$ while a and c are much smaller than $1/N$. This dynamics describes a system in which the generations are overlapping and individuals are continuously being born (and die) (first term in Eq. (5)), diffusing between the sub-populations (second term) and compete for resources (third term).

The dynamics Eq. (5) describes equally well the evolution of the wealth $w_i(t)$ of the individuals i in a financial market. More precisely Eq. (5) represents the wealth $w_i(t+1)$ of the individual i at time $t+1$ in terms his/her wealth $w_i(t)$ at time t:

- The first (and most important) term in Eq. (5) expresses the auto-catalytic property of the capital: its contribution to the capital $w_i(t+1)$ at time $t+1$ is equal to the capital $w_i(t)$ at time t multiplied by the random factor $\lambda(t)$ which reflects the relative gain/loss which the individual incurred during the last trade period. (This property is consistent with the actual phenomenological data which indicate that the distribution of individual incomes is proportional to the distribution of individual wealth).
- The second term $+ a(t) \, w(t)$ expresses the auto-catalytic property of wealth at the social level and it represents the wealth the individuals receive as members of the society in subsidies, services and social benefits. This term is proportional to the general social wealth (index) $w(t)$.
- The last term $- c(t) \, w(t) \, w_i(t)$ in Eq. (5) originates in the competition between each individual i and the rest of the society. It has the effect of limiting the growth of $w(t)$ to values sustainable for the current conditions and resources. The effects of inflation , or proportional taxation are well taken into account by this term.

With these assumptions, it turns out that Eq. (5) leads to a power law distribution of the instantaneous $w_i(t)$ values i.e. the probability $P(w.)$ for one of the $w_i(t)$'s to take the value $w.$ is:

$$P(w.) \sim w.^{-1-\alpha} \text{ with typically } 1 < \alpha < 2. \tag{6}$$

Generically, the origin of the distribution $P(w.)$ in Eq. (6) can be traced to its scaling properties. More precisely, the probability distribution of the form Eq. (6) is the only one whose shape (parameter α) does not change at all upon a rescaling transformation

$$w_i(t) \rightarrow 2 w_i (t) \tag{7}$$

In fact, by a rescaling Eq. (7), the Eq (6) transforms into itself with the same α:

$$P_\alpha (w) \rightarrow P_\alpha(2 w) \sim (2 w)^{-1-\alpha} \sim w^{-1-\alpha} \sim P_\alpha(w)$$

in contrast to say the Gaussian $Q_k (r)$ whose shape (parameter k) changes $(k \rightarrow 4k)$:

$$Q_k(r) \rightarrow Q_k(2 r) \sim e^{-k(2r)^{**2}} \sim e^{-4k\,r^{**2}} \sim Q_{4k} (r) \neq Q_k (r).$$

It is therefore expected that such distributions Eq. (6) will be the result of dynamics which is invariant itself under the rescaling Eq. (7). This turns out to be the case of the generalized Lotka-Volterra dynamics generated by Eq. (5). Indeed, if one applies the scaling transformation Eq. (7) on one of the $w_i (t)$'s in Eq. (5) one obtains:

$$2 w_i (t+1) = 2 \lambda(t)\ w_i (t) + 2 a (t)\ w_i (t) - 2 c(t)\ u_i (t)\ w_i (t)$$
$$+ a(t)\quad u_i(t)\quad - 4 c (t)\ w_i^{2}(t) \tag{8}$$

where we noted $u_i (t) = w(t) - w_i (t)$.

One sees that $w_i (t+1)$ updated according to Eq. (8) has the same dynamics as before the rescaling transformation (updating according to the Eq. (5)) except for the last 2 terms which are not scaling invariant. Therefore, one expects the scaling power law Eq. (6) to hold for values of the $w_i (t)$'s for which these last 2 terms are negligible in comparison with the other terms in Eq. (8) (recall $a, c << 1/N$):

$$w/N < w_i (t) < w \tag{9}$$

This is quite a considerable range if the system has a large number of elements $i=1,...,N$. Note that for the single variable Lotka Volterra Eq. (3) the scaling range Eq. (9) does not exist as $N=1$ and there is no differentiation between $w_i (t)$ and $w (t)$.

The explicit simulation of Eq. (5) confirms this prediction [18]. The dynamics is best visualized in terms of the logarithm [9] of the investors relative wealth (normalized to the index w): $v_i (t) = \ln (w_i(t)/w(t))$. If one starts with all the traders having the same wealth (delta function distribution at $v_i(0)= -\ln N$), after a relatively short time, the distribution will diffuse into a spreading log-normal distribution. Upon drifting into the lower cut-off induced by the term $\ln a$ (cf. Eq. (5)), the shape of the v_i's distribution $\wp(v)$ will change into a decreasing exponential. In fact if the diffusion coefficient is σ and the drift coefficient is $-\mu$, then $\wp(v)$ fulfills the master equation :

$$\partial \wp(v)/\partial t = \sigma \partial^2 \wp(v)/\partial v^2 - \mu \partial \wp(v)/\partial v$$

which admits the exponential solution $\wp(v)\, dv \sim e^{-v\mu/\sigma}\, dv$. This exponential distribution for the $v_i(t)$'s corresponds to a power law Eq. (6) with exponent $\alpha = \mu/\sigma$ in the original w_i variables [19]:

$$\wp(\ln w)\, d \ln w \sim e^{-(\ln w)\mu/\sigma}\, 1/w\, d w = w^{-1-\mu/\sigma} d w$$

In spite of the fact that the terms non homogenous in $w_i (t)$ in the Eq. (8) are negligible in the scaling range Eq. (9), they do play a crucial role in fixing the boundary conditions for the scaling dynamics. This in turns determine the effective parameters σ and $-\mu$ and therefore the value of the scaling exponent α. More precisely, upon substituting the instantaneous ideal value $<w(t)>$ of $w(t)$ (the currently expected value of $w(t)$ neglecting fluctuations and relaxation time Eq.(5)):

$$< w (t) > = (< \lambda (t) > -1 + N <a (t) >)/ <c(t)> \tag{10}$$

into the Eq. (5), one obtains:

$$w_i (t+1) =(\lambda (t) - < \lambda (t) > +1 - N <a (t) >)\ w_i (t) + a (t)\ w(t) \tag{11}$$

The exponent α in Eq. (6) is then fixed (neglecting in the region Eq. (9) the term $a(t)w(t)$) by the condition that the distribution $P (w)\, d w$ is unchanged by the updating Eq. (11). I.e. the flow of traders leaving a certain wealth level w to become poorer or richer equals the total flow of traders arriving at the wealth w from poorer or richer wealth stations $w/(\lambda-<\lambda >+1-N a)$ upon undergoing the transformation Eq. (11):

$$w^{-1-\alpha}\ dw = \int \Pi(\lambda)\ [w/(\lambda - <\lambda > + 1 - N a)]^{-1-\alpha}\ d w/(\lambda - <\lambda > + 1 - N a)\ d\lambda \tag{12}$$

where $\Pi(\lambda)$ is the distribution of λ used in Eq. (5). This leads to the transcendental equation for α [11]:

$$\int \Pi(\lambda)(\lambda(t) - < \lambda (t) > +1 - N <a (t) >)^\alpha\ d\lambda = 1 \tag{13}$$

which, given N, a and the distribution $\Pi(\lambda)$ of λ does not depend on c or on an overall shift in $\lambda : \Pi(\lambda) \to \Pi(\lambda-\lambda_0)$. This equation can be either solved numerically for α, or approximately by expanding the bracket around 1 in powers of $\lambda (t) - < \lambda (t) > - N <a (t) >$. This leads for $N a << (<\lambda^2 > - < \lambda >^2) = \sigma^2 << 1$ to the approximate solution :

$$\alpha \approx 1+ 2 N a /[\sigma^2 + (N a)^2] \tag{14}$$

One sees from Eq. (10) that upon changes in the external conditions (resources, predators, etc.), represented by variations in $<c(t)>$, the total population can change by orders of magnitude without affecting the Eq. (13) which determines the exponent α. Therefore the distribution of the individual wealth fulfills the power law Eq. (6) even in non-stationary conditions when $<w(t)>$ varies continuously in time. In fact, even for $c=0$, when an instantaneous ideal value does not exists and the total wealth (/market index) $w(t)$ increases indefinitely, one observes in each particular moment t a very precise power law distribution among the current $w_i (t)$ values, with a stable α exponent. This is confirmed both by simulations and by the observation of experimental data. If w 's are town populations or sub-species, a power law distribution which survives large ecological fluctuations in Eq. (10) is predicted.

Note also that the limit $c= 0$, $a \rightarrow 0$ is not uniform: Eq. (14) gives then $\alpha = 1$ while it is known that in the total absence of the lower bound term a, the multiplicative dynamics leads to an ever-flattening log-normal distribution which approaches $\alpha = 0$. This is of practical importance as indeed most of the systems in nature which display power laws have exponents α between 1 and 2 .

A similar situation holds for the case in which the term a (t) $w(t)$ is substituted by a reflecting wall [11] which disallows any $w_i(t)$ to assume values lower than $\varepsilon(t) \equiv \omega_0 w(t)/N$:

$$w_i \ (t) > \ \varepsilon \ (t) \equiv \omega_0 \ w(t) \ /N \tag{15}$$

where $0 < \omega_0 < 1$.
In the typical western economies $\omega_0 \sim 1/3$, this corresponds to a social policy where no individual is allowed to slump below the fraction ω_0 of the average wealth w (t) $/N$. More specifically, during the simulation of the linearized ($a= 0$, $c= 0$) Eq. (5) each time that w_i $(t+1)$ comes out less then $\varepsilon(t)$, its value is actually updated to $\varepsilon(t)$. In this case, the exponent α turns out totally independent on $\Pi(\lambda)$ and for a wide range is determined only by the approximate formula [11]:

$$\alpha=1/(1-\omega_0). \tag{16}$$

Note again that the limit of no lower bound $\omega_0 \rightarrow 0$ leads to $\alpha=1$ while in reality for finite N in the absence of lower bound effects, the distribution approaches for $\omega_0= 0$ an infinitely flat log-normal distribution corresponding to $\alpha=0$. However, the value $\alpha=1$ is relevant for firms sizes, towns populations and words frequencies where a very small but finite lower bound is provided by the natural discretization of w_i (number of firm employees, town residents, word occurrences cannot be lower than 1). The Eq. (16) can be obtained starting form the expressions for the total probability and the total wealth. First, using the total probability $= 1$, one fixes (assuming $N/\omega_0 >>1$) the constant of proportionality in Eq. (6):

$$1= C\int_\varepsilon x^{-1-\alpha} \ dx \Rightarrow \ \ 1 \approx C \varepsilon^{-\alpha} \ /\alpha \Rightarrow \ \ C \approx \alpha \ [\omega_0 w/N]^\alpha \tag{17}$$

Then, using the expression for C in the formula of the total wealth w one gets:

$$w = NC\int_\varepsilon x^{-\alpha} \ dx \Rightarrow w \approx \ NC \ \varepsilon^{1-\alpha} \ /(\alpha-1) = \ \alpha\omega_0 w/(\alpha-1) \tag{18}$$

which means

$$1 \approx \alpha\omega_0/(\alpha-1) \tag{19}$$

which by solving with respect to α leads to (16). For very low values of $\omega_0 << 1/N$ the upper bound w in the integral in (18) becomes relevant and the value of α does depend on N:

$$\alpha \approx - \ln N / (\ln \omega_0 - \ln N) \tag{20}$$

which in particular has the correct limit $\alpha = 0$ for $\omega_0 = 0$. For intermediate values, one can solve numerically the couple of equations (17) and (18) with the correct upper bounds (*w*) in the integrals and the result agrees with the actual simulations of the linearized random system Eq. (5) submitted to the lower bound constraint (15). This concludes the deduction of the truncated Pareto power law 1.1 in generic markets (and in general systems consisting of auto-catalyzing parts, ecologies, etc.).

2.2 Pareto Power Wealth Distribution implies Intermittent Levy-Stable Returns

Let us now understand the emergence of the property *1.2*: the fluctuations of the *w(t)* around its ideal instantaneous value $< w(t) >$ Eq. 10 are not Gaussian. The "Gaussian" distribution is intuitively visualized by imagining a person ("drunkard") taking at each time *t* a step (of approximate unit size) to the left or to the right with equal probability ½. The Gaussian probability distribution Q (*r*) is then approximately defined by the probability for the person ("drunkard") to end-up after *T* steps, at the distance *r (T)* from the starting point . For instance, the probability for the largest fluctuations (say *r (T)= T*) to occur is easy to compute: it is the probability that all the *T* steps will be in the same direction. This equals the product of the probabilities ½ for each of the *T* steps separately to be in that direction i.e. $(½)^T$. At the first sight, this Gaussian random walk description fits well the time evolution of the sum *w* Eq. (4) under the dynamics Eq. (5): at each time step one of the $w_i(t)$'s is updated to a new value $w_i(t+1)$ and the sum *w(t)* changes by the random quantity $w_i(t+1) - w_i(t)$. Consequently, the dynamics of *w(t)* consists of a sequence of random steps of magnitude $w_i(t+1) - w_i(t)$. The crucial caveat is that according to the Eq. (5) , for the range Eq. (9) in which the last 2 terms in Eq. (7) are negligible, the steps $w_i(t+1)-w_i(t)$ are proportional to the w_i *(t)*'s themselves. Consequently, *w(t)* evolves by random steps whose magnitude is not approximately equal to any given unit length. Rather, the random steps $w_i(t+1) - w_i(t)$ have various magnitudes with probabilities distributed by a power law probability distribution Eq. (6). Random walks with steps whose sizes are not of a given scale [3] but are distributed by a power law probability distribution Eq. (6) $P (w.) \sim w.^{-1-\alpha}$ are called Levy flights. The associated probability distribution $Q_\alpha(r)$ that after *T* such steps the distance from an initial value *w(t)* will be $r = (w(t+T)- w(t))/w(t)$ is called a Levy-stable[1] distribution of index α.

The Levy-stable distribution[2] has very different properties from a Gaussian distribution. For instance the probability that after *T* steps, the walker will be at a distance *r= T* from the starting point is this time dominated by the probability that

---

[1] The name "stable" has to do with another property of these distributions which is not directly relevant to this letter.

[2] There is a cut-off in the Levy-stable distribution for large values of *r*. This is discussed in Section 3 below.

one of the steps is of size T. This will happen (according to Eq. (6)) with probability of order $T^{-1-\alpha}$. To see the dramatic difference between the time fluctuations $r = (w(t+T)- w(t))/w(t)$ predicted by the Levy flights vs. the ones predicted by the Gaussian, consider the typical numerical example $\alpha = 1.5$ and $T=25$. The probability that after a sequence of 25 steps, a Levy flyer will be at a distance 25 from the starting point is $25^{-2.5}$ i.e. about 1000 times larger than the corresponding Gaussian walk probability estimated above: $1/2^{25}$.

Therefore, our model Eq. (5), predicts the emergence with significant probability of very large (intermittent) Levy-stable distributed market fluctuations.

In fact we reach a more general conclusion: ANY quantity which is a sum of random increments proportional to the wealths $w_i(t)$ will have fluctuations described by a Levy-stable distribution of index β equal to the exponent α of the wealth power distribution Eq. (6) of the w_i's.

In particular, if one assumes that the individual investments are stochastically proportional to the investor's wealth (which is consistent with the empirical fact that the income distribution is proportional to the wealth distribution) then one predicts [11] that the stock market fluctuations will be described (effect 1.2) by a Levy stable distribution of index equal to the measured exponent $\alpha =1.4$ of the Pareto wealth distribution Eq. (6) (effect 1.1). This highly nontrivial relation between the wealth distribution and the market fluctuations is confirmed by the comparison of the latest available experimental data [12] .

In principle alternative mechanisms exploiting the Lotka-Volterra mechanism could take place: the investors could be roughly of the same wealth but act in "herds" [13-16] of magnitude w_i which evolve according the generalized Lotka-Volterra Eq. (5). This would lead to power law distribution in the size of these herds and consequently to a Levy stable distribution in the market fluctuations. However unless all the investors in a herd make their bid at the same time, the herding will show in time correlations of the stock evolution. Presently, there is no evidence for such correlations nor for the presence of scaling herds. Still, one should keep an open mind [16,22] about the significance of the $w_i(t)$'s involved in the Eq. (5).

2.3 Levy-Stable fluctuations may look like noisy, drifting, deterministic Chaos

In usual stochastic systems in which the elementary degrees of freedom $w_i(t)$ are of the same order of magnitude, the fluctuations around the mean value are the result of a large number of random contributions of the same size: Gaussian noise.

In the case in which the elementary degrees of freedom are distributed according to Eq. (6) the largest degrees of freedom are macroscopic and, in certain cases (especially for low α), the dynamics is dominated by the few largest elements.

This might look locally as a chaotic process of low dimensionality (small number of parameters and of degrees of freedom). However, the relevant $w_i(t)$'s may change in time and the smaller $w_i(t)$'s do imply additional fluctuations not related with the dominating degrees of freedom. Therefore, while in certain limits one may obtain deterministic low dimensional chaos, this is only an extreme idealization.

2.4 Market Crashes; Market Strategies Changes; How Generic is Scaling ?

The model Eq. (5) was initially proposed as a mezoscopic description of a wide series of simulation experiments on the (Levy-Levy-Solomon [8,20-22]) **LLS** microscopic representation model. The LLS model considers [8] individual investors with various procedures of deciding the amount of stock to sell/buy at each time and studies the resulting market dynamics. The variants of the basic model displayed always the central features of Eq. (5). In particular, for a very wide range of wealth Eq. (9) the gain/loss of each investor was stochastically proportional to its current wealth. So was its influence on the market changes. Therefore the ingredients necessary to obtain the effects 1.1.-1.3 through the mechanisms described above were always in place in the realistic LLS market models.

Moreover, a very simple mechanism for booms and crashes (effect 1.4) was naturally present in many of the LLS runs [8]: each investor had the tendency to assume that the future behavior of the market is going to be similar to the past one. This meant that prices had the tendency to rise beyond the value justified by the expected dividends (the investors expected gain from the sheer increase in the stock price). This lead to a quite unstable situation as the discrepancy between the dividends and the market price level became more and more severe. At a certain stage, an usual, relatively mild downwards fluctuation would take place. As this downwards fluctuation was internalized as part of the traders past experience, it lead to a lowering of the future expectations, followed by a further decrease in prices. This triggered eventually an avalanche effect. The down trend would stop only as the market price became so low that the expectation of the dividends alone justified buying the stock. Therefore, even the simplest versions of the LLS model are capable to generate in addition to the universal features 1.1-1.3 also the cycles of crashes and booms characteristic for the real markets.

The simple LLS model was also capable to create interesting dynamics in the strategies of the investors. Indeed, as it happened often [20], the investors having a particular investing policy would be occasionally advantaged by the current dynamics of the market. This would cause them to earn more from the market fluctuations. As they became richer, they influenced increasingly the market changing thereby its dynamics. In the new dynamical state, another group would become advantaged and start to become richer thereby changing in its turn the character of the market. The new market behavior would be advantageous for yet another group and so on. Therefore the market would pass through various epochs without external influence and without any of the investors changing its strategy [20].

Recently, models considering strategy changes have been proposed [5,16,22], which may lead to yet richer results. The inclusion of adaptive agents, transaction costs, herding effects etc. in the LSS model is quite straightforward but may lead to further uncovering of unexpected and highly non-trivial relationships and results.

Finally, one can consider the possible extensions of the dynamics Eq. (5) to even more generic systems. First, one can use instead of the average $w(t)$ Eq. (4) any combination of the $w_i(t)$'s with positive coefficients or a general function $W(w_1, ... w_N)$ which depends monotonically (increasingly) in each of the $w_i(t)$'s. Secondly the random distribution of the λ's, and the constants a and c can be included in a more general form [7]:

$$w_i(t+1) = \Phi(t,W) w_i(t) + \Psi(t,W) \tag{21}$$

where Φ and Ψ are such that there exists an "equilibrium region" of W's for which the function $<\Phi(W)> - 1$ changes sign and for which $<\Psi(W)>$ is much smaller than 1. Assuming the w_i's very small compared with W, one can consider a generic stochastic updating procedure:

$$w_i(t+1) - w_i(t) = \partial \Lambda(t,W) / \partial w_i \tag{22}$$

where Λ is a random potential whose partial derivatives admit Eq. (21) as an approximate linear expansion in the w_i's around its (dynamical) ground state. The properties 1.1-1.3 will then still hold for a wide range of parameters.

3   Corrections to Levy-flight behavior. Relation to (G)ARCH models

Let us now return to the dynamics of the system Eq. (5) and study the departures from a perfect uncorrelated Levy-flight behavior. This is of more than academic interest in as far as real markets display clearly the existence of such departures both in the market returns distribution and in the time correlations (especially of the market "volatility").

Let us first discuss the departures from the ideal Levy-stable shape of the market fluctuations (returns) assuming for the moment that the individual steps $w_i(t+1) - w_i(t) \sim (\lambda-1) w_i(t)$ are independent In order to obtain a perfect Levy-stable shape it is necessary that the sizes of the individual steps of the Levy-flights are distributed perfectly by the power law Eq. (6) up to arbitrary large steps sizes. This is obviously inconsistent with the wealth truncation Eq. (9) which implies that steps of size $(\lambda-1) w_i(t) > (\lambda-1) w(t)$ have 0 probability to appear. Therefore, steps of arbitrary size expected from the Levy-flight model fail to appear in the model Eq. (5): the Pareto Power-law in w_i Eq. (6) is truncated and consequently the corresponding Levy-stable distribution in $r(t)$ Eq. (2) is truncated. This starts to be quantitatively relevant for times T for which according to the untruncated distribution, the probability of elements of size w to appear is of order 1. This T can be estimated by estimating the probability (in the absence of truncation) for a w_i to equal or exceed the entire wealth w in the system (cf. Eq. (17)):

$$P(w) = C w^{-\alpha} / \alpha \approx w^{-\alpha} [\omega_0 w / N]^\alpha = [\omega_0 / N]^\alpha \tag{23}$$

Therefore, in a non-truncated Levy flight, one would expect for times $T \geq [N/\omega_0]^\alpha$ the appearance, with high probability, of $w_i(t)$'s of order $w(t)$ and larger. Since such $w_i(t)$'s will fail to show up, the distribution looks truncated. For T's of the order $T \sim [N/\omega_0]^\alpha$, the truncation will just consist in the probability being 0 for fluctuations beyond the magnitude $(\lambda_{max} -1)$ w (t). For even larger times, the truncation will appear trough the fact that the largest fluctuations will be dominated by the probability to have a few individual steps of the largest allowed size $(\lambda_{max} -1)$ w (t) rather than one single step of larger (un-allowed by Eq. (9)) magnitude. This will lead to an exponential tail rather than the naively expected untruncated Levy-stable law. For times $T > N^{1+\alpha}$ this Gaussian mechanism replaces the Levy-flight dynamics over the entire distribution.

These departures from the Levy-stable shape are actually compounded with deviations from the assumption of stochastic independence of the successive $w(t)$ increments $w_i(t+1) - w_i(t)$. Indeed, the value of the $w_i(t+1)$ depends through the linear term a and especially through the bilinear term $-cw_i(t)w(t)$ on the other $w_i(t)$'s at previous times. In particular, if the updating of a large $w_i(t)$ induces a large departure of $w(t)$ from its ideal value $< w(t) >$, this departure will survive for a while and it will influence the dynamics of the updatings of the subsequent $w_i(t)$'s . Therefore, one expects that the dynamics Eq. (5) will lead to time correlations in the fluctuations amplitudes. This kind of effects are recorded in actual market measurements and it is desirable to take advantage of the various possible mechanisms to generate and control them.

In particular, a very important extension of (5) is to make the distribution $\Pi(t,\lambda)$ of the λ's in Eq.(5) dependent on the w_i' s or of their time variations. For instance, one can dynamically update the distribution Π (t,λ) to equal the distribution of the returns r during the time period preceding t. This would induce time correlations in the "volatility" and clustering similar to the ones observed in nature and mimed by the various ARCH models [23]. The difference would be that, in our case, the distribution will also reproduce more realistically the (truncated) Levy-stable character of the fluctuations.

Another dependence of the λ's on the previous dynamics is suggested by the intuition that the actual increase or decrease $(\lambda-1)$ $w_i(t)$ in the capital invested in stock by an individual trader i is a result of the actual trends (returns r) in the market in the time passed since his/her last trade(s). This can take place both because the direct influence of the market on the trader's wealth as well as through the market trends influence on his/her investment decisions. Limiting oneself only to the influence of the return since the last trade (this can be relaxed by taking into account longer memories [8,20]) one is lead to the dynamics:

$$w_i(t+1) = (\eta(t) + \mu(t) r_i(t)) w_i(t) + a(t) w(t) - c(t) w(t) w_i(t) \qquad (24)$$

where μ and η are parameters and the return $r_i(t)$ since the last trade is defined by :

$$r_i(t) = (w(t) - w(t_i))/w(t_i) \qquad (25)$$

where the time t_i in Eq. (25) is the last time the element i was updated. Recall that at each time t , there is one single element i which is randomly selected for being updated by the Eq. (5) respectively Eq. (24)). Therefore the term $w(t)-w(t_i)$ couples the past fluctuations in the market to the individual capital fluctuations.

The random character of the terms $\mu(t)$ and $\eta(t)$ is not mandatory. In its absence, the random selection of the updated element i is the only source of randomness in (24). The new multiplicative term r_i (t) in Eq. (24) introduces positive feedback in the dynamics of the w_i's: an increase in w_i leads to an increase in w, which leads to an increase in r which leads to an increase in w_i closing the positive feedback loop. In certain cases this can lead to crashes in other macroscopic events. Following the dynamics Eq. (24)-Eq. (26), both r_i and w_i will acquire long power-like tails and one expects a 2-powers tail in the market price $w(t)$ fluctuations of the type lately measured in real markets [13].

A variety of sub-models can be constructed with "personalized" (i-dependent) investment strategies $X_i(t,(r(.),w(.))$ which are functionals of the past market **history** $w(.)$. In particular the X_i's may simulate adaptive technical trading strategies and/or portfolio optimization (by investing in more than one instrument w_i $^K)$. Moreover, one may introduce an active monetary policy by making the all terms adaptive/history dependent:

$$w_i^{\ K}\ (t+1) = X_i^K(t,,\ w_j^L\ (.))(\ 1+r_i^K(t))\ w_i^K\ (t)\ +\ E(w_j^L\ (.))\ -\ F(w_j^L\ (.))\ w_i^K(t)$$
(26)

This would constitute a middle ground efficient compromise between the microscopic representation LLS model [8,20]and the mezoscopic effective model Eq.(5).

4   Acknowledgments

This research was supported in part by the USA-Israel Binational Science Foundation, the Germany-Israel Foundation. I thank the co-authors of my papers quoted in this report: O. Biham, H. Levy, M. Levy, O.Malcai, N. Persky. Dietrich Stauffer provided much of the energy for this quite long series of papers. Tito Arecchi suggested the dynamics of the type Eq. (22) for the study of chaotic systems.

5   References

1) S. Solomon, in *Annual Reviews of Computational Physics* I, Ed. D. Stauffer, p. 243 (World Scientific, 1995).

2) Pareto, V. Cours d'Economique Politique}, Vol 2, (1897).} *Manual of Political Economy*, Macmilan. G.K. Zipf, *Human Behaviour and the Principle of Least Effort* (Addison Wesley Press, Cambridge MA 1949).

3) P. Levy, *Theorie de l'Addition des Variables Aleatoires* Gauthier-Villiers, Paris, 1937 . E.W. Montroll and M.F. Shlesinger, Proc. Nat. Acad. Sci. USA 79 (1982)3380. R.N. Mantegna and H.E. Stanley in *Levy Flights and Related Topics in Physics*, Eds. M.E. Shlesinger, G. Zaslavsky and U. Frisch, Springer 1995.

4) Mandelbrot, B. B. J. Business 36, 394-419 (1963); *The Fractal Geometry of Nature*, Freeman, San Francisco, 1982), Econometrica 29 (1961) 517.

5) P.W. Anderson, J. Arrow and D. Pines, eds. *The Economy as an Evolving Complex System*, Redwood City, Calif.: Addison-Wesley,1988

6) J. Lotka, *Elements of Physical Biology*, Williams and Wilkins, Baltimore 1925.
   V. Volterra, Nature 118 (1926) 558; R.M. May, Nature 261 (1976) 207.

7) S. Solomon and M. Levy International Journal of Modern Physics C , Vol. 7, No.5 (1996) 745; O. Biham, M. Levy, O. Malcai and S. Solomon preprint.

8) M. Levy, H. Levy and S. Solomon, Econ. Let. 45(1994)103;J.Phys 5(1995)1087.

9) H.Simon, Biometrika, vol42, Dec.1955;Y. Ijiri and H.Simon, *Skew Distributions and the Sizes of Business Firms*,(North Holland, Amsterdam, 1977).

10) Gell-Mann, M. ,*The Quark and the Jaguar*, Little Brown and Co.,London 1994.

11)M. Levy and S. Solomon Int. J. Mod. Phys. C , Vol. 7 (1996) 595;

12)R. N. Mantegna and H. E. Stanley, Nature 383 (1996) 587; 376 (1995) 46.

13)Potters, M., Cont, R. and Bouchaud, J.P. Europhys. Lett 41 (1998) 3

14)Bak, P; Paczuski, M; Shubik, M. Physica A 3-4 (1997) 430.

15)D. Sornette and R. Cont J. Phys. I France 7, (1997) 431; Kesten, Acta. Math. 131 (1973) 207 .

16)M Marsili, S. Maslov and Y-C Zhang, cond-mat/ 9801239, Caldarelli, G; Marsili, M; Zhang, YC., Europhysics Letters 40 (1997) 479, Challet, D; Zhang, YC., Physica A 246 (1997) 407

17)M. Levy and S. Solomon Physica A 242 (1997) 90.

18)Takayasu et al., Phys. Rev.Lett. 79, 966 (1997)

19)M. Levy and S. Solomon, Int. J. Mod. Phys. C, Vol. 7, No.1 (1996) 65-72.

20)M. Levy, N. Persky and S. Solomon Int. J. of High Speed Computing 8 (1996)93

21)T. Hellthaler, Int. J. Mod. Phys. C 6 (1995) 845; D. Kohl to appear in Int. J. Mod. Phys. C.

22)S. Moss De Oliveira, P.M.C de Oliveira, D. Stauffer, *Sex, Money, War and Computers: Nontraditional Applications of Computational Statistical Mechanics*, in press 1998

23) BaillieR. and Bollerslev T. Review of Economic Studies 58 (1990) 565; Engle R.F., Ito T. and Lin W.-L. Econometrica 58 (1990) 525

PART 2

TRADING AND ARBITRAGE STRATEGIES

CONTROLLING NONSTATIONARITY IN STATISTICAL ARBITRAGE USING A PORTFOLIO OF COINTEGRATION MODELS

A. N. BURGESS

Department of Decision Science
London Business School
Sussex Place, Regents Park, London, NW1 4SA, UK
E-mail: N.Burgess@lbs.ac.uk

We present an analysis of time-series modelling which allows for the possibility of an "unmodelled" component which is present in the underlying generating process, but is not captured in a particular "model" of the time-series. Within this framework, "nonstationarity" is a relative, rather than an absolute, property, which is conditional on a given data representation, model and/or set of parameters. We apply this perspective to the problem of trading statistical arbitrage models which are based on the econometric notion of weak cointegration between asset prices. We show how a modelling framework which supports multiple models may reduce the out-of-sample performance degradation which is caused by non-stationarities in the relative price dynamics of the set of target assets. A necessary condition is shown to be that the unmodelled components of the individual models must be less than perfectly correlated, thus motivating the use of a population-based algorithm which jointly optimises a portfolio of decorrelated models. We describe an application of this methodology to trading statistical arbitrage between equity index futures and present empirical results, before concluding with a brief discussion of the issues raised and an outline of ongoing developments.

1 Introduction

In economic, and in particular, financial, time-series any single model can typically only explain a small fraction of the total variability; for instance forecasting models of financial asset prices can account for between 0 and 5% of the total variability in returns. Not only is it plausible to hypothesize multiple *models* of such time-series, it is also plausible that there are a number of factors at play in *creating* the dynamics. For instance, movements in the FTSE100 may be partly due to movements in the Dow Jones, partly due to movements in oil prices, partly due to short-term inefficiencies, partly due to sentiment, partly due to political factors, and so on. In addition, the relative importance of these different factors is likely to vary over time. Thus the performance of any single model is likely to suffer from instabilities, indicating the presence of non-stationarities.

In this paper, we present an analytic framework for modelling time-series which are generated by processes which are partially stochastic and partially deterministic in nature. A key feature of the framework is that it allows for the possibility of an "unmodelled" component which is present in the underlying generating process which produces an observed time-series, but is not captured in a particular "model" of the time-series. This unmodelled component arises partly

A.-P.N. Refenes et al. (eds.), Decision Technologies for Computational Finance, 89–107.

from the use of a restricted information set which does not necessarily contain all the relevant information, and partly from the choice of a particular family of models which may only be able to capture the underlying dynamics imperfectly. We show how the presence of such an "unmodelled" component can lead to "nonstationarity" in the behaviour of the system. This nonstationarity manifests itself in the form of a performance degradation during an "out of sample" period which is non-identical to the data sample used for parameter optimisation. From this perspective "nonstationarity", rather than an absolute, is a relative property which is conditional on a given data representation, model and/or set of parameters.

We apply this perspective to the problem of trading statistical arbitrage models which are based on the econometric notion of weak cointegration between asset prices. We show how a modelling framework which supports multiple models may reduce the impact, in terms of out-of-sample performance degradation, of non-stationarities in the relative price dynamics of the set of assets. A necessary condition is shown to be that the *unmodelled components* of the individual models must be less than perfectly correlated. This provides a motivation for the population-based algorithm of Burgess (1997) which is used to jointly optimise a portfolio of decorrelated and hence complementary models. Further results of this approach, and a discussion of the issues which they raise, are presented in this paper.

The paper is organised as follows. In section 2 we present the analytic framework for examining the relationship between non-stationarity and the unmodelled component of a time-series. In section 3 we present a definition of "statistical arbitrage" and describe a four-stage cointegration-based methodology for building statistical arbitrage models. In section 4 we describe an application of this methodology to trading statistical arbitrage between equity index futures and present empirical results. The paper concludes with a brief discussion and an outline of ongoing developments.

2   Nonstationarity

In this section we introduce a perspective on time-series modelling which allows for the possibility of an "unmodelled" component, which is present in the data-generating process of the time-series but is not captured in a specific model of a time-series. The following is a condensed and simplified presentation of the issues which arise in this context; for a fuller discussion see (Burgess, 1998).

2.1   Decomposition of model error

We can consider any random variable y_t as being the result of a data-generating process which is partially deterministic and partially stochastic:

$$y_t = g(\mathbf{z}_t) + \varepsilon(\mathbf{v}_t)_t \tag{1}$$

where the deterministic component is a function 'g' of the vector of independent variables $\mathbf{z}_t = \{\ z_{1,t}\ ,\ z_{2,\,t}\ ,\ \dots\ ,\ z_{nz,t}\ \}$ and the stochastic component is drawn from a distribution 'ε' which may vary as a function of variables $\mathbf{v}_t = \{\ v_{1,t}\ , v_{2,\,t}\ ,\ \dots\ ,\ v_{nv,t}\ \}$. Under the assumptions that the stochastic term is homoskedastic and normally distributed, the data-generating process would reduce to:

$$y_t = g(\mathbf{z}_t) + N(0, \sigma_y^2) \tag{2}$$

The purpose of modelling the data-generating process is to construct an estimator of the target series, y_t of the form:

$$\hat{y}_t = f(\mathbf{x}_t) \tag{3}$$

In general the function 'f' will not be identical to the true function 'g'. Similarly the "explanatory" variables $\mathbf{x}_t = \{\ x_{1,t}\ ,\ x_{2,\,t}\ ,\ \dots\ ,\ x_{nx,t}\ \}$ will not be identical to the truly influential variables $\mathbf{z}$. We can then define the model error η_t:

$$
\begin{aligned}
\eta_t &= y_t - \hat{y}_t \\
&= \big[g(\mathbf{z}_t) + \varepsilon(\mathbf{v}_t)_t\big] - f(\mathbf{x}_t) \\
&= \big[g(\mathbf{z}_t) - f(\mathbf{x}_t)\big] + \varepsilon(\mathbf{v}_t)_t
\end{aligned}
\tag{4}
$$

i.e. the model error, η_t, consists of one component which is due to the inherent stochastic component $\varepsilon(\mathbf{v}_t)$, and a second component which is due to the discrepancy between the true function 'g' of variables $\mathbf{z}$ and the estimated function 'f' of variables $\mathbf{x}$.

By considering the various steps of the modelling procedure it is possible to break down the model error into a number of components. Firstly, we define $g_R^*(\mathbf{x}_t)$ which is the "optimal" estimator of $g(\mathbf{z}_t)$ in the case where the information set is restricted to variables $\mathbf{x}$, and where "optimal" is defined as the function with minimal average loss over the probability distribution $p(\mathbf{y}, \mathbf{z})$:

$$g_R^*(\mathbf{x}_t) = \min_{g_R} \int L\big(y_t, g_R(\mathbf{x}_t)\big)\, dp \tag{5}$$

We can then define an "unmodelled" component $u(\mathbf{z}_t, \mathbf{x}_t)$ which corresponds to the difference between the true function $g(\mathbf{z}_t)$ and the estimator $g_R^*(\mathbf{x}_t)$ which is "optimal" with respect to the restricted information set $\mathbf{x}$:

$$u(\mathbf{z}_t, \mathbf{x}_t) = g(\mathbf{z}_t) - g_R^*(\mathbf{x}_t) \tag{6}$$

A further source of potential error is that in practice the optimisation of the function $g_R^*(\mathbf{x}_t)$ cannot be over all possible functions, but must be limited to a particular family of models 'f'. In the case of the least squares loss function, we define the asymptotically-optimal estimator f^* and parameter vector θ^*:

$$f^*(x_t, \theta^*) = \min_\theta \int L(y_t, f(x_t, \theta)) \, dp \qquad (7)$$
$$= \min_\theta \int (y_t - f(x_t, \theta))^2 \, dp$$

We can define the "bias" which is due to choosing a particular family of models:

$$b(f, x_t) = g_R^*(x_t) - f^*(x_t, \theta^*) \qquad (8)$$

In practice, we obtain a potentially different estimator $f(x_t, \theta)$ by optimising with respect to a particular empirical sample:

$$f(x_t, \theta) = \min_\theta \sum (y_t - f(x_t, \theta))^2 \, dp \qquad (9)$$

We can quantify this effect by defining the function $v(f, x_t, \theta)$ as the difference between the asymptotically optimal estimator $f^*(x_t, \theta^*)$ and the empirically optimised estimator $f(x_t, \theta)$:

$$v(f, x_t, \theta) = f^*(x_t, \theta^*) - f(x_t, \theta) \qquad (10)$$

We can now relate these quantities to the expected loss (mean-squared error) of the model $\hat{y} = f(x_t, \theta)$:

$$
\begin{aligned}
E[L(y_t, \hat{y}_t)] &= E[(y_t - \hat{y}_t)^2] \\
&= E[(f(x_t, \theta) + v(f, x_t, \theta) + b(f, x_t) + u(z_t, x_t) + \varepsilon(v_t)_t - f(x_t, \theta))^2] \\
&= E[v(f, x_t, \theta)^2] + E[b(f, x_t)^2] + E[u(z_t, x_t)^2] + E[\varepsilon(v_t)_t^2]
\end{aligned}
\qquad (11)
$$

Where the result is obtained under the assumption that the four sources of error are all independent, thus allowing the cross-terms within the expectation to disappear.

2.2 *Performance Degradation due to Nonstationarity*

The first two terms of (11) comprise the well known "bias-variance tradeoff": model variance is high for flexible functions and low for more restricted model families; conversely model bias is low for flexible functions and high for more-restricted function classes. Similarly, the implications of the fourth term, the inherent noise in the target variable, are relatively well understood. However, the third term, relating to the "unmodelled" component in the underlying generating process, is typically brushed aside with the assumptions that models should be both "well specified" and "stationary" before any meaningful statistical analysis can be conducted. We now investigate the implications of this additional source of model error, specifically the extent to which a particular model is indeed both "well specified" and "stationary".

In particular we demonstrate that traditional performance metrics and model selection criteria will, in general, over-estimate model performance and under-estimate generalisation error, when there is an unmodelled component in the deterministic part of the generating process. This performance degradation may occur in a number of forms but from the perspective of the limited information set **x** will have the common characteristic that the underlying process will appear to "change" in some way from one sample to another. As these samples are typically taken over different time periods, these changes will appear as **nonstationarities** in that certain properties of the data will appear to vary with time.

As an illustration of the effect which an unmodelled component has on the model error, consider the trivial but illustrative example:

$$y_t = x_t + z_t + \varepsilon_t \tag{12}$$

Where y_t is the target variable, x_t is an observed independent variable, z_t is an unobserved independent variable, and ε_t is a stochastic component. Choosing the model family provided by linear regression, the associated model is:

$$y_t = \alpha + \beta x_t + e_t \tag{13}$$

The forecast error can be broken down into the unmodelled component z_t, the inherent stochastic term ε_t and the model variance (sampling error) term $-\alpha + (1-\beta)x_t$. In this case, there is no model bias because the family of linear regression models contains the ideal (restricted) function: $\hat{y}_t = x_t$.

Given a sample $Z = \big((y_1, z_1, x_1), (y_2, z_2, x_2), \ldots\ldots, (y_n, z_n, x_n)\big)$, the parameters '$\alpha$' and '$\beta$' will be optimised using the ordinary-least squares (OLS) loss function, with respect to the restricted information set: $X = \big((y_1, x_1), (y_2, x_2), \ldots\ldots, (y_n, x_n)\big)$. Now, consider the "out of sample" error obtained by applying the model to a second set of data $X^{OS} = \big((y_{\tau+1}, x_{\tau+1}), \ldots, (y_{\tau+m}, x_{\tau+m})\big)$ which corresponds to the unrestricted information set $Z^{OS} = \big((y_{\tau+1}, z_{\tau+1}, x_{\tau+1}), \ldots, (y_{\tau+m}, z_{\tau+m}, x_{\tau+m})\big)$.

It is easy to show that the out-of-sample bias, i.e. the average value of the out-of-sample error is given by:

$$\mathrm{E}\big[e_{t,OS}\big] = \mathrm{E}\big[z_{t,OS}\big] - \mathrm{E}\big[z_t\big] = \Delta\,\mathrm{E}\big[z_t\big] \tag{14}$$

Thus, we can see that any change in the average value of the unobserved variable z_t will lead to a bias in the out-of-sample error. Similarly the "performance degradation" or increase in the expected loss is given by:

$$E\left[e_{t,os}{}^2\right] - E\left[e_t{}^2\right] = \Delta s_\varepsilon^2 + \Delta s_z^2 + E\left[(1-\beta)^2\right]\Delta s_x^2 + \Delta E\left[z_t\right]^2 + E\left[(1-\beta)^2\right]\Delta E\left[x_t\right]^2 \quad (15)$$

The first three terms lead to changes in the forecast error variance (heteroskedasticity) which may be either positive or negative. On the other hand, changes in the <u>average</u> value of either the observed or unobserved variable can only increase the forecast error. Of the two, changes in the unobserved variable have a *greater* impact on the model errors because they are not compensated for within the model. Even in the case where there is no actual change in the probability distribution of any of the variables, the expected performance bias is given by the standard equation for the variance of the difference of two sample means:

$$E\left[\left\{E[z_t] - E[z_{t,os}]\right\}^2\right] = \sigma_z^2 \frac{n+m}{nm} \quad (16)$$

In the case where there is no systematic deviation in the unobserved variables, then this increase in the expected generalisation error can be considered as analogous to model variance, i.e. a source of sampling error which is due to variables which are not included in the model itself. The more serious case is where there is some systematic deviation in the unobserved variable, leading to a bias not just in squared error shown in (15), but also in the mean error itself as shown in equation (14).

In the general case, the expected out-of-sample bias in mean error is equal to the change in the expected value of the unmodelled component:

$$E\left[e_{t,os}\right] = E\left[u(z_t,x_t)_{os}\right] - E\left[u(z_t,x_t)\right] = \Delta E\left[u(z_t,x_t)\right] \quad (17)$$

and the expected performance degradation is given by:

$$E\left[e_{t,os}{}^2\right] - E\left[e_t{}^2\right] = \Delta E\left[u(z_t,x_t)\right]^2 + (heteroskedasticity) + (model\ variance) \quad (18)$$

Being a squared term, the performance degradation due to the "nonstationarity" component is at best zero and in general will be greater than zero and **any** estimate of prediction error, for **any** model, will suffer from a downward bias if there is an unmodelled component in the data-generating process of the time-series.

2.3   Reduction of performance degradation via model combination

Just as the effects of model bias and variance can be reduced through model combination , so can the effects of nonstationarity. However, a key consideration in this context is that the nonstationarity effect is not so much dependent on the parameters of a model (like model variance), or even the chosen family of models (like model bias) but rather on the nature of the unmodelled component: i.e. the net effect of everything which is omitted from the model, in particular the omission of some of the variables which are part of the true data-generating process[1]. Thus model combination approaches which are based on resampling within a particular functional family will have little value for controlling the effects of nonstationarity. To illustrate this insight, consider a simple example of combining two models.

$$\text{Model 1:} \quad y_t = f_1(\mathbf{x}_t, \theta) + v_1(f, \mathbf{x}_t, \theta) + b_1(f, \mathbf{x}_t) + u_1(\mathbf{z}_t, \mathbf{x}_t) + \varepsilon_1(\mathbf{v}_t), \tag{19}$$

$$\text{Model 2:} \quad y_t = f_2(\mathbf{x}_t, \theta) + v_2(f, \mathbf{x}_t, \theta) + b_2(f, \mathbf{x}_t) + u_2(\mathbf{z}_t, \mathbf{x}_t) + \varepsilon_2(\mathbf{v}_t),$$

Then the expected loss of the combined model is given by:

$$
\begin{aligned}
\mathrm{E}\!\left[\left(y_t - \hat{y}_t\right)^2\right] &= \mathrm{E}\!\left[\left(y_t - \left\{w f_1(\mathbf{x}_t,\theta) + (1-w) f_2(\mathbf{x}_t,\theta)\right\}\right)^2\right] \\
&= \mathrm{E}\!\left[\left(\begin{array}{l} w\{v_1(f,\mathbf{x}_t,\theta) + b_1(f,\mathbf{x}_t) + u_1(\mathbf{z}_t,\mathbf{x}_t) + \varepsilon_1(\mathbf{v}_t)_t\} \\ +(1-w)\{v_2(f,\mathbf{x}_t,\theta) + b_2(f,\mathbf{x}_t) + u_2(\mathbf{z}_t,\mathbf{x}_t) + \varepsilon_2(\mathbf{v}_t)_t\} \end{array}\right)^2\right]
\end{aligned}
\tag{20}
$$

Defining $\sigma_{V,1}^2 = \mathrm{E}\!\left[v_1(f,\mathbf{x}_t,\theta)^2\right], \sigma_{V,2}^2 = \mathrm{E}\!\left[v_2(f,\mathbf{x}_t,\theta)^2\right]$, etc. this simplifies to:

$$
\begin{aligned}
\mathrm{E}\!\left[\left(y_t - \hat{y}_t\right)^2\right] &= w^2\sigma_{V,1}^2 + (1-w)^2\sigma_{V,2}^2 + 2w(1-w)\rho_V\sigma_{V,1}\sigma_{V,2} \\
&\quad + w^2\sigma_{B,1}^2 + (1-w)^2\sigma_{B,2}^2 + 2w(1-w)\rho_B\sigma_{B,1}\sigma_{B,2} \\
&\quad + w^2\sigma_{U,1}^2 + (1-w)^2\sigma_{U,2}^2 + 2w(1-w)\rho_U\sigma_{U,1}\sigma_{U,2} \\
&\quad + \sigma_{E,1}^2
\end{aligned}
\tag{21}
$$

In the case where the two models are identical, $\rho_V = \rho_B = \rho_U = 1$ and the expected loss (MSE) reduces to the single-model case shown in equation (11). Combining resampled models within the same family reduces the average loss by the extent to which the model variances are uncorrelated ($\rho_V < 1$), but has no effect on errors due to model bias ($\rho_B = 1$), unmodelled components ($\rho_U = 1$), and the inherent stochastic term. Combining models from different functional families, but based on the same set of variables/representations, may reduce errors due to model bias ($\rho_B < 1$), but not those related to unmodelled components ($\rho_U = 1$). In order to reduce the effects of the unmodelled components, and in particular the associated degradation in out-of-sample performance, we can define the "degree of nonstationarity" in a manner analogous to equation (18):

$$
\begin{aligned}
\Delta\mathrm{E}\!\left[e_t^2\right] &= w^2\Delta\mathrm{E}\!\left[u_1(\mathbf{z}_t,\mathbf{x}_t)\right]^2 + (1-w)^2\Delta\mathrm{E}\!\left[u_2(\mathbf{z}_t,\mathbf{x}_t)\right]^2 \\
&\quad + 2w(1-w)\mathrm{E}\!\left[\Delta u_1(\mathbf{z}_t,\mathbf{x}_t)\Delta u_2(\mathbf{z}_t,\mathbf{x}_t)\right]
\end{aligned}
\tag{22}
$$

---

[1] In principle, it may be difficult (and not necessarily useful) to distinguish between a variable which is completely omitted and one which is merely "misrepresented"

If the models are from the same functional family, or even based on the same information set $\mathbf{x}_t$, then $u_1(\mathbf{z}_t, \mathbf{x}_t) = u_2(\mathbf{z}_t, \mathbf{x}_t)$ and model combination will not result in any reduction in the degradation of performance due to nonstationarity.

In this section we have presented a partial analysis of the implications of modelling time-series which may contain an unmodelled yet in principle deterministic component. In order to do so we have had to vastly simplify a number of issues; in particular we have presented the analysis as if the issues of parameter, model and variable selection are independent decisions rather than, in principle at least, inter-related aspects of the modelling process as a whole.

We find the simplification justified in that it serves to highlight the risks which are involved in building models which must by definition be misspecified, as is typically the case in the complex dynamical systems which exist in finance. In particular the analysis serves as a motivation for the use of modelling approaches which exploit not only resampling and the combination of different functional forms but also diversification of the information sets upon which the different models are based. An example of such an approach is the population-based algorithm described in (Burgess, 1997) and which forms part of the statistical arbitrage methodology described below.

3   A Methodology for Statistical Arbitrage

We define statistical arbitrage as a generalisation of traditional "zero-risk" arbitrage. Zero-risk arbitrage consists of constructing two combinations of assets with identical cash-flows, and exploiting any discrepancies in the price of the two equivalent assets. The portfolio Long(combination1) + Short(combination2) can be viewed as a synthetic asset, of which any price-deviation from zero represents a "mispricing" and a potential risk-free profit[2]. In statistical arbitrage we again construct synthetic assets in which any deviation of the price from zero is still seen as a "mispricing", but this time in the statistical sense of having a predictable component to the price-dynamics.

Our methodology for exploiting statistical arbitrage involves four stages:

- constructing "synthetic assets" and testing for cyclicity in the price-dynamics
- selecting exogenous variables which influence the price-dynamics
- modelling the error-correction mechanism using nonparametric models
- jointly optimising and combining the models using a portfolio approach

---

[2] Subject to transaction costs, bid-ask spreads and price slippage

3.1   Testing for cyclicity in synthetic asset prices

Within the statistical arbitrage methodology we consider a "synthetic asset" to be any linear or nonlinear combination of tradable assets. Many options exist for constructing such combinations. One option is to use a regression methodology similar to that used in cointegration analysis, the synthetic asset can then be defined as the target asset (left hand side of the regression) together with a negative weighting of the cointegrating portfolio (right-hand side off the cointegrating regression). Another approach is to construct synthetic assets based on a factor analysis of price changes, resulting in combinations which represent exposure to different risk factors within the market, e.g. curvature factor of the yield curve (Burgess, 1996).

In order for opportunities for statistical arbitrage to exist within a set of asset prices, it is not necessary that the assets are strictly cointegrated in the statistical sense. For a set of variables (asset prices) to be cointegrated implies that whilst the individual series are random walks (integrated of order 1), there exists a linear combination of the assets which is stationary (integrated order 0). Thus the tests for cointegration are tests for the stationarity of the residual of a cointegrating regression[3]. Clearly, a combination of assets with a stationary price represents a straightforward opportunity for statistical arbitrage: if the "mispricing" is above (below) zero then sell (buy) the synthetic asset and realize a profit as the price reverts downwards (upwards) towards zero.

However tests for stationarity tend to be very restrictive, with low power against the null hypothesis of a random walk. Instead, we prefer to use more-powerful tests which can distinguish the situation where the price dynamics are technically nonstationary but which nevertheless contain a "cyclical" component.

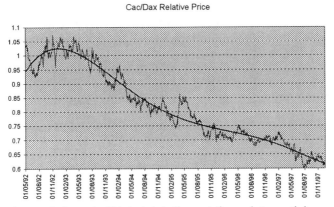

Cac/Dax Relative Price

Figure 1: a synthetic asset which is technically nonstationary but nevertheless contains a predictable cyclical component: the relative prices of the French Cac and German Dax indices

---

[3] see (Granger, 1983), (Engle and Granger, 1987)

98

Whereas a standard Dicky-Fuller test[4] of the price series fails to reject the null hypothesis of non-stationarity ('t'-statistic of 2.34 against a 10% critical value of 2.84), a more powerful "Variance Ratio" test[5] strongly rejects the random walk hypothesis, as shown in table 1 below:

Test	Test Statistic	p-value	Conclusion
Dicky-Fuller	2.34	> 0.10	fail to reject random walk
10-period VR	0.754	0.04	cyclical effect
100-period VR	0.295	0.01	strong cyclical effect
Sharpe (Cyc50)	1.15	0.009	tradable statistical arbitrage

Table 1: the standard Dicky-Fuller test (for stationarity) fails to reject the null hypothesis that the Cac/Dax relative price is nonstationary; in contrast, the more general Variance Ratio tests indicate the presence of a cyclical component in the price dynamics, and the opportunities for statistical arbitrage are confirmed by the performance of a simple trading rule

As the table also indicates, the presence of cyclical effects can be turned into profitable statistical arbitrage through the use of a simple technical trading rule (here based on reversion of the price, not towards, zero, but towards the value of the series 50 time-steps into the past).

3.2   Identifying Exogenous Influences

Innovations in the mispricing of the synthetic asset may be caused by random factors, or may be related to exogenous "unmodelled" factors. In the latter case the forecasting performance may be improved by including these exogenous factors in the model of price dynamics. The functional relationship between these exogenous factors and the price dynamics will typically not be known in advance, necessitating the use of a "model-free" variable selection methodology.

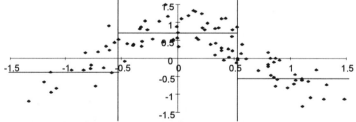

Figure 2: An example of a non-linear relationship which may be identified by means of a bin smoother (3 bins in the example) but which would give zero correlation and hence be missed by a linear test

---

[4] see (Dicky and Fuller, 1979)

[5] for use of the variance ratio to test against a random walk, see, for example, (Lo and MacKinley, 1988)

In our case we choose to use an analysis of variance approach, which is described in (Burgess, 1995) and (Burgess and Refenes, 1996) and is based on the use of non-parametric smoothing techniques, such as the bin-smoother illustrated above. The use of such techniques is motivated by the fact that the smoothing kernels can be chosen to be similar to the flexible "equivalent kernels" which are constructed by neural networks during the learning procedure.

3.3 Modelling conditional cointegration with neural networks

In real financial time-series, the "error-correction" effect which acts to restore the cointegration may be relatively weak, perhaps because the short term dynamics of the mispricing may be determined by a large number of factors, of which the cointegration effect is only one. In such a scenario the high bias of linear models can cause them to fail to capture a deterministic component of the price dynamics even when it does exist. Advanced modelling methodologies, such as neural networks and other non- or semi-parametric techniques such as generalised additive models (Hastie and Tibshirani, 1990), projection pursuit regression (Friedman and Stuetzle, 1981), and classification and regression trees (Breiman et al., 1984) offer the ability to optimise the bias-variance tradeoff in a more flexible manner.

The notion of *conditional cointegration* becomes particularly relevant when we consider the increasing efficiency of the financial markets. Cointegration effects that are strong enough to prevail under all market conditions are relatively easy to detect using conventional techniques, and thus are unlikely to generate excess profits for very long. On the other hand, more subtle conditional cointegration effects may be invisible to conventional analysis and hence are less likely to be eliminated by market activity. To illustrate this effect, consider the set of time series described by the following system of equations:

$$Ln(X_t) = Ln(X_{t-1}) + d + \eta_t \qquad \eta_t \sim NID(0, 1) \qquad (23)$$

$$N_t = \gamma.N_{t-1} + e_t \qquad (|\gamma| < 1) , \ e_t \sim NID(0, 1) \qquad (24)$$

$$R_{t-1} = Ln(Y_{t-1}) - Ln(X_{t-1}) \qquad (25)$$

$$\Delta Ln(Y_t) = \alpha.\Delta Ln(Y_{t-1}) - \beta.R_{t-1}.(1-N_{t-1}) + \varepsilon_t \qquad \varepsilon_t \sim NID(0, 1) \qquad (26)$$

The target time-series, Y_t, is essentially a random walk, with some momentum, which is cointegrated with the non-stationary variable 'X_t'. The influence of a second exogenous variable 'N_t', a proxy for "market news", introduces a nonlinearity into the error-correction mechanism. For a sample of 1000 observations, the variance of Y was found to be 14.7% deterministic and 85.3% due to the random innovations. This level of signal/noise is realistic for financial time-series, given that it refers to the "ideal" model and any empirical model would be expected to capture only a proportion of the deterministic component.

The first half of the sample was used to estimate a set of predictive models. The specification of the models differed in the flexibility of functional form (linear regression versus feedforward neural networks) and in the representation of the independent variables (autoregressive versus error-correction). The performance of the models on the remaining 500 observations is reported in table 2, below:

Model	Model Specification	Correl (jn-sample)	Correl (out-sample)	Correct Direction	Profit
	Linear Models				
A	$\Delta Y_t = \alpha_1 \Delta Y_{t-1} + \alpha_2 \Delta X_{t-1} + \alpha_3 N_{t-1} + \varepsilon_t$	0.20	0.01	49.2%	3.2%
B	$\Delta Y_t = \alpha_1 \Delta Y_{t-1} + \alpha_2 \Delta X_{t-1} + \alpha_3 N_{t-1} + \alpha_4 R_{t-1} + \varepsilon_t$	0.31	0.09	51.0%	9.9%
	Neural network models				
C	$\Delta Y_t = NN(\Delta Y_{t-1}, \Delta X_{t-1}, N_{t-1}) + \varepsilon_t$	0.34	0.02	51.0%	5.3%
D	$\Delta Y_t = NN(\Delta Y_{t-1}, \Delta X_{t-1}, N_{t-1}, R_{t-1}) + \varepsilon_t$	0.46	0.28	59.4%	26.9%
	Benchmark	0.43	0.31	59.8%	29.5%

Table 2: performance of different models on artificial data

The price dynamics are driven largely by the error-correction effect on the residual R_t which is invisible within the traditional representation (models A and C). The linear error-correction model (B) also fails to capture the underlying dynamics due to the inability to model the conditioning effect of the "news" variable N_t. Only Model D combines the flexible modelling capability of the neural network with the additional information regarding the relative mispricing R_t, allowing it to capture the underlying dynamics of the system to a high level of accuracy (90%+ correlation with the "ideal" model).

This simple example serves to motivate the use of a nonlinear modelling methodology based on neural networks, which is capable of capturing subtle "conditional cointegration" effects. Empirical experiments with real data, which are reported elsewhere[6], have provided substantial evidence for the existence of similar relationships in the relative price dynamics of international equity indices.

3.4   A portfolio approach to model combination

As indicated in section 2, no matter how rigourous the methodology adopted, the presence of non-stationarity ensures that no individual model can be optimal for modelling a time-series which evolves through time. This realisation is reflected in a recent trend towards model combination approaches.

---

[6] See (Burgess and Refenes, 1996)

Weigend and Mangeas (1996) consider the case of "multi-stationary" time-series where the dynamics oscillate between a number of different regimes. This "switching" approach, based on the "mixture of experts" model of Jacobs et al (1991), is most appropriate when there is a distinct shift from one regime to another, the dynamics of the individual regimes are stationary, and only a small number of regimes are active at a given time.

Where the non-stationarity is more significant, for instance when the regimes are not distinct, are changing through time, and may be all active simultaneously, a more robust approach is to combine independent models. Rehfuss et al (1996) motivate a "committee" approach where the model forecasts are combined according to a fixed weighting, in fact they suggest that the most robust approach is to assign an equal weight to each model, particularly in the case where models may be invalidated due to non-stationarity.

In Burgess (1997), we suggested that, in a model combination approach, it is appropriate to **jointly** optimise the individual models, rather than doing so on a purely individualistic basis. This was achieved using a population-based methodology, where the "fitness" of individual models was adjusted by a novel penalty term based on the correlations between the profit and loss patterns of the individual models. This served to generate a portfolio of complementary models which were explicitly decorrelated and hence could be expected to be more robust to the effects of nonstationarity.

In our statistical arbitrage methodology, we combine the population based methodology of Burgess (1997) with the suggestion of Refenes et al (1994), that an appropriate framework for weighting individual models is provided by traditional portfolio optimisation theory, such as Markovitz mean-variance optimisation. In the mean-variance approach, the vector of optimal portfolio weights is given by:

$$\mathbf{w}^* = \arg\max_{\mathbf{w}} \left\{ \sum_i w_i r_i - \frac{1}{2\theta} \sum_i \sum_j w_i w_j \sigma_i \sigma_j \rho_{ij} \right\}$$

$$= \arg\max_{\mathbf{w}} \left\{ \mathbf{w}^T \mathbf{r} - \frac{1}{2\theta} \mathbf{w}^T \mathbf{V} \mathbf{w} \right\}$$

(27)

where θ is a "risk appetite" parameter, $\mathbf{w} = \{w_1, w_2, \ldots, w_n\}^T$ is the vector of portfolio weights, $\mathbf{r} = \{r_1, r_2, \ldots, r_n\}^T$ the vector of expected returns and $\mathbf{V}$ the covariance matrix of the returns. Within our framework, we apply the optimisation to a portfolio of **models** rather than of underlying assets. The resulting portfolio weights are based on both the expected performance of individual models, and the correlations in the profits and losses of the individual models. We use the optimised model weights as our measure of model fitness and are thus effectively evaluating each model in the context of the entire "portfolio" of models within the current population.

At each new iteration of the optimisation the least fit models are eliminated from the population and replaced with new models which are randomly generated. The new models will only be allocated significant weights if so doing will improve the overall risk adjusted return of the portfolio as a whole. Thus by only retaining models which are deemed fit, *within the current context*, we are jointly optimising the overall performance of the population, and generating a set of complementary and decorrelated models which will be more robust to the effects of nonstationarity.

4   Empirical Results

In this section, we describe the results of applying the methodological framework described in the previous section, to the problem of modelling and trading the relative returns of the following set of international equity indices:

- Dow Jones Industrial Average, Standard and Poors 500 Index (US)
- FTSE 100 (UK)
- DAX 30 (Germany)
- CAC 40 (France)
- SMI (Switzerland)
- IBEX (Spain)
- OMX (Sweden)
- Hang Seng (Hong Kong)
- Nikkei 225 (Japan)

4.1 Experimental Data

The data used in the experiment were daily closing prices for the period 1st August 1988 to 8th October 1997. From the total of 2419 observations the first 1419 were used for estimating the parameters of the statistical arbitrage models and the most recent 1000 were withheld for out-of-sample testing and evaluation. In order to avoid the "data snooping" bias which enters the performance estimate when the out-of-sample data is used for model selection, the evaluation data was further divided in two: the earlier 500 observations (9th December 1993 to 9th November 1995) were used to evaluate models within the context of the population based optimisation procedure, and the final 500 observations (10th November 1995 to 8th October 1997) were withheld for a one-off evaluation of out-of-sample performance.

4.2   Statistical Arbitrage Models

The individual models within the population are what might be described as "implicit" statistical arbitrage models, because there is no explicit "forecasting" involved. The models exploit any cyclicity in the relative prices of a set of underlying assets by taking positions which will be profitable if the prices move in such a way as to reduce the current "mispricing" between the assets.

The "mispricing" between a set of assets is defined as the residual r_t of the dynamic regression between a chosen target asset $y_{1,t}$ and the remaining assets $y_{2,t}$ ... $y_{n,t}$. The models are thus based on the concept of cointegration between asset prices but can accommodate nonstationarities in the equilibrium "fair price" relationship through the use of a time-varying "cointegration" vector:

$$y_{1,t} = \beta_{2,t}.y_{2,t} + \beta_{3,t}.y_{3,t} + \text{.......} + r_t \tag{28}$$

where $r_t \sim NID(0, \sigma^2)$ and the parameters β_i are generated by the process:

$$\beta_{i,t} = \beta_{i,t-1} + \eta_{i,t} \qquad \eta_{i,t} \sim NID(0, \sigma^2 q_i) \tag{29}$$

This is a state-space model in which the states are the cointegration coefficients β_i and which can easily be implemented within the framework of a standard Kalman filter. The scale parameters q_i determine the rate at which the coefficients may evolve through time; in the special case of all the q_i's = 0 the model collapses to a (fixed coefficient) regression model.

4.3   Model Parameters

The first set of parameters which define an individual model serve to define the "arbitrage model" and comprise the choice of target asset (y_1); the choice of the cointegrating assets (y_2....y_n), and the "sensitivity" coefficient, which in this case is constrained to be identical for all the cointegrating assets (q_2 ... $q_n = q$). These parameters are used to generate the time-series which represents the "synthetic asset":

$$SA_t = \beta_{2,t}.y_{2,t} + \beta_{3,t}.y_{3,t} + \text{.......} + \beta_{n,t}.y_{n,t} \tag{30}$$

and the "mispricing" is then simply the difference between the target and the synthetic asset:

$$M_t = y_{1,t} - (\beta_{2,t}.y_{2,t} + \beta_{3,t}.y_{3,t} + \text{.......} + \beta_{n,t}.y_{n,t}) = r_t \tag{31}$$

The second set of parameters define the "trading model" and describe the size of the position which should be taken, in terms of a weighting coefficient w_F for a "fixed" trading strategy where the position depends only upon the **sign** of the mispricing, against a "relative" strategy which also depends on the **magnitude** of the mispricing:

$$P_t = -\left(y_{1,t} - \left[\beta_{2,t} y_{2,t} + ... + \beta_{n,t} \cdot y_{n,t}\right]\right)\left(w_F \; SIGN(r_t) + \; [1 - w_F] \, r_t\right) \qquad (32)$$

Notice that the position P_t is opposite in sign to the mispricing because we are expecting the relative prices to change so as to **reduce** the mispricing. The second component of the trading model is a "horizon" parameter which determines the length of time for which the position should be held in order to allow the mean-reversion to take effect.

The empirical results presented below correspond to a single experiment, in which a portfolio of ten models was optimised over 5000 iterations of the population-based algorithm.

4.4   Results

The performance of the statistical arbitrage models is summarised in Table 3 below. In addition to the performance of the individual models, the table reports the performance of two portfolios: one formed from a fitness-weighted average, and one from an unweighted average of the individual models.

	Evaluation Period			Out-sample (1-250)			Out-sample (251-500)		
	Direction	Sharpe	Profit	Direction	Sharpe	Profit	Direction	Sharpe	Profit
WtAv	**60.2%**	**4.42**	**82.7**	**51.2%**	**1.79**	**13.3**	**52.0%**	**0.58**	**8.8**
SimAv	**61.8%**	**3.88**	**73.9**	**49.2%**	**1.60**	**11.8**	**49.6%**	**0.29**	**4.7**
Model1	53.2%	1.93	75.4	46.4%	-0.31	-4.5	47.6%	-0.51	-8.4
Model2	54.6%	2.22	60.7	52.4%	3.18	20.4	50.8%	2.17	41.4
Model3	51.8%	0.44	8.7	50.4%	0.57	6.8	55.6%	2.86	39.6
Model4	53.6%	1.84	106.4	50.8%	0.79	21.2	49.6%	0.28	11.6
Model5	52.8%	1.06	88.1	54.8%	1.04	19.8	47.6%	-0.52	-33.8
Model6	51.8%	1.97	112.1	55.2%	2.08	38.8	51.2%	0.35	15.9
Model7	58.4%	2.59	69.0	51.6%	-0.01	-0.1	53.6%	0.00	0.0
Model8	53.0%	1.45	80.0	46.4%	-1.11	-26.3	48.0%	-0.30	-10.1
Model9	50.4%	1.31	39.9	45.6%	-0.06	-0.6	43.6%	-1.53	-59.5
Model10	54.0%	1.56	98.6	53.2%	2.15	42.8	55.2%	1.96	50.3

Table 3: Performance of statistical arbitrage models of international equity indices; the performance of both individual models and the portfolios formed by constructing either a weighted or unweighted average of the models is very high during the "evaluation period" but suffers from model selection bias; although some individual models suffer a severe performance degradation in the true out-of-sample period, the performance of the combined portfolios is more robust.

The performance metrics reported are the correctness of the directional forecasts, the trading performance expressed as an annualised Sharpe-ratio, and the total profit (or loss) earned during the period. Notice the wide diversity of the performance of the individual models, warning of the high level of risk which is inherent in choosing a single *best* model. In contrast, the two portfolios constructed by combining the individual models, whether by fitness weighted average or a simple unweighted average, both have a similar level of performance - less profitable than the best models, but a long way from making the losses of the worst models, and significantly positive over the out-of-sample period as a whole.

The performance degradation from the evaluation period to the out-of-sample period is due to two factors. Firstly, even though no model parameters are actually *fitted* to the data from the evaluation period, the models are *selected* on the basis of performance during this period. This creates a "selection bias" which leads to an inflated estimate of the true model performance. The second cause of performance degradation is nonstationarity in the relative price dynamics of the various indices. Furthermore, we see an increase in the performance degradation as we move from the first half to the second half of the out-of-sample period, indicating that the effects of nonstationarity grow with time.

As a final point, note that although the performance of the models is not spectacular, this is a very crude analysis which neglects the potential for leveraged trading, de-selection of underperforming models, periodic refreshing of the portfolio and many other enhancements that would be open to a potential trader of such a system.

5   Concluding Remarks

In this paper we have described a methodology in which advanced modelling techniques are employed to exploit opportunities for "statistical arbitrage" between financial instruments. Market-neutral combinations of assets are constructed in such a way that any price deviations from zero can be considered a "mispricing"; however, unlike traditional arbitrage, in which the "mispricing" can be locked in as "risk free" profit, the profitability of statistical arbitrage trades is contingent upon the continuation of statistical relationships between the relative prices of the assets within the arbitrage portfolio.

In the second section we presented a novel perspective on the concept of "nonstationarity", illustrating that the out-of-sample performance degradation which is often ascribed to "nonstationarity" is a logical consequence of the fact that, in practice, many models must, of necessity, be misspecified. This misspecification arises from the fact that any given model will contain only a subset of the many factors which drive asset price dynamics. In particular, our analysis shows that **any** estimate of prediction error, for **any** model, will suffer from a downward bias[7] if there is an unmodelled component in the data-generating process of the time-series.

In the third section, we have outlined a methodology for exploiting statistical arbitrage opportunities. The methodology is inspired by the econometric notion of

---

[7] conversely, any estimate of performance will show an **upward** bias

cointegration, whilst benefitting from the recognition that for statistical arbitrage opportunities to exist it is not necessary that the assets be strictly cointegrated in the statistical sense. The methodology is based on four stages of identifying weak cointegration, or "cyclicity" in relative price movements, identifying exogenous influences, modelling the mechanism which acts to eliminate statistical "mispricings", and combining sets of models within a portfolio in order to reduce the effects of nonstationarity.

Finally we reported the results of applying the methodology to a particular set of assets, namely the major international equity indices. Whilst a wide spread of performance was achieved within a set of ten individual models, the combined portfolios showed a consistently profitable performance over a true out-of-sample period.

The paper raises a number of issues which are worthy of further study. Firstly we have only just begun to explore the relationship between model misspecification, in the presence of "unmodelled" components, and out-of-sample performance degradation; and the implications of this effect for forecasting models in general and trading models in particular. Secondly, many opportunities exist for further refining the methodological framework, in particular with respect to cyclicity testing and model-free variable selection but also with regard to neural network model selection and the most appropriate objective function for the joint optimisation procedure. Finally, there is the empirical issue of searching for, and exploiting, statistical arbitrage opportunities between different sets of financial instruments, at a wide range of time-scales from monthly prices changes down to intra-day effects. All of these issues are currently the subject of ongoing research.

6   Acknowledgements

The author would like to gratefully acknowledge the support for this work from the Economic and Social Research Council (Award number R022250057).

7   References

Breiman, L., Friedman, J. H., Olshen, R. A., and Stone C. J., 1984, Classification and Regression Trees, Wadsworth and Brooks/Cole, Monterey.

Burgess, A. N., 1995, Non-linear model identification and statistical significance tests and their application to financial modelling, in IEE Proceedings of the 4th International Conference on Artificial Neural Networks, Cambridge, 312-317

Burgess, A. N., 1996, Statistical yield curve arbitrage in eurodollar futures using neural networks, in Refenes et al (eds), Neural Networks in Financial Engineering, World Scientific, Singapore, 98-110

Burgess, A. N., 1997, Asset allocation across European equity indices using a portfolio of dynamic cointegration models, in Weigend et al (eds) Neural Networks in Financial Engineering, World-Scientific, Singapore, 276-288

Burgess, A. N., 1998, A new perspective on nonstationarity, Technical Report, Decision Technology Centre, London Business School

Burgess, A. N. and Refenes, A. N., 1996, Modelling non-linear cointegration in international equity index futures, in Refenes et al (eds), Neural Networks in Financial Engineering, World Scientific, Singapore, 50-63

Dickey, D. A. and Fuller, W. A., 1979, Distribution of the estimators for autoregressive time-series with a unit root, Journal of the American Statistical Association, 74, 427-431.

Engle, R. F. and Granger, C. W. J., 1987, Co-integration and error-correction: representation, estimation and testing, Econometrica, 55, 251-276

Friedman, J.H. and Stuetzle, W., 1981. Projection pursuit regression. Journal of the American Statistical Association. Vol. 76, pp. 817-823.

Granger, C. W. J., 1983, Co-integrated variables and error-correcting models, UCSD Discussion Paper.

Hastie, T.J. and Tibshirani, R.J., 1990. Generalised Additive Models. Chapman and Hall, London

Jacobs, R. A., Jordan, M. I., Nowlan, S. J. and Hinton, G. E., 1991, Adaptive mixtures of local experts, Neural Computation, 3, 79-87

Lo, A. W., and MacKinley, A. C., 1988, Stock market prices do not follow random walks: evidence from a simple specification test, The Review of Financial Studies, Vol 1, Number 1, pp. 41-66

Refenes, A. N., Bentz, Y. and Burgess, N., 1994, Neural networks in investment management, Journal of Communications and Finance, 8, April 95-101

Rehfuss, S., Wu, L., and Moody, J. E., 1996, Trading using committees: A comparative study, in Refenes et al (eds), Neural Networks in Financial Engineering, World Scientific, Singapore, 612-621

Weigend A. S., and Mangeas, M., 1996, Analysis and prediction of multi-stationary time series, in Refenes et al (eds), Neural Networks in Financial Engineering, World Scientific, Singapore, 597-611

NONPARAMETRIC TESTS FOR NONLINEAR COINTEGRATION

JÖRG BREITUNG
Institute for Statistics and Econometrics
Humboldt University Berlin
Spandauer Strasse 1, D-10178 Berlin, FRG
E-mail: breitung@wiwi.hu-berlin.de

A test procedure based on ranks is suggested to test for nonlinear cointegration. For two (or more) time series it is assumed that there exist monotonic transformations such that the normalized series can asymptotically be represented by independent Brownian motions. Rank test procedures based on the difference between the sequences of ranks are suggested. If there is no cointegration between the time series, the sequences of ranks tend to diverge, whereas under cointegration the sequences of ranks evolve similarly. Monte Carlo simulations suggest that for a wide range of nonlinear models the rank test performs better than parametric competitors. To test for nonlinear cointegration a variable addition test based on the ranks is suggested. As empirical illustrations we consider the term structure of interest rates and the relationship between common and preferred stock prices. It turns out that for this applications there is only weak evidence for a nonlinear long run relationship.

1 Introduction

Since the introduction of the concept of cointegration by Granger (1981) the analysis of cointegrated models was intensively studied in a linear context, whereas the work on the extension to nonlinear cointegration is still comparatively limited. Useful reviews of recent work in the analysis of nonlinear cointegration are provided by Granger and Teräsvirta (1993), Granger (1995) and Granger, Inoue and Morin (1997).

In many cases, economic theory suggests a nonlinear relationship as for the production function or the Phillips curve, for example. However, theory does not always provide a precise specification of the functional form so that it might be desirable to have nonparametric tools for estimation and inference. In this paper rank test procedures are considered to test whether there is a cointegration relation among the variables and whether this relationship is nonlinear.

The rank test procedures for cointegration are based on a measure for the differences between the rank sequences of the series. If there is no cointegration between the series, the ranks tend to diverge as the sample size increase,

A.-P.N. Refenes et al. (eds.), Decision Technologies for Computational Finance, 109–123.
© 1998 *Kluwer Academic Publishers. Printed in the Netherlands..*

whereas under cointegration the rank sequences evolve similarly. Assuming that the series are uncorrelated random walks under the null hypothesis, it is shown that the rank differences can be asymptotically represented as a linear combination of arcsine distributed random variables.

2 A rank test for cointegration

Let $\{x_t\}_1^T$ and $\{y_t\}_1^T$ be two real valued time series. Following Granger and Hallman (1991a) we assume that there exist two monotonic increasing transformations $z_{1t} = f(x_t)$ and $z_{2t} = g(y_t)$ such that z_{1t} and z_{2t} are random walk sequences with constant means and stationary increments. If it is unknown whether the functions are increasing or decreasing, a two sided version of the test is applicable.

If x_t and y_t are (nonlinearly) cointegrated, there exists a relationship of the form

$$u_t = g(y_t) - f(x_t),\tag{1}$$

where u_t is short memory in mean as defined in Granger and Hallman (1991a).

As demonstrated by Granger and Hallman (1991b), the Dickey-Fuller test may perform poorly if $f(x_t)$ and $g(y_t)$ are nonlinear functions. We therefore construct a robust test based on the ranks of the series. Let

$$R_T(x_t) = \text{Rank[of } x_t \text{ among } x_1, \ldots, x_T \text{]}$$

and define $R_T(y_t)$ accordingly. The following proposition generalizes a result given in Breitung and Gouriéroux (1997).

Proposition 1: *Let* $x_t = \mu + \sum_{i=1}^{t} v_i$, *where it is assumed that (i)* $E(v_t) = 0$, *(ii)* $\sup_t E|v_t|^\delta < \infty$ *for some* $\delta > 2$ *and (iii)* $\{v_t\}$ *is strong mixing with mixing coefficients* α_m *that satisfy* $\sum \alpha_m^{1-2/\delta} < \infty$. *Then, as* $T \to \infty$, *the limiting process of the ranks can be represented as*

$$T^{-1} R_T(x_{[aT]}) \Rightarrow a\mathcal{A}_1 + (1-a)\mathcal{A}_2 ,$$

where $\mathcal{A}_1$ *and* $\mathcal{A}_2$ *are two independent random variables with an arcsine distribution.*

PROOF: Let $[\cdot]$ represent the integer part, "$\Rightarrow$" denotes weak convergence of the associated probability measure and $W(a)$ is a standard Brownian motion. Then,

$$T^{-1} R_T(x_{[aT]}) = T^{-1} \sum_{t=1}^{T} \mathbb{1}(x_t < x_{[aT]})$$

$$= \sum_{t=1}^{T} \mathbb{1}\left(\frac{1}{\sqrt{T}}z_{[\frac{t}{T}T]} < \frac{1}{\sqrt{T}}z_{[aT]}\right)\left[\frac{t}{T} - \frac{t-1}{T}\right]$$

$$\Rightarrow \int_0^1 \mathbb{1}[W(u) < W(a)]\mathrm{d}u$$

$$= \int_0^a \mathbb{1}[W(u) < W(a)]\mathrm{d}u + \int_a^1 \mathbb{1}[W(u) < W(a)]\mathrm{d}u.$$

Since the increments of the Brownian motion are independent, the two parts of the integral are independent as well.

Using $\stackrel{d}{=}$ to indicate equality in distribution we have

$$\int_0^a \mathbb{1}[W(u) < W(a)]\mathrm{d}u = \int_0^a \mathbb{1}[W(a) - W(u) > 0]\mathrm{d}u$$

$$\stackrel{d}{=} \int_0^a \mathbb{1}[W(a - u) > 0]\mathrm{d}u$$

$$\stackrel{d}{=} \int_0^a \mathbb{1}[W(u) > 0]\mathrm{d}u$$

$$\stackrel{d}{=} a\int_0^1 \mathbb{1}[W(u) > 0]\mathrm{d}u$$

$$\stackrel{d}{=} a\mathcal{A}_1,$$

where $\mathcal{A}_1 = \int_0^1 \mathbb{1}[W(u) > 0]\mathrm{d}u$ is a random variable with an arcsine distribution (cf. Breitung and Gouriéroux, 1997). Similarly, we find

$$\int_a^1 \mathbb{1}[W(u) < W(a)]\mathrm{d}u = (1 - a)\mathcal{A}_2,$$

where $\mathcal{A}_2$ is another random variable with an arcsine distribution independent of $\mathcal{A}_1$. □

The rank statistic is constructed by replacing $f(x_t)$ and $g(y_t)$ by $R_T(x_t)$ and $R_T(y_t)$, respectively. Since we assume that $f(x_t)$ and $g(y_t)$ are two random walk series, it follows that $R_T(x_t) = R_T[f(x_t)]$ and $R_T(y_t) = R_T[g(y_t)]$ behave like ranked random walks for which the limiting distribution is given in Proposition 1. The advantage of a statistic based on the sequence of ranks is that the functions $f(\cdot)$ and $g(\cdot)$ need not be known.

We consider two "distance measures" between the sequences $R_T(x_t)$ and $R_T(y_t)$:

$$\kappa_T = T^{-1}\sup_t |d_t| \tag{2}$$

$$\xi_T = T^{-3}\sum_{t=1}^{T} d_t^2, \tag{3}$$

where $d_t = R_T(y_t) - R_T(x_t)$. It should be noted that d_t is $O_p(T)$ and, thus, the normalisation factors are different from other applications of these measures. The statistic κ_T is a Kolmogorov-Smirnov type of statistic considered by Lo (1991) and ξ_T is a Cramer-von Mises type of statistic used by Sargan and Bhargava (1983). The null hypothesis of no (nonlinear) cointegration between x_t and y_t is rejected if the test statistics are too small.

It is interesting to note that the statistic ξ_T allows for different interpretations. Let $\tilde{b}_T$ denote the least-squares estimate from a regression of $R_T(y_t)$ on $R_T(x_t)$. Using $\sum R_T(x_t)^2 = \sum R_T(y_t)^2 = T^3/3 + O(T^2)$ we have

$$
\begin{aligned}
\xi_T &= \frac{1}{T^3} \sum_{t=1}^{T} [R_T(y_t)^2 - 2R_T(y_t)R_T(x_t) + R_T(x_t)^2] \\
&= \frac{2 - 2\tilde{b}_T}{T^3} \sum_{t=1}^{T} R_T(x_t)^2 \\
&= \frac{2}{3}(1 - \tilde{b}_T) + o_p(1).
\end{aligned}
$$

If y_t and x_t are not cointegrated, then $\tilde{b}_T$ has a nondegenerate limiting distribution (see Phillips (1986) for the linear case). On the other hand, if y_t and x_t are cointegrated, then $\tilde{b}_T$ converges to one in probability and therefore ξ_T converges to zero.

Second, consider a Cramer-von Mises type of statistic based on the residuals of a cointegration regression on the ranks:

$$
\begin{aligned}
\tilde{\xi}_T &= \frac{1}{T^3} \sum_{t=1}^{T} [R_T(y_t) - \tilde{b}_T R_T(x_t)]^2 \\
&= \frac{1}{T^3} \sum_{t=1}^{T} [R_T(y_t)^2 - 2\tilde{b}_T R_T(y_t)R_T(x_t) + \tilde{b}_T^2 R_T(x_t)^2] \\
&= \frac{1 - \tilde{b}_T^2}{T^3} \sum_{t=1}^{T} R_T(x_t)^2 \\
&= \frac{1}{3}(1 - \tilde{b}_T^2) + o_p(1).
\end{aligned}
$$

Hence, a two-step approach similar to the one suggested by Engle and Granger (1987) can be seen as a two-sided version of a test based on ξ_T.

Third, the statistic ξ_T is related to "Spearman's rho", that is, the usual rank correlation coefficient considered in Kendall and Gibbons (1990), for example. Spearman's rho is defined as

$$
r_s = 1 - \frac{6}{T^3 - T} \sum_{t=1}^{T} d_t^2 \tag{4}
$$

(cf. Kendall and Gibbons (1990, p.8)). The statistic r_s can therefore be seen as a mapping of ξ_T into the interval $[-1, 1]$. If x_t and y_t are cointegrated, Spearman's rho converges in probability to one as $T \to \infty$.

Proposition 1 implies that, if $f(x_t)$ and $g(y_t)$ are independent random walk sequences we have

$$T^{-1}d_{[aT]} \Rightarrow a(\mathcal{A}_1 - \mathcal{A}_3) + (1 - a)(\mathcal{A}_2 - \mathcal{A}_4) ,$$

where $\mathcal{A}_1, \ldots, \mathcal{A}_4$ are independent random variables with an arcsine distribution. Hence, the increments of random walk sequences x_t and y_t may be allowed to be heteroscedastic and serially correlated as long as Assumption 1 is satisfied.

Under the alternative of a cointegration relationship as given in (1) we have

$$\begin{aligned}
T^{-1}d_{[aT]} &= T^{-1}\left\{R_T[T^{-1/2}g(y_t)] - R_T[T^{-1/2}f(x_t)]\right\} \\
&= T^{-1}\left\{R_T[T^{-1/2}f(x_t) + o_p(1)] - R_T[T^{-1/2}f(x_t)]\right\} \\
&\Rightarrow 0.
\end{aligned}$$

Hence, κ_T and ξ_T converge to one in probability as $T \to \infty$, i.e., both rank tests are consistent.

The asymptotic theory for correlated random walk sequences x_t and y_t turns out to be much more complicated. However, the dynamic properties of the sequence $T^{-1/2}d_t$ are similar to a random walk, although it was shown in Proposition 1 that d_t possesses a different limiting distribution. Nevertheless, we may adopt a nonparametric correction suggested by Phillips (1987). The "long run variance" of the sequence d_t is estimated as

$$\hat{\sigma}_m^2 = c_0 + 2\sum_{j=1}^{m} w_j c_j ,$$

where $w_j = (m - j + 1)/(m + 1)$ and $c_j = T^{-2} \sum_{t=j+2}^{T} \Delta d_t \Delta d_{t-j}$, where Δ is the first difference operator. It is important to notice that c_j involves a factor of T^{-2}. This is due to fact that the covariances between ranks are $O(T)$.

For $m = 0$ we let $\hat{\sigma}_0^2 = c_0$. The modified test statistics result as

$$\begin{aligned}
K_T(m) &= \kappa_T/\hat{\sigma}_m & (5) \\
Z_T(m) &= \xi_T/\hat{\sigma}_m^2. & (6)
\end{aligned}$$

Although there is no thorough asymptotic justification for this correction, Monte Carlo simulations suggest that the corrections performs reasonable in practice.

The rank statistic can be generalized to test for cointegration among the $k + 1$ variables $y_t, x_{1t}, \ldots, x_{kt}$, where it is assumed that $g(y_t)$ and $f_j(x_{jt})$

Table 1: Critical Values

T	0.10	0.05	0.01
κ_{100}	0.610	0.520	0.400
κ_{500}	0.644	0.552	0.422
ξ_{100}	0.059	0.042	0.024
ξ_{500}	0.057	0.042	0.024
$K_{100}(m)$	0.400	0.370	0.320
$K_{500}(m)$	0.394	0.364	0.316
$Z_{100}(m)$	0.027	0.022	0.016
$Z_{500}(m)$	0.023	0.019	0.013
$\widetilde{Q}_{100}[1]$	−3.15	−3.55	−4.35
$\widetilde{Q}_{500}[1]$	−3.27	−3.67	−4.44
$\widetilde{Q}_{100}[2]$	−3.58	−3.97	−4.75
$\widetilde{Q}_{100}[2]$	−3.65	−3.99	−4.66
$\widetilde{Q}_{100}[3]$	−4.00	−4.35	−5.13
$\widetilde{Q}_{100}[3]$	−4.06	−4.40	−5.04
$\widetilde{Q}_{100}[4]$	−4.33	−4.69	−5.41
$\widetilde{Q}_{100}[4]$	−4.44	−4.73	−5.33

Note: Critical values resulting from 10,000 replications of two independent random walk sequences. The nonparametric correction for the statistic $Z_T(m)$ was computed letting $m = 0$. The statistic $\widetilde{Q}_T[k]$ represents a residual based Dickey-Fuller t-test with k regressors. The regressions do not include a constant term.

$(j = 1, \ldots, k)$ are monotonic functions. Let $R_T(\mathbf{x}_t) = [R_T(x_{1t}), \ldots, R_T(x_{kt})]'$ be a $k \times 1$ vector and $\tilde{\mathbf{b}}_T$ is the least-squares estimate from a regression of $R_T(y_t)$ on $R_T(\mathbf{x}_t)$. A two-step test procedure based on the Cramer-von Mises type of statistic for the residuals yields the test statistic

$$\widetilde{Q}_T[k] \;=\; \frac{1}{T^3} \sum_{t=1}^{T} [R_T(y_t) - \tilde{\mathbf{b}}_T' R_T(\mathbf{x}_t)]^2. \tag{7}$$

Using Monte Carlo simulations, the critical values for the test statistics κ_T, ξ_T, $K_T(m)$, $Z_T(m)$ and $Q_T[k]$ are computed for $T = 100$ and $T = 500$ (see Table 1).

3 A rank test for neglected nonlinearity

Whenever the rank test for cointegration indicates a stable long run relationship, it is interesting to know whether the cointegration relationship is linear or nonlinear. For a convenient representation of such null and alternative hypotheses we follow Granger (1995) and write the nonlinear relationship as

$$y_t = \gamma_0 + \gamma_1 x_t + f^*(x_t) + u_t \; , \tag{8}$$

where $\gamma_0 + \gamma_1 x_t$ is the linear part of the relationship. Under the null hypothesis it is assumed that $f^*(x_t) = 0$ for all t. If $f^*(x_t)$ is unknown it may be approximated by Fourier series (Gallant (1981)) or a neuronal network (Lee, White and Granger (1993)). Here we suggest to use the multiple of the rank transformation $\theta R_T(x_t)$ instead of $f^*(x_t)$.

It is interesting to note that the rank transformation is to some extent related to the neural network approach suggested by Lee, White and Granger (1993). If x_t is a $k \times 1$ vector of "input variables" and α is a corresponding vector of coefficients, the neural network approach approximates $f^*(x_t)$ by $\sum_{j=1}^{q} \beta_j \psi(x_t' \alpha_j)$, where $\psi(\cdot)$ has the properties of a cumulated distribution function. A function often used in practice is the logistic $\psi(x) = x/(1 - x)$. In our context, x_t is a scalar variable, so that the neuronal network term simplifies to $\beta \psi(\alpha x_t)$. Since $T^{-1} R_T(x_t) = \widehat{F}(x_t)$, where $\widehat{F}(x_t)$ is the empirical distribution function, it follows that, asymptotically, the rank transformation of x_t renders the (unconditional) c.d.f. of x_t. Hence, using the rank transformation can motivated as a convenient choice of $\psi(\alpha x_t)$ with the attractive property, that the parameter α can be dropped due to the invariance of the rank transformation.

If it is assumed that x_t is exogenous and u_t is white noise with $u_t \sim N(0, \sigma^2)$, a score test statistic is obtained as the $T \cdot R^2$-statistic of the least-squares regression

$$\tilde{u}_t = c_0 + c_1 x_t + c_2 R_T(x_t) + e_t \; , \tag{9}$$

where $\tilde{u}_t = y_t - \tilde{\gamma}_0 - \tilde{\gamma}_1 x_t$ and $\tilde{\gamma}_0$ and $\tilde{\gamma}_1$ are the least-squares estimates from a regression of y_t on a constant and x_t.

A problem with applying the usual asymptotic theory to derive the limiting null distribution of the test statistic is that the regression (9) involves the nonstationary variables x_t and $R_T(x_t)$. However under some (fairly restrictive) assumptions, Proposition 2 shows that under the null hypothesis $c_2 = 0$ the score statistic is asymptotically χ^2 distributed.

Proposition 2: *Let* $x_t = \displaystyle\sum_{j=1}^{t} v_j$ *and*

$$y_t = \gamma_0 + \gamma_1 x_t + u_t \; ,$$

where v_t *satisfies the assumptions (1) – (3) of Proposition 1 and* u_t *is white noise with* $E(u_t) = 0$ *and* $E(u_t^2) = \sigma_u^2$. *As* $T \to \infty$, *the score statistic* $T \cdot R^2$ *of the regression (9) has an asymptotic* χ^2 *distribution with one degree of freedom.*

PROOF: It is convenient to introduce the matrix notation:

$$\mathbf{X_1} = \begin{bmatrix} 1 & x_1 \\ \vdots & \vdots \\ 1 & x_T \end{bmatrix} \quad \text{and} \quad \mathbf{X_2} = \begin{bmatrix} R_T(x_1) \\ \vdots \\ R_T(x_T) \end{bmatrix},$$

$\mathbf{y} = [y_1, \ldots, y_T]'$ and $\tilde{\mathbf{u}} = [\tilde{u}_1, \ldots, \tilde{u}_T]'$. With this notation, the score statistic can be written as

$$T \cdot R^2 = \frac{1}{\tilde{\sigma}^2}(\hat{\beta}_2)^2[\mathbf{X_2'X_2} - \mathbf{X_2'X_1}(\mathbf{X_1'X_1})^{-1}\mathbf{X_1'X_2}],$$

where $\hat{\beta}_2$ is the least-squares estimator of β_2 in the regression $\mathbf{y} = \mathbf{X_1}\beta_1 + \mathbf{X_2}\beta_2 + \mathbf{u}$ and $\tilde{\sigma}^2 = \tilde{\mathbf{u}}'\tilde{\mathbf{u}}/T$. As shown by Park and Phillips (1988), the least-square estimators in a regression with strictly exogenous $I(1)$ regressors is conditionally normally distributed, so that conditional on $\mathbf{X} = [\mathbf{X_1}, \mathbf{X_2}]$, $\tilde{\beta}_2$ is asymptotically distributed as $N(\mathbf{0}, \mathbf{V_2})$, where

$$\mathbf{V_2} = \sigma_u^2[\mathbf{X_1'X_2} - \mathbf{X_2'X_1}(\mathbf{X_1'X_1})^{-1}\mathbf{X_1'X_2}]^{-1}.$$

From $\tilde{\sigma}_u^2 \xrightarrow{p} \sigma_u^2$ it follows that $T \cdot R^2$ has an asymptotic χ^2 distribution with one degree of freedom. $\square$

Unfortunately, the assumptions for Proposition 2 are too restrictive to provide a useful result for practical situations. Frequently, the errors u_t are found to be correlated and the regressor x_t may be endogenous. However, using standard techniques for cointegration regressions (Saikkonen (1991), Stock and Watson (1993)) the test can be modified to accommodate serially correlated errors and endogenous regressors.

4 Small sample properties

To investigate the small sample properties of the rank tests we follow Gonzalo (1994) and generate two time series according to the model equations

$$\begin{aligned} y_t &= \beta z_t + u_t, & u_t = \alpha u_{t-1} + \epsilon_t \\ z_t &= z_{t-1} + v_t \end{aligned} \tag{10}$$

where

$$\begin{bmatrix} \epsilon_t \\ v_t \end{bmatrix} \sim \text{iid } N\left(\mathbf{0}, \begin{bmatrix} 1 & \rho \\ \rho & 1 \end{bmatrix}\right)$$

The variable x_t is obtained from random walk z_t by using the inverse function $x_t = f^{-1}(z_t)$.

Under the null hypothesis

$$H_0: \quad \beta = 0 \quad \text{and} \quad \alpha = 1$$

Table 2: Size and power for uncorrelated random walks ($\theta = 0$)

$f(x) =$		x		x^3	e^x	$\tan^{-1}(x_t)$
α	κ_T	ξ_T	CDF	CDF	CDF	CDF
1.00	0.049	0.049	0.050	0.098	0.051	0.077
0.98	0.594	0.616	0.057	0.310	0.156	0.186
0.95	0.733	0.792	0.137	0.491	0.229	0.295
0.90	0.861	0.930	0.549	0.730	0.323	0.474
0.80	0.953	0.993	1.000	0.866	0.410	0.616

Note: Empirical sizes resulting from 10,000 replications of the process given in (10). The sample size is $T = 200$. Under the null hypothesis ($\alpha = 1$) we let $\beta = 0$ and under the alternative ($|\alpha| < 1$), $\beta = 1$. The nominal size is 0.05. The test statistic κ_T and ξ_T are defined in (2) and (3). CDF indicates a Dickey-Fuller t-test on the residuals of a cointegrating regression including a constant term.

there is no cointegration relationship between the series. If in addition $\rho = 0$, then x_t and y_t are two independent random walk sequences. For this specification Table 2 reports the rejection frequencies of different cointegration tests. The rank tests κ_T and ξ_T are computed as in (2) and (3) and "CDF" indicates the Dickey-Fuller t-test for the residuals from a linear regression of y_t on x_t and a constant. The results for the linear process is given in the left half of Table 2 indicated by $f(x) = x$. It might be surprising to see that the rank test is much more powerful than the CDF test if α is close to one. There are two main reasons for this gain in power. First, the rank test does not require to estimate the cointegration parameter β. Accordingly, this test has the same power as for the case of a known cointegration relationship. Second, the rank test procedures impose the *one-sided* hypothesis that $f(x_t)$ is an *increasing* function.

Since the rank tests are invariant to a monotonic transformation of the variables, the power function is the same as for the linear case. Comparing the power of the CDF test with the rank counterparts, it turns out that the power of CDF test may drop dramatically for nonlinear alternatives (see also Granger and Hallman, 1991b), while the rank test performs as well as in the linear case. In particular, for the case $f(x_t) = exp(x_t)$ the parametric CDF test performs quite poorly.

To investigate the effects of a correlation between x_t and y_t, we generate correlated random walks using different values of ρ. Table 3 presents the empirical sizes for testing the null hypothesis of no cointegration. It turns out that for a substantial correlation all tests possess a serious size bias. Among the rank tests, the statistic $K_T(0)$ turns out to perform best. In sum, the results suggest that the correction works satisfactory for small and moderate correlation only.

Table 3 Testing correlated random walks

ρ	$K_T(0)$	$Z_T(0)$	$\widetilde{Q}_T[1]$
−0.9	0.123	0.010	0.004
−0.6	0.065	0.017	0.013
−0.4	0.051	0.026	0.023
−0.2	0.050	0.036	0.034
0.0	0.045	0.048	0.051
0.2	0.048	0.062	0.068
0.4	0.053	0.084	0.091
0.6	0.064	0.114	0.124
0.9	0.104	0.252	0.267

Note: Empirical sizes resulting from 10,000 replications of the process given in (10) with $T = 100$ and $\theta = 0$ (no serial correlation). The nominal size is 0.05. The parameter ρ measures the correlation coefficient between the innovations of the random walks.

Next we consider the small sample properties of the rank test for nonlinear cointegration suggested in Section 3. It is assumed that y_t and x_t are cointegrated so that $y_t - \beta f(x_t)$ is stationary. By setting $\alpha = 0.5$ we generate serially correlated errors and letting $\rho = 0.5$, the variable x_t is correlated with the errors u_t, that is, x_t is endogenous. The rank test for nonlinear cointegration is obtained by regressing y_t on $x_t, y_{t-1}, \Delta x_{t+1}, \Delta x_t, \Delta x_{t-1}$ and a constant. The score statistic is computed as $T \cdot R^2$ from a regression of the residuals on the same set of regressors and the ranks $R_T(x_t)$.

To study the power of the test we consider three different nonlinear functions. As a benchmark we perform the tests using $f(x_t)$ instead of the ranks $R_T(x_t)$. Of course, using the true functional form, which is usually unknown in practice, we expect the test to have better power than the test based on the ranks. Surprisingly, the results of the Monte Carlo simulations (see Table 4) suggest that the rank test may even be more powerful than the parametric test, whenever the nonlinear term enter the equation with a small weight ($\beta = 0.01$). However, the gain in power is quite small and fall in the range of the simulation error. In any case, the rank test performs very well and seems to imply no important loss of power in comparison to the parametric version of the test.

5   Empirical applications

The rank test is applied to test for a possible nonlinear cointegration between interest rates with different time to maturity and the relationship between common and preferred stocks.

Recent empirical work suggests that interest rates with a different time

Table 4: Power against nonlinear cointegration relationships

$f(x) =$	x^3		$exp(x)$		$\tan^{-1}(x)$	
regressor:	$R_T(x_t)$	$f(x_t)$	$R_T(x_t)$	$f(x_t)$	$R_T(x_t)$	$f(x_t)$
$\beta = 0.01$	0.267	0.252	0.246	0.216	0.237	0.226
$\beta = 0.05$	0.473	0.485	0.701	0.676	0.549	0.548
$\beta = 0.1$	0.714	0.746	0.957	0.955	0.834	0.855
$\beta = 0.5$	0.974	0.988	1.000	1.000	0.999	1.000

Note: Simulated power from a score tests using $R_T(x_t)$ and $f(x_t)$ as additional regressors. The sample size is $T = 200$.

to maturity are nonlinearly related.[1] The data set consists of monthly yields of government bonds at different time to maturity as published by the German *Bundesbank*. The sample runs from 1967(i) through 1995(xii) yielding 348 observations for each variable.

The nonlinear relationship between yields for different times to maturity can be motivated as follows. Let r_t denote the yield of a one-period bond and R_t represents the yield of a two-period bond at time t. The expectation theory of the term structure implies that

$$R_t = \phi_t + 0.5r_t + 0.5E_t(r_{t+1}) , \qquad (11)$$

where E_t denotes the conditional expectation with respect to the relevant information set available at period t and ϕ_t represents the risk premium. Letting $r_{t+1} = E_t(r_{t+1}) + 2\nu_t$ and subtracting r_t from both sides of (11) gives

$$R_t - r_t = 0.5(r_{t+1} - r_t) + \phi_t + \nu_t .$$

Assuming that r_t is $I(1)$ and $\phi_t + \nu_t$ is stationary implies that R_t and r_t are (linearly) cointegrated (Wolters (1995)). However, if the risk premium depends on r_t such that $\phi_t = f^*(r_t) + \eta_t$ with η_t stationary, then the yields are nonlinearly cointegrated:

$$R_t - f(r_t) = u_t \sim I(0) ,$$

where $f(r_t) = r_t + f^*(r_t)$ and $u_t = 0.5(r_{t+1} - r_t) + \eta_t + \nu_t$. Note that u_t is correlated with r_t and, therefore, r_t is endogenous. Furthermore, if the sampling interval is shorter than the time to maturity, then the errors are serially correlated even if ν_t and η_t are white noise.

To test whether interest rates possess a (nonlinear) cointegration relationship we first apply various tests for unit roots to the series. The Dickey-

---

[1] See, e.g., Campbell and Galbraith (1993), Pfann et al. (1996), and the reference therein.

Table 5: The cointegration relationship with R1

Regr.	CDF	$\widetilde{Q}_T[1]$	$K_T(0)$	$Z_T(0)$	nonlin	corr
R2	−4.138*	−5.246*	0.347*	0.010*	0.003	0.935
R3	−3.591*	−4.362*	0.357*	0.014*	0.012	0.873
R4	−3.373*	−4.083*	0.366*	0.015*	0.034	0.817
R5	−3.213	−3.829*	0.380*	0.017*	0.107	0.774
R10	−2.702	−3.216	0.471	0.024	0.489	0.675

Note: "CDF" denotes the Dickey-Fuller t-test applied to the residuals of the cointegration regression, $\widetilde{Q}_T[1]$ is the same test applied to the ranks (7), $Z_T(m)$ is given in (6), "nonlin" indicates the test for nonlinearity using the ranks as additional regressors, "corr" denotes the mutual correlation between the differenced series. "*" indicates significance at the 0.05 significance level.

Fuller test and the rank test suggested in Breitung and Gouriéroux (1997) cannot reject the hypothesis that interest rates behave like a random walk.[2]

The results presented in Table 5 highlight the cointegration properties of yields with different time to maturity. The parametric as well as the rank tests indicate a cointegration relationship between the short term bonds, while the evidence for cointegration between short run and long run bonds (R1 and R10) is much weaker. Furthermore, the rank test for nonlinear cointegration does not reveal evidence against a linear cointegration relationship.

The second application concerns common and preferred stocks of several German companies. The preferred stocks do not imply voting rights but usually receive a higher dividend payment than the respective common stocks. However, since any information about the company affect both kinds of stocks similarly, it is expected that there exists a stable relationship between both stock prices.

The stock prices are the daily closing prices running from 1/2/1996 to 3/27/1997 and are taken from the Teledata database. At some trading days, no stock price is reported so that the sample sizes depend on the company and range from 281 (*Herlitz*) to 290 (*VW*).

The application of various kind of unit root tests (not reported) suggest that all stock prices behave like random walks. The evidence for cointegration between common and preferred stocks is mixed. For *VW*, *Herlitz* and *Strabag* the cointegration tests clearly indicate a stable long run relationship (see Table 6). The rank test for nonlinearity suggests that the cointegration relationship is linear. For *MAN* the evidence for a cointegration relationship is much weaker. At a significance level of 0.05 the CDF, $\widetilde{Q}_T[1]$ and $K_T(0)$ tests cannot reject the hypothesis that common and preferred stocks are cointegrated, whereas the statistic $Z_T(0)$ indicates a cointegration relationship. Again the rank test for nonlinearity does not reveal evidence for a possible nonlinear cointegration

---

[2]For reasons of space the results are not presented.

Table 6: Cointegration between common and preferred stocks

	CDF	$\tilde{Q}_T[1]$	$K_T(0)$	$Z_T(0)$	nonlin	corr
VW	−3.618*	−4.381*	0.365*	0.013*	0.950	0.919
Herlitz	−7.155*	−8.344*	0.260*	0.004*	0.696	0.768
Strabag	−6.654*	−8.578*	0.252*	0.004*	0.241	0.354
MAN	−3.156	−3.604	0.421	0.017*	0.009	0.623

Note: see Table 5.

relationship in all cases.

These results have important implications for the efficient market hypothesis. As argued by Granger (1986) a linear cointegration relationship implies that at least one of the series is forecastable by using lagged error correction terms. Therefore, the efficient market hypothesis is empirically rejected for *Herlitz* and *Strabag*.

6 Concluding Remarks

We have considered rank tests for a nonlinear cointegration relationship. Under the hypothesis that $T^{-1/2}g(y_{[aT]})$ and $T^{-1/2}f(x_{[aT]})$ converge weakly to two independent Brownian motions $W_1(a)$ and $W_2(a)$, the limiting distribution of $d_{[aT]} = R_T(y_{[aT]}) - R_T(x_{[aT]})$ can be derived. Tests based on the sequence d_t appear to have good power properties against cointegration relationships of the form of the form $g(y_t) - f(x_t) \sim I(0)$. However, if the cointegration relationship has a more general form, for example $h(y_t, x_t) = x_t/y_t \sim I(0)$, the rank test may lack power. Therefore, it seems desirable to construct nonparametric tests against a more general form of nonlinear cointegration. Furthermore, we have no asymptotic theory for the case that x_t and y_t are mutually correlated.

The rank test procedures were applied to test for a possible nonlinear cointegration between interest yields with different time to maturity and to common and preferred stocks of several German companies. In both cases we found evidence for cointegration but the evidence for a nonlinear relationship is weak.

Acknowledgements

I am indebted to Professor Halbert White for many helpful comments and suggestions. Of course, I am responsible for all remaining errors and deficiencies. Furthermore, I gratefully acknowledge financial support from the *Sonderforschungsbereich 373* at the Humboldt University Berlin.

References

Breitung J., Gouriéroux C., Rank Tests for Unit Roots, Journal of Econometrics 1997; 81:7–28.

Campbell B., Galbraith J.W., Inference in Expectations Models of the Term Structure: a non-parametric approach, Empirical Economics 1993; 18:623–638.

Gallant A.R., Unbiased Determination of Production Technologies, Journal of Econometrics 1981; 30:149–169.

Gonzalo J., Five Alternative Methods of Estimating Long Run Relationships, Journal of Econometrics 1994; 60:203–233.

Granger C.W.J., Some Properties of Time Series Data and Their Use in Econometric Model Specification, Journal of Econometrics 1981; 16:121–130.

Granger C.W.J., Developments in the Study of Co-integrated Economic Variables, Oxford Bulletin of Economics and Statistics 1986; 48:213–228.

Granger C.W.J., Modelling nonlinear relationships between extended-memory variables, Econometrica 1995; 63:265–279.

Granger C.W.J., Hallman J., Long Memory processes with attractors, Oxford Bulletin of Economics and Statistics 1991a; 53:11–26.

Granger C.W.J., Hallman J., Nonlinear Transformations of Integrated Time Series, Journal of Time Series Analysis 1991b; 12:207–224.

Granger C.W.J., Inoue T., Morin N., Nonlinear Stochastic Trends, Journal of Econometrics 1997; 81:65–92.

Granger C.W.J., Teräsvirta T., Modelling Nonlinear Economic Relationships, Oxford: Oxford University Press, 1993.

Kendall M., Gibbons J.D., Rank Correlation Methods, London: Edward Arnold, 1990.

Lee T.-H., White H., Granger C.W.J., Testing for Neglected Nonlinearity in Time Series Models: a comparison of neural network methods and alternative tests, Journal of Econometrics 1993; 56:269–290.

Lo A.W., Long-term Memory in Stock Market Prices, Econometrica 1991; 59:1279–1314.

Park J.Y., Phillips P.C.B., Statistical Inference in Regressions with Integrated Processes: Part 1, Econometric Theory 1988; 4:468–497.

Phillips P.C.B., Understanding Spurious Regressions in Econometrics, Journal of Econometrics 1986; 33:311–340.

Phillips P.C.B., Time Series Regression with a Unit Root, Econometrica 1987; 55:277–301.

Pfann G., Schotman P., Tschernig R., Nonlinear Interest Rate Dynamics and Implications for the Term Structure, Journal of Econometrics 1995; 74:149–176.

Saikkonen, P., Asymptotically Efficient Estimation of Cointegration Regressions, Econometric Theory 1991; 7:1–21.

Sargan J.D., Bhargava A., Testing Residuals from Least Squares Regression for Being Generated by the Gaussian Random Walk, Econometrica 1983; 51:153–174.

Stock J.H. Watson M.W., A Simple Estimator of Cointegrating Vectors in Higher Order Integrated Systems, Econometrica 1993; 61:783–820.

Wolters J., On the Term Structure of Interest Rates – emprical results for Germany, Statistical Papers 1995; 36:193–214.

Comments on "A Nonparametric Test For Nonlinear Cointegration" By Jörg Breitung

HALBERT WHITE

Department of Economics
University of California, San Diego
La Jolla, CA 92093-0508
email: hwhite@weber.ucsd.edu

This paper provides a very appealing approach to testing for nonlinear cointegration in a way that avoids a drawback faced by standard tests, which will often reject the null of cointegration in the presence of nonlinear cointegration. Unlike previous work on nonlinear cointegration (e.g. Granger and Teräsvirta, 1993; Granger, 1995; Granger, Inoue, and Morin, 1997; Swanson, Corradi, and White, 1997), the test is based on ranks. For a time series $x_t, t = 1, ..., T$, $R_T(x_t)$ is the rank of x_t in the sample of size T. To test the null of no nonlinear cointegration between $\{x_t\}$ and $\{y_t\}$, one forms

$$K_T = T^{-1} \sup_t |d_t| \text{ or}$$

$$\xi_T = T^{-2} \sum_{t=1}^{T} d_t^2,$$

where $d_t = R_T(y_t) - R_T(x_t)$ is the difference in ranks. More sophisticated statistics are proposed, based on standardizing in reasonable ways, but it suffices for the present discussion to limit attention to these straightforward statistics.

Under the null of no cointegration, we expect the ranks of y_t and x_t to be unrelated, so that K_t and ξ_t will tend to be large. We reject the null if K_t and ξ_t are small. The author provides useful critical values in Table 1.

These tests are applied to examine possible cointegrating relations among various German Bond yields at different maturities and among the returns of various German firms' stocks. The testing approach is analogous to that standard in the literature, in that a sequence of tests is performed. First, one tests for unit roots. If the series are found to have a unit root, one proceeds to test for cointegration. In the present context, one applies the new tests for nonlinear cointegration.

There is, however, a potentially serious drawback to proceeding in the sequential manner, as Elliott (1995) has pointed out for standard (linear) cointegration testing. Elliott documents the facts that unit root tests (such as the Dickey-Fuller, applied here) tend to have low power, and that a joint test of a unit root/no cointegration null exhibits significantly superior performance, except for a few cases in which one has an extremely strong prior that the underlying series possess unit roots.

Elliott provides an example, directly relevant in the present context, examining cointegrating relations between three and six month U.S. Treasury Bill rates. He finds that a sequential testing approach accepts the unit root null and rejects the null of no cointegration. Nevertheless, a joint test rejects the unit root/no

A.-P.N. Refenes et al. (eds.), Decision Technologies for Computational Finance, 125–127.
© 1998 *Kluwer Academic Publishers. Printed in the Netherlands..*

cointegration null in favor of a levels vector autoregression. Elliott concludes that this rejection is plausibly linked to the failure of U.S. interest rates to be truly integrated.

Similar conclusions may well apply in the present application, where the unit root test does not reject the unit root null, but the cointegration test does reject the no cointegration null for short term bonds. There is no particular reason to think that the nonlinear elements in the current approach would materially affect Elliott's point about the low power of Dickey-Fuller-type tests. Further, U.S. and German interest rates are not likely to behave so disparately that German rates would be integrated while U.S. rates are not. It is rather more plausible that neither are integrated.

This suggests taking Elliott's suggestion to heart in the present context by fashioning a joint test for the null hypothesis of unit root/no cointegration. In keeping with the spirit of the appealing use of ranks in the cointegration test, one might also base the unit root test on ranks, using statistics like ξ_T, but with d_t defined as $R_T(y_t) - R_T(y_{t-1})$ or as $R_T(x_t) - R_T(x_{t-1})$. Finding the proper joint distribution of the statistics involved constitutes an interesting challenge, however.

Alternatively, one can attempt to accommodate the sequential testing framework by conditioning the distribution of the cointegration test on the outcome of the unit root test. This also will present non-trivial challenges.

The author performs Monte Carlo experiments to investigate the size and power of his new rank tests for nonlinear cointegration, using nonlinearly cointegrated data generating processes of the type considered by Granger and Hallman (1991a,b). That is, for time series $\{x_t\}$ and $\{y_t\}$, there exist monotone functions f and g such that $\{f(x_t)\}$ and $\{g(y_t)\}$ are long memory ($I(1)$), but $\{f(x_t) - g(y_t)\}$ is short memory ($I(0)$). These experiments show the tests have reasonable size and power for the null and alternative models considered. An alternative form of nonlinear cointegration has been proposed and studied by Swanson, Corradi, and White (1997), in which a ($p \times 1$) vector x_t obeys

$$x_t = A x_{t-1} + g_0(\theta_0' x_{t-1}) + \varepsilon_t,$$

where g_0 is bounded and non-zero, $\{x_t\}$ is a non-ergodic Markov process, $\{\theta_0' x_t\}$ is an ergodic Markov process for some ($p \times r$) matrix θ_0, and A is a ($p \times p$) matrix, $A = \alpha \theta_0'$ for ($p \times r$) matrix α. It seems plausible that the author's rank test should have power against this sort of nonlinear alternative as well, and it would be interesting to see further Monte Carlo evidence on this point.

Finally, it is important to note that cointegration, linear or not, is not necessarily an all or nothing phenomenon. The Stochastic Permanent Break (STOPBREAK) processes of Engle and Smith (1998) provide an alternative to cointegration that can be viewed as a form of temporary cointegration. For the STOPBREAK process, data are generated according to

$$y_t - \delta x_t = m_t + \varepsilon_t$$

$$m_t = m_{t-1} + q_{t-1}\varepsilon_{t-1}$$

$$q_t = q(\varepsilon_t),$$

where q maps into the unit interval, $[0, 1]$, and is nondecreasing in the absolute value of its argument, e.g.

$$q(\varepsilon_t) = \varepsilon_t^2 / (\gamma + \varepsilon_t^2).$$

The key idea is that mean reversion is less likely after a large shock than it is after a small shock.

It is plausible that the author's new rank test will have power against STOPBREAK processes as well as against non-cointegrated alternatives. Investigation of this possibility is an interesting avenue for future research. Moreover, the STOPBREAK model suggests an interesting extension to models with temporary nonlinear cointegration. Following Granger and Hallman (1991a, b) we can replace $y_t - \delta x_t$ with $g(y_t) - f(x_t)$ in the data generating equations for the STOPBREAK process. One might then test for temporary nonlinear cointegration of the sort afforded by this modified STOPBREAK process against more general non-cointegrated alternatives.

Additional References

Elliott, G., "Tests for the Correct Specification of Cointegrating Vectors and the Error Correction Model," UCSD Department of Economics Discussion Paper 95-42 (1995).

Engle, R.F. and Smith, A.D., "Stochastic Permanent Breaks," UCSD Department of Economics Discussion Paper 98-03 (1998).

Swanson, N.R., Corradi, V., and White, H., "Testing for Stationarity-Ergodicity and for Comovements Between Nonlinear Discrete Time Markov Processes," UCSD Department of Economics Discussion Paper (1997).

Reinforcement Learning for Trading Systems and Portfolios: Immediate vs Future Rewards

John Moody,[*] Matthew Saffell, Yuansong Liao and Lizhong Wu
Oregon Graduate Institute, CSE Dept.
P.O. Box 91000, Portland, OR 97291–1000
{moody, saffell, liao, lwu}@cse.ogi.edu

Abstract

We propose to train trading systems and portfolios by optimizing financial objective functions via reinforcement learning. The performance functions that we consider as value functions are profit or wealth, the Sharpe ratio and our recently proposed *differential Sharpe ratio* for online learning. In Moody & Wu (1997), we presented empirical results in controlled experiments that demonstrated the efficacy of some of our methods for optimizing trading systems. Here we extend our previous work to the use of Q-Learning, a reinforcement learning technique that uses approximated future rewards to choose actions, and compare its performance to that of our previous systems which are trained to maximize immediate reward. We also provide new simulation results that demonstrate the presence of predictability in the monthly S&P 500 Stock Index for the 25 year period 1970 through 1994.

1 Introduction: Reinforcement Learning for Trading

The investor's or trader's ultimate goal is to optimize some relevant measure of trading system performance, such as profit, economic utility or risk-adjusted return. In this paper, we propose to use reinforcement learning to directly optimize such trading system performance functions, and we compare two different reinforcement learning methods. The first uses immediate rewards to train the trading systems, while the second (Q-Learning (Watkins 1989)) approximates discounted future rewards. These

---

[*] John Moody is also with Nonlinear Prediction Systems.

A.-P.N. Refenes et al. (eds.), Decision Technologies for Computational Finance, 129–140.
© 1998 *Kluwer Academic Publishers. Printed in the Netherlands..*

methodologies can be applied to optimizing systems designed to trade a single security or to trade a portfolio of securities. In addition, we propose a novel value function for risk adjusted return suitable for online learning: the *differential Sharpe ratio*.

Trading system profits depend upon sequences of interdependent decisions, and are thus path-dependent. Optimal trading decisions when the effects of transactions costs, market impact and taxes are included require knowledge of the current system state. Reinforcement learning provides a more elegant means for training trading systems when state-dependent transaction costs are included, than do more standard supervised approaches (Moody, Wu, Liao & Saffell 1998). The reinforcement learning algorithms used here include maximizing immediate reward and Q-Learning (Watkins 1989).

Though much theoretical progress has been made in recent years in the area of reinforcement learning, there have been relatively few successful, practical applications of the techniques. Notable examples include Neuro-gammon (Tesauro 1989), the asset trader of Neuneier (1996), an elevator scheduler (Crites & Barto 1996) and a space-shuttle payload scheduler (Zhang & Dietterich 1996). In this paper we present results for reinforcement learning trading systems that outperform the S&P 500 Stock Index over a 25-year test period, thus demonstrating the presence of predictable structure in US stock prices.

2 Structure of Trading Systems and Portfolios

2.1 Traders: Single Asset with Discrete Position Size

In this section, we consider performance functions for systems that trade a single security with price series z_t. The trader is assumed to take only long, neutral or short positions $F_t \in \{-1, 0, 1\}$ of constant magnitude. The constant magnitude assumption can be easily relaxed to enable better risk control. The position F_t is established or maintained at the end of each time interval t, and is re-assessed at the end of period $t + 1$. A trade is thus possible at the end of each time period, although nonzero trading costs will discourage excessive trading. A trading system return R_t is realized at the end of the time interval $(t - 1, t]$ and includes the profit or loss resulting from the position F_{t-1} held during that interval and any transaction cost incurred at time t due to a difference in the positions F_{t-1} and F_t.

In order to properly incorporate the effects of transactions costs, market impact and taxes in a trader's decision making, the trader must have internal state information and must therefore be recurrent. An example of a single asset trading system that could take into account transactions costs and market impact would be one with the following decision function: $F_t = F(\theta_t; F_{t-1}, I_t)$ with $I_t = \{z_t, z_{t-1}, z_{t-2}, \ldots; y_t, y_{t-1}, y_{t-2}, \ldots\}$

where θ_t denotes the (learned) system parameters at time t and I_t denotes the information set at time t, which includes present and past values of the price series z_t and an arbitrary number of other external variables denoted y_t.

2.2 Portfolios: Continuous Quantities of Multiple Assets

For trading multiple assets in general (typically including a risk-free instrument), a multiple output trading system is required. Denoting a set of m markets with price series $\{\{z_t^a\} : a = 1, \ldots, m\}$, the market return r_t^a for price series z_t^a for the period ending at time t is defined as $((z_t^a/z_{t-1}^a) - 1)$. Defining portfolio weights of the ath asset as $F^a()$, a trader that takes only long positions must have portfolio weights that satisfy: $F^a \geq 0$ and $\sum_{a=1}^m F^a = 1$.

One approach to imposing the constraints on the portfolio weights without requiring that a constrained optimization be performed is to use a trading system that has softmax outputs: $F^a() = \{\exp[f^a()]\}/\{\sum_{b=1}^m \exp[f^b()]\}$ for $a = 1, \ldots, m$. Here, the $f^a()$ could be linear or more complex functions of the inputs, such as a two layer neural network with sigmoidal internal units and linear outputs. Such a trading system can be optimized using unconstrained optimization methods. Denoting the sets of raw and normalized outputs collectively as vectors $\mathbf{f}()$ and $\mathbf{F}()$ respectively, a recursive trader will have structure $\mathbf{F}_t = \text{softmax} \{\mathbf{f}_t(\theta_{t-1}; \mathbf{F}_{t-1}, I_t)\}$.

3 Financial Performance Functions

3.1 Profit and Wealth for Traders and Portfolios

Trading systems can be optimized by maximizing performance functions $U()$ such as profit, wealth, utility functions of wealth or performance ratios like the Sharpe ratio. The simplest and most natural performance function for a risk-insensitive trader is profit. We consider two cases: additive and multiplicative profits. The transactions cost rate is denoted δ.

Additive profits are appropriate to consider if each trade is for a fixed number of shares or contracts of security z_t. This is often the case, for example, when trading small futures accounts or when trading standard US$ FX contracts in dollar-denominated foreign currencies. With the definitions $r_t = z_t - z_{t-1}$ and $r_t^f = z_t^f - z_{t-1}^f$ for the price returns of a risky (traded) asset and a risk-free asset (like T-Bills) respectively, the additive profit accumulated over T time periods with trading position size $\mu > 0$ is then defined as:

$$P_T = \sum_{t=1}^{T} R_t = \mu \sum_{t=1}^{T} \left\{ r_t^f + F_{t-1}(r_t - r_t^f) - \delta |F_t - F_{t-1}| \right\} \tag{1}$$

with $P_0 = 0$ and typically $F_T = F_0 = 0$. Equation (1) holds for continuous quantities also. The wealth is defined as $W_T = W_0 + P_T$.

Multiplicative profits are appropriate when a fixed fraction of accumulated wealth $\nu > 0$ is invested in each long or short trade. Here, $r_t = (z_t/z_{t-1} - 1)$ and $r_t^f = (z_t^f/z_{t-1}^f - 1)$. If no short sales are allowed and the leverage factor is set fixed at $\nu = 1$, the wealth at time T is:

$$W_T = W_0 \prod_{t=1}^{T} \{1 + R_t\} = W_0 \prod_{t=1}^{T} \left\{ 1 + (1 - F_{t-1})r_t^f + F_{t-1}r_t \right\} \{1 - \delta |F_t - F_{t-1}|\}. \tag{2}$$

When multiple assets are considered, the effective portfolio weightings change with each time step due to price movements. Thus, maintaining constant or desired portfolio weights requires that adjustments in positions be made at each time step. The wealth after T periods for a portfolio trading system is

$$W_T = W_0 \prod_{t=1}^{T} \{1 + R_t\} = W_0 \prod_{t=1}^{T} \left\{ \left(\sum_{a=1}^{m} F_{t-1}^a \frac{z_t^a}{z_{t-1}^a} \right) \left(1 - \delta \sum_{a=1}^{m} |F_t^a - \tilde{F}_t^a| \right) \right\}, \tag{3}$$

where $\tilde{F}_t^a$ is the effective portfolio weight of asset a before readjusting, defined as $\tilde{F}_t^a = \{F_{t-1}^a(z_t^a/z_{t-1}^a)\} / \{\sum_{b=1}^{m} F_{t-1}^b(z_t^b/z_{t-1}^b)\}$. In (3), the first factor in the curly brackets is the increase in wealth over the time interval t prior to rebalancing to achieve the newly specified weights F_t^a. The second factor is the reduction in wealth due to the rebalancing costs.

3.2 Risk Adjusted Return: The Sharpe and *Differential* Sharpe Ratios

Rather than maximizing profits, most modern fund managers attempt to maximize risk-adjusted return as advocated by Modern Portfolio Theory. The Sharpe ratio is the most widely-used measure of risk-adjusted return (Sharpe 1966). Denoting as before the trading system returns for period t (including transactions costs) as R_t, the Sharpe ratio is defined to be

$$S_T = \frac{\text{Average}(R_t)}{\text{Standard Deviation}(R_t)} \tag{4}$$

where the average and standard deviation are estimated for periods $t = \{1, \ldots, T\}$.

Proper on-line learning requires that we compute the influence on the Sharpe ratio of the return at time t. To accomplish this, we have derived a new objective function called the *differential Sharpe ratio* for on-line optimization of trading system performance (Moody *et al.* 1998). It is obtained by considering exponential moving averages of the returns and standard deviation of returns in (4), and expanding to first order in the decay rate η: $S_t \approx S_{t-1} + \eta \frac{dS_t}{d\eta}|_{\eta=0} + O(\eta^2)$. Noting that only the first order term in this expansion depends upon the return R_t at time t, we define the *differential Sharpe ratio* as:

$$D_t \equiv \frac{dS_t}{d\eta} = \frac{B_{t-1}\Delta A_t - \frac{1}{2}A_{t-1}\Delta B_t}{(B_{t-1} - A_{t-1}^2)^{3/2}} \; . \tag{5}$$

where the quantities A_t and B_t are exponential moving estimates of the first and second moments of R_t:

$$
\begin{aligned}
A_t &= A_{t-1} + \eta\Delta A_t = A_{t-1} + \eta(R_t - A_{t-1}) \\
B_t &= B_{t-1} + \eta\Delta B_t = B_{t-1} + \eta(R_t^2 - B_{t-1}) \; .
\end{aligned}
\tag{6}
$$

Treating A_{t-1} and B_{t-1} as numerical constants, note that η in the update equations controls the magnitude of the influence of the return R_t on the Sharpe ratio S_t. Hence, the *differential Sharpe ratio* represents the influence of the return R_t realized at time t on S_t.

4 Reinforcement Learning for Trading Systems and Portfolios

The goal in using reinforcement learning to adjust the parameters of a system is to maximize the expected payoff or reward that is generated due to the actions of the system. This is accomplished through trial and error exploration of the environment. The system receives a reinforcement signal from its environment (a *reward*) that provides information on whether its actions are good or bad. The performance functions that we consider are functions of profit or wealth $U(W_T)$ after a sequence of T time steps, or more generally of the whole time sequence of trades $U(W_1, W_2, \ldots, W_T)$ as is the case for a path-dependent performance function like the Sharpe ratio. In either case, the performance function at time T can be expressed as a function of the sequence of trading returns $U(R_1, R_2, \ldots, R_T)$. We denote this by U_T in the rest of this section.

4.1 Maximizing Immediate Utility

Given a trading system model $F_t(\theta)$, the goal is to adjust the parameters θ in order to maximize U_T. This maximization for a complete sequence of T trades can be done off-line using dynamic programming or batch versions of recurrent reinforcement learning algorithms. Here we do the optimization on-line using a standard reinforcement learning technique. This reinforcement learning algorithm is based on stochastic gradient ascent. The gradient of U_T with respect to the parameters θ of the system after a sequence of T trades is

$$\frac{dU_T(\theta)}{d\theta} = \sum_{t=1}^{T} \frac{dU_T}{dR_t} \left\{ \frac{dR_t}{dF_t} \frac{dF_t}{d\theta} + \frac{dR_t}{dF_{t-1}} \frac{dF_{t-1}}{d\theta} \right\} . \tag{7}$$

The above expression as written with scalar F_i applies to the traders of a single risky asset, but can be trivially generalized to the vector case for portfolios.

The system can be optimized in batch mode by repeatedly computing the value of U_T on forward passes through the data and adjusting the trading system parameters by using gradient ascent (with learning rate ρ) $\Delta\theta = \rho dU_T(\theta)/d\theta$ or some other optimization method. A simple on-line stochastic optimization can be obtained by considering only the term in (7) that depends on the most recently realized return R_t during a forward pass through the data:

$$\frac{dU_t(\theta)}{d\theta} = \frac{dU_t}{dR_t} \left\{ \frac{dR_t}{dF_t} \frac{dF_t}{d\theta} + \frac{dR_t}{dF_{t-1}} \frac{dF_{t-1}}{d\theta} \right\} . \tag{8}$$

The parameters are then updated on-line using $\Delta\theta_t = \rho dU_t(\theta_t)/d\theta_t$. Such an algorithm performs a stochastic optimization (since the system parameters θ_t are varied *during* each forward pass through the training data), and is an example of *immediate reward* reinforcement learning. This approach is described in (Moody *et al.* 1998) along with extensive simulation results.

4.2 Q-Learning

Besides explicitly training a trader to take actions, we can also implicitly learn correct actions through the technique of *value iteration*. In value iteration, an estimate of future costs or rewards is made for a given state, and the action is chosen that minimizes future costs or maximizes future rewards. Here we consider the specific technique named Q-Learning (Watkins 1989), which estimates future rewards based on the current state and the current action taken. We can write the Q-function version of Bellman's equation as

$$Q^*(x,a) = U(x,a) + \gamma \sum_{y=0}^{n} p_{xy}(a) \left\{ \max_b Q^*(y,b) \right\} , \tag{9}$$

where there are n states in the system and $p_{xy}(a)$ is the probability of transitioning from state x to state y given action a. The advantage of using the Q-function is that there is no need to know the system model $p_{xy}(a)$ in order to choose the best action. One simply calculates the best action as $a^* = \arg\max_a(Q^*(x, a))$. The update rule for training a function approximator is $Q(x, a) = Q(x, a) + \rho\gamma\max_b Q^*(y, b)$, where ρ is a learning rate.

5 Empirical Results

5.1 Long/Short Trader of a Single Artificial Security

We have tested techniques for optimizing both profit and the Sharpe ratio in a variety of settings. We present results here on artificial data comparing the performance of a trading system, "RTRL", trained using real time recurrent learning with the performance of a trading system, "Qtrader", implemented using Q-Learning. We generate log price series of length 10,000 as random walks with autoregressive trend processes. These series are trending on short time scales and have a high level of noise. The results of our simulations indicate that the Q-Learning trading system outperforms the "RTRL" trader that is trained to maximize immediate reward.

The "RTRL" system is initialized randomly at the beginning, trained for a while using labelled data to initialize the weights, and then adapted using real-time recurrent learning to optimize the *differential Sharpe ratio* (5). The neural net that is used in the "Qtrader" system starts from random initial weights. It is trained repeatedly on the first 1000 data points with the discount parameter γ set to 0 to allow the network to learn immediate reward. Then γ is set equal to 0.9 and training continues with the second thousand data points being used as a validation set. The value function used here is profit.

Figure 1 shows box plots summarizing test performances for ensembles of 100 experiments. In these simulations, the data are partitioned into a training set consisting of the first 2,000 samples and a test set containing the last 8,000 samples. Each trial has different realizations of the artificial price process and different random initial parameter values. The transaction costs are set at 0.2%, and we observe the cumulative profit and Sharpe ratio over the test data set. We find that the "Qtrader" system, which looks at future profits, significantly outperforms the "RTRL" system which looks to maximize immediate rewards because it is effectively looking farther into the future when making decisions.

136

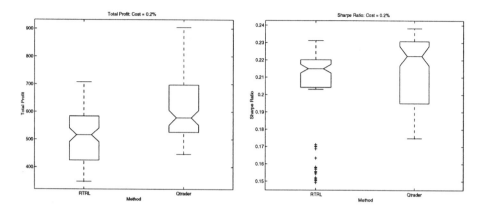

Figure 1: Boxplot for ensembles of 100 experiments comparing the performance of the "RTRL" and "Qtrader" trading systems on artificial price series. "Qtrader" outperforms the "RTRL" system in terms of both (a) profit and (b) risk-adjusted returns (Sharpe ratio). The differences are statistically significant.

5.2 S&P 500 / TBill Asset Allocation System

5.2.1 Long/Short Asset Allocation System and Data

A long/short trading system is trained on monthly S&P 500 stock index and 3-month TBill data to maximize the differential Sharpe ratio. The S&P 500 target series is the total return index computed by reinvesting dividends. The S&P 500 indices with and without dividends reinvested are shown in Figure 2 along with the 3-month treasury bill and S&P 500 dividend yields. The 84 input series used in the trading systems include both financial and macroeconomic data. All data are obtained from Citibase, and the macroeconomic series are lagged by one month to reflect reporting delays.

A total of 45 years of monthly data are used, from January 1950 through December 1994. The first 20 years of data are used only for the initial training of the system. The test period is the 25 year period from January 1970 through December 1994. The experimental results for the 25 year test period are true *ex ante* simulated trading results.

For each year during 1970 through 1994, the system is trained on a moving window of the previous 20 years of data. For 1970, the system is initialized with random parameters. For the 24 subsequent years, the previously learned parameters are used to initialize the training. In this way, the system is able to adapt to changing market and economic conditions. Within the moving training window, the "RTRL" systems use the first 10 years for stochastic optimization of system parameters, and the subsequent

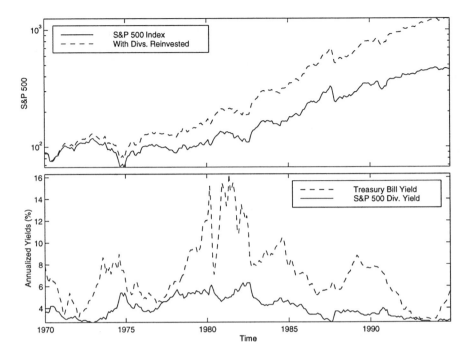

Figure 2: Time series that influence the return attainable by the S&P 500 / TBill asset allocation system. The top panel shows the S&P 500 series with and without dividends reinvested. The bottom panel shows the annualized monthly Treasury Bill and S&P 500 dividend yields.

10 years for validating early stopping of training. The networks are linear, and are regularized using quadratic weight decay during training with a regularization parameter of 0.01. The "Qtrader" systems use a bootstrap sample of the 20 year training window for training, and the final 10 years of the training window are used for validating early stopping of training. The networks are two-layer feedforward networks with 30 tanh units in the hidden layer.

5.2.2 Experimental Results

The left panel in Figure 3 shows box plots summarizing the test performance for the full 25 year test period of the trading systems with various realizations of the initial system parameters over 30 trials for the "RTRL" system, and 10 trials for the "Qtrader" system[1]. The transaction cost is set at 0.5%. Profits are reinvested during trading, and multiplicative profits are used when calculating the wealth. The notches in the box plots indicate robust estimates of the 95% confidence intervals on the hypothesis that the median is equal to the performance of the buy and hold strategy. The horizontal lines show the performance of the "RTRL" voting, "Qtrader" voting and buy and hold strategies for the same test period. The annualized monthly Sharpe ratios of the buy and hold strategy, the "Qtrader" voting strategy and the "RTRL" voting strategy are 0.34, 0.63 and 0.83 respectively. The Sharpe ratios calculated here are for the excess returns of the strategies over the 3-month treasury bill rate.

The right panel of Figure 3 shows results for following the strategy of taking positions based on a majority vote of the ensembles of trading systems compared with the buy and hold strategy. We can see that the trading systems go short the S&P 500 during critical periods, such as the oil price shock of 1974, the tight money periods of the early 1980's, the market correction of 1984 and the 1987 crash. This ability to take advantage of high treasury bill rates or to avoid periods of substantial stock market loss is the major factor in the long term success of these trading models. One exception is that the "RTRL" trading system remains long during the 1991 stock market correction associated with the Persian Gulf war, though the "Qtrader" system does identify the correction. On the whole though, the "Qtrader" system trades much more frequently than the "RTRL" system, and in the end does not perform as well on this data set.

From these results we find that both trading systems outperform the buy and hold strategy, as measured by both accumulated wealth and Sharpe ratio. These differences are statistically significant and support the proposition that there is predictability in the U.S. stock and treasury bill markets during the 25 year period 1970 through 1994. A more detailed presentation of the "RTRL" results is presented in (Moody *et al.* 1998).

---

[1]Ten trials were done for the "Qtrader" system due to the amount of computation required in training the systems

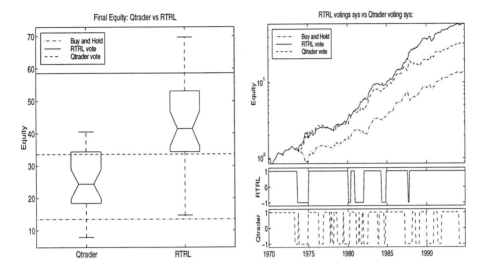

Figure 3: Test results for ensembles of simulations using the S&P 500 stock index and 3-month Treasury Bill data over the 1970-1994 time period. The solid curves correspond to the "RTRL" voting system performance, dashed curves to the "Qtrader" voting system and the dashed and dotted curves indicate the buy and hold performance. The boxplots in (a) show the performance for the ensembles of "RTRL" and "Qtrader" trading systems when transaction costs are set at 0.5%. The horizontal lines indicate the performance of the voting systems and the buy and hold strategy. Both systems significantly outperform the buy and hold strategy. (b) shows the equity curves associated with the voting systems and the buy and hold strategy, as well as the voting trading signals produced by the systems. Initial equity is set to 1. In both simulations, the traders avoid the dramatic losses that the buy and hold strategy incurred during 1974. In addition, the "RTRL" trader makes money during the crash of 1987, while the "Qtrader" system avoids the large losses associated with the buy and hold strategy during the same period.

6 Conclusions and Extensions

In this paper, we have trained trading systems via reinforcement learning to optimize financial objective functions including our recently proposed *differential Sharpe ratio* for online learning. We have also provided simulation results that demonstrate the presence of predictability in the monthly S&P 500 Stock Index for the 25 year period 1970 through 1994. We have previously shown with extensive simulation results (Moody *et al.* 1998) that the "RTRL" trading system significantly outperforms systems trained using supervised methods for traders of both single securities and portfolios. The superiority of reinforcement learning over supervised learning is most striking when state-dependent transaction costs are taken into account. Here we show that the Q-Learning approach can significantly improve on the "RTRL" method when trading single securities, as it does for our artificial data set. However, the "Qtrader" system does not perform as well as the "RTRL" system on the S&P 500 / TBill asset allocation problem, possibly due to its more frequent trading. This effect deserves further exploration.

Acknowledgements

We gratefully acknowledge support for this work from Nonlinear Prediction Systems and from DARPA under contract DAAH01-96-C-R026 and AASERT grant DAAH04-95-1-0485.

References

Crites, R. H. & Barto, A. G. (1996), Improving elevator performance using reinforcement learning, *in* D. S. Touretzky, M. C. Mozer & M. E. Hasselmo, eds, 'Advances in NIPS', Vol. 8, pp. 1017–1023.

Moody, J. & Wu, L. (1997), Optimization of trading systems and portfolios, *in* Y. Abu-Mostafa, A. N. Refenes & A. S. Weigend, eds, 'Neural Networks in the Capital Markets', World Scientific, London.

Moody, J., Wu, L., Liao, Y. & Saffell, M. (1998), 'Performance functions and reinforcement learning for trading systems and portfolios', *Journal of Forecasting* 17. To appear.

Neuneier, R. (1996), Optimal asset allocation using adaptive dynamic programming, *in* D. S. Touretzky, M. C. Mozer & M. E. Hasselmo, eds, 'Advances in NIPS', Vol. 8, pp. 952–958.

Sharpe, W. F. (1966), 'Mutual fund performance', *Journal of Business* pp. 119–138.

Tesauro, G. (1989), 'Neurogammon wins the computer olympiad', *Neural Computation* 1, 321–323.

Watkins, C. J. C. H. (1989), Learning with Delayed Rewards, PhD thesis, Cambridge University, Psychology Department.

Zhang, W. & Dietterich, T. G. (1996), High-performance job-shop scheduling with a time-delay td(λ) network, *in* D. S. Touretzky, M. C. Mozer & M. E. Hasselmo, eds, 'Advances in NIPS', Vol. 8, pp. 1024–1030.

An Evolutionary Bootstrap Method for Selecting Dynamic Trading Strategies

Blake LeBaron
Department of Economics
University of Wisconsin - Madison
1180 Observatory Drive
Madison, WI 53706
(608) 263-2516
blebaron@ssc.wisc.edu

March 1998

Abstract

This paper combines techniques drawn from the literature on evolutionary optimization algorithms along with bootstrap based statistical tests. Bootstrapping and cross validation are used as a general framework for estimating objectives out of sample by redrawing subsets from a training sample. Evolution is used to search the large space of potential network architectures. The combination of these two methods creates a network estimation and selection procedure which aims to find parsimonious network structures which generalize well. Examples are given from financial data showing how this compares to more traditional model selection methods. The bootstrap methodology also allows more general objective functions than usual least squares since it can estimate the in sample bias for any function. Some of these will be compared with traditional least squares based estimates in dynamic trading settings with foreign exchange series.

A.-P.N. Refenes et al. (eds.), Decision Technologies for Computational Finance, 141–160.
© 1998 *Kluwer Academic Publishers. Printed in the Netherlands..*

1 Introduction

Two recent techniques are gaining respect in nonlinear modeling. First, evolutionary methods have proved to a be a useful tool in network construction and estimation.[1] Second, Efron's bootstrap has been shown to be a useful tool for network diagnostics, and forecast combination.[2] This paper combines the two into a new model selection/estimation procedure. The bootstrap allows the estimation of off training set objectives for a very wide range of functions, while a population based search facilitates a search over the huge space of potential network structures. These procedures are applied to foreign exchange data with the objective of finding useful dynamic trading strategies through the combination of simple trend following strategies along with interest rate information.[3] The basic philosophy here is to take simple tools from each area and combine them into a more automatic network construction and selection system.

The next section describes in detail the objectives used, the bootstrap procedures, and the evolutionary network selection. Section 3 describes the results of some initial tests on foreign exchange data, and section 4 concludes, cautions the reader on how to interpret the results, and gives suggestions for future research.

2 Model Selection and Estimation

2.1 Ojective Functions

Several new techniques for estimating and evaluating trading models will be used in this paper. No one of these is particularly novel, but the combination provides interesting improvements in the performance of trading strategies.

The first major change comes in using an objective function inspired more by economic objectives than statistical goals.[4] A simple trading objective is used where it is assumed that the desire is to generate a signal, s_t that will be used to take a position at time t in a zero cost strategy. The payoff to such a

---

[1] See surveys in (Balakrishnan & Honavar 1995), (Mitchell 1996), and (Yao 1996).

[2] For examples of bootstrap applications to neural networks see (Connor 1993), (LeBaron & Weigend 1998), (Paaß 1993), and (Tibshirani 1994).

[3] Early results show them to be an effective tool in simulated time series forecasts using Henon data (LeBaron 1997).

[4] The recent papers by (Bengio 1997), (Choey & Weigend 1997), and (Moody & Wu 1997) are clearly inspirational here. Other recent examples looking at the importance of other loss functions can be found in (Granger & Pesaran 1996).

strategy at time $t + 1$ would be

$$s_t r_{t+1}, \tag{1}$$

where r_{t+1} is the payoff to the zero cost strategy. In general s_t will be constrained to be 1 or -1. However, it could in principle take on any value indicating a larger or smaller position. Taking the mean of this over a sample gives the obvious sample objective,

$$\frac{1}{T-1} \sum_{t=1}^{T-1} s_t r_{t+1}. \tag{2}$$

More traditional metrics will also be used such as a squared error loss function. In this case the objective is to forecast the value of the future return. It is estimated by,

$$\frac{1}{T-1} \sum_{t=1}^{T-1} (o_t - r_{t+1})^2, \tag{3}$$

where o_t is the output of a forecasting network at time t.

2.2 Bootstrap cross-validation

Model selection is obtained through the use of both bootstrap and cross-validation techniques. Candidate networks are evaluated according to their in sample objective functions adjusted by an estimate of the in sample bias.

In the case of the bootstrap a method known as the 632 bootstrap is used.[5] The basic idea is to estimate the in sample bias by drawing a new sample from the original sample with replacement, and using this as a training set with the original sample taking the role of a test set. This follows the traditional bootstrap estimators in spirit, but it turns out to have some problems. It is clear that this estimator will be biased since there is a large overlap between the training and test sets since they were drawn from the same finite population. The 632 bootstrap is one possible adjustment to account for this bias. This is a quick overview of this type of bootstrapping. Squared error is used in the following examples, but other measures could be used as well.

Define the squared forecast error for an approximating function, f, and estimated parameters, $\hat{\beta}$, as,

$$\hat{e}^2 = 1/n \sum_{i=1}^{n} (y_i - f(x_i, \hat{\beta}))^2, \tag{4}$$

---

[5]The idea of the bootstrap originated in (Efron 1979). Details on this can be found in (Efron 1983) and (Efron & Tibshirani 1993).

144

where $\hat{\beta}$ is estimated on the entire sample of length, n. The 0.632 bootstrap estimates the bias adjustment to this in sample error as

$$\hat{\omega}^{(0.632)} = 0.632(\hat{\epsilon}^{(0)} - \hat{e}^2). \tag{5}$$

$\hat{\epsilon}^{(0)}$ is the estimated squared error for points not in the training set. This is defined for B bootstrap replications as,

$$\hat{\epsilon}^{(0)} = \frac{1}{B} \sum_{b=1}^{B} \frac{1}{\#(i \notin K)} \sum_{i \notin K} (y_i - f(x_i, \beta^{(K)}))^2, \tag{6}$$

where K represents the set of points in each bootstrap draw, which are drawn with replacement. β is estimated on each draw, and the error is estimated over points not in K. The adjusted error estimate is

$$\hat{e}^{(0.632)} = \hat{e}^2 + \hat{\omega}^{(0.632)} \tag{7}$$

$$\hat{e}^{(0.632)} = 0.368\hat{e}^2 + 0.632\hat{\epsilon}^{(0)} \tag{8}$$

This gives an estimate that is a weighted average of the in sample error, and the "out of sample" error from $\hat{\epsilon}^{(0)}$. The weighting, 0.632, is derived from the probability that a given point is actually in a given bootstrap draw,

$$\alpha = 0.632 = 1 - (1 - (1/n))^n \approx 1 - e^{-1}. \tag{9}$$

We will also consider drawing less than the entire sample at times.[6] This gives a different weighting factor for equation 9. If the sample is drawn of length $m < n$ then the weighting factor becomes,

$$\alpha = 1 - (1 - (1/n))^m, \tag{10}$$

$$\hat{e}^{(0.632)} = (1 - \alpha)\hat{e}^2 + \alpha\hat{\epsilon}^{(0)} \tag{11}$$

A second technique, which is used, is monte-carlo crossvalidation. This is standard K-fold crossvalidation where the subsets are drawn at random. The estimated error is again the mean over a set of monte-carlo simulations,

$$\hat{\epsilon}^{MC} = \frac{1}{B} \sum_{b=1}^{B} \frac{1}{\#(i \notin K)} \sum_{i \notin K} (y_i - f(x_i, \beta^{(K)}))^2.$$

However, in this case the sets K are drawn without replacement from the underlying distribution. Further descriptions, and some examples of performance for monte-carlo crossvalidation can be found in (Shao 1993).

---

[6]This idea of using less than a full sample bootstrap has been introduced in a slightly different context in (Hall 1990).

2.3 Network Evolution

Approximating functions $f()$ will be standard feedforward, single hidden layer, neural networks with hyperbolic tangent activation functions. Hidden units values are given by,

$$h_{t,j} = \tanh(\beta_{0,j}^x + \sum_{i=1}^{N_i} \beta_{i,j}^x x_{t,i}), \tag{12}$$

where $\beta_{0,j}^x$ is a bias or constant term, and $x_{t,i}$ are the inputs. For standard forecasts, the weighted sum of the hidden units is used as the output,

$$o_t = \sum_{j=1}^{N_h} \beta_j^h h_{t,j} \tag{13}$$

where β_j are the output weights on the hidden units.[7]

In the case of the dynamic strategy objectives the output is fed through a final tanh unit to constrain the output signal to $[-1, 1]$. Using the notation of section 2.1 gives,

$$s_t = \tanh(o_t). \tag{14}$$

This gives a smooth trading rule function. In final evaluation this will be mapped into a "hard" rule where s_t takes on the sign of o_t as its value. This objective, being discontinuous, causes problems for the hill climbing based estimation procedure, so the tanh function is used as a stand in. Surprisingly, the tanh results are very close to the "hard" rule, and they are not reported.

Network weights are estimated by hill climbing. However, the network architecture is determined through an evolutionary procedure. There is a large and growing literature on evolving neural networks.[8] This paper uses a very simple evolutionary structure. Obviously, improvements may be obtained using more sophisticated methods in the future.

A population of 50 network architectures is given by $(s_j, w_j^0; w_j)$ where j is the population index. s_j is a vector of binary variables representing each connection in a network. Let L be the number of nonzero entries in s_j. w_j^0 is a real vector of length L that gives the starting values used in hill climbing, and w_j is a real vector of length L representing the final "optimized" network weights. A picture of this flat binary representation and the corresponding network is given in figure 1.

---

[7]No aggregate bias term is used. The maximum number of active hidden units is set to 8, which turned out not to be a binding constraint.

[8]Useful surveys on this field can be found in (Balakrishnan & Honavar 1995) and (Yao 1996).

146

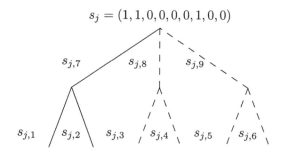

$$s_j = (1, 1, 0, 0, 0, 0, 1, 0, 0)$$

Figure 1: Single hidden unit, 2 inputs

New networks are evolved using tournament selection and two mutation operators, micro and macro mutation. A parent network is selected by choosing 10 networks at random, and then using the fittest of these in the mutation stage that follows. Micro mutation involves looking at the connections between the hidden units and inputs. The mutation operator sweeps through all input lines and with probability 0.1 it flips their bits from 0 to 1. Macro mutation involves choosing one hidden unit at random. Its connection to the output is then flipped from 0 to 1, or 1 to 0. If it is activated, then each of its input lines are activated with probability, 0.9. Both types of mutations occur exclusively with probability 1/3. The remaining 1/3 of the time, the network structure is simply copied to create a new network with the same structure, but new starting values will be chosen for hill climbing. Once the child's architecture is decided through mutation, and the starting values are drawn, its final weights, w_j, are set using a hill climbing algorithm on the full training sample.[9]

---

[9]Optimization uses the BFGS algorithm described in (Press, Flannery, Teukolsky & Vetterling 1986) with numeric derivatives. For the case of squared error loss it would probably be more efficient to use the Levenberg-Marquardt algorithm, but this would make comparisons difficult, so the same hill climbing algorithm will be used in all cases. All the algorithms have been hand coded in Matlab to maintain control, but they have been compared with the Matlab optimization toolbox routines for testing. Also, starting values use a technique suggested in (Kuan & White 1994) where the initial weights on the hidden unit outputs are set using an OLS regression on the target value. This accepts that the initial weights guide the general direction of the sensitivity of the hidden units to different patterns, and the output

Ten new networks are chosen in this fashion. New networks have an initial startup number of bootstrap simulations of 5. This prevents many simply lucky, but not very good, networks from invading the population. Also, new networks must be better than the parents they replace. This is similar to $\mu + \lambda$ selection described in (Bäck 1996), and the election operator of (Arifovic 1994). In other words, after the child fitness values are estimated from the bootstraps, the best 50 out of the current pool of 60 networks will become the new population. This selection method has the property of slowing down evolution as the population improves which allows it to concentrate on getting good bootstrap bias estimates for the current set of networks. New networks are started at randomly drawn initial weights.

Bias estimates proceed according to the bootstrap or cross validation methods described earlier. However, it is important to be clear just what the timing is. Bootstrapping is a computationally intensive algorithm, and it would be infeasible to perform many bootstraps on many population members. Therefore, a single bootstrap iteration is performed on the entire population at each evolutionary time step. This means that the bias estimates are continuously being updated over time, and the stochastic fitness values will be changing. For each bootstrap bias estimate, a new subsample, K is drawn, and β is estimated through hill climbing using randomly drawn starting values.[10]

A serious problem for neural networks is that of local minima. The possibility of having candidate solutions that have stopped at a local, and not a global minimum adds a troubling aspect of imprecision.[11] An attempt is made to avoid these local minimum solutions in the population. New networks can be direct copies of old network structures subject only to a change in the startup vector, w^0. This new candidate network is simply a retry of an old network structure at new starting weights. If this network out performs its parent in the population in terms of in sample objectives, then it shows that the parent was at a local minimum in terms of that objective. When this happens this child directly replaces the parent. In this way the system strives for networks that, subject to their architecture constraints, minimize in sample objectives. Architecture decisions are made according to the bias adjustments previously described. This is in contrast to techniques such as "stop training" which may

should be quickly moved to reflect this. Many experiments have indicated that the only real impact of this is a very significant speed improvement.

[10]It is important to remember that the candidate network weights from the full training set are used in out of sample forecasting. The estimated weights from the bootstrap draws and corresponding estimates of in sample bias are used in model selection fitness only.

[11]A small experiment with the networks and data used in this paper showed that this variability could be significant. Objective functions varying by as much as 150 percent about their mean for different starting values in the weight vector were common. Also, for some starting values the objective changed sign.

often stop at a local minimum on the training or cross validation sample.[12]

All networks are initialized with 70 percent of their connections activated. This amounts to roughly 50 percent of the connections on since many of these bits may be connected to deactivated hidden units.[13] The starting weights for the inputs are all set to uniform values on $[-0.05, 0.05]$. This is used for all starting value initializations. The results have been generally robust to changes in this distribution. Finally, evolution is run for 30 generations. New networks are not allowed during the first and last 5 generation to get better bootstrap estimates during these periods.

3   Foreign exchange example

3.1   Data Preliminaries

This section gives a quick example of this procedure applied to foreign exchange data. See (LeBaron 1997) for more extensive applications to simulated test time series.

The series used is the British pound from January 1979 to October 25, 1993, daily with 3500 points.[14] Forecasting is done in a rolling manner in order to capture potential nonstationarities in the series. The first 1000 points will be used to estimate and evaluate networks which will be used on the next 500 out of sample data points. After these forecasts are completed the blocks will be rolled forward by 500, and the procedure is repeated. This is done five times to give a total forecast time series length of 2500.

The objective is to forecast the one day continuously compounded return corrected for the interest differential. P_t is the foreign exchange price in dollars per pound.

$$r_{t+1} = \log P_{t+1} - \log P_t - (r_t^{US} - r_t^{UK}) \tag{15}$$

Given uncovered interest parity this should be unforecastable given time t information. The strategies estimated will report

$$\frac{1}{T-1} \sum_{t=1}^{T-1} s_t r_{t+1}, \tag{16}$$

---

[12]The concern for avoiding local minimum is approached in another bootstrapping context by (Tibshirani & Knight 1995).

[13]Everytime a new network structure is set up it must be run through a specification check to make sure that it is a valid network. This eliminates hidden unit inputs for hidden units that are not active, and makes sure that active hidden units have at least one input.

[14]The sample was chosen to enable the rolling sample lengths to come out even.

an estimate of the dynamic trading strategies reported earlier. This would be a strategy of borrowing in one currency, and then investing in the other one. Given covered parity conditions hold this is also the payoff to a strategy of forward speculation where a forward position long or short is taken at t and then unwound at time $t + 1$.

The inputs for forecasting are a sequence of price moving average ratios. Inputs are constructed from a commonly used set of predictor variables. These are listed in table 1.[15] Ideally, this table would be much bigger to test out the

Table 1: Information Variables

1.	Two price/moving average ratios. (150 and 5 day)
2.	One lag of the interest adjusted return series defined in equation 15.
3.	A local average of squared returns (10 days) as a volatility estimate.
4.	The interest differential at time t, $r_t^{US} - r_t^{UK}$.
5.	The interest rate differential less its 30 week moving average.

evolutionary system's ability to weed out irrelevant predictors, but this hasn't been done. These have not been individually tested for relevance, so several of these may be useless.

There is some preprocessing performed before networks are estimated. All preprocessing uses only information in the training set. All the inputs are divided by the training set standard deviation for each value. The volatility and interest rate series are demeaned using the training set. Finally, the output target, or future return is demeaned in the training set alone using the mean from the training set. This is done to keep the trading rule objective from trying to just "fit the mean" of the sample. If the sample mean was positive then the trading rule might find it optimal to go long all the time. Setting this mean to zero makes sure that it goes after a dynamic switching strategy.

The data are then formed into pairs, (r_{t+1}, x_t), where x_t is the vector of prediction variables. It is this set of pairs that will serve as the pool for drawing new values during bootstrapping. The x_t are mapped into s_t using the fitted networks, and a hyperbolic tangent in the estimation stage. This is converted to a hard $[-1, 1]$ function for the actual reported results.[16]

---

[15]The technical predictors have been used in many papers including, (Dooley & Shafer 1983), (Sweeney 1986), (LeBaron 1998), (Levich & Thomas 1993), and (Taylor 1992). Volatility based correlation forecasts were introduced in (Bilson 1990) and (LeBaron 1992). The inclusion of the interest differential reflects the large literature on the forward bias in foreign exchange markets, (Engel 1996) and (Lewis 1995). The interest rate differential moving average is inspired by recent work in (Eichenbaum & Evans 1995) that indicates that the impact of large interest rate differentials may drop off over time.

[16]Fitted tanh objectives turned out to be very close to the hard trading rule objective,

3.2 Results

Table 2 presents the out of sample forecast and trading results. These are the values of the dynamic trading strategies evaluated out of sample on each of the 500 test periods, and averaged over all 5 of these. These test periods are used for running the strategies, and play no roll in model selection or estimation. Several numbers are reported giving estimates of the usefulness of the dynamic strategy, and its significance.

The first row reports the bootstrap results using a half sample selection rule. 500 points are drawn from the 1000 length training sample with replacement, and this is used as a bootstrap draw in the bias adjustment procedure.[17] In the first row of the table, the mean percentage return is given as 0.067 percent with a standard error of 0.015 which is clearly significantly different from zero.[18] Zero is what would be expected in the case where uncovered parity held, or foreign exchange markets were unpredictable. Also, reported is the fraction of correct sign predictions which is also significantly different from 0.5, but not too far from it in magnitude at 0.54. Finally, the annual Sharpe ratio is given. This is the mean return divided by the standard deviation of the return. It is not a dimensionless number, but under independent returns it scales as $\sqrt{n}$ or the length of the period. It is reported for the annual horizon here which is common. The reported value of 1.39 is very large relative to other strategies and portfolios available to investors.[19] Also, reported are the 95% confidence bounds for the bootstrapped Sharpe ratio distribution. These indicate that its large value is quite significant, but also reminds us how imprecise the estimated Sharpe ratios are.

Moving to the next row of the table, labeled Bootstrap 1.0, we see the results for the traditional 632 bootstrap where the full sample length, 1000, is used as the number for the training set. While the numbers here are still significantly large, they appear to be smaller than the ones for the 0.5 sample sizes.

$[-1, 1]$ in the results they produced. This indicates that the tanh function output is very close to -1 or 1 in most cases. This finding is relevant to the problem of whether a an objective that looked at other criteria, such as the Sharpe ratio, would have changed the results. If the tanh function is giving -1 or $+1$ as output, and if there is no forecastibility in the conditional variance, then maximizing expected returns will maximize the Sharpe ratio, since the denominator of the Sharpe ratio is minimized by maximizing the expected return. To see this remember that the standard deviation is $\sqrt{E(s_t r_{t+1}^2) - E(s_t r_{t+1})^2}$. See (Skouras 1997) for more information on this.

[17] The weightings are adjusted as in equation 10.

[18] Standard errors are estimated using a bootstrap procedure where the dynamic returns themselves are redrawn with replacement. The block bootstrap was also used to simulate dependence in the series, but the results were the same, so they are not reported.

[19] A well diversified aggregate stock portfolio has a Sharpe ratio of between 0.3 and 0.4 depending on the securities and time period.

Table 2: Comparisons

Description	Mean Payoff (percent)	Sign Probablity	Sharpe	Sharpe (0.025)	Sharpe (0.975)
Bootstrap 0.5	0.067 (0.015)	0.540 (0.009)	1.39 (0.31)	0.80	2.02
Bootstrap 1.0	0.042 (0.016)	0.526 (0.009)	0.86 (0.32)	0.20	1.47
Monte-carlo Cross Validation	0.047 (0.015)	0.529 (0.009)	0.98 (0.32)	0.37	1.62
No Adjust	0.044 (0.014)	0.527 (0.009)	0.91 (0.30)	0.28	1.45
No adjust Full Connection	0.021 (0.015)	0.512 (0.010)	0.43 (0.32)	-0.19	1.04
MSE	0.027 (0.015)	0.511 (0.009)	0.55 (0.31)	-0.10	1.15
MSE BIC	0.020 (0.015)	0.513 (0.009)	0.41 (0.31)	-0.19	1.02
MA(150)	0.030 (0.015)	0.527 (0.010)	0.61 (0.32)	-0.02	1.20

Dynamic trading strategy results. All numbers are estimated using the 5, 500 length testing periods. These were not used for model estimation or selection. Mean payoff is the mean payout on the dynamic strategy over the out sample period, see equation 16. Sign Probability is the probability of a correct sign prediction, and Sharpe is the annual Sharpe ratio. Numbers in parenthesis are standard errors from a 1000 length bootstrap. Sharpe (0.025) and (0.975) are the respective quantiles of the bootstrap distribution.

The next few rows present several other methods for comparison. The first is monte-carlo cross validation. For this a training set is drawn without replacement from the sample, and the remaining data is used for testing in network selection. The numbers are reported using a 50/50 training/testing split. They are generally not very different from the bootstrap using the full sample.

The next row, labeled "no adjust", presents a very crucial comparison. In these runs the bootstrap adjustment is turned off completely, and the system evolves toward the network which fits best in the entire training set. This should be very sensitive to over fitting problems. Interestingly, it doesn't do all that badly. It is comparable to the monte-carlo cross validation and the full sample bootstrap. Also, it should be noted that the mean return is not significantly different from the 0.5 bootstrap either.[20] The row labeled, "Full Connection", evaluates the usefulness of lean networks. Here a fully connected network is used. The best network over 1000 different starting values is chosen for out of sample forecasting, with no bias adjustment on the in sample fitness. The performance of the fully connected nets drops dramatically to 0.0208 which is significantly different from the bootstrap 0.5 forecasts.

The next two rows report numbers using traditional MSE estimates. These networks are then used as trading rules by taking the sign of the forecast. In the first case no adjustment is made in fitting. This gives a much smaller mean return of 0.0267 which is significanly different from the bootstrap case with a t-test value of 1.89 which is significant at the 5 percent level using a one tailed test.[21] The Sharpe ratio of 0.55 is less than half that for the first bootstrap. The next row adds a standard BIC (Schwarz 1978) penalty to the network fitness value. This penalizes the network for extra parameters. It is clear that this is over penalizing since the estimated networks do not even give a significantly positive return or Sharpe ratio. With a link percentage of only 0.03 these networks cannot be doing very much.

The final row presents a comparison with a simple dynamic trading strategy using a 150 day moving average. For this strategy the signal s_t is set to 1 if the price is above a 150 day moving average and -1 otherwise. This simple strategy is one of the inputs to the neural network, but it is often used on its own. The eyeball test again sees a big difference. The Sharpe ratio for this strategy is only 0.61 which compares to 1.38 for the bootstrap. The means are again significantly different with a t-value of 1.79.[22]

The dynamic trading strategies cannot really be evaluated as to whether they should be used until some account is taken of transaction costs. Here, a relatively conservative estimate of 0.05 percent for a one way trade will be used. This actually means that each time a strategy changes sign it imposes a 0.1 percent cost since changing positions involves both unwinding the foreign position, and setting up a new domestic position, or the reverse.

Adjusted returns and Sharpe ratios are given in table 3. It is clear that for most of the rules there is an impact from transaction costs. For the bootstrap they fall from 0.0667 to 0.0513, but the Sharpe ratios that are commanded by

---

[20] A rough judge of significance here would be a t-test on the means. Given their estimated standard errors the standard error on the difference would be $\sqrt{(s_1^2 + s_2^2)}$ which is 0.02 for these showing that the difference between any of the means reported so far is not significantly different from zero.

[21] Again caution should be used in interpreting this test since the difference is being measured off the best performing rule.

[22] These tests would be an interesting application for the Reality Check of (White 1997). Without a framework like that it is still difficult to interperet the difference between values that may have been preselected.

Table 3: Transaction Cost Adjustment

Description	Mean Payoff (percent)	Trade Probability	Sharpe
Bootstrap 0.5	0.0513	0.1536	1.0682
MCV 0.5	0.0327	0.1448	0.6787
No adjust	0.0247	0.1904	0.5127
MA(150)	0.0263	0.0328	0.5462

Dynamic strategy figures adjusted for transaction costs. MCV stands for monte-carlo cross-validation. Trade probability is the estimated probability of the strategy trading.

the best strategies are still in a range that would be thought of as interesting. This table also reports the probability of trade. It is clear that the network strategies trade more frequently then the simple moving average trading rule which only trades about 3 percent of the time.[23]

Table 4: Subsamples

Period	Training Boot 0.5	Test Boot 0.5	Test Boot 1.0	Test No adjust
831003-851008	0.0629	0.0947	0.1025	0.0330
851009-871009	0.0948	0.0911	0.0190	0.0429
871012-891004	0.0914	0.0447	0.0132	0.0348
891005-911007	0.0428	0.0376	0.0295	0.0318
911008-931025	0.0546	0.0654	0.0439	0.0762

Table 4 presents some results from subsamples to show how the network fitting and trading rule profitability changes over subsamples. The values are taken from the 0.5 bootstrap. The range is pretty big with some periods showing dramatic one day returns of nearly 0.1 percent, but other periods drop off to only 0.037 percent. This is reflective of the large noise in financial data, and in the trading rule objective. The table also gives a comparison across several of the methods. Interestingly, the 0.5 bootstrap performs the best in 3 of the 5 subsamples, and second best in the other two. This is supportive of consistently good performance of this method, and also that it might have been able to have been selected using past data.

Table 5 displays the time variation in the fitted networks when applied to further distant future subsamples. Each entry shows the initial objective from

---

[23] It should be noted that the inclusion of transaction costs eliminates the significant difference between the bootstrap and MA(150) rules. This is due to the fact that the first strategy incurs larger costs from more frequent trading.

154

the 500 days following the training period, the test set, along with the objective evaluated further out in the future. This gives a view of how time varying the predictability is. Most of the network trading objectives do decay as the horizon is moved farther out in the future.

Table 5: Future Subsamples

Period	831003-851008	851009-871009	871012-891004	891005-911007	911008-931025
831003-851008	0.0947	0.0889	0.0034	0.0091	0.0209
851009-871009		0.0911	0.0158	0.0206	0.0570
871012-891004			0.0447	0.0312	0.0571
891005-911007				0.0376	0.0070

Subsample variation is also displayed in figure 2. This picture shows the evolution in network structure for the bootstrap and no adjustment cases. Link fraction refers to the number of connections that are active divided by the total number possible, or the overall connectedness of the networks. It is clear in the bootstrap case the networks are getting leaner as they evolve. This is not necessarily the case for no adjustments. Some networks are getting leaner, and others are expanding. It is interesting that any network would be eliminating connections in the no adjustment case. However, it is possible that the difficulty of estimating this objective function may get larger as nodes are added making it more unlikely that they will hit a set of starting values that leads to good networks. This puts some pressure towards leaner networks even without an explicit bias adjustment.

4   Conclusions and Future Work

These results show promise for some of the methods introduced here. As mentioned in the introduction the combination of several things, trading objectives, bootstrap bias adjustment, and evolutionary network selection, appears to be helpful in forecasting experiments. The results should still be viewed with some caution as this was one problem and one time period of observation. Also, while the method clearly dominates some simpler forecasting methods, and random walk guessing, statistically significant differences across several methods was not seen.

In terms of methodology this work is pushing closer to handing a larger part of the network selection, and parameter choice problems over to a mechanized system. The objective is obviously to take more of the guess work out of

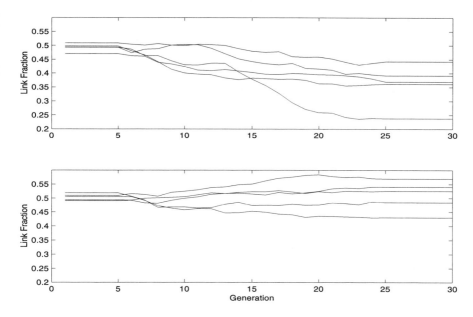

Figure 2: Linkage Fraction: Bootstrap (top) and No adjustment (bottom), 30 Generations each run

nonlinear model selection and fitting. There is still a long ways to go, and this is far from a fully automatic black box forecasting system. The system analyzed here brings along some new problems of its own. First, it introduces many new parameters for which theory gives little guidance on how they should be set. Second, the bootstrap procedure is very computationally burdensome. On current levels of machinery it remains a constraint on what can be done. The use of relatively small simple networks, small populations, and input lists was a constraint imposed by computational size.

Since the philosophy was to take the simplest components from each area the possibilities for improvement are quite large. As mentioned earlier the evolutionary structure for the networks is crude. Crossover like operations are not used, and the actual data structure of the nets as a flat bitstring could certainly be changed. A network structure that was better suited to evolution would be useful. Also, the value added of bootstrapping and crossvalidation is still not entirely clear here. This is the area of greatest uncertainty in terms of structure and parameter choice. A good question that remains is why did the half sample bootstrap do so much better than the full sample approach advocated in the bootstrapping literature. This remains a serious mystery for future research, and bigger computers. It is always possible that financial series may just be too noisy to give a firm answer here. Finally, direct application of greater computing horsepower is also an obvious area for improvement. It would be easy to simply extend population sizes and generation lengths. Also, a very delicate issue that is not directly addressed is the rate of evolution versus the bootstrap. Since evolution is occurring over an essentially noisy fitness value it is possible that the system can be evolving over noise in some cases. This can be lessened by increasing the amount of bootstrapping relative to evolution, by reducing the number of new rules coming in, or running several bootstrap iterations for every population step. Another method for increasing the precision of the bootstrap at each step is to reduce the in sample draw on the bootstrap. This method appeared successful here in that the best performing bootstrap used a 50 percent sample draw.

Another methodological question that this paper asks concerns the value of population based search. Several arguments for evolutionary search have been offered including, combinations of building blocks and endogenous annealing schedules. This paper offers a more direct reason for using population based search. In the case where the computational time for estimating an objective is very costly, and noisy objectives can be slowly improved through extra function evaluations, the use of a population based search may helpful. It allows the search to concentrate scarce computing resources on the most likely useful candidate solutions. It would be impossible to cover the entire sample computationally, but the population defines a subset where the searcher should work hard to get better fitness values from the bootstrap iterations. This is a much more direct and practical benefit to population based search than the previously mentioned benefits. However, it does not negate their possible contribution in the search process. A second aspect of populations that is not used here, is that the final forecasting rule could be a combination of several of the best rules, or the trading signal could be a vote from several nets. These methods have been tried by many others in different contexts, and they might prove useful here. One complication, is that it is a little difficult to judge the bootstrap bias estimates if the actual forecast is going to be a function of several networks.

This paper has shown the possibility for using a new evolutionary bootstrap process in selecting dynamic trading strategies. It should be reminded that this process remains somewhat preliminary, and further complete out of sample periods need to be checked before this should be taken live as a trading strategy. Also, the troubling lack of significant differences between several of the methods should also suggest proceeding with some caution as well. However, it suggests that there many be value added to this procedure and further explorations in this directions may prove fruitful.

5 Acknowledgments

The author is would like to thank Andreas Weigend, and other participants at CF97 for useful comments. Also, the Mathworks provided some of the software used in this study. Much of this research was completed while the author was visiting the Center for Biological and Computational Learning (CBCL) at MIT, and the author is grateful for the many comments and suggestions from the CBCL community. Finally, the author thanks the Sloan Foundation, and the Wisconsin Alumni Research Foundation for financial support.

References

Arifovic, J. (1994), 'Genetic algorithm learning and the cobweb model', *Journal of Economic Dynamics and Control* **18**, 3–28.

Bäck, T. (1996), *Evolutionary Algorithms in Theory and Practice*, Oxford University Press, Oxford, UK.

Balakrishnan, K. & Honavar, V. (1995), Evolutionary design of neural architectures: A preliminary taxonomy and guide to the literature, Technical report, Dept. of Computer Science, Iowa State University, Ames, Iowa.

Bengio, Y. (1997), Training a neural network with a financial criterion rather than a prediction criterion, *in* 'Decision Technologies for Financial Engineering: Proceedings of the Fourth International Conference on Neural Networks in the Capital Markets', World Scientific, Singapore, pp. 36–48.

Bilson, J. F. (1990), "Technical" currency trading, *in* L. R. Thomas, ed., 'The Currency-Hedging Debate', IFR Publishing Ltd., London.

Choey, M. & Weigend, A. S. (1997), Nonlinear trading models through sharpe ratio maximization, *in* A. S. Weigend, Y. S. Abu-Mostafa & A. P. N. Refenes, eds, 'Decision Technologies for Financial Engineering: Proceedings of the Fourth International Conference on Neural Networks in the Capital Markets', World Scientific, Singapore, pp. 3–22.

Connor, J. T. (1993), Bootstrap methods in neural network time series prediction, *in* J. Alspector, R. Goodman & T. X. Brown, eds, 'International Workshop on applications of neural networks to telecommunications', Erlbaum, Hillsdale, NJ, pp. 125–131.

Dooley, M. P. & Shafer, J. (1983), Analysis of short-run exchange rate behavior: March 1973 to november 1981, *in* D. Bigman & T. Taya, eds,

'Exchange Rate and Trade Instability: Causes, Consequences, and Remedies', Ballinger, Cambridge, MA.

Efron, B. (1979), 'Bootstrap methods: Another look at the jackknife', *The Annals of Statistics* **7**, 1–26.

Efron, B. (1983), 'Estimating the error rate of a prection rule: improvement on cross validation', *Journal of the American Statistical Association* **78**, 316–331.

Efron, B. & Tibshirani, R. (1993), *An Introduction to the Bootstrap*, Chapman and Hall, New York.

Eichenbaum, M. & Evans, C. L. (1995), 'Some empirical evidence on the effects of shocks to monetary policy on exchange rates', *Quarterly Journal of Economics* **110**, 975–1009.

Engel, C. (1996), 'The forward discount anomaly and the risk premium: A survey of recent evidence', *Journal of Empirical Finance* **3**, 123–192.

Granger, C. & Pesaran, M. H. (1996), A decision theoretic approach to forecast evaluation, Technical report, University of California, San Diego, La Jolla, CA.

Hall, P. (1990), 'Using the bootstrap to estimate mean squared error and select smoothing parameter in nonparametric problems', *Journal of Multivariate Analysis* **32**, 177–203.

Kuan, C. M. & White, H. (1994), 'Artificial neural networks: An econometric perspective', *Econometric Reviews* **13**, 1–91.

LeBaron, B. (1992), 'Forecast improvements using a volatility index', *Journal of Applied Econometrics* **7**, S137–S150.

LeBaron, B. (1997), An evolutionary bootstrap approach to model selection and generalization, Technical report, The University of Wisconsin - Madison, Madison, Wisconsin.

LeBaron, B. (1998), Technical trading rules and regime shifts in foreign exchange, *in* E. Acar & S. Satchell, eds, 'Advanced Trading Rules', Butterworth-Heinemann, pp. 5–40.

LeBaron, B. & Weigend, A. S. (1998), 'A bootstrap evaluation of the effect of data splitting on financial time series', *IEEE Transactions on Neural Networks* **9**(1), 213 – 220.

Levich, R. M. & Thomas, L. R. (1993), 'The significance of technical trading-rule profits in the foreign exchange market: A bootstrap approach', *Journal of International Money and Finance* **12**, 451–474.

Lewis, K. (1995), Puzzles in international financial markets, *in* G. M. Grossman & K. Rogoff, eds, 'Handbook of International Economics', Vol. 3, North Holland, Amsterdam, pp. 1913–1971.

Mitchell, M. (1996), *An Introduction to Genetic Algorithms*, MIT Press, Cambridge, MA.

Moody, J. & Wu, L. (1997), Optimization of trading systems and portfolios, *in* 'Decision Technologies for Financial Engineering: Proceedings of the Fourth International Conference on Neural Networks in the Capital Markets', World Scientific, Singapore, pp. 23–36.

Paaß, G. (1993), Assessing and improving neural network predictions by the bootstrap algorithm, *in* S. J. Hanson, J. D. Cowan & C. L. Giles, eds, 'Advances in Neural Information Processing Systems', Vol. 5, Morgan Kaufmann, San Mateo, CA, pp. 196–203.

Press, W. H., Flannery, B. P., Teukolsky, S. A. & Vetterling, W. T. (1986), *Numerical Recipes: The art of scientific computing*, Cambridge University Press, Cambridge, UK.

Schwarz, G. (1978), 'Estimating the dimension of a model', *Annals of Statistics* **6**, 461–464.

Shao, J. (1993), 'Linear model selection by cross-validation', *Journal of the American Statistical Association* **88**, 486–494.

Skouras, S. (1997), An (abridged) theory of technical analysis, Technical report, European University Institute, Florence, Italy.

Sweeney, R. J. (1986), 'Beating the foreign exchange market', *Journal of Finance* **41**, 163–182.

Taylor, S. J. (1992), 'Rewards available to currency futures speculators: Compensation for risk or evidence of inefficient pricing?', *Economic Record* **68**, 105–116.

Tibshirani, R. (1994), A comparison of some error estimates for neural network models, Technical report, Dept. of Preventive Medicine and Biostatistics, University of Toronto, Toronto, Ontario.

160

Tibshirani, R. & Knight, K. (1995), Model search and inference by bootstrap "bumping", Technical report, Dept of Statistics, University of Toronto, Toronto, Ontario.

White, H. (1997), A reality check for data snooping, Technical report, University of San Diego, La Jolla, CA.

Yao, X. (1996), 'A review of evolutionary artificial neural networks', *International Journal of Intelligent Systems* **8**, 539–567.

DISCUSSION OF "AN EVOLUTIONARY BOOTSTRAP METHOD FOR SELECTING DYNAMIC TRADING STRATEGIES"

A. S. WEIGEND

Department of Information Systems
Leonard N. Stern School of Business
New York University
44 West Fourth Street, MEC 9-74
New York, NY 10012
aweigend@stern.nyu.edu
www.stern.nyu.edu/~aweigend

This note summarizes the remarks as discussant of Blake LeBaron's paper *An Evolutionary Bootstrap Strategy for Selecting Dynamic Trading Strategies* at NNCM/CF97 in London. First, the main contributions of the paper are placed in a general modeling framework. Second, some ideas for further analysis are given. Third, possible relationships between minimal architectures and poor local minima are discussed.

1   Placing the paper in the seven step framework of modeling

I would like to start the discussion by placing LeBaron's insightful and well-written paper in a general framework of modeling. This framework consists of the following steps: (1) Task, (2) Data, (3) Architecture, (4) In-sample objective, (5) Optimization, (6) Out-of-sample evaluation, and (7) Analysis.

1.1 Problem / Task

The goal of LeBaron's paper is to find a dynamic strategy for trading in the UK/US foreign exchange market. The strategy is to provide daily recommendations for the position size, restricted to be either fully long (+1) or fully short (-1).

1.2 Data / Representation

The inputs are derived from two time series, the daily foreign exchange price in US Dollars per Pound Sterling, and the daily interest rate differential between the US and the UK. LeBaron corrects the daily returns with the interest rate

A.-P.N. Refenes et al. (eds.), Decision Technologies for Computational Finance, 161–164.
© 1998 *Kluwer Academic Publishers. Printed in the Netherlands..*

differential—an excellent example of incorporating domain knowledge into the model.

Determining a good set of inputs remains one of the hard problems in financial modeling. The number of potentially useful technical indicators is in the hundreds, and the number of subsets grows exponential with the number of individual indicators. A reasonable set of variables inspired by trading and economic ideas has to suffice. LeBaron chooses six inputs derived from the two time series.

1.3 Model Class / Architecture

The model class considered consists of simple feed-forward networks with one layer of up to eight hidden tanh units, and one tanh output unit.

1.4 Cost Function / In-sample Objective

The networks are trained to optimize in-sample profit.

1.5 Model Selection / Optimization

The networks are selected using bootstrap and cross-validation techniques.

1.6 Evaluation (Out-of-sample)

The evaluation is very transparent: build a model on 1000 days, evaluate it on the subsequent 500 days. This setup is subsequently rolled forward by 500 days, resulting in 50% overlap in the training set between adjacent runs, but no overlap in the test set.

While trained on profit maximization, the resulting trading models are evaluated on a number of statistics that include the Sharpe ratio and the probability of predicting the direction of the price change correctly.

1.7 Analysis / Interpretation

One of the issues raised in the discussion of the paper in London was how long inefficiencies in the market persist. This question can be addressed by evaluating a model not only on the 500 days immediately following its the training set, but also on test sets that are further away from the training set. Table 5, included in the printed version of LeBaron's paper, shows that in nine of the ten comparisons that can be made for fixed test periods, the profit of a strategy deteriorates monotonically as the time between training set and test set increases. This probability of obtaining this result by chance is about 1%. This indicates that trading models in this market deteriorate significantly over two years.

LeBaron's conclusion section is clear, full of good ideas, and needs no further debate. I will use the remainder of this discussion to give a couple of suggestions for further analysis, and will close with some remarks on the implicit desire for sparse networks and the relation to the problem of local minima.

2   Suggestions for further analysis

It is well known[1] that the weights of networks that are trained on profit maximization tend to grow quite large, saturating the tanh output. The following simple post-training experiment might be interesting. Let, as in LeBaron's Eq. (13), $o(t)$ denote the network-input into the output tanh unit, i.e., the sum of the hidden unit activations multiplied with the weights between the hidden units and the output. Define an additional parameter, a, that determines the slope of the tanh output. The position size at day t, $s(t)$, is then given by

$$s(t) = tanh\,(\,a\,o(t)\,)\,.$$

LeBaron uses $a=1$ in the training phase, and lets a go to infinity in the evaluation phase. A suggestion would be to analyze several performance measures as function of a. In my experience, such performance-vs.-a curves are rarely monotonically increasing—which would indicate that the binary strategy is indeed the best—but usually show an inverse U-shaped curve. This is often true for the symmetric Sharpe ratio, as well as for asymmetric risk measures such as lower partial moments. Choosing, after training, a value of a that corresponds to the maximum performance can have particularly large effects when the transaction costs are large.

The second suggestion is to analyze how the network uses the inputs: Are some of them always chosen? Are there others that never survive? The seven steps of modeling mentioned in the first section only describe one pass through the data. The beauty of modern modeling approaches is that they generate new insights and hypotheses. This is at the very heart of the iterative nature of modeling. For example, the two suggestions may result in a problem modification that allows for non-binary position sizes, or may guide an exploration of different input variables.

---

[1] The fact that a profit objective leads to binary position sizes was to my knowledge first pointed out by Alan Yamamura (1993, private communication). It can be related back to the concept of *overconfidence* used by David Rumelhart and Bo Curry (1989, private communication), and is also discussed in Choey and Weigend (1997; see the reference section of LeBaron's paper).

3   Smaller networks give worse local minima

LeBaron combines state-of-the-art search techniques with evaluation techniques. It is interesting that the resulting networks are very sparse and extremely robust against overfitting. Note that the out-of-sample profit average over the five periods is within 4% of the corresponding in-sample profit average (computed from LeBaron's Table 4).

But, is it possible that this impressive tracking of out-of-sample and in-sample performance is achieved at the expense of otherwise possibly better out-of-sample performance? Weigend (1994) reported a set of experiments that tried to shed some light on the relation between ease-of-search and network size. On a classification task, networks with 0 to 15 hidden units were trained, and the out-of-sample performance was monitored as a function of training time. It was not surprising that larger networks had better in-sample performance. What was surprising was that their best out-of-sample performance (defined as the best performance on the test set, before overfitting) was also better.

This was interpreted as the gradient search becoming easier with increased dimensionality: high-dimensional hidden unit spaces offer more directions out of a local minimum than low-dimensional hidden unit spaces. A parallel might be drawn to solid state physics where the number of essentially equally good (local) (energy-) minima increases with the number of interacting elements. The fact that LeBaron reports a factor of 1.5 between good solutions (in Footnote 11) might also indicate that the search in such sparse networks is just plain hard.

I would like to thank Blake LeBaron for kindly sharing his insights.

4   Reference

Weigend, A. S. "On Overfitting and the Effective Number of Hidden Units." In *Proceedings of the 1993 Connectionist Models Summer School*, Mozer, M. C., P. Smolensky, D. S. Touretzky, J. L. Elman, and A. S. Weigend, eds., pp. 335-342. Hillsdale, NJ: Erlbaum. 1994.

MULTI-TASK LEARNING
IN A NEURAL VECTOR ERROR CORRECTION APPROACH
FOR EXCHANGE RATE FORECASTING

F. A. RAUSCHER

Daimler-Benz AG
Research and Technology – FT3/KL
P.O. Box 2360, 89013 Ulm, Germany
E-mail: folke.rauscher@dbag.ulm.daimlerbenz.com

Recent studies on exchange rate forecasting showed that the cointegration concept for economic time series analysis proved to be fruitful. The Johansen procedure in particular, with its evolving multiple-equation Vector Error Correction models, is able to capture more complex, higher-order cointegrated relationships between financial market time series than single-equation, semi-reduced models following the Engle/Granger approach. Following promising results achieved by the application of Neural Networks to predict financial data, this study additionally uses Neural Networks for modeling any non-linearities within the estimated cointegration systems. To make full use of the interdependencies among economic time series and to pay attention to the increased integration of international financial markets, this paper presents research on Multi-Task Learning. The idea is that by learning different, yet related, tasks simultaneously, underlying interdependencies between the various learning outputs can be exploited. The paper presents a neural Vector Error Correction approach with multiple output units as a Multi-Task Learning methodology of practical use in finance. By focusing on forecasting the DEM/USD-exchange rate, the performance is compared and evaluated out-of-sample.

1   Introduction

Investigations into the increased integration of international financial markets clearly state that forecasting models focusing only on one isolated market segment independently, suffer certain drawbacks.[1] Because there exist a lot of interdependencies between various markets and their prices, this information about the mode of interaction should not be wasted for economic modeling. Therefore, this paper presents a Multi-Task Learning methodology in a neural Vector Error Correction (VEC) approach for exchange rate forecasting.

Starting off with the cointegration framework in general, the multivariate maximum likelihood approach for cointegration modeling by Johansen[2] is identified as being best applicable to the financial market situation. Section 3 gives the motivation in this econometric modeling context for non-linear models like neural networks. Then the fact of financial market integration is addressed and in

---

[1] e.g., Rehkugler et al. (1996), Bartlmae (1997)
[2] Johansen (1988)

A.-P.N. Refenes et al. (eds.), Decision Technologies for Computational Finance, 165–179.
© 1998 *Kluwer Academic Publishers. Printed in the Netherlands..*

Section 5 the concept of Multi-Task Learning is presented. The main part of the paper consists of an empirical in-depth analysis to compare linear single-task, neural single-task and neural multi-task approaches within a cointegration framework for predicting the DEM/USD-exchange rate one month in advance. Finally a summary is presented and concluding remarks are provided.

2 Cointegration[3]

Looking at international financial markets, most time series follow a random walk. Those time series can be described as possessing the following statistical characteristics:

- an alternating mean μ depending on time

- a variance σ which is not necessarily limited

- the expected period of time by which the process returns to a previous value is infinite

Time series with the features mentioned above are called non-stationary. Usually economic variables become stationary when differences are taken once. Thus, the variables are integrated of order one, $I(1)$, i.e., each variable has a unit root or stochastic trend or random walk element. The employment of non-stationary variables or the modeling of time series with different orders of integration gives rise to several econometric problems.[4] To use only stationary data for regression techniques, the standard procedure is to take the first differences for time series analysis. However, the information embodied in the level of the variables is lost. The concept of cointegration helps to overcome this conflict.

In the economic context considered here, a group of first-order integrated time series is cointegrated if there is a combination of them that is stationary, i.e., the combination does not have a stochastic trend. The basic statement is that if, in the long run, two or more non-stationary time series move jointly or closely together, and therefore the difference between them is constant and stationary, the variables within that data set are called cointegrated.

For example, consumption and income are likely to be cointegrated. If they were not, consumption might drift well above income which ultimately would be unfeasible, or consumption might fall so far below income that consumers would be irrationally piling up savings.

The following subsections will describe briefly the two most commonly known frameworks within which one can test hypotheses about cointegration.

---

[3] For this cointegration exposition also see Rauscher (1997).

[4] Muscatelli and Hurn (1992), Granger and Newbold (1979)

2.1   Engle/Granger procedure

The concept of cointegration following Engle and Granger (1987) is a two-step methodology.[5]

In the first step of this regression-based approach a model is estimated to describe the long-term relationship. This first cointegration model is determined by fundamental economic variables according to, e.g., a monetary exchange rate model. As an equilibrium model it postulates that the underlying set of first-order integrated variables move together in the long run. The residuals of this cointegration regression should be stationary if the regressand and the regressors are cointegrated. The assumed unique cointegration vector or the corresponding residual are also called error correction term because it describes the actual deviation of the endogenous variable from its theoretical equilibrium.

If such a set of cointegrated time series exists, the Granger representation theorem[6] states that there is a valid error correction representation. Thus, the second step of the methodology takes up the stationary error correction term with reversed sign as well as the other stationary variables, for this reason being in first differences, according to economic theory. The final error correction model describes the dynamic short-term process and is used for calculating forecasts.

2.2   Johansen procedure

The second concept of cointegration considered in this paper was established by Johansen (1988). It is a multivariate framework based on a maximum likelihood approach and allows one to estimate several cointegration vectors simultaneously in contrast to prior limitations of the cointegration vector space. The following approach will give a brief discussion of the Johansen procedure.[7]

The data generating process of a p-dimensional vector X can be presented as a vector autoregressive (VAR) system taking levels of the variables which may look as follows:

$$X_t = \mu + \Pi_1 X_{t-1} + \ldots + \Pi_k X_{t-k} + \varepsilon_t \qquad t = 1,2,\ldots \qquad (1)$$

where ε_t are Gaussian errors, μ is a vector of constants and all p elements of X are $I(1)$ variables.

To obtain an error correction representation of the above VAR model, equation (1) can be re-arranged:[8]

---

[5] For an exchange rate application see Steurer (1997).

[6] Engle and Granger (1987)

[7] For more complete expositions see Johansen (1988, 1991) as well as Johansen and Juselius (1990).

[8] Gardeazabal and Regúlez (1992), p. 44

$$\Delta X_t = \mu + \Pi_1 X_{t-1} + \Gamma_1 \Delta X_{t-1} + ... + \Gamma_{k-1} \Delta X_{t-k+1} + \varepsilon_t \qquad (2)$$

where $\Gamma_i = -\left(\Pi_{i+1} + ... + \Pi_k\right)$ and $\Pi = I - \Pi_1 - ... - \Pi_k$.

The long run impact matrix Π makes up the equilibrium condition for equation (2), looking as follows:

$$\Pi X = 0 \qquad (3)$$

The aim of the procedure is to identify if the matrix Π contains information about long run relationships between the p elements of X. Because every term in equation (2) is stationary, except X_{t-1}, the expression ΠX_{t-1} must be stationary, too. This zero-order integration of ΠX_{t-1} is expressed by the rank r of the matrix Π. For the only case of interest here, i.e., $0 < r < p$, there are r cointegration relationships inherent in the model. The long run impact matrix Π can be re-written as the product of two matrices α and β, each of the form $(p \times r)$, such that:

$$\Pi = \alpha \cdot \beta' \qquad (4)$$

Here the loading matrix α contains the loading factors in its columns. The rows of β' form the r distinct cointegration vectors so that:

$$\beta_i' \cdot X_{t-1} \sim I(0) \qquad (5)$$

where β_i' is the i-th row of the matrix β' .

Now a maximum likelihood approach allows testing for the number of cointegration vectors and estimating the coefficients.[9]

2.3   Financial market implication

The simpler regression-based two-step methodology by Engle and Granger (1987) suffers from a number of deficiencies. One major restriction of this concept is that only one single cointegration vector is assumed, which is not necessarily correct. However, using ordinary least squares to estimate a cointegration relationship for a p-dimensional vector does not clarify whether one is dealing with a unique cointegration vector or simply with a linear combination of the *(p-1)* possible distinct cointegration vectors that may exist within the time series system. Another drawback stems from the fact that there is a separate estimation of the long run equilibrium and the short run dynamic of the cointegrated variables.

---

[9] For details see Johansen (1988, 1991), Johansen and Juselius (1990) and Cuthbertson et al. (1992).

The multivariate cointegration technique proposed by Johansen (1988) avoids some of the disadvantages mentioned above. Within a dynamic vector auto-regressive model both the short run and the long run relationships are estimated simultaneously. Furthermore, the Johansen procedure is superior because it fully captures the underlying time series properties of the data, provides estimates of all cointegration vectors that exist within a vector of variables, and offers a test statistic for the number of cointegrating vectors. Again, this contrasts with the regression-based methodology. However, a possible disadvantage of the Johansen procedure is the higher number of parameters required.

Looking at financial markets and exchange rates in particular, it becomes clear that applied cointegration techniques must move away from single-equation, semi-reduced models towards more complex, higher-order integrated, multivariate models to make full use of all interdependencies among financial market variables and to capture the complex phenomena underlying the determination of exchange rates.[10] Therefore, accounting for the dynamic interrelationship of all variables,[11] the multivariate cointegration concept of Johansen is the right means to combine time series analysis, econometric theory and financial market properties for successful exchange rate forecasting.

3　Non-linearity

Besides cointegration, one of the most popular applications for predicting financial data are neural networks.[12] Though promising results have been achieved with both approaches, the performance of neural networks is hardly ever related to conventional econometric methodologies, such as Vector Error Correction models. The question which arises is, can non-linear methods such as neural networks help in modeling any non-linearities inherent within the estimated cointegration system.

For the "chaotic" financial markets a purely linear approach for modeling cointegration relationships does not reflect the reality. In particular, the foreign exchange market and its time series can be characterized as follows:

- no obvious distinction between endogenous and exogenous variables
- a high number of potential influential factors on, e.g., exchange rates
- a distortion of underlying causalities by external random effects
- no rationally motivated operating
- a very complex mode of action

---

[10] Gandolfo et al. (1990), p. 966

[11] Kugler and Lenz (1993), p. 181

[12] Refenes (1995), Rehkugler and Zimmermann (1994), Weigend et al. (1991)

• non-linear dependencies and relationships

For example, if interest rates do not react to a small change in inflation in the first instance, but after crossing a certain interval or threshold react all the more, a non-linear relationship between interest rates and inflation exists.

This study, therefore, as a first objective tries to improve the purely linear combination of cointegrated time series within the comprehensive Johansen procedure by using neural networks for modeling.

4   Financial market integration

Because on international financial markets the mode of action mentioned above is very much about multi-lateral interdependencies in both causal directions and between all market determinants simultaneously, economic modeling approaches must pay attention to this increased market integration. Due to trade liberalization, advanced information technologies and high capital mobility, international financial markets grow together and a rising level of integration is observable.[13] So all single markets, as well as their driving forces, influence each other and are influenced by each other. This happens at the same time and in altering directions.

The actual degree of market integration can be tested upon the existence and validity of parity relations. In this context parity relations are theoretical approaches[14] – starting from an arbitrary point of view – to describe the relationships between, e.g., inflation, interest rates and exchange rates. Examinations of cointegration relations as described in Section 2 show that there are statistically supported multi-layer interrelations between different international markets as well as interdependencies between the various financial prices.

Therefore, forecasting procedures which focus only on one isolated financial market or one single magnitude independently, waste the auxiliary information inherent in the observed financial market integration.

5   Multi-Task Learning

An estimation methodology which solves different but related tasks simultaneously can use these interdependent tasks to better identify the causality or determinants which all tasks have in common. By incorporating prior knowledge in the form of auxiliary information about integrated markets, domain-specific hints provide the estimation model with an inductive bias which leads towards better

---

[13] Poddig and Rehkugler (1996)

[14] Well known models include the Purchasing Power Parity, Monetary Models and the International Fisher Relation.

representations of the domain's underlying regularities. Using this information about interdependencies and related tasks helps to improve the generalization performance on unseen or future data.

The Multi-Task Learning[15] approach presented in this paper is an inductive transfer method which incorporates prior knowledge about integrated financial markets in the form of related tasks. These tasks are presented to the learning system in a shared representation and manifested by hints[16] to guide the learning process towards better solutions of the main problem.

5.1 *Neural Network representation*

The application of Multi-Task Learning to neural networks has a straight forward realization.[17] In the case, e.g., of a three layer feedforward backpropagation neural network (Fig. 1)[18], the simplest way for incorporating prior knowledge in the form of hints into the inductive learning system is to add extra outputs. Each additional output unit, fully connected to the hidden layer, represents an extra task related to the primary one.

---

[15] First introduced as "a knowledge-based source of inductive bias" to the machine learning community by Caruana (1993).

[16] Abu-Mostafa (1990, 1994, 1995)

[17] For the implementation of Multi-Task Learning in different learning algorithms see Caruana (1997).

[18] Bartlmae et al. (1997)

172

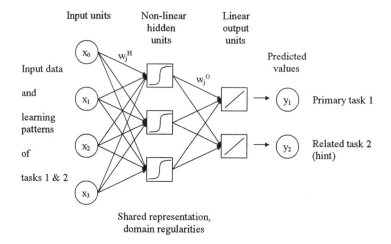

Fig. 1: Multi-Task Learning neural network with two related tasks.

The basic idea is that these extra tasks are used as hints or a knowledge-based source of inductive bias. As a result, the shared hidden layer is moved towards representations that better reflect regularities of the domain as a whole. As a consequence, these extra tasks support learning the main task better[19] and the training signals of related tasks are used as an inductive bias or hints to improve generalization.[20] Multi-Task Learning adds additional tasks only to improve and stabilize the performance of the main task. The outputs of the related tasks are ignored when making predictions. Thus, the major goal is not to find a good model for all tasks, but to find an improved neural network for the primary task.

5.2   Theoretical implementation and economic application

Coming back to the theoretical implementation,[21] the idea underlying neural Multi-Task Learning is that the related tasks in the form of additional output units influence the hidden layer through their additional gradient information. This is leading to an improved shared representation of the domain's underlying regularities. Because the gradient of a hidden-layer weight w_j^H is just a weighted

[19] Caruana (1996), p. 87

[20] Abu-Mostafa (1990, 1995), Caruana (1995)

[21] See Caruana (1995) for details, who identified five mechanisms by which multi-task backpropagation improves generalization.

sum of the gradient information of each single task, it points to a direction which decreases the error over all tasks simultaneously. After the learning procedure the network weights represent a better overall relationship between the input variables and all output variables. So Multi-Task Learning results in the property of a shared domain's regularity and an improved generalization performance, if correct additional hints are chosen and introduced to the neural network as additional output units.

Supportive hints can be derived from theoretically supported dependencies or extra tasks can correspond to important learnable features of the main task. Because the usefulness of additional tasks depends on their information value, it is crucial for the Multi-Task Learning methodology to identify relevant ones.[22] Following the earlier discussion of financial market integration and its verification upon the existence of statistically significant cointegration relations, the auxiliary information in the form of related tasks are taken from the set of cointegrated time series according to the Vector Error Correction representation to improve the main task: forecasting the future DEM/USD-exchange rate.

6   Empirical investigation

Following the aspects mentioned so far, the idea is to combine the multivariate cointegration framework, a neural network modeling methodology, and Multi-Task Learning aspects to better forecast financial market time series. In this context the final objective of the paper is to carry out an in-depth empirical investigation to evaluate linear single-task, neural single-task and neural multi-task forecasting approaches within a cointegration framework. The following paragraphs will describe the methodology of the empirical investigation.

6.1   Data and model

To carry out the empirical study, monthly data ranging from January 1980 to October 1997 was taken. For calculating the forecasts, data from 1980 through to 1992 was taken to estimate or train the various models and neural networks. The out-of-sample period covered January 1993 until October 1997. For the latter period, DEM/USD-exchange rate forecasts were made one month ahead. Performance results presented below focus on this magnitude for evaluation purposes.

---

[22] Multi-Task Learning does not always improve the performance and some inductive biases might hurt (Caruana (1997), p. 71).

The time series focused on for estimating the exchange rate determination followed a flexible price monetary model,[23] which can be written as follows:

$$s = \left(m - m^*\right) - \alpha \cdot \left(y - y^*\right) + \beta \cdot \left(i - i^*\right) \tag{6}$$

where lower case letters indicate natural logarithms and asterisks denote the corresponding foreign variables, here this means US-magnitudes. The variables in detail are:

s spot exchange rate measured in domestic currency units per one unit foreign currency, DEM/USD

m money supply, aggregate M 3

y industrial production index

i short-term interest rate, 3-month LIBOR

Various studies[24] have shown that the above mentioned determinants can be sustained by econometric research in order to analyze exchange rates. In the following this model will be used to form the basis for the empirical investigation.

6.2   Vector Error Correction system

To estimate a Vector Error Correction (VEC) model, one first has to test for non-stationarity and cointegration of the time series focused on, as well as to determine the number of cointegration vectors. The augmented Dickey-Fuller test[25] as well as the Phillips-Perron test[26] indicate that the time series focused on are first-order integrated when levels are taken, but are stationary when first differences are considered. Testing for the cointegration rank, both likelihood-ratio-tests[27] indicated the presence of three statistically significant cointegration vectors among the series.[28]

After having confirmed that the variables are cointegrated and determined the number of cointegrating equations, it is possible to estimate a VEC model.

A VEC model is a specialized vector autoregressive system applied to the first difference of the data, in which every equation has the same right hand variables. The estimation of the VEC model proceeds by regressing the first

---

[23] According to the theoretical framework delivered by Frenkel (1976) / Bilson (1987) and as investigated in MacDonald and Taylor (1993).

[24] e.g., Kim and Mo (1995), Gerhards (1994)

[25] Said and Dickey (1984)

[26] Phillips (1987)

[27] See Johansen (1988) for details.

[28] The λ_{max}-test as well as the Trace-test were calculated using the CATS procedure in the RATS software (Hansen and Juselius (1995)).

difference of each endogenous variable on a one period lag of the estimated cointegration vectors involving levels of the series and lagged first differences of all of the endogenous variables in the system. To estimate the system, in our example a lag length of two proved to satisfy the normal specification for the residuals. Furthermore, economic interpretation as well as statistical criteria guided to assume the series to have means and linear trends, but the cointegrating equations to have only intercepts. To keep the number of parameters low and in line with the amount of data in the estimation period, no other exogenous variables were included in the VEC model.

Because initially the aim was to calculate a system purely according to the economic theory mentioned earlier, no insignificant parameters, e.g., showing small t-statistics, were taken out.

As a result, the estimated VEC model had seventeen input time series and an output vector containing the seven time series mentioned. According to the form of equation (2) the final VEC system looks as follows:

$$\Delta \begin{pmatrix} s \\ m \\ m* \\ y \\ y* \\ i \\ i* \end{pmatrix}_t = \mu + \Gamma_1 \Delta \begin{pmatrix} s \\ m \\ m* \\ y \\ y* \\ i \\ i* \end{pmatrix}_{t-1} + \Gamma_2 \Delta \begin{pmatrix} s \\ m \\ m* \\ y \\ y* \\ i \\ i* \end{pmatrix}_{t-2} + \alpha\beta' \begin{pmatrix} s \\ m \\ m* \\ y \\ y* \\ i \\ i* \end{pmatrix}_{t-1} \tag{7}$$

where α is the loading matrix and β' consists of three rows, each making up one of the three cointegration vectors determined earlier.

6.3   Linear approach versus neural single-task learning

To compare linear single-task, neural single-task and neural multi-task forecasting approaches, the focus is solely on predicting the main task. Therefore, to carry out the first comparison between a linear approach versus neural single-task learning, the linear Vector Error Correction (VEC) model following the Johansen cointegration procedure mentioned earlier versus its neural counterpart is evaluated. Focusing on the line of the matrix system (Equation 7) where Δs stands on the left hand side, the application of single-task learning (STL) is represented by a neural network with the predictor for the future exchange rate being the only output unit.

The following table (Tab. 1) shows the results:[29]

---

[29] To evaluate the different forecasting results in the out-of-sample period ranging from January 1993 to October 1997, five performance measures are reported here: hit rate (HR), coefficient of inequality of Theil (TU), realized potential (Pot.), annualized return (Ret.) and Sharpe ratio (SR). The naive prediction states that the exchange rate change at times t is the best predictor of the change at time-step $t+1$.

	HR	TU	Pot.	Ret.	SR
Perfect forecast	1	0	1	0.27	15.43
Naive prediction	0.57	1	0.29	0.08	2.19
Lin. VEC mod.	0.59	1.35	0.29	0.09	2.54
Neural STL appr.	0.60	1.08	0.35	0.11	2.96

Tab. 1: Linear approach versus neural single-task learning.

Up to here the calculated results strongly suggest that there is an empirical validity of cointegration in modeling economic and financial variables. Furthermore, the assumption of non-linearities within the set of cointegrated time series considered in this study can be empirically sustained by applying neural networks.

6.4   Neural single-task versus neural Multi-Task Learning

So far, the forecasting procedure applied was limited to the focus on the future change of the DEM/USD-exchange rate being the exclusive output unit. However, as outlined in the paper, adding related tasks represented to the neural network by further output units for simultaneous learning in a Multi-Task Learning approach should prove beneficial.

To evaluate a neural single-task approach versus neural Multi-Task Learning (MTL), all other variables contained in the output vector of the initial error correction representation (Equation 7) are represented as further related tasks. These auxiliary hints are incorporated into the neural learning system in the form of additional output units.

The results from empirical investigations carried out are reported in the table overleaf (Tab. 2).

	HR	TU	Pot.	Ret.	SR
Neural STL appr.	0.60	1.08	0.35	0.11	2.96
Neural MTL appr.	0.60	0.98	0.41	0.12	3.21

Tab. 2: Neural single-task versus neural Multi-Task Learning.

The performance evaluation of the presented forecasting methodology indicates that paying attention to interdependencies between related tasks in a Multi-Task Learning approach, following the prior cointegration analysis, can prove fruitful for forecasting the magnitude focused on.

7 Conclusion

The empirical investigations conducted here and their results show that, within the domain of forecasting financial market time series, there exists a high number of interdependencies due to increased market integration which are ignored whilst applying only partial prediction models. However, these relationships, which exist between related tasks, can help to better model the task focused on. In the context of integrated financial markets, Multi-Task Learning is presented as a mechanism that improves generalization by using the domain-specific information contained in the learning patterns of related tasks as an inductive bias. In our approach the information inherent in interrelations between cointegrated financial time series is not neglected, but used to improve the forecasting quality.

Further research should consider a quantification of the information value of hints to identify supportive tasks. In addition, a weighting procedure of multiple tasks in respect to the error function as well as the specific model selection of Multi-Task Learning neural networks are still to be investigated.

8 Acknowledgements

In writing this paper, I benefited greatly from the research of my colleague Kai Bartlmae. Furthermore, the guidance of Dr. Steurer and the support of our research group led by Prof. Nakhaeizadeh are acknowledged. I also want to thank Dr. Fahling and the Daimler-Benz treasury department for providing valuable assistance.

9 References

Abu-Mostafa, Y. S. (1990): Learning from Hints in Neural Networks. Journal of Complexity, 6(2):192–198.
Abu-Mostafa, Y. S. (1994): Learning from Hints. Journal of Complexity, 10(1):165–178.
Abu-Mostafa, Y. S. (1995): Hints. Neural Computation, 7:639–671.
Bartlmae, K. (1997): Multi-Task Lernen bei neuronalen Netzen zur Aktienkurs- prognose. Master Thesis, University of Karlsruhe, Institute of Logic, Complexity and Deduction Systems, Karlsruhe, Germany.

Bartlmae, K., Gutjahr, S., Nakhaeizadeh, G. (1997): Incorporating prior knowledge about financial markets through neural multitask learning. Poster Presentation, Fifth International Conference on Computational Finance, London Business School, London, England.

Bilson, J. F. O. (1987): The monetary approach to the exchange rate - some empirical evidence. IMF Staff Papers, 25:48–75.

Caruana, R. (1993): Multitask Learning: A Knowledge-Based Source of Inductive Bias. Proceedings of the 10th International Conference on Machine Learning, Amherst, USA, 41–48.

Caruana, R. (1995): Learning Many Related Tasks at the Same Time With Backpropagation. Advances in Neural Information Processing Systems, 7:657–664.

Caruana, R. (1996): Algorithms and Applications for Multitask Learning. Proceedings of the 13th International Conference on Machine Learning, Bari, Italy, 87–95.

Caruana, R. (1997): Multitask Learning. Machine Learning, 28:41–75.

Cuthbertson, K., Hall, S., Taylor, M. P. (1992): Applied econometric techniques. Phillip Allan, London, England.

Engle, R., Granger, C. W. J. (1987): Co-integration and error-correction: representation, estimation and testing. Econometrica, 49:251–276.

Frenkel, J. A. (1976): A monetary approach to the exchange rate: doctrinal aspects and empirical evidence. Scandinavian Journal of Economics, 78:200–224.

Gandolfo, G., Padoan, P. C., Paladino, G. (1990): Exchange rate determination: single-equation or economy-wide models?. Journal of Banking and Finance, 14:965–992.

Gardeazabal, J., Regúlez, M. (1992): The monetary model of exchange rate - estimation, testing and prediction. Springer, Berlin, Germany.

Gerhards, T. (1994): Theorie und Empirie flexibler Wechselkurse. Physica, Heidelberg, Germany.

Granger, C. W. J., Newbold, P. (1979): Spurious regression in econometrics. Journal of Economics, 2:111–120.

Hansen, H., Juselius, K. (1995): CATS in RATS - cointegration analysis of time series. Software Manual, Estima, Evanston, USA.

Johansen, S. (1988): Statistical analysis of cointegration vectors. Journal of Economic Dynamics and Control, 12:231–254.

Johansen, S. (1991): Estimation and hypothesis testing of cointegration vectors in gaussian vector autoregressive models. Econometrica, 59:1551–1580.

Johansen, S., Juselius, K. (1990): Maximum likelihood estimation and inference on cointegration - with applications to the demand for money. Oxford Bulletin of Economics and Statistics, 52:169–210.

Kim, B. J. C., Mo, S. (1995): Cointegration and long-run forecast of exchange rates. Economic Letters, 48:353–359.

Kugler, P., Lenz, C. (1993): Multivariate cointegration analysis and the long-run validity of PPP. The Review of Economics and Statistics, 75:180–184.

MacDonald, R., Taylor, M. P. (1993): The monetary approach to the exchange rate - rational expectations, long-run equilibrium and forecasting. IMF Staff Papers, 40:89–107.

Muscatelli, A., Hurn, S. (1992): Cointegration and dynamic time series models. Journal of Economic Surveys, 6:1–43.

Phillips, P. C. B. (1987): Time series regression with a unit root. Econometrica, 55:277–301.

Poddig, T., Rehkugler, H. (1996): A "World" Model of Integrated Financial Markets using Artificial Neural Networks. Neurocomputing, 10:251–273.

Rauscher, F. A. (1997): Exchange Rate Forecasting: a Neural VEC Approach. Neural Network World Journal, 4/5:461–471.

Refenes, A.-P. N. (1995): Neural Networks in Capital Markets. Wiley, Chichester, England.

Rehkugler, H., Poddig, T., Jandura, D. (1996): Einsatz integrierter Modelle für die simultane Prognose von Aktienkursen, Zinsen und Währungen für mehrere Länder mit Neuronalen Netzen, in: Bol, G. et al. (Eds.): Finanzmarktanalyse und -prognose mit innovativen quantitativen Verfahren. Physica, Heidelberg, Germany, 207–236.

Rehkugler, H., Zimmermann, H. G. (1994): Neuronale Netze in der Ökonomie. Vahlen, Munich, Germany.

Said, S. E., Dickey, D. A. (1984): Testing for unit roots in autoregressive moving average models of unknown order. Biometrica, 59:599–607.

Steurer, E. (1997): Ökonometrische Methoden und maschinelle Lernverfahren zur Wechselkursprognose - theoretische Analyse und empirischer Vergleich. Physica, Heidelberg, Germany.

Weigend, A. S., Huberman, B. A., Rumelhart, D. E. (1991): Predicting Sunspots and Exchange Rates with Connectionist Networks, in: Casdagli, M., Eubank, S.: Nonlinear Modeling and Forecasting. Addison-Wesley, Reading, USA, 395–432.

SELECTING RELATIVE - VALUE STOCKS WITH NON LINEAR COINTEGRATION

Christos Kollias
Hughes Financial Analytics
e-mail: hfa@clara.net

Kostas Metaxas
University of Athens
e-mail: konstantinos.n.metaxas@usa.net

Abstract

The cointegration between individual stocks and the index is conditional on a number of variables to account for company-specific fundamentals and non-linear dynamics. This paper describes a methodology for selecting relative value stocks using the principle of non linear cointegration. The forecast of the cointegration residuals is being made using neural networks in order to capture any short-run dynamics in the estimation process. The trading rules that were applied indicate that consistent profits can be realised.

However, the magnitude of the profits that most stocks have generated was relatively small. A closer look in the results justified that the performance was heavily penalised due to the effect of trading costs. The reason appears to be that too many buy/sell signals were suggested by the model which conceal the real performance of the cointegration model. The above may be attributed to the fact that market imperfections such as trading costs are not incorporated within the cointegration relationship and the forecasting model. We are introducing some preliminary ideas on the problem of incorporating market imperfections in the modeling process and the need for tests and measures (such as cyclicity tests) that may accomplish that.

I. Introduction

Cointegration is an economic and financial phenomenon which has been attracting increasing attention amongst both academics and practitioners

A.-P.N. Refenes et al. (eds.), Decision Technologies for Computational Finance, 181–191.
© 1998 *Kluwer Academic Publishers. Printed in the Netherlands..*

over recent years. The basic idea behind cointegration is that there are markets and/or economic variables which in the long run share a common stochastic trend but from which there may be temporary divergences. The short term deviations from the long run equilibrium relationship between financial assets can be exploited by investors. In section II of this paper a statistical arbitrage strategy is developed using a non-linear methodology to exploit the arbitrage opportunities in the Athens Stock Exchange. Section III discuss the empirical findings and introduces some ideas of incorporating trading costs in the modeling process.

II. Cointegration and Relative Value – Methodology and Results

A statistical arbitrage opportunity occurs when a price discrepancy exists between two or more highly related assets. The opportunity can be exploited by buying the underpriced asset and selling the overpriced one. Many different arbitrage relations have been identified in financial assets. For example triangular, geographic and derivative arbitrage in the foreign exchange markets; index, geographic and derivative arbitrage in the equity markets, represent common cases of riskless arbitrage. Statistical arbitrage or relative value trading occurs when short-run deviations appear from established long-run relationships.

The residuals of an estimated long run cointegrating relationship represent the short term deviations from the long run equilibrium. In order to identify the presence or not of a long run cointegrating relationship the following regression is estimated:

$$Y_t = a + bX_t + u_t \qquad (1)$$

It has been shown that if two variables Xt and Yt are integrated of the same order, I(1), then any linear combination of these series $u_t = Y_t - bX_t$ may be I(0). It follows that $\mathbf{u_t}$ in equation (1) is the equilibrium error that measures the short term deviations from equilibrium and may itself be stationary (Granger 1986; Engle and

Granger 1987). If this is the case, then the disequilibrium errors will tend to move towards their mean value, thus correcting the disequilibria that have appeared. The assumption that the residuals from a cointegrating regression are inclined to move towards their mean, implies that the time series involved do not permanently drift away from their equilibrium relationship. If this happens then the residuals will no longer tend to move towards their mean. In a sense the residuals u_t can be regarded as temporary mispricings between two or more assets. Such mispricings may be exploited by investors.

Burgess and Refenes (1995) introduced the concept of conditional cointegration. In this particular application we examined the presence or not of cointegration between a representative set of stocks (25) and the general index in the ASE.

The stocks were selected on the basis of their market capitalization. The selected stocks are also representative of the various industrial sectors traded in the ASE. The sample size covers the period of 3/1/94 to 2/4/96 that allows a maximum of 576 observations.

Graph 1 : Cointegrating residuals.

184

Cointegrating Residuals - Stock: Ethniki

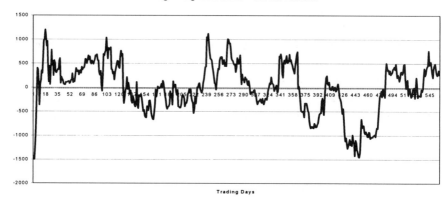

Graph 2: Cointegrating residuals

Equation (1) was estimated for each of the selected stocks using a rolling window regression of 120 days. The obtained residuals were tested for their stationarity using the standard DF and ADF tests. Of the 25 estimated cointegrating regressions only the residuals of 19 regressions passed the relevant tests. Graphs 1 and 2 are representative of the mean reversion tendency of the obtained cointegrating residuals.

A crude exploitation strategy of the cointegrating residuals mean reversion tendency is the following:

if the residuals are higher than their mean, the asset relatively to the general index is overpriced and therefore its price is expected to fall. In such a case investors will sell the asset. The reverse is the case if the residuals are below their mean value. The asset relatively to the general index is underpriced and therefore its price will tend to go up. In this case investors will buy the asset.

Having estimated the residuals from the cointegrating regressions, the issue at hand is to develop a forecasting method for the residuals that accounts for company specific reasons and dynamics. To account for the possibility of I) a time varying relationship between the cointegration residuals and market factors and II) possible nonlinearities accruing from the interaction between these factors, we use neural networks.

Equation 2, describes the forecasting model for the cointegration residuals. The model attempts to capture the behavior of the cointegration residuals due to company specific factors and short-term dynamics. PE and Gearing ratios can represent company specific factors, and oscillators such as RSI, MFI and MACD can be used in order to model short-term dynamics.

$$\frac{1}{5}\sum_{i=t}^{t+4} u_t = \phi(u_{t-n}, RSI(u_t), \frac{1}{m}\sum_{n=t}^{t-m-1} n, vS, vI, PE_t, PE_{t-n}, G_t, G_{t-n},$$

$$RSI(S)_t, RSI(I)_t, MFI(S)_t, MACD(S)_t, MACD(I)_t)$$

(2)

where:

$\frac{1}{5}\sum_{i=t}^{t+4} u_i$ is the depended variable

vS, vI volume Stock, Index

PE price to earning ratio

G gearing ratio

RSI Relative strength index

MFI Money Flow Index

The residuals were then expressed as a function of several factors as it can be seen in (2). A moving window modeling approach was used with 100 training observations, 20 cross validation and further 20 for out-of-sample testing. The window was then shifter forward 20 observations and the process repeated until the end of data set.

The network was trained to forecast the average value of u_t for the next five time periods as seen in (2).

186

Graphs 3 and 4 are representative of network performance in terms of actual and fitted values.

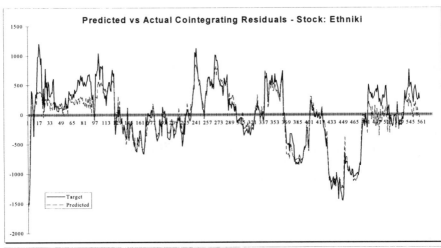

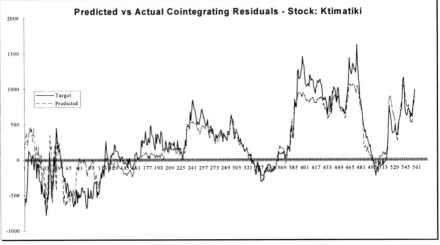

Graphs 3 and 4: Predicted Vs Actual.

Based on the predictions by the networks the following trading strategy was implemented:

Trading Strategy
If $\hat{u}_i > u_i + \delta$ then buy stock and sell index
Else if $\hat{u}_i < u_i - \delta$ then sell stock and buy index
Else Stay neutral

Where $\hat{u}_i$: prediction of the neural net

δ : constant

In order to exploit the neural networks predictions, we construct portfolios of the underlying assets and the general index. Since we assume that a trader would take opposite positions (long-short) in the stock and the general index a characteristic of this portfolio is that the sum of portfolio weights is zero. i.e.:

$$P_i = \pm Stock_i \pm Idx_i = 0$$

Graphs 5, 6 and 7 are representative P&L curves while the results of our trading strategy for all the stocks in the sample are shown in Table 2. Overall the average profit obtained for this time period was 12,27%. Of the 19 stocks traded 14 ended with a profit and 5 with a loss.

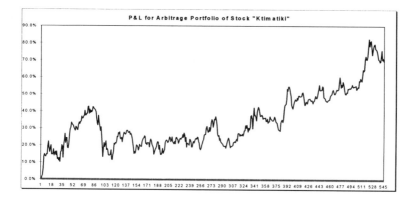

188

Graphs 5,6,7: Representative P&Ls

Table 2: Profits per Stock

| Stock | No of trades | With transaction costs (0.6%) | | | | No transaction costs | | | |
		Profit	Max Profit	Min Profit	St. Dev.	Profit	Max Profit	Min Profit	St. Dev.
Ktimatiki	84	63.33%	7.28%	-6.85%	2.20%	83.39%	7.29%	-7.04%	2.32%
Geniki	120	26.26%	8.73%	-6.16%	1.87%	48.46%	9.41%	-6.56%	2.00%
Hraklis	113	-13.50%	6.98%	-6.23%	1.72%	-2.01%	7.04%	-6.43%	1.80%
Moyzka	119	33.40%	5.74%	-4.78%	1.68%	52.92%	5.86%	-4.78%	1.78%
Mathra	128	50.18%	13.18%	-7.87%	2.11%	84.07%	15.66%	-7.96%	2.29%
Pireos	129	30.75%	5.52%	-5.77%	1.39%	52.23%	6.07%	-5.77%	1.46%
Ergas	407	8.73%	3.96%	-3.25%	1.08%	13.19%	4.04%	-3.35%	1.10%
Iatri-ko	107	7.27%	5.43%	-6.68%	1.60%	19.72%	5.46%	-6.95%	1.68%
Epilek-k	105	18.12%	6.92%	-6.89%	1.74%	34.11%	6.95%	-6.94%	1.82%
Titan-k	78	19.19%	6.61%	-6.48%	1.47%	31.36%	6.73%	-6.49%	1.52%
Ethniki	112	59.86%	12.69%	-6.34%	2.22%	95.24%	14.56%	-7.66%	2.45%
Ioniki	111	36.19%	7.90%	-8.08%	2.10%	61.21%	8.05%	-8.79%	2.23%
Intra-pa	208	10.41%	6.94%	-9.36%	1.89%	40.36%	7.10%	-9.40%	2.03%
Naouk	402	3.38%	4.66%	-3.12%	1.25%	9.58%	4.83%	-3.04%	1.29%
Eboriki	79	-53.74%	4.73%	-6.42%	1.03%	-51.02%	4.90%	-6.43%	1.06%
Petzet-k	161	-7.05%	6.85%	-6.21%	1.41%	7.99%	6.86%	-6.19%	1.51%
Aegek	289	27.76%	5.59%	-4.16%	1.24%	37.31%	6.00%	-4.26%	1.30%
Delta-k	77	-34.59%	4.89%	-4.81%	1.12%	-30.40%	4.93%	-4.82%	1.14%
mhxanikh	87	-52.93%	6.23%	-5.66%	1.28%	-49.51%	6.41%	-5.70%	1.32%
Average	153	12.27%	6.89%	-6.06%	1.60%	28.33%	7.27%	-6.24%	1.69%
St.Dev.	102	33.46%	2.45%	1.56%	0.39%	41.73%	3.04%	1.67%	0.44%

I. Conclusion – further research

The paper developed a statistical arbitrage methodology in the Athens Stock Exchange based on the notion of cointegration. The profits obtained using a non-linear forecasting methodology indicate that arbitrage opportunities exist and that consistent profits can be realised.

However, the magnitude of the profits that most stocks have generated was quite small. The average profit across all stocks was 12,27%, which is certainly not satisfactory for a sample period of two and a half years. A first thought might be that small profits are realised simply because the theoretically suggested cointegrating relationship does not exist and therefore the results are within the bounds of any statistical error. Another explanation may also be that the model **does** capture the relationship but this relationship cannot be forecasted.

A closer look in the results justified to us that the resulting performance was heavily penalised due to the effect of trading costs. When trading costs have been assumed to be zero the P&Ls have been outstandingly better (see Table 2). Therefore, the reason appears to be that too many buy/sell signals were suggested by the model which conceal the real performance of the cointegration model.

The above may be attributed to the fact that market imperfections such as trading costs are not incorporated within the cointegration relationship and the forecasting model. It is a common practice between analysts and researchers not to include market imperfections in the modeling process most probably because there isn't any concise framework to do so. On the other hand, many authors consider the effect of transaction costs on the execution of trades and the fact that transaction costs may influence expected returns (Wilcox 1993, Jarrow & O'Hara 1989, Amihud & Mendelson 1986).

We think that a natural extension to this paper is to investigate how market imperfections such as trading costs can be incorporated in the modeling process and more specifically in the cointegrating relationship and/or the forecasting NN model of the cointegration residuals. The need of tests and measures that account for market imperfections within any analytical framework provided by finance nowadays becomes more and more interesting.

References

Burgess A.N. and Refenes A.P. (1995) "Modelling non-linear cointegration in international equity index futures" in Neural Networks in Financial Engineering A.P. Refenes et al.

Engle, R.F and C.W.J Granger (1987) "Co-integration and error correction: representation, estimation and testing", Econometrica, Vol. 55, pp.251-276.

Granger, C.W.J. (1986) "Developments in the study of cointegrated economic variables", Oxford Bulletin of Economics and Statistics, Vol. 48, pp. 213-228.

Holden, K and J. Thompson (1992) "Cointegration: an introductory survey", British Review of Economic Issues, Vol. 14, No.3

Refenes, A.P. (1995) Neural Networks in the Capital Markets, Wiley

Refenes A.P., Abu-Mostafa Y., Moody J., Weigend A., Neural Networks in Financial Engineering Proc. Of the 3rd NNCM, World Scientific

PART 3

VOLATILITY MODELING AND OPTION PRICING

OPTION PRICING WITH NEURAL NETWORKS
AND
A HOMOGENEITY HINT

RENÉ GARCIA

Département de Sciences Économiques et C.R.D.E., Université de Montréal
C.P. 6128, Succ. Centre-Ville, Montréal, Québec, H3C 3J7, Canada
E-mail: garcia@plgcn.umontreal.ca

and

RAMAZAN GENÇAY

Department of Economics, University of Windsor, Windsor, Ontario, N9B 3P4, Canada
Department of Economics, Bilkent University, Bilkent, Ankara, 06533, Turkey
E-mail: gencay@uwindsor.ca

As soon as one is ready to accept the homogeneity of degree one of the option price with respect to the underlying stock price and the strike price, the resulting option pricing formula keeps the *main functional shape* of the usual Black-Scholes formula. The generalized option pricing formula nests most of the usual parametric option pricing formulas. We show that pricing accuracy gains can be made by exploiting the implications of this homogeneity property in a nonparametric framework. The results indicate that the homogeneity hint always reduces the out-of-sample mean squared prediction error compared with a feedforward neural network with no hint.

1 Introduction

Garcia and Renault (1995) have shown that, as soon as one is ready to accept the homogeneity property of option prices, the resulting option pricing formula keeps the *main functional shape* of the usual Black-Scholes formula. Their generalized option pricing formula nests most of the usual parametric option pricing formulas and rests on a very general stochastic framework in a dynamic asset pricing equilibrium model.

We show that pricing accuracy gains can be made by exploiting the implications of this homogeneity property. Instead of setting up a learning network mapping the ratio S/K and the time to maturity (T-t) directly into the derivative price, we break down the pricing function into two parts, one controlled by the ratio S/K, the other one by a function of time to maturity. In each part, a learning network is fit with S/K and T-t as inputs.

To assess the empirical relevance of this additional structure consistent with homogeneity, we estimate pricing functions for European call options on the S&P 500 index for various sampling periods between 1987 and 1994. The homogeneity hint always reduces the out-of-sample mean squared prediction

A.-P.N. Refenes et al. (eds.), Decision Technologies for Computational Finance, 195–205.

error compared with a feedforward neural network with no hint. Garcia and Gençay (1997) also evaluated the pricing model in terms of hedging performance for simulated data and the S&P 500 index.

Section 2 discusses the nonparametric approach to option pricing and presents the restrictions implied by the generalized option pricing formula. Section 3 is on the nonparametric learning with hints. Empirical results are presented in section 4. We conclude afterwards.

2 Nonparametric Option Pricing with Homogeneity

A natural nonparametric function for pricing a European call option on a non-dividend paying asset is

$$C_t = f(S_t, K, \tau) \tag{1}$$

where S_t is the price of the underlying asset, K is the strike price and τ is the time to maturity. This function will also be valid to learn prices generated by a Black-Scholes model since the interest rate and volatility parameters present in the formula are constant and cannot be identified by a nonparametric estimator of $f(.)$. Since it is generally more difficult to estimate nonparametrically this function when the number of input variables is large, Hutchinson, Lo and Poggio (1994) reduce the number of inputs by one by dividing the function and its arguments by K. Therefore, the pricing function takes the following form:

$$\frac{C_t}{K} = f(\frac{S_t}{K}, 1, \tau) \tag{2}$$

This form assumes the homogeneity of degree one in the asset price and the strike price of the pricing function f. Another technical reason for dividing by the exercise price is that the process S_t is nonstationary while the variable $\frac{S_t}{K}$ is stationary as exercise prices bracket the underlying asset price process, as Ghysels et al. (1997) emphasize. The crucial question is to determine to what extent this homogeneity property is restrictive for the nonparametric learning of the option pricing function. From Merton (1973), we know that the call pricing function is homogeneous of degree one in the asset price and the strike price when the unconditional distribution of returns is independent of the level of the asset price. In Garcia and Renault (1995), Proposition 2 establishes that a necessary and sufficient condition for homogeneity is the conditional independence (under the pricing probability measure) between future returns and the current price, given the currently available information other than the history of the underlying asset price. This property must be understood as a noncausality relationship in the Granger sense from the current price to future returns and not as an independence property. This characterization of homogeneity is more general than the sufficient condition proposed by Merton (1973), not only since the independence requirement is replaced by a more specific noncausality assumption, but also since it is stated in terms of the pricing probability measure rather than the data generating process. This allows a possible dependence of the risk premiums on the asset price S_t. This setting admits very general processes for the underlying asset, such as for example a stochastic volatility model except that the volatility function cannot be a function of the asset price level as in implied tree models.

3 Nonparametric Learning with Hints

All nonparametric estimation techniques share the same fundamental premise of learning from input and output pairs. For a nonparametric method to learn an unknown function from data, it must be able to make generalizations to the out-of-sample setting from the limited input-output pairs upon which it is trained. A method which provides additional information to the learning algorithm is the method of *hints*. A method with hints describes a situation where, in addition to the set of input-output pairs of an unknown function, there is additional prior information about the properties of the unknown function which is provided to the learning algorithm. In general, hints provide auxiliary information about the unknown function which can be used to guide the learning process. The idea of using auxiliary information about the target function to help the learning process is clearly a basic one, and has been used in the literature under different names such as hints, prior knowledge and explicit rules. Because hints impose additional constraints on the set of allowable solutions to which the learning process may converge, the hints may tend to worsen the in-sample performance by excluding some solutions that might otherwise fit the data better. This clearly helps to avoid overfitting in the learning algorithms. The main purpose of using hints is to improve the out-of-sample performance of the learning algorithms.

There are different types of hints common to different applications. Invariance hints of Duda and Hart (1973), Hinton (1987), Hu (1962) and Minsky and Papert (1988) are the most common types of hints in pattern recognition applications. An invariance hint asserts that the target function is invariant under certain transformations of the input. Monotonicity hints, as in Abu-Mostafa (1993), are common in applications such as medical diagnosis and credit-rating where the target function is assumed to be monotonic in certain variables. Symmetry hints are commonly used in foreign exchange predictions by technical analysts. Abu-Mostafa (1994, 1995) indicate that appropriately placed restrictions may lead to improved out-of-sample generalizations.

The architecture of our networks with and without the homogeneity hint are presented below. We will estimate the following two models, respectively for the model without hint (3) and with hint (4):

$$f^{NN}(x,\theta) = \beta_0 + \sum_{j=1}^{d} \beta_j \frac{1}{1 + \exp(-\gamma_{j0} - \sum_{i=1}^{p} \gamma_{ji}x_i))} \tag{3}$$

$$f^{WH}(x,\theta) = \beta_0 + \frac{S_t}{X}\left(\sum_{j=1}^{d}\beta_j^1\frac{1}{1+\exp(-\gamma_{j0}^1 - \sum_{i=1}^p \gamma_{ji}^1 x_i))}\right) \tag{4}$$

$$-e^{-\alpha\tau}\left(\sum_{j=1}^{d}\beta_j^2\frac{1}{1+\exp(-\gamma_{j0}^2 - \sum_{i=1}^p \gamma_{ji}^2 x_i))}\right)$$

Theoretical restrictions such as the absence of arbitrage opportunities impose that the two blocks between parentheses in (4) approximate the same function (for example the normal distribution function in the Black-Scholes formula), with possibly different signs for the same inputs in each block. We account for this by allowing for the same number of hidden units in each block and letting the sign of the inputs unconstrained within each block.

From a statistical point of view, one drawback of the feedforward neural network technique is the virtual absence of inferential procedures to determine the best model specification. There are a number of information theoretic criteria such as the Schwarz Information Criteria (SIC) or the Akaike's Information Criteria (AIC) to be used for this purpose. The shortcoming of the SIC and the AIC is that they indicate feedforward network models which do not generalize well. Swansson and White (1995) report that the SIC fails to select sufficiently parsimonious models in terms of being a reliable guide to the out-of-sample performance. Cross-validation based methods are also available and require heavy computational time to determine the network complexity. In this paper, we do not use any model selection criteria in choosing a particular network complexity. Our methodology is to estimate the feedforward network models with different hidden units with and without the homogeneity hint and compare their performance across these hidden units over a validation period.

Since the networks for the model with hint will always have about twice as many parameters as the networks without the hint for a given number of hidden units, it is important to compare the performance of the two networks with a strategy that accounts for this fact, even if we assess the models based on out-of-sample performance. We will therefore proceed in three steps. First, we will estimate networks with 1 to 9 hidden units for the regular neural networks and 1 to 5 hidden units for the networks with hint over half of the data points for a particular sample, the training period. Next, we will choose the network in each family that gives the best mean square prediction error (MSPE) over half of the remaining data points in the sample, called the validation period. Finally, we assess the prediction performance (MSPE) of the best model chosen in the previous step for the models with and without the homogeneity hint over the last quarter of data, the prediction period. Since the estimation result of the networks depends on the random seed from which initial values are drawn for the parameters, we repeat the same experiment five times for each sample. We compare the performance in terms of mean and variance of these five MSPEs for each family of networks. This will assess the pricing performance of the formula for each type of model.

As for the inputs, we will limit our investigation to two inputs, namely $\frac{S_t}{K}$ and τ, to gauge the improvement achieved with the homogeneity hint in a model kept as simple as possible. It will also make our results comparable to previous studies such as Hutchinson, Lo and Poggio (1994) who used the same inputs. Of course, the introduction of various estimates of the volatility of the underlying assets could further improve results but this avenue will not be pursued here. The interest rate is estimated by the parameter α in the model with hint (4) but is absent from (3). Again, introducing the observed interest rate could bring useful information.

4 Empirical Results

The data are daily S&P 500 Index European options obtained from the Chicago Board Options Exchange for the period January 1987 to October 1994. The S&P 500 index option market is extremely liquid as it is one of the most active options markets in the United States. This market is the closest to the theoretical setting of the Black-Scholes model. In constructing the data used in the estimation, the options with zero volume are not used. For each year, the sample is split into three parts: a training period (first half of the year), a validation period (third quarter) and a prediction period (fourth quarter). One possible drawback of such a setup is that we will always evaluate the predictive ability of our networks on the last quarter of the year. The advantage is that it will facilitate comparison between years, especially with reference to the last quarter of 1987, where a market crash occurred. Since our main purpose is to compare the feedforward networks with and without the homogeneity hint, the last quarter of each year is as good for prediction purposes as any other period. Moreover, since our methodology for choosing the best architecture involves estimating numerous networks for each family of models and repeating the estimation for five different seeds, it requires a lot of computations and limits somewhat the scope of our investigation. In the next two subsections, we will analyze the results in terms of predictive performance for pricing and hedging respectively.

For pricing, our network performance measure will be the Mean Squared Prediction Error (MSPE) in the prediction sample. Results are presented in Table 1. For each year, we report the MSPE obtained for the five experiments for each family of networks, along with the number of hidden units selected. For each experiment and each network (1 to 5 units for the networks with the homogeneity hint and 1 to 9 units for the networks without the hint), we draw 200 sets of parameters starting from a picked seed and select the best as the starting values for our nonlinear least square estimation over the first half of the sample for each year. The number of units reported in the table corresponds to the networks that obtained the lowest MSPE over the validation period, the third quarter of the year.

A first general result is that the average MSPE for the models with the homogeneity hint (WH) is always smaller than the MSPE of the models with no hint (NN). The average MSPE ratios of the models with and without hint for 1987 to 1993 are 46, 89, 98, 92, 93, 92 and 72 percent, respectively. Furthermore, the ratio of the MSPE standard deviations across the five experiments substantially favours the model with the homogeneity hint. In most years, this ratio is lower than 50 percent, the lowest being in 1987 (22%) and the largest in 1992 (91%). This robust feature of the networks with hint is as important as the fact that they produce a lower average MSPE. The measure η, which combines the mean and the variance in a single statistic, delivers basically the same message as the mean statistic. The WS test supports in general the model with the homogeneity hint. For five years out of 7, the p-value is below 16%. Only in 1989 and 1990 is the hypothesis not supported by the results. This is confirmed by the WR test.

The performance of the linear and the Black-and-Scholes models are also presented in Table 1. Not surprisingly, the linear model provides the poorest performance in terms of MSPE. The MSPE performance of the Black and Scholes (BS) model is significantly better than the linear model but worse than the feedforward network models. Over all years except 1987, the BS MSPE is 3 to 10 times larger than the feedforward networks. The result in 1987 might then appear surprising. It is less so when one realizes that the BS model incorporates information from the third quarter of the year that is not part of the training sample of the networks. Indeed, the volatility in the BS model is based on the stock returns over the last sixty days preceding the first day of the last quarter. If we give a comparable information to the networks, in the sense that we train them over the first nine months of 1987 and forecast the option prices over the last quarter, the MSPEs are 6.50 and 4.11 for the NN and WH models respectively. Therefore, with comparable information, the model with hint does slightly better than the BS model in 1987. This emphasizes the fact that in Table 1 the BS model is given an informational advantage compared with the other three models. The relative pricing performance of the networks is all the more remarkable.

To conclude this assessment of the pricing performance of the competing feedforward network models, we can say that the networks with hint show undoubtedly more robustnesss than the networks without hint. In most years, there is also statistical evidence in support of the hypothesis of a lower MSPE for the model based on the homogeneity hint.

5 Conclusions

In this paper, we show that pricing accuracy gains can be made by exploiting the implications of the homogeneity property of the options prices in a neural network nonparametric framework. Instead of setting up a learning network mapping the ratio S/X and the time to maturity (T-t) directly into the derivative price, we break down the pricing function into two parts, one controlled by the ratio S/X, the other one by a function of time to maturity. The results indicate that the homogeneity hint always reduces the out-of-sample mean squared prediction error compared with a feedforward neural network with no hint.

6 Acknowledgements

René Garcia gratefully acknowledges financial support from the Fonds de la Formation de Chercheurs et l'Aide à la Recherche du Québec (FCAR) and the Natural Sciences and Engineering Council of Canada.

Ramazan,Gençay thanks to the Social Sciences and Humanities Research Council of Canada and the Natural Sciences and Engineering Research Council of Canada for financial support. We are grateful to Sami Bengio, Yoshua Bengio, Nour Meddahi and Yaser Abu-Mostafa for useful discussions and comments.

7 References

Abu-Mostafa, Y. (1993), A method for learning from hints, In *Advances in Neural Information Processing Systems*, S. Hanson et al., eds., Vol. 5, 73-80, Morgan Kaufmann, San Mateo, CA.

Abu-Mostafa, Y. (1994), Learning from hints, *Journal of Complexity*, 10, 165-178.

Abu-Mostafa, Y. (1995), Financial market applications of learning from hints, *Neural Networks in the Capital Markets*, A. Refenes, ed., 221-232, Wiley, London, UK.

Duda, R. and P. Hart (1973), Pattern classification and scene analysis, John Wiley, New York.

Garcia, R. and R. Gençay (1998), Pricing and hedging derivative securities with neural networks and a homogeneity hint, *Journal of Econometrics*, forthcoming.

Garcia, R. and E. Renault (1995), Risk Aversion, Intertemporal Substitution and Option Pricing, Working paper, Université de Montréal.

Ghysels, E., V. Patilea, E. Renault and O. Torrès (1997), Nonparametric methods and option pricing, CIRANO working paper 97s-19, Montréal.

Hinton, G. (1987), Learning translation invariant recognition in a massively parallel network, *Proceedings of Conference on Parallel Architectures and Languages Europe*, 1-13.

Hu, M., 1962, Visual pattern recognition by moment invariants, *IRE Transactions of Information Theory*, 8, 179-187.

Hutchinson, J. M., A. W. Lo and T. Poggio (1994), A Nonparametric approach to pricing and hedging derivative securities via learning network, *Journal of Finance*, 3, 851-889.

Merton, R. C. (1973), Rational Theory of Option Pricing, Bell Journal of Economics and Management Science 4, 141-183.

Minsky, M. and S. Papert, 1988, Perceptrons, MIT Press, Cambridge, MA.

Swanson, N. and H. White, 1995, A Model-Selection Approach to Assessing the Information in the Term Structure Using Linear Models and Artificial Neural Networks, *Journal of Business and Economics Statistics*, 13, 265-275.

Table 1
Out-of-Sample Mean Square Prediction Errors
S&P 500 Call Options

Year	Number of Observations	Hidden Units	MSPE WH	Hidden Units	MSPE NN	MSPE LIN / BS
87	TS - 3610	1H	13.32	5H	32.14	98.96/4.38
	VS - 2010	3H	10.91	6H	5.83	
	PS - 2239	3H	13.44	3H	16.67	
		4H	12.23	9H	14.87	
		2H	33.62	6H	111.64	Ratio
	Mean		16.70		36.23	0.46
	St. Dev.		9.51		43.20	0.22
	$\eta = \sqrt{M^2 + SD^2}$		19.22		56.38	0.34
	WS		3	(0.16)		
	WR		23	(0.21)		
88	TS - 3434	2H	0.6713	8H	0.7135	8.41/2.07
	VS - 1642	4H	0.7800	7H	0.8905	
	PS - 1479	5H	0.6806	6H	0.9035	
		4H	0.7061	7H	0.7463	
		5H	0.7188	8H	0.7258	Ratio
	Mean		0.7114		0.7959	0.89
	St. Dev.		0.0429		0.0931	0.46
	$\eta = \sqrt{M^2 + SD^2}$		0.7126		0.8013	0.89
	WS		0	(0.03)		
	WR		19	(0.05)		
89	TS - 3052	2H	0.4120	7H	0.4354	3.75/1.42
	VS - 1565	3H	0.4177	9H	0.4106	
	PS - 1515	5H	0.4233	9H	0.4034	
		3H	0.4055	6H	0.4140	
		5H	0.4106	8H	0.4398	Ratio
	Mean		0.4138		0.4206	0.98
	St. Dev.		0.0068		0.0160	0.43
	$\eta = \sqrt{M^2 + SD^2}$		0.4139		0.4209	0.98
	WS		4	(0.22)		
	WR		25	(0.34)		

Table 1 (Cont'd)
Out-of-Sample Mean Square Prediction Errors
S&P 500 Call Options

Year	Number of Observations	Hidden Units	MSPE WH	Hidden Units	MSPE NN	MSPE LIN/BS
90	TS - 3605	4H	0.6640	5H	0.6812	8.15/2.62
	VS - 2075	3H	0.6581	9H	0.6168	
	PS - 2166	1H	0.8027	7H	0.8269	
		4H	0.5950	4H	0.8820	
		3H	0.6605	4H	0.6198	Ratio
	Mean		0.6761		0.7253	0.92
	St. Dev.		0.0763		0.1222	0.62
	$\eta = \sqrt{M^2 + SD^2}$		0.6804		0.7356	0.92
	WS		7	(0.50)		
	WR		24	(0.27)		
91	TS - 4481	3H	0.3505	5H	0.3475	3.45/1.73
	VS - 1922	4H	0.3393	8H	0.3910	
	PS - 2061	5H	0.3478	8H	0.4023	
		4H	0.3743	6H	0.4108	
		3H	0.3370	6H	0.3360	Ratio
	Mean		0.3498		0.3775	0.93
	St. Dev.		0.0148		0.0336	0.44
	$\eta = \sqrt{M^2 + SD^2}$		0.3501		0.3790	0.92
	WS		3	(0.16)		
	WR		23	(0.21)		
92	TS - 4374	5H	0.1589	7H	0.1497	2.39/1.36
	VS - 1922	5H	0.1666	9H	0.1626	
	PS - 1848	3H	0.1464	9H	0.1598	
		3H	0.1458	4H	0.1840	
		3H	0.1377	5H	0.1683	Ratio
	Mean		0.1511		0.1649	0.92
	St. Dev.		0.0115		0.0126	0.91
	$\eta = \sqrt{M^2 + SD^2}$		0.1515		0.1653	0.92
	WS		3	(0.16)		
	WR		19	(0.05)		

Table 1 (Cont'd)
Out-of-Sample Mean Square Prediction Errors
S&P 500 Call Options

Year	Number of Observations	Hidden Units	MSPE WH	Hidden Units	MSPE NN	MSPE LIN/BS
93	TS - 4214	3H	0.0686	9H	0.1019	2.28/0.74
	VS - 1973	4H	0.1265	3H	0.0878	
	PS - 2030	5H	0.1057	6H	0.2028	
		5H	0.1081	7H	0.1827	
		2H	0.1179	7H	0.1514	Ratio
	Mean		0.1054		0.1453	0.72
	St. Dev.		0.0222		0.0498	0.44
	$\eta = \sqrt{M^2 + SD^2}$		0.1077		0.1536	0.70
	WS		3	(0.16)		
	WR		23	(0.21)		

Notes: This table presents the out-of-sample mean square prediction error (MSPE) performance of a neural network with a homogeneity hint (WH), of a regular feedforward network (NN), of a linear model (LIN) and of the Black-Scholes (BS) model for S&P 500 European call option prices. The five MSPEs correspond to five estimated networks starting from five different seeds. MSPEs are 10^{-4}. In the number of observations column, TS stands for training sample, VS for validation sample and PS for prediction sample. The number of units refers to the number of units in the network that produced the best MSPE performance over the validation period for the WH or the NN family of networks. The test statistics WS and WR refer to the Wilcoxon signed rank test and the Wilcoxon-Mann-Whitney test respectively. The corresponding p-values are in parentheses.

BOOTSTRAPPING GARCH(1,1) MODELS

G. MAERCKER

Institut für Techno- und Wirtschaftsmathematik (ITWM)
Erwin-Schrödinger-Straße, D-67663 Kaiserslautern, Germany
E-mail: maercker@itwm.uni-kl.de

In this paper we propose a bootstrap method for quasi-maximum likelihood (QML) estimators in GARCH(1,1) models. The wild bootstrap is used to bootstrap GARCH(1,1) processes and construct bootstrap QML estimators. It is shown that this bootstrap procedure "works" in the sense that it is consistent. Simulation results demonstrate the small sample behaviour of the proposed bootstrap method.

1 Introduction

Many time series exhibit non-constant conditional variance (conditional heteroskedasticity). That is why in recent years nonlinear processes capable of modelling such volatility have come into particular interest in time series analysis, especially in econometrics and finance. In financial time series the autoregressive conditional heteroskecastic (ARCH) models by Engle (1982) and the generalized ARCH (GARCH) models by Bollerslev (1986) are frequently used. Especially the GARCH(1,1) model has served as an appropriate model in many applications.

Over the past years, many extensions and applications of the ARCH model have been studied, see e.g. Engle (1995).

This paper discusses a bootstrap method for the quasi-maximum likelihood estimators in GARCH(1,1) models. For a bootstrap method for Yule-Walker type estimators see Maercker (1997).

The bootstrap is a method for estimating or approximating the distribution of a statistic and its characteristics. The bootstrap is based on a resampling method of the observed data. Since its introduction by Efron (1979) for models with i.i.d. observations, there have been many applications and extensions of the bootstrap principle, also in case of dependent data. An alternative to Efron's classical bootstrap is the so-called wild bootstrap, see Mammen (1992).

In empirical application usually maximum likelihood (ML) or quasi-maximum likelihood (QML) estimators are used for the estimation of GARCH models. These estimators are consistent and asymptotically normal as was shown for ARCH models by Weiss (1986) and for GARCH models by Lee and Hansen (1994), among others.

QML estimators are obtained by maximizing a likelihood function constructed under the assumption of normality of the error structure. The QML estimator, which falsely assumes normality, is asymptotically normal, but less efficient than the ML estimator. That is why a semiparametric procedure might be useful, see Engle and González-Rivera (1991) and Drost and Klaassen (1996), and also Maercker (1997) for semipararmetric ARCH models.

A.-P.N. Refenes et al. (eds.), Decision Technologies for Computational Finance, 207–218.
© 1998 *Kluwer Academic Publishers. Printed in the Netherlands..*

However, as QML estimators are commonly used in practice, we will present a wild bootstrap procedure for these estimators and prove its (weak) consistency. For the proof we shall make use of results of Lee and Hansen (1994), who derived consistency and asymptotic normality of QML estimators in GARCH(1,1) models under fairly weak conditions on the model.

The article is organized as follows. Section 2 introduces the notation, defines the estimator, and states the main results of Lee and Hansen (henceforth LH) (1994). In Section 3 we present the bootstrap procedure. Simulation results for the small sample behaviour are presented in Section 4.

2 Quasi-maximum likelihood estimators

Let $\{\varepsilon_t : t \in \mathbb{Z}\}$ are i.i.d. mean zero innovations with unit variance. Consider the GARCH(1,1) model

$$X_t = \sigma_t \varepsilon_t, \quad t = 0, 1, 2, \ldots \tag{1}$$

where

$$\sigma_t^2 = \sigma_t^2(\theta) = \omega(1-\beta) + \alpha X_{t-1}^2 + \beta \sigma_{t-1}^2, \quad \omega > 0, \alpha, \beta \geq 0 \tag{2}$$

with parameter $\theta = (\omega, \alpha, \beta)'$.

Assume that the conditional variance process is started in the infinite past, so it may be equivalently expressed by

$$h_t(\theta) := \sigma_t^2(\theta) = \omega + \alpha \sum_{k=0}^{\infty} \beta^k X_{t-1-k}^2. \tag{3}$$

We want to exclude the pure ARCH or even i.i.d. case. Hence define the compact parameter space

$$\Theta = \{\theta : 0 < \omega_l \leq \omega \leq \omega_u, 0 < \alpha_l \leq \alpha \leq \alpha_u, 0 < \beta_l \leq \beta \leq \beta_u < 1\}.$$

Let $\{X_0, \ldots, X_n\}$ be observations from a GARCH(1,1) process with underlying parameter $\theta_0 = (\omega_0, \alpha_0, \beta_0)' \in \Theta$.

For the calculation of the likelihood function we need to compute $\sigma_t(\theta)$ and therefore we need a start-up condition. Let us introduce $\{\tilde{\sigma}_t\}$ as conditional variance process with start-up condition

$$\tilde{\sigma}_0^2 \equiv \omega.$$

By iteration of (2) with this initial value we get the convenient expression

$$\tilde{\sigma}_t^2(\theta) = \omega + \alpha \sum_{k=0}^{t-1} \beta^k X_{t-1-k}^2.$$

Under the assumption that the innovations are standard normally distributed, i.e. $\varepsilon_t \sim \mathcal{N}(0,1)$, we then may compute the likelihood function and as log likelihood function we obtain (ignoring constants)

$$L_n(\theta) = \frac{1}{n} \sum_{t=1}^{n} l_t(\theta) \quad \text{where} \quad l_t(\theta) = -\left(\ln \tilde{\sigma}_t^2(\theta) + \frac{X_t^2}{\tilde{\sigma}_t^2(\theta)} \right).$$

This is called the quasi-maximum likelihood function as the true error density need not be normal. We state the following assumption, compare LH (1994) (Assumption A.1).

ASSUMPTION 1

(i) $E\varepsilon_t^4 < \infty$;

(ii) ε_t^2 is nondegenerate;

(iii) $E\left[\ln\left(\beta_0 + \alpha_0\varepsilon_t^2\right)\right] < 0$;

(iv) θ_0 is in the interior of Θ.

Assumption 1(iii) guarantees the stationarity and ergodicity of the conditional variance process $\sigma_t^2(\theta_0)$.

The fourth moments of the innovations are needed for asymptotic normality, whereas no moment conditions on the process $\{X_t\}$ are required. As is shown in LH (1994), most expressions can be reduced to ratios of geometric averages in the squared innovations.

Note that Condition 1(ii) does not require $\beta_0 + \alpha_0 < 1$. This implies that even the so-called integrated GARCH(1,1) (IGARCH(1,1)), models with $\alpha_0 + \beta_0 = 1$ are allowed (Engle and Bollerslev (1986)).

As in LH (1994) we introduce the unobserved likelihood function, where the "unobserved" variance $h_t(\theta) = \sigma_t^2(\theta)$ as defined in (3) without any start-up condition is used. We set

$$L_n^u(\theta) = \frac{1}{n}\sum_{t=1}^n l_t^u(\theta) \quad \text{where} \quad l_t^u(\theta) = -\left(\ln h_t(\theta) + \frac{X_t^2}{h_t(\theta)}\right).$$

While $l_t(\theta)$ is not stationary due to the presence of the start-up condition, the unobserved process $l_t^u(\theta)$ is stationary, see LH (1994).

Since also IGARCH models are allowed, i.e. the case $\alpha_0 + \beta_0 = 1$, Lee and Hansen need to restrict the parameter space to $\Theta_2 \subset \Theta$ for showing consistency of the QML estimator. For details we refer to LH (1994).

Define the QML estimator by

$$\hat{\theta}_n = \arg\max_{\theta \in \Theta_2} L_n(\theta).$$

$\hat{\theta}_n$ is the parameter value which maximizes the likelihood in the restricted region $\Theta_2 \subset \Theta$.

Denote the vector of derivatives and matrix of second derivatives of l_t^u by ∇l_t^u and $\nabla^2 l_t^u$, respectively. Set

$$\begin{aligned} A(\theta) &= E\left(\nabla l_t^u(\theta)\nabla l_t^u(\theta)'\right), \quad A_0 = A(\theta_0), \\ B(\theta) &= -E\nabla^2 l_t^u(\theta), \quad B_0 = B(\theta_0). \end{aligned}$$

The main result of LH (1994) then is

Proposition 1 *Under Assumption 1 we have*

$$\sqrt{n}\left(\hat{\theta}_n - \theta_0\right) \xrightarrow{D} \mathcal{N}(0, V_0),$$

where $V_0 = B_0^{-1} A_0 B_0^{-1}$.

PROOF: Lee and Hansen (1994), Theorem 3. □

Define

$$\hat{A}_n(\theta) = \frac{1}{n} \sum_{t=1}^{n} \nabla l_t(\theta) \nabla l_t(\theta)', \quad \hat{A}_n = \hat{A}_n(\hat{\theta}),$$

$$\hat{B}_n(\theta) = -\frac{1}{n} \sum_{t=1}^{n} \nabla^2 l_t(\theta), \quad \hat{B}_n = \hat{B}_n(\hat{\theta}).$$

The following lemma shows that $\hat{A}_n$, $\hat{B}_n$ are consistent estimates for A_0 and B_0 respectively.

Lemma 2 *Under Assumption 1 we have*

$$\hat{V}_n = \hat{B}_n^{-1} \hat{A}_n \hat{B}_n^{-1} \xrightarrow{P} V_0 = B_0^{-1} A_0 B_0^{-1}.$$

PROOF: Lee and Hansen (1994), Lemma 12. □

In empirical application the QML estimator is found by a Newton iterative procedure. Let $\theta^{(i)}$ denote the parameter estimate after the i-th iteration. $\theta^{(i+1)}$ is then calculated from

$$\theta^{(i+1)} = \theta^{(i)} + \frac{1}{n} \hat{B}_n \left(\theta^{(i)}\right)^{-1} \sum_{i=1}^{n} \nabla l_t \left(\theta^{(i)}\right). \tag{4}$$

Observe that, denoting $\theta = (\theta_1, \theta_2, \theta_3)'$, we have

$$\nabla l_t(\theta) = \left(\frac{\partial l_t(\theta)}{\partial \omega}, \frac{\partial l_t(\theta)}{\partial \alpha}, \frac{\partial l_t(\theta)}{\partial \beta}\right)'$$

with

$$\frac{\partial l_t}{\partial \theta_i}(\theta) = \left(\frac{X_t^2}{\tilde{\sigma}_t^2(\theta)} - 1\right) \frac{\partial \tilde{\sigma}_t^2(\theta)}{\partial \theta_i} \frac{1}{\tilde{\sigma}_t^2(\theta)}$$

and the analogous expressions for ∇l_t^u with

$$\frac{\partial l_t^u}{\partial \theta_i}(\theta) = \left(\frac{X_t^2}{h_t(\theta)} - 1\right) \frac{\partial h_t(\theta)}{\partial \theta_i} \frac{1}{h_t(\theta)}.$$

For the second derivatives we get

$$\frac{\partial^2 l_t^u}{\partial \theta_i \partial \theta_j} = \left(\frac{X_t^2}{h_t} - 1 \right) \left(\frac{\partial^2 h_t}{\partial \theta_i \partial \theta_j} \frac{1}{h_t} - 2 \frac{\partial h_t}{\partial \theta_j} \frac{1}{h_t} \frac{\partial h_t}{\partial \theta_i} \frac{1}{h_t} \right) - \frac{\partial h_t}{\partial \theta_i} \frac{1}{h_t} \frac{\partial h_t}{\partial \theta_j} \frac{1}{h_t}.$$

In particular, since $E\left(\frac{X_t^2}{h_t(\theta_0)} - 1 \right) = E\left(\frac{X_t^2}{\sigma_t(\theta_0)^2} - 1 \right) = E\left(\varepsilon_t^2 - 1 \right) = 0$, we have

$$B_0 = B(\theta_0) = E\left(\frac{1}{h_t^2(\theta_0)} \frac{\partial h_t(\theta_0)}{\partial \theta_i} \frac{\partial h_t(\theta_0)}{\partial \theta_j} \right)_{i,j=1,2,3} \tag{5}$$

3 The bootstrap procedure

The joint asymptotic normal distribution of the estimator $\hat{\theta}_n$ might be used to construct confidence sets for $\hat{\omega}_n$, $\hat{\alpha}_n$, and $\hat{\beta}_n$. However, the exact distribution of the estimators is unknown. This distribution can as well be estimated by a bootstrap approximation. The bootstrap can be used to obtain a confidence set simply by replacing the unknown distribution with its bootstrap estimator. In small sample sizes the bootstrap estimator might be a better approximation to the exact distribution than the normal approximation.

We now discuss a bootstrap method for estimating the distribution of $\sqrt{n}\left(\hat{\theta}_n - \theta\right)$. We propose an appropriate resampling method and construct bootstrap estimators. It will be shown that the (conditional) distribution of these bootstrap estimators converges in probability to the same asymptotic distribution as given in Proposition 1 for the original estimator, that is, the bootstrap procedure is (weakly) consistent.

To this aim, we represent the squared process $\{X_t^2\}_{t \geq 1}$ in the following equivalent way. Denoting for $t = 1, 2, \ldots$

$$\eta_t = \sigma_t^2(\varepsilon_t^2 - 1),$$

we have

$$X_t^2 = \sigma_t^2 + \eta_t.$$

Observe that the innovations $\{\eta_t\}$ are uncorrelated but not i.i.d.. Because of $E\varepsilon_t^2 = 1$ we have

$$E[\eta_t | \mathcal{F}_{t-1}] = \sigma_t^2 E[\varepsilon_t^2 - 1] = 0,$$

where $\mathcal{F}_{t-1} = \sigma(\sigma_0, X_0, X_1, \ldots, X_{t-1})$ and ε_t is independent of $\mathcal{F}_{t-1}$, thus $\{\eta_t\}$ forms a martingale difference sequence.

The idea of the bootstrap procedure now is the following.

Suppose we have observations $X_1, \ldots, X_n$ with underlying parameter θ_0. Calculate the QML estimator $\hat{\theta}_n$, compute $\hat{\sigma}_t^2 = \tilde{\sigma}_t^2(\hat{\theta}_n)$, and the empirical residuals

$$\hat{\eta}_t = X_t^2 - \hat{\sigma}_t^2, \quad t = 1, \ldots, n.$$

Now generate an independent resample $\eta_1^*, \ldots, \eta_n^*$, where η_t^* has (conditional) mean zero, variance $\hat{\eta}_t^2 = (X_t^2 - \hat{\sigma}_t^2)^2$, and third moment $\hat{\eta}_t^3 = (X_t^2 - \hat{\sigma}_t^2)^3$, i.e.

$$E^*\eta_t^* = 0, \quad E^*\eta_t^{*2} = (X_t^2 - \hat{\sigma}_t^2)^2, \quad E^*\eta_t^{*3} = (X_t^2 - \hat{\sigma}_t^2)^3, \quad t = 1, \ldots, n.$$

Here E^* denotes the conditional expectation given a sample $X_1, \ldots, X_n$.

This resampling technique, which is based on an estimated residual distribution, is called *wild bootstrap*. In this method n different distributions are estimated by only n observations. This method was introduced by Wu (1986), for extensions and applications see e.g. Mammen (1992). In Härdle and Mammen (1993) the wild bootstrap is used in nonparametric regression, for further applications see also Franke, Kreiss and Mammen (1997), and Neumann and Kreiss (1998).

The bootstrap innovations $\eta_1^*, \ldots, \eta_n^*$ can be constructed by generating an i.i.d. sample $\bar{\eta}_1, \ldots, \bar{\eta}_n$ with $E\bar{\eta}_t = 0, E\bar{\eta}_t^2 = 1, E\bar{\eta}_t^3 = 1$, and then setting

$$\eta_t^* = (X_t^2 - \hat{\sigma}_t^2)\bar{\eta}_t.$$

E.g. put $\bar{\eta}_t = U_t/\sqrt{2} + (V_t^2 - 1)/2$ with U_t, V_t being independent standard normally distributed random variables, $t = 1, \ldots, n$. Of course, other constructions are possible, for a detailed description see Mammen (1992).

After resampling of the innovations, define the bootstrap observations

$$X_t^{2*} = \hat{\sigma}_t^2 + \eta_t^*, \quad t = 1, \ldots, n.$$

Then use the one-step Newton iteration with $\hat{\theta}_n$ as starting value to calculate the bootstrap estimator

$$\hat{\theta}_n^* = \hat{\theta}_n + \frac{1}{n}\check{B}_n(\hat{\theta}_n)^{-1} \sum_{t=1}^{n} \nabla l_t^*(\hat{\theta}_n) \tag{6}$$

where the bootstrap score function is defined by

$$\nabla l_t^*(\hat{\theta}_n) = \left(\frac{\partial l_t^*}{\partial \omega}, \frac{\partial l_t^*}{\partial \alpha}, \frac{\partial l_t^*}{\partial \beta} \right)'$$

with

$$\begin{aligned}
\frac{\partial l_t^*}{\partial \theta_i} &= \left(\frac{X_t^{2*}}{\hat{\sigma}_t^2} - 1 \right) \frac{\partial \tilde{\sigma}_t^2(\hat{\theta}_n)}{\partial \theta_i} \frac{1}{\hat{\sigma}_t^2} \\
&= \frac{1}{\hat{\sigma}_t^2} \eta_t^* \frac{\partial \tilde{\sigma}_t^2(\hat{\theta}_n)}{\partial \theta_i} \frac{1}{\hat{\sigma}_t^2},
\end{aligned}$$

and the matrix estimator $\check{B}_n(\hat{\theta}_n)$, based on (5), is defined by

$$\check{B}_n(\hat{\theta}_n) = \frac{1}{n} \sum_{t=1}^{n} \frac{1}{\hat{\sigma}_t^4} \left(\frac{\partial \tilde{\sigma}_t^2(\hat{\theta}_n)}{\partial \theta_i} \frac{\partial \tilde{\sigma}_t^2(\hat{\theta}_n)}{\partial \theta_j} \right)_{i,j=1,2,3}$$

In this bootstrap procedure, having in mind the representation $X_t^2 = \sigma_t^2 + \eta_t$ with a martingale difference sequence $\{\eta_t\} = \{\sigma_t^2 (\varepsilon_t^2 - 1)\}$, the empirical residuals $X_t^2 - \hat{\sigma}_t^2$ which show up in the score function are imitated by the bootstrap residuals η_t^*.

For the proof of weak consistency of this wild bootstrap method we need a slighty stronger moment condition on the innovations than for asymptotic normality of the QML estimator.

ASSUMPTION 1 (i)' $E |\varepsilon_t|^{4+\delta} < \infty$ for some $\delta > 0$.

Now we are ready to state the weak consistency result. Let $\mathcal{L}^*(\ldots)$ denote the conditional law $\mathcal{L}(\ldots | X_1, \ldots, X_n)$ and d_∞ the Kolmogorov distance, i.e. $d_\infty(P, Q) = \sup_{x_1, x_2 \in R} |F_P(x_1, x_2) - F_Q(x_1, x_2)|$, where F_P, F_Q denote the distribution functions of P and Q, respectively.

Theorem 3 *Suppose Assumptions 1(ii) to (iv) and 1(i)'. Then the wild bootstrap procedure for the QML estimator $\hat{\theta}_n$ is weakly consistent, i.e.*

$$d_\infty \left(\mathcal{L}^* \left(\sqrt{n} \left(\hat{\theta}_n^* - \hat{\theta}_n \right) \right), \mathcal{L} \left(\sqrt{n} (\theta_n - \theta_0) \right) \right) \longrightarrow 0 \quad \text{in probability.}$$

PROOF: We will prove asymptotic normality of the bootstrap distribution, i.e.

$$\mathcal{L}^* \left(\sqrt{n} \left(\hat{\theta}_n^* - \hat{\theta}_n \right) \right) \xrightarrow{D} \mathcal{N}(0, V_0) \quad \text{in probability.}$$

By construction (6) we have

$$\sqrt{n} \left(\hat{\theta}_n^* - \hat{\theta}_n \right) = \frac{1}{\sqrt{n}} \check{B}_n(\hat{\theta}_n)^{-1} \sum_{t=1}^{n} \nabla l_t^*(\hat{\theta}_n).$$

As is shown in LH (1994), Lemma 11, $\hat{B}_n(\hat{\theta}_n)$ is a consistent estimate for B_0. In view of (5) $\check{B}_n(\hat{\theta}_n)$ is a consistent estimate for $B(\theta_0)$ as well. Therefore it suffices to show

$$\frac{1}{\sqrt{n}} \sum_{t=1}^{n} \nabla l_t^*(\hat{\theta}_n) \xrightarrow{D} \mathcal{N}(0, A_0) \quad \text{in probability.}$$

We will verify the Lindeberg condition

$$\frac{1}{n} \sum_{t=1}^{n} E^* \left[\left(c' \nabla l_t^*(\hat{\theta}_n) \right)^2 1_{\{|c' \nabla l_t^*(\hat{\theta}_n)| > n^{-1/2}\varepsilon\}} \right] \xrightarrow{P} 0 \quad \text{for all } \varepsilon > 0, \ c \in R^3, \quad (7)$$

and, furthermore,

$$\text{Var}^* \left(\frac{1}{\sqrt{n}} \sum_{t=1}^{n} \nabla l_t^*(\hat{\theta}_n) \right) \longrightarrow A_0 \quad \text{in probability.} \quad (8)$$

To see (8), observe that

$$
\begin{aligned}
\text{Var}^* \left(\frac{1}{\sqrt{n}} \sum_{t=1}^{n} \nabla l_t^*(\hat{\theta}_n) \right) &= \frac{1}{n} \sum_{t=1}^{n} E^* \left(\nabla l_t^*(\hat{\theta}_n) \nabla l_t^*(\hat{\theta}_n)' \right) \\
&= \frac{1}{n} \sum_{t=1}^{n} \nabla l_t(\hat{\theta}_n) \nabla l_t(\hat{\theta}_n)' \\
&= \hat{A}_n \longrightarrow A_0 \quad \text{in probability}
\end{aligned}
$$

by Lee and Hansen (LH (1994), Lemma 12).

In order to verify the Lindeberg condition (7) choose a $\delta > 0$ such that $E|\varepsilon_1|^{4+\delta} < \infty$ according to Assumption 1(i)'. Then we get for $\varepsilon > 0$, $c \in R^3$

$$
\begin{aligned}
\frac{1}{n} \sum_{t=1}^{n} E^* &\left[\left(c' \nabla l_t^*(\hat{\theta}_n) \right)^2 1_{\{|c' \nabla l_t^*(\hat{\theta}_n)| > n^{1/2}\varepsilon\}} \right] \\
&\leq \frac{1}{n^{1+\delta/2}\varepsilon^\delta} \sum_{t=1}^{n} E^* \left| c' \nabla l_t^*(\hat{\theta}_n) \right|^{2+\delta} \\
&= \frac{1}{n^{1+\delta/2}\varepsilon^\delta} \sum_{t=1}^{n} \left| c' \nabla l_t(\hat{\theta}_n) \right|^{2+\delta} E |\bar{\eta}_t|^{2+\delta} \\
&= o_P(1)
\end{aligned}
$$

with the same arguments as in LH (1994) for the proof of Proposition 1 and as $E|\varepsilon_t|^{4+\delta} < \infty$. This concludes the proof of the theorem. $\qquad\square$

4   Simulations

In order to illustrate the performance of the bootstrap procedures described in the preceding section, we show some results of simulation experiments. We simulated GARCH(1,1) processes of length $n = 300$ with standard normal error distribution and with parameter $(\omega, \alpha, \beta) = (0.05, 0.2, 0.6)$. The parameter is estimated by the QML estimator. The distribution of the standardized estimator is approximated by the estimated density calculated from Monte Carlo replications. Then the bootstrap approximation and the normal approximation, based on one sample, are calculated. All approximations are based on 1000 Monte Carlo replications.

Figure 1 compares the distribution of $\sqrt{n}(\hat{\alpha}_n - \alpha)$ with the bootstrap distribution of $\sqrt{n}(\hat{\alpha}_n^* - \hat{\alpha}_n)$. Note that the bootstrap procedure is based on only one (randomly chosen) sample of the underlying GARCH process. For comparison, also the normal approximation is calculated.

Figure 2 and Figure 3 show the results for the parameters β and ω, respectively.

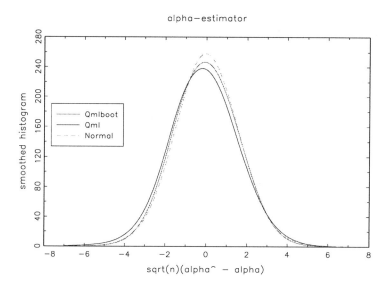

Fig. 1: Distribution of $\sqrt{n}(\hat{\alpha}_n - \alpha)$ with bootstrap approximation and normal approximation for simulated GARCH(1,1) processes with $(\omega, \alpha, \beta) = (0.05, 0.2, 0.6)$, sample size $n = 300$. All plots are based on 1000 Monte Carlo replications.

216

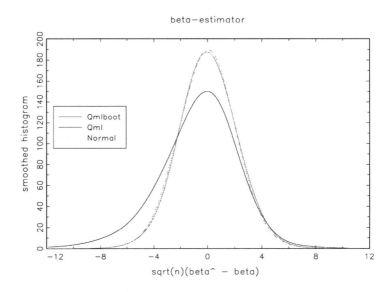

Fig. 2: Distribution of $\sqrt{n}(\hat{\beta}_n - \beta)$ with bootstrap approximation and normal approximation. Parameter as in Figure 1.

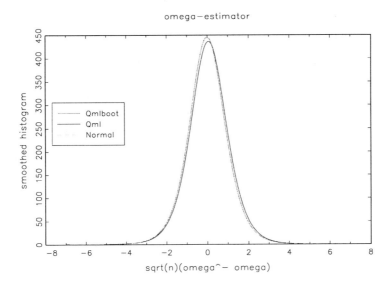

Fig. 3: Distribution of $\sqrt{n}(\hat{\omega}_n - \omega)$ with bootstrap approximation and normal approximation. Parameter as in Figure 1.

5 Acknowledgements

I am very grateful to my supervisor J.-P. Kreiss for many helpful discussions.

6 References

Bollerslev, T. Generalized autoregressive conditional heteroskedasticity, *J. Econometrics* 1986, 31:307–327.

Drost, F. C., Klaassen, C. A. J. Efficient estimation in semiparametric GARCH models, Preprint, 1996, to appear in *J. Econometrics*.

Efron, B. Bootstrap methods: Another look at the jackknife, *Ann. Statist.* 1979, 7:1–26.

Engle, R. F. Autoregressive conditional heteroscedasticity with estimates of the variance of U.K. inflation, *Econometrica* 1982, 50:987–1007.

Engle, R. F. (ed.) *ARCH: Selected Readings*, Oxford University Press, Oxford, 1995.

Engle, R. F., Bollerslev, T. Modelling the persistence of conditional variances, *Econometric Reviews* 1986, 5:1–50, 81–87.

Engle, R. F., Gonzáles-Rivera, G. Semiparametric ARCH models, *J. Business and Economic Statist.* 1991, 9:345–359.

Franke, J., Kreiss, J.-P., Mammen, E. Bootstrap for kernel smoothing in nonlinear time series, Preprint 97/03, Technical University Braunschweig, 1997, submitted to *Bernoulli*.

Härdle, W., Mammen, E. Comparing nonparametric versus parametric regression fits, *Ann. Statist.* 1993, 21:1926–1947.

Lee, S.-W., Hansen, B. E. Asymptotic theory for the GARCH(1,1) quasi-maximum likelihood estimator, *Econometric Theory* 1994, 10:29–52.

Maercker, G. *Statistical Inference in Conditional Heteroskedastic Autoregressive Models*, Shaker, Aachen, 1997.

Mammen, E. *When Does Bootstrap Work?* Lecture Notes in Statistics 77, Springer, New York, 1992

Neumann, M. H., Kreiss, J.-P. Regression-type inference in nonparametric autoregression, Preprint, 1998, submitted to *Ann. Statist.*

Weiss, A. A. Asymptotic theory for ARCH models: estimation and testing, *Econometric Theory* 1986, 2:107–131.

Wu, C. F. J. Jackknife, bootstrap and other resampling methods in regression analysis, *Ann. Statist.* 1986, 14:1261–1343.

USING ILLIQUID OPTION PRICES TO RECOVER PROBABILITY DISTRIBUTIONS

F. GONZÁLEZ MIRANDA

Department of Finance
Swedish School of Economics and
Business Administration
Arkadiagatan 22, 00101, Helsinki, Finland
E-mail: gonzalez@shh.fi

A. N. BURGESS

Department of Decision Science
London Business School
Sussex Place, Regents Park, London, NW1 4SA, UK
E-mail: N.Burgess@lbs.ac.uk

This paper describes a method for recovering the risk neutral market's perceived probability distribution (RND) of European options on the FTSE100 Index on an hourly time basis. A nonparametric procedure is used to choose probabilities that minimise an objective function subject to requiring that the obtained probabilities comply with observed option prices. The procedure is based on the idea that probability distributions of asset returns can be expressed as a mixture of lognormal variables. The use of a lognormal mixture provides a natural and robust way to model distributions with fat tails, a key feature of financial returns. The optimisation technique for estimating probability distributions incorporates a "smoothness" and a "variability" factor in the objective function to account for situations where little smoothness and high variability in the posterior distributions are plausible due to problems in the data, such as illiquidity. With this method we are able to resolve some of the numerical difficulties presented by earlier procedures, plot consistent pictures in a timely fashion of the implied distribution and measure the first four implied moments of the future probability distribution implied by the FTSE 100 option market.

1   Introduction

The use of derivative prices to obtain information about future asset prices is common. Because option prices are formed by the interaction among option market participants they can give a collective expression of expectations about future price distributions of the underlying asset. European call options on the same underlying asset can be combined to form state-contingent claims whose returns are dependent on the "state" of the economy at a particular time, T, in the future. The prices of such assets reflect investors' assessments of the probabilities of particular states occurring in the future.

An important class of state contingent claims is the elementary claim introduced by Arrow (1964) and Debreu (1959). The elementary claim, also known as the Arrow-Debreu security, is a derivative security that pays $1 at future time T

A.-P.N. Refenes et al. (eds.), Decision Technologies for Computational Finance, 219–232.
© 1998 *Kluwer Academic Publishers. Printed in the Netherlands..*

if the underlying asset takes a particular value, or "state", S_T, at that time, and zero otherwise. The prices of Arrow-Debreu securities at each possible state are directly proportional to the risk-neutral probabilities of each of the states taking place (Cox and Ross (1976))[1]. In a continuum of states, the prices of Arrow-Debreu securities are defined by the "state-price density" (SPD). Unfortunately the Arrow-Debreu security is not traded on any exchange and hence its price is not directly observable. However, we can replicate such a security from the prices of traded financial securities[2].

Breeden and Litzenberger (1978) demonstrated that if the underlying price at time T has a continuous probability distribution, then the state price at state S_T is proportional to the second derivative of a related call option with respect to its strike price, $\partial^2 c/\partial X^2$, evaluated at an exercise price of $X=S_T$. When applied across the continuum of states, $\partial^2 c/\partial X^2$ equals the state price density (and hence the risk neutral density, RND).

Four related techniques have been used in the literature to estimate risk neutral densities. All these approaches can be related to the Breeden and Litzenberger (1978) result. In the first approach assumptions are made about the stochastic process that governs the price of the underlying asset and the RND function is inferred from it. For example, if asset prices follow geometric Brownian motion and the risk-free rate is constant, the RND is lognormal (the Black-Scholes case). Generally the RND cannot be computed in closed form and numerically intensive methods must be used. In the second type of techniques, the RND is derived in some parametric form[3]. Shimko (1993) provides a method of implementing it by fitting a smooth quadratic function of strike prices to the implied volatilities of market option prices. He then uses the Black-Scholes formula to invert the interpolated smile curve, solving for the call price as a continuous function of the strike price. The problem with Shimko's extrapolation procedure is that it arbitrarily assigns a constant volatility structure to the area outside the traded strike range. Since the final distribution is pieced together it is not always possible to ensure a smooth transition from the observable part of the distribution to the tails. A third approach would consist of interpolating a call pricing function $c(X, t)$, that is consistent with the monotonicity and convexity conditions and that can be differentiated twice[4]. This can be implemented by applying nonparametric kernel regression to estimate the entire call pricing function[5]. The fact that the

[1] The constant of proportionality is the present value of a zero-coupon bond that pays $1 at time T, with the discount rate being the risk-free rate of interest.

[2] See Banz and Miller (1978), Breeden and Litzenberger (1978) and Ross (1976).

[3] See Jarrow and Rudd (1982), Shimko (1993), Longstaff (1995), Derman and Kani (1994) and Madan and Milne (1994).

[4] See Bates (1991) and Aït-Sahalia and Lo (1995).

[5] See Härdle (1991)

nonparametric regression approach involves a large number of regressors, makes this technique particularly data-intensive. Since we are working with very limited numbers of quoted prices, this approach is practically unimplementable for most of the option markets with which we are concerned. A fourth line of research is to specify a prior parametric distribution as a candidate RND function, generally the log-normal density[6]. The RND is then estimated by minimising its distance to the prior parametric distribution under the constraints that it correctly prices a selected set of derivative securities. As opposed to the first approach cited, it is more general to start with an assumption about the terminal RND function rather than assuming a stochastic process by which the underlying price evolves. This is because a given stochastic process implies a unique terminal distribution, but the converse is not true, that is, any given RND function is consistent with many different stochastic processes.

In this paper, we adopt the latter method as our preferred approach. We develop this methodology incorporating new features to existing systems in the literature to account for the relatively limited number of prices quoted across strikes at any one point in time. The fact that many option markets only trade a small range of exercise prices makes it extremely difficult to obtain an implied RND for the asset under consideration in a consistent manner. Our method tries to overcome this difficulty by introducing in the optimisation program penalty factors such as "smoothness" and "variability" factors that will account for situations where little smoothness and high variability in the posterior RND are plausible due to problems in the data. Following Ritchey (1990) we propose a mixture of weighted lognormal distributions as the prior parametric distribution[7]. Given that observed financial asset price distributions are in the neighbourhood of the lognormal distribution, it seems plausible to use such assumption. Moreover, the functional form assumed provides a natural and robust way to model distributions with fat tails and skewness, a key feature of financial returns[8].

The paper is organised as follows. In section 2 we examine the relationship between RND functions and derivative securities. In section 3 we describe our methodology for estimating RND functions. We then present results of simulations carried out on FTSE European option data. We describe the data used and show how the proposed method works, emphasising how the methodology can be modified to account for peculiarities in the data. Section 5 concludes by analysing the potential advantages that derived RND functions present to decision- makers in the market place.

---

[6] See Rubinstein (1994), Jackwerth and Rubinstein (1995), Melick and Thomas (1994), Bahra (1997).

[7] Finite mixture of distributions have been used as models throughout the history of modern statistics. For an excellent monograph on the use of finite mixture distributions and its possible practical uses see Titterington, Smith and Makov (1985).

[8] These features are mainly caused by continuous jumps in prices and stochastic volatility. See for example Duffie and Pan (1997).

2   Derivative Securities and RND functions.

We now review the relationship between RND functions and the pricing of derivative securities in a no-arbitrage framework. As suggested by Breeden and Litzenberger (1978), we can price state-contingent claims within a time-state preference framework. The one-unit payoff to an elementary claim at a given future state, $S_T = X$ can be obtained by selling two call options with exercise price $X = S_T$ and buying two call options, one with exercise $S_T - \Delta S_T$ and one with exercise price $S_T + \Delta S_T$, where ΔS_T is the step size between adjacent calls. This portfolio of call options is a butterfly spread with centre at X. The butterfly pays nothing outside the interval $[\ S_T - \Delta S_T\ ,\ S_T + \Delta S_T\ ]$. Letting the step size, ΔS_T , tend to zero, the payoff function of the butterfly tends to a Dirac delta function with mass at $X = S_T$, implying that in the limit the butterfly becomes and Arrow-Debreu security paying \$1 if $S_T = X$ and zero for all other states. By denoting an option contract $c(X, \tau)$, as the payoff to an European call with strike price at X and time to maturity, $\tau = T\text{-}t$, we can define a butterfly spread as:

$$\frac{\left[c(S_T + \Delta S_T, \tau) - c(S_T, \tau)\right] - \left[c(S_T, \tau) - c(S_T - \Delta S_T, \tau)\right]}{\Delta S_T}\Bigg|_{X=S_T} = 1 \qquad (1)$$

Now, if we define $P(S_T, \tau, \Delta S_T)$ as the price of an elementary claim (i.e. a butterfly spread) centred on state $S_T = X$, then $P(S_T, \tau; \Delta S_T)$ divided by the step size between adjacent calls, ΔS_T , may be written in terms of a portfolio of call options as the following equation:

$$\frac{P(S_T, \tau; \Delta S_T)}{\Delta S_T} = \frac{\left[c(S_T + \Delta S_T, \tau) - c(S_T, \tau)\right] - \left[c(S_T, \tau) - c(S_T - \Delta S_T, \tau)\right]}{(\Delta S_T)^2} \qquad (2)$$

In the limit, as the step size tends to zero, the price of the butterfly spread at state $S_T = X$ tends to the second derivative of the call pricing function with respect to the exercise price at $X = S_T$.

$$\lim_{\Delta S_T \to 0} \frac{P(S_T, \tau; \Delta S_T)}{\Delta S_T} = \frac{\partial^2 c(X, \tau)}{\partial X^2}\Bigg|_{X=S_T} \qquad (3)$$

By quoting butterfly spreads across the continuum of possible states, each with very small step sizes between exercise prices, we can obtain the complete state pricing function, the SPD. In a similar way, we can express Arrow-Debreu prices as expected future payoffs by multiplying the present value of \$1 by the risk-neutral probability of the state that gives rises to the payoff occurring at $S_T = X$. This produces the result that the second derivative of the call pricing function with respect to the exercise price is equal to the discounted risk neutral distribution function, RND, of S_T conditioned on the underlying price at time t, S,

$$\frac{\partial^2 c(X,\tau)}{\partial X^2} = e^{-r\tau} g(S_T) \tag{4}$$

where r is the risk free rate of return over the time period $\tau = T\text{-}t$, and $g(S_T)$ is the RND function of S_T.

The Breeden and Litzenberger result does not make any assumptions about the underlying price generating process[9]. The only requirement needed to estimate a continuous $g(S_T)$ density function is that $c(X, \tau)$ will be twice differentiable. Under no arbitrage conditions, $c(X, \tau)$ is convex and monotonic decreasing in exercise price. For example, consider the Black-Scholes formula where the underlying asset S_t follows a geometric Brownian motion process with constant volatility, σ, and interest rate, r, and dividend yield, d, are also constant.

$$c_{BS}(S_t, X, \tau, r_\tau, d; \sigma) = S_t N(d_1) - e^{-r\tau} N(d_2) \tag{5}$$

The Black-Scholes assumption implies that the RND function of S_T, $g(S_T)$, is lognormal with mean $((r_\tau - d_\tau) - \frac{1}{2}\sigma^2)\tau$ and variance $\sigma^2(\tau)$.

$$g(S_T) = \frac{1}{S_T \sqrt{2\pi\sigma^2\tau}} e^{-\frac{(\ln(S_T/S_t) - ((r-d) - \frac{1}{2}\sigma^2)\tau)^2}{2\sigma^2\tau}} \tag{6}$$

Cox and Ross (1976) show that for the existence of no-arbitrage opportunities in an economy we need an artificial distribution called the risk neutral valuation measure, and that an equilibrium asset price is the properly discounted expected value of its payoffs. In this way, we can represent the value of an European call option as

$$c(S, X) = e^{-r\tau} \int_0^\infty g(S_T) \max(S_T - x, 0) dS_T \tag{7}$$

This approach of valuation does not require particular assumptions about the dynamics of price change or other information about the time path of prices. The only required condition is that there are no arbitrage opportunities in the complex of options and underlying assets. In the Black and Scholes world as discussed above

---

[9] The result only assumes perfect markets, i.e., no restrictions on short sales, no transaction costs or taxes and infinite borrowing at the risk free rate of interest.

the RND function is the lognormal but in theory other functional forms for the density function could be used.

3   Fitting the implied RND as a mixture of log-normal distributions

As discussed in the previous section, we can define the price of a European call option at any time t as the discounted sum of all expected future payoffs (equation (7). Rather than specifying the asset price dynamics to infer the RND function, it is possible to make assumptions about the functional form of the RND function itself and to recover its parameters by minimising the distance between observed option prices and those generated by the proposed parametric function.

As mentioned in the first section, assuming a functional form for the terminal RND, rather than a stochastic generating process for the underlying asset, is a more general approach and therefore preferred. The reason is that a given stochastic process corresponds in a unique manner to a terminal distribution. However, the opposite is not true, that is, any given RND function is consistent with many different stochastic price processes.

In this way, any density function, $g(S_T)$, can be used in equation (7) and its parameters recovered by optimisation methods. Posed with the question of which density function could be a good proxy for obtaining RND functions, we should be aware, as pointed out by Bahra (1997), that using finite variance models other than the Gaussian could provoke the underlying price distribution to change as the holding period changes. In the case of being in a Gaussian world, if daily prices are lognormally distributed then other arbitrary length holding period price distributions must also be lognormal. No other variance distribution is stable under addition. Moreover, there is another important factor that favours the use of the Gaussian family type of distributions, specifically the lognormal distribution. Financial asset price distributions behave similarly to the lognormal distribution. Ritchey (1990) proposes as the underlying distribution a weighted sum of k-component lognormal density functions.

$$g(S_T) = \sum_{i=1}^{k} \left[\theta_i L(\alpha_i, \beta_i; S_T) \right] \tag{8}$$

where $L(\alpha_i, \beta_i; S_T)$ is the i-th lognormal density component in the k-component mixture with parameters α_i and β_i. Where,

$$\alpha_I = ((r_\tau - d_\tau) - \tfrac{1}{2}\,\sigma^2)\tau \qquad \text{and} \quad \beta_I = \sigma^2(\tau)$$

The mixture is guaranteed to have a nonnegative value and satisfy the unitary condition of its sum, that is,

$$\sum_{i=1}^{k} \theta_i = 1, \text{ and } \theta_i > 0$$

An interesting property about the use of a k-mixture of lognormal functions is that it serves as a robust way to model distributions with high kurtosis and skewness, key features in financial price distributions. This is important since it will help us in identifying those aspects of the data that are more prominent such as the so-called "volatility smile". Each lognormal density function is completely defined by two parameters. The values of these parameters, its mean and variance, together with the relative weighting applied to each component density function, determines the overall shape of the implied RND function.

The choice of the number of k components in the k-mixture of lognormals is not clear cut. The fact that many option markets are thinly traded and trade across a relatively small range of exercise prices imposes some restrictions on the number of components that can be included. This limits the number of parameters that can be estimated from the data since we do not want to overparameterise our mixture. In any case, this overparameterisation can be controlled by introducing a series of penalty factors in our minimisation problem as we do later.

The general optimisation method given by equation (7) can be formalised as follows:

$$f(X) = Min_t \sum_{i=1}^{n} \left(\left(c(X_i, \tau) - e^{-r\tau} \int_0^{\infty} g(S_T)(S_T - X_i)dS_T \right)^2 \right) \tag{9}$$

where n is equal to the number of strikes traded and $g(S_T)$ is equal to a weighted sum of lognormal density functions as in (8). It follows that the minimisation criterion is of the quadratic type. For fixed values of X and τ and for a set of values for the distributional parameters and r, the free interest rate, equation (9) can be used to provided fitted values of $c(X_i, \tau)$, the European call prices observed at time t. In this article we only make use of call prices but put prices can be used similarly since both are priced from the same underlying distribution.

With this approach we would expect the parameters in equation (9) to move over time as news and option prices adjust to incorporate changing beliefs about future events. The interesting advantage of this method is that it can accommodate almost any shape for the implied distributions, even those cases in which the market has a bi-modal view about the terminal value of the underlying asset.

The implied density functions derived are risk neutral, that is, they are equivalent to the true market density functions only when investors are risk neutral. In practice this is not likely to happen since investors will incorporate certain degrees of risk aversion as well as beliefs about future outcomes into option prices. However as Rubinstein (1994) points out, even if the market does demand a premium for taking on risk, the true market implied density function may not differ very much from the true RND[10].

The problem with using the simple objective function in (9) to obtain the parameters that form the mixture of lognormals, is that it could occasionally lead to posterior distributions that have little smoothness with respect to price and high variability with respect to time. This is sometimes the result of noise and "staleness" in option data and not genuine changes in investors' beliefs about future outcomes for the price of the underlying asset. We have to be aware that in many of the markets with which we are concerned, option trading is not yet conducted in a fluent manner, that is, a small range of exercise prices are traded with considerable time gaps between trades. Infrequent intra-day quotes and limited range of exercise prices pose serious difficulties to the researcher who tries to disentangle different aspects of option markets. To account for this we add to the objective function in (9) three penalty factors: a "smoothness" or curvature component, a "variability" or change component and a "arbitrage" component or difference between the forward price implied by the RND and the observed forward price.

In general, the augmented version of the objective function will be in discrete time:

$$\alpha f(x) + \alpha' h(x) + \alpha'' k(x) + \alpha''' l(x) \tag{10}$$

The smoothness component $h(x)$ will account for situations when little smoothness is considered to be implausible. To accomplish this we need to select the posterior implied probabilities, Pj, which minimise the following equation:

$$h(x) = \sum_j (P_{j-1} - 2P_j + P_{j+1})^2 \tag{11}$$

with $P_{-1} = P_{n+1} = 0$ and $\sum_j P_j = 1$,

The implied posterior probabilities, Pj, are the risk neutral probabilities that the underlying asset price will be Sj on the expiration date of the options. The objective of equation (11) is to find the smoothest distribution in the sense of minimising the second derivative of Pj with respect to the underlying asset level and in this sense minimising the curvature exhibited in the implied probability distribution[11]

The variability component is denoted as:

---

[10] Rubinstein (1994) found that for assumed market risk premia of between 3.3 per cent and 5 per cent, the subjective distribution is only slightly shifted to the right relative to the risk-neutral distribution and that the shapes of these two distributions are quite similar.

[11] Each term in equation (11) corresponds to the value of a butterfly option spread, which is the finite difference approximation of the second derivative $\partial^2 Pj / \partial S^2 j$

$$k(x) = \sum_j \left(P_j^t - P_j^{t-1} \right)^2 \qquad (12)$$

In much the same way, $k(x)$, has to be minimised. The variability component of equation (12) will account for situations when changes in final implied distributions are considered implausible. For example, in the case that in an illiquid hour of trade two market participants perform a trade that is not considered representative, the obtained implied distribution will change accordingly but will not really represent the overall perception of the market. We want to avoid this type of unrepresentative situations by penalising noise trades in the context of illiquid trading periods.

Finally, in the absence of arbitrage opportunities, the mean of the implied RND function should equal the forward price of the underlying asset. We can treat the underlying asset as a zero-strike option and use the incremental information it provides by including its forward price as an additional observation in the minimisation procedure. Formally,

$$l(x) = \left(\hat{S}_T \, e^{-r\tau} - S_t \right)^2 \qquad (13)$$

where,

$$\hat{S}_T = \sum_j \ln(S_j / S_t) \times P_j \qquad (14)$$

The implied forward price of the underlying asset given by the implied distribution is denoted by $\hat{S}_T$ and S_t is the current index level at time t. This value is obtained by the sum across all possible future states j of the resulting Pj risk neutral probabilities multiplied to the logarithm of the underlying asset price, Sj, divided by the current value of the underlying at time t, S_t.

The penalty parameters in equation (10), α's, are selected based on the trade-off between increasing the accuracy in obtaining the observed option prices and avoidance of overfitting the observed prices that leads to probability distributions that are unrepresentative not smooth and change much over time. The typical values for α's will vary for each particular experiment. For example, sometimes we will demand more control on the "variability" component than for the rest of components, increasing the relative penalty of the variability component, α'', with respect to the other penalty factors, α, α' and α'''. The non-linear optimisation problem in equation (10) is implemented using a quasi-Newton method with a tolerance error level of 10^{-2}. In general, the optimisation is achieved within the prespecified tolerance and iterations parameters making this method appealing to a fast and robust discovery of market's probabilities.

In the following section we will describe the method at work using intraday market data from the FTSE European option market in LIFFE.

4 Extracting implied distributions from LIFFE FTSE 100 index options.

We apply the finite mixture distribution approach presented above to derive the implied probability distributions of LIFFE European options on the FTSE 100 index. In this section we describe the data, some institutional characteristics of the FTSE 100 option market, and how the proposed methodology can be implemented and modified to account for singular features of the data.

The empirical research is based on a database which contains all reported trades and quotes covering the FTSE100 European index option traded at the LIFFE from January 1, trough December 31, 1997. This data was supplemented by the FTSE 100 European index option settlement price dataset[12]. The data was then used to create a subset of hour-by hour records showing the last available transaction, quote and accumulated hourly volume closest to each time limit.

The FTSE 100 European index option trades between 8:35 to 16:10 GMT. This translates into nine succeeding hourly time limits during the trading day. The interval between exercise prices is determined by the time to maturity of a particular expiry month and is either 50 or 100 index points (i.e. 5225, 5275, ...). The contract is cash settlement based on the exchange delivery settlement price.

As opposed to previous studies on intraday RND extraction it is not possible to obtain a minute-by-minute option price records using our dataset[13]. Although an automatic autoquote system is in place in LIFFE similar to that of the Chicago Board Options Exchange's AutoQuote system[14] there is no indication by examining the updates made on normal trading sessions that these updates take place in a frequent and timely manner. Besides, LIFFE does not keep a record of the quotes supplied to its local autoquote system. This leaves us with a dataset with an incomplete set of strike prices and with many possible non-simultaneous observations within the hourly time basis framework set for the study. In most cases this is the typical situation we would have in option datasets since infrequent trading is the norm rather than the exception of option markets around the world.

The fact that we can encounter non-simultaneity in our dataset is important because a critical requirement for the method proposed for recovering RND is simultaneity in option price observations. Within our framework, there is a

---

[12] Both datasets were generously supplied by MarketData services of LIFFE.

[13] Jackwerth and Rubinstein (1996) used the S&P500 European index dataset traded on the Chicago Board Options Exchange. They were able to use a minute-by-minute dataset with a sufficiently large number of traded strike prices.

[14] The automated quotes are supplied by market makers. A market maker is assigned to update quoted options starting with a deep in the money option. The market maker in charge of the update will with different volatilitities use the Black Scholes formula to set prices for all quoted options.

maximum possible gap between prices of 59 minutes which exacerbates the non-simultaneity problem in observed prices. In this sense, the selection of an hour time framework is somewhat arbitrary. We could have reduced the size of the window, resulting in periods without any observations, or we could have eliminated the time window restriction all together using observations as they came along. In any case, we can modify our system by increasing for example the variability penalty as discussed in the previous section when we suspect the existence of a non-simultaneity problem. The flexibility and strength of the proposed system is evident in this case since we can adapt the optimisation to account for situations of noisy data.

In order to implement the minimisation system we require a risk free interest rate and a dividend yield for the FTSE 100 index. Here we opted for using the implied interest rates and implied dividend yield imbedded in the European put-call parity relation, in much the same way as in Shimko (1993). The implied dividend yield and the implied interest rate calculated in this way fall close to the historical values[15]. The index level used in these calculations is the reported cash FTSE 100 index recorded in the LIFFE dataset.

Finally, in the process of setting up the database, we checked for errors and more specifically for general arbitrage violations. These violations must be eliminated from the data for an implied risk-neutral distribution to exist. With this objective, puts were translated into calls using European put-call parity. For all options we checked that the following condition holds:

$$S_t e^{-d\tau} \geq C_i \geq \max\left[0, S e^{-d\tau} - X_i e^{-r\tau}\right] \qquad (15)$$

We also checked that general spread arbitrage conditions were complied with by the data. As discussed earlier for most of the option markets with which we are concerned there exist a fairly limited number of prices quoted across strikes. The FTSE 100 is not an exception to this rule. Because of this, we prefer to optimise the objective function given in equation (9) as:

$$f(X) = Min_t \sum_{i=1}^{8} \left(\left(c(X_i, \tau) - e^{-r\tau} \int_0^\infty g(S_T)(S_T - X_i) dS_T \right)^{2 \times n_i} \right) \qquad (16)$$

Note the subtle change in the objective function. Now we enter into the minimisation program a new component, n_i, the accumulated traded volume within the hour of a specific strike price. For example, if a specific strike i is not traded at all during the preceding hour (i.e. $n_i=0$) the objective function will ignore the particular strike price. On the contrary when a specific strike is frequently traded,

---

[15] The difference between the implied interest rate and Libor rates over specified time periods are generally unsignificant.

that is investors incorporate new beliefs about the underlying, the program will reinforce that extra knowledge into the system. This feature will also help in reducing the non-simultaneity problem in option price observations exposed above.

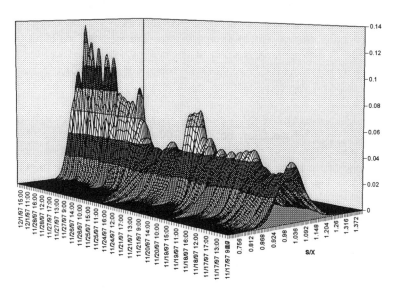

Fig. 1: Hourly implied probability distributions from December 1997 FTSE 100 European Index options. Period Nov. 17, 9:00 AM- Dec. 1, 17:00 PM.

Figure (1) illustrates a typical implied probability distribution. The graph shows 95 hourly implied probability distributions for the December FTSE 100 European index option contract as a function of S/X. Figure 1 also shows that as expiration approaches, the distributions become less dispersed since the market, all other things being equal, becomes more certain about the terminal value due to the smaller likelihood of extreme events occurring. Much of the information contained in the RND functions can be summarised through a range of statistics. Clear candidates are the mean (i.e. the expected future value of the underlying asset), median, mode, standard deviation (analogous to the implied volatility of an option price), skewness, interquartile range and kurtosis. All these statistics are fully defined by the distributions, providing a useful way of tracking the behaviour of the RND functions over the life of a single contract.

4   Conclusion

In this article we have presented the theory that underlines the relationship between option prices to risk-neutral distribution functions and have described a method for estimating such functions. The approach assumes that probability distributions of asset returns can be modelled as a weighted mixture of independent lognormal functions. Using this methodology we have estimated implied probability distributions for FTSE 100 European index options.

By looking at the index probabilities the market participant can track down the behaviour of a market using simple descriptive statistics. It provides a unique measure of volatility and a unique measure for the mean of the distribution, resolving the paradox that volatility implied by options with the same maturity date varies with strike price. We can also check for inconsistencies and suitability of the Black-Scholes model for pricing options. Our analysis with FTSE 100 option data indicates that while Black-Scholes performs well in normal market conditions, it does not behave well in extreme market situations (i.e. long maturity options, when approaching expiration dates). The technique is useful to analyse changes in implied RND functions around specific events, for example in the advent of sudden unexpected movements in the market. In this way, the analysis of implied distributions can help for example in the management of financial risk, forecasting, in assessing monetary or economic policy or in the identification of market anomalies.

An important issue tackled in this paper is the quality and limitations of the data that is available from option markets. This factor can affect considerably the extraction of RND functions. Many options markets are fairly illiquid especially at deep in the money and out of the money strike prices. There is a considerable "staleness" at these outer strikes making them less informative about market expectations. These limitations may sometimes cause irregular changes in the degree of convexity of the option pricing function. We have tried to account for this by introducing several penalty factors in our optimisation program. The bottom line is deciding whether to place reliance on the information extracted. The expectations obtained should be believable in light of the news reaching the market. In the case of the implausible RND functions that on occasion result when there are relatively few data observations across strike prices, we can make use of the mechanisms described above to temper the sensitivity of the lognormal mixture distribution. These mechanisms are mainly the "variability" and the "smoothness" penalties in equation (10). In this sense, a good deal of further research is required to investigate more fully the potential benefit of the proposed method. For example, typical values used for α, α', α'' and α''' in our experiments are 10^4, 10^5, 10^3 and 10^2. This does not mean that we should always have to use the same parameters. Depending on market situations or data availability the values of the parameters would change. As a first step towards solving this problem, it is necessary to define when a particular change in an implied probability distribution is considered significant from a historical point of view. This could be done by establishing appropriate benchmarks such as long term averages for the different summary statistics extracted from the implied RND functions, or by using event studies.

Acknowledgements

The authors wish to thank the British Council and the Finnish CIMO for financial support. The first author acknowledges financial support from a training project by the EU TMR.

References

Aït-Sahalia, Y. and Lo, A., Nonparametric estimation of state price densities implicit in financial asset prices. NBER, working paper, No. 5351, 1995.

Arrow, K.J., The role of securities in the optimal allocation of risk-bearing, Review of Economics Studies 1964, No.2, 91-96.

Bahra, B., Implied risk-neutral probability density functions from option prices: theory and application. Working paper series, n. 66. Bank of England 1997.

Banz, C.A. and Torous, W.N., On jumps in common stock prices and their impact on call option pricing, Journal of Finance 1985, 40, 155-73.

Bates, D.S., The crash of 87: was it expected? The evidence from options markets, Journal of Finance 1991, 46, 1099-44.

Black, F. and Scholes, M., The pricing of options and corporate liabilities, Journal of Political Economy 1973, 81, 637-59.

Breeden, D. and Litzenberger, R., Prices of state-contingent claims implicit in options prices, Journal of Business 1978, 51, 621-651.

Cox, J. and Ross, S., The valuation of options for alternative stochastic processes, Journal of Financial Economics 1976, 3, 145-66.

Debreu, G, *Theory of value*, Wiley, NY, 1959.

Derman, E. and Kani, I., Riding on a smile, RISK 1994, 2, No. 7, 32-38.

Duffie, D. and Pan, J., An overview of value at risk. Journal of Derivatives 1997, Spring, 7-49.

Härdle, W, *Smoothing techniques with implementation in S*, Sp.-Verlag, NY, 1991.

Jackwerth, J. and Rubinstein, M., Recovering probability distributions from contemporaneous security prices, Journal of Finance 1996,51, No. 5, 1611-1631.

Jarrow, R. and Rudd, A., Approximate option valuation for arbitrary stochastic processes, Journal of Financial Economics 1982, 10, 347-69.

Longstaff, F., Option pricing and the martingale restriction, Review of Financial Studies 1995, vol. 8, No. 4, 1091-1124.

Melick, W.R. and Thomas, C.P., Recovering an asset's implied PDF from option prices: an application to crude oil during the gulf crisis, working paper Federal Reserve Board, Washington, 1994.

Ritchey, R.J., Call option valuation for discrete normal mixtures, Journal of Financial Research, vol XIII, No. 4, 285-96, 1990.

Rubinstein, M., Implied binomial trees, Journal of Finance 1994, 49, 771-818.

Shimko, D., Bounds of probability, RISK 1993, 6, No. 4, 33-37.

Titterington, D.M., Smith, A.F.M., Makov, U.E., *Statistical analysis of finite mixture distributions*. John Wiley & Sons, Chichester 1985.

MODELING FINANCIAL TIME SERIES

USING STATE SPACE MODELS

Jens Timmer

Fakultät für Physik, Universität Freiburg
Hermann-Herder Strasse 3, D–79104 Freiburg, Germany

jeti@fdm.uni-freiburg.de
www.fdm.uni-freiburg.de/~jeti

Andreas S. Weigend

Department of Information Systems, Leonard N. Stern School of Business
New York University, 44 West Fourth Street, MEC 9-74 , New York, NY
10012, USA

aweigend@stern.nyu.edu
www.stern.nyu.edu/~aweigend

Abstract. In time series problems, noise can be divided into two categories: dynamic noise which drives the process, and observational noise which is added in the measurement process, but does not influence future values of the system. In this framework, empirical volatilities (the squared relative returns of prices) exhibit a significant amount of observational noise. To model and predict their time evolution adequately, we estimate state space models that explicitly include observational noise. We obtain relaxation times for shocks in the logarithm of volatility. We compare these results with ordinary autoregressive models and find that autoregressive models underestimate the relaxation times by about two orders of magnitude due to their ignoring the distinction between observational and dynamic noise. This new interpretation of the dynamics of volatility in terms of relaxators in a state space model carries over to stochastic volatility models and to GARCH models, and is useful for several problems in finance, including risk management and the pricing of derivative securities.

A.-P.N. Refenes et al. (eds.), Decision Technologies for Computational Finance, 233–246.
© 1998 *Kluwer Academic Publishers. Printed in the Netherlands..*

1   Introduction

Modeling and predicting the volatility of financial time series has become one of the central areas in finance and trading; examples range from pricing derivative securities to computing the risk of a portfolio. Volatility is usually predicted using generalized autoregressive conditional heteroskedastic (GARCH) models; Bollerslev, Engle and Nelson (1995) guide through the GARCH literature, and Engle (1995) collects some of the key papers.

Here we present an alternative to GARCH that models the underlying dynamics using a state space model. This allows us to describe the hidden process in terms of variables natural for a dynamic system, such as decay times for shocks. Stochastic volatility models (see Shephard (1996) for a review) are a variant of the general state space approach presented here. They differ in that the mapping from the hidden variable to the observed variable is nonlinear.

Section 2 defines and explains the formalism of state space models. Section 3 describes the data set used in this study. The results are presented in Section 4. Section 5 summarizes the findings and discusses some of the applications of this approach for noisy time series in finance.

2   Formalism of linear state space models

In time series modeling, one crucial question is whether or not observational noise is present in the data. Observational noise of a high level can pose a severe problem if it is not treated properly, leading to models that underestimate the functional relation between past and future values.

A simple way of generating a time series is through an autoregressive (AR) process of order p, AR[p]

$$x(t) = \sum_{i=1}^{p} a_i \, x(t-i) + \epsilon(t) \quad , \tag{1}$$

where $\epsilon(t)$ denotes an uncorrelated Gaussian distributed random variable with mean zero and constant variance σ^2, $\mathcal{N}(0, \sigma^2)$. Through the eyes of a physicist, such a process can be interpreted as a combination of *relaxators* and *damped oscillators* (Honerkamp 1993). The simplest case is an AR[1] process

$$x(t) = ax(t-1) + \epsilon(t) \tag{2}$$

It can be characterized in the time domain as a relaxator by an exponentially decaying impulse response, proportional to $\exp(-t/\tau)$, with the relaxation time

$$\tau = -\frac{1}{\log a} \tag{3}$$

After this time, the amplitude of an impulse will have decayed to $1/e$ or 37% of its initial value.

In the frequency domain, an AR process can be interpreted as a filter responding to white noise. The power spectrum of an AR[1] process drops off with

$$S(\omega) = \frac{\sigma^2}{|1 - ae^{-i\omega}|^2} = \frac{\sigma^2}{1 + a^2 - 2\cos\omega} \tag{4}$$

By increasing the model order, an AR[2] process can describe an oscillator or two relaxators, an AR[3] process can combine a relaxator with an oscillator, etc.

Despite the simplicity and multiple interpretability of AR models, not all processes in the world are linear autoregressive. Examples of generalizations without hidden states consist of including past q driving noise terms in the dynamics, yielding an autoregressive moving average ARMA[p, q] processes, as well as including nonlinearities. Here we extend autoregressive models in a different direction, by allowing for a hidden state.

In Eq. (1) the $x(t)$ served two roles: it was the variable that was observed, and it was the variable in which the dynamics was expressed. However, there are processes where the dynamics cannot be observed directly because it is masked by observational noise. This requires the notion of a *hidden state*. In terms of notation, we keep the letter x as the variable that contains the dynamics, and use $y(t)$ for the observed variable. The state, characterized by the vector $\vec{x}(t)$, captures all the information needed to characterize the state of the linear state space model (LSSM) at time t:

$$\vec{x}(t) = \mathbf{A}\,\vec{x}(t-1) + \vec{\epsilon}(t), \qquad \vec{\epsilon}(t) \in \mathcal{N}(0, \mathbf{Q}) \tag{5}$$

$$y(t) = \mathbf{C}\,\vec{x}(t) + \eta(t), \qquad \eta(t) \in \mathcal{N}(0, R) \tag{6}$$

Eq. (5) describes the dynamics. Eq. (6) maps the dynamics to the observation and includes the observational noise $\eta(t)$.

As in the case of the observable linear autoregressive model describing the process via physical quantities can yield important insights. The spectrum of a LSSM is given by

$$S(\omega) = \mathbf{C}(1 - \mathbf{A}e^{-i\omega})^{-1}\mathbf{Q}\left((1 - \mathbf{A}e^{i\omega})^{-1}\right)^T \mathbf{C}^T + R \quad . \tag{7}$$

The superscript $(\cdot)^T$ denotes transposition. The spectra of AR processes are a subset of Eq. (7). Note that LSSM spectra include shapes that cannot be generated by AR processes. An important example of such a shape is a spectrum where for low frequencies the power drops similarly to an AR[1] process (see Eq. (4)), but for higher frequencies the power remains constant and does not continue to fall, as an AR model would require it to. This low-frequency signal above a flat noise floor is the crucial *spectral signature* of a LSSM that cannot be emulated by an ordinary autoregressive model.

While parameter estimation in AR models is well established (e.g., by the Burg or the Durbin-Levinson algorithms), it is more cumbersome in the case of state space models . A standard approach uses the expectation maximization (EM) algorithm (Dempster, Laird and Rubin 1977), a general iterative procedure for estimating parameters for models with hidden variables. In the E-step, it is assumed that the parameters of the model are known, and the hidden variables are estimated. In the M-step, the estimates of the hidden variables are taken literally and the values of the parameters are adjusted. This approach was first applied to LSSM by Shumway and Stoffer (1982).

Specifically for the case of the LSSM, the first E-step starts from the initial values of the parameters $\mathbf{A}, \mathbf{Q}, \mathbf{C}, R$, and estimates the hidden dynamic variable $\vec{x}(t)$ using a Kalman filter. With the following definitions

- $z_{t|t'} :=$ the predicted value of a quantity $z(t)$ based on the data $y(1), ..., y(t')$,

- $\Omega_{t|t'} :=$ the covariance matrix of the estimated $\vec{x}(t)$, and

- $\Delta_{t|t'} :=$ the variance of the prediction errors $(y(t) - y_{t|t'})$,

the equations for the Kalman filter are (Kalman 1960):

$$\Omega_{t|t-1} = \mathbf{A}\Omega_{t-1|t-1}\mathbf{A}^T + \mathbf{Q} \tag{8}$$

$$\Delta_{t|t-1} = C\Omega_{t|t-1}C^T + R \tag{9}$$

$$K = \Omega_{t|t-1}C^T\Delta_{t|t-1}^{-1} \tag{10}$$

$$\Omega_{t|t} = (1 - KC)\Omega_{t|t-1} \tag{11}$$

$$\vec{x}_{t|t-1} = A\vec{x}_{t-1|t-1} \tag{12}$$

$$y_{t|t-1} = C\vec{x}_{t|t-1} \tag{13}$$

$$\vec{x}_{t|t} = \vec{x}_{t|t-1} + K(y(t) - y_{t|t-1}) \tag{14}$$

In the subsequent M-step, the parameters A, Q, C, R are updated; the derivation of the equations can be found in Honerkamp (1993). The iterative model fitting process ends when a convergence criterion is met. This concludes the description of how the model parameters are updated in the M-step.

Once a model has been built, its quality can be evaluated by several different criteria, including:

- **Predictive accuracy.** True out-of-sample predictions are generated using Eq. (13) on a test set that comes after the training period.

- **Whiteness of the prediction errors.** The model should explain all temporal correlations in the data: a perfect model takes the signal and turns it into white noise. Statistically, the question is whether we can reject (at a certain level of significance) the null hypothesis that the residuals are uncorrelated. We use the Kolmogorov-Smirnov test to determine whether the periodogram of the residuals is consistent with a flat white noise spectrum.

For linear models, two additional criteria are useful:

- **Behavior in the time domain** (relaxation times). The parameters in linear models are related to relaxation times of the corresponding oscillators and relaxators. When the relaxation times are too small (of order of one time step), they usually only fit noise, indicates that the order of the model is too large.

- **Behavior in the frequency domain** (spectrum). The spectrum of the linear process can be computed from the parameters of the estimated

238

models through Eq. (7). Since the spectrum of the model should correspond to the expectation of the periodogram of the data, comparing the spectrum to the periodogram is another important qualitative criterion.

The suggestions listed here are just some of the useful general criteria that will be used in this article. For any specific problem, there are additional, more specific smoke alarms and sanity checks.

3 Data

This article reports results on the high frequency DEM/USD foreign exchange rates.[1] We began with eight years of data (through June 29, 1995) spaced apart 30 minutes in ϑ-time (Theta-time). We dropped all points with missing values, and then took every fourth of the remaining points for our analysis, effectively downsampling to two hours in ϑ-time. ϑ-time removes daily and weekly seasonality: times of day with a high mean volatility are expanded, and times of day and weekends with low volatility are contracted (Dacorogna, Gauvreau, Müller, Olsen and Pictet 1996).

The top panel of Fig. 1 graphs the level of DEM/USD for the first half of 1995. Its periodogram, shown in the left panel of Fig. 2, drops to first approximation as the spectrum of a random walk whose $1/f^2$ line is also indicated. (f denotes the frequency.) The signature of observational noise—a noise floor masking the signal at high frequencies—is absent: the periodogram continues to drop to the highest time scale. The result is that *price levels* $p(t)$ of financial instruments do not exhibit significant observational noise; all the "noise" on prices is dynamical.

The central panel of Fig. 1 shows the difference of the logarithm of the price levels

$$\log p(t) - \log p(t-1) = \log \frac{p(t)}{p(t-1)} \approx \frac{p(t) - p(t-1)}{p(t-1)} \qquad (15)$$

This quantity can be interpreted as the logarithm of the geometric growths, i.e., as the logarithm of the ratio of the prices which can also be interpreted as the

---

[1]We thank Michel Dacorogna (Olsen & Associates, Zurich) for the high frequency DEM/USD exchange rate data.

returns normalized by the levels, i.e., the *relative returns*. Note in the central panel of Fig. 1 that the width of the "band" varies over time; regimes with larger shocks alternate with regimes with smaller widths. The corresponding periodogram of the relative returns is shown in the right panel of Fig. 2. Note that it is essentially flat: the subsequent returns on the two-hour time scale in ϑ-time appear to be (linearly) uncorrelated.

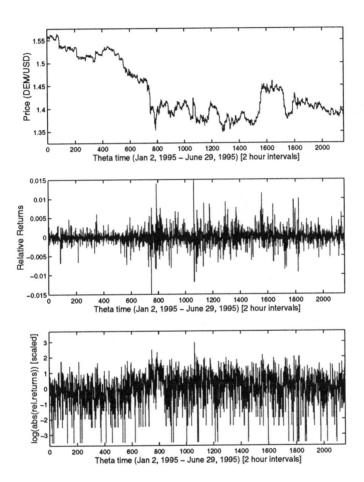

Figure 1: This figure displays a six-month window of the high frequency foreign exchange data, sampled at two hour intervals in ϑ-time. The top panel shows the prices, the middle panel shows the relative returns, and the bottom panel shows the series used in our analysis, i.e., after applying the logarithm and scaling it to zero mean and unit variance.

240

To exploit this observed structure in the absolute values of the relative returns, we square the relative returns, i.e., ignoring their signs. The distribution of the squared returns is very skewed. To make it less skewed, we take their

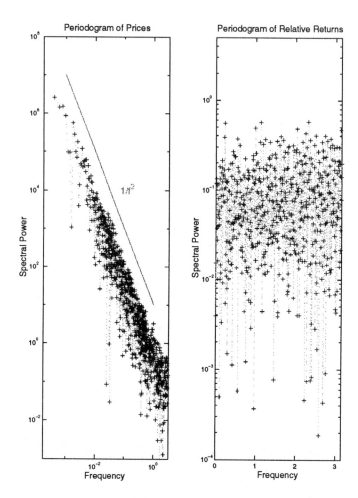

Figure 2: Periodogram of the DEM/USD prices (left), and of the relative returns (right). Expressed in 1/time, the leftmost points correspond to 1/(8 years), 1/(4 years), 1/(2.6 years), 1/(2 years). To guide the eye, we also plotted the $1/f^2$ drop in spectral power of a random walk over six orders of magnitude. The periodogram of the returns on the right hand side is essentially flat. Neither the prices nor the returns indicate the presence of observational noise, in contrast to Fig. 3.

logarithm,

$$y(t) = \log \left[\log \frac{p(t)}{p(t-1)} \right]^2 . \tag{16}$$

The *logarithm of the squared relative returns*, $y(t)$, is shown for the DEM/USD data in the the bottom panel of Fig. 1.

The squared relative returns can be interpreted as independent realizations of a random variable with a slowly changing mean. If the relative returns $\log p(t)/p(t-1)$ were normally distributed with unit variance, their squares would follow a χ_1^2 distribution. The variance of this χ^2 distribution is twice its mean, implying that the realizations are very noisy indeed! This is the source of the observational noise for volatility. On empirical data, it is well known that the relative returns $\log p(t)/p(t-1)$ are not normally distributed, but have fatter tails. However, the spirit of the explanation for the observational noise still applies; see also Diebold and Lopez (1995).

Fig. 3 shows this effect. The periodogram of the data contains most of its power at low frequencies. Subsequently, as the frequency increases, it begins to drop. Finally, it flattens out as the signal gets masked by this "observational noise," stemming from the noisy realizations of the slowly changing means of the squared returns.

4 Results

Table 1 summarizes the results for the high frequency DEM/USD data, comparing linear state space models with ordinary AR models. The linear state space models differ crucially from the AR models in the decay times τ: while the decay times of the state space models are significant, they are negligible for the AR models where the processes typically decay within one time step. Since the state space model is fitted to $y(t)$ as defined in Eq. (16), the decay times characterize when the logarithm of the squared relative returns has decayed to 37% of its initial value.

For first order models describing a single relaxator, there is a huge difference in decay time between 156 time steps for the LSSM in contrast to an insignificant 0.45 time steps for the AR process. The eigenvalues of the second order models turn out to be real; the process thus corresponds to the superposition of two relaxators. The slower one of the two relaxators settles to around 240 of the 2-hour steps and corresponds to 20 days, whereas the slower AR relaxator still decays in a single time step. Using third order an oscillator emerges whose resonance frequencies $1/T$ correspond to about one day. This might indicate a tiny amount of periodicity left after the transformation of the

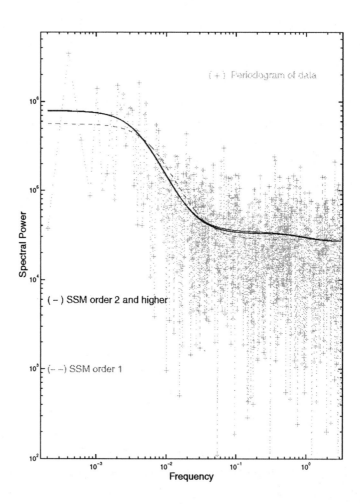

Figure 3: Periodogram ("+") of the DEM/USD exchange rates, and spectra of the estimated state space models (SSM) of order one (dashed line) and orders two and three (solid lines).

raw data to ϑ-time, but they do not contribute significantly to the dynamics since its relaxation time is a few time steps only.

Models	τ (decay times) 1 step = 2 hours	Coefficients			Prob white noise	E
$LSSM(1)$	156	0.994			0	0.960
$LSSM(2)$	240, 1.09	0.996 0 0 0.399			0.72	0.957
$LSSM(3)$	236 $[T = 17\ \tau = 1.6]$	0.966 0 0 0 0.507 −0.188 0 0.188 0.507			0.57	0.957
$AR(1)$	0.45	0.107			0	0.988
$AR(2)$	0.85, 0.64	0.100 0.066			0	0.984
$AR(3)$	1.25 $[T = 6.5\ \tau = 0.86]$	0.097 0.062 0.044			2e-6	0.982

Table 1: Results for the volatilities of the DEM/USD exchange rates. While linear state space models (LSSM) of order two and three fit the data well, ordinary AR models cannot explain the structure of the data.

The decay constants presented here are defined for the logarithm of the squared relative returns. Nonlinear transformations do not allow for an amplitude-independent interpretations of decay times in general. However, fitting state space models directly to the absolute or squared relative returns (without taking the logarithm) yields similar decay constants. This implies that our characterization also hold for stochastic volatility models.

The fourth column in Table 1 shows that the residuals of the state space model of order one are not consistent with white noise, implying that a first order LSSM does not describe the data adequately. However, the higher order LSSMs produce residuals consistent with white noise at a significance level of 0.05 for the Kolmogorov-Smirnov test on the whiteness of the residuals (Brockwell and Davis 1991). None of the residuals of the AR models are consistent with white noise.

The last column gives the normalized mean squared error, E, between the observed $y(t)$ and the predictions obtained via Eq. (13). Whereas for LSSM, the error drops quickly to a constant level of 0.957 at order 2, it decreases for AR models at a much slower rate, and also remains at a higher level. In an

AR(1) model, for example, E takes the value of 0.973, still significantly above the value of the second order LSSM.

The curves in Fig. 3 are the power spectra of the state space models They are computed using Eq. (7). There is a clear difference between the first order spectrum and the higher order spectra. The higher orders ($\geqslant$ 2) are very similar, indicating that the second order state space model is indeed sufficient. The spectra of the state space models correspond well to the periodogram of the data.

The failure of AR models is a consequence of the observational noise that is present in the volatility data and not considered by the AR models. In presence of observational noise the parameters in AR models are underestimated. This effect is known from linear regression as the problem of *errors-in-variables* (Fuller 1987).

5   Summary and Applications

This article showed the important distinction between observational and dynamic noise. When observational noise is present, an autoregressive approach cannot model the data adequately—a state space approach is needed to capture the hidden dynamics. Volatilities do exhibit signature of observational noise in the periodogram: for low frequencies, there is structure above the noise floor of observational noise.

We showed on an examplary financial data sets that a linear state space model can describe volatilities well. We also showed that the resulting models can be nicely interpreted, both from the perspective of physics as a superposition of two simple relaxators, and from the perspective of finance as volatility clustering with a decay time of about three weeks These results are in strong contrast to AR models that ignore observational noise. The more promising modeling approach using state space models over AR models for volatility suggests several applications in financial markets, including

- **Estimating risk.** Knowing the evolution of the volatility is important for determining the risk associated with a position on a financial instrument: the volatility can be interpreted as the conditional standard deviation of the returns.

- **Pricing derivative securities.** Using financial theory, discrepancies between the predicted volatility and the implied volatility can be translated into mispricings, which can in turn be exploited in trading.

- **Information for regime switching models.** The predicted volatility can be an important input for trading models based on the "gated experts" architecture (Weigend, Mangeas and Srivastava 1995). In this case, the hidden state is offered as an additional input to the gate to help determine the current region.

Acknowledgments

Jens Timmer gratefully acknowledges the hospitality of the Information Systems Department of NYU's Leonard N. Stern School of Business. Andreas Weigend thanks Joel Hasbrouck and Steve Figlewski for their comments, as well as the participants of the NBER/NSF Forecasting Seminar for discussions at the NBER 1997 Summer Institute, and acknowledges support from the National Science Foundation (ECS-9309786) and the Air Force Office of Scientific Research (F49620-96-1-0240).

References

Bollerslev, T., Engle, R. F. and Nelson, D. B. (1995). ARCH models, *in* R. F. Engle and D. L. McFadden (eds), *Handbook of Econometrics*, Vol. 4, North-Holland, New York, NY, chapter 49.

Brockwell, P. J. and Davis, R. A. (1991). *Time Series: Theory and Methods*, Springer-Verlag, New York.

Dacorogna, M. M., Gauvreau, C. L., Müller, U. A., Olsen, R. B. and Pictet, O. V. (1996). Changing time scale for short-term forecasting in financial markets, *Journal of Forecasting* **15**: 203–227.

Dempster, A., Laird, N. and Rubin, D. (1977). Maximum likelihood from incomplete data via EM algorithm, *J. Roy. Stat. Soc.* **39**: 1–38.

246

Diebold, F. X. and Lopez, J. A. (1995). Modeling volatility dynamics, *in* K. Hoover (ed.), *Macroeconometrics: Developments, Tensions, and Prospects*, Kluwer Academic Press, Boston, pp. 427–472.

Engle, R. F. (ed.) (1995). *ARCH: Selected Readings*, Oxford University Press, Oxford, UK.

Fuller, W. A. (1987). *Measurement Error Models*, John Wiley, New York.

Honerkamp, J. (1993). *Stochastic Dynamical Systems*, VCH, New York.

Kalman, R. E. (1960). A new approach to linear filtering and prediction problems, *Trans. ASME J. Basic Eng. Series D* **82**: 35–45.

Shephard, N. (1996). Statistical aspects of ARCH and stochastic volatility, *in* D. R. Cox, D. V. Hinkley and O. E. Barndorff-Nielsen (eds), *Time Series Models In Econometrics, Finance and Other Fields*, Chapman and Hall, London, pp. 1–67.

Shumway, R. and Stoffer, D. (1982). An approach to time series smoothing and forecasting using the EM algorithm, *J. Time Ser. Anal.* **3**: 253–264.

Weigend, A. S., Mangeas, M. and Srivastava, A. N. (1995). Nonlinear gated experts for time series: Discovering regimes and avoiding overfitting, *International Journal of Neural Systems* **6**: 373–399.

FORECASTING PROPERTIES OF NEURAL NETWORK GENERATED VOLATILITY ESTIMATES

PARVEZ AHMED
Department of Finance and Business Law
The Belk College of Business Administration
University of North Carolina at Charlotte
Charlotte, NC 28223, USA
E-mail: pahmed@email.uncc.edu
http://www.uncc.edu/~pahmed/

STEVE SWIDLER[1]
Department of Finance and Real Estate
College of Business Adminstration
University of Texas at Arlington
Arlington, TX 76019, USA
E-mail: swidler@uta.edu

The price of an option, from an arbitrage pricing model, as an estimate of the option's fair market value is only as good as the volatility measures being used. Investors having access to superior forecasts of future volatility are likely to devise trading strategies that would generate profits by identifying mispriced options. The extant literature considers informational efficiency and finds that implied volatility is not an unbiased forecast of future volatility. The analysis suggests that implied volatility is related to moneyness, time to maturity and the ratio of put-to-call trading volume, however, the exact functional relation is unknown. In the absence of a known functional form, artificial neural networks (ANN) can generate a model that captures this systematic relationship. Results using equity option data show that, in general, neural networks do not produce superior estimates of future volatility.

1   Introduction

An unbiased estimate of the future volatility of asset returns is of great interest to investors in general and option traders in particular. A model's option price as an estimate of the option's fair market value is only as good as the volatility measure being used. Thus, investors having access to superior forecasts of future volatility are likely to devise trading strategy that could generate profit by identifying mispriced options.

---

[1] Currently visiting at Southern Methodist University, Dallas, Texas.

A.-P.N. Refenes et al. (eds.), Decision Technologies for Computational Finance, 247–258.
© 1998 *Kluwer Academic Publishers. Printed in the Netherlands.*.

If volatility is constant over time then historical or past volatility will simply be the best estimate of future volatility. However, if volatility is stochastic then neither historical volatility nor the volatility implied by constant volatility option pricing models (such as the Black-Scholes) can provide unbiased estimates of future volatility. Although stochastic volatility models provide an alternative to the limitations imposed by the Black-Scholes model, they are difficult to implement. (Canina and Figlewski 1993) argue that it is appropriate to use implied volatility from constant volatility models as it is most likely to be used by traders. The constant volatility option pricing models do suffer from some systematic biases with respect to moneyness and time to maturity. Moreover, they do not incorporate other information contained in the market such as historical volatility and trading volume. This study argues that by empirically modeling the information ignored by option pricing models it may be possible to estimate future volatility whose information is superior to that of volatility implied by option prices.

(Canina and Figlewski 1993, Rubinstein 1994, Derman and Kani 1994 and Dumas and Fleming 1995) find implied volatility is a U-shaped function with respect to moneyness. The in- and out-of-the money options have higher implied volatility than the at-the-money options. Further, (Canina and Figlewski 1993 and Clarke 1994) find implied volatility to be a decreasing function of time to expiration. Moreover, (Ahmed and Swidler 1996) show that implied volatility for Norwegian equity options has lower informational content during periods when the put trading volume is very high relative to the trading volume in calls. They attribute this to the restriction on selling Norwegian stocks short on the Oslo Stock Exchange.

(Figlewski 1989) notes, the market uses all information contained in the market to form an estimate of future volatility and does not necessarily conclude that implied volatility is an unbiased forecast of future volatility. While it is empirically known that implied volatility has systematic relation to moneyness, time to maturity and ratio of put-to-call trading volume their exact functional relation is unknown. In the absence of a known functional form, artificial neural networks (ANN) can generate a model that captures this systematic relationship.

Artificial neural networks (ANN) are mathematical, algorithmic software models that acquires knowledge through a learning process. ANN can provide an accurate approximation of any function of the input vector. Neural networks do not make any rigid assumption about the structure of the model but estimate it from the available data. Thus, ANN is merely a non-linear multiple regression model with coefficients estimated through minimization of the usual mean squared estimation error (White 1989a, 1989b).

2   Data

Data for the study consists of transactions prices for stock and call options traded on the Oslo Stock Exchange. This paper analyzes stock and options on Norsk Hydro (NHY), Saga Petroleum (SAG) and Bergesen (BEB) for the time period May, 1990-June, 1993. Data for Hafslund Nycomed A (HNA) covers the period December, 1991-June, 1993. The data for this study reflects the universe of options trading on the OSE for the period May 1990 to June 1993.

The data set first matches a call with the underlying stock transaction price that immediately precedes the option trade. The analysis then calculates the implied volatility for each call option using the methodology described in (Jarrow and Rudd 1983). Call options that violate the lower boundary condition i.e., their market price is less than the current dividend adjusted stock price minus the strike price, have a negative implied volatility and are excluded from the study. The study also eliminates options with fewer than 7 days to expiration and those that are more than 20% in- or out-of-the money.

3   Research Design

3.1   Variable Selection

Most studies on forecasting volatility assume future volatility to depend solely on implied volatility or historical volatility. However, the more recent evidence shows implied volatility to be only one element of the information set that explains future volatility. Results from (Ahmed and Swidler 1996) show implied volatility for the Norwegian options has systematic relationship with moneyness M, time to maturity, τ, and ratio of put-to-call trading volume over the previous three days, PC3. In the presence of short selling restrictions on the OSE, the ratio of put-to-call volume may proxy for the negative sentiment of the market. While the variable PC3 captures the immediate negative concerns of market participants it may fail to account for more persistent concerns over relatively longer time periods. Persistent negative concerns about a stock will translate into higher put-to-call trading volume over relatively longer time periods. This persistence in negative sentiment, may be captured by the put-to-call trading volume over the previous ten days, PC10. (Stein 1989) show volatility of stock returns to be mean reverting i.e. over longer periods of time, volatility reverts to its long run mean. The implication is that in the long run, history will repeat itself. But markets are forward looking and (Choi and Wohar 1992) show that past or historical volatility, do not always anticipate future volatility. So like implied volatility, historical volatility is unlikely to be an unbiased predictor of future volatility in the short run. However, in the long run, the mean reversion characteristic of volatility is likely to make historical volatility an important element of the information set used to predict future volatility.

This study conjectures that some of the factors that may be part of a trader's information set in forming an expectation of future volatility are implied volatility, IV, moneyness, M, time to maturity, τ, standard deviation of stock returns over previous thirty trading days (historical volatility), HV30, ratio of average put to call trading volume over previous three trading days, PC3 and ratio of average put to call trading volume over previous ten trading days, PC10. However, implied volatility, IV, is also a function of moneyness, M and time to maturity, τ. The proper model is then to have IV as a dependent variable. This introduces a new dependent variable volatility bias, VB, which is the difference of FV and IV. Volatility bias indicates the error made by implied volatility as a forecast of future volatility. The ANN model estimates VB:

$$FV - IV = VB = \mathcal{F}(M, \tau, HV30, PC3, PC10). \tag{1}$$

Adding IV to forecasts of VB on out of sample data gives the neural network's forecast of future volatility, NNV:

$$NNV = IV + VB. \tag{2}$$

3.2 Volatility Measures

The Norwegian equity options are American options with known discrete dividend payments. Given the possibility of early exercise, the appropriate model to price these American options is the (Cox-Ross-Rubinstein 1979) Binomial Option Pricing Model.

3.3 Tests for Linearity

The current financial literature do not provide any insight into the nature of the relationship, linear or nonlinear, between volatility bias, VB, and the other variables, X = (M, τ, HV30, PC3, PC10). Just fitting a flexible nonlinear model may lead to data mining if nonlinearity is not present. Hence the study first tests for the presence of nonlinearity between VB_t and X_t using three methods from (Lee, White and Granger 1993).

3.4   Artificial Neural Network (ANN)

This study uses a particular type of ANN--the Multi-Layer Perceptrons (MLP), with feedforward back propagation training algorithm. The three layers are the input, middle (hidden) and output layers. Each neuron in the network transmits a signal to each neuron in the succeeding layer over a weighted connection. Thus the network is fully connected between layers.

To test the proposition, implied volatility is the "best" estimate of future volatility, the study will compare the forecasting properties of implied volatility (IV) to those computed by the neural network (NNV). Comparison between IV and NNV will be made on out of sample data.

The neural network trains using the following steps. In step one, randomly choose ten observations spanning approximately a week's option prices. These ten observations are set aside and form the *production set*. Twenty such production sets will test the forecasting properties of the neural network. Moreover, the observations in the production set do not have options expiring after the first trading date in the remaining data. The sample on which the neural network "trains" consists of 110 observations spanning approximately a quarter of a year. From these 110 observations, 12.5% are assigned to the *test set* and the remaining observations belong to the *training set*. This process is repeated twenty times. Finally, the network "trains" on the training sets, validates its training on the test sets and forecasts on the production sets. Thus, out of sample forecasts are generated for two hundred observations for each production set.

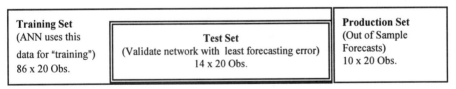

Figure 1: Stratification of the data for each stock

The neural network for this study employs the back propagation training algorithm. Back propagation, a supervised learning technique, requires a training set of input-output pairs. The net behaves as a functional imitator, mapping each of the 5 input vectors (HV30, PC3, PC10, M and τ) in X_p to their corresponding output vector, VB_p. Thus, there are P input-output pairs (patterns) and the network will have $n = 5$, input and $m = 1$, output nodes. The control parameter is the single hidden layer with h nodes. In the learning algorithm, the individual neurons have a sigmoidal response curve to their respective inputs. The sigmoidal response function chosen here is the *logistic* function.

Training consists of presenting an input pattern, X_p with a known, desired output, VB_p. Comparing output, y_p, to the desired response, VB_p shows the error made due to the network's current weighted inputs. Back propagation involves computing this error and sending it back to the middle layer across connections and then letting the network readjust the weighted inputs. The network aims at minimizing this error or cost function, E:

$$E = \frac{1}{2Pm}\sum_{p=1}^{P}\sum_{i=1}^{m}(y_{p,i} - VB_{p,i})^2,$$

(3)

where $y_{p,i}$ is the network's estimated output and $VB_{p,i}$ is the desired response for the output node i for pattern p. For each input-output pair the process repeats 10,000 times allowing completion of the learning process. At pre-specified intervals, the network uses the test set to generate forecasts and again estimate an average error. With readjusted weighting of the input vector, the error in the test set decreases and then starts increasing. The "best" model is then the one for which the average error is lowest on the test set.

The "best trained" network now forecasts the volatility bias on the out-of-sample production sets. Averaging the volatility bias over all neural networks yields average forecasts. Adding implied volatility to the average forecast yields an estimate of the neural networks prediction of future volatility, NNV. Tests of informational content of NNV follow the informational content and encompassing regression with bootstrapping to account for serial correlation.

3.5   Comparison of Forecasts

Mean absolute error (MAE) for IV or NNV is the mean of the absolute deviation of implied volatility or NNV from future volatility. However, the mean square error (MSE) measures the mean of the squared deviations of IV or NNV from future volatility. Both measures provide a way of detecting superiority of forecast among competing estimates (Malliaris and Salchenberger 1994).

4   Results

Table 1 reports the average implied volatility in various sub-samples stratified on moneyness and time to maturity. The results show a systematic relationship of implied volatility with moneyness and time to maturity. On average, the out- and in-the-money sub-samples have higher implied volatility than the at-the-money sub-samples. The general form of these relationships are in figures 2 and 3. In figure 2, implied volatility is U shaped ('smile') with respect to moneyness. However, for options with the same number of days to expirations, future volatility is a constant. Thus, future volatility graphs as a horizontal line with respect to moneyness. Volatility bias, the difference between future volatility and implied volatility will then have an inverted U shape with respect to moneyness.

Table 1: Implied Volatility Across Subsamples on Moneyness and Maturity

This table provides estimates of average implied volatility of the various aggregated sample for all stock options. Column one and five refer to the sample used (e.g., BEB-O implies it is the out-of-money sample for the option on BEB, BEB-A implies it is the at-the-money sample for the option on BEB, BEB-I implies it is the in-the-money sample for the option on BEB. BEB-T1, BEB-T2 and BEB-T3 are for BEB subsamples with time to maturity 7-30 days, 31-90 days and greater than 90 days respectively.

Sub-Sample	IV	Average Maturity	Average Moneyness	Sub-Sample	IV	Average Maturity	Average Moneyness
A. Implied volatility by moneyness group				*B. Implied volatility by time to maturity group*			
BEB-O	0.4093	78.24	0.92	BEB-T1	0.4094	26.29	1.00
BEB-A	0.3890	70.02	1.00	BEB-T2	0.3956	65.91	0.98
BEB-I	0.3928	67.42	1.08	BEB-T3	0.3976	118.82	0.97
HNA-O	0.2947	79.31	0.94	HNA-T1	0.3724	26.28	1.00
HNA-A	0.2984	62.22	1.00	HNA-T2	0.2895	64.97	0.98
HNA-I	0.3321	66.78	1.07	HNA-T3	0.2648	120.61	0.98
NHY-O	0.2977	81.28	0.93	NHY-T1	0.3144	29.92	1.00
NHY-A	0.2895	61.66	1.00	NHY-T2	0.2902	64.96	1.00
NHY-I	0.3018	61.12	1.06	NHY-T3	0.2865	116.46	0.99
SAG-O	0.4361	78.62	0.92	SAG-T1	0.4430	27.19	1.00
SAG-A	0.4181	69.18	1.00	SAG-T2	0.4162	66.33	0.99
SAG-I	0.4334	65.93	1.09	SAG-T3	0.4328	117.01	0.99

Table 1 also shows that the implied volatility of options with greater than 90 days to maturity are generally lower than options expiring in less than 30 days.

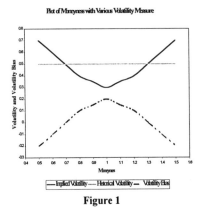

Figure 1

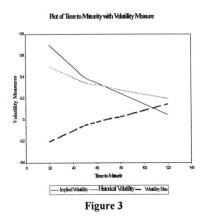

Figure 3

Moreover, volatility when computed over longer periods of time is generally lower. Figure 3, plots the general form of this relationship. Both future volatility and implied volatility are shown to be decreasing functions of time to maturity. Thus, volatility bias will be increasing at a decreasing rate for increases in to time to maturity. In the rare case, when both implied and future volatility are parallel, volatility bias will be a horizontal line. Figure 3, shows volatility bias to have a positive slope. This is true when implied volatility has a higher slope and intersects future volatility from above. However, for instances when implied volatility has a lower slope than future volatility and intersects the curve for future volatility from below, volatility bias will be downward sloping. In other words, the exact shape of volatility bias with respect to time to maturity depends on the relative slopes of future and implied volatility.

Table 2 reports the relative importance of the input variables in explaining the dependent variable, volatility bias. The variables that contribute the least are M and τ. The variables that contribute the most are HV30 and put-call trading volume ratios. This seems a little counter-intuitive. Much of the extant literature has shown that implied volatility has a significant systematic relationship with moneyness and time to maturity. However, (Ahmed and Swidler 1996) shows that for the Norwegian market put-to-call trading volume is indeed a significant variable in explaining the information content of implied volatility. They attribute this mainly to the restriction on OSE for short-selling Norwegian stocks.

Table 2: Average Rank of the Input Variables Showing Their Relative Contribution in Explaining Variation in Volatility Bias

PC3 = ratio of the three day put-to-call trading volume, PC10 = ratio of the ten day put-to-call trading volume, HV30 = thirty day historical volatility, τ = days to maturity and M = moneyness are ranked by their contribution in explaining volatility bias in each of the ten models.

Stock	Input Variables				
	PC3	PC10	HV30	τ	M
BEB	2	3	1	4	5
HNA	3	2	1	4	5
NHY	2	1	3	4	5
SAG	1	2	4	3	5

RESET statistics from the models in (Lee, White and Granger 1993) allow determination of possible non-linearity in relationship between volatility bias and the input vectors. Table 3 reports the RESET statistics. With RESET statistics being greater than the critical values, the null hypothesis of a linear relationship between volatility bias and the five input variables is rejected. This shows that the relationship between input and output variables are non-linear. In the absence of theory based understanding of modeling the non-linear relationship between volatility bias and the set of input vectors, this study uses ANN to empirically model this relationship.

Table 3: Tests for Non-Linearity

Tests for the presence of nonlinearity between VB and X = (M, τ, HV30, PC3, PC10), using three methods are from Lee, White and Granger (1993). The first test statistics is RESETk, where k = 2, 3, 4 and where n is the number of observations, follows a $F(k-1, n-k)$ distribution. RESETp$_m$ also follows $F(p_m, n-k)$ where p_m is number of principal components. RESETR^2 follows $\chi^2(p_m)$. * Significant at the 5% level

	BEB	HNA	NHY	SAG
RESET2	14.698*	19.830*	30.055*	18.270*
RESET3	7.499*	14.562*	22.829*	12.491*
RESET4	14.421*	9.724*	18.199*	13.457*
RESETp$_m$	10.321*	27.042*	21.965*	20.629*
RESETR^2	32.137*	12.300*	38.640*	18.220*

Mean squared errors (MSE) and mean absolute error (MAE) allow comparison between various forecasts (IV and NNV) of future volatility. Table 4 reports the MSE and MAE for the forecasts of future volatility IV and NNV. The results show that the neural networks forecast of future volatility, NNV, is insignificantly different from implied volatility, IV, in 2 out of the 4 stocks studied. In only one case NNV is superior to IV. However, NNV is also seen to be inferior to IV in one instance. This study shows that implied volatility, though not an unbiased estimate of future volatility, often remains the "best" estimate.

Table 4: Comparison of Forecast Bias for Production Set

Mean Square Error (MSE) and Mean Absolute Errors (MAE) allow comparison between the forecasting power of implied volatility, IV and neural network's estimate of volatility, NNV. SD = Standard Deviation for MSE or MAE and t-statistics = t-statistics for the difference in MSE or MAE between IV and FV. * Significant at the 5% level

	NNV	IV		NNV	IV
		BEB			
MSE	0.0478	0.0458	*MAE*	0.1819	0.0783
SD	0.0138	0.0134	*SD*	0.0406	0.0343
t-statistics	-0.0204		*t-statistics*	-0.0362	
		HNA			
MSE	0.3011	0.0070	*MAE*	0.3544	0.0008
SD	0.0531	0.0035	*SD*	0.0446	0.0230
t-statistics	-12.353*		*t-statistics*	-12.811*	
		NHY			
MSE	0.0138	0.0106	*MAE*	0.1014	0.0872
SD	0.0083	0.0041	*SD*	0.0258	0.0228
t-statistics	-1.0909		*t-statistics*	-1.2223	
		SAG			
MSE	0.0199	0.0300	*MAE*	0.1140	0.1451
SD	0.0091	0.0156	*SD*	0.0102	0.0470
t-statistics	1.9025*		*t-statistics*	1.5762	

5   Conclusions

Current ANN technology does not permit estimates of future volatility that is superior to implied volatility. However, in the future, with more advanced neural networks it may be possible to produce estimates that are superior to implied volatility. If volatility is stochastic then it makes forecasting very difficult using the tools currently available to traders. However, if volatility is relatively deterministic (as was the case for SAG) then it is indeed possible to improve on the estimate of future volatility coming from implied volatility alone. But for cases with stochastic volatility a simple feed forward network is unlikely to yield better volatility forecasts. Future work in this area should perhaps focus on some type of recurrent architecture and try to incorporate any time series properties of volatility within the neural network model.

6   References

Ahmed, P. and S. Swidler, "The Relation Between the Informational Content of Implied Volatility and Arbitrage Costs: Evidence from the Oslo Stock Exchange", forthcoming in *International Review of Economics and Finance*.

Canina, L. and S. Figlewski, "The Information Content of Implied Volatility", *The Review of Financial Studies,* 1993; 6, 659-681

Choi, S., and M.E. Wohar, "Implied Volatility in Options Markets and Conditional Heteroscedasticity in Stock Markets", *The Financial Review*, 1992; 27, 503-530

Clarke, R.G., "Estimating and Using Volatility: Part 2", *Derivatives Quarterly*, 1994; 35-40

Cox, J.C., S.A. Ross, and M. Rubinstein "Option Pricing: A Simplified Approach", *Journal of Financial Economics,* 1979; 7, 229-263

Derman, E., and I. Kani Riding on a Smile, *Risk*, 1994; 7(4), 2-9

Dumas, B., J. Fleming, and R.E. Whaley "Implied Volatility Smiles: Empirical Tests", *Duke University Working Paper*, 1995

Figlewski, S. "What Does an Option Pricing Model Tell Us About Option Prices", *Financial Analysts Journal*, 1989; 12-15

Jarrow, R.A., and A. Rudd, *Option Pricing*, 1983; Richard D. Irwin, IL.

Lee, T,. H. White, and C.W.J. Granger "Testing for Neglected Nonlinearity in Time

258

Series Models", *Journal of Econometrics*, 1993; 56, 269-290

Malliaris, M. And L. Salchenberger, "Neural Networks for Predicting Options Volatility", in *Proceedings of World Congress on Neural Networks*, 1994; Vol 2, San Diego, Lawrence Earlbaum Associates, Hillsdale, NJ, 290-295

Rubinstein, M. "Implied Binomial Tree", *Journal of Finance*, 1994; 49 (3), 771-818

Stein, J. "Overreaction in the Options Market", *Journal of Finance*, 1989; 44, 1011-1023

White, H. "Learning Artificial Neural Network Models: A Statistical Perspective", *Neural Computation*, 1989a; 1, 425-464

White, H. "An additional Hidden Unit Test for Neglected Non-Linearity in Multilayer Feedforward Networks", *Proceedings of the International Joint Conference on Neural Networks*, 1989c; Washington DC. IEEE Press, New York, 2, 451-455

INTEREST RATES STRUCTURE DYNAMICS: A NON PARAMETRIC APPROACH

MARIE COTTRELL
Université de Paris 1
SAMOS
90 rue de Tolbiac, F-75634 Paris Cedex 13, France
E-mail : cottrell@univ-paris1.fr

ERIC DE BODT
Université de Lille 2 - ESA
Université catholique de Louvain - CGEF
1 pl. des Doyens, B-1348 Louvain-la-Neuve, Belgium
E-mail : debodt@fin.ucl.ac.be

PHILIPPE GRÉGOIRE
University of Namur
CeReFim
8 Rempart de la Vierge, 5000 Namur, Belgium
E-mail : philippe.gregoire@fundp.ac.be

The rapid growth of new "exotic" interest rate derivatives, especially the important classes of path-dependent, has required the introduction of models capable of pricing and hedging these instruments which are dependent on correlated movements of the different maturity of the yield curve. Beyond the valuation models, financial institutions have a crucial need for risk management tools. One of the most important contribution to risk management in the 90s has been the development and implementation of the so called Value at Risk (VaR). To estimate VaR numbers, one needs to establish specific assumptions about the future behavior of the prices or of the factors (yield curve) that explain the prices in the case of an existing model that links the factors to the prices. In this paper, we use the Kohonen algorithm together with a Monte-Carlo simulation to generate long term path of the yield curve. To test the accuracy of our method to reproduce future paths that has the same stochastic properties than the historical path, we use both Cox, Ingersoll and Ross and Longstaff and Schwartz interest rate model to generate such an "historical" path. We then use the Generalized Method of Moments to verify if the simulated paths have the same properties than the "historical" ones.

1   Introduction

The valuation of interest rate contingent claims is a field of importance due to the growth of their use. A common approach starts with the specification of the dynamics of the factors that drive the interest rates structure movements. The one-factor model (for example, Vasiceck [1977], Cox, Ingersoll Ross [1985]) assumes a

A.-P.N. Refenes et al. (eds.), Decision Technologies for Computational Finance, 259–266.

dynamic for the instantaneous interest rate and the two-factors model (for example, Longstaff, Schwartz [1992]) assumes the dynamics of both the instantaneous interest rate and its volatility. Another approach considers that the initial term structure is known and that its dynamic is exogenously given. For example, Ho and Lee [1986] assume that of the term structure follows a binomial process. Most recently, Heath, Jarrow and Morton [1992] have developed a new methodology to price interest rates contingent claims. They obtain necessary and sufficient conditions that ensure that the dynamic of the forward rates are arbitrage-free. With this family of process and the no-arbitrage condition, one can price any contingent claim by discounting the future payoffs. Beyond the valuation, there is a crucial need for risk management. One of the most important contribution to risk management in the 90s has been the development and implementation of the so called Value at Risk (VaR), largely known through the promotion of RiskMetrics par JPMorgan. VaR is defined as the maximum possible loss for a given position or portfolio within a known confidence interval over a specific time horizon (in the case of a one day horizon, VaR is called Daily Earnings at Risk (DeaR)). To estimate VaR numbers, one needs to establishe specific assumptions about the future behavior of the prices or of the factors that explain the prices in the case of an existing model that links the factors to the prices. For example, as the price of a coupon bond is given by discounting future coupons and principal by the interest rate prevailing for each payment date, VaR numbers will be obtained by assuming the behavior of the interest rates.

In recent studies, the authors have proposed a new methodology to generate future paths of interest rates structure that have the same properties as the historical data (Cottrell, de Bodt, Grégoire [1996], [1997]). This methodology is called a non-parametric approach because we do not impose any functional form for the interest rates process or the underlying factors. The aim of this paper is to test the accuracy of the method to reproduce interest rates paths that are compatible with the observed historical data. To achieve this, we will generate a single path of the interest rates structure with the one-factor model of Cox, Ingersoll and Ross [1985] and another path with the two-factors model of Longstaff and Schwartz [1992]. With these "theoretical" data and the proposed non parametric approach we will generate several future paths for the interest rates structure. Then, we will test whether or not these paths have the same properties as the dynamic underlying both the one and two-factors models.

2   Methodology

2.1   Algorithm

To simulate the future behavior of a process using historical data, we start from a matrix composed by observations of the process at different times (each row corresponds to a point in time). The process can be characterized by one or several state variables (in other words, it can be one or multi dimensional). The initial matrix, denoted **D**, is of size $[r \times c]$, where r is the number of observations and c the number of state variables. The first step of our approach is, as for a lot of classical time series analysis methods, to choose a lagging order. The initial data matrix, **D**, is then modified to incorporate, for each row, the vector of the observed variables as well as the past realizations of those ones. The new data matrix, **LD**, is of size $[(r - \lambda) \times (c \times \lambda)]$, where λ is the lagging order. Rows of **LD** are denoted $x_t = (x_{t,1}, \cdots, x_{t,n})$, where t is the time index and $n \in (c \times \lambda)$. The **LD** matrix is then decomposed into a number of homogeneous clusters, using the Kohonen algorithm[1]. To each unit of the Kohonen map is associated, after learning, a number of individuals for which this unit is the winning one. The clusters are so formed. For each unit, the mean profile $\bar{x}_i$ of the attached individuals is calculated. As λ, the choice of the number of clusters will depend on the features of the analyzed process. The observation of the homogeneity of the clusters (for example, the Fisher statistics or one of its multidimensional extensions) obtained after learning is a good indicator.

For each row x_t of the **LD** matrix, the associated deformation is then computed. It is denoted y_t and is obtained by the following calculation: $y_t = x_{t+\tau} - x_t$, where τ is a time delay. On this basis, for each cluster of the **LD** matrix, a P_i matrix, composed by the y_t corresponding to the x_t of the cluster i, is formed.

For each P_i matrix, as for the **LD** matrix, the decomposition into a number of homogeneous clusters is realized, once again using the Kohonen algorithm (a one-dimensional Kohonen map is also used). The mean profiles of the formed clusters are then determined and denoted by $\bar{y}_j$.

The last step to characterize the analyzed process is to establish the empirical frequencies of $\bar{y}_j$ conditionally to $\bar{x}_i$. They are denoted by $P(\bar{y}_j | \bar{x}_i)$.

The simulation procedure takes the following form:

- Choice of a starting point x_t (for example, the initial individual in the **LD** matrix).
- Determination of the winning $\bar{x}_i$ using $\text{ArgMin} \| x_t - \bar{x}_i \|$.
- Picking an $\bar{y}_j$ at random according to the conditional distribution $P(\bar{y}_j | \bar{x}_i)$.
- Computation of x_{t+1} by $x_t + \bar{y}_j$.
- Iteration of the procedure to simulate the dynamics of the process on a specific time horizon.

For stochastic processes, the procedure can be iterated and the results averaged.

---

1 For the justification of this choice, see Cottrell, de Bodt and Verleysen (1996).

2.2   The construction of the data set.

To construct the first theoretical interest rates structure path, we use the general equilibrium model of Cox, Ingersoll and Ross (1985b). In this one-factor model, the dynamic of the state variable is given by :

$$dr(t) = (a - br(t))dt + \sigma\sqrt{r(t)}dz(t) \tag{1}$$

where a, b et σ are positive and constant. $\{z(t),\ t \geq 0\}$ is a standard Wiener process. This definition ensure that interest rates are all positive (if $r(0) \geq 0$) and display mean reverting towards a/b.

Cox, Ingersoll and Ross (1985) have shown that the interest rate at time t for a maturity τ is :

$$R(r,\tau) = -\frac{1}{\tau}(A(\tau) + B(\tau)r) \tag{2}$$

To generate the second theoretical interest rate path, we use the two-factors model of Longstaff and Schwartz (1992). In this model, the state variables are non observable and their dynamics are :

$$dX(t) = (a - bX(t))dt + c\sqrt{X(t)}dz_1(t) \tag{3}$$

$$dY(t) = (d - eY(t))dt + f\sqrt{Y(t)}dz_2(t) \tag{4}$$

where a, b, c, d, e, $f > 0$ and z_1 and z_2 are uncorrelated Wiener process. Theorem 1 of Cox, Ingersoll and Ross (1985a) and a simple rescaling[2] of the state variables lead to the expression of the instantaneous rate :

$$r(t) = \alpha x(t) + \beta y(t) \tag{5}$$

The instaneous variance of changes in $r(t)$, $V(t)$ can be obtained by applying Ito's lemma to $r(t)$ and taking the appropriate expectation :

$$V(t) = \alpha^2 x(t) + \beta^2 y(t) \tag{6}$$

Longstaff and Schwartz have shown that the interest rate at time t for a maturity τ is :

---

2 $x = X/c^2$ and $y = Y/f^2$ The dynamics are $dx(t) = (\gamma - \delta x(t))dt + \sqrt{x(t)}dz_2(t)$ and $dy(t) = (\eta - \xi y(t))dt + \sqrt{y(t)}dz_2(t)$

$$R(r, \tau) = -\frac{1}{\tau}\left(A(\tau) + B(\tau)r + C(\tau)V\right) \tag{7}$$

To generate a path for the interest rates structure, we use the discrete form of Eq. (1) for the first data set, Eq. (3) and (4) for the second one as well as Eq. (2) and (7) for the interest rate of any maturity τ. With a step equal to one business day, $dt = 1/250$, the discrete form of the dynamic of the instantaneous spot rate is given by :

$$r(t+1) = r(t) + (a - br(t))(1/250) + \sigma\sqrt{r(t)}\sqrt{1/250}\,\varepsilon \tag{8}$$

in the case of the one-factor model and by :

$$x(t+1) = x(t) + (\gamma - \delta x(t))(1/250) + \sqrt{x(t)}\sqrt{1/250}\,\varepsilon_1 \tag{9}$$

$$y(t+1) = y(t) + (\eta - \xi y(t))(1/250) + \sqrt{y(t)}\sqrt{1/250}\,\varepsilon_2 \tag{10}$$

in the case of the two-factor model. ε_t are drawn from uncorrelated normal distribution; $N(0,1)$.

At any time t, the interest rate structure is totally defined by the value of the parameters a, b, σ and by the level of the instantaneous rate, $r(t)$ in the case of the one-factor model. For the two-factor model, six parameters are needed (α, β, γ, δ, η, ξ) and both the level of the short rate $r(t)$, and its instantaneous variance $V(t)$. In this study, we use the values of the parameters found in Dahlquist (1996) for the one-factor model and from Longstaff, Schwartz (1992) for the two-factor model.

2.3 Validation of the simulation procedure

For each model, we generate one path of 2.000 steps for 15 maturity ranging from 1 to 15 years. To form the first "theoretical" data sets, we add to the 2.000 vectors of 15 dimensions (interest rates with maturity ranging from 1 to 15 years) the level of the instantaneous spot rate at each step. The second "theoretical" data sets includes 2.000 vectors of 15 dimensions and the level of both the instantaneous spot rate and its variance at each step.

On each data set, we determine the interest rates shocks that are defined as the interest rates structure at date t minus the interest rates structure at date t-1. We form respectively 9 and 30 homogenous clusters out of the 2.000 interest rates structure and the 1999 interest rates shocks. The mean profile of these clusters are denoted $\overline{x}_i$ and $\overline{y}_j$. The mean profiles in the case of the one-factor model are of dimension 16 and those in the case of the two-factors model are of dimension 17. To generate the future interest rates paths we apply the procedure described in section 2.1.

In this study, we are showing the simulation procedure leads to future paths that generate yield curve with the same properties than the "theoretical" data. More precisely we verify, at each step, if the shape of the yield curve has the same properties than the theoretical yield curve induce by the used models. As the "theoretical" data result from known diffusion process with respectively one and two

264

state variables and from a model that gives an analytical expression of the interest rate structure, it is possible to test whether or not the generated yield curves result from the same diffusion process. To do this, we will use the General Method of Moments proposed by Hansen (1982).

3   Results

Using the simulation procedure described in section 2.1, we have generated several paths of the entire term structure with maturity ranging from 1 year up to 15 years in the case of the one-factor model of Cox, Ingersoll and Ross [1985b]. These paths have been calculated with Eq. (8) for the 1-year rate and Eq. (2) for the rates with maturity ranging from 2 to 15 years. The parameters a, b and σ are given in table 1. The path of the short generated by the one factor model is presented in figure 1. To generate this path, we have used Eq. (8) for the dynamic of the state variable. The parameters are given in table 1. Figure 2 shows an example of the paths generated by the simulation procedure for the one factor model. From these paths of 2.000 steps and the yield curve at each step, we estimated the parameters by the Generalized Method of Moments. The comparison of the estimated parameters and the input parameters are given in table 1.

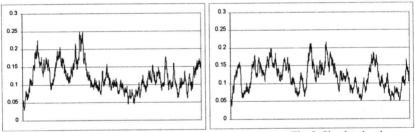

Fig.1: Theoretical paths   Fig. 2: Simulated paths

Parameter	Input	Estimate	Error	t-statistic
TWO FACTORS MODEL				
β	0.151325	0.151325	0.761217E-08	.198793E+08
v^*	1.50000	1.50000	0.216064E-06	.694239E+07
α	0.001149	0.114900E-02	0.682133E-08	168443.
δ	0.05658	0.056580	0.229353E-07	.246694E+07
γ	3.5	3.49999	0.201851E-04	173395.
η	0.121582	0.121582	0.238796E-07	.509146E+07
ONE-FACTOR MODEL				
B	0.7037	0.703700	0.574202E-08	0.122553E+09
σ^2	0.0144	0.014400	0.269731E-08	0.533864E+07
A	0.0902	0.090200	0.606020E-09	0.148840E+09

Table 1: estimates of the parameters of both the Cox, Ingersoll Ross and the Longstaff-Schwartz model.

These impressive results seem clearly confirm that our procedure respects the nature of the model that describes the interest rate structures. However, it is important to note that in this study we did verify on a sample that the generated yield curves have the same properties that the theoretical one. To complete the tests, it is important to verify if the simulated paths of the state variables have the same properties than the paths generated by the assumed stochastic processes. This work shall be achieve in a future study.

4   Conclusion

In this paper, we have analyzed the accuracy of an algorithm to reproduce paths that have the same stochastic properties than a given path. The procedure involves an algorithm that captures the properties, especially the conditional distribution of probability, of a process dynamic observed through a data set. This algorithm, described at section 2.1, uses two Kohonen maps to form clusters of yield curves and of shocks that applied to it. The empirical distribution of frequency of deformations conditional to the initial vector is then computed for each data set generated with the models of Cox-Ingersoll-Ross and Longstaff-Schwartz. Given that, we used a Monte-Carlo simulation to generate several paths. To test the accuracy of the procedure we have used the General Method of Moment to verify if the simulated yield curves have the same properties than the theoretical yield curve, that is, if the simulated yield curve are described by the model equations. The results are encouraging as long as we analyze the compatibility between the shape of the simulated yield curve and the model equations. Further research should be done to test whether or not the simulated dynamics of the state variables have the same

266

properties than the assumed dynamics of the theoretical models. Moreover, this study should be enlarge to other interest rates structure.

References

Chan K.G., Karolyi G.A., Longstaff F.A., Sanders A.B. (1992), An Empirical Comparison of Alternative Models of the Short-Term Interest Rate, Journal of Finance 48, p. 1209-1227.

Cox J.C., Ingersoll J.E., Ross S.A. (1985a), An Intertemporal General Equilibrium Model of Asset Prices, Econometrica 53, p. 363-384

Cox J.C., Ingersoll J.E., Ross S.A. (1985a), A Theory of the Term Structure of Interest Rates, Econometrica 53, p. 385-407

Clewlow L., Caverhill A. (1994), On the Simulation of Contingent Claims, Journal of Derivatives, Winter, p. 66-74.

Cottrell M., de Bodt E., Grégoire Ph., Simulating Interest Rate Structure Evolution on a Long Term Horizon : A Kohonen Map Application, Proceedings of Neural Networks in The Capital Markets, Californian Institute of Technology, World Scientific Ed., Passadena, 1996.

Cottrell M., de Bodt E, Verleysen M., Kohonen maps versus vector quantization for data analysis, Proceedings of European Symposium on Artificial Neural Networks, Dfacto Ed., Brugge, 1997.

Cottrell M., Fort J.C., Pagès G. (1997), Theoretical aspects of the SOM algorithm, Proc. of WSOM'97, Helsinki, p. 246-267

Dahlquist M. (1996), On alternative interest rate processes, Journal of Banking & Finance, vol. 20, p. 1033-1119.

Hansen L.P. (1982), Large Sample Properties of Generalized Method of Moments Estimator, Econometrica 50, 1029-1054.

Heath D., Jarrow R. , Morton A. (1992), Bond Pricing and the Term Structure of Interest Rates : A New Methodology for Contingent Claims Valuation, Econometrica 60, p. 77-105.

Ho T.S., Lee S.-B. (1986), Term Structure Movements and Pricing Interest Rate Contigent Claims, The Journal of Finance 41, p. 1011-1029.

Kohonen T. (1995), Self-Organizing Maps, Springer Series in Information Sciences Vol 30, Springer, Berlin.

Longstaff F.A., Schwartz E.S. (1992), Interest Rates Volatility and the Term Structure : a Two-factor General Equilibrium Model, The Journal of Finance 47, 1259-1282.

Pagès G. (1993), Voronoï tesselation, Space quantization algorithms and numerical integration, Proc. ESANN'93, M.Verleysen Ed., Editions D Facto, Bruxelles, p. 221-228.

Rebonato R. (1996), Interest-Rate Option Models, John Wiley & Sons Ltd, England.

Vasiceck O.A. (1977), An Equilibrium Characterization of the Term Structure, Journal of Financial Economics 5, p. 177-188.

STATE SPACE ARCH:
FORECASTING VOLATILITY WITH A STOCHASTIC
COEFFICIENT MODEL

ÁLVARO VEIGA   *MARCELO C. MEDEIROS*   *CRISTIANO FERNANDES*
alvf@ele.puc-rio.br   *mcm@ele.puc-rio.br*   *cris@ele.puc-rio.br*

Laboratório de Estatística Computacional
Departamento de Engenharia Elétrica, PUC- Rio
Rua Marquês de São Vicente, 225
22453-900, Rio de Janeiro - Brazil

This article investigates the use of AR models with stochastic coefficients to describe the changes in volatility observed in time series of financial returns. Such models can reproduce the main stylised facts observed in financial series: excess kurtosis, serial correlated square returns and time-varying conditional variance. We first cast the model in a state space form. Then the EM algorithm is used to estimate the parameters of the model. With the state-space formulation one can use the Kalman filter to evaluate the conditional variance of future returns. The model is tested using daily returns of TELEBRÁS-PN, one of the main stocks of the brazilian market.

keywords: volatility, stochastic coefficient models, Kalman filter, EM algorithm, GARCH.

1   Introduction

Financial time series present a number of features that make their modelling a challenge. First of all, its unconditional distribution is leptokurtic or, equivalently, it has *fat tails*. This means that one observes more extreme values than those predicted by the normal distribution. Next, the series usually present virtually no serial correlation which precludes the use of the traditional linear models, such as ARMA (Box, Jenkins & Reinsel 1994) and Gaussian state space models (see, e.g., Harvey & Shephard 1993). In spite of the lack of serial correlation, the square or the absolute value of the series do present significant autocorrelation, which entails a time varying conditional variance or, the so called *volatility*.

A.-P.N. Refenes et al. (eds.), Decision Technologies for Computational Finance, 267–274.
© 1998 *Kluwer Academic Publishers. Printed in the Netherlands..*

The correct evaluation of the volatility of financial series is of paramount importance in portfolio management, options pricing and risk management. Since the seminal work of Engle (1982), where the ARCH (autoregressive conditional heteroskedasticity) model was first proposed a profusion of new volatility models has appeared both in the Time Series and Econometrics literature.

These models may be organised into two distinct classes: the ARCH models (GARCH, M-GARCH, E-GARCH, MACH) - in which the volatility is explained by its dependence on past volatilities and a positive function of past observations (Engle 1995, Gourieóux 1997) - and the stochastic volatility models - where the dynamics of the volatility is captured by an unobserved stochastic process (see, e.g., Shephard 1994).

This work investigates a third approach, denominated State Space ARCH (SS-ARCH), where the changes in volatility comes from stochastic variations in the coefficients of an AR model. This idea has been apparently first suggested by Tsay (1987) whom remarked that random coefficients autoregressions (RCA) could produce time varying volatility just as an ARCH model.

The model proposed in this article moves a step further by considering an autoregressive model with coefficients varying as a Vector Autogression (VAR). The hyperparameters of the model are estimated by maximum likelihood using an adaptation of EM algorithm formulated by Shumway and Stoffer (1982).

The article is organized as follows: in section 2 we present the model in state space form. Section 3 presents the main properties of the SS-ARCH process. Section 4 describes an EM algorithm to estimate the hyperparameters of the model. Finally, section 5 evaluates the performance of the SS-ARCH model with respect to a GARCH model.

2   The SS-ARCH model

The SS-ARCH(p) model assumes that the returns y_t are produced by a time-varying autoregressive process of order p described by:

$$y_t = a_{1t}y_{t-1} + a_{2t}y_{t-2} + \ldots + a_{pt}y_{t-p} + \varepsilon_t, \quad t = 1, \ldots, T \tag{1}$$

$$\varepsilon_t \sim N(0, R) \quad and \quad E[\varepsilon_t \varepsilon_s] = 0 \quad if \quad t \neq s$$

with the $p \times 1$ vector of coefficients $a_t = [a_{1t}, \ldots, a_{pt}]^T$ following a first order autoregressive (VAR) process with mean μ_a, expressed by:

$$(a_t - \mu_a) = \phi(a_{t-1} - \mu_a) + \omega_t \tag{2}$$

$$\omega_t \sim N_p(0, Q), \quad E[\omega_t \omega_s^T] = 0 \quad if \quad t \neq s, \quad E[\varepsilon_t \omega_s^T] = 0 \quad \forall \ t, s$$

The model can be cast in the state-space form:

$$y_t = M_t \alpha_t + v_t \tag{3}$$

$$\alpha_t = F\alpha_{t-1} + G\omega_t \tag{4}$$

with

$$F = \begin{bmatrix} \phi & 0 \\ 0 & I \end{bmatrix}, \quad G = \begin{bmatrix} I \\ 0 \end{bmatrix}, \quad M_t = \begin{bmatrix} Y_{t-1}^T & Y_{t-1}^T \end{bmatrix} \quad and \quad Y_{t-1}^T = \begin{bmatrix} y_{t-1}, \ldots, y_{t-p} \end{bmatrix}$$

A physical interpretation can be given to the variation of the AR coefficients. In fact, as it is well known, the coefficients of linear system determines its dynamic properties. Consequently, in the SS-ARCH formulation, the source of volatility variation can be ascribed to the changes in the dynamics with which the market processes the incoming information.

3   Conditional moments of an SS-ARCH process

Asymptotic distribution of the SS-ARCH process y_t, as in other volatility models, is very complex to be deduced and has no closed form. From the point of view of volatility forecasting, only the conditional variance is of interest and these are much easier to obtain. First, let's note that, by Eq. (1), that the SS-ARCH process is conditionally normal. The conditional mean and variance can be obtained by taking conditional expectations on both sides of Eq. (4):

$$E(y_t \mid y_{t-1}, y_{t-2}, ...) = \hat{y}_{t|t-1} = M^T_t \, \hat{\alpha}_{t|t-1} \tag{5}$$

$$h_t = E[(y_t - \hat{y}_{t|t-1})(y_t - \hat{y}_{t|t-1})^T / y_{t-1}, y_{t-2}, ...] = M_t \, P_{t|t-1} \, M^T_{t-1} + R \tag{6}$$

with $\hat{\alpha}_{t|t-1}$ and $P_{t|t-1}$, being respectively, the conditional mean and conditional

variance of the state vector, which can be recursively evaluated by the Kalman filter (see, e.g., Anderson and Moore 1979).

Unlike others volatility models, the SS-ARCH can produce a time-varying conditional mean. This will happen if either $\phi \neq 0$ or $\mu_a \neq 0$. If $\mu_a \neq 0$, there would be serial correlation and a linear model should be able to reduce the forecasting error variance. This is in contradiction with the concept of efficient markets. However, in practice, it is often the case that small, although significant, serial correlation is observed in financial series and this must be taken into account.

We now examine the conditional variance, given by Eq. (6). It is clear that the state space model in Eqs (3) and (4) is time varying and does not admit, in the general case, a solution to the Riccati equation and, consequently, $P_{t|t-1}$ will not converge. Note also that Eq. (6) is nothing more than a generalisation of the traditional ARCH expression to the evolution of the variance with additional cross products (the terms $y_{t-i}y_{t-j}$) and time varying coefficients, as shown below:

$$h_t = \sum_{i=1}^{p} \sum_{j=1}^{p} c_{ij} \, y_{t-i} y_{t-j} + R$$

where c_{ij} is the element (i, j) of the forecasting error covariance of the vector a_t,

given by, $c_{ij} = p_{i,j} + p_{i+p,j} + p_{i,j+p} + p_{i+p,j+p}$ with $p_{i,j}$ being the

element i, j of the state covariance matrix $P_{t/t-1}$.

The expression for the variance h_t becomes exactly the expression given by an ARCH model if $\mu_a = 0$, $\phi = 0$ and Q is a diagonal matrix as bellow:

$$h_t = Y^T_{t-1} Q Y_{t-1} + R = q_1 y^2_{t-1} + q_2 y^2_{t-2} + ... + q_p y^2_{t-p} + R$$

where q_i is the ith element of the diagonal of Q.

4   Parameter estimation: the EM algorithm

The parameters σ_0^2, μ_a, Σ, ϕ, Q and R are unknown and must be estimated from the data. In the present work, we use the Expectation-Maximisation (EM) algorithm proposed by Dempster, Laird and Rubin (1977). The EM algorithm is an alternative approach to the iterative computation of maximum likelihood estimates in a large range of problems, where traditional algorithms such as Newton-Raphson may turn out to fail. An approach of the EM algorithm to state space smoothing and forecasting has been proposed by Shumway and Stoffer (1982) and adapted in this work to take into account the special structure of the matrix F.

Basically, the EM algorithm maximizes the likelihood of the set of complete data (the asset returns y_t and the non-observable coefficients a_{it}, $(i=1,...,p)$ by maximizing the expected value of the likelihood conditional on the incomplete data (the asset returns y_t).

Each iteration of the algorithm is performed in two steps. First,. the expected value of the likelihood is evaluated conditionally on the observed returns (the incomplete data) and the current values to σ_0^2, μ_a, Σ, ϕ, Q and R. The expected value of the likelihood depends on the smoothed state vector $\alpha_{t/T}$ and its covariance $P_{t/T}$ with $t=1,...,T$ given by the Kalman smoother. Based on these values,

σ_0^2, μ_a, Σ, ϕ, Q and R are estimated so as to maximise the expected conditional likelihood of the incomplete data. For state space models with normal random components, this involves simple mean square problems and an analytical solutions is available.

Other quantities of interest like the one step ahead predictions and smoothed values of the state and observed series are obtained as a by-product of the application of the Kalman smoother - which includes the Kalman filter in its forward iterations. Also, the corresponding covariances, mainly the conditional variance of y_t , are obtained by the Kalman filter.

5   Application

Our data consist of the daily returns of TELEBRÁS-PN, one of the main stocks on the brazilian market. The period considered was from 06/30/94 to 12/30/96, see figure 1, with 617 observations. The series was split into two parts. The first one, containing 517 observations, was used to estimate the model, and the remaining 100 observations were used for testing. The series kurtosis is 18.277 and the Jarque-Bera test for normality is 6177 (p-value < 10^{-5}), indicating a clear excess of kurtosis and rejection of normality for the returns.

Figure 1: returns of TELEBRAS-PN from 06/30/94. to 12/30/96.

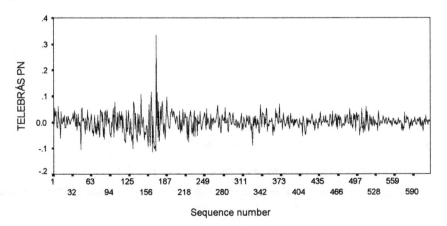

Table 1 compares the performance of a SS-ARCH with p=2 and a GARCH(1,1). In the estimation period the models have a similar performance, while in the out-of-sample period the GARCH model presents both a better RMSE and MAE, although the SS-ARCH achieved a higher value for the log of the likelihood.

Table 1. Goodness-of-fit statistics for the estimation and testing periods.

	SS-ARCH(2)		GARCH(1,1)	
	estim.	test	estim.	test
RMSE$_1$[1]	0.0051	$6.565.10^{-4}$	0.0051	$4.273.10^{-4}$
RMSE$_2$[2]	0.0250	0.0190	0.0248	0.0138
MAE[3]	0.0013	$6.267.10^{-4}$	0.0014	$3.694.10^{-4}$
LKLHD[4]	$-1.474.10^3$	-338.956	$-1.535.10^3$	-363.316
% of obs. outside 95% conf. interval	5.03	0.0	4.84	0.0

6 Conclusions

This work has investigated the use of autoregressive models with stochastic coefficients to describe the variation of volatility in financial series of returns. This formulation, denominated SS-ARCH, differs from the usual volatility models (GARCH and Stochastic Volatility) by attributing the variations in change of volatility to variations to changes in the dynamics with which the market processes the incoming information.

---

[1] $RMSE_1 = \sqrt{1/T \, \Sigma \, (y_t^2 - h_t)^2}$

[2] $RMSE_2 = \sqrt{1/T \, \Sigma \, (|y_t| - h_t^{1/2})^2}$

[3] $MAE = 1/T \, \Sigma \, (y_t - h_t^{1/2})^2$

[4] $LKLHD =$ likelihood kernel $= \Sigma \, \{ \ln(h_t^{1/2}) + \frac{1}{2} \, (y_t^2 / h_t) \}$

The model was evaluated in comparison to a GARCH model using real data. Although not conclusive, the example shows that their performance are quite similar with some advantage to the GARCH model.

The SS-ARCH model offers some advantages in comparison to the other volatility models, the main one being the facility in specifying an EM algorithm to estimate a multivariate volatility model. The main drawback is probably its non parsimonious nature and the slow convergence of the EM algorithm. Also, the asymptotic theory for the SS-ARCH process is not yet established.

The results obtained in this work are encouraging enough to justify further research on the SS-ARCH formulation.

7   References

Anderson B. D. O.; Moore J. B. *Optimal Filtering*, Prentice-Hall, 1979.

Box,G.E.P.; Jenkins, G.W.; Reinsel, G.C. *Time Series Analysis- Forecasting and Control.* 3rd edition. Prentice Hall, 1994.

Dempster, A. P., N. M Laird,. and D. B. Rubin *Maximum Likelihood from Incomplete Data via The EM Algorithm*, J. R. Statist. Soc B 39, 1-38m 1989.

Engle, R. F. *Autoregressive Conditional Heterocedasticity with Estimates of the Variance of UK Inflation.* Econometric Reviews, 5: 1-50, 1982.

Engle, R. F. *ARCH Selected Readings.* Oxford University Press, 1995.

Gouriéroux, C. *ARCH Models and Financial Applications.* Springer-Verlag, 1997.

Harvey, A. C.; Shephard, N. *Structural Time Series Models.* Handbook of Statistics, vol. 11, 10, 261-302, 1993.

Shephard, N. *Local scale models.* Journal of Econometrics 60, 181-202, 1994.

Shumway, R. H. and Stoffer, D.S. *An Approach to Time Series Smoothing and Forecasting Using the Em Algorithm*, Journal of Time Series Analysis Vol. 3, No. 4, 1982.

Tsay, R.S. *Conditional Heteroscedastic Time Series Models*, JASA, Vol. 82, No. 398, 590-604, 1987.

PART 4

TERM STRUCTURE AND FACTOR MODELS

Empirical Analysis of the Australian and Canadian Money Market Yield Curves: Results Using Panel Data

S. H. BABBS
First Chicago NBD and University of Warwick
First National Bank of Chicago,
1 Triton Square,
London NW1 3FN, UK
E-mail: sbabbs@uk.fcnbd.com

K. B. NOWMAN
Department of Investment, Risk Management and Insurance &
Centre for Mathematical Trading and Finance,
City University Business School,
Frobisher Crescent,
London EC2Y 8HB, UK
E-mail: K.B.Nowman@city.ac.uk

In this paper we estimate one and two factor models of the term structure of interest rates using Australian and Canadian panel data from the yield curve. We use Kalman filtering econometrics to estimate the parameters of the model and our empirical results indicate that the two factor model provides a good description of the Australian and Canadian money market yield curves.

1   Introduction

The econometrics of the Kalman filter is now well developed and documented by for example, Harvey (1989). Their application in finance is a more recent development and over the last few years the Kalman filtering methodology has been applied to a number of different term structure of interest rates models by for example, Chen and Scott (1995), Geyer and Pichler (1996), Jegadeesh and Pennacchi (1996) and Lund (1997a,b). In a more recent application the Kalman filter has been applied to the term structure of interest rate model considered by Babbs and Nowman (1997). In Babbs and Nowman (1997) and subsequent applications in Babbs and Nowman (1998a,b) they obtained supportive empirical results for a

A.-P.N. Refenes et al. (eds.), Decision Technologies for Computational Finance, 277–289.
© 1998 *Kluwer Academic Publishers. Printed in the Netherlands..*

number of markets for their model. In this paper we use Australian and Canadian term structure of interest rate data to estimate one and two factor models of Babbs and Nowman (1997).

The organisation of this paper is as follows. In Section 2 we briefly discuss the term structure model of Babbs and Nowman (1997) and estimation of its parameters. Section 3 discusses the data sets used and presents the empirical results. Concluding remarks are presented in Section 4.

2   One-Two Factor Interest Rate Models and Estimation

The model considered by Babbs and Nowman (1997) is a special case of the general term structure model of Langetieg (1980). In the two factor case the model assumes that the spot interest rate, r, is given by

$$r(t) = \mu - X_1(t) - X_2(t) \tag{1}$$
$$dX_1 = -\xi_1 X_1 dt + c_1 dW_1 \tag{2}$$
$$dX_2 = -\xi_2 X_2 dt + c_2 dW_2 \tag{3}$$

where μ is the long-run average rate, and $X_1(t)$ and $X_2(t)$ represent the current effect of streams of short and long term economic news. The arrival of each type of news is modelled by the innovations of standard Brownian motions, which may be correlated with dynamics given by Ornstein-Uhlenbeck processes represented by Eq. (2) and Eq. (3). In this framework, the price for a pure discount bond, $B(M,t)$ can be easily derived for the general case of n-factors with correlated state variables (see Babbs and Nowman (1997) for full details and its exact functional form). The theoretical yield curve for the model is given by

$$R(t+\tau,t) \equiv -\log B(t+\tau,t)/\tau \tag{4}$$

where $\tau \equiv M - t$ is the time to maturity of the bond. To estimate the underlying parameters of the term structure model we rewrite the model in the standard state space form comprising the measurement and transition equations (see Harvey (1989)) below:

$$R_k = d(\psi) + Z(\psi)X_k + \varepsilon_k \qquad \varepsilon_k \sim N(0, H(\psi)) \tag{5}$$
$$X_k = \Phi_k(\psi) X_{k-1} + \eta_k \qquad \eta_k \sim N(0, V_k(\psi)) \tag{6}$$

where the i'th row of the matrices d and Z are defined in Babbs and Nowman (1997); $\Phi_k(\psi) = e^{-\xi_J(t_k - t_{k-1})}$ $j = 1,2$ and X_k is shorthand notation for X_{t_k} where we have N observed interest rates at time t_k. The parameter vector ψ contains $\mu, \xi_j, c_j, \rho, \theta_q$ and the variances of the distribution of the measurement errors $H = h_1, ..., h_N$. The Kalman filter algorithm is then applied to the above state space form (see Harvey (1989) and Babbs and Nowman (1997)).

3 Data and Empirical Results

The data used in this empirical study consists of weekly (wednesdays) zero-coupon yields for the Australian and Canadian term structure curves obtained from the First National Bank of Chicago, London. At each date we have the N-interest rates. To estimate the state space model, we have chosen the following maturities: 3 months, 6 months and 1, 2, 3, 5, 7 and 10 years. Summary sample means and standard deviation information for the rates are reported in Table I below. The sample periods are: October 1994 to January 1998 for Australia giving a total of 173 observation dates; June 1993 to January 1998 for Canada giving a total of 244 observation dates.

Table I: Data Summary: Sample Means (%) and Standard Deviations

	Nobs	3M	6M	1Y	2Y	3Y	5Y	7Y	10Y
AUS	173	6.68	6.73	6.77	7.25	7.50	7.93	8.20	8.42
		1.08	1.19	1.26	1.32	1.27	1.23	1.22	1.21
CAN	244	4.95	5.14	5.42	6.07	6.43	6.97	7.32	7.71
		1.39	1.38	1.35	1.33	1.25	1.16	1.13	1.09

We now discuss the estimates of the one and two factor models on the Australian and Canadian data. The corresponding estimation results are presented in Table II. We also report the implied factor loadings generated by the model. Finally, the historical tracking performance of the one and two factor models are compared to the observed rates.

Table II: Australian and Canadian Empirical Estimates

	AUSTRALIA One Factor	AUSTRALIA Two Factor	CANADA One Factor	CANADA Two Factor
ξ_1	0.0196 (0.0008)	0.2151 (0.0612)	0.0750 (0.0051)	0.6010 (0.0356)
ξ_2		0.0103 (0.0005)		0.0232 (0.0048)
c_1	0.0158 (0.0006)	0.0238 (0.0010)	0.0449 (0.0031)	0.0234 (0.0039)
c_2		0.0196 (0.0014)		0.0137 (0.0029)
ρ		-0.7475 (0.0675)		-0.3461 (0.0043)
μ	0.0603 (0.0005)	0.0587 (0.0254)	0.0420 (0.0048)	0.0268 (0.0223)
θ_1	0.2611 (0.0515)	0.6093 (0.5192)	0.2818 (0.0033)	0.5106 (0.0676)
θ_2		0.5971 (0.5318)		0.4119 (0.0491)
$\sqrt{h_1}$	0.0087 (0.0020)	0.0069 (0.0001)	0.0080 (0.0001)	0.0070 (0.0002)
$\sqrt{h_2}$	0.0068 (0.0008)	0.0048 (0.00005)	0.0064 (0.0001)	0.0052 (0.0003)
$\sqrt{h_3}$	0.0062 (0.0013)	0.0028 (0.0001)	0.0043 (0.0001)	0.0029 (0.00002)
$\sqrt{h_4}$	0.0031 (0.0014)	0.0010 (0.00004)	0.0014 (0.00001)	0.0004 (0.0001)
$\sqrt{h_5}$	0.0016 (0.0002)	<0.0001 (0.000004)	0.00001 (0.00001)	0.0008 (0.00002)
$\sqrt{h_6}$	0.0013 (0.0021)	0.0003 (0.00001)	0.0017 (0.00002)	0.0005 (0.00002)
$\sqrt{h_7}$	0.0015 (0.0026)	0.0004 (0.00001)	0.0026 (0.0001)	0.00001 (0.000002)
$\sqrt{h_8}$	0.0020 (0.0005)	0.0006 (0.00004)	0.0035 (0.0002)	0.0008 (0.0001)
LogL	7346	8232	10085	11410

Australia

In both one and two factor models the estimates of the mean reversion and diffusion parameters as well as most of the measurement errors are statistically significant. The long-run average rate is significant in both models also. The market price of risks are not significant in the two factor model whereas it is in the one factor model. The standard deviation of the measurement errors in the one factor model for the 3 month rate is 87 basis points and 68 basis points for the 6 month rate. This compares to 69 basis points for the 3 month rate and 48 basis points for the 6 month rate in the two factor model. In the remaining maturities the measurement errors in the two factor model are 28 basis points for the 1 year rate, 10 basis points for the 2 year rate, less than one basis point for the 3 year rate, 3 basis points for the 5 year rate, 4 basis points for the 7 year rate and 6 basis points for the 10 year rate. This compares to 62 basis points for the 1 year rate, 31 basis points for the 2 year rate, 16 basis points for the 3 year rate, 13 basis points for the 5 year rate, 15 basis points for the 7 year rate and 20 basis points for the 10 year rate in the one factor model. Overall the two factor models measurement errors are much smaller than the one factor model. Both models have large measurement errors in the very short end of the curve (less than one year).

The mean reversion parameters represent the mean half-lives for the interest rate process, i.e. the expected time for the process to return halfway to its long term mean. For the two factor model the mean half lives are 3.2 years for the first factor and 67 years for the second factor (see Chen and Scott (1995) for mean half lives for a CIR two factor model on weekly US data). The correlation coefficient is strongly negative at -75 percent. The estimate of the long-run average rate is 6.03 percent for the one factor model and 5.87 percent for the two factor model and are within the range of plausible values. The log-likelihood values for the one factor model are 7346 and for the two factor model 8232. The likelihood ratio test of the one factor versus the two factor gives a value of 1772 and one can reject the null hypothesis of a one factor model at the 5 percent significance level. Overall the estimates have plausible values.

Canada

In both one and two factor models the estimates of the mean reversion, diffusion as well as most of the measurement errors are statistically significant. The long-run average rate is not statistically significant in the two factor model whereas it is in the one factor model. The standard deviation of the measurement errors in the one factor model for the 3 month rate are 80 basis points and 64 basis points for the 6 month rate. This compares to 70 basis points for the 3 month rate and 52 basis points for the 6 month rate in the two factor model. In the remaining maturities the measurement errors in the two factor model are 29 basis points for the 1 year rate, 4 basis points for the 2 year rate, 8 basis points for the 3 year rate, 5 basis points for the 5 year rate, less than 1 basis point for the 7 year rate and 8 basis points for the 10 year rate. This compares to 43 basis points for the 1 year rate, 14 basis points for the 2 year rate, less than 1 basis point for the 3 year rate, 17 basis points for the 5 year rate, 26 basis points for the 7 year rate and 35 basis points for the 10 year rate in the one factor model. Overall the two factor models measurement errors are smaller than the one factor model. For the one factor model the mean half life is 9.2 years and for the two factor model it is just over a year for the first factor and 30 years for the second factor. The correlation coefficient is -35 percent and is less nagative than the results reported in Babbs and Nowman (1997, 1998a,b). The estimate of the long-run average rate is 4.2 percent for the one factor model and 2.7 percent for the two factor model. The log-likelihood values for the one factor model are 10085 and for the two factor model 11410. The likelihood ratio test of the one factor versus the two factor gives a value of 2650 and one can reject the null hypothesis of a one factor model at the 5 percent significance level. Overall the estimates have plausible values.

Litterman and Scheinkman (1991) used principal components analysis on US yields and identified three factors which they interpreted as changes in level, steepness and curvature of the yield curve. Following the findings of Litterman and Scheinkman (1991, Table 2) we impose that factor two has approximately zero impact on the term structure at the 5 year maturity and show in Fig. 1 and Fig. 2 the factor loadings generated by the two factor model as a function of maturity.

For Australia the impact of the first factor on yield curve changes has an equal positive effect on the maturities. We conclude, that the first factor can be associated to a *level* factor. The second factor lowers the yields for zeros up to five years and than raises the yields for zeros of longer maturities. We notice that the impact on yields is still rising at ten years and is line with Litterman and Scheinkman whose yields peaked at around eighteen years. Thus the second factor represents a *steepness* factor.

For Canada the impact of the first factor on yield curve changes has an equal positive effect on the maturities. We conclude, that the first factor can be associated to a *level* factor. The second factor lowers the yields for zeros up to five years and than has approximately an equal positive impact on yields for zeros of longer maturities. Thus the second factor represents a *steepness* factor. Overall, the model generates factor loadings similar to those obtained by Litterman and Scheinkman (1991) for US data, as well as those obtained in Babbs and Nowman (1997, 1998a,b) for other currencies.

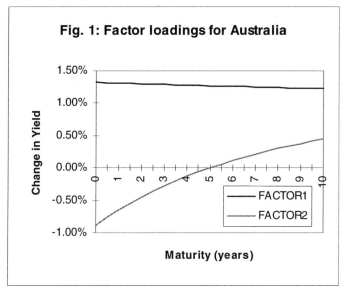

Fig. 1: Factor loadings for Australia

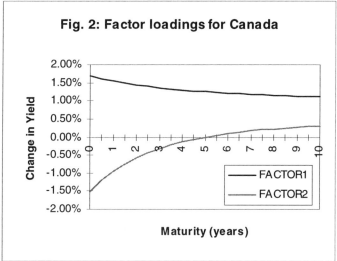

Fig. 2: Factor loadings for Canada

We now plot the estimated time series implied by the measurement equation for the one and two factor models where the unobserved state variables are represented by the filtered estimates and compare them with the observed rates for a few selected maturities.

284

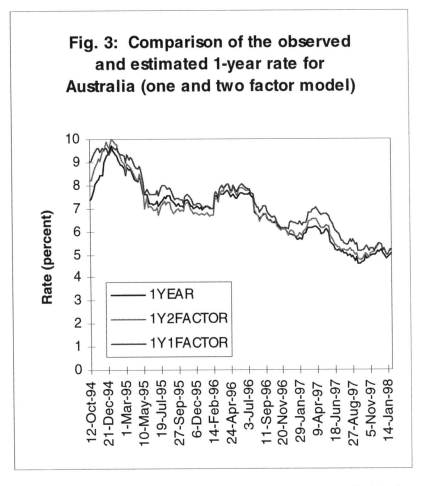

Fig. 3: Comparison of the observed and estimated 1-year rate for Australia (one and two factor model)

Above we have plotted in Fig. 3 for Australia the one year rates implied by the one and two factor models. The one factor models tracking performance tends to over predict generally whereas the two factor model tends to closely track the data and turning points.

We have plotted now the implied 10 year rates in Fig. 4 for Australia implied by the one and two factor models. Both the one and two factor models track the data well capturing the main turning points during the sample period. The two factor models tracking performance through is much better since its measurement error was only 6 basis points compared to 20 basis points in the one factor model.

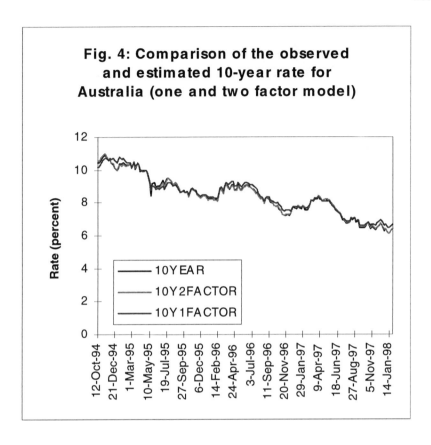

Fig. 4: Comparison of the observed and estimated 10-year rate for Australia (one and two factor model)

Turning to Canada now we have plotted the implied 1 year rates in Fig. 5 for the one and two factor models. The one factor models tracking performance tends to be more volatile than the two factor model and tends to over and under predict during the sample period. The two factor models performance with measurement error of 29 basis points tends to track the data well especially given the more volatile nature of the series.

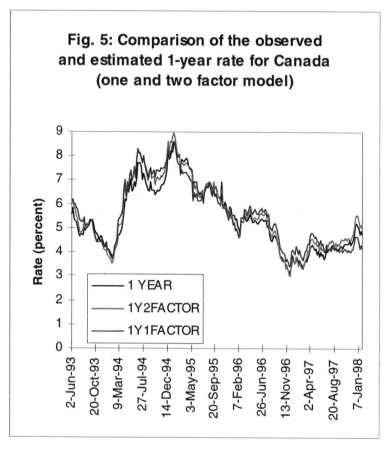

Fig. 5: Comparison of the observed and estimated 1-year rate for Canada (one and two factor model)

Turning to the implied 10 year rates in Fig. 6 for Canada the one factor models performance tends to track well until 1997 when there is a large deviation from the observed rate. The two factors performance is more impressive with a measurement error of only 8 basis points being reflected in the tracking of major turning points over the sample period.

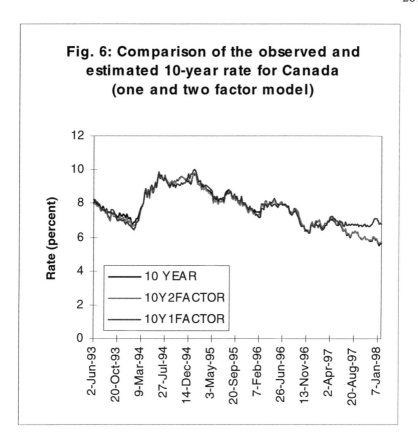

Fig. 6: Comparison of the observed and estimated 10-year rate for Canada (one and two factor model)

Overall we find that the two factor models tracking performance is more impressive for both the Australian and Canadian term structures.

4   Conclusion

In this paper we have obtained further empirical results for the one and two factor models of the term structure of interest rates recently considered by Babbs and Nowman (1997). Using a state space formulation we have applied Kalman filtering econometrics to obtain estimates of the parameters of the models. In Babbs and Nowman (1997) they applied the model to the US term structure and their results indicated that the model could explain movements in the US yield curve. Our results in this paper have plausible values and the measurement errors in the two factor model indicate that it provides a good description of the Australian and Canadian money market yield curves. These results provide further support for the model in addition to the range of other markets the model has recently been applied to (see Babbs and Nowman (1998a,b)).

Acknowledgements

We thank the editors of this volume for their advice and the First National Bank of Chicago, London for providing the data. The views expressed are those of the authors and not necessarily those of any organisation they are affiliated.

References

Babbs, S. H. and Nowman, K. B, Kalman Filtering of Generalized Vasicek Term Structure Models, Financial Options Research Centre, University of Warwick, Preprint 97/80, 1997.

Babbs, S. H. and Nowman, K. B, An Application of Generalized Vasicek Term Structure Models to the UK Gilt-Edged Market: A Kalman Filtering Analysis. Forthcoming in *Applied Financial Economics*, 1998a.

Babbs, S. H. and Nowman, K. B, Econometric Analysis of a Continuous Time Multi-Factor Generalized Vasicek Term Structure Model: International Evidence. Forthcoming in *Asia-Pacific Markets: Journal of Japanese Association of Financial Econometrics and Engineering*, 1998b.

Chen, R. and Scott, L, Multi-factor Cox-Ingersoll-Ross Models of the Term Structure: Estimates and Tests from a Kalman Filter Model. Unpublished paper, 1995.

Geyer, A. L. J. and Pichler, S, A State-Space Approach to Estimate and Test Multi-Factor Cox-Ingersoll-Ross Models of the Term Structure. Unpublished paper, 1996.

Harvey, A. C. *Forecasting, Structural Time Series Models and the Kalman Filter*, Cambridge University Press, 1989.

Jegadeesh, N. and Pennacchi, G. G, The Behaviour of Interest Rates Implied by the Term Structure of Eurodollar Futures. *Journal of Money, Credit, and Banking, 1996; 28:* 426-46.

Langetieg, T. C, A Multivariate Model of the Term Structure. *Journal of Finance*, 1980; 35; 71-91.

Litterman, R. and Scheinkman, J, Common Factors Affecting Bond Returns. *Journal of Fixed Income*, 1991; 1: 54-61.

Lund, J, A Model for Studying the Effect of EMU on European Yield Curves. Manuscript, The Aarhus School of Business, 1997a.

Lund, J, Econometric Analysis of Continuous-Time Arbitrage-Free Models of the Term Structure of Interest Rates. Manuscript, The Aarhus School of Business, 1997b.

TIME-VARYING FACTOR SENSITIVITIES
IN EQUITY INVESTMENT MANAGEMENT

Y. BENTZ, J. T. CONNOR

Department of Decision Science
London Business School
Sussex Place, Regents Park, London, NW1 4SA, UK
E-mail: Y.Bentz@lbs.ac.uk

This article shows how state space models and the Kalman filter can advantageously be used to estimate time-varying factor sensitivities. The common alternative to stochastic parameter regression, rolling regression, is shown to be biased in situations where the actual factor sensitivities are not constant but vary over time. We propose a state space approach estimating time-varying factor sensitivities. The models are applied to typical asset management tasks such as exposure monitoring, performance attribution, style analysis and portfolio tracking. The assets used in this study are individual stocks, stock portfolios and currencies. Typical factors are economic ones (such as interest and exchange rates, commodity prices for instance), statistical ones (obtained by factor analysis) and style indices (e.g. growth/value and large/small capitalisation stock indices). The models are compared to traditional rolling estimation both in terms of reliability and flexibility. Sensitivity instability tests are also discussed. The models are applied to both European and American market data.

1   Introduction

Financial markets have dramatically changed over the last three decades. Money management has evolved from art into science, from the "have a hunch, buy a bunch" approach into an approach that is more systematic, objective, controllable and quantitative, in one word: "scientific". Underlying this transformation have been theoretical advances in modelling and controlling risk, essentially by using the key concepts of "sensitivity", "factor exposure" and "diversification". Many practitioners would name factor modelling as the single most important tool in modern investment management. Investment diversification, hedging, factor betting, index tracking, portfolio replication, performance attribution, style monitoring and management all necessitate at some stage an accurate estimation of sensitivities.

Sensitivity estimation can be simple or complex, depending on the assumptions made about the sensitivities to be estimated. In most instances, OLS (Ordinary Least Squares) linear regression is used to estimate factor model coefficients (sensitivities). OLS requires several assumptions, in particular, that the relationship between variables does not vary according to the "context", i.e. that sensitivities are constant over the estimation set. If these assumptions are violated, for example when the explanatory variables represent only some of the influences

A.-P.N. Refenes et al. (eds.), Decision Technologies for Computational Finance, 291–308.
© *1998 Kluwer Academic Publishers. Printed in the Netherlands..*

(e.g. interacting variable missing) or when the functional form of the relationship changes over time, OLS regressions produce a systematic error and attribute effects that are partially deterministic and predictable to random noise.

Although OLS estimates can be biased and can become very hazardous to use in the cases where sensitivities change over time, many practitioners use them. Yet, more advanced models have become technically available thanks to the recent improvements in computer technology. Such models do not assume parameter constancy and are more adequate for monitoring and predicting factor sensitivities. They are generally known as stochastic parameter regressions. State space models and the Kalman provides a powerful and flexible framework to perform stochastic parameter regressions. Widely used in control engineering sciences for the last two decades, adaptive models such as the Kalman filter meet an increasing success in time series modelling and economics (Harvey et al. 1986, Cuthbertson and Taylor 1986).

The purpose of this paper is to describe state space models for estimating time-varying sensitivities and to show the advantages such models can offer in the context of quantitative investment management. Not only does the model optimally estimate the current factor sensitivities but it also enables to forecast future sensitivity levels, provided they follow a univariate process (trending or mean reverting processes, for instance).

2. Estimating factor sensitivities in changing markets: problems and solutions.

Essentially, factor models are used to relate the return from an asset or a portfolio of assets to one or several factors. In general, this return is generated by an unknown process, involving endogenous and exogenous influences. Reality is often far to complex to be fully understood and an exhaustive knowledge of these influences and the relationships between them is often impossible. The task of the analyst is then to propose simplifying assumptions both about the number and the choice of factors and about the nature of the relationships between the studied outcome and those variables. In most instances the relationships between the variables are assumed to belong to a special class of functions, namely those who follow a linear additive form, such as equation 1:

$$R_t = \alpha + \sum_{i=1}^{N} \beta_i F_{it} + \varepsilon_t \qquad (1)$$

where Y_t is the return of the asset in period t α is the intercept term
            X_{it} are the factors β_i are the factor sensitivities
            ε is a residual random term

The choice of equation 1 is convenient since β_i directly represent the joint factor sensitivities of asset returns. It is also locally valid since any continuous and differentiable function can be locally approximated by a linear function. A natural question is then to ask how small the dataset needs to be for the estimation to be 'local'. Practically, this depends on how constant the true sensitivities are over the dataset. In the limit, when sensitivities do not vary according to the 'context' and over time, equation 1 holds also globally. In cases where they do vary, however, for instance when the factors represent only some of the influences (e.g. interacting variable missing) or when the functional form of the relationship is not linear or time-varying, the model provides only a partial description of the reality. Some systematic error is made and attributed to the random error term ε.

Unfortunately, markets evolve, and so do the dynamics of asset prices, their volatility, their covariances and their sensitivities to economic and financial factors. Markets are significantly affected by economic, political and social events as well as by anticipations of these events. At a macro level, institutional regulations, tax laws, inflation, growth in the economy, the fast progress in information technology, the emergence of the global economy, the changing public attitude towards consumer durables and pollution may have, among many other factors, a critical influence on the way markets react and behave. At a micro-economic level, changes in the operating and the financial leverage, mergers and acquisitions, market expansion, product diversification, change of technology or management, may affect the pattern of exposures of the firm, if not the actual one, at least its financial market's perception. At a portfolio level, shifts in holdings, market timing and stock selection may influence the portfolio sensitivity to economic and financial factors.

While much attention has been given to the choice of factors and to the applications of factor modelling, little research has addressed testing and modelling of time-varying sensitivities, with the notable exception of the instability of beta measures. Important contributions in this field are, among others, those of Blume (adjusting historical estimates of beta by univariate regression taking their mean reversion into account, Blume 1975), Vacicek (Bayesian adjustment technique toward 1, Vacicek 1973), Rosenberg and Guy (Prediction of Beta from Investment fundamentals, Rosenberg and Guy 1976) and Fabozzi and Francis (stability test and estimation of beta with a stochastic parameter regression procedure, Fabozzi and Francis 1978, Ohlson and Rosenberg 1982, Bos and Newbold 1984). However, factor models should not be reduced to the sole market model and other sensitivities than beta are of interest. It is not the purpose of this article to detail the numerous applications of factor models in equity investment. The interested reader can find partial reviews in investment handbooks (see, for instance, Elton and Gruber 1995) or, for a more exhaustive survey, Bentz 1997. Table 1 proposes a brief summary of factor models' applications in equity investment management. The addressed estimation issues as well as the proposed solutions can naturally be generalised to most, if not all, applications listed in table 1.

Application type	Inputs	Estimation technique	Factor model utilisation	Outputs
Equity Investment Diversification Risk decomposition	· Security returns · Market returns · Economic factors	· Simple or multiple Time-series regression	• Estimating the correlation structure of security returns • Decomposing investment risk into systematic Vs specific components • Portfolio diversification • Benchmark for estimating fair asset return and cost of capital	$·\beta s$ $·\rho s$ $·\alpha$ $·\varepsilon$ $·R^2$
Exposures measurement and management Hedging	· Security returns Economic factors, (GDP growth, default risk, interest and exchange rates…)	· Simple or multiple Time-series regression	• Factor exposures estimation • Portfolio immunisation and hedging • Factor replication, factor betting • Pricing of factor exposures	$·\beta s$
Index tracking Portfolio profiling	· Security returns · Indices returns · Economic factors	· Multiple Time-series regression	• Portfolio and index tracking • Portfolio profiling • Strategic Portfolio planning	$·\beta s$
Equity Style analysis and management	· Security returns · Style indices · Sector indices	· Time-series regression	• Investment style monitoring • Performance attribution • Active style management	$·\beta s, \alpha$ $·\varepsilon$ $·R^2$
Evaluation of portfolio performance	· Security returns · Market returns · Economic factors · Style indices	· Simple or multiple Time-series regression	• Adjusting performance for Risk • Performance decomposition and attribution • Evaluation of Market timing ability	$·\beta s$ $·\alpha$ $·\varepsilon$
Return and risk Forecasting	· Security returns · Economic, variables · Accounting ratios · Broker estimates	· Cross-sectional regression · Time-series regression	• Forecasting asset returns • Scenario simulation • Generating buy/sell signals • Forecasting securities' beta • Pricing of factor exposures	$·E(r)$ · Signals $·\beta s$
Cointegration analysis	· Security or portfolio prices · Indices levels	· Time-series regression	• Statistical arbitrage • Residual trading	· Residuals $·\beta s$
Statistical factor modelling	· Security returns	· Principal Component Analysis	• Identification of pervasive factors • Stock clustering, pair trading • Portfolio replication	$·Fs$ $·\beta s$
Scoring / screening of securities	· Fundamental variables · Broker estimates · Ranking variables	· Weighted averages · Threshold averages	• Security selection by scoring • Security selection by screening	· Buy / sell signals

Table 1: a review of the applications of factor modelling in the setting of equity investment management

As market dynamics change over time, any fixed parameter model will only be valid for a certain period of time. This is not a major problem since it is always possible to periodically re-estimate the model (*rolling estimation*). More serious, however, is the fact that model estimation may be biased. This may have serious consequences for risk management, portfolio diversification and asset selection. It is probably in the 1980's, with the emergence of ARCH models (Engle 1982), that practitioners have realised the relevance of stochastic parameter models and adaptive estimation. The advantages are numerous and can be shown by studying the shortcomings of fixed parameter regression models estimated on rolling windows of observations. These shortcoming are now analysed.

- **Estimation bias.** The problem is illustrated in figure 1. The sensitivity $\partial Y/\partial X$ of an asset return (say Y) to a factor (say X) is represented on the vertical axis. The actual sensitivity is not constant but varies over time. The reason for the variability is not known. An important interacting variable may be missing, or there could be a structural change. The cause does not really matter. In figure 1, the average sensitivity is close to zero and would probably appear as statistically insignificant. However, the true sensitivity is far from being insignificant. For instance, at time t, the sensitivity of Y to X is strongly negative although the model's prediction is slightly positive.

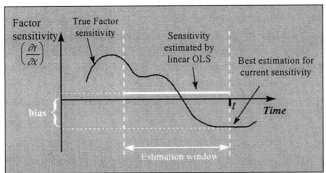

Figure 1: Actual sensitivity (in black) and sensitivity measured by linear OLS estimation (in white). When the true sensitivity is not constant but varies over time, OLS estimation, which measures an average sensitivity over the estimation period, is biased. The amplitude of the bias depends on the variability and the nature of the true sensitivity as well as the length of the estimation window.

The violation of the assumption of sensitivity constancy engenders an estimation bias. The model attributes an effect that is largely deterministic to the stochastic residual ε_t. This is usually not a serious problem when the researcher is interested in measuring past average effects between variables. However, when the estimated sensitivities are to be used in the future, the problem is more serious and can lead to unfortunate decisions. This is a common situation in equity investment management where measuring past sensitivities is far less important than predicting future ones.

- **Shadow effects and lag of estimated sensitivities.** Because rolling regression measures an average sensitivity over the estimation period the measured sensitivity is lagging the true sensitivity, especially when this last one is trending. This effect is well known by technical analysts that use moving averages of security prices or rates (a moving average lags the current value). The size of the lag depends on the size of the rolling window. This effect gives rise to shadows in sensitivity time series as events influence sensitivity estimates as long as they are part of the estimation window. There is no guidance about how to choose this size, apart from guessing how unstable the true underlying sensitivities are. Furthermore, the difference between two consecutive measures depends only on two data points, i.e. the date entering the estimation window and the date leaving it. While it is legitimate that the most recent data point has an effect on this difference, there is no reason for the most remote point in the window to have more effect than any other observation, especially so because the size of the window has been chosen somehow arbitrarily. A solution to this problem consists of weighting the data points in order to attribute more credibility to recent observations than to more remote ones. This is however not ideal since the question of choosing the decay rate and the form of the weighting function remains.

- ***Poor prediction ability***. The sensitivity is predicted to be the same in the future as it is today. The underlying sensitivity time structure is not modelled, reflecting the inability of the model to separate transitory effect from permanent ones. For mean-reverting sensitivities (e.g. market βs), or trending ones (e.g. exposures to exchange rates for a firm that increasingly relies on exports), the rolling estimation procedure does not take full advantage of the information available in the data.

The approach used in this paper overcome most of these problems as it is recursive and optimally updates sensitivity levels each time a new data point become available. This approach, generally known as stochastic parameter regression analysis, is the most suitable in many cases.

3. A state space approach of estimating time-varying factor sensitivities

Originally developed by control engineers in the 1960's (Kalman 1960), and in particular for application concerning spacecraft navigation and rocket tracking, state space models have since attracted considerable attention in economics, finance, the social sciences and have been found to be useful in many non-stationary problems and particularly for time series analysis (Harvey 1984, Engle and Watson 1987). The Kalman filter is a powerful method for handling these state space models.

The Kalman filter consists of a system of equations for recursively and optimally estimating the current state (usually non-observable) of a dynamic system, from an ordered set of observations (usually a time series) contaminated by noise. This current state is described as a linear combination of state variables. State variables can represent unobservable components such as trends, cyclical and random components, seasonal factors, latent variables or factor sensitivities. Clear introductions to state space models and the Kalman filter can be found in Harvey 1989, Chatfield 1989, Hamilton 1994, Wells 1995 and Gourieroux and Monfort 1997. The original description of the filter and its derivation can be found in Kalman 1960.

The stochastic coefficient regression model expressed in a state space form can be defined by a system of two equations. The first equation is referred to as the "*observation equation*" and relates the observable dependent variables to the independent variables through the unobservable states variables:

$$Y_t = \mathbf{H}_t(\mathbf{s}_t + d) + \varepsilon_t \qquad for\ t = 1, \dots, T \qquad (2)$$

where Y_t is the dependent observable variables (e.g. an asset return) at time t
$\quad \mathbf{s}_t$ is a K vector that describes the state of the factor sensitivities of the asset returns at time t
$\quad d$ is a K non-random vector that can account for the long term mean is sensitivities
$\quad \mathbf{H}_t$ is a K vector that contains the factor values at time t.
$\quad \varepsilon_t$ is a serially uncorrelated perturbation with zero mean and variance R_t, i.e.:
$\quad E(\varepsilon_t) = 0$ and $Var(\varepsilon_t) = R_t$, R_t being non-random. It is not observable.

The exact representation of $\mathbf{H}_t$ and $\mathbf{s}_t$ will depend on the model specification for the factor sensitivities. A random trend model, for instance, will require more state variables ($K=2N$, N being the number of factors) than a random coefficient or a random walk model ($K=N$). Equation 8 can be easily extended to a multivariate dependent time series of m observations at each point in time. Y_t would then represent a m vector, $\mathbf{H}_t$ would be K×m matrix and ε_t would be an m vector. State space models and the Kalman filter can deal multivariate series without any theoretical complication.

In general, the elements of $\mathbf{s}_t$ are not observable. However, their time structure is assumed to be known. The evolution through time of these unobservable states is a first order Markov process described by a "*transition equation*":

$$\mathbf{s}_t = \Phi \mathbf{s}_{t-1} + c_t + \eta_t \qquad for\ t = 1, \dots, T \qquad (3)$$

where Φ is a non-random $K×K$ state transition matrix
$\quad c_t$ is a non-random K vector
$\quad \eta_t$ is an $m×1$ vector of serially uncorrelated disturbances with zero mean and covariance $\mathbf{Q}_t$, i.e.:
$\quad E(\eta_t) = 0$ and $Var(\eta_t) = \mathbf{Q}_t$, $\mathbf{Q}_t$ being non-random. It is not observable.

The initial state vector $\mathbf{s}_0$ has a mean of s and a covariance matrix $\mathbf{P}_0$. Furthermore, the disturbances ε_t and η_t are uncorrelated with each other in all time periods, and uncorrelated with the initial state

The system matrices, Φ, P and $\mathbf{Q}$, the vectors η, c and d and the scalar R are non-random although some of them may vary over time (but they do so in a predetermined way). Furthermore, the *observation noise* ε_t and the *system noise* η_t are Gaussian white noises.

Various time structures for the sensitivities are considered:

- **The Random Walk**

  The random walk model dictates that the best estimate of future sensitivities is the current sensitivity. To specify this model, vectors *d* and *c* are set to zero and the system matrices for the random walk model are given by equations 4

$$
\begin{aligned}
\mathbf{s}_i(t) &= \left[\beta_{i,1}, \beta_{i,2}, \cdots, \beta_{i,N}\right]', \\
\mathbf{H}(t) &= \left[1, F_1, \cdots, F_{N-1}\right], \\
\Phi &= \mathbf{I}
\end{aligned}
\tag{4}
$$

  where, Φ is $N \times N$, $\mathbf{H}_t$ $1 \times N$, and s_t is $N \times 1$, N being the number of independent variables, including the constant.

- **The Random Trend**

  The random trend model dictates that the best estimate of future sensitivities is the current sensitivity plus the trend. In the presence of a trend, sensitivities at $t+1$ are not equally likely to be above or under the value at t. A simple model which allows the sensitivities to trend is the random trend model. In a state space form, it can be written as:

$$
\begin{pmatrix} \beta_i(t) \\ \delta_i(t) \end{pmatrix} = \Phi_0 \begin{pmatrix} \beta_i(t-1) \\ \delta_i(t-1) \end{pmatrix} + \begin{pmatrix} \varepsilon_i(t) \\ \gamma_i(t) \end{pmatrix}
\tag{5}
$$

  where the individual sensitivity random trend state transition matrix is given by $\Phi_0 = \begin{bmatrix} 1 & 1 \\ 0 & 1 \end{bmatrix}$.

  To specify this model, vectors *d* and *c* are set to zero and the collection of factor sensitivities and trends are expressed as:

$$
s(t) = \left[\beta_1(t), \delta_1(t), \beta_2(t), \delta_2(t), ..., \beta_N(t), \delta_N(t)\right]'
\tag{6}
$$

$$
\mathbf{H}(t) = \left[1, 0, 1, 0, ..., 1, 0\right]
\tag{7}
$$

$$
\Phi = \begin{bmatrix} \Phi_0 & 0 & \cdots & 0 \\ 0 & \Phi_0 & & 0 \\ \vdots & & \ddots & \\ 0 & 0 & & \Phi_0 \end{bmatrix}
\tag{8}
$$

  where the dimensions of the state of sensitivities has been doubled to include trends in the sensitivities, i.e. Φ is $2N \times 2N$, s_t is $2N \times 1$, and H_t is $1 \times 2N$.

The Kalman filter

The objective of state space modelling is to estimate the unobservable states of the dynamic system from observations in the presence of noise. The Kalman filter is recursive method of doing this, i.e. filtering out the observation noise in order to optimally estimate the state vector at time t, based on the information available at time t (i.e. the observations up to and including Y_t). What makes the operation difficult is the fact that the states (e.g. the sensitivities) are not constant but change over time. The assumed amount of observation noise vs. system noise is used by the filter to optimally determine how much of the variation in Y_t should be attributed to the system, and how much is caused by observation noise. The filter consists of a system of equations which allow to update the estimate of the state s_t when new observations become available. More precisely, we want to estimate $\hat{s}_{t|t}$ (eq. 9) and the state error covariance matrix $P_{t|t}$ (eq. 10):

$$\hat{s}_{t|t} = E(s_t | Y_1, \ldots, Y_t) \tag{9}$$

$$P_{t|t} = E\left((s_t - \hat{s}_{t|t})(s_t - \hat{s}_{t|t})'\right) = \mathrm{var}(s_t - \hat{s}_{t|t}) \tag{10}$$

where the notation $\hat{a}_{b|c}$ denotes an estimate of a at time b conditional on the information available at time c.

Perhaps the most important part of a model is the predictions it yields. The predicted state of sensitivities $\hat{s}_{t|t-1}$ and the corresponding forecasting error covariance matrix $P_{t|t-1} = E\left((s_t - \hat{s}_{t|t-1})(s_t - \hat{s}_{t|t-1})'\right)$ are given by the *prediction equations*. 11 and 12:

$$\hat{s}_{t|t-1} = \Phi \hat{s}_{t-1|t-1} + c_t \tag{11}$$

$$P_{t|t-1} = \Phi P_{t-1|t-1} \Phi' + Q_t \tag{12}$$

and the predicted dependent variable is given by equation 13:

$$\hat{Y}_{t|t-1} = H_t \hat{s}_{t|t-1} + d \tag{13}$$

The forecast error e_t at time t and its variance f_t can be calculated by equations 14 and 15 respectively:

$$e_t = Y_t - \hat{Y}_{t|t-1} \tag{14}$$

$$f_{t|t-1} = \Phi P_{t|t-1} \Phi' + R_t \tag{15}$$

The new information is represented by the prediction error, e_t. It can be the result of several sources: random fluctuations in the returns, changes in the underlying states, or error in previous state estimates. Given this new information, the estimate $\hat{s}_{t|t}$ of the state vector and its covariance $P_{t|t}$ can now be updated through the *updating equations* 16 and 17 respectively. The Kalman filter takes the new information from each return to adjust estimates of the underlying states, where the new information is simply the prediction error of the returns. The Kalman gain matrix, K_t, adjusts the state estimates optimally to reflect the new information.

$$\hat{s}_{t|t} = \hat{s}_{t|t-1} + K_t e_t \tag{16}$$

$$P_{t|t} = \left(I - K_t H_t'\right) P_{t|t-1} \tag{17}$$

The Kalman gain matrix is calculated with the state error covariance $P_{t|t-1}$ and the predicted state error covariance $P_{t|t-1}$ with the recursive equation 18:

$$K_t = P_{t|t-1} H_t' \left(H_t P_{t|t-1} H_t' + R_t\right)^{-1} \tag{18}$$

300

In order to clarify the sequence of the Kalman filter equations, figure 2 presents a flowchart for the filter.

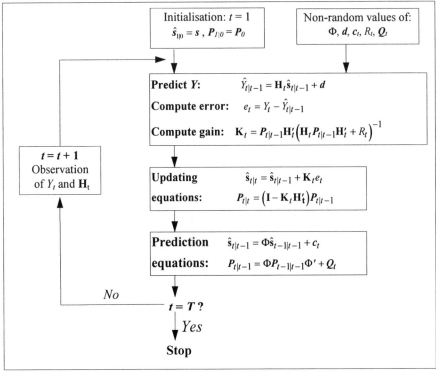

Figure 2: Flowchart of the Kalman filter

The recursive nature of the Kalman filter is a major computational advantage. It enables the model to update the conditional mean and covariance estimates of the states at time t based only on the estimate obtained at time $t-1$. Although it takes into account the entire history, it does not need an expanding memory.

The model requires initial values of the mean and the covariance of the states. These can be set by some prior knowledge. For instance, one can start with a prior value of 1 for a stock's beta, and a prior value of 0 for the sensitivity of the return to exchange rates. Alternatively, the OLS estimates of sensitivity (estimate and covariance matrix) could be used as initial values. A third possibility would be to use a diffuse prior for the initial state estimate (practically, initial state values of zero and a diagonal covariance matrix with large values is a good approximation of the diffuse prior) so that the filter would give little credibility to the initial state value and converge quickly to sensitivity values suggested by the data.

Estimation of the filter's hyper-parameters

Up to this point, some of the state space model coefficients were assumed to be known. This is not specific to state space models. Alternative regression models also require some parameters to be known (or assumed) *a priori*. For instance, weighted regression requires a decay parameter for the weighting function while rolling regression requires the size of the rolling window of observations. In each case, the sensitivities estimated will change with the choice of such hyper-parameters.

The values for these *hyper-parameters* (Φ, Q_t, R_t, d and c_t in the case of the general stochastic parameter regression model) can be set arbitrarily, according to some prior information or can be estimated by maximum likelihood, i.e. be optimised from the data. Two sets of hyper-parameters are particularly important as they have a major impact on the smoothness of the sensitivity estimates. These are the observation and system noises. It is important to balance well these quantities because they affect the weight of recent observations vs. the weight of more remote ones, the smoothness of the sensitivity estimates as well as their standard errors. Ideally, such parameters should be related to the data rather than being assigned *a priori* values.

Other parameters can also influence the estimated sensitivities, such as the elements of the state transition matrix Φ, as well as the parameter vectors d and c_t. Depending on the model specification such values are either set or estimated from the data along with the noise variances.

The models considered having Gaussian residuals, the log-likelihood function $\mathcal{L}$ can be written in terms of the prediction errors e_t and their variances $f_{t|t-1}$ defined in equations 14 and 15:

$$\mathcal{L}(\theta|Y_1,Y_2\cdots,Y_T) = -\frac{T}{2}\left(\ln(2\pi)+\ln(R)\right) - \frac{1}{2}\sum_{t=1}^{T}\ln(f_{t|t-1}) - \frac{1}{2R}\sum_{t=1}^{T}\frac{e_t^2}{f_{t|t-1}} \qquad (19)$$

and the maximum likelihood estimate $\hat{\theta}$ of the parameter vector θ is:

$$\hat{\theta} = \underset{\theta}{\text{argmax}}\ \mathcal{L}(\theta|Y_1,Y_2,...,Y_T) \qquad (20)$$

The likelihood can then be optimised with conjugate gradient techniques.

4. Examples of time-varying factor sensitivities in financial time series

As an example, we apply the state space approach to the monitoring of beta for one of the stocks in the data set. Second, the pattern of exposures of the British market portfolio to the US stock market, the trade-weighted currency exchange rate, the Brent oil prices and the short term interest rates is monitored over a period of

302

thirteen years by unconstrained stochastic parameter regression analysis. Third, constrained stochastic parameter regression is used to analyse the investment style of an American Mutual Fund. Finally, the sensitivities of the British pound and the French franc to the German mark and the US dollar are estimated and analysed over a 13-year period.

The variability of stock **beta.** *The example of Accor*

The Accor Group is a major player in the hotels industry and the business services. The company runs hotels in the traditional sector with chains such as Mercure or Ibis as well as in the economy sector with Formule 1 hotel and Motel 6 chains. The business services sector includes Ticket Restaurant lunch vouchers, institutional catering, restaurants chains and car rental.

Market risk can be measured for a stock by the sensitivity of its returns to market returns. This sensitivity is called the stock's "beta". An accurate estimation of beta is important in asset management because beta accounts for a large part of systematic risk that can not be diversified away. However, betas are additive. It is therefore possible to construct a portfolio with any level of beta, provided the investor can short some of the stocks, and provided future betas are reasonably well estimated. Accor's beta seems to vary substantially. There is a large swing in β at the beginning of the 1990's when profits are at a record high and debt start to increase sharply, along with financial gearing. The β reverts to its long term average of 1 in late 1992 after disappointing profits partly du to a fall in hotel occupancy in the catastrophic summer 1992 when many roads where blocked because of a lorry driver's strike, and an unfavourable court ruling involving Accor's take over of Wagon-Lits. The variation of beta is illustrated in figure 3.

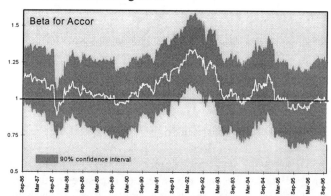

Figure 3: The movements in Accor's beta over an 11 year period (in white). The dark band corresponds to the 90% confidence level of the sensitivity estimate.

The variability of portfolio sensitivities. The example of the British market portfolio

It is conceivable, in principle, to measure the exposures of assets or portfolio of assets to any quantity that is perceived to be related to their value. Monitoring factor sensitivities enables the investor to take conscious exposures to sources of risk. Measuring the pattern of sensitivity provides the investor with a quick insight into the portfolio structure and returns' dynamics. Furthermore it enables him/her to tune the pattern of risk in order to profile the portfolio to the client's needs and desires and to hedge against some sources of risk while taking advantage of others.

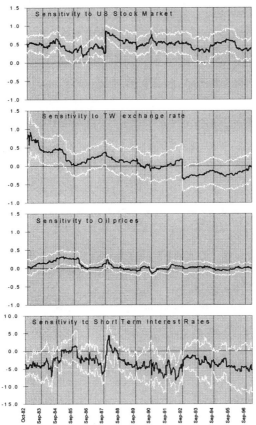

Figure 4: Sensitivity of the British stock index to the US stock market, the British pound trade weighted exchange rate, to oil prices and to short term exchange rates. The white bands correspond to the 90% confidence intervals for the estimated sensitivity coefficients (in black).

Here, we estimate the exposure of the British stock index (weekly logarithmic returns on the all share index, Datastream) to four factors over a 12-year period. The first factor is the US stock market (weekly logarithmic returns on the all share index, Datastream); the second factor is the British pound (weekly logarithmic changes in the Trade Weighted Currency index computed by the Bank of England); the third factor is oil prices (weekly logarithmic changes in the price of Brent oil); the fourth factor represents short term interest rates (first differences in 3 months Euro-currency middle rate for the Pound). Figure 4 presents the results of the analysis.

Short term interest rates and the American stock market seem to be the more important factors, especially since the 1987 market crash. Oil prices stopped being a major determinant in 1986 after the price of the barrel of Brent Oil had dropped from $30 in December 1985 to $13 in April 1986. Since this period, the sensitivity to oil prices has continuously fallen, with the notable exception of August 1990 to autumn 1991 during which most stock markets gyrated at the pace of the news coming from the Gulf region. The sensitivity to the British pound, petro-currency in the early 1980's has fallen until the pound left the ERM in September 1992.

Constrained factor models for style monitoring and performance attribution.

Style management has become a common practice among pension funds (Sharpe 1992). Typically, style can be viewed as a mixed exposure to several basic market segments, e.g. growth/value, large/small capitalisation, domestic/international. Some managers are specialised in a style, enabling sponsors to diversify their holdings according to investment styles. This makes it very important for a manager to fit explicitly into its style category. A reputation as a manager who drifts between styles can be extremely harmful to future marketing efforts. In this context, factor modelling provides a fast and simple way to monitor manager's investment styles. The sensitivities of the fund's returns to those of style indices give the average style mix of the fund over the estimation period. A major shortcoming of the method is its incapacity to provide instantaneous measures of managers' styles.

A passive fund manager provides an investor with an investment style while an active manager provides both style and selection. Therefore, fund selection returns can be measured as the difference between the fund's returns and those of a passive mix with the same style. Practically, the selection skills are given by the α of the factor model while the style contributions are given by the various βs. Results associated with the choice of investment style should be attributed to the investor, not to the manager. An accurate estimation of the sensitivities is crucial to performance attribution.

In this context of active and passive asset management an accurate estimation of the future, or at least, instantaneous sensitivity is important. If sensitivities are not properly estimated, managers may not realise the expected profit even though their factor anticipations were right.

In order to estimate the managed portfolio's sensitivities to style indexes, either unconstrained or constrained parameter models can be applied. The first model does not constrain the coefficients and provides an unbiased estimate of the current portfolio style. The second model constrains the sensitivity coefficients to be positive and to sum up to one. Although this model is biased, because of the limitation of its degrees of freedom, it is usually preferred because its coefficients can be interpreted in terms of portfolio weights on the style indexes.

Figure 5 shows the estimation results obtained by the two estimation methods. Unconstrained sensitivities can be interpreted in much the same way as beta. For instance, in October 1991, for a one percent increase in the Large Caps / Growth index, the fund's value was expected to go up by 0.5 percent. Because these sensitivities are unconstrained, some values can be negative. For instance, a large exposure to value stocks coincided with a negative exposure to growth stocks between October 1992 to December 1995. This is not surprising since, value and growth stocks have opposite behaviours relative to the large capitalisation index.

For constrained regression (right hand side chart), however, all exposures are positive and sum up to one. Here, sensitivity figures can be interpreted in terms of portfolio holdings. Although exposure coefficients can be biased, the alpha (the fund's benchmark adjusted performance) is comparable for both regression techniques. This might not always be the case, especially when actual sensitivities are outside the range [0,1]. The bias introduced by constraints may then affect more seriously the alpha.

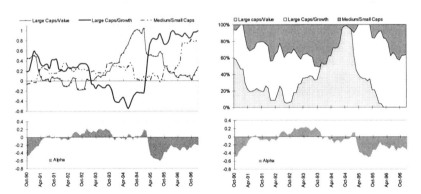

Figure 5: Effective style mix measured for the same fund with unconstrained regression (left hand side) and constrained regression (right hand side).Unconstrained stochastic parameter regression provides unbiased estimates of the fund's style exposures. Exposures can be interpreted as any sensitivity measures. Because these sensitivities are unconstrained, some values can be negative. A large exposure to value stocks can lead to a negative exposure to growth stocks, as it is the case between October 1992 to December 1995.

The variability of currency exposures. The example of a British pound and the French franc.

The sensitivity of currencies to other currencies can be estimated by regression of exchange rate variations. For instance, the coefficients α and β of the equation $\Delta \frac{FF}{X} = \alpha \cdot \Delta \frac{USD}{X} + \beta \cdot \Delta \frac{DM}{X}$ represent the sensitivities of the French franc to the US dollar and the German mark. X is a reference currency and $\Delta Y/X$ is the logarithmic variation of the exchange rate between currency Y and X.

The results of the study for the franc and the pound between January 1984 and February 1997 are presented in figure 6. The exposures of the franc to the dollar and the deutschmark vary very little over the period considered (standard deviations for these sensitivities are 0.03 and 0.05 respectively). Variations are almost imperceptible apart from March 1986 (devaluation of the franc), September 1992 (EMS crisis, the British pound and the Italian Lira leave the ERM), July 1993 (the fluctuation bands of the ERM are enlarged for the FF/DM rate) and beginning 1995 (pre- and post-election speculations about the monetary intentions of the new government).

In contrast, sensitivities for the British pound fluctuate greatly (standard deviations for these sensitivities are 0.10 and 0.20 respectively), suggesting a bigger independence from the deutschmark. These sensitivities reflect the market participants' perceptions of the implicit relationships between currencies and the convergence/divergence of fiscal and monetary policies. With the planned fall of the US dollar, March 1985 marks the beginning of a closer connection between the pound and the mark. Sensitivity levels vary after the Plaza Accords in September 1985 and the Louvre Accords in February 1987. Between 1988 and 1990, the sensitivity to the German mark gyrates at the pace of the declarations by the British government about a possible joining of the ERM. Between October 1990 (the pound joins the EMS) and September 1992 (the pound leaves the EMS) sensitivities are relatively stable. From 1993, with Britain's independent monetary policy, the sensitivities to both currencies decrease.

A fixed parameter model would have done reasonably well for estimating the exposures of the French franc. In contrast, such a model would have done quite poorly on the British pound, because of the instability of its sensitivity pattern.

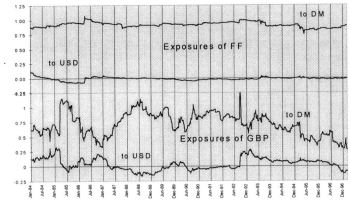

Figure 6: Exposure of the French franc and the British pound to the US dollar and the Deutschmark over a 13-year period. While the sensitivity pattern of the franc is quite stable over time, the one for the pound fluctuates more significantly, except for the period when the pound was part of the ERM.

Conclusion

This article proposed an alternative approach to rolling OLS regression analysis for estimating sensitivity of assets returns to economic and financial factors. We showed that OLS estimation of future sensitivity levels is biased if sensitivities are not stable through time. This shortcoming is particularly serious in quantitative equity investment management where past sensitivities are of relative importance compared to future ones. We proposed to use parameter constancy tests to evaluate whether factor sensitivities are reasonably constant (in which case rolling OLS estimation can be used), or whether they vary over the sample (in which case more complex model should be used to predict factor sensitivities). A state space approach to sensitivity modelling has been proposed and the unconstrained as well as constrained estimation by Kalman filtering has been described and discussed.

Finally, the proposed approaches have been applied to financial data. They provided a good insight in market dynamics and proved to be useful not only when sensitivity levels are varying but also when they are constant. The advantage of general models, not assuming parameter constancy, is obvious in a field like equity management where much is assumed and little is known about the dynamics of returns.

Given the many applications of factor modelling in equity management, stochastic parameter regression models and sensitivity constancy tests should be added to the asset manager's toolbox.

References

Bentz, Yves, "Identifying and Modelling Conditional Factor Sensitivities: an Application to Equity Investment Management", Doctoral Thesis, *London Business School*, 1997

Blume, Marchall, "Betas and their Regression Tendencies", *Journal of Finance*, 10, No.3 (June 1975), pp. 785-795

Bos, Paul and Newbold, Theodore, "An empirical investigation of the possibility of stochastic systematic risk in the market model", *Journal of Business*, **57** (1984), pp.35-41

Chow, G. C., "Tests of Equality between sets of Coefficients in two Linear Regressions", *Econometrica* **28**, (1960), pp. 591-605

Cooley, T.F. and Prescott, E.C., "Varying parameter regression: A theory and some applications", *Annals of Economic and Social Measurement*, **2**, pp. 463-474, 1973

Cuthbertson, K. and Taylor, M. P., "Anticipated and unanticipated variables in the demand for M1 in the UK", *Manchester School*, **57** (4), 319-39.

Doran, Howard, .E., "Constraining Kalman filter and smoothing estimates to satisfy time-varying restrictions", *The Review of Economics and Statistics*, August 1991, pp.568-572

Elton, Edwin J. and Gruber, Martin, J., *Modern Portfolio Theory and Investment Analysis*, John Wiley and Sons, Inc, 1995

Fabozzi, Frank, J. and Francis, J.C., "Beta as a random coefficient", *Journal of financial and Quantitative Analysis*, **13** (1978), pp.101-116

Goldfeld, S.M. and Quandt, R.E., "The estimation of structural shifts by switching regressions", *Annals of Economic and Social Measurement*, **2**, pp. 475-485, 1973

Hansen, Bruce, E., "Testing for Parameter Instability in Linear Models", *Journal of Policy Modeling*, **14**, No.4, (1992), pp. 517-533

Harvey, Andrew C., Henry, S. G. B., Peters, S. and Wren-Lewis, S., "Stochastic trends in dynamic regression models: an application to the employment-output equations", *Economic Journal*, **96** (1986), pp. 975-85.

Jazwinski, Andrew H., *Stochastic Processes and Filtering Theory*, Academic Press, 1970

Lintner, John, "The valuation of Risk Assets and the Selection of Risky Investments in Stock Portfolios and Capital Budgets", *Review of Economics and Statistics*, 47:13-37 February 1965

McGee, V.E. and Carlton, T.W., "Piecewise regression", *Journal of the American Statistical Association*, **65**, pp. 1109-1124, 1970

Mossin, Jan, "Equilibrium in a Capital Asset Market", *Econometrica*, October 1966

Nyblom, J., "Testing for the Constancy of Parameters over Time", *Journal of the American Statistical Association,* **84**, 1989, pp.223-230

Ohlson, J. and Rosenberg, Barr, "Systematic risk of the CRSP equal-weighted common stock index: a history estimated by stochastic parameter regression", *Journal of Business*, **55** (1982), 121-145

Rosenberg, Barr and Guy,James, "Predictions of Beta from Investment Fundamentals", *Financial Analyst Journal*, **32** (May-June 1976), pp.60-72, **33**(July-August 1976), pp.62-70

Rosenberg, Barr, "Random coefficient models: the analysis of a cross section of time series by stochastically convergent parameter regression", *Annals of Economic and Social Measurement*, **2**, pp. 399-428, 1973

Sharpe, William, F., "Asset Allocation: Management Style and Performance Measurement", *Journal of Portfolio Management*, **18**, No.2, (Winter 1992), pp. 7-19

Vasicek, O. "A Note on Using Cross-Sectional Information in Bayesian Estimation of Security Betas", Journal of Finance, 8 (December 1973)

DISCOVERING STRUCTURE IN FINANCE USING INDEPENDENT COMPONENT ANALYSIS

ANDREW D. BACK
Brain Science Institute
The Institute of Physical and Chemical Research (RIKEN)
2-1 Hirosawa, Wako-shi, Saitama 351-0198, Japan
back@brain.riken.go.jp
www.bip.riken.go.jp/absl/back

ANDREAS S. WEIGEND
Department of Information Systems
Leonard N. Stern School of Business
New York University
44 West Fourth Street, MEC 9-74
New York, NY 10012, USA
aweigend@stern.nyu.edu
www.stern.nyu.edu/~aweigend

Independent component analysis is a new signal processing technique. In this paper we apply it to a portfolio of Japanese stock price returns over three years of daily data and compare the results obtained using principal component analysis. The results indicate that the independent components fall into two categories, (i) infrequent but large shocks (responsible for the major changes in the stock prices), and (ii) frequent but rather small fluctuations (contributing little to the overall level of the stocks). The small number of major shocks indicate turning points in the time series and when used to reconstruct the stock prices, give good results in terms of morphology. In contrast, when using shocks derived from principal components instead of independent components, the reconstructed price does not show the same results at all. Independent component analysis is shown to be a potentially powerful method of analysing and understanding driving mechanisms in financial time series.

1 Introduction

What drives the movements of a financial time series? In this paper, we focus on a new technique which to our knowledge has not been used in any significant application to financial or econometric problems[1] called *independent component analysis* (ICA)

---

[1] We are only aware of Baram and Roth (1995) who use a neural network that maximizes output entropy and of Moody and Wu (1996), Moody and Wu (1997a), Moody and Wu (1997b) and Wu and Moody (1997) who apply ICA in the context of state space models for interbank foreign exchange rates to improve the separation between observational noise and the "true price."

A.-P.N. Refenes et al. (eds.), Decision Technologies for Computational Finance, 309–322.

which is also referred to as *blind source separation* (Herault and Jutten 1986, Jutten and Herault 1991, Comon 1994).

The central assumption is that an observed multivariate time series (such as daily stock returns) reflects the reaction of a system (such as the stock market) to a few statistically independent time series. ICA provides a mechanism of decomposing a given signal into statistically *independent components* (ICs).

ICA can be expressed in terms of the related concepts of entropy (Bell and Sejnowski 1995), mutual information (Amari, Cichocki and Yang 1996), contrast functions (Comon 1994) and other measures of the statistical independence of signals. For independent signals, the joint probability can be factorized into the product of the marginal probabilities. Therefore the independent components can be found by minimizing the Kullback-Leibler divergence between the joint probability and marginal probabilities of the output signals (Amari et al. 1996).

Independent component analysis can also be contrasted with principal component analysis (PCA) and so we give a brief comparison of the two methods here. Both ICA and PCA linearly transform the observed signals into components. The key difference however, is in the type of components obtained. The goal of PCA is to obtain principal components which are uncorrelated. Moreover, PCA gives projections of the data in the direction of the maximum variance. The principal components (PCs) are ordered in terms of their variances: the first PC defines the direction that captures the maximum variance possible, the second PC defines (in the remaining orthogonal subspace) the direction of maximum variance, and so forth. In ICA however, we seek to obtain statistically independent components.

PCA algorithms use only second order statistical information. On the other hand, ICA algorithms may use higher order[2] statistical information for separating the signals (see for example Cardoso 1989, Comon 1994). For this reason non-Gaussian signals (or at most, one Gaussian signal) are required for ICA. For PCA algorithms however, the higher order statistical information provided by such non-Gaussian signals is not required or used, hence the signals in this case can be Gaussian.

The goal of this paper is to explore whether ICA can give some indication of the underlying structure of the stock market. The hope is to find interpretable factors of instantaneous stock returns. Such factors could include news (government intervention, natural or man-made disasters, political upheaval), response to very large trades, and, of course, unexplained noise. Ultimately, we hope that this might yield new ways of analyzing and forecasting financial time series, contributing to a better understanding of financial markets.

---

[2] ICA algorithms based on second order statistics have also been proposed (Belouchrani, Abed Meraim, Cardoso and Moulines 1997, Tong, Soon, Huang and Liu 1990).

2 ICA in General

2.1 Independent Component Analysis

ICA denotes the process of taking a set of measured signal vectors, x, and extracting from them a (new) set of statistically independent vectors, y, called the independent components or the sources. They are estimates of the original source signals which are assumed to have been mixed in some prescribed manner to form the observed signals.

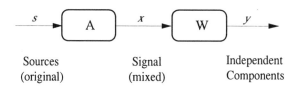

Figure 1: Schematic representation of ICA. The original sources s are mixed through matrix $\mathbf{A}$ to form the observed signal x. The demixing matrix $\mathbf{W}$ transforms the observed signal x into the independent components y.

Figure 1 shows the most basic form of ICA. We use the following notation: We *observe* a multivariate time series $\{x_i(t)\}$, $i = 1, ..., n$, consisting of n values at each time step t. We *assume* that it is the result of a mixing process

$$x_i(t) = \sum_{j=1}^{n} a_{ij} s_j(t) \quad .$$
(1)

Using the instantaneous observation vector $\mathbf{x}(t) = [x_1(t), x_2(t), ..., x_n(t)]$, the problem is to find a *demixing matrix* $\mathbf{W}$ such that

$$\begin{aligned} \mathbf{y}(t) &= \mathbf{W}\mathbf{x}(t) \\ &= \mathbf{W}\mathbf{A}\mathbf{s}(t) \end{aligned}$$
(2)

where $\mathbf{A}$ is the unknown mixing matrix. We assume throughout this paper that there are as many observed signals as there are sources, hence $\mathbf{A}$ is a square $n \times n$ matrix. If $\mathbf{W} = \mathbf{A}^{-1}$, then $\mathbf{y}(t) = \mathbf{s}(t)$, and perfect separation occurs. In general, it is only possible to find $\mathbf{W}$ such that $\mathbf{W}\mathbf{A} = \mathbf{P}\mathbf{D}$ where $\mathbf{P}$ is a permutation matrix and $\mathbf{D}$ is a diagonal scaling matrix (Tong, Liu, Soon and Huang 1991).

To find such a matrix $\mathbf{W}$, the following assumptions are made:

- The sources $\{s_j(t)\}$ are statistically independent. While it might sound strong, this is not an unreasonable assumption when one considers for example sources of very different origins ranging from foreign politics to microeconomic variables that might impact a stock price.

- At most one source has a Gaussian distribution. In the case of financial data, normally distributed signals are so rare that only allowing for one of them is not a serious restriction.

- The signals are stationary. Stationarity is a standard assumption that enters almost all modeling efforts, not only ICA.

In this paper, we only consider the case when the mixtures occur instantaneously in time. This appears to be a reasonable assumption to make since it implies that at each time instant, the observed stock price is comprised of all currently available information from all sources and is acted on immediately. It is also of interest to consider models based on multichannel blind deconvolution (Jutten, Nguyen Thi, Dijkstra, Vittoz and Caelen 1991, Weinstein, Feder and Oppenheim 1993, Nguyen Thi and Jutten 1995, Torkkola 1996, Yellin and Weinstein 1996, Parra, Spence and de Vries 1997) however we do not do this in the present paper.

2.2 Algorithms for ICA

The earliest ICA algorithm that we are aware of and one which started much interest in the field is that proposed by Herault and Jutten (1986).

Since then, a wide variety of ICA algorithms have been proposed using on-line and batch methods. In addition, various approaches for obtaining the independent components have been proposed, including: minimizing higher order moments (Cardoso 1989) or higher order cumulants (Cardoso and Souloumiac 1993), maximization of mutual information of the outputs or maximization of the output entropy (Bell and Sejnowski 1995), minimization of the Kullback-Leibler divergence between the joint and the product of the marginal distributions of the outputs (Amari et al. 1996).

Neurally inspired algorithms have also been proposed which incorporate a nonlinear function to introduce higher order statistics (see for example Cichocki and Moszczyński 1992, Choi, Liu and Cichocki 1998, Cichocki, Unbehauen and Rummert 1994, Girolami and Fyfe 1997, Hyvärinen 1996, Karhunen 1996, Oja and Karhunen 1995). An important development recently is the field of ICA algorithms which are referred to as *natural gradient* algorthms (Amari et al. 1996, Amari 1998). A similar approach was independently derived by Cardoso and Laheld (1996) who referred to it as a *relative gradient* algorithm. This theoretically sound modification to the usual on-line updating algorithm overcomes the problem of having to perform matrix inversions at each time step and therefore permits significantly faster convergence. Another extension includes contextual ICA (Pearlmutter and Parra 1997) where a method utilizing spatial and temporal information was proposed based on maximum likelihood estimation to separate signals having colored Gaussian distributions or low kurtosis. The ICA framework has also been extended to allow for nonlinear mixing (Burel 1992, Yang, Amari and Cichocki 1997, Yang, Amari and Cichocki 1998, Lin, Grier and Cowan 1997).

A batch ICA algorithm, sometimes referred to as "decorrelation and rotation" (Pope and Bogner 1996), is given by the following two stage procedure (Bogner 1992, Cardoso and Souloumiac 1993).

1. *Decorrelation or whitening.* Here we seek to diagonalize the covariance matrix of the input signals.

2. *Rotation.* The second stage minimizes a measure of the higher order statistics which will ensure the non-Gaussian output signals are as statistically independent as possible. It can be shown that this can be carried out by a unitary rotation matrix (Cardoso and Souloumiac 1993). This second stage provides the higher order independence.

Note that this approach relies on the measured signals being non-Gaussian. For Gaussian signals, the higher order statistics are zero already and so no meaningful separation can be achieved by ICA methods.

The empirical study carried out in this paper uses the JADE (Joint Approximate Diagonalization of Eigenmatrices) algorithm (Cardoso and Souloumiac 1993) which is an efficient batch algorithm computed in stages. The first stage whitens the data by computing the sample covariance matrix, giving the second order statistics of the signals. The second stage consists of finding a rotation matrix which jointly diagonalizes eigenmatrices formed from the fourth order cumulants of the whitened data. The outputs from this stage are the independent components.

3 Analyzing Stock Returns with ICA

3.1 Description of the Data

To investigate the effectiveness of ICA techniques for financial time series, we apply ICA to data from the Tokyo Stock Exchange. We use daily closing prices from 1986 until 1989[3] of the 28 largest firms.

Figure 2(a) shows the stock price of the first company in our set, the Bank of Tokyo-Mitsubishi, between August 1986 and July 1988.

The preprocessing consists of three steps: we obtain the daily stock returns, subtract the mean of each stock, and normalize the resulting values to lie within the range $[-1, 1]$. The stock returns are obtained by taking the difference between successive values of the prices $p(t)$, as $x(t) = p(t) - p(t-1)$. Given the relatively large change in price levels over the few years of data, an alternative would have been to use relative returns, $\log(p(t)) - \log(p(t-1))$, describing geometric growth as opposed to additive growth. Figure 3 shows these normalized stock returns.

---

[3] We chose a subset of available historical data on which to test the method. This allows us to reserve subsequent data for further experimentation.

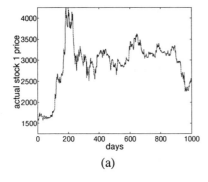 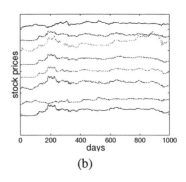

(a)   (b)

Figure 2: (a) The price of the Bank of Tokyo-Mitsubishi stock for the period 8/86 until 7/88. This bank is one if the largest companies traded on the Tokyo Stock Exchange. (b) The largest eight stocks on the Tokyo Stock Exchange over the same period, offset for clarity. The lowest line displays the price of the Bank of Tokyo-Mitsubishi.

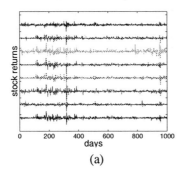 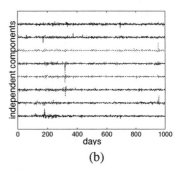

(a)   (b)

Figure 3: (a) The stock returns (differenced time series) of the first eight stocks for the period 8/86 until 7/88. The large negative return at day 317 corresponds to the crash of 19 October 1987. The lowest line again corresponds to the Bank of Tokyo-Mitsubishi. The question is: can ICA reveal useful information about these time series? (b) The first eight ICs, resulting from the ICA of all 28 stocks.

3.2   Structure of the Independent Components

We performed ICA on the stock returns using the JADE algorithm (Cardoso and Souloumiac 1993) described in section 2.2. In all the experiments, we assume that the number of stocks equals the number of sources supplied to the mixing model.

In the results presented here, all 28 stocks are used as inputs in the ICA. However for clarity, the figures only display the first few ICs. Figure 3(b) shows a subset of eight ICs obtained from the algorithm. Note that the goal of statistical independence forces the 1987 crash to be carried by only a few components.

We now present the analysis of a specific stock, the Bank of Tokyo-Mitsubishi. The contributions of the ICs to any given stock can be found as follows.

For a given stock return, there is a corresponding row of the mixing matrix $\mathbf{A}$ used to weight the independent components. By multiplying the corresponding row of $\mathbf{A}$ with the ICs, we obtain the weighted ICs. We define *dominant* ICs to be those ICs with the largest maximum signal amplitudes. They have the largest effect on the reconstructed stock price. In contrast, other criteria, such as the variance, would focus not on the largest value but on the average.

Figure 4(a) weights the ICs with the the first row of the mixing matrix which corresponds to the Bank of Tokyo-Mitsubishi. The four traces at the bottom show the four most dominant ICs for this stock.

From the usual mixing process given by Eq. (1), we can obtain the reconstruction of the ith stock return in terms of the estimated ICs

$$\hat{x}_i(t-j) \;=\; \sum_{k=1}^{n} a_{ik}y_k(t-j) \quad j = 0, .., N-1 \tag{3}$$

where $y_k(t-j)$ is the value of the kth estimated IC at time $t-j$ and a_{ik} is the weight in the ith row, kth column of the estimated mixing matrix $\mathbf{A}$ (obtained as the inverse of the demixing matrix $\mathbf{W}$). We define the weighted ICs for the ith observed signal (stock return) as

$$\bar{y}_{ik}(t-j) \;=\; a_{ik}y_k(t-j) \quad k = 1, .., n; j = 0, .., N-1. \tag{4}$$

In this paper, we rank the weighted ICs with respect to the first stock return. Therefore, we multiply the ICs with the first row of the mixing matrix and so we use a_{1k} $k = 1, .., n$ to obtain the weighted ICs. The weighted ICs are then sorted[4] using an L_∞ norm, since we are most interested in showing just those ICs which cause the maximum price change in a particular stock.

The ICs obtained from the stock returns reveal the following aspects:

- Only a few ICs contribute to most of the movements in the stock return.

- Large amplitude transients in the dominant ICs contribute to the major level changes. The nondominant components do not contribute significantly to level changes.

- Small amplitude ICs contribute to the change in levels over short time scales, but over the whole period, there is little change in levels.

Figure 4(b) shows the reconstructed price obtained using the four most dominant weighted ICs and compares it to the sum of the remaining 24 nondominant weighted ICs.

---

[4]ICs can by sorted in various ways. For example, in the implementation of the JADE algorithm Cardoso and Souloumiac (1993) used a Euclidean norm to sort the rows of the demixing matrix $\mathbf{W}$ according to their contribution across all signals.

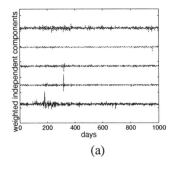 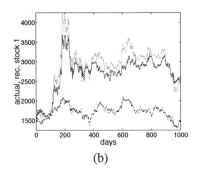

(a)   (b)

Figure 4: (a) The four most dominant weighted ICs (corresponding to the Bank of Tokyo-Mitsubishi) are shown starting from the bottom trace. The top trace is the summation of the remaining 24 least dominant ICs for this stock. (b) *Top* (dotted) line: original stock price. *Middle* (solid) line: reconstructed stock price using the four most dominant weighted ICs. *Bottom* (dashed) line: reconstructed residual stock price obtained by from remaining 24 weighted ICs. Note that the major part of the true 'shape' comes from the most dominant components; the contribution of the non-dominant ICs to the overall shape is only small.

3.3 Thresholded ICs Characterize Turning Points

The preceding section discussed the effect of a lossy reconstruction of the original prices, obtained by considering the cumulative sums of only the first few dominant ICs. In this section we examine the reconstructed prices using the dominant ICs after they have been thresholded to remove all values smaller than a certain level.

The thresholded reconstructions are described by

$$\bar{x}_i(t-j) \;=\; \sum_{k=1}^{n} g\left(\bar{y}_{ik}(t-j)\right) \quad j=0,..,N-1, \tag{5}$$

$$g(u) \;=\; \begin{cases} u & |u| \geq \xi \\ 0 & |u| < \xi \end{cases} \tag{6}$$

where $\bar{x}_i(t-j)$ are the returns constructed using thresholds, $g(\cdot)$ is the threshold function and ξ is the threshold value. The threshold was set arbitrarily to a value which excluded almost all of the lower level components.

The reconstructed stock prices are found as

$$\begin{aligned} \hat{p}_i(j+1) &= \hat{p}_i(j) + \bar{x}_i(j) \quad j=t-N,..,t-1 \\ \hat{p}_i(t-N) &= p_i(t-N) \end{aligned} \tag{7}$$

For the first stock, the Bank of Tokyo-Mitsubishi, $p_1(t-N) = 1550$.

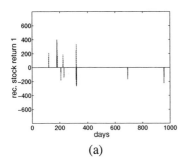 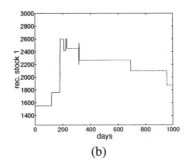

(a) (b)

Figure 5: ICA results for the Bank of Tokyo-Mitsubishi: (a) thresholded returns constructed from the four most dominant weighted ICs, (b) reconstructed prices obtained by computing the cumulative sum of only the thresholded values. Note that the price for the 1,000 points plotted is still characterized well by only a few innovations.

The thresholded returns of the four most dominant ICs are shown in Figure 5(a), and the stock price reconstructed from the thresholded return values are shown in Figure 5(b). The figures indicate that the thresholded ICs provide useful morphological information and can extract the turning points of original time series.

3.4 Comparison with PCA

PCA is a well established tool in finance. Applications range from Arbitrage Pricing Theory and factor models to input selection for multi-currency portfolios (Utans, Holt and Refenes 1997). Here we seek to compare the performance of PCA with ICA using singular value decomposition (SVD).

The results from the PCs obtained from the stock returns reveal the following aspects:

- The distinct shocks which were identified in the ICA case are much more difficult to observe.

- While the first four PCs are by construction the best possible fit in a quadratic error sense to the data, they do not offer the same insight in structure in the data compared to the ICs.

- The dominant transients obtained from the PCs, ie., after thresholding, do not lead to the same overall shape of the stock returns as the ICA approach. Hence we cannot make the same conclusions about high level and low level signals in the data. The effect of thresholding is shown in Figure 7.

For the experiment reported here, the four most dominant PCs are the same, whether ordered in terms of variance or using the L_∞ norm as in the ICA case. Beyond that the orders change.

318

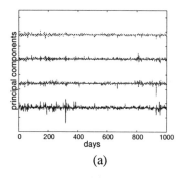 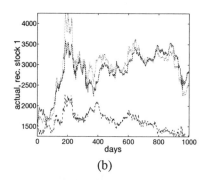

(a)   (b)

Figure 6: For the Bank of Tokyo-Mitsubishi: (a) the four most dominant PCs corresponding to stock returns, (b) *Top* (dotted) line: original stock price. *Middle* (solid) line: reconstructed stock price using the four most dominant PCs. *Bottom* (dashed) line: reconstructed residual stock price obtained by from remaining 24 PCs. The sum of the two lower lines corresponds to the true price. In this case, the error is smaller than that obtained when using ICA. However, the overall shape of the stock is not reconstructed as well by the PCs.

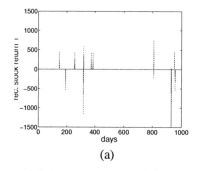 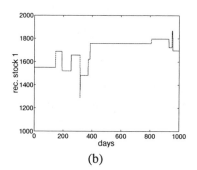

(a)   (b)

Figure 7: PCA results for the Bank of Tokyo-Mitsubishi: (a) thresholded returns constructed from the four most dominant PCs, (b) reconstructed prices. In this case, the model does not capture the large transients observed in the ICA case and fails to adequately approximate the shape of the original stock price curve.

Figure 7(b) shows the reconstructed stock price from the thresholded returns are a poor fit to the overall shape of the original price. This implies that key high level transients that were extracted by ICA are not obtained through PCA.

In summary, while PCA also decompose the original data, the PCs do not possess the high order independence obtained of the ICs. A major difference emerges when only the largest shocks of the estimated sources are used. While the cumulative sum up the largest IC shocks retains the overall shape, this is not the case for the PCs.

4   Conclusions

This paper applied independent component analysis (ICA) to decompose a portfolio of 28 instantaneous stock returns into statistically independent components (ICs). The components of the instantaneous vectors of observed daily stock are statistically dependent; stocks on average move together. In contrast, the components of the instantaneous daily vector of ICs are constructed to be statistically independent. This can be viewed as decomposing the returns into statistically independent sources. On three years of daily data from the Tokyo stock exchange, we showed that the estimated ICs fall into two categories, (i) infrequent but large shocks (responsible for the major changes in the stock prices), and (ii) frequent but rather small fluctuations (contributing only little to the overall level of the stocks). The October 1987 crash, for example, is given by only a few ICs in the first group and does not appear in the other group.

We have shown that by using a portfolio of stocks, ICA can reveal some underlying structure in the data. Interestingly, the 'noise' we observe may be attributed to signals within a certain *amplitude* range and not to signals in a certain (usually high) *frequency* range. Thus, ICA gives a fresh perspective to the problem of understanding the mechanisms that influence the stock market data.

In comparison to PCA, ICA is a complimentary tool which allows the underlying structure of the data to be more readily observed. There are clearly many other avenues in which ICA techniques can be applied to finance. Implications to risk management and asset allocation using ICA are explored in Chin and Weigend (1998).

Acknowledgements

We are grateful to Morio Yoda, Nikko Securities, Tokyo for kindly providing the data used in this paper, and to Jean-François Cardoso for making the source code for the JADE algorithm available. Andrew Back acknowledges support of the Frontier Research Program and RIKEN and would like to thank Seungjin Choi and Zhang Liqing for helpful discussions. Andreas Weigend acknowledges support from the National Science Foundation (ECS-9309786) and would like to thank Fei Chen, Elion Chin and Juan Lin for stimulating discussions.

References

Amari, S. (1998). Natural gradient works efficiently in learning, *Neural Computation* **10**(2): 251–276.

Amari, S., Cichocki, A. and Yang, H. (1996). A new learning algorithm for blind signal separation, *in* G. Tesauro, D. S. Touretzky and T. K. Leen (eds), *Advances in Neural Information Processing Systems 8 (NIPS*95)*, The MIT Press, Cambridge, MA, pp. 757–763.

Baram, Y. and Roth, Z. (1995). Forecasting by density shaping using neural networks, *Proceedings of the IEEE/IAFE 1995 Conference on Computational Intelligence for Financial Engineering (CIFEr)*, IEEE Service Center, Piscataway, NJ.

Bell, A. and Sejnowski, T. (1995). An information maximization approach to blind separation and blind deconvolution, *Neural Computation* **7**: 1129–1159.

Belouchrani, A., Abed Meraim, K., Cardoso, J. and Moulines, E. (1997). A blind source separation technique based on second order statistics, *IEEE Trans. on S.P.* **45**(2): 434–44.

Bogner, R. E. (1992). Blind separation of sources, *Technical Report 4559*, Defence Research Agency, Malvern.

Burel, G. (1992). Blind separation of sources: a nonlinear neural algorithm, *Neural Networks* **5**: 937–947.

Cardoso, J. (1989). Source separation using higher order moments, *International Conference on Acoustics, Speech and Signal Processing*, pp. 2109–2112.

Cardoso, J. and Laheld, B. (1996). Equivariant adaptive source separation, *IEEE Trans. Signal Processing*.

Cardoso, J. and Souloumiac, A. (1993). Blind beamforming for non-Gaussian signals, *IEE Proc. F.* **140**(6): 771–774.

Chin, E. and Weigend, A. S. (1998). Asset allocation: An independent component analysis, *Technical report*, Information Systems Department, Leonard N. Stern School of Business, New York University.

Choi, S., Liu, R. and Cichocki, A. (1998). A spurious equilibria-free learning algorithm for the blind separation of non-zero skewness signals, *Neural Processing Letters* **7**: 1–8.

Cichocki, A. and Moszczyński, L. (1992). New learning algorithm for blind separation of sources, *Electronics Letters* **28**(21): 1986–1987.

Cichocki, A., Unbehauen, R. and Rummert, E. (1994). Robust learning algorithm for blind separation of signals, *Electronics Letters* **30**(17): 1386–1387.

Comon, P. (1994). Independent component analysis – a new concept?, *Signal Processing* **36**(3): 287–314.

Girolami, M. and Fyfe, C. (1997). An extended exploratory projection pursuit network with linear and nonlinear anti-hebbian connections applied to the cocktail party problem, *Neural Networks* **10**(9): 1607–1618.

Herault, J. and Jutten, C. (1986). Space or time adaptive signal processing by neural network models, *in* J. S. Denker (ed.), *Neural Networks for Computing. Proceedings of AIP Conference*, American Institute of Physics, New York, pp. 206–211.

Hyvärinen, A. (1996). Simple one-unit algorithms for blind source separation and blind deconvolution, *Progress in Neural Information Processing ICONIP'96*, Vol. 2, Springer, pp. 1201–1206.

Jutten, C. and Herault, J. (1991). Blind separation of sources, part I: An adaptive algorithm based on neuromimetic architecture, *Signal Processing* **24**: 1–20.

Jutten, C., Nguyen Thi, H., Dijkstra, E., Vittoz, E. and Caelen, J. (1991). Blind separation of sources, an algorithm for separation of convolutive mixtures, *Proceedings of Int. Workshop on High Order Statistics*, Chamrousse (France), pp. 273–276.

Karhunen, J. (1996). Neural approaches to independent component analysis and source separation, *Proceedings of 4th European Symp. on Artificial Neural Networks (ESANN'96)*, Bruges, Belgium, pp. 249–266.

Lin, J. K., Grier, D. G. and Cowan, J. D. (1997). Faithful representation of separable distributions, *Neural Computation* **9**: 1305–1320.

Moody, J. E. and Wu, L. (1996). What is the "true price"? – State space models for high frequency financial data, *Progress in Neural Information Processing (ICONIP'96)*, Springer, Berlin, pp. 697–704.

Moody, J. E. and Wu, L. (1997a). What is the "true price"? – State space models for high frequency FX data, *in* A. S. Weigend, Y. S. Abu-Mostafa and A.-P. N. Refenes (eds), *Decision Technologies for Financial Engineering (Proceedings of the Fourth International Conference on Neural Networks in the Capital Markets, NNCM-96)*, World Scientific, Singapore, pp. 346–358.

Moody, J. E. and Wu, L. (1997b). What is the "true price"? – State space models for high frequency FX data, *Proceedings of the IEEE/IAFE 1997 Conference on Computational Intelligence for Financial Engineering (CIFEr)*, IEEE Service Center, Piscataway, NJ, pp. 150–156.

Nguyen Thi, H.-L. and Jutten, C. (1995). Blind source separation for convolutive mixtures, *Signal Processing* **45**(2): 209–229.

Oja, E. and Karhunen, J. (1995). Signal separation by nonlinear hebbian learning, *in* M. P. et al. (ed.), *Computational Intelligence - A Dynamic System Perspective*, IEEE Press, New York, NY, pp. 83–97.

Parra, L., Spence, C. and de Vries, B. (1997). Convolutive source separation and signal modeling with ML, *International Symposium on Intelligent Systems (ISIS'97)*, University of Reggio Calabria, Italy.

Pearlmutter, B. A. and Parra, L. C. (1997). Maximum likelihood blind source separation: A context-sensitive generalization of ICA, *in* M. C. Mozer, M. I. Jordan and T. Petsche (eds), *Advances in Neural Information Processing Systems 9 (NIPS*96)*, MIT Press, Cambridge, MA, pp. 613–619.

Pope, K. and Bogner, R. (1996). Blind signal separation. I: Linear, instantaneous combinations, *Digital Signal Processing* **6**: 5–16.

Tong, L., Liu, R., Soon, V. and Huang, Y. (1991). Indeterminacy and identifiability of blind identification, *IEEE Trans. Circuits, Syst.* **38**(5): 499–509.

Tong, L., Soon, V. C., Huang, Y. F. and Liu, R. (1990). AMUSE: A new blind identification algorithm, *International Conference on Acoustics, Speech and Signal Processing*, pp. 1784–1787.

Torkkola, K. (1996). Blind separation of convolved sources based on information maximization, *Proc. of the 1996 IEEE Workshop Neural Networks for Signal Processing 6 (NNSP96)*, IEEE Press, New York, NY.

Utans, J., Holt, W. T. and Refenes, A. N. (1997). Principal component analysis for modeling multi-currency portfolios, *in* A. S. Weigend, Y. S. Abu-Mostafa and A.-P. N. Refenes (eds), *Decision Technologies for Financial Engineering (Proceedings of the Fourth International Conference on Neural Networks in the Capital Markets, NNCM-96)*, World Scientific, Singapore, pp. 359–368.

Weinstein, E., Feder, M. and Oppenheim, A. (1993). Multi-channel signal separation by de-correlation, *IEEE Trans. Speech and Audio Processing* **1**(10): 405–413.

Wu, L. and Moody, J. (1997). Multi-effect decompositions for financial data modelling, *in* M. C. Mozer, M. I. Jordan and T. Petsche (eds), *Advances in Neural Information Processing Systems 9 (NIPS*96)*, MIT Press, Cambridge, MA, pp. 995–1001.

Yang, H., Amari, S. and Cichocki, A. (1998). Information-theoretic approach to blind separation of sources in non-linear mixture, *Signal Processing* **64**(3): 291–300.

Yang, H. H., Amari, S. and Cichocki, A. (1997). Information back-propagation for blind separation of sources in non-linear mixtures, *IEEE International Conference on Neural Networks, Houston TX (ICNN'97)*, IEEE-Press, pp. 2141–2146.

Yellin, D. and Weinstein, E. (1996). Multichannel signal separation: Methods and analysis, *IEEE Transactions on Signal Processing* **44**: 106–118.

FITTING NO ARBITRAGE TERM STRUCTURE MODELS USING A REGULARISATION TERM

N. TOWERS, J. T. CONNOR

Department of Decision Sciences
London Business School
Sussex Place, Regents Park,
London, NW1 4SA, UK.
E-mail: ntowers@lbs.ac.uk

In this paper we develop a generic, flexible fitting method that can be applied to no arbitrage term structure models. Flexibility in the model fitting methodology is generated by assuming that observed prices are not exact but have a bid/ask spread. A regularisation term is incorporated into the model's fitting algorithm in order to generate smoother expected interest rates while still enforcing the no arbitrage constraint. The regularisation term acts as a roughness penalty term by measuring the smoothness of the models expected future interest rates. This fitting technique more closely reflects the market expectation of a smooth transition between consecutive points on the yield curve. We demonstrate this model fitting approach by applying it to the single factor Black-Derman-Toy interest rate model. The model is calibrated to observed quarterly term structure data from the US treasury market. The results compare this new fitting method using a regularisation term with the traditional calibration method of matching the observed mid prices. Graphs show how this new approach to model fitting more closely reflects market expectation leading to a smoother evolution of the term structure of interest rates.

1   Introduction

Term structure models describe the evolution of the entire term structure of interest rates. They form a relationship between the term to maturity and the yield to maturity for comparable bonds through time. There are two main classes of term structure models: equilibrium models and no-arbitrage models. Equilibrium models, also known as absolute pricing models, approximate typical occurrences of the term structure, however, the model is not constrained to be exactly consistent with the observed term structure. In contrast, no arbitrage models, also known as relative pricing models, optimise model parameters so that the estimated bond prices match observed market prices. In practice, equilibrium models are normally used to value straight bonds while no arbitrage models are used to price interest rate derivatives relative to the underlying bonds. This paper focuses on the no-arbitrage class of models.

A.-P.N. Refenes et al. (eds.), Decision Technologies for Computational Finance, 323–332.
© 1998 *Kluwer Academic Publishers. Printed in the Netherlands..*

324

A number of no arbitrage term structure models have been developed within the literature. These involve modelling either the instantaneous forward rates (Heath, Jarrow, Morton, 1992) or the short term interest rate (Ho and Lee 1986; Black, Derman, Toy, 1990; Black and Karasinski, 1991; Hull and White 1990). In this paper we restrict our attention to the simplest class of no arbitrage models, the one factor term structure models of the short term interest rate.

The continuous-time version of the short term interest rate process, r, is the solution of the general stochastic differential equation of the form

$$dr = \mu(r,t)dt + \sigma(r,t)dW \qquad (1)$$

where r is the short rate, W is a standard Brownian motion process under the risk neutral probability measure, and $\mu(r, t)$ and $\sigma(r, t)$, are time dependent functions relating to the drift and volatility of the short rate process. The drift function describes the level and speed of mean reversion.

Equation (1) possesses the Markov property as functions, $\mu(r, t)$ and $\sigma(r, t)$, are not dependent on past history. This class of models, based solely on the short term interest rate, are called single factor models as they contain only one source of uncertainty, W_t. The different types of term structure models are determined by the choice of the drift and volatility functions, $\mu(r, t)$ and $\sigma(r, t)$. In general, due to the complexity of single factor term structure models, they do not possess closed form analytical solutions and so discrete time models are built to provide approximate numerical solutions.

Numerical implementations of no-arbitrage models need optimisation of parameters so that estimated prices match the observed term structure. This feature of price matching, known as model calibration, is a requirement of no-arbitrage models. This allows an interest rate derivative to be valued as if one had constructed a portfolio which replicates the cash flows. The cost of the replicating portfolio must be the value of the original security. Practitioners can then use these models for pricing and hedging many types of interest rate derivatives which depend on the yield curve.

The purpose of this paper is to further develop the model fitting methodology that maintains the no-arbitrage condition. The flexibility in the model fitting process is generated by assuming that the observed prices are not exact points but defined by their respective bid/ask prices. The methodology aims to allow generation of the smoothest possible interest curve which more closely reflects market expectation of a smooth transition between consecutive points on the yield curve. The regularisation term maximises the degree of smoothness in the estimated term structure while still enforcing the no arbitrage condition. We demonstrate the effectiveness of this methodology by applying it to the fitting of the single factor Black-Derman-Toy (BDT) interest rate model.

2   Modelling using Numerical Approximation

There are various well known numerical procedures which form an approximate representation of equation (1) in the literature. These include binomial trees, trinomial trees, finite differences and Monte Carlo simulation. All these numerical methods approximate the continuous time nature of the short term interest rate within a discrete time framework.

In the discrete state-time representation, the stochastic process for the short rate can be modelled as an interest rate tree. If the time step on the tree is Δt, then the rates are continuously compounded Δt-period rates. In this paper we apply our model fitting approach to the binomial approximation of the interest rate process. In principle the methodology can be applied to any lattice based model. The construction of a binomial tree can lead to two different types of branching shown in Figure 1.

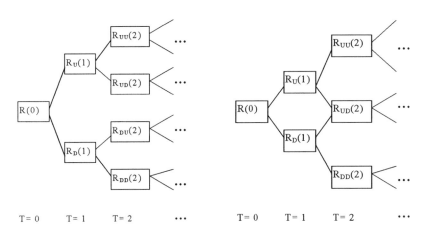

Figure 1 depicts two different types of interest rate tree. The tree on the left is non-recombining while the tree on the right recombines at each node.

The interest rate tree begins at a given state, R(0), which defines the value of the interest rate from the current time (T=0) to the start of the next time step. The binomial interest rate tree then divides into two states, an up state, $R_U(1)$, and a down state, $R_D(1)$. The values of these two states are determined by the evolution of the short term interest rate process defined by the drift and volatility functions in equation (1). For the next step (T=2) the nodes continue to divide but will recombine if the tree describes a Markov process. The Markov nature of equation

(1) enables lattice based modelling approaches to form a recombining state-time framework. This has the advantage that the size of the tree increases linearly with the number of time steps against exponential growth for non-recombining trees.

Once the tree has been constructed the values of all the states can be modified by a set of parameters, two for each time step, that control the drift and volatility rates. These parameters describe the drift and volatility functions defined in equation (1).

3   Black-Derman-Toy Interest Rate Model

The Black-Derman-Toy model has become an industry standard for single factor interest rate models. It is popular as it allows the fitting of a term structure of volatilities and as well as short term interest rates. In addition, the assumption of a log normal distribution for the interest rate process guarantees that interest rates remain non-negative.

In the continuous time version of this model, the instantaneous short rate, r, follows a risk adjusted process of the form

$$d \ln r(t) = \alpha(t)dt + \sigma(t)dW \tag{2}$$

where the function $\alpha(t)$ describes the drift rate and $\sigma(t)$ the stochastic volatility.

In the discrete state-time approximation of equation (2) the up and down states in the interest rate tree are described by

$$
\begin{aligned}
R(t+1, j+1) &= R(t, j)\exp(\mu(t)+\sigma(t)/2) \\
R(t+1, j-1) &= R(t, j)\exp(\mu(t)-\sigma(t)/2)
\end{aligned}
\tag{3}
$$

where $R(t,j)$ describes the value of the interest rate for a node at state j, and time step t, within the tree.

The interest rates within the binomial tree constructed from equation (3) are then governed by a set parameters, λ, two for each time step, that describes the one time step drift rates and volatility rates as follows

$$\lambda = \left\{\mu_1, \cdots, \mu_N, \sigma_1, \cdots, \sigma_N\right\} \tag{4}$$

4   Pricing Method: Forward Induction

Once the interest rate tree has been constructed it is necessary to calculate the value of each state within the tree. One of most elegant pricing methods, developed by Jamishidian (1991), constructs another tree of state-prices which correspond to states within the interest rate tree. The values of the state-price tree are found using forward induction and by the principle of risk-neutral pricing. The state-price tree then defines the probability weighted value of each state within the interest rate tree. For example, in state $UD(2)$ of the recombining interest rate tree of the state-price can be expressed as follows

$$P_{UD(2)} = 0.5*\frac{P_{U(1)}}{1+R_{U(1)}} + 0.5*\frac{P_{D(1)}}{1+R_{D(1)}} \tag{5}$$

where $P_{U(1)}$ and $P_{D(1)}$ are values from the state-price tree that have been calculated in a similar way. Equation (5) shows how the values of price-states are dependent on the value of state-prices in the previous time step and the value of states the interest rate tree in the current time step. Note that $P_{(0)}=1$, by definition the value of 1\$ at time T=0. Figure 2 shows conceptually how the state-price tree is constructed for the recombining interest rate tree.

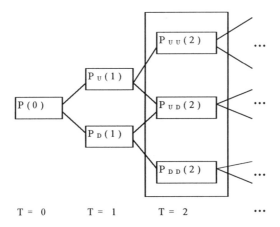

Figure 2 depicts the construction of the state price tree. The rectangular box indicates which prices are used to estimate the zero coupon bond at time step T=2.

The state-price tree is used to calculate the model's estimated price of the zero coupon bond for each time step. These are directly comparable to the observed zero bond prices at different maturities. The estimated zero bond price is simply calculated as the sum of all the state-prices in a given time step. The estimated and observed prices can then be compared and the model's estimated zero price modified by changing the parameters that govern the values of the states in the interest rate tree. The process of adapting model parameters requires the implementation of an optimisation algorithm which minimises a cost function. The cost function is a measure of the fit between the estimated and observed zero bond prices for all maturities. The traditional method and the alternative method suggested in this paper of implementing this optimisation are discussed the next sections.

5 Model Fitting: Traditional Calibration

The traditional calibration approach to fitting term structure models involves optimisation of a cost function. The optimisation process aims to modify each of the model's drift and volatility parameters in order to minimise the sum of squared deviations between estimated and observed zero bond prices for all maturities. As stated, the models estimated zero bond prices are calculated by summing the values of all the states in the state-price tree for a given time step. The optimisation procedure can be restated as the minimisation of the model fitting cost function, C, defined by

$$C = \sum_{i=1}^{N} (P_k - \hat{P}_k)^2 \tag{4}$$

where N is the number of observed zero bonds, P_k, is the observed zero bond price with maturity i, and $\hat{P}_k$ the equivalent discount bond price estimated from the ith time step in the term structure model. As the number of degrees of freedom in the data matches that of the model the cost function will tend to zero as the number of iterations increases to infinity. When the value of the cost function is close to zero the model is thought to be calibrated and optimisation is halted.

6 Model Fitting: Using a Regularisation Term

The new fitting approach uses the same basic procedure to price the states of the interest rate tree (i.e. using the forward induction method) but minimises a different cost function. The new cost function measures the smoothness of the model's drift and volatility parameters. These parameters are proportional to the implied forward rates and forward volatility rates from the models zero bond prices. Smoothing the changes in these parameters is then equivalent to smoothing the term structure models expected change in the short term interest rates and expected short term volatility rates. The no-arbitrage condition is maintained by constraining minimisation of regularisation term, the new cost function, to be within the bounds of the observed bid/ask prices. The cost function acts as a roughness penalty term by penalising the deviation of neighbouring parameters. This fitting approach relates to a regularisation term commonly used in statistical modelling to control a models "goodness of fit". The new cost function, C, is minimised

$$C = \left\{ \sum_{i=1}^{N} \left(\mu_t - \mu_{t-1} \right)^2 + \sum_{i=1}^{N} \left(\sigma_t - \sigma_{t-1} \right)^2 \right\} \tag{5}$$

where μ_t represents the drift parameter and σ_t the volatility parameter at time step t, subject to the following constraint on the models estimated zero prices

$$P_k^{bid} \leq \hat{P}_k \leq P_k^{ask} \quad \forall k \in T(k) \tag{6}$$

where P_k^{bid} and P_k^{ask} denotes the observed zero bond bid and ask price with time to maturity k, and $\hat{P}_k$ the models estimated price. The new cost function will bias the model in favour of a smooth transition between neighbouring interest rates and volatility rates.

7   Results

To test the model fitting process a "snapshot" of observe term structure prices were taken from the US Treasury market. 40 observations were obtained for bid and ask prices of US treasury discount bonds with equally spaced maturities from 3 months to 10 years. The zero prices were converted to minimum and maximum values of annualised 3 month forward rates which maintain the no arbitrage condition. The range of acceptable forward rates for each maturity are shown in Figure 3.

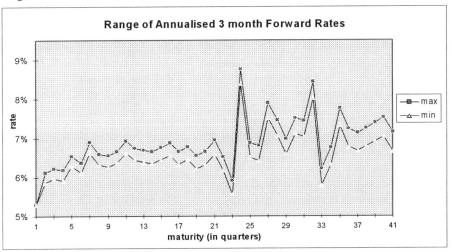

Figure 3 shows the range of annualised 3 month forward rates that maintain the no arbitrage condition for each maturity in the observed term structure.

Black-Derman-Toy models using the two cost functions described by equations (4) and (5) were optimised. The zero prices generated from the two different cost functions were compared. The annually compounded 3 month forward rate curves for the estimated zero bond prices are shown in figure 4. These forward rates are generally considered to be the market expectation of the risk-adjusted term structure of the short term interest rate. As expected the two curves fulfilled the no arbitrage condition, as shown by comparing the results with the acceptable range in figure 3. For the new fitting method, equation (5), the constraint on the cost function, equation (6) ensured that the estimated prices had forward rates that were within the rate spread. Figure 4 shows how the new fitting methodology allows more flexibility in the curve fitting process. For the traditional method the estimated forward rates match the observed rates. The new shows a slightly smoother fit of the forward rates compared to the traditional method.

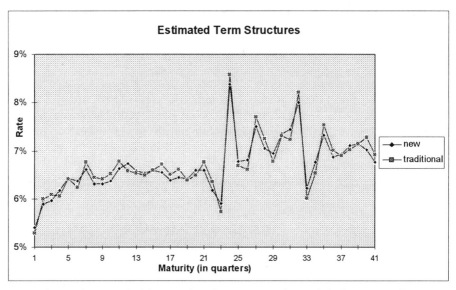

Figure 4 show a graph of the two estimated term structures from optimisation of the traditional and the new model fitting process.

Model calibration using a regularisation parameter was implemented using a non-linear optimisation algorithm to minimise the cost function. During each iteration the models parameters were re-estimated simultaneously. Figure 5 shows how the measure of smoothness, the roughness penalty term (RPT), decreases during the model fitting process. Note that the value at iteration zero is the measure of smoothness obtained from the standard method of calibrating the model to the observed mid price.

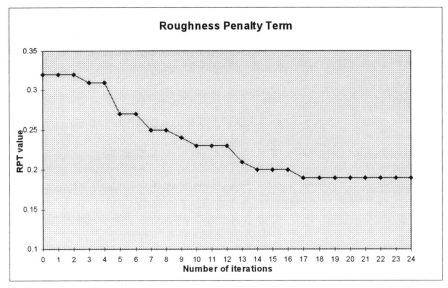

Figure 5 shows how the measure of the smoothness, the roughness penalty term decreases as the regularised model is optimised.

8   Conclusions

We have presented an alternative approach to the fitting of no arbitrage term structure models. The standard approach is enhanced by allowing the model fitting procedure to use two observed prices at each maturity, the bid and ask values, rather than only one. These two values are considered to be the bounds of the no arbitrage condition at each maturity. The extra information provides flexibility in the model calibration procedure. A new methodology is presented which takes advantage of the price spread to give a smoother term structure by using a regularisation term. The model fitting cost function is adapted to smooth the term structure rather than calibrate the model to observed prices. The no arbitrage condition is maintained during the model fitting approach by using constrained optimisation.

The methodology is applied to the calibration of the Black-Derman-Toy interest rate model. The interpolated curve is constrained to maintain the no arbitrage condition. The optimisation method converges and results show a smoother fit to the observed data compared to the traditional approach to calibration.

A fitted model can then be used to price interest rate derivatives relative to the observed underlying term structure including both bid and ask prices at each maturity. This new fitting methodology will give a slightly different valuation compared to a term structure model calibrated using only one observed price at each maturity. The price differential between the two fitting methods is dependent on the amplitude of the bid/ask spread and the type of derivative. It is thought that this new methodology may provide a more accurate valuation of interest rate derivatives. Further work is necessary to discover under what conditions the price differential for various interest rate derivatives is significant.

9   References

Black, F., Derman, E., Toy, W., "A One-Factor Model of Interest Rates and its Application to Treasury Bonds," *Financial Analysts Journal*, 1990.

Black, F., Karasinski, P., "Bond and Option Pricing when Short Rates are Lognormal." *Financial Analysts Journal*, July-August, pages 52-59, 1991.

Connor, J., Bolland, P., Lajbcygier, P., "Intraday Modelling of the Term Structure of Interest Rates,", *Proceedings of the Neural Networks in the Capital Markets*, 1996.

Connor, J., Towers, N., "Modelling the term structure of interest rates: A neural network perspective", *unpublished technical report, London Business School*, 1997.

Duffie, D., "State space models of the term structure of interest rates" in *Vasicek and Beyond, 1990*.

Heath, D., Jarrow, R., Morton, A., "Bond Pricing and the Term Structure of Interest Rates: A New Methodology for Contingent Claims Valuation" *Econometrica*, 1991.

Ho, S. Y. and Lee, S., "Term Structure Movements and Pricing Interest Rate Contingent Claims," in *Vasicek and Beyond: Journal of Finance*, 1990.

Hull, J., White, A., "The pricing of options on interest rate caps and floors using the Hull-White model", *Journal of Financial Engineering*, Vol. 2, 1993

Jamshidian, F., "Forward induction and construction of yield curve diffusion models", *Journal of Fixed Income*, June 1991.

QUANTIFICATION OF SECTOR ALLOCATION AT THE GERMAN STOCK MARKET

DR. ELMAR STEURER

Daimler-Benz AG
Forschung und Technik - FT3/KL
Postfach 2360
89013 Ulm
E-Mail:steurer@dbag.ulm.daimlerbenz.com

This paper reports upon a quantitative sector allocation of the German stock market, represented by the DAX (Deutscher Aktienindex). The purpose is to present an approach how to identify an appropriate sector allocation of the 10 DAX sectors quantitatively in advance to outperform the DAX. Fundamental and technical factors are used for the explanation of each of the 10 DAX sectors. With these models forecasts for each sector are given one month ahead. Two methodologies are used for forecasting the monthly returns: linear regression and neural networks. The next step is to take in addition to these forecasts the 24-month volatilities of the considered sectors and the corresponding correlation matrix to carry out a portfolio optimisation. With these received sector weights an out-of-sample performance comparison for the out-of sample range from January 1996 until June 1997 is conducted. Thus the focus of this study lies on two points: First, whether it is possible to outperform the benchmark DAX with a quantitative method. And second, whether nonlinear methodologies deliver added value to classical econometric methods.

1 Introduction

All active managers intend to beat a given benchmark. But for active management of equities it is extremely difficult to solve this task. There are several basic types of active investment strategies. They include country selection, sectoral emphasis and stock selection. The focus given here lies on sectoral emphasis. Manager following sectoral emphasis attempt to increase residual return through analysing the influence of common factor exposure. The use of a sector allocation model permits the manager to efficiently capture expected returns by ensuring that there are no incidental risks in the portfolio. Against this background the predictability of an appropriate sector allocation should have important implications for investors who are willing to use tactical asset allocation strategies. The article is organised as follows: In section 2 the data used is presented. Particularly some transformations of market data into discrete data provide a certain degree of forecasting ability for stock market performance one month in advance. In section 3 the combination of the proposed data is carried out by multiple linear regression to receive valid and robust models for forecasting the monthly return of each sector contained in the DAX. Only available information is used to forecast the monthly return of the next month which is used as an estimate of the expected sector return. Together with these forecasts monthly volatilities and correlations are taken to carry

A.-P.N. Refenes et al. (eds.), Decision Technologies for Computational Finance, 333–351.
© 1998 *Kluwer Academic Publishers. Printed in the Netherlands..*

334

out an optimisation of a DAX portfolio with a special focus on practical investment restrictions. Finally the quality of this implementable investment strategy is examined by backtesting the historical performance in a realistic „out-of-sample" setting. As a nonlinear methodology neural networks are taken to analyse their forecasting capabilities.

2   Data

The sector models are built recognising that different sectors are driven by different factors. Rather than using the same factors for each, the model analyses sectors separately, capturing each one's characteristics. One sector is considered as a combination of different factors. Figure 2.1 displays that these factors are separated into three groups, namely macroeconomic data, sector specific data and performance consideratios.

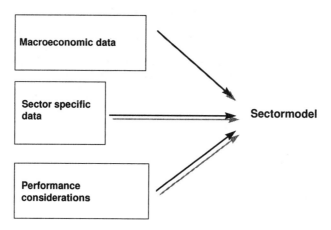

Fig. 2.1: Sector model - structure

The macroeconomic data consists mainly of fundamental variables which have the potential to influence the whole market as well each sector. Due to the problem of non stationarity the data is transformed to yearly and monthly returns, respectively. Hereinafter these transformations are abbreviated with the extensions JR and D (table 2.1). Sector specific data consists of data on orders, production and climate indices of each sector (table 2.2). Performance variables reflect mainly the relative attractiveness of the asset classes equities, bonds and cash. Other variables of this group quantify the risk aversion of the stock market approximatively and the technical situation of the bond markets. (see for more Illmanen (1995)). According to him „investors are more risk averse (afraid) when their curent wealth is low relative to their past wealth. The higher risk aversion makes them demand higher risk premia (larger compensations for holding risky assets) near business cycle troughs. Conversely, higher wealth near business cycle peaks makes investors less risk averse (more complacent and greedy); therefore, they bid down the required risk premia (by bidding up the asset prices). Thus, the observed time-variation in risk premia may be explained by the old Wall Street adage about the cycle of fear and greed." (Illmanen (1995 p. 1 / 2)). Table 2.3 gives an overview about the variables reflecting performance considerations. Finally the variable DTBOMOM „simulates a simple moving average trading rule to exploit the persistence (positive autocorrelation) in bond returns." (Illmanen (1995), p. 3) The disadvantage of such a moving average is that this indicator lags behind the market action. The time lag is reduced with the shorter averages, but can never be completely eliminated. The consequence is that moving averages are worthless in sideways trends, but work properly in upwards or downwards trends. „Thus the rule is to take a long (short) position in the bond market when the long-term bond yield declines (increases) to more than five basis points below (above) its six-month average; ... The dummy variable takes value 1, -1, or 0 if the strategy is long, short, or neutral, respectively." (Illmanen (1995), p. 3).

Time-series	Abbreviation
REX Performance Index	REXP
German interest years 10 years	DTBO
German interest years 3 months	DT3M
Dollar/Mark	USD
US interest years 3 months	US3M
German consumer price index	DTCPI
German producer price index	DTPPI
German money supply M1	DTM1
German money supply M3	DTM2
German producer price index	DTPPI
German producer price index	DTIMPPR
German wages	DTWAGES
German capacity utilisation	DTCAPA
German industrial production	DTINDP
German outputgap[1]	OUTPUTGAP
	OUTGAPPOS
	OUTGAPNEG
German orders	DTORDER
German current account	DTLB
German foreign orders	AUFAUS
German exports 3 months average	EXPORTS
German Ifo-Business climate	IFO
German employment	DTBES
DAX price earning ratio	DAXKGV
German unemployment rate	DTARL
German supply M3	DTM3
German retail sales	DTRETA
German loans, long-term	DTKREDLA
German loans, short-term	DTKREDKU

Table 2.1: Macroeconomic data

---

[1] See for more Clark et al. (1996), Dicks (1996)

Time-series	abbreviation
Chemical industry, orders	CHEMAUF
Automotive industry, orders	AUTOORD
Mechanical industry, orders	MASCHORD
German Ifo-consumer climate	IFOKONSKLI
German term structure, 10 years - 3 months	DTST
German term structure, monthly change	DTSTD
German durable good orders	INVESTAUF

Table 2.2: Sector specific data

Abbreviation	Description
DT3MMAX	Performance of German money market If DT3M > (DAXJR or REXPJR) $\Rightarrow$ DT3MMAX =1 else 0
DAXMAX	Performance of German stock market If DAX > (DT3M oder REXPJR) $\Rightarrow$ DAXMAX =1 else 0
REXMAX	Performance of German bond market If REX > (DAXJR oder REXPJR) $\Rightarrow$ DEXMAX =1 else 0
DTBOMOM	Momentum of German bond market Falling yields: Current yield < (average yield 6 months -0,05) $\Rightarrow$ DTBOMOM = 1 Rising yields: Current yield > (average yield 6 months +0,05) $\Rightarrow$ DTBOMOM = -1 else: 0
DAXWEA	DAX Riskaversion (DAX 24 months average) / current DAX

Table 2.3: Used time series of the group: performance considerations

The purpose of the described approach is to provide a valuation of the 10 sectors of the DAX. Table 1 reports the sector weighting of the DAX by adding up the companies' weighting according to their sector classification on 16 January 1997. Unfortunately there are no historical sector sub-indices available. Therefore the Composite DAX (CDAX) is regarded in this study because this index is split into sector sub-indices which are published by the Deutsche Börse AG on a daily basis. Thus the CDAX index provides the desired historical prices of each sub-sector for empirical studies. The CDAX can be considered as an enhancement of the DAX as this index consists of 356 companies with the objective to represent the whole German stock market. A common feature between DAX and CDAX is that both indices are performance indices, which means that dividends and rights are reinvested. (see for more details Beilner et el. (1990)). Remarkable is that the correlation between DAX and CDAX is very high as the large market capitalisation of the DAX stocks dominate the CDAX. The DAX stocks' weighting is around 67 % in the CDAX.

Sector	Weighting in %	Minimum weighting in %	Maximum weighting in %
Chemicals	24,0	10	25
Utilities	20,5	10	25
Insurances	12,8	5	20
Banks	9,3	5	25
Automotives	12,5	5	25
Elektricals	9,9	5	15
Mechanical Engineering	6,7	2	10
Retail	2,6	0	6
Steel	2,0	0	6
Transport	0,5	0	6

Table 2.4: Sector weightings of the DAX sectors on 16 January 1997, Investment restrictions

Although the DAX is not split into these sector sub-indices table 2.4 reports the sector weighting of the DAX by adding up the companies' weighting according to their sector classification. Concerning the sector breakdown there are major differences between the CDAX and DAX. Compared to the CDAX, the DAX sector weightings are clearly higher for chemicals (24 % compared to 20,1 %) and utilities (20,5 vs 15,6)[2]. Some CDAX sectors are not contained in the DAX. Thus these sectors - construction, textile, paper, holdings and breweries - are not considered hereinafter. An important restriction fund managers have to regard in practice is given by transactions costs and large turnover, respectively. Therefore in practice fund managers have to take care about investment limits to the given sectors. Table 2.4 shows the limits concerning the minimum and maximum sector weightings applied in this study.

3   Sector analysis

3.1   Motivation

Recent research shows that movements of equities of one sector are not fully unpredictable (Burgess (1997)). Using quantitative techniques it should be possible to spot times when markets are cheap or expensive by identifying the factors that are important in determining market returns. Earlier empirical research (Graf et al. (1996)) shows that the expected excess returns of stocks and long-term bonds vary over the business cycle; they tend to be high at the end of the recession and low at the end of the expansion. As an illustrative example figure 3.1 shows the different outperformance of the typical cyclical automotive sector and the liquidity driven bank sector in the period from January 1984 to January 1997. In addition the yearly

---

[2] Weightings on 16 January 1997

growth rate of the German industrial production as the most important economic variable representing the cylical waves is presented. In general, the typical different performance of these two sectors depending on the economic up- and downswing can be seen. In particular, cyclical stocks in Germany provide a good investment opportunity with increasing signs of an economic upswing (e. g. in 1993 and 1996). Then typically banks underperform the automotive sector due to tougher monetary and liquidity conditions. But the underperformance of bank equities should come to an end in a later stage of the economic cycle (e. g. in 1992). These visually drawn hypotheses are confirmed by quantitative analysis, described in the following sections. All models are estimated by using the time period form December 1980 until December 1995.

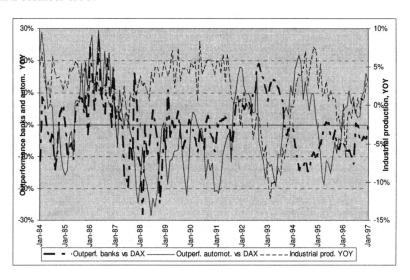

Fig. 3.1: Outperformance of automotive sector and bank sector from January 1984 to January 1997 vs German industrial production (YOY)

3.2   Total market

The model covering the total market exhibits cyclicals and export sensitivity (table 3.1). The influence of the cyclicals is indicated by the growth rate of wages and the positive correlation between the change in 10 year interest rates and monthly changes of the market. Export sensitivity is shown by the importance of exports and the Dollar/Mark exchange rate. In addition the influence of exports and Dollar/Mark gives evidence that an considerable part of German industry earnings is generated by foreign orders. The relation between the predicted and the realised monthly returns may not appear very impressive, reflecting the fact that most of the monthly fluctuations are unpredictable The negative signs before German industrial production and the wages coefficients indicate performance pressure during the late stage of the economic cycle. Such an situation should favour smaller companies with domestic market orientation whereas the DAX with the German blue chips is more biased towards early cyclical stocks. Recovery in Germany is very often export led. Thus an early stage of recovery should be positive for the industrial blue chips and the interest sensitive stocks of the DAX. In addition liquidity conditions are very important for the financial sectors as banks, insurances and utilities. Due to their holdings of fixed income assets these sectors will benefit of an expansive monetary policy in a recession. As a result some sectors of the stock market, such as banks, insurances and utilities should deliver better performance during a recession than the cylical sectors, such as automotives, mechanical engineering or steel.

Variable	Coefficient	Std. Error	t-Statistic	Prob.
DTBOD(-2)	0.028942	0.013422	2.156295	0.0323
USDLND(-1)	0.266146	0.094692	2.810666	0.0055
DTINDJR(-3)	-0.150749	0.097044	-1.553412	0.1220
DTBOMOM(-1)	0.010684	0.004215	2.534948	0.0121
DAXMAX(-1)	0.032110	0.012061	2.662191	0.0084
REXMAX(-1)	0.023460	0.013441	1.745440	0.0825
DT3MMAX(-1)	0.024640	0.017294	1.424799	0.1559
DTPPILND(-2)	1.307163	1.179062	1.108647	0.2690
DTIMPPRLND(-2)	-0.309048	0.449564	-0.687440	0.4926
US3MD(-1)	-0.004063	0.004543	-0.894427	0.3722
DTWAGESJR(-1)	-0.668368	0.322310	-2.073682	0.0395
AUFAUSJR(-2)	-0.094160	0.065931	-1.428159	0.1549
EXPORTEJR(-2)	0.098990	0.059625	1.660203	0.0985
R-squared	0.131560	F-statistic		2.398595
Adjusted R-squared	0.076711	Prob(F-statistic)		0.006557

Table 3.1: Total market model

3.3   Automotives

Table 3.2 displays the model of the automotive sector and exhibits the typical cyclical character of this sector. A lot of factors will favour this sector with a stabilisation of the economic upswing. For example higher capacity utilisation, positive growth rates and even increasing interest rates are positive for the automotive stocks. Due to intensive just-in-time production orders and production of this sector are highly correlated. Thus only orders of the automotive sector are included in this model.

Variable	Coefficient	Std. Error	t-Statistic	Prob.
DTINDJR(-2)	-0.457966	0.183129	-2.500782	0.0132
USDLND(-1)	0.530822	0.143997	3.686348	0.0003
DTBOD(-1)	0.014699	0.022697	0.647628	0.5180
DT3MD(-2)	0.029869	0.013998	2.133837	0.0342
DTIMPPRLND(-2)	-0.345242	0.659049	-0.523849	0.6010
DAXMAX(-1)	0.022669	0.015877	1.427785	0.1550
REXMAX(-1)	0.010023	0.017786	0.563531	0.5737
DT3MMAX(-1)	0.003691	0.020284	0.181969	0.8558
AUTOORDJR(-4)	0.035286	0.046906	0.752276	0.4528
DTPPILND(-2)	3.111435	1.668218	1.865125	0.0637
DTBOMOM(-1)	0.023771	0.007033	3.380177	0.0009
DTWAGESJR(-4)	-0.212371	0.422011	-0.503236	0.6154
DTCAPAJR(-1)	0.266148	0.184933	1.439160	0.1518
IFOKONKLIJR(-2)	0.000510	0.000426	1.196328	0.2331
R-squared	0.182360	F-statistic		3.225397
Adjusted R-squared	0.125822	Prob(F-statistic)		0.000205

Table 3.2: Sector model: Automotives

3.4 Chemicals

In practice this sector will especially benefit from a weakening Deutsch Mark. This is empirically evident by the significant positive correlation between Dollar/Mark and the monthly changes of this sector (table 3.3). Only one specific factor - namely the orders of the chemical industry - is included in this model.

Variable	Coefficient	Std. Error	t-Statistic	Prob.
DTINDLND(-3)	-0.306203	0.188767	-1.622124	0.1064
DT3MD(-1)	0.016985	0.008640	1.965761	0.0508
DTIMPPRJR(-2)	0.115792	0.066335	1.745571	0.0825
OUTPUTGAP(-3)	-0.001344	0.000864	-1.556060	0.1214
DAXMAX(-1)	0.010966	0.005084	2.157023	0.0323
REXMAX(-1)	0.012848	0.006821	1.883461	0.0612
DT3MMAX(-1)	0.008912	0.007338	1.214535	0.2261
CHEMAUFJR(-4)	-0.228938	0.084106	-2.722008	0.0071
DTBOMOM(-1)	0.010332	0.003599	2.870485	0.0046
USDLND(-1)	0.310782	0.087771	3.540835	0.0005
INVESTAUFJR(-5)	0.117293	0.050927	2.303168	0.0224
IFOJR(-1)	0.039513	0.027201	1.452658	0.1480
R-squared	0.152220	F-statistic		3.085025
Adjusted R-squared	0.102879	Prob(F-statistic)		0.000780

Table 3.3: Sector model: Chemicals

3.5   Electricals

Variable	Coefficient	Std. Error	t-Statistic	Prob.
USDLND(-1)	0.315779	0.109099	2.894433	0.0042
DT3MD(-2)	0.029266	0.011437	2.558796	0.0113
DTINFL(-2)	0.438753	0.269753	1.626495	0.1055
REXPLND(-2)	-0.088424	0.383808	-0.230385	0.8180
DAXMAX(-1)	0.028352	0.013159	2.154529	0.0325
REXMAX(-1)	0.026979	0.014125	1.910001	0.0576
DT3MMAX(-1)	0.021465	0.017301	1.240698	0.2162
DTBOMOM(-1)	0.013855	0.004788	2.893577	0.0043
AUFAUSJR(-2)	-0.169515	0.075618	-2.241728	0.0261
DTWAGESJR(-4)	-0.647268	0.347604	-1.862084	0.0641
DTCAPAJR(-1)	0.310331	0.124457	2.493479	0.0135
DTRETAJR(-1)	-0.136470	0.096085	-1.420304	0.1572
R-squared	0.156885	F-statistic		3.214061
Adjusted R-squared	0.108073	Prob(F-statistic)		0.000493

Table 3.4: Sector model: Electricals

By analysing the model (table 3.4) it is remarkable that electricals will benefit from higher inflation rates and rising three-months interest rates. Thus the sector is characterised by late-cycle dependencies. This is underlined by the important positive influence of yearly change of the capacity utilisation (DTCAPAJR). In such an environment capacity utilisation has started to rise consistently. This means an improvement in the imvestment trend and a major stepping up of investment plans, respectively. Besides this, electricals are especially affected by the wages situation. Higher wages tend to influence negatively the sector performance.

3.6   Banks

The model shown in table 3.5 indicates that two typical monetary factors are important for bank perfomance: On the one hand the impact of interest rates and on the other hand the changing shape of the yield curve. Historically up until 1994 there was generally a good correlation between German bank share price perfomance and long bonds, although best performance for the German banks was in anticipation of interest rate changes or the early stages of interest rate movements. Traditionally the mortgage banks have benefited from a positive yield curve and falling rate environment, due to volume benefits and timing differences between loan approvals and taking up the funding of the loan. Basically rising short rates and a flatter yield curve should impact more negatively on the banks. The flatter yield curve will squeeze spreads arising from mismatches of fixed rate loan books funded by short term borrowing. Given the empirical evidence that a flat yield curve corresponds with high economic growth rates and a steep yield curve with weakening or even negative growth rates the consequence is that bank stocks should perform particularly well in a negative economic environment. Along with the overall weakening economy core business is under pressure due to falling interest margins and weak credit demand. But other areas of business were able to compensate for this. Supported by the lowering level of interest rates trading profits from playing the yield curve will be increasing then.

Variable	Coefficient	Std. Error	t-Statistic	Prob.
DTINDLND(-1)	-0.614216	0.248673	-2.469979	0.0144
USDJR(-1)	0.073451	0.035814	2.050926	0.0416
DTBOD(-1)	-0.028051	0.017659	-1.588426	0.1138
REXPLND(-2)	-0.326802	0.384619	-0.849677	0.3966
DAXMAX(-1)	0.030434	0.008716	3.491716	0.0006
REXMAX(-2)	0.008181	0.009457	0.865117	0.3881
DT3MMAX(-1)	0.024661	0.013813	1.785368	0.0758
DTPPIJR(-1)	0.257838	0.302041	0.853652	0.3944
DTINFL(-1)	-0.701580	0.412201	-1.702034	0.0904
DTBOMOM(-1)	0.009997	0.005967	1.675435	0.0955
DTSTD(-3)	0.008613	0.009730	0.885179	0.3772
R-squared	0.118112	F-statistic		2.571466
Adjusted R-squared	0.072180	Prob(F-statistic)		0.006098

Table 3.5: Sector model: Banks

3.7 Transport

Variable	Coefficient	Std. Error	t-Statistic	Prob.
DTINDLND(-2)	0.420765	0.274188	1.534585	0.1265
DTBOD(-2)	0.039374	0.017582	2.239414	0.0263
DT3MD(-2)	0.023952	0.012369	1.936474	0.0543
DAXMAX(-1)	0.000318	0.007699	0.041244	0.9671
REXMAX(-2)	0.022698	0.009053	2.507239	0.0130
DT3MMAX(-1)	0.001762	0.011367	0.155046	0.8769
DTPPILND(-3)	-2.208794	1.531524	-1.442220	0.1509
DTIMPPRJR(-2)	0.040586	0.140082	0.289726	0.7723
DTBOMOM(-1)	0.016295	0.005649	2.884574	0.0044
IFOJR(-1)	0.059702	0.033340	1.790742	0.0749
USDJR(-1)	0.085969	0.052261	1.644972	0.1016
AUFAUSJR(-3)	-0.079934	0.078723	-1.015385	0.3112
R-squared	0.135184	F-statistic		2.714205
Adjusted R-squared	0.085378	Prob(F-statistic)		0.002828

Table 3.6: Sector model: Transport

The sector is mainly influenced by Dollar/Mark, producer price index and Ifo business climate index (table 3.6). In addtion to these factors three months interest rates, the performance variable of the REX (REXMAX) and the technical situation of the German bond market (DTBOMOM) are remarkable. Given the positive correlation with three months interest rates and the Ifo business climate this sector exhibits typical cyclical characteristics. The negative sign before the producer price index indicates the high dependency of this sector to changes in producer prices. This trade-off can be explained by the high sensitivity of the transport sector to changes in oil prices.

3.8 Mechanical Engineering

The sector mechanical sector is mainly affected by movements of Dollar/Mark (table 3.7). This feature is highlighted in practice. The sector recovered at the beginning of the first quarter 1997 on the back of a weakening of the Deutsch Mark. Furthermore mechanical engineering receives a major impulse from capital investment. Increasing capital investment should lead to good sector performance.

Variable	Coefficient	Std. Error	t-Statistic	Prob.
USDLND(-1)	0.445410	0.115903	3.842966	0.0002
DT3MD(-2)	0.012881	0.010226	1.259711	0.2093
DAXMAX(-1)	0.006066	0.006469	0.937789	0.3495
REXMAX(-1)	-0.008059	0.007634	-1.055630	0.2925
DT3MMAX(-1)	-0.010714	0.009497	-1.128176	0.2607
DTIMPPRLND(-1)	-0.687333	0.542828	-1.266208	0.2070
OUTPUTGAP(-1)	-0.001831	0.001000	-1.830795	0.0687
REXPLND(-3)	0.406530	0.313961	1.294841	0.1970
DTPPILND(-1)	2.413973	1.357739	1.777936	0.0770
MASCHORDLND(-4)	0.091939	0.068549	1.341227	0.1815
DTBOMOM(-1)	0.007366	0.004503	1.635872	0.1035
INVESTAUFJR(-2)	0.109859	0.065676	1.672732	0.0960
EXPORTEJR(-1)	-0.083621	0.067006	-1.247965	0.2136
R-squared	0.163413	F-statistic		3.076493
Adjusted R-squared	0.110296	Prob(F-statistic)		0.000543

Table 3.7: Sector model: Mechanical Engineering

3.9 Steel

This sector is considered as high cyclical (table 3.8). Empirical evidence supports this view. Share performance of steel shares is positively driven to a large extent by rising 10-year interest rates as well as a rising producer price index. Both developments are typical for an economic upswing in an early stage. If the cycle has become more mature, this sector is negatively affected. Then the turnover of this industry will continue to be dampened for weaker demand and falling prices of base products. The model shows that higher growth in capacity utilisation and wages - corresponding with a mature cycle - will cause performance pressure to this sector.

Variable	Coefficient	Std. Error	t-Statistic	Prob.
DTBOD(-2)	0.023584	0.016119	1.463133	0.1451
DAXMAX(-1)	0.000474	0.019306	0.024572	0.9804
REXMAX(-1)	-0.015198	0.023238	-0.654039	0.5139
DT3MMAX(-1)	-0.008224	0.022629	-0.363415	0.7167
DTPPIJR(-2)	0.385854	0.181010	2.131668	0.0343
DTINDLND(-2)	0.549830	0.250542	2.194563	0.0294
DTBOMOM(-1)	0.007704	0.005169	1.490246	0.1378
DTWAGESJR(-3)	-0.802472	0.373961	-2.145869	0.0331
DAXWEA(-2)	0.040199	0.019271	2.085964	0.0383
MASCHORDLND(-2)	0.058175	0.076157	0.763883	0.4459
DTCAPAJR(-3)	-0.097683	0.128575	-0.759739	0.4483
USDLND(-1)	0.345126	0.115937	2.976847	0.0033
R-squared	0.132825	F-statistic		2.659580
Adjusted R-squared	0.082883	Prob(F-statistic)		0.003413

Table 3.8: Sector model: Steel

3.10 Utilities

The analysis of this sector (table 3.9) gives evidence for either cyclical and monetary aspects. On the one hand cyclical dependencies are evident by the importance of orders to the mechanical engineering sector - a typical cyclical variable. A cyclical upswing will yield to higher electricity consumption and thus earnings upgrades of shares of this sector. On the other hand the significant negative correlation between changes in ten year German interest rates indicates that this industry is able to decouple from a generally weaker economic situation due to their large holdings of fixed income assets. Such an exposure will benefit from an environment of falling interest rates.

Variable	Coefficient	Std. Error	t-Statistic	Prob.
DTBOD(-1)	-0.029687	0.010284	-2.886661	0.0043
DAXMAX(-1)	0.011990	0.008329	1.439528	0.1516
REXMAX(-1)	0.003516	0.008642	0.406856	0.6846
DT3MMAX(-1)	-0.000525	0.006850	-0.076650	0.9390
USDLND(-1)	0.179922	0.078772	2.284083	0.0235
DTINDLND(-1)	-0.270869	0.163595	-1.655730	0.0994
REXPJR(-2)	0.057892	0.075087	0.771005	0.4417
DTBOMOM(-2)	-0.002743	0.003257	-0.842294	0.4007
MASCHORDJR(-4)	0.177980	0.053979	3.297218	0.0012
INVESTAUFJR(-4)	-0.158266	0.070454	-2.246381	0.0258
R-squared	0.128976	F-statistic		3.158904
Adjusted R-squared	0.088146	Prob(F-statistic)		0.001405

Table 3.9: Sector model: Utilities

3.11 Insurance

This sector is mainly driven by financial and monetary factors (table 3.10). An environment of falling interest and inflation rates, respectively, favours this sector. Given weak economic growth with low inflation rates will generate high liquidity by an expansive monetary policy of the Bundesbank. Against this background insurance companies will achieve high profits and earning upgrades due to their large holdings of fixed income assets.

Variable	Coefficient	Std. Error	t-Statistic	Prob.
DTBOD(-1)	-0.046314	0.022086	-2.097011	0.0373
DAXMAX(-1)	0.013660	0.014999	0.910730	0.3636
REXMAX(-1)	-0.010783	0.014415	-0.747999	0.4554
DT3MMAX(-1)	-0.006394	0.018751	-0.340970	0.7335
DTINFL(-2)	0.565219	0.329679	1.714451	0.0881
DTBOMOM(-1)	0.006380	0.006824	0.934847	0.3510
USDLND(-1)	0.473151	0.145979	3.241224	0.0014
DTCAPAJR(-1)	0.192329	0.141432	1.359871	0.1755
REXPLND(-3)	0.588259	0.429351	1.370112	0.1722
DTM3JR(-3)	-0.143164	0.132528	-1.080260	0.2814
R-squared	0.123826	F-statistic		3.030663
Adjusted R-squared	0.082968	Prob(F-statistic)		0.002068

Table 3.10: Sector model: Insurance

3.12 Retailing

Hopes for higher consumption should deliver good sector performance. This hypothesis is proven by data analysis (table 3.11). Hopes for a recovery in retail sales are primarily based on a rise in disposable income and better job security. These expectations are measured by the Ifo consumer climate index - the popular German consumer sentiment - which shows an positive significant correlation to the monthly returns of this sector. In addition yearly growth of money supply correspond with the theme of disposable income. High growth rates of German money supply M3 will support the performance of this sector.

Variable	Coefficient	Std. Error	t-Statistic	Prob.
DTBOD(-2)	0.033021	0.016193	2.039275	0.0428
DAXMAX(-1)	0.001798	0.013800	0.130264	0.8965
REXMAX(-1)	0.011195	0.015356	0.729028	0.4669
DT3MMAX(-1)	-0.004810	0.018851	-0.255140	0.7989
DTPPIJR(-2)	0.311189	0.178999	1.738492	0.0837
DTBOMOM(-1)	0.009253	0.005188	1.783666	0.0760
DTWAGESJR(-1)	-0.567225	0.416756	-1.361048	0.1751
IFOKONKLIJR(-1)	0.000717	0.000356	2.016482	0.0451
DTM3JR(-3)	0.231950	0.127329	1.821665	0.0701
USDLND(-1)	0.320938	0.116506	2.754687	0.0064
R-squared	0.103370	F-statistic		2.472261
Adjusted R-squared	0.061558	Prob(F-statistic)		0.010852

Table 3.11: Sector model: Retailing

4 Optimisation

4.1 Concept

This quantitative approach identifies valuation and economic factors that are expected to determine market performance over the next month. It uses these factors to forecast asset returns and then tailors a portfolio to risk/return objectives. The optimisation is carried out by the classical approach of Markowitz (1952) or Elton / Gruber (1991). The optimisation process builds an efficient frontier which shows how expected returns increase with the risk level. Optimisation then selects the next point on efficient frontier that corresponds to the appropriate level of risk. This point on the efficient frontier represents a specific portfolio described by the sector weigthings x_i. To optimise a portfolio estimates of the sector returns μ_i, the standard deviations σ_i of each of the DAX sectors, i. e. the monthly volatilities, and the correlations ρ_{ij} are necessary. Basically a portfolio of assets that provides the highest return at a given level of risk, or, alternatively the minimum risk at a given level of return can be constructed. Due to two reasons the first approach is considered in this study.

- Typically in asset management outperformance of a certain benchmark means achieving a higher return rather than a lower risk.
- The quality of the forecasts given by the sector models can be better checked out with the target of a higher return. Then the chosen level of risk has to be included into the constraints.

Thus the following optimisation problem is solved every month:

Maximize

$$\sum_{j=1}^{n} x_i \mu_i \tag{1}$$

with following constraints:

$$\sum_{i=1}^{n} x_i = 1 \tag{2}$$

x_i denotes the portfolio weighting of one sector. The sum of the weightings x_i is restricted to 1. That means that no cash is hold and the portfolio is fully invested in sectors of the DAX. The target of the proposed methodology is to deliver outperformance in terms of higher return over a given benchmark. The expected portfolio return largely depends on the chosen level of risk. In this study the level of risk is restricted to the market risk σ_P, i. e. the volatility of the optimised portfolio σ_M is the same as the volatility of the DAX over the last 24 months:

$$\sigma_P \leq \sigma_M \tag{3}$$

whereas

$$\sigma_P{}^2 = \sum_{i=1}^{n} \sum_{j=1}^{n} x_i{}^2 \sigma_i{}^2 + 2\sum_{i=1}^{n} \sum_{j=1}^{n} x_i x_j \, \rho_{ij} \sigma_i \, \sigma_j \tag{4}$$

The forecasts of the quantitative sector models are used in place of the historical mean. Due to the high linear correlation of the second moments of financial time series (see Bollerslev (1986), Engle (1982), Moftakhar (1994)) the historical standard deviation is considered as the best predictor for the future standard deviation. The recommended asset allocation depends directly on the estimated parameters. In other words: The better the quality of the parameters the better the quality of the recommendation. An important influence to the quality of the estimates has the estimation period chosen. Basically, the more historical data available the better the quality of the estimates in the sense of robustness and reliability. In this study volatilities of each sector and correlations between the regarded sectors based on the previous 24 months.

4.2   Backtest January 1996 until May 1997

Finally, the objective of this study is to check out the forecasting ability of the quantitative sector allocation by an out-of-sample comparison covering the period from January 1996 until May 1997. Every month the sector models are recalculated and the portfolio is optimised. Table 4.2 reports the statistics of the backtest. The monthly and cumulated performance of the optimised sector model and the two benchmarks DAX and CDAX are shown. Both methodologies of the sector models, the linear regression as well the neural nets outperformed both benchmarks mainly due to following reasons:

- Using linear regression the steady overweighting of the sector chemicals from March 1996 until June 1996 together with an overweighting of the utilities achieved an advantage of about 4 %. Another interesting allocation succeeded in April 1997. An overweighting of the electricals was the reason that the optimised portfolio lost only 0.8 % (linear regression) in comparison to -1.6 % of the DAX and -1.3 % of the CDAX, respectively. Linear regression results lead to an overweighting of the utilities with a good performance of VEBA and Deutsche Telekom in May 1997. That was the reason to decouple further.

- Considering neural networks the key asset allocation was an steady overwheighting of the interest rate sensitive sectors insurance and utilities from August 1996 to May 1997. Given an environment of falling interest rates in this period both sectors outperformed the market.

As a result the performance of the linear regression was 7 % better than the DAX and 13 % better than the CDAX performance at the end of the backtest period. More impressive are the figures of the neural networks: They had an advantage of 33.3 % against the DAX and 39.6 % against the CDAX. Thus the neural nets could beat both benchmarks and the linear regression. This examination suggests that neural networks tend to forecast better than linear stastical methods and corresponds to the findings of Hill et al. (1994), that artificial neural networks dominate standard statistical techniques when the data are (i) of a financial nature, (ii) seasonal or (iii) non-linear. These very encouraging results are visualised in figure 4.1.

Performance	DAX	CDAX	Linear regression	Neural net
Dec 95				
Jan 96	8.81%	7.39%	8.45%	10.41%
Feb 96	0.61%	-0.42%	0.40%	1.19%
Mar 96	0.16%	-0.03%	1.44%	1.68%
Apr 96	0.12%	0.02%	0.99%	1.90%
May 96	1.24%	1.56%	2.78%	3.04%
Jun 96	1.86%	2.93%	2.14%	3.51%
Jul 96	-3.05%	-3.28%	-3.03%	-0.68%
Aug 96	2.91%	2.50%	2.52%	3.86%
Sep 96	3.43%	3.38%	3.83%	4.52%
Oct 96	0.74%	0.03%	0.83%	1.34%
Nov 96	5.38%	3.84%	3.87%	5.37%
Dec 96	2.31%	2.65%	2.44%	3.97%
Jan 97	5.71%	6.25%	6.33%	7.58%
Feb 97	7.07%	5.58%	6.34%	7.16%
Mar 97	5.20%	4.99%	5.57%	7.10%
Apr 97	-1.60%	-1.27%	-0.82%	-1.68%
May 97	5.15%	5.56%	6.22%	5.65%

Table 4.1: Backtest: Monthly performance of the optimised models and the two benchmarks DAX and CDAX

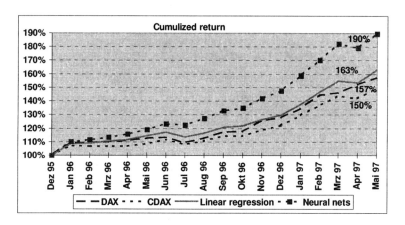

Fig. 4.1: Cumulized return, backtest period

Performance	DAX	CDAX	Linear regression	Neural net
Dec 95	100.00%	100.00%	100.00%	100.00%
Jan 96	108.81%	107.39%	108.45%	110.41%
Feb 96	109.47%	106.94%	108.88%	111.72%
Mar 96	109.65%	106.91%	110.45%	113.60%
Apr 96	109.78%	106.93%	111.54%	115.76%
May 96	111.15%	108.60%	114.64%	119.28%
Jun 96	113.22%	111.78%	117.09%	123.47%
Jul 96	109.76%	108.11%	113.55%	122.63%
Aug 96	112.95%	110.81%	116.41%	127.37%
Sep 96	116.82%	114.56%	120.86%	133.13%
Oct 96	117.68%	114.60%	121.86%	134.91%
Nov 96	124.01%	118.99%	126.57%	142.16%
Dec 96	126.87%	122.14%	129.66%	147.80%
Jan 97	134.12%	129.77%	137.87%	159.00%
Feb 97	143.60%	137.02%	146.61%	170.39%
Mar 97	151.06%	143.85%	154.79%	182.49%
Apr 97	148.64%	142.02%	153.52%	179.43%
May 97	156.29%	149.92%	163.08%	189.57%

Table 4.2 : Backtest: Cmulated performance of the optimised sector models and the two benchmarks DAX and CDAX

5   Conclusion

This approach analyses straightforward relationships between factors and sector performance of the German stock market. Following points are worth noting:

- The backtest results suggest that German stock market investors could enhance their performance substantially by exploiting the forecasting ability of a quantitative sector allocation. Based on this analysis, the proposed quantitative strategy that adjust the portfolio sector weighting dynamically using the signals from predictor variables should earn substantially higher long-run returns than did static strategies which do not actively adjust the portfolio weightings.

- In addition to this findings with this quantitative method it is possible to see precisely which factors are driving market forecasts. Thus even if some investors find the proposed approach too mechanical or too risky to be used systematically, they may want to use it selectively. As a result this approach delivers at least worthful insights into sources of risk and return of the German stock market.

- The empirical results indicate that nonlinear methods for forecasting sector returns of the DAX are able to deliver added value to the common used linear regression. Thus neural networks are an interesting alternative to linear models. But further research is necessary to confirm these findings.

Literature

Beilner, T., Mathes, H. D., DTB DAX-Futures: Bewertung und Anwendung, Die Bank, 1990; 7: 388 - 395

Bollerslev, T., Generalized Autoregressive Conditional Heteroscedasticity, Journal of Econometrics, 1986; 31: 307 - 327

Burgess, A. N., Modelling Asset Prices using the Portfolio of Cointegration Models Approach, London Business School, Department of Decision Science, Working Paper, 1997

Clark, P., Laxton, D., Rose, D., Asymmetry in the U.S. Output-Inflation Nexus, IMF Staff Papers, Vol. 43, No.1, S. 216 - 251

Dicks, M., Output Gaps And All That, Lehman Brothers, June 1996

Elton, E. J. , Gruber, M. J., *Modern Portfolio Theory and Investment Analysis*, New York, 1991

Engle, R., Autoregressive Conditional Heteroscedasticity With Estimates of the Variance of U.K. Inflation, Econometrica, 1982; 50: 987 - 1007

Graf, J., Zagorski, P., Westphal, M., Knöller, S. „Strategische Asset Allocation mit Neuronalen Netzen: Prognosegesteuertes Portfoliomanagement", in *Quantitative Verfahren im Finanzmarktbereich*, Schröder, M., ZEW-Wirtschaftsanalysen, Nomos, Band 5, 1996

Hill, T., Marquez, M., O'Conner, Remus, W., Artificial neural network models for forecasting and decision making, International Journal of Forecasting, 1994; 10: 5 - 15

Illmanen, Forecasting U.S. Bond Returns, Salomon Brothers Inc., United States Fixed-Income Research, Portfolio Strategies, August 1995

Markowitz, H. M., Portfolio Selection, Journal of Finance, 1952; 7: 67 - 91

Moftakhar, V., Varianzminimale Portefeuilles am deutschen Aktienmarkt, Beiträge zur Theorie der Finanzmärkte, Institut für Kapitalmarktforschung, J. W. Goethe-Universität, Frankfurt, Working Paper, 1994

PART 5

CORPORATE DISTRESS MODELS

PREDICTING CORPORATE FINANCIAL DISTRESS USING QUANTITATIVE AND QUALITATIVE DATA: A COMPARISON OF STANDARD AND COLLAPSIBLE NEURAL NETWORKS

QUEEN BOOKER, JOHN D. JOHNSON and ROBERT E. DORSEY

School of Business Administration
University of Mississippi
Holman Hall, University, MS 38677

The intent of this study is to compare the predictive strength of two neural network models –a standard feedforward neural network trained using a genetic algorithm and the more recently developed collapsible neural network using genetic algorithms - to determine corporate financial distress (bankruptcy). This research expands existing bankruptcy models on several levels. First, it utilizes financial ratios based on the cash flow statements in addition to the usual ratios based on balance sheets and income statements. It also incorporates qualitative data that may indicate financial distress such as change in management and change in auditor. Lastly, it provides a promising algorithm using collapsible neural networks to provide parsimony in the model structure and insight into the process used by the neural network in its decision making process.

1 Introduction

U. S. business failure has reached levels not seen since the great depression of the 1930s. Unlike the failures of the depressions, current business failures are materializing during periods of economic growth. This environment requires computational tools to assist auditors and potential creditors in determining if a firm is potentially headed for financial distress which may include but is not limited to insolvency, failure, default, and bankruptcy. In addition to the impact on creditors' and shareholders' wealth, business bankruptcy impacts labor and governmental agencies and, ultimately could effect the entire economy. Given the magnitude of the resulting harm of business failure, stakeholders have an intrinsic interest in utilizing a better methodology to assist in making decisions about investments and alerting them if a firm is having financial distress.

Historically, statistical methods such as logistic regression analysis and multiple discriminant analysis have been used to determine financial risk.

A.-P.N. Refenes et al. (eds.), Decision Technologies for Computational Finance, 355–363.
© 1998 *Kluwer Academic Publishers. Printed in the Netherlands..*

Many of these methods are based on models developed in the late 1960s by noted financial analysts/accountants such as Edward I. Altman and William H. Beaver, who recognized the relationship between a firm's balance sheet and its proclivity for financial distress. A new statistical method called Artificial Neural Networks (ANN) was introduced in the early 1990s and has since been proven to be a strong tool in determining financial distress in studies such as Raghupathis, Schakde, and Raju (1991), Coats and Fant (1992), Altman, Marco and Varetto (1994), Dorsey, Edmister and Johnson (1995), and Wilson and Sharda (1996). Using various topologies and training algorithms, each of these studies conclude that the neural network performs at least as well if not better than the applied statistical method. Hence the improvement of predictability of neural networks over applied statistical models has been well documented. For this reason, this study emphasizes the comparison of the standard neural network models to the more recently developed collapsible model.

2 Neural network models

Artificial neural networks were patterned after the processing capabilities of the human brain and nervous system (Hawley, Johnson, and Raina, 1992). This "mimicking" of brain processes is what makes the neural network unique in that it can recognize patterns in the presence of incomplete or noisy data. This ability makes it useful for providing decision support when the decision maker has limited knowledge about the appropriate forecasting method. While neural networks can overcome the problem of determining what model or functional form to use when designing the decision analysis process and can limit the need for a priori information, the decision maker must still be cognizant as to which variables to include in the ANN.

2.1 Standard Neural Networks

Neural network computing has been offered as a solution to the statistical problems of many other classification techniques. Artificial neural networks represent a different form of computation from the more common algorithmic models. The neural network models, in a simplified way, the biological systems of the human brain. Simulated neurons serve as the basic functional unit of the ANN in much the same way that the binary electronic switches serve as the basic units in digital computers (Hawley et al, 1992). A neuron is a simple structure that performs three basic functions: the input, processing, and output of signals. Neural networks take advantage of this structure by combining one or more hidden layers of nodes between the input and output neurons (nodes), and developing correspondingly a large number of weights (connectors).

An important consideration in ANNs is the use of training (learning) algorithms. Among the more popular algorithms are back propagation, gradient descent techniques, simulated annealing, tabu search and genetic search.

Another consideration is the number of hidden nodes and layers needed for successful classification. Most studies involving financial distress use only one hidden layer. This is supported by Haykin (1994) who concluded after training and testing several levels of complexity with hidden layers that the simple models generalized better than complicated models. The number of nodes in the hidden layer differed according to the number of variables used in the model, with a minimum of

$$\frac{(n+1)}{2}$$

and a maximum of

$$n+1$$

where n is the total number of input variables (nodes). These results are supported by Ripley (1993). However, with the addition of one hidden node the complexity of the system increases by n additional weights.

2.1.1   Genetic Algorithm

The genetic algorithm (GA) was introduced by John Holland in 1975 (Blankenship, 1994). He provided a general framework for viewing all types of adaptive systems and how the evolutionary process can be applied to artificial systems (Koza, 1992). The GA is an "intelligent" probabilistic search algorithm that is based on the evolutionary process of biological organisms in nature. The GA simulates the mutative generation process by taking an initial population of observations and applying genetic operators in each reproduction. In terms of optimization, each observation in the group is encoded into a string or *chromosome* which represents a possible *solution* to a given problem. The fitness of an individual observation is evaluated with respect to a given objective function. Highly fit solutions reproduce by exchanging pieces of their genetic information in a crossover procedure with other highly fit solutions (observations). This produces new "offspring" solutions, which share some characteristics taken from both parents. Mutation is often applied after crossover by altering some genes in the strings. The offspring can either replace the whole population (generational approach) or replace less fit individuals (steady state approach). This evaluation-selection-reproduction cycle is repeated until a satisfactory solution is found, that is, until the population converges.

Though a neural network trained with the genetic algorithm can reduce the amount of information the decision maker must know in order to analyze the data, the decision maker is still responsibile for the analysis of the output from the ANN. For this reason, this research explores the concept of the collapsible neural network.

2.2 Collapsible Neural Networks

The collapsible neural network (CNN) demonstrates potential for improving on the existing technology behind the ANN trained by a genetic search algorithm. The CNN is a feedforward neural network that dynamically eliminates connectors that are not significant to the decision made by the system. This is much like the decision making process in the human brain where several connections are made when the brain is learning a new idea and connectors are lost when their significance is reduced or eliminated. Hence, the power behind the CNN is its ability to reduce the number of connections or weights in the weight matrix such that further analysis can be made regarding the significance of variables as well as the process of decision making.

A more complex model which includes a dynamic reconfigurable neurons which include dynamic feedback were investigated in a recent study by Johnson and Dorsey (1997). The dynamic reconfigurable neural networks using a genetic algorithm based training methodology, quickly identified a set of weights to solve the objective function for energy surface optimality by generating penalties for extraneous nodes and connections. This study extended the previous work of Harold Szu in solving the training problem and developed a novel methodology that uses genetic algorithms to select structures that are optimal in the sense of minimizing an energy function. The CNN uses a similar methodolgy to the one presented in the work of Dorsey and Johnson but uses a simpler feedforward unidirectional structure. That is, it takes a standard feedforward network and uses a modified genetic procedure to evolve not only the connection weights but also the underlying connection structure.

3 Model for the study

The topology of the neural networks used in this study had one output node, one hidden layer with eight nodes, and fourteen input nodes, and uses a genetic algorithm training method. The basic neural network model for this study used both the ratios described by using Z-score analysis (Altman, 1968) as well as additional ratios selected from the cash flow statement. Additionally, we include significant corporate events like change in management and change in auditors as additional qualitative measures to test improvements in the reduction of Type I and Type II errors. A Type I error is defined as classifying a bankrupt firm as non bankrupt and a Type II error is defined as classifying a non bankrupt firm as bankrupt.

3.1 Data

In the current study, corporate financial distress is defined as a Chapter 7 bankruptcy or complete liquidation of a firm's assets. Additional firm population constraints are: (1) publicly-traded firms; (2) minimum activity of five years; and, (3) activity period from 1990 to 1997. A further constraint regarding the bankrupt firms in this study is that the financial data used were obtained for the period preceding bankruptcy by three years. A total of 100 firms are included. Half of the firms are active, healthy firms and the other half must have declared bankruptcy under Chapter 7 or otherwise ceased trading due to complete liquidation. Financial information on changes in management or directorship was obtained from *Compact Disclosure's* 10-K reports filed with the Securities Exchange Commission.

Financial ratios used for the current study were adopted because of their proven or suspected usefulness in earlier research in the area of financial distress prediction. Each ratio was calculated from the financial data contained in the 10-K reports on *Compact Disclosure*. In addition to the financial ratios, qualitative variables believed to be indicative of financial distress were ascertained from the 10-K reports. These qualitative variables include changes in auditor and in management. Changes in management include resignation, dismissal or replacement of the chief executive officer, chief financial officer, or other key positions within the organization. Similar changes for the auditor were included.

The use of ratios for financial analysis began during the last stages of the American industrial revolution. Beginning with the *current ratio* which was established by Horrigan in 1968, researchers have developed numerous ratios as a measure of efficiency as predictors of financial distress. (See Booker, Greer, Sudderth 1997 for further discussion on financial distress ratios). The widespread use of financial ratios in predicting business failure continued to stimulate research for building the base of possible predictors. Beaver (1966) focused on cash flow, liquidity and profitability ratios, adding cash flow to total debt, net income to total assets, and total debt to total assets to the list of predictors for failure. Altman (1968) found that earnings before interest and taxes to total assets and sales to total assets were the largest contributors to group separation between bankrupt and nonbankrupt firms. Similar to Beaver's focus on cash flows, research has shown cash flow to current liabilities and cash flow to total assets to be important indicators of bankruptcy (Gentry et. al. 1985, Ward 1995, Aziz, et. al. 1988). More recent research compared firm ratios to indicate when a company is more likely to file bankruptcy. These studies confirmed the importance of previously cited ratios and extended the list to include earnings before interest and tax to sales. Based upon these studies, the aforementioned ten financial ratios were selected for the models in the current experiment as potential predictors of bankruptcy.

For change in management, Roger Mills (1996) noted two unfinished business areas in determining the strength of a firm: whether the firm's major assets are human rather than physical capital, and whether the firm is global or not. At its extreme, financial distress corresponds with complete failure in the form of administration. Also, if a firm is unhappy with an audit report given by its auditor, particularly if it indicates a possible financial problem, it is likely that a firm may seek to change auditors. Hence, a change in management at the upper levels and a change in auditor may indicate financial weakness or a predictor of failure. Given that possibility, these criteria were chosen as possible qualitative evidence of bankruptcy for this study. Thus, the qualitative indicators used in the current study include changes in management and changes in auditor. A summary of the variables and their descriptions are listed in Table 3.1.

Table 3.1: Quantitative and qualitative variables used in study

Variables	*Interpretation*
CFOTL	Cash flow from operations to total liabilities
CLCA	Current liabilities to current assets
CPACHG	Change in CPA (Certified Public Accountant)
EBITNS	Earnings before interest and tax to net sales
EBITTA	Earnings before interest and tax to total assets
MGTCHG	Change in management or directorship
NCFCL	Net cash flow to current liabilities
NCFTA	Net cash flow to total assets
NITA	Net income to total assets
NSTA	Net sales to total assets
TLTA	Total liabilities to total assets
WCTA	Working capital to total assets

4   Methodology

The use of ANN to predict financial distress has been the basis of several research studies during the past few years. This attention can be attributed to the ability of the ANN to deal with unstructured problems, inconsistent information and real time output (Hawley, et al 1992)   One of the unique abilities of a artificial neural network is its ability to map non-linear functions. The training method used in this study is the genetic algorithm. The networks consisted of three layers, the input, output, and hidden nodes. The input layer had twelve input nodes, not including the bias term, with each node corresponding to one of the independent variables. The output layer had only one node: 1 if the firm is bankrupt or 0 if they are solvent. The hidden layer of the final model consisted of three (3) nodes which were derived through sucessive evaluations of several architectures. Each network was allowed to train on 80% of the cases, in which 50% filed for bankruptcy and the others were healthy. The network was then tested using the remaining twenty (20) cases.   A bootstrapping method was used to generate multiple data sets for testing and training.   The bankrupt and non bankrupt firms were randomized and forty (40) of each group were selected for training and the remaining were used for testing. A total of ten data sets was used for both the standard and collapsible neural network. Details of the training process are available on request.

4   Results

The training converged for all of these samples without any misclassifications. When testing these trained networks on the holdout sample, they were able to classify all of the firms in accordance to their actual financial situation when using all variables. The major difference, however, was in the time taken to converge. The standard neural network took between 750,000 iterations and over 1,000,000 iterations to converge whereas the collapsible network require at most 400,000 iterations.   This significant decrease in iterations was due to the reduction in search space allowed by setting variables to zero. The reduction in weights by the collapsible model varied which variables remained in the model and which were eliminated by a complete lost of weight connections. However, current liabilities to current assets, earnings before interest and tax to net sales, total liabilities to total assets and working capital to total assets were consistently among those variables to retain at least one weight connection to the hidden layer. In the best collapsible model, all the variables remained except cash flow from operations, earnings before interest and tax to total assets, net cash flow to total assets, and one of the hidden layer nodes. This would indicate that the best network requires only one hidden node, and can sucsessfully model and classify firms with only eight of the selected ratios, but more than the five originally used by Altmann. Overall, the results are promising and clearly demonstrates a new level of development of neural networks in corporate financial distress prediction.

362

5 Bibliography

E. I. Altman, "Financial Ratios Discriminant Analysis, and the Prediction of Corporate Bankruptcy." *Journal of Finance,* (September 1968), pp. 589-609.

E. I. Altman, *Corporate Financial Distress.* New York: John Wiley and Sons. 1993.

E.I. Altman, G. Marco, F. Varetto, "Corporate distress diagnosis: Comparisons using linear discriminant analysis and neural networks (the Italian experience)," *Journal of Banking & Finance,* 18 no. 3 (May 1994), pp. 505-529.

A. Aziz, D. Emanuel, and G. H. Lawson, "Bankruptcy Prediction -- An Investigation of Cash Flow Based Models," *Journal of Management Studies* 25 no. 5 (September 1988), pp. 419-437.

W. H. Beaver, "Financial Ratios as Predictors of Failure," *Empirical Research in Accounting: Selected Studies, (*1966), pp. 71-111.

R. Blankenship, *Modeling Consumer Choice: An Experimental Comparison of Concept Learning System, Logit, and Artificial Neural Network,* dissertation (August 1994).

Q. Booker, T. Greer, T. Sudderth, "Predicting Corporate Bankruptcy Using Qualitative and Quantitative Variables: A Comparison of Traditional Statistical Methods and Neural Networks," forthcoming Advances in Artificial Intelligence in Economics, Finance, and Management, 1997.

P. K. Coats, L. F. Fant, "A Neural Network Approach to Forecasting Financial Distress," *Journal of Business Forecasting* 10 no. 4 (Winter 1991-1992), pp. 9-12

R. A. Collins and R. D. Green, "Statistical Method for Bankruptcy Forecasting, " *Journal of Economics and Business* 32 (1982), pp. 349-54.

Robert E. Dorsey Robert O. Edmister, and John D. Johnson, *Financial Distress Prediction Using Multi-Layered Feed Forward Neural Nets,* Charlotte: Research Foundation of the Chartered Financial Analysts, 1995.

John D. Johnson and Robert E. Dorsey, "Evolution of Dynamic Reconfigurable Neural Networks: Energy Surface Optimality Using Genetic Algorithms," Optimality in Biological and Artificial Networks, 1997.

B. S. Everitt and G. Dunn, *Applied Multivariate Data Analysis*. New York: Halsted Press. 1991.

J. A. Gentry, P. Newbold, and D. T. Whitford, "Classifying Bankrupt Firms with Funds Flow Components," *Journal of Accounting Research* 23(Spring 1985), pp. 146-60.

D. Hawley, J. Johnson, and D. Riana, " Artificial Neural Systems: A New Tool for Financial Decision-Making," *Financial Analysts Journal,* (November/December, 1992), pp. 63-72.

C. Klimasauskas., 1992, 'Applying Neural Networks,' in Trippi, R.R. and E.Turban (Eds.), Neural Networks in Finance and Investing.

R. Mills, "Developments in Corporate Finance," *Manager Update* 7 no. 22 (October 28, 1996), pp. 161-2.

J. R. Koza, *Genetic Programming: On the Programming of Computers by Means of Natural Selection,* The MIT Press, 1992.

W. Raghupathi, L. Schkade, and B. S. Raju, "A Neural Network Application for Bankruptcy Prediction," *IEEE,* 1991, pp. 147-55.

E. Rahimian, S. Singh, T. Thammachote, and R. Virmani, "Bankruptcy Prediction by Neural Network, " *Neural Networks in Finance and Investing,* Chicago: Irwin Professional Publishing, 1996.

B. D. Ripley, 1993, 'Statistical Aspects of Neural Networks,' in O.E.Barndorff-Nielsen, J.L. Jensen and W.S. Kendall (Eds.), Networks and Chaos -Statistical and Probabilistic Aspects, Chapman and Hall, 40 - 123.

K. Y. Tam and M. Kiang, "Predicting Bank Failures: A Neural Network Approach, "*Applied Artificial Intelligence* 4 no. 4 (1990) pp. 265-82.

R. Wilson and R. Sharda, "Bankruptcy Prediction Using Neural Networks," *Neural Networks in Finance and Investing,* Chicago: Irwin Professional Publishing, 1996.

CREDIT ASSESSMENT USING EVOLUTIONARY MLP NETWORKS

E. F. F. MENDES, A. C. P. L. F. CARVALHO
Computing Department
University of São Paulo
C.P. 668,C.E.P. 13560-970, São Carlos, SP, Brazil
E-mail: {prico, andre} @icmsc.sc.usp.br

A. B. MATIAS
Business Department
University of São Paulo
Ribeirão Preto, SP, Brazil
E-mail: fmatias@netsite.com.br

Credit assessment, in the form of credit card, direct credit to consumer and check card, is usually carried out either empirically or through a credit scoring system based on discriminate or logistical regression analysis. In the past years, a growing number of finance institutions has been looking for new techniques to improve the profit of their services, reducing the delinquency rates. For such, new techniques have been proposed, among them, neural networks. In neural networks design, a few parameters must be adequately set in order to achieve an efficient performance. The setting of these parameters is not a trivial task, since different applications may require different values. The "trial-and-error" or traditional engineering approaches for this task do not guarantee that an optimal set of parameters is found. Recently, genetic algorithms have been used as a heuristic search technique to define these parameters. This article presents some results achieved by using this technique to search optimal neural architectures for credit assessment.

1   Introduction

In most of the cases of credit assessment, bank managers must deal with a large number of information, from very different sources. Much of this information can be incomplete, ambiguous, partially incorrect, or with doubtful relevance. The traditional approaches used by bank managers are dependent on the experience. Frequently, bank managers analyses the credit application in a subjective way and they usually cannot explain the decision process, i.e. they are not able to point out the factors which influenced their decisions. Besides, credit assessment is a very dynamic task, with constant modifications due to economic factors and where decisions need to be fast. Artificial Neural Networks, ANN are a potential technique for credit assessment. They offer an efficient alternative to the numerical formulas used in the last decade.

A.-P.N. Refenes et al. (eds.), Decision Technologies for Computational Finance, 365–371.
© 1998 *Kluwer Academic Publishers. Printed in the Netherlands..*

ANN are already being used in a large number of financial tasks as bankruptcy prediction, exchange rate forecasting, stock market prediction and commodity trading (Carter and Catlett 1987, Richeson, Zimmerman and Barnett 1994, Trippi and Turban 1996).

This paper analyses the performance of Multi-Layer Perceptron networks, MLP, trained with the Backpropagation algorithm (Rumelhart, Hinton and Williams 1986), to create a model to evaluate risks in credit applications, from examples of past applications. The performance these neural models, strongly depends on the topology of the network used (size, structure and connections), along with the parameters of its learning algorithm (learning rate, momentum term).

It is a common sense that the design of efficient Neural Networks is not a simple task. For such, techniques based on empirical knowledge have been proposed (Caudill 1991).

A very common approach is the design of networks from standard architectures, or based on another architecture previously used. In these cases, the network is tested for the desired function; and modifications in the architecture are carried out until one architecture suitable for the application is found (Bailey and Thompson 1990). However, this approach requires a long time, may present a very high cost and does not guarantee the best results, because the performance criterion is based on a complex arrangement of factors. This is a typical problem of "multi-criterial" optimization.

Aiming to solve this problem, several techniques to automate neural architectures design for particular classes of problems have been investigated. One of the most successful of these techniques involves the search for optimal architecture through genetic algorithms (Holland 1975), which is called evolutionary design.

2 Evolutionary Design of Neural Architectures

In the evolutionary design of neural architectures, each individual usually corresponds to a neural network candidate to solve the problem. The evolutionary process starts with a population of genotypical representations of, randomly generated, valid networks. The networks (phenotypes) are derived from their representations (genotypes) through a transformation function. A neural simulator trains all the networks with the same training data set, and their performances are evaluated. A fitness function is then used to evaluate the present state of the population, establishing the fitness, an aptitude grade, for each network, according to its performance regarding all the other networks. The best networks go to the next generation, where reproduction operators like elitism, crossover and mutation, produce new individuals. This process is repeated until there is no further improvement in the performances achieved by the networks.

The choice of the genotypical representation is crucial in the design of an evolutionary system. The representation or codification used determines not only the classes of neural architectures which can evolve, but also the functioning of both the decoding process and the reproduction operators (Whitley, Schaffer and Eshelman 1992, Balakrishnan and Honavar 1995).

The genotypical representation of the Neural Network structure is not so direct. Several factors must be considered: if the representation allows approximately optimal solutions to be represented; how invalid structures could be excluded; how the reproduction operators should act so that the new generation would have only valid Neural Networks; and how the representation would support the growth of neural architectures. The ideal would be that the genetic space of the neural networks did not have genotypes of invalid networks and that this space could be expanded to all genotypes of potentially useful networks (Branke 1995).

The representation used in this work is a simplification of the representation proposed in (Mandisher 1993). It describes the components in a parameter area and a layer area. The parameter area specifies the learning rate and the momentum term for all network connections. The layer area specifies the number of units in each layer (up to three layers can be used). In this representation, invalid structures could be generated in just one case: when there were not any units in the second intermediate layer although they could be found in the third hidden layer. However, this case is easily detectable, and they are not generated in the initialisation phase.

The networks can only be evaluated after their training using the same data set. The training and validation error rates can be used to determinate the performance of these networks. In some applications, such as financial forecasting and credit assessment, for which the proposed approach has been used, it is possible to specify heuristics for performance evaluation that take into account the error costs made by the networks, through a cost matrix, or the calculation of loss caused by the networks in each transaction. Thus, the evaluations can be more specific and precise, and the given fitness can be more representative of the networks performance to solve these problems.

3   Experiments

During the development of this work, a prototype for the evolutionary design of neural architectures was created, the NeurEvol, using the C language. This prototype consists of two main modules: the Evolutionary Module and the Neural Module, as illustrated in Figure 1. The Evolutionary Module includes a genetic algorithm and it has evaluation and reproduction sub-modules. The Neural Module works by exchanging files with the SNNS simulator (Zell, et al. 1995) for the neural network training and validation. This module embodies a network generator sub-module, a *batchman* program generator sub-module and a sub-module for reading the results generated by the simulator.

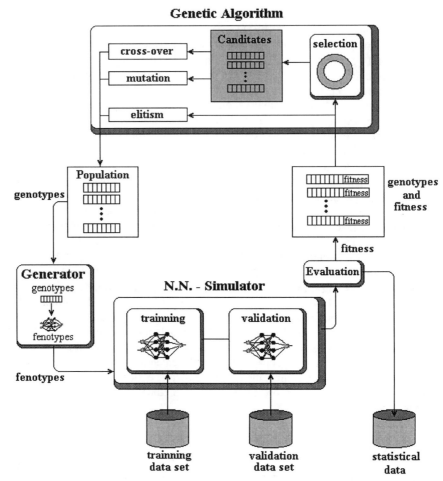

Figure 1: Evolutionary approach process for Neural Network architecture design.

In the experiment using NeurEvol presented in this paper, a data set of real world credit applications of the *Banestado,* a Brazilian state bank, was employed. This data set was composed by customers personal and professional information, besides information about the intended credit application. The model main objective was to evaluate the risk of new credit applications.

NeurEvol was set with a crossover rate of 80% and mutation of 10%. During the network training the smallest value of the Mean Squared Error in the training and validation sets were used as a early stopping criterion. A population of 20 individuals was used during 10 generations. A maximum of 20 units in the hidden layers and 800 training cycles were specified. Figure 2 presents the fitness of the best individual and Figure 3 presents the average fitness of the population in each generation. It can be observed that the fitness of the best individual improved in the generations 4, 8 and 10; whereas the average fitness was evolved gradually. These results also show that several good architectures were obtained in few generations.

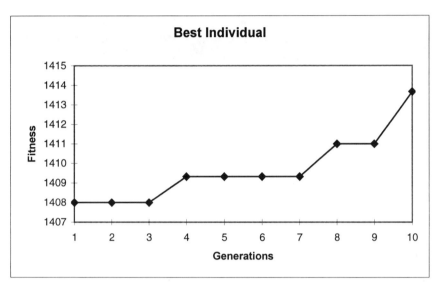

Figure 2: Evolution of the best individual during 10 generations.

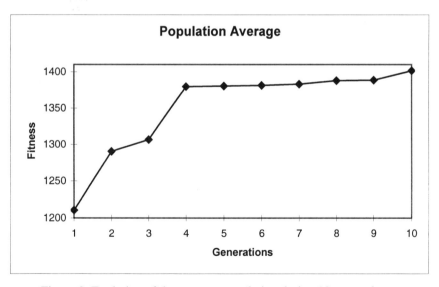

Figure 3: Evolution of the average population during 10 generations.

The results achieved in this experiment were compared to previous results obtained using the statistical method Discriminate Analysis, and a neural network generated by an empirical approach. Table 1 presents the number of patterns wrongly classified and the costs of these errors using each of these methods.

Table 1 – Results of this experiment x previous results.

METHOD	NPWC – C1	NPWC – C2	Costs
ANN – NeurEvol	2	15	47
ANN – Empirical	4	16	52
Discriminate Analysis	52	219	709

4   Conclusion

The results obtained confirm the efficiency of the model and the methodology used. The selected ANN was inserted in a mangers aid tool. This system can be used to forecast the risk of new customers credit application, which is very useful tool for aid the management of large amount of credit applications.

The optimisation of Neural Networks using Genetic Algorithms is usually carried out using toy problems. In this paper, the optimisation for a real world application was investigated. In the experiments, restrictions related to the application were considered in the optimisation process. These restrictions were useful to reduce the search space used by the genetic algorithm. The results presented in this paper, and results obtained in a previous experiment (Mendes and Carvalho 1997) show that is possible to automate the design of neural architectures using an evolutionary approach.

It was shown that this approach is able to improve the set of network parameters towards an optimal architecture. This work was concerned only with the optimisation of Multilayer Perceptrons networks trained with the Backpropagation algorithm. However, the method proposed is general enough to be used with other connectionist models or different training algorithms.

For future work, it is planned an increase in the number of generations, the removal of the restrictions of fully connected and strictly layered networks, the use of alternative fitness functions, the investigation of other representation approaches, the use of the proposed method for other neural models and the analysis of the performance achieved by NeurEvol for other data sets.

5   Acknowledgements

The authors would like to thanks CNPq and FAPESP for the financial support.

6   References

Carter C., Catlett J. Assessing Credit Card Applications Using Machine Learning, IEEE Expert Fall 1987, 71-79.

Richeson L., Zimmerman R., Barnett K., Predicting Consumer Credit Performance: Can Neural Networks Outperform Traditional Statistical Methods. International Journal of Applied Expert Systems 1994; 2: 116-130.

Trippi R., Turban E. *Neural Networks in Finance and Investing*, Irwin Professional Publishing, 1996.

Rumelhart D.E., Hinton G.E., Williams R.J., "Learning internal representation by error propagation", In *Parallel Distributed Processing*, 318-362, Cambridge: MIT Press, 1986.

Caudill M., Neural Network Training Tips and Techniques. AI Expert - January 1991; 6: 56-61.

Bailey D.L., Thompson D.M., Developing Neural Network Applications, AI Expert - September 1990; 5: 34-41.

Holland J.H. *Adaptation in Natural and Artificial Systems*, Ann Arbor: The University of Michigan Press, 1975.

Whitley D., Schaffer J.D., Eshelman L.J. "Combinations of Genetic Algorithms and Neural Networks: A Survey of the State of the Art", In *Proceedings of the International Workshop on Combinations of genetic algorithms and neural networks*, 1-37. IEEE Press, 1992.

Balakrishnan K., Honavar V. "Evolutionary Design of Neural Architectures - a Preliminary Taxonomy and Guide to Literature", A. I. Research Group, Iowa State University, *Technical Report CS TR #95-01*, 1995.

Branke J. "Evolutionary Algorithms for Network Design an Training", Institute AIFB, University of Karlsruhe, *Technical Report n.322*, 1995.

Mandisher M., "Representation and Evolution of Neural Networks", University of Dortmund, Germany, *Technical Report*, 1993.

Zell A. et al., "SNNS Stuttgart Neural Network Simulator - User Manual, Version 4.1", I.P.V.R., Universität Stuttgart, Germany, *Technical Report: 6/95*, 1995.

Mendes E.F.F., Carvalho A.C.P.L.F., "Evolutionary Design of MLP Neural Network Architectures", In *Proceedings of the IV Brazilian Symposium on Neural Networks*, 58-65. IEEE Computer Society, 1997.

EXPLORING CORPORATE BANKRUPTCY WITH TWO-LEVEL SELF-ORGANIZING MAP

K. KIVILUOTO

Laboratory of Computer and Information Science
Helsinki University of Technology
P.O. Box 2200, FIN-02015 Espoo, Finland
E-mail: Kimmo.Kiviluoto@hut.fi

P. BERGIUS

Kera Ltd.
P.O. Box 559, FIN-33101 Tampere, Finland
E-mail: Pentti.Bergius@kera.fi

The Self-Organizing Map is used in the analysis of the financial statements, aiming at the extraction of models for corporate bankruptcy. Using data from one year only often seems to be insufficient, but straightforward methods that utilize data from several consecutive years typically suffer from problems with rule extraction and interpretation. We propose a combination of two Self-Organizing Maps in a hierarchy to solve the problem. The results obtained with our method are easy to interpret, and offer much more information of the state of the company than would be available if data from one year only were used. Using our method, three different types of corporate behaviour associated with high risk of bankruptcy can be recognized, together with some characteristic features of enterprises that have a very low bankruptcy risk.

1 Introduction

The Self-Organizing Map (SOM) of Kohonen (1995) has been found to be a valuable tool for analyzing financial statements. In a number of earlier studies (Martín-del-Brío and Serrano-Cinca 1993; Back et al. 1994; Shumsky and Yarovoy 1997; Kiviluoto and Bergius 1997), the SOM has been used for data visualization, and in some cases also for classification of companies into healthy and bankruptcy-prone ones.

A.-P.N. Refenes et al. (eds.), Decision Technologies for Computational Finance, 373–380.
© 1998 *Kluwer Academic Publishers. Printed in the Netherlands..*

A common feature to the studies referenced above is that they are based on data from financial statements given either for a single year or for two consecutive years. However, the practice that has long been preferred by the analysts of Kera Ltd., a Finnish financing company, is to use data from several consecutive years – it has been found that single year data is simply not enough to give a reliable idea of the state of an enterprise. A straigthforward application of this philosophy would be to concatenate financial ratios from several years into a single input vector, which then could be visualized using SOM. The problem with this approach is that the map thus obtained is difficult to interpret: there are no simple explications for the different areas of the map.

The solution that we propose in this paper is to proceed in two phases. First, the instantaneous or single-year state of the enterprise is found using the SOM in a standard manner (see below); the instantaneous state is hence encoded as a position on the map. Then, the change in the corporate state can be analyzed using another SOM that is trained with vectors obtained by concatenating the position vectors on the first SOM from several consecutive years. Now each point on this second-level SOM corresponds to a *trajectory* on the first-level SOM, while the first-level SOM is well-suited for further analysis because its "coordinate axes" turn out to have very natural interpretations.

2   Self-Organizing Map for "semi-supervised" learning

Basically, the SOM associates each unit of a (usually two-dimensional) map with a point in the data space, and the SOM algorithm is capable to find these "links" between the map units and the data space in such a manner, that map units located near each other have also their associated data space points near each other (see figure 1). The mapping from data space onto the map is defined as follows: a data point is mapped to that map unit which has its link closer to the data point than any other map unit.

The SOM algorithm is usually used in the context of unsupervised learning, in which there are no known target variables – the data is first mapped to the SOM and then analyzed using e.g. some of the visualization methods discussed by Kohonen (1995). However, here we have also an output variable: the possible bankruptcy of the company. The solution is to train the SOM in a "semi-supervised" manner, used e.g. by Heikkonen et al. (1993): only the information that can be found from the financial statements is used for determining the shape of the map, other attributes of interest are just carried along with the weight vectors so that they can be later used for analysis.

Specifically, denote the set of financial indicators with vector $\mathbf{x}^{(f)}$ and other attributes of interest, such as a binary bankruptcy indicator, with $\mathbf{x}^{(a)}$; concatenating these, vector $\mathbf{x} \equiv [\mathbf{x}^{(f)T}\ \mathbf{x}^{(a)T}]^T$ is obtained. The weight vector $\mathbf{m}_j$ associated with each map unit j correspondingly has two parts: $\mathbf{m}_j = [\mathbf{m}_j^{(f)T}\ \mathbf{m}_j^{(a)T}]^T$.

The learning algorithm consists of first finding the *best-matching unit* index c for the present data vector using the rule

$$c = \operatorname*{argmin}_{j} ||\mathbf{x}^{(f)} - \mathbf{m}_j^{(f)}|| \qquad (1)$$

and then updating weight vectors using the rule

$$\mathbf{m}_j := \mathbf{m}_j + \alpha h(j,c)(\mathbf{x} - \mathbf{m}_j), \quad \forall j \qquad (2)$$

where α is the learning rate, and $h(j,c)$ is a neighborhood function which here has the form of a Gaussian.

The next phase is to teach a second-level SOM with data vectors obtained by concatenating annual positions of enterprises on the first-level SOM; this is shown schematically in figure 2.

Now the relative values of the first- or second-level SOM unit components are easily visualized

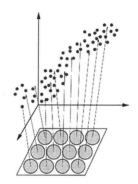

Figure 1: The SOM algorithm finds links between the data space and the map so that the topological relations are preserved as well as possible

as gray-level pictures for each component separately. In such a picture, the gray-level value of a map unit reflects the smoothed average value of the component in question of the data vectors mapped to that particular map unit or near it. For instance, if in such a picture some unit is almost black, the data vectors that are mapped to that map unit or to its neighbors have, on the average, very low relative values of the corresponding component.

3 Material

The material used in the present study consists of Finnish small and medium-sized enterprises, using the line of business, age, and size as the selection criteria. It was also required that the history and state of the enterprise be known well enough: if there were no data available for a longer period than two years before the bankruptcy, or if the last known financial statements were very poor,

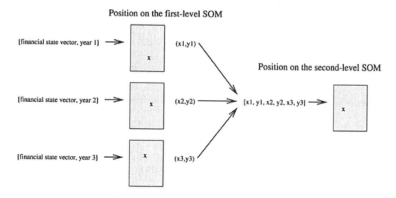

Figure 2: The second-level SOM input vectors consist of a company's position vectors on the first-level SOM during several consecutive years.

the company was rejected from the sample. However, in excess to these criteria, no data were rejected from the original population because it was "atypical", or looked like an outlier. In the final sample, there were 8 484 financial statements given by 2 116 companies, of which 568 have gone bankrupt.

The financial indicators used for training the first-level SOM are three commonly used ratios that measure the profitability and solidity of a company: (i) operating margin and rents, (ii) net income, and (iii) equity ratio. In addition to these, (iv) net income of the previous year is also included; together with the net income of the present year, it reflects the change in profitability.

Before training, the indicators were first preprocessed using histogram equalization separately for each indicator.

4   Results

The first-level SOM is shown in figure 3. In each subfigure, one component of the weight vectors associated with the map units is displayed. The gray-level coloring shows the relative values of that component in different parts of the map, black corresponding to "bad" values – either low values of financial ratios, or high proportion of bankruptcies. Note how the profitability generally increases when going downwards, while solidity generally increases to the right. The bankruptcies are concentrated in the upper left-hand corner of the map, where both profitability and solidity are low.

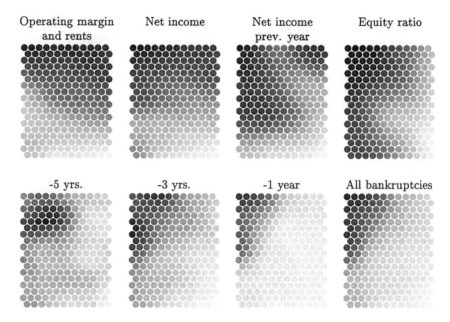

Figure 3: The first-level SOM. Shown are the relative values of the financial indicators, proportion of enterprises with varying number of years to bankruptcy, and proportion of all enterprises that went bankrupt within five years after giving the financial statement.

Examples of trajectories formed by an enterprise during several consecutive years are depicted in figure 4. Generally, the trajectories tend to move counter-clockwise: a decrease in profitability, which shows as an upward movement, eventually results in a decrease in solidity, thus producing a leftward movement as well. Exceptions to this rule indicate abnormalities, such as sudden changes in the capital structure of the enterprise.

The second-level SOM is shown in figure 5, together with examples of the trajectories on the first-level SOM that correspond to different parts of the second-level SOM. There seem to be at least three different types of enterprise behavior that are associated with an increased risk of bankruptcy. The *first* of these is mapped to the upper right part of the second-level SOM: the enterprise is constantly in the low profitability, low solidity area. The *second* is in the upper middle part of the second-level SOM. These enterprises seem to be poorly

378

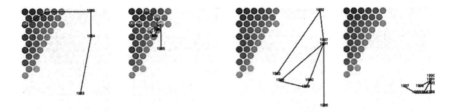

Figure 4: Trajectories of four companies on the first-level SOM – the two companies on the left went eventually bankrupt. The year the enterprise was mapped to each trajectory point is plotted next to the trajectory; the area with a high bankruptcy risk is marked with a (thresholded) darker shade.

controlled by the management, and so they experience large changes – long jumps on the first-level SOM – from year to year. This kind of behaviour becomes risky especially when it coincides with a decrease in solidity.

The *third* type of enterprise behaviour that is associated with an increased risk of bankruptcy can be found in the bottom-right corner of the second-level SOM. Almost all of the bankruptcies that fall into this group took place during the recession of the early nineties, and a common trait of the collapsed corporations here was that they typically had large loans in foreign currencies. First, the devaluation of the Finnish currency caused the solidity of these enterprises to weaken even though their profitability was very good; then the sales plummeted with the overall economic slump, which proved fatal for those firms that could not react fast enough and were already plagued by a relatively low solidity.

On the other hand, in the middle and on the lower left of the second-level SOM, the bankruptcy risk is very low. The first-level SOM trajectories here can be characterized as either having very small changes from year to year, or, if there are longer jumps, letting none of these notably weaken the solidity.

5 Discussion

The two-level self-organizing map can be applied to the qualitative analysis of financial statements with success. Its main advantage is that it is a very effective way to visualize higher-dimensional input data: among other things, it can be used to detect regions of increased risk of failure, to view the time

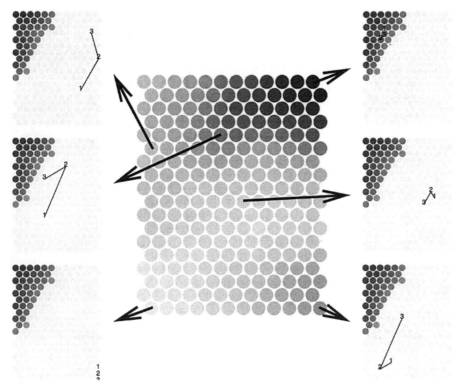

Figure 5: The second-level SOM and some first-level SOM trajectories that correspond to the indicated second-level SOM units.

evolution of the state of an enterprise, or to explore some typical corporate trajectories.

It seems plausible that this methodology could be extended also to quantitative analysis. The first step could be the classical "bankruptcy prediction problem", in which one tries to answer the question whether or not some company will go bankrupt, given its financial statements. This has become something of a benchmark problem and has been widely studied, so it could be used to get an idea of the performance level of the methodology introduced here; in the preliminary tests, the method has performed roughly at the same level as the popular Linear Discriminant Analysis (see Altman 1968).

380

Further steps in the quantitative analysis, and perhaps more interesting ones than the blind classification of bankruptcy prediction, might be estimating the probability of bankruptcy and testing different bankruptcy models or hypotheses. An interesting application of the latter would be contrasting the "failure trajectories" discussed above to those introduced by Argenti (1976); an initial examination hints that Argenti's bankruptcy trajectories might indeed have their representation also on the second-level SOM.

References

Altman, E. I. (1968, September). Financial ratios, discriminant analysis, and the prediction of corporate bankruptcy. *The Journal of Finance* (4), 589–609.

Argenti, J. (1976). *Corporate collapse – the causes and symptoms*. McGraw-Hill.

Back, B., G. Oosterom, K. Sere, and M. van Wezel (1994). A comparative study of neural networks in bankruptcy prediction. In *Multiple Paradigms for Artificial Intelligence (SteP94)*. Finnish Artificial Intelligence Society.

Heikkonen, J., P. Koikkalainen, and E. Oja (1993, July). Self-organizing maps for collision-free navigation. In *World Congress on Neural Networks*, Volume III of *International Neural Network Society Annual Meeting*, pp. 141–144. Neural Network Society.

Kiviluoto, K. and P. Bergius (1997, June). Analyzing financial statements with the self-organizing map. In *Proceedings of the workshop on self-organizing maps (WSOM'97)*, Espoo, Finland, pp. 362–367. Neural Networks Research Centre, Helsinki University of Technology.

Kohonen, T. (1995). *Self-Organizing Maps*. Springer Series in Information Sciences 30. Berlin Heidelberg New York: Springer.

Martín-del-Brío, B. and C. Serrano-Cinca (1993). Self-organizing neural networks for the analysis and representation of data: Some financial cases. *Neural Computing & Applications 1*, 193–206.

Shumsky, S. A. and A. Yarovoy (1997, June). Neural network analysis of Russian banks. In *Proceedings of the workshop on self-organizing maps (WSOM'97)*, Espoo, Finland. Neural Networks Research Centre, Helsinki University of Technology.

The Ex-ante Classification of Takeover Targets
Using Neural Networks

David Fairclough
The Business School, Buckinghamshire Chiltern University
Chalfont St. Giles, U.K.

John Hunter
Department of Economics, Brunel University,
Uxbridge, U.K.

In this article we use a net with a single hidden layer and back-propagation to discriminate between targets and non-target firms. The model is estimated on a state-based sample, though the best net is selected and subsequently analysed on the basis of a cross-validation sample which is representative of the true population. Tests of model performance are constructed on the basis of performance in the cross-validation sample. In addition to the usual asymptotic assumptions commonly made we also use a bootstrap pairs sampling algorithm, and a residual based sampling algorithm to generate alternative standard errors and confidence intervals

1. Introduction

Since 1971 there has been an increasing empirical interest in the ex-ante identification of takeover targets. More recently, papers by Dietrich and Sorensen (1984) and Palepu (1986) have used discrete choice models to predict takeover targets. Applications using neural networks to classify discrete data have, in the main, been confined to the prediction of bankruptcy; e.g. Tam and Kiang (1990), Alici[1] (1995), Tyree & Long[1] (1995). Such studies have consistently suggested that neural networks are superior as classifiers to multiple discriminent analysis (MDA) or logit. The network used in this article nests within it logit regression and as is explained in White (1989) can be viewed as a semi-parametric estimator.

As yet, the neural network literature has not produced a generally agreed procedure for inference. In this study we use a secondary (cross-validation) sample of firms for model selection and testing. Sample performance is based on the categorisation rate which is used first of all with a fixed net design and asymptotic standard errors. Then we look at the sensitivity of net performance via the exclusion of an input, and by constructing bootstrap standard errors and 95th percentile points.

Next we discuss sampling and data selection, in section 3 motives and methodology, and in section 4 the bootstrap. The net results are presented in section 5, in section 6 the bootstrap results and in section 7 we offer our conclusions.

2. Sampling and Data

The issue of sample selection is critical to our discussion. In essence we have selected at random the sub-samples analysed and the set of non-acquired companies. Although the acquired

---

[1] See Refenes et al (1995).

A.-P.N. Refenes et al. (eds.), Decision Technologies for Computational Finance, 381–388.
© 1998 *Kluwer Academic Publishers. Printed in the Netherlands..*

companies are known in advance, as is the sample proportion for the state based sample, the companies used in the training, cross-validation and holdout samples are all drawn randomly.

Predictive performance has become an issue in this literature, but this often relates to the performance within sample where the overall classification rate can be considered as a pseudo R^2 (Maddala 1983). In discriminating between target and non-target firms, the overall classification accuracy achieved in the literature to date ranges from 63% reported by Simkowitz and Monroe (1971) to 91% reported by Dietrich and Sorensen (1984). While Sen et al[1] (1995), who also use a neural network achieve a classification rate of 63%. Palepu (1986) has suggested that state-based samples can overstate classification accuracy or within sample predictive performance. Palepu used logit with a representative holdout sample of 1117 firms (30 targets and 1087 non-targets) and found that he could correctly identify 80% of the targets and 45% of the non-targets giving an overall classification rate of 45.95%. This highlights a key problem with this type of discreet classification, that a highly asymmetric structure produces a large number of Type II errors (i.e. the misclassification of a non-target firm). In a representative sample, this inevitably leads to low overall classification rates and poor predictive performance. Accordingly, we use population-representative cross-validation and holdout samples and attempt to define a model which minimises Type II errors.

We obtained a sample of firms listed on the London Stock Exchange for the period 1987 to 1996 from the Datastream Database. In addition to the 140 target firms (identified using the Investors Chronicle) a further sample of non-target firms was selected at random. producing 1480 company-years of data. To permit temporal variation, all variables were standardised using the mean and standard error of the non-target group relative to the appropriate year. Then each variable was further re-scaled to lie in the range [0 1]. In common with other cross-sectional studies, the sample was divided into three sub-samples. Firstly a state-based training set of 120 firms was randomly selected for model specification. Secondly a cross-validation sample of 150 was randomly drawn from the remaining observations to evaluate net performance. The remaining 1350 observations were used as the holdout sample.

3. Variable Selection and Methodology

A number of hypotheses exist to explain merger activity. In particular, the paper by Dietrich and Sorensen (1984) emphasises the investment potential of acquired firms. They differentiate between variables which are net present value enhancing, such as growth and profitability, relative to what might be viewed as poisoned pills, such size and leverage, which reduce the risk of acquisition. Also acquisition might be viewed as a mechanism for restructuring distressed companies (Clark et al 1993). However, preliminary work that we have undertaken did not lead us to select inputs based on this type of hypothesis. To some extent the above literature suggests, that the market has a problem with appropriately valuing companies at the margin. In a sense beauty is always in the eye of the beholder. Theories such as synergy (Healy et al 1992) suggest that an acquired company has a peculiar value in time and space to its partner which might differ considerably from the markets average. Table 1 presents the selection of 17 initial variables which we considered to be influential in explaining takeover behaviour, they are mainly drawn from the existing literature.

Variable	Dimension	Description
POUT	Div Policy	Dividend per Sh./Net. EPS
PE	Performance	Sh. Pr./EPS
X(737)	Leverage	Loan Capital/Equity+Reserves
PTBV	Valuation	Market Value/Net Tangible Assets
LN(104)	Size	Natural Log of Sales
X(707)	Performance	Return on Capital Employed
X(713)	Profitability	Operating Profit/Tot Sales
X(721)	Activity	Tot Sales/Assets Employed
X(732)	Int Cover	Tot Interest/Tot profit
X(741)	Liquidity	Current Assets/current Liab.
EI:(3)	Growth	Ind. Earnings:-Avg Annual 3Yr Gr
X(104)(1G)	Growth	Sales:- 1Yr Growth
X(211)(1G)	Growth	Earnings per Share:-1Yr Growth
P-PI^(1)	Performance	1Yr Sh Pr Growth Rel To FTA Index
NP/MV	Valuation	Net Profit/Market Value
S/MV	Valuation	Sales/Market Value
ASS/MV	Valuation	Assets Emp./Market value

Table 1. List of Input Variables.

Clearly a number of hypotheses might be addressed when one looks at the Table 1, but, net weights do not have a straight forward parametric interpretation. However, we can generate a pseudo-parametric measure of responsiveness by looking at the local variation in the output associated with a 1% perturbation of an input variable. This is described by Hunter and Fairclough (1998) as a pseudo-elasticity. We can also determine whether a particular input has an important influence on the results by looking at the effect of its exclusion on the over-all predictability.

A fully connected network[2] with all 17 inputs from Table 1 was trained to minimum error, though the network actually produces a family of such results. Following our suggestion in section 2, the net with the lowest Type II error is the one which is finally selected. This is then pruned by eliminating the variable with the smallest input loading. and a new network trained using the surviving inputs. The final model has one output neuron and one hidden layer containing seven neurons. The 8 input variables finally selected were: PE, PTBV, X(713), EI:(3), X(211)(1G), S/MV, ASS/MV. The PE ratio, X(713) and PTBV were also used by Palepu (1986) and Dietrich and Sorensen (1984), while Sen et al[1] (1995) included PE, X(713) and S(ales)/ASS(ets). The other variables in the model measure growth and performance, while the excluded variables were found not to affect classification accuracy.

The net discussed here learns how to approximate a generalised non-linear function $g(x)$ by searching a family of net architectures $f(x,w)$ where x is a k vector of net inputs and w is an l vector of net weights. The net error is defined as:

$$e = y - f(x,w) \qquad (1)$$

The net selects a set of optimal weights w^* by minimising a residual sum of squares function $\lambda(w)$ based on (1). It follows from White (1989) that this, also minimises the distance $E([g(x)-f(x,w)]^2)$. For the categorical variable used here this is the same as minimising $E([\gamma(x) - f(x,w)]^2)$ which implies that

---

[2] Network computations were carried out using NeuDesk supplied by Neural Computer Sciences. The net algorithm used here has a sigmoid transfer function and standard back propagation.

$\mathbf{w}^*$ is selected so that $f(\mathbf{x},\mathbf{w})$ best approximates a conditional probability $(\gamma(.))$. Optimal values of the output function, are then also conditional probabilities:

$$y^* = \gamma(\mathbf{x}) = f(\mathbf{x},\mathbf{w}^*) \qquad (2)$$

A problem with neural nets as semi-parametric estimators is the nature of support which depends on regularity or the existence of an implicit likelihood associated with the estimator. White (1989) argues that a net with one hidden layer and standard back-propagation has an information theoretic interpretation:

> "*More specifically when the learning behaviour embodied in the structure of the net is viewed as Kullback-Leibler Information, learning is a quasi-maximum likelihood statistical estimation procedure.*" (White 1989).

The network weights also satisfy standard asymptotics as does any measure of predictive accuracy (π) based on (2). Any well defined linear function of the weights is also asymptotically normal and as a result:

$$z = \frac{\pi_i - p_i}{SE(\pi_i) \; asy} \sim N(0,1). \qquad (3)$$

can be used to undertake inference on the categorisation rate in large samples.

4. Ex-ante Bootstrap Analysis

The notion of the bootstrap was introduced by Ephron (1979). While Weigend and Le Baron (1994) first applied the bootstrap to neural nets using time series data. It is standard to re-estimate the models on the basis of the bootstrap sample, but this is complicated when a neural net is analysed. Notice, that any re-estimation could violate some of the regularity conditions as smoothness is not guaranteed once the weights change as each weight vector implies a different semi-parametric form. Maerker (1997) solves this problem using what she refers to as a wild bootstrap which operates by re-sampling the hessian or rather looks at a non-linear problem within a neighbourhood of the solution. Here, we operate in a neighbourhood of the optimal value by fixing the net weights and analysing the behaviour of the model in response to the statistical variability associated with variation in both the data and a randomly re-sampled output variable. This approach is consistent with the view espoused by Weigend and LeBaron (1994), that variance estimates are more sensitive to the inputs, than the initial selection of the weights. In what follows, small sample approximations to standard errors are defined using bootstrap pairs sampling discussed by Tibshirani (1995) and the re-sampling approach designed for use with binary variables by Adkins (1990).

If we look at the bth paired sample selected at random from a holdout sample, then there are $b=1, ... B$ sub-samples of paired observations $(y,x)^b$ drawn at random. We then define the pair $(y,y^b) = (y,f(\mathbf{x}^b,\mathbf{w}^*))$ which is used to produce a categorisation rate $\pi(b)$ that defines the proportion of times $y = y^b$. From the categorisation rate we construct estimates of the variance and the mean:

$$\hat{se}_B = \sqrt{\sum_{b=1}^{B} \frac{(\pi(b) - p(.))^2}{B-1}} \text{ , where } p(.) = \sum_{b=1}^{B} \frac{\pi(b)}{B} . \qquad (4)$$

An approach which is closer to the spirit of the bootstrap due to Ephron (1979) was devised by Adkins (1990) to define small sample approximations of standard errors for the probit estimator. If we draw B monte-carlo samples from a uniform distribution for ε^b such that $0 \leq \varepsilon^b \leq 1$, then we use the following criterion to select the bootstrap samples for y^b:

$$y^b = 1 \; if \; 0 \leq \varepsilon^b \leq y^*$$
$$y^b = 0 \; if \; y^* < \varepsilon^b \leq 1.$$

We then use the pair (y, y^b) to determine the categorisation rate and (4) to construct similar mean and variance estimates to those described in the bootstrap pairs case.

5. Neural Network Results

For the model discussed in section 3 we look at the net performance relative to other net selections and alternative estimators. We generate pseudo-elasticities associated with a 1% change in the inputs and look at the effect of variable exclusion on predictive performance.

	Cross-val Sample:		
	Total	Targets	Non-T
226N1	0.9400	0.1250	0.9859
	Holdout Sample:		
	Total	Targets	Non-T
226N1	0.9333	0.0417	0.9836
MDA	0.2430	0.8750	0.2074
SNN	0.5993	0.4306	0.6088

Table 2: Classification Results.

	Cross-val Sample:		
	Total	Targets	Non-T
Mean	0.93360	0.08586	0.98889
St Err	0.04090	0.18650	0.01642
95%CI:UB	1.01380	0.45175	1.02107
95%CI:LB	0.85343	-0.28000	0.95671
$H_o(1)$: z=	-0.27140	0.17442	2.56950
$H_o(2)$: z=		0.45993	

Table 3: Model Validation Results.

In Table 2 the cross-validation and holdout sample results are presented for the final model (Net 226N1). That this model is the best overall classifier (94%) relative to the other net models is not surprising as it was selected on this basis. The reason for this is the classification of non-targets (Non-T) which is 98.59%, though only 12.5% of targets are classified correctly. Alternatively, net 226N5, which in the cross-validation sample was much better at classifying the targets (87.5%), turned out to be a poor classifier of non-targets (23.94%) and as a result produced a poor overall classification rate (27.33%). Similarly (MDA) and the single layer net (SNN) are poor at identifying non-targets. Such models may well have produced better predictions had they been trained using the cross-validation sample, but typically representative samples are not used to generate such results.

The main advantage of a single representative cross-validation sample is in constraining the potential for overtraining, though here it is used to select our preferred net. A more rigorous test of a models performance follows from assessing its ability to classify in a holdout sample. As can be seen from the second block of results in Table 2, it also appears to select a model which performs well in the holdout sample.

In Table 3 we extend the results by resampling the cross-validation sample to measure classification variance and model performance. To do this, 50 sub-samples of n=50 were drawn at random, then the average classification rate and its standard error were calculated. Table 3 gives

95% confidence intervals in which the overall classification rate and target classification rates for the holdout sample lie, though the non-target rate is just outside the lower bound.

We also compare the model performance relative to randomness as a randomly selected sub-sample should reflect the structure of the overall sample, that is 5.3% targets and 94.7% non-targets. The test $H_0(1)$ of random performance is constructed using the re-sampled standard errors and the normal test (3). Classifying at random one would expect to be correct 94.7% of the time. The first test result in row $H_0(1)$ of Table 3, shows that the overall classification rate 93.36% is not significantly different from randomness based on a two tailed test at the 5% level. A similar result holds for the classification of targets (column 2), while the classification of non-targets at 98.89% is significantly better than that suggested by random selection as $z=2.5695$ exceeds 1.96. We also test whether the target classification is significantly different from 0, that is row $(H_0(2)$. Using a one-sided test at the 5% level we cannot reject the null that the classification of targets is not significantly different from 0. It is important to realise, that none of the existing studies have addressed such issues and were they to do so the results in Table 2 suggest that the randomness test would fail.

Though the net weights do not have the usual parametric interpretation, a local approximation of the slope can be defined by looking at the percentage output response associated with a one percent change in each input. This defines a pseudo elasticity within a neighbourhood of the optimum. The responses are negative for PE (-2.72%), X(713) (-.85%), X(211)(1G) (-2.4%) and ASS/MV (-1.56%). This suggests, that the risk of being a target is reduced by high values of price relative to earnings as this increases the cost of acquisition; assets employed relative to market value which suggests over-valuation; operating profit relative to sales which implies little chance of restructuring; and earnings per share to 1 year growth which suggests poor growth potential. The response is positive for MV (5.51%), PTBV (4.96%), EI:(3) (1.64%) and S/MV (.22%). The risk of being a target is increased by high market valuation and market to book value which would appear to have an obvious interpretation. A similar effect is associated with earnings to average three year growth and sales to market value which both suggest that targets are relatively profitable.

To evaluate the importance of the variables, we dropped each in turn and retrained the network using the remaining seven. Each new networks classification rate was compared with the full model. The reduction in overall classification rate ranges from 5.56% for PTBV to 39.33% for X(732). The significance of such classification rates was tested by comparing performance in the holdout sample with that of the final model. The null of equal classification rate was rejected in all cases at the 1% level. Hence, each of these 8 variable makes a significant contribution to model performance. The interested reader is directed to Hunter and Fairclough (1998) for further details.

6. Bootstrap Results

Predictive performance is evaluated here using two bootstrap procedures. First of all the resampling procedure (Boot 1) used in Section 5 is extended to B=1000 replications based on sub-samples of 50 and a cross validation sample of 150. The second bootstrap (Boot2) uses B=1000 replications based on the method of Adkins (1990) discussed at the end of section 4. While the third procedure (Boot3), re-samples from the combined cross-validation and holdout samples (1500), using B=1000 realisations of equivalents to the cross-validation sample (n=150). These results are shown in Table 4 below.

In row 2, we repeat the initial estimates of the categorisation rate and asymptotic standard errors obtained for the cross-validation sample. In addition to means and standard errors, the subsequent rows present 95% confidence intervals (CI). The 95% confidence interval for model predictive performance is estimated in two ways. First by adopting standard procedures under the assumption of normality (Table 4 col.5-6). Secondly, based on the method in Ephron and Tibshirani (1986) which uses $\alpha/2$ and $(1-\alpha/2)$ percentile points from the empirical distribution (Table 4 col.7-8).

	Mean	Bias	Std Err	95%CI (Standard)		95%CI (Percentile)	
				LB	UB	LB	UB
"True" Value	0.9340						
Static X-Val Samp	0.9400	0.0060	0.0194				
Boo11(B=1000)	0.9379	0.0039	0.0336	0.8739	1.0061	0.8600	1.0000
Boot2(B=1000)	0.5439	-0.3901	0.0397	0.8622	1.0178		
Boot3(B=1000)	0.9351	0.0011	0.0186	0.9035	0.9765	0.8933	0.9667

Table 4. Bootstrap Standard Errors and Confidence Intervals.

Comparing the standard errors in the second row of Table 4 with the row for Boot 3, there is little to choose between re-sampling the population using sub-samples of n=150 and using the binomial approximation. However, comparison of these results with either the row marked Boot2 and that based on resampling within the cross-validation sample, Boot1, produces a standard error which is approximately double that obtained from the other two methods at 3.36%. There also appears to be little difference in the confidence intervals obtained by standard calculations and those obtained from the empirical bootstrap distribution.[3]

The other point of interest here, is the extent to which the sample estimation of mean classification rate is biased. Though the true classification rate is unknown, an estimate of the "true" value is obtained from the classification rate within the combined cross-validation and holdout samples (93.4%). Assuming that this is a good estimate, then the biases shown in Table 4, column 3 are under .5% except for Boot 2 the method due to Adkins (1990) which uses a very different approach.

7. Conclusions

These results would appear to support the view that artificial neural networks are better at the ex-ante classification of a representatively selected sample of non-target and target firms than either MDA or Logit. Furthermore, the strategy of minimising Type II errors seems to lead to a better overall classification rate than currently achieved in the existing studies. The quasi-elasticity results provide a local approximation which appears consistent with theory and all the variables have a significant influence on the classification rate in the cross-validation sample.

The method of resampling the cross-validation sample not only provides a mechanism for inference, but it also allows us to measure the sensitivity of the results to the selection of that sample.

---

[3] As the empirical distribution for Boot 2 is not correctly centred, then we do not use it to define $\alpha/2$ and $1-\alpha/2$ percentiles.

We intend to extended these results by testing the robustness of the validation procedures and improving the joint classification rates of targets and non-targets.

8. References.

Adkins, L. "Small Sample Inference in the Probit Model." Oklahoma State University, Working paper, 1990.

Clark, K., Ofek, E. "Mergers as a Means of Restructuring Distressed Firms: An Empirical Investigation", Journal of Financial and Quantitative Analysis, December 1993; 29:541-561.

Dietrich, J.K., Sorensen, E. "An Application of Logit Analysis to Prediction of Merger Targets", Journal of Business Research, 1984; 12:393-412.

Ephron, B. "Bootstrap Methods: Another Look at the Jackknife.", Annals of Statistics, 1979; 7:1-26.

Ephron, B., Tibshirani, R. "Bootstrap Methods for Standard Errors, Confidence Intervals and Other Methods of Statistical Accuracy.", Statistical Science, 1986, 1: 54-77.

Healy, P.M., Palepu., K.G., Ruback, R.S. " Does Corporate Performance Improve after Mergers? ", Journal of Financial Economics, 1992; 31:135-175.

Hunter, J., Fairclough, D. "A Local Interpretation of Neural Net Outputs", Brunel University Discussion Paper , 1998.

Maerker, G. "Bootstrapping GARCH(1,1) Models", paper presented at the Computational Finance 97 Conference, held at the LBS December 1997.

Maddala, G.S. Limited - Dependent and Qualitative Variables in Econometrics. Cambridge University Press, 1983.

Palepu, K.G. "Predicting Takeover Targets: A Methodological and Empirical Analysis", Journal of Accounting and Economics, 1986; 8:3-35.

Refenes, A.N., Abu-Mostafa, Y., Moody, J., Weigend, A, (Ed's). Neural Networks in Financial Engineering; Proceedings of the Third International Conference on Neural Networks in the Capital Markets. World Scientific, 1995.

Simkowitz, M.A., Monroe, R.M. "A Discriminant Analysis Function for Corporate Targets", Southern Journal of Business, November 1971; 1-16.

Tam, K.Y ., Kiang, M. "Predicting Bank Failures; a Neural Network Approach." Applied Artificial Intelligence, 1990; 4:265-282.

Tibshirani, R. "A Comparison of Some Error Estimates for Neural Network Models." Dept. of Preventive Medicine and Biostatistics, University of Toronto, 1995.

Weigend, A.S., LeBaron, B. "Evaluating Neural Network Predictors by Bootstrapping." Proc.of Int'l Conference on Neural Information Processing, Seoul, 1994.

White, H. "Learning in Artificial Neural Networks: A Statistical Perspective", Neural Computation, 1989; 1:425-464.

PART 6

ADVANCES ON METHODOLOGY – SHORT NOTES

FORECASTING NON-STATIONARY FINANCIAL DATA
WITH OIIR-FILTERS AND COMPOSED THRESHOLD MODELS

MARC WILDI

Institut for Empirical Economic Research
University of St-Gallen
9000 St. Gallen, Switzerland
E-mail : marc.wildi@few.unisg.ch

The paper proposes a forecasting-technique well suited to stationary and non-stationary economic or financial data. Two methods are used which together generalize the Box-Jenkins ARIMA-technique : Optimized-Infinite-Impuls-Response-Filters generalize difference-filters and composed-threshold (piecewise linear) models generalize linear ARMA-models.

1 Introduction

The two essential methodological extensions of the proposed method when compared to ARIMA-models is given by the ability of OIIR-(Optimized Infinite Impuls Response) filters to extract stationary components from non-stationary trends, without altering or distorting the former, and by the ability of CT-(Composed Threshold) models to take account of unconditional as well as conditional first and second order moments in the extracted stationary components. Section 2 introduces filter concepts together with an example in which frequency characteristics of an OIIR-filter are compared to the difference filter of the ARIMA-model. It will be shown that the obtained characteristics very well match the detrending problem of economic time series. Section 3 briefly introduces CT-models used in estimation as well as forecasting of the extracted stationary component of a non-stationary time series. In section 4 we give an example which illustrates the forecasting accuracy of the proposed method, when compared to ARIMA-modelling. In section 5 we shall give insight into the extraction problem of the stationary component resulting in the design of OIIR-filters and finally section 6 concludes with some general remarks about signal extraction, forecasting, long memory and random-walks in economic time series

2 Filters

2.1 The transfer function

A filter is a device which transforms a given input X_t to an output Y_t such that the latter exhibits some intended characteristics. Filters can be defined in the time

A.-P.N. Refenes et al. (eds.), Decision Technologies for Computational Finance, 391–402.
© 1998 *Kluwer Academic Publishers. Printed in the Netherlands..*

domain as well as the frequency domain : the so called Fourier- and inverse Fourier-transforms map from one space into the other. The transfer function of a filter is the functional expression relating the input to the output.The transfer function of an IIR-

filter for example is given by: $\quad H(B) = b \dfrac{\prod\limits_{k=1}^{n}(B-z_k)(B-\bar{z}_k)}{\prod\limits_{k=1}^{m}(B-p_k)(B-\bar{p}_k)}\quad$, where B is the

backward operator : $B(X_t)=X_{t-1}$ and z_k and p_k designate the parameters or the zeroes and poles of H and b is a normalization constant. To analyze the properties of a filter given by H in the frequency domain, one replaces B by the exponential $e^{-i\omega}$ so that $H(\omega)$ will become a function of ω. $H(\omega)$ is completely determined by its absolute value or amplitude function $|H(\omega)|$ together with its argument or phase function $\arg(H(\omega))$: the former is the weight the filter assigns to a given frequency whereas the latter is a measure for the time delay of the filter response at a given frequency. Designing a filter consists in constructing a filter which best fits some intended characteristics defined in the time domain or the frequency domain. The difference filter for example is a high pass filter, as can be seen in fig. 2 : low frequencies are attenuated and the frequency zero is stopped because the amplitude function of the filter (AMP-D) becomes small when $\omega\rightarrow0$. The rather trivial design of the difference filter permits transformation of a non-stationary random-walk into a stationary time series describing the evolution of the increments of the random-walk. Often filters are designed in the time domain : difference filters (including seasonal filters) and (exponential) moving-average filters are such examples, where the latter define a low-pass design (high frequencies are attenuated). Though intuitively appealing, the time domain approach often implies bad filter characteristics when analyzed in the frequency domain. Although the structures of the two domains or spaces match into each other, the previous discrepancy is not surprising since elementary operations like addition or multiplication are not preserved by the Fourier-transform: our natural time-domain intuition fails in designing appropriate frequency domain characteristics. However, frequency characteristics have a strong intuitive appeal in the time domain. For example, in order to deseasonalize, to detrend or to smooth (extract the trend) a given economic series, it is sufficient to remove seasonal cycles, cycles of infinite length (frequency 0) or short (high frequency) cycles respectively. These tasks should be executed separately or simultaneously by designing a corresponding filter, which perfectly removes the intended frequency areas and does not affect the remaining ones. Such filters, which perfectly met some specification, are called ideal filters. We shall see in section 2.2 that they can only be approximated, so that our time domain problem will become an optimization problem in the frequency domain. As a result, we feel that design in the frequency domain is often (much) more natural than design in the time domain, which at least often reduces to heuristic or intuitively motivated arguments.

In the following, we list some properties an ideal filter should have, when used in an economic context and compare an OIIR-filter with the difference filter subject to these constraints.

2.2 Selection of an appropriate filter class

First let X_t be a given (non-stationary) discrete time series beginning at $t=1$ and ending at $t=N$. In order to select among possible design techniques of filters applicable to X_t, we list some properties that the ideal and hence the realized filter should have :

P1. Delay of the filter response (i.e. phase function) is zero over the whole frequency spectrum.

P2. Perfect amplitude function (0 in stoppband, 1 in passband).

P3. Upper edge stability (at t=N).

P4. Flexibility.

P5. Fast and easy implementation.

P1 implies that the filter "answers" immediately to a given input and together with P2 they implie that the filter does neither add information not contained in the data nor remove too much information. In economic applications one is very often interested in forecasts of a given time series so that the delay of a filter becomes a very important parameter subject to minimization. Since P1 cannot be realized until the filter "degenerates", our goal will be to minimize the phase response. Like P1, P3 is somehow specific to economic applications. It implies that past filter values must not be reactualized when new data becomes available. In economic time series retroactive behaviour (of trend, of season,...) is in fact unlike. Moreover, upper edge stability ensures better forecasting ability by avoiding additional uncertainty of the signal extraction procedure at $t=N$. It should be noted that P1, P2 and P3 are opposed (they underly a kind of uncertainty principle), so that filter design in frequency domain becomes an optimization procedure. P4 not only means that a given filter class should be able to approximate many design shapes (see section 4 and 5), but also that the class should be able to handle n-th order zeroes for example, since many non-stationary time series (like simulated random-walks for example) have infinite variance. All in all P1-P5 seem to be rather strongly antagonistic but we shall see in our example that the class of IIR-filters provides a good tool for approximating our idealized purposes. We now briefly analyze a few well known filter design techniques and evaluate them with respect to P1-P5. First of all, non-linear filters, where the output is a non-linear function of the input, are often (strongly) worse than linear filters with respect to P1 or P3 and P5. Often even P2 is not met satisfactorily, while linear IIR-filters offer a good approximation to arbitrary amplitude functions with few parameters beeing estimated (parsimony). From electrical sciences and/or physics we know of a lot of preoptimized analog filter designs such as Butterworth- Tchebychev- or elliptic filters for example, which may be digitized by appropriate techniques (see for example Rabiner and Gold (1975)). Unfortunately, besides essentially contradicting P4 and P1 (in fact

394

corresponding optimization procedures do not minimize the phase-response), these often are in more or less strong conflict with all other intended properties. All-pole designs like Butterworth or Tchebychev class I filters are for example inappropriate for integrated (i.e. infinite variance) time series. Two important techniques remain: ad hoc optimization of FIR- (finite impulse response) and IIR- (infinite impulse response) filter designs. Since the latter is a generalization of the former we shall concentrate on IIR-filters. Recall that an IIR-filter is completely determined by its poles, zeroes and the parameter b. The need for real filter coefficients implies that complex poles or zeroes occur in conjugate pairs. Replacing any conjugate pair of poles (P_1,P_2 for example) or zeroes (Z_1,Z_2 for example) by their reciprocals $1/P_1,1/P_2$ and $1/Z_1,1/Z_2$ respectively leaves the amplitude function of the filter invariant. However, in order to obtain a design which is stable, the poles must strictly lie within the unit circle. The transfer function H of the filter is said to be minimal-phase if all its zeroes and poles are less than one in absolute value. Such designs are not always desirable, because the input process X_t may be unstable (non stationary) so that some frequencies must be eliminated (i.e. set to zero) in order to obtain stationarity of the filtered output, which in turn implies that some zeroes of H must lie on the unit circle. We therefore extend the definition of minimum-phase to transferfunctions with zeroes and poles strictly lying within the unit circle except perhaps for some zeroes lying on it. We now illustrate the results of an optimization of an IIR-filter design in figs. 1 and 2:

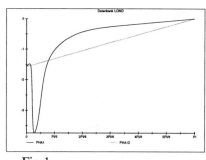

Fig 1

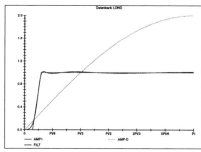

Fig 2

AMP1 and PHA1 are the amplitude and phase functions of the optimized filter and FILT is the ideal amplitude function, which are compared to the corresponding frequency characteristics of the difference filter. The sharp amplitude function shows a narrow cutoff-band and the phase becomes nearly flat, tending to zero : taken together, the properties of filter 1 will ensure a very good signal extraction (see section 4) while the time delay, beeing zero at frequency π, will ensure efficient forecasting-ability. We defer to section 5 a discussion of OIIR-filters, but before let us very briefly define the CT-model-class used in section 4 to estimate and forecast stationary components.

3   CT-MODELS

Suppose Y_t is an extracted stationary component of X_t. An ARMA-model of Y_t is defined by

$$Y_t + a_1 Y_{t-1} + a_2 Y_{t-2} + \ldots + a_p Y_{t-p} = \epsilon_t + b_1 \epsilon_{t-1} + \ldots + b_{t-q} \epsilon_{t-q}$$

where ϵ_t is an uncorrelated white noise process. It is well known that ARMA-models represent a good approximation to the Wold-decomposition of Y_t, meaning that ARMA-models approximate well the covariance structure of a stationary regular process. However, by the linearity assumption, they define a model class with passive dynamics and uncorrelated innovations only. CT-models generalize the linear ARMA-models to piecewise linear ARMA-models with active dynamics (limit-cycle-behaviour of the skeleton) and innovations approximating second-order martingal-difference-sequences. The following is an example of a CT-model which will be used in the examples of section 3 :

$$Y_t = \begin{cases} \displaystyle\sum_{k=1}^{p_1} a_{k1} Y_{t-k} + \sum_{k=0}^{q_1} b_{k1} \epsilon_{t-k,1} \ , \ Y_{t-d_1} \leq r_1, \ Y_{t-d_{11}} \leq r_{11} \\[3mm] \displaystyle\sum_{k=1}^{p_2} a_{k2} Y_{t-k} + \sum_{k=0}^{q_2} b_{k2} \epsilon_{t-k,2} \ , \ Y_{t-d_1} \leq r_1, \ Y_{t-d_{11}} > r_{11} \\[3mm] \displaystyle\sum_{k=1}^{p_3} a_{k3} Y_{t-k} + \sum_{k=0}^{q_3} b_{k3} \epsilon_{t-k,3} \ , \ Y_{t-d_1} > r_1, \ Y_{t-d_{12}} \leq r_{12} \\[3mm] \displaystyle\sum_{k=1}^{p_4} a_{k4} Y_{t-k} + \sum_{k=0}^{q_4} b_{k4} \epsilon_{t-k,4} \ , \ Y_{t-d_1} > r_1, \ Y_{t-d_{12}} > r_{12} \end{cases}$$

For estimation, diagnostic-cheking and forecasting of such models we refer to Wildi (1997). Let us just say that these models are very powerfull, since they can capture periodic as well as non linear quasi periodic or chaotic behaviour of stationary time series. By combining CT-models with OIIR-filters we shall now show the forecasting ability of the method and compare it to classical ARIMA-forecasting.

4   EXAMPLE : BONDJP

BONDJP or Japanese bond yield, is a daily series, from 1. April 1986 upwards with N=260 observations, whose realization is shown in fig. 3 (see Mills (1996)).

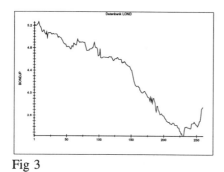

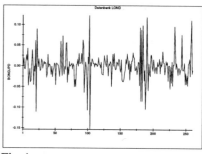

Fig 3   Fig 4

4.1   ARIMA-model

The estimated ARIMA-model is $\Delta X_t = -0.001 - 0.194 \Delta X_{t-1} + \epsilon_t$, where Δ means the difference operator. The differenced series is seen in fig. 4. It makes X_t a random-walk with negative drift, which seems inappropriate to the forecasting period in which the trend has reversed. Of course, modifications of the model could allow for non linear adaptive estimation of the intercept term, but the problem of the smoothing factor (i.e. the memory of the estimation procedure) would nevertheless persist. We shall see in 4.4 how the problem can be solved by our technique.

4.2   high pass design

We saw in section 2 the amplitude and phase functions of a sharp high pass filter (filter 1) with cutoff frequency at $\pi/15$. The filter is given by the linear recursive formula :

$$y_t - 3.31 y_{t-1} + 4.4 y_{t-2} - 2.93 y_{t-3} + 0.99 y_{t-4} - 0.14 y_{t-5} =$$

$$-.76 x_t + 2.94 x_{t-1} - 4.43 x_{t-2} + 3.3 x_{t-3} - 1.26 x_{t-4} + 0.24 x_{t-5} - 0.02 x_{t-6}$$

The output of the filter is seen in fig. 5. A comparison with the original data in fig. 6 suggests that the pass-band of the stationary component is almost unaltered by the filter because the ideal amplitude function is sharply approximated by filter 1 (with a mean-square error approximation of $O(10^{-5})$) and because the phase is small in the pass band. A direct comparison of the differenced series in fig. 4 with the optimized filter output in fig. 5 reveals a more erratic behaviour of the former, because the amplitude function of the difference filter amplifies high frequencies, i.e. the noise, and damps down the low frequencies (see fig. 2) . Since the time delay of filter 1 is as small as the delay of the simple difference filter (and less than many common

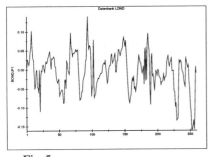

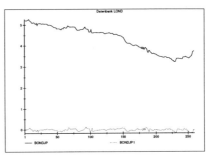

Fig 5   Fig 6

high pass filter designs) the output is well suited to forecasting purposes. A comparison of the spectra of the differenced series with the OIIR-output in fig. 7 reveals that the spectral part of low frequencies belonging to the stationary component has been partially destroyed by the difference filter.

Remark : Once the filter coefficients have been computed, filtering of the non-stationary series becomes a very fast procedure. Note also that coefficients of IIR-filters are independent of the input, so that they may be used for any non-stationary series of integration order 1 with the same cutoff-frequency. We shall see in section 5 why this is (partially) not true for OIIR-filters

4.3 CT-model

For the ex ante estimation we through away the last ten values of the filter output bondjp1 (fig. 5) and estimate a CT model with N'=250 data points to obtain

$$
X_t = \begin{cases}
0.003+0.84X_{t-1}+\epsilon_t \ , & X_{t-12}\leq0.023,\ X_{t-6}\leq0.058 \\[2em]
-0.032+0.187X_{t-1}+\epsilon_t \ , & X_{t-12}<0.023,\ X_{t-6}>0.058 \\[2em]
0.011+0.28X_{t-1}-0.68X_{t-2}+\epsilon_t, & X_{t-12}>0.023,\ X_{t-4}\leq-0.029 \\[2em]
0.05+0.89X_{t-1}-0.49X_{t-2}-0.73X_{t-3}+\epsilon_t, & X_{t-12}>0.023,\ X_{t-4}>0.029
\end{cases}
$$

in which delays of 12, 6 and 4 time units correspond to apparent seasonalities revealed by the small peaks of the estimated spectral density in fig. 7.

398

4.4   Low-pass design

In order to extract the trend, we construct an optimized low-pass filter with cutoff frequency $\pi/15$ (see section 5 for a motivation of this choice).

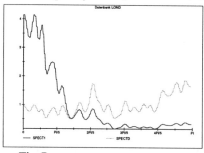

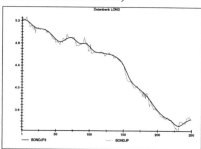

| Fig 7 | Fig 8 |

We obtain the output of fig. 8 in which the trend is compared with the original series. In contrast to the negative slope of the ARI-model corresponding to the negative intercept term of the AR-model, the extracted low frequency component moves upwards at the upper end (N'=250) of the series or in other words : trend reversion was captured very early by the filter (in fact the filter was optimized with respect to trend reversions by taking account of its phase function). The filter has a time delay of about 2-3 time units, which is very small when compared to other low-pass filter-designs with such narrow pass-band.

4.5   Forecasts

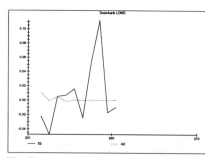

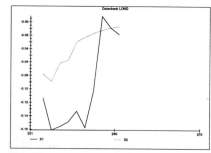

| Fig 9 | Fig 10 |

An ex ante forecast simulation from 1 to 10 steps ahead of the differenced series Bondjpd is seen in fig. 9. The estimated AR-model is $X_t = -0.001 - 0.194 X_{t-1} + \epsilon_t$.

A similar forecast simulation of the filter output Bondjp1 with the above CT-model is seen in fig. 10. A comparison with the realized filter output shows the goodness of the forecasts. We now simply invert the difference filter to obtain the ARI-forecast (i.e. we add the forecasts of the AR-model together in order to obtain the intended random-walk behaviour). The CTOIIR forecasts are obtained by extending linearly the trend obtained in section 4.4 over the forecasting period and overlapping the CT-forecasts (see fig. 11 for a comparison with the true process values). The ARI-forecasts behave almost constant, moving down very slowly whereas the CTOIIR-forecasts move up closely to the original series, offering a much better approximation to the original time series behaviour.

5 Signal-extraction-optimization with OIIR-filters

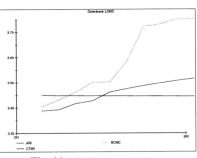

Fig 11

First of all, why did we extract the low frequencies or detrend the non-stationary series? An intuition of this can be given in the frequency domain : in order to include waves of a given frequency (or length) in a statistical model (i.e. to estimate parameters), we need some sample of this wave, which means that in the intervall t=1,...,N the wave should replicate itself several times. This in turn implies that waves of high length or very low frequencies cannot be included in the estimation of a stationary model when their amplitude (or energy) exceeds a certain amount : they must be considered separately and in fact in the above examples they represented the trend component. In the above examples we choose $\pi/15$ as cutoff frequency of filter 1. This choice was not arbitrary since it corresponds to the resolution of the estimated spectral density : in fact, based on a single realisation of sample-length N, the estimated spectral density cannot dicriminate neighbouring peaks of the theoretical spectral density of the process, if the distance between these two peaks is too small. Ultimately the reason for this is the well known bias-variance problem which runs into an uncertainty principle. The resolution partially depends on the choice of window used in smoothing the periodogramm and on a priori information (for example the presence of seasonalities) but roughly the band considered ($\pi/15$) corresponds to this resolution (see for example the peaks of the estimated spectrum in fig 7 : the width of these peaks corresponds to the width of the respective cutoff band). Filter 1 is an OIIR-filter : besides the poles and zeroes of the IIR-filter, it has one additional complex conjugate pair of poles, say P_1 and P_2 and one additional complex conjugate pair of zeroes ,say Z_1 and Z_2, on a radius with argument (or angle) ±half the cutoff frequency (in our example ±$\pi/30$). Together with the IIR-part of the filter they approximate an ideal high pass filter, but in addition they account for the low frequency part of the spectrum of the stationary component : the pole-zero combination is moved on the radius until the in-sample forecasting performance of the stationary model is maximized (maximization of a modified signal to noise ratio). It can be shown that the pole-zero combination is not uniquely determined, so that the undeterminacy can be used to optimize phase and amplitude characteristics of the resulting OIIR-filter. Through these considerations we see now what we intended when requesting flexibility of the filter design in section 2.2 (property P.4).

Imagine the cutoff-band is choosen larger than the spectral resolution : then we should include additional poles and zeroes in order to account for possibly more than one peak in the estimated spectrum. But additional poles and zeroes would affect the phase response of the filter and hence possibly increase the time delay of the filter response, which must be avoided when forecasting is intended. If the cutoff-band is too narrow, frequencies which do not belong to the stationary component would pass through the lower end of the pass band and alter the estimation of the stationary component. Therefore all parameters of the OIIR-filter become uniquely determined by an optimization principle based on signal extraction, ultimately motivated by forecasting considerations : we call such a filter design an OIIR-filter.

Remark : From the above we see that filter coefficients of IIR-filters only depend on the length of a given input series (determining the Nyquist sampling rate or the width of the stop-band of the filter), whereas the pole-zero combination of OIIR-filters additionally depends on the forecasting ability of the stationary model within the sample.

6   Conclusion

It has become common in ARIMA-modelling that both the detrending procedure (difference filter) and the estimation of a stationary component (ARMA-models) are intimately linked together, forming a whole called an ARIMA-model. By our approach, the separation of these procedures becomes obvious. Note that OIIR-filters and CT-models can be used independently of each other, because as for ARIMA-models, there is ultimately no intimate reason linking both techniques together. In fact, in implementing the above forecasts we used CT-models with difference filters as well as linear models with OIIR-filters. In both examples OIIR filters best harmonized with CT-models and conversely. This must not be true generally, but our experience about this very new subject is rather limited. By the close relationship between CT-models and artificial neural nets, we think that OIIR-filters might well harmonize with the latter technique too.

Since difference filters and ARMA models trivially belong to IIR filter- and CT model-classes respectively, the proposed CTOIIR-technique is a generalization of the well known Box-Jenkins ARIMA-forecasting technique (see Box and Jenkins,

(1970)). Note that by using OIIR filters in approximating the shape of ideal filters, we introduce an approach which splits economist's believes about the nature of economic and/or financial data : are these time series integrated or not? Our procedure is able to deal equally well with both hypotheses, since forecasting considerations alone determine the best possible model. If the process-generating mechanism is a random-walk without any signal overlapping it (say a "pure" random-walk), the best filter would naturally be given by the difference filter. In fact, by allowing the additional pol-zero combination to monitor the attenuation level of the low frequencies, OIIR-filters ultimately degenerate to all-pass filters when applied to random-walks. Which pratical relevance should we accord to such processes? It is clear that most economic data like prices, interest rates, bonds, exchange rates,etc... are not completely random and therefore subject to a process with a memory that can be very long. This reflects nothing else than the rigidity of our economies or the inertial force or persistency of their states. If one supposes the existence of a pure random-walk generating a time series, then the memory of the process becomes infinite: any shock at any time will shift the whole future series (that means for the eternity!) by its proper amount. This intuitively very unappealing behaviour then becomes opposed to the efficient market hypothesis, which gives an economic foundation to the random-walk hypothesis (recall however the idealized assumptions underlying that hypothesis). In the light of these comments, we think that pure random-walks do not correctly reflect economic behaviour. Of course, short-memory processes or signals could overlap a random-walk. There is a lot of literature treating the signal extraction problem in this case, but, as we know, these approaches all rely on more or less strong model constraints, which define the kind of extraction procedure a priori. In a sense, our approach tends towards a non-parametric estimation of the trend as well as of the stationary component, subject to optimization of the forecasting accuracy. By its flexibility, our method provides a forecasting tool capable of handling univariate stationary or non-stationary, integrated or non-integrated series: the additional pol-zero combination provides a continuous solution between qualitatively different non-stationarities.

Why is differencing so successfull? It suggests an immediate time domain interpretation and it is a very simple and very effective detrending procedure which, in fact, forms the basic block of high-pass IIR filters. Unfortunately, a difference filter distorts components it should extract. Ultimately, by constructing OIIR filters which match ideal filters, we do nothing else than equalize this distortion and by allowing a pole-zero combination varying allong a given radius, we incorporate the possibility of real valued integration orders of non-stationary time series. By optimizing the filters with respect to the phase response and the extracted signal, we provide a powerfull tool, primarily designed for forecasting, whose output can be used by any statistical estimation procedure as linear ARMA, non linear CT- or non linear artificial neural net models. In our view, CT-models take their advantage from beeing motivated by statistical considerations -powerful linearity tests, consistent estimation (learning), diagnostic (pruning) and forecasting procedures- without loosing in generality when compared to artificial neural nets.

References

Box G.E.P., Jenkins G.M : Time series analysis, forecasting and control. Holden-Day, San Francisco (1970).

Mills T.C. : The econometric modelling of financial time series. Cambridge University Press, Cambridge (1996).

Rabiner L.R., Gold B. : Theory and application of digital signal processing. Prentice Hall, Englewood Cliffs (1975).

Wildi M : Schätzung, Diagnose und Prognose nicht-linearer SETAR-Modelle. Physica Verlag, Heidelberg (1997).

PORTFOLIO OPTIMISATION WITH CAP WEIGHT RESTRICTIONS

NIKLAS F. WAGNER

Bayerische Vereinsbank AG, Treasury,
80311 Munich, Germany
E-mail: debvmnfw@ibmmail.com

The practical application of the Markowitz portfolio optimisation framework faces the problem of noise when historical estimates are used as input parameters. In this paper I propose a simple modification for portfolio optimisation that allows for the incorporation of a priori information in the portfolio optimisation process. Capital market theory and empirical results indicate that capitalisation weights are a reasonable source of information. The modified framework can be interpreted as an approach to practical portfolio optimisation, which refers to the Bayesian principle of using prior information in decision making under uncertainty.

1   Introduction

The practical application of the MARKOWITZ (1952) portfolio optimisation framework has been criticised due to the problem of deriving subjective estimates of the covariances, variances and expectations of asset returns. According to MICHAUD (1989), for example, the estimation problem has limited the acceptance of mean-variance models in the investment community.

Estimation risk in portfolio selection problems has led to the development of several methods for practical application. BAWA, BROWN, AND KLEIN (1979) – apart from discussing other approaches to the problem of noise – support a rigorous Bayesian approach to the portfolio selection problem with estimation risk. Other authors propose intuitive rules in order to reduce the effect of estimation error. BLUME (1975) suggests that estimation error in beta coefficients can be reduced by accounting for a mean reversion effect. ELTON AND GRUBER (1973) implement simplified models of the correlation structure of asset returns. VASICEK (1973) uses a Bayesian approach to modify sample estimates. ROSENBERG (1974) proposes to use fundamental characteristics of the firm to predict equity return behaviour. FISHER (1975) uses the optimisation framework in order to derive estimates of expected returns under the assumption that a given portfolio is mean-variance efficient. JOBSON AND KORKIE (1981) apply results of James/Stein estimation to generate expected returns. BLACK AND LITTERMAN (1992) cope with the problem of deriving return expectations by applying the CAPM equilibrium model as a neutral reference point. Another approach,

A.-P.N. Refenes et al. (eds.), Decision Technologies for Computational Finance, 403–416.
© 1998 *Kluwer Academic Publishers. Printed in the Netherlands..*

following COHEN AND POGUE (1967), is setting constraints on the portfolio weights, which is frequently recommended for practical implementations of mean-variance optimisation (see FROST AND SAVARIO (1988), among others).

In this paper a simple modification for portfolio optimisation that allows for the incorporation of prior information is proposed. It is assumed that this information can e.g. be gained by using capitalisation weights as additional input to the optimisation procedure. The proposed modification does not necessarily alter given point estimates. In contrast to other approaches, instead of imposing constraints on single weights, it imposes a loss function over all weights in the optimisation.

2   The basic portfolio selection model

The MARKOWITZ (1952, 1959)/TOBIN (1958) single period portfolio selection model assumes an individual that possesses subjective information about the distribution of returns on a universe of N risky assets, $i = 1, ..., N$. In this setting, a portfolio allocation is characterised by the vector of portfolio weights, denoted by $\mathbf{x} = (x_i)_{N \times 1}$. The set of feasible decisions is given as $C = \{\mathbf{x} \in \mathbb{R}^N : \mathbf{x}^T \mathbf{1} = 1, \mathbf{x} \geq \mathbf{0}\}$, with $\mathbf{1} \equiv (1)_{N \times 1}$, $\mathbf{0} \equiv (0)_{N \times 1}$. Alternatively, short sales may not be ruled out in C. In any case, the vector of portfolio weights is called admissible if and only if $\mathbf{x} \in C$. Applying axioms of rational behaviour under uncertainty, the individual seeks an optimal allocation that maximises the expectation of a given von Neumnann/Morgenstern-utility function U. This function is assumed to be twice differentiable, increasing and strictly concave, which implies nonsatiation and risk averse behaviour. The random vector of asset returns is $\tilde{\mathbf{r}} = (R_i)_{N \times 1}$ and has a probability density $f(\tilde{\mathbf{r}} | \theta)$ which depends on a set of parameters included in $\theta \in \mathbb{R}^K$. Under these basic assumptions the optimal allocation $\mathbf{x}_0 \in C$ is chosen as to maximise

$$E\left[U(\mathbf{x}^T \tilde{\mathbf{r}}) | \theta\right] = \int U(\mathbf{x}^T \tilde{\mathbf{r}}) f(\tilde{\mathbf{r}} | \theta) d\tilde{\mathbf{r}}. \tag{1}$$

The expectation in (1) is dependent on the value of θ. Assuming a quadratically approximable utility function U or normally distributed returns R_i, the above maximisation is equivalent to the well known mean-variance portfolio selection problem. In this case we have $\theta = (\mu, \Omega)$, where $\Omega = (\sigma_{i,j})_{N \times N}$ is the positive definite covariance matrix of returns and $\mu = [E(R_i)]_{N \times 1}$ represents the vector of expected returns, both having finite elements. The portfolio selection problem can then be written as

$$\mathbf{x}^T \Omega \mathbf{x} \rightarrow \min \tag{2.1}$$
$$\text{s.t.:} \ \mathbf{x}^T \mu = E(R_p) \tag{2.2}$$
$$\mathbf{x} \in C. \tag{2.3}$$

The term $E(R_P)$, $R_P = \mathbf{x}^T \tilde{\mathbf{r}}$, is a constant representing the individual's expected portfolio return for a given $\mathbf{x}$. For this portfolio problem, the subjective information input consists of a risk component Ω and an expected return component μ.

3 Bayesian approaches to portfolio selection

Within the classical model (2) it is assumed that the distribution parameters Ω and μ are known with certainty. The question is, however, how this subjective information is inferred. In general, the input to the decision process is some set of information, available prior to the holding period. Whereas the return component might be generated by some expert team, the risk component is frequently estimated from a sample of realised asset returns. Therefore, in most practical applications the parameter vector θ is subject to *estimation risk*. In this case, other than sample information might be useful for choosing $\mathbf{x}$ in order to maximise the individual's expected utility (1). Such information is referred to as prior information. The Bayesian approach allows for considering both, sample and prior information, in the decision process.

3.1 Bayesian estimation of the distributional parameters

In the following the density $f(\theta)$ represents the prior information concerning the whole distribution of $\tilde{\mathbf{r}}$. Sample information is given by a random returns sample $\tilde{\mathbf{R}} = (\tilde{\mathbf{r}}_t)_{N \times T}$, $t = 1, ..., T$. To employ the Bayesian approach, the likelihood function for the sample observations $f(\tilde{\mathbf{R}} | \theta)$ and $f(\theta)$ are required. Then prior and sample information can be combined into what is termed the posterior distribution of θ, denoted $f(\theta | \tilde{\mathbf{R}})$. It follows from Bayes law

$$f(\theta | \tilde{\mathbf{R}}) \propto f(\tilde{\mathbf{R}} | \theta) f(\theta) . \tag{3}$$

A Bayesian decision is taken on the basis of a given loss function $L(\theta_B, \theta)$ which measures the cost of choosing the parameter to be θ_B when the true value is θ. The optimal decision minimises the posterior expected loss. The maximisation of (1) is then carried out with $\theta = \theta_B$. For a quadratic loss function, θ_B is chosen identical to the expectation of the marginal posterior distribution of θ (see GREENE (1997, pp. 311-317), for example). The above approach has been proposed e.g. by VASICEK (1973) within the simplified single-index portfolio selection model. Assuming a normally distributed prior for the cross section of asset betas, he uses the posterior mean as a modified estimate of the beta parameter of a single asset.

3.2 Bayesian incorporation of estimation risk in the expected utility function

BAWA, BROWN, AND KLEIN (1979) show that apart from the approach mentioned above, it is possible to use Bayes rule in order to incorporate all available information into a *predictive distribution*. Furthermore, it is possible to define the individual's expected utility function explicitly with respect to this distribution.

The predictive distribution is defined as the expectation of the probability density of $\tilde{r}$ conditioned on θ, denoted $f(\tilde{r}|\theta)$, with respect to the posterior distribution of θ, denoted $f(\theta | \tilde{R})$. Thus we have

$$g(\tilde{r}) = \int f(\tilde{r}|\theta) f(\theta|\tilde{R}) d\theta . \tag{4}$$

Then the Bayesian optimal allocation x_B is chosen as to maximise

$$E[U(x^T\tilde{r})] = \int U(x^T\tilde{r}) g(\tilde{r}) d\tilde{r} . \tag{5}$$

The maximisation of the individual's expected utility is carried out with respect to the density of the predictive distribution $g(\tilde{r})$ which is conditioned on sample and prior information. Estimation error is taken into account with the formation of the posterior distribution. The fact that estimates of the return distribution of risky assets are subject to sampling error, should lead individual investors to minimise the overall portfolio risk including estimation risk.

A solution to this approach within the single-index model is provided by CHEN AND BROWN (1983). In general, the predictive distribution is „both difficult to derive and to work with" (BAWA, BROWN, AND KLEIN (1979, p. 119)). Without question, this method is the most rigorous way of incorporating estimation risk in the portfolio selection problem. Assuming noninformative priors, estimation risk can be evaluated explicitly within the individuals' expected utility function: Facing estimation risk, risk averse individuals should adopt a more conservative investment strategy. However, there remains the question of how an informative prior concerning the distribution of $\tilde{r}$ can be derived in practice. Additionally, only information concerning the distribution of $\tilde{r}$ is considered, although the relevant choice variable is the vector of portfolio weights x.

3.3 Bayesian choice of the decision variable

Problem (1) is concerned with the choice of a decision variable x. Since we require the maximisation of an expected utility function, the problem description is basically equivalent to the Bayes principle of minimising expected loss.

Consider that the individual has some prior about the optimal choice of x represented by a prior distribution of the optimal decision. This distribution is denoted by $f(x_0)$. Assume further that given a sample $\tilde{R}$, the likelihood $f(\tilde{R}|x_0)$ and finally the posterior distribution $f(\mathbf{x}_0|\tilde{\mathbf{R}})$ can be derived. Given a loss function $L(\mathbf{x}_B, \mathbf{x}_0)$, an optimal Bayes decision $\mathbf{x}_B$ is chosen as to minimise posterior expected loss

$$E\left[L(\mathbf{x}_B,\mathbf{x}_0)|\tilde{\mathbf{R}}\right] = \int_C L(\mathbf{x}_B,\mathbf{x}_0)f(\mathbf{x}_0|\tilde{\mathbf{R}})d\mathbf{x}_0 . \tag{6}$$

In the portfolio selection problem, we can define the loss function as a distance measure D that depends on the utilities of choosing $\mathbf{x}_B$ rather than $\mathbf{x}_0$ (see e.g. FIRCHAU (1986))

$$L(\mathbf{x}_B,\mathbf{x}_0) = D\left[U(\mathbf{x}_B^T\tilde{\mathbf{r}}),U(\mathbf{x}_0^T\tilde{\mathbf{r}})\right]. \tag{7}$$

This approach interprets the portfolio selection problem as a problem of Bayesian inference. The focus does not lie on the estimation risk referring to the parameters of the return distribution, but on the choice of the decision variable. As above, the approach will be difficult to apply; in this case this will be especially due to calculation of the posterior density. Additionally, in contrast to the other Bayesian approaches estimation risk is not explicitly encountered for.

4 Practical approaches

From a practical viewpoint, a portfolio manager's goal is to perform an investment strategy that keeps the actual portfolio close to some desirable optimal. In the above section, applications of the Bayesian method to the portfolio problem have been described. In this section, traditional approaches to estimation risk are considered. These approaches start off from the so called *parameter certainty equivalent method*; i.e. the subjective characterisation of the returns distribution is based on realised point estimates calculated from a given returns sample. Using this method, a lost of the sample error information is incurred. Traditional approaches then develop heuristical methods of coping with estimation risk. Within this context, referring to the idea of subsection 3.3, this section continues with the description of a framework that uses sources of prior information in optimal portfolio choice.

4.1 Traditional versions of the parameter certainty equivalence method

Assume, $\theta = \hat{\theta}$, i.e. each solution to the portfolio problem (1) is a solution as if the point estimate of the parameter vector was identical to the true parameter vector. The decision problem (1) becomes maximisation of:

$$E\left[U(\mathbf{x}^T\tilde{\mathbf{r}})|\hat{\theta}\right] = \int U(\mathbf{x}^T\tilde{\mathbf{r}})f(\tilde{\mathbf{r}}|\hat{\theta})d\tilde{\mathbf{r}} . \tag{8}$$

This method is used in standard applications of the portfolio selection framework and ignores estimation risk. It could be justified asymptotically when all estimation risk vanishes. Intuitive methods which aim to cope with estimation risk within this model enter the portfolio selection problem at this stage: Possible methods include (i) using modified estimates for θ which have superior predictive power. This can be achieved by altered point estimates, estimating simplified structures of the covariance matrix (i.e. index-models) or including external prior information that is useful in predicting the return behaviour. It is also possible to incorporate estimation risk via the approach of section 3.1. Another method is (ii) to restrict the set of admissible decisions C. This is frequently done in such way that it imposes a correction towards an equally weighted portfolio.

4.2 Imposing moment restrictions within the parameter certainty equivalence method

While x_0 conditional on θ is a deterministic solution, solving problem (8) by the choice of an optimal weights vector x_0 can be interpreted as the result of a random experiment: Assuming multivariate normally distributed asset returns $\tilde{r} \sim N(\mu, \Omega)$ with $\theta = (\mu, \Omega)$ and a random sample $\tilde{R}$ from which $\hat{\theta}$ can be computed, JOBSON AND KORKIE (1980) show that the estimated optimal solution conditional on the parameter estimates, $\hat{x}_0$, is asymptotically normally distributed. For the characterisation of the distributional parameters refer to JOBSON AND KORKIE (1980, pp. 545-547). This observation leads to the assumption that an individual may see its decision variable x to be randomly distributed (see JOBSON AND KORKIE (1981)).

In the decision process $\hat{x}_0$ is a realised point estimate, i.e. information that is given prior to the choice of x. Assume that the individual can postulate some prior for the distribution of x_0. In the Bayesian approach this information about the optimal choice of x is represented by a prior density $f(x_0)$. Assume further that the individual's prior information does not represent the entire distribution of x_0 but is restricted to distributional moments. In particular, we may simplify the model by assuming that only expectation and variance of the distribution of x_0 are known. In this case, we can more precisely describe our prior by stating that the prior expectation of the optimal portfolio weight x_{i0} is equal to b_i. Hence, for the vector of optimal weights we have the prior expectation

$$E(x_0) = \int_C x_0 f(x_0) dx_0 = b,$$ (9)

with $b = (b_i)_{N \times 1}$. For the variance of optimal weights we can write

$$Var(x_0) = \int_C (x_0 - b)(x_0 - b)^T f(x_0) dx_0 = \delta^2 I,$$ (10)

where I is the $N \times N$ unity matrix and δ denotes the admissible standard deviation in the choice of the portfolio weights x_{i0}. As a simplification, the parameter δ is assumed to be equal for all portfolio weights. The choice of δ by the individual should be inversely related to the magnitude of estimation error in the parameter estimates of μ and Ω. Estimation risk will lead the individual to reduce the admissible standard deviation between the chosen optimal and the given prior weight expectations.

The approach of this section is to incorporate the prior information about x_0 into the portfolio selection problem by restricting problem (8) with the moment restrictions (9) and (10). Expectation (9) holds for the average of all N weights in the portfolio selection problem. Within the optimal portfolio weights, some deviation from the expected value will occur. These deviations depend on the realisation of the parameter estimates of θ and the parameter δ. The optimal choice of x will face a trade off between choosing $\hat{x}_0$, i.e. ignoring prior information, versus b, i.e. ignoring sample information. This trade off can be quantified by the variance of the of the distribution of x_0 given by (10).

In the case of a single portfolio optimisation process δ can be interpreted as a cross-sectional average admissible deviation for the optimal portfolio weights. Therefore, δ^2 can be estimated by the sample variance, $s^2 = (N-1)^{-1} (x-b)^T(x-b)$. Imposing the moment restrictions according to (9) and (10) and defining $d \equiv s^2 (N-1)$ (i.e.: d is the sum of squared deviations, SSD), model (2.1-3) can be extended to

$$x^T \Omega x \to \min \tag{11.1}$$
$$\text{s.t.: } x^T \mu = E(R_p) \tag{11.2}$$
$$x \in C \tag{11.3}$$
$$(x-b)^T(x-b) = d . \tag{11.4}$$

The non-linear restriction in the above optimisation problem leads to the question of whether additional assumptions are necessary for the existence of a solution. Setting up the Lagrangian for problem (11)

$$\mathcal{L}(x,\lambda) = \frac{1}{2} x^T \Omega \, x - \lambda_1\left(x^T \mu - E(R_p)\right) - \lambda_2\left(x^T 1 - 1\right) - \frac{\lambda_3}{2}\left((x-b)^T(x-b) - d\right), \tag{12}$$

differentiating with respect to x and equating the result to zero yields

$$\left(\Omega - \lambda_3 I\right)x - \left(\lambda_1 \mu + \lambda_2 1 - \lambda_3 b\right) = 0 . \tag{13}$$

This condition, together with the constraints (11.2-4), must hold for an optimal vector of portfolio weights. If a solution to this non-linear system of equations exists, it can be derived computationally by applying numerical methods.[1] In cases of practical optimisation with a strictly convex target function (Ω is assumed p.d.) it will be straightforward to get numerical results. A survey of standard algorithms is given in GREENE (1997). Available software is described e.g. in SCHOENBERG (1995).

---

[1] The inverse of the first multiplicative term in equation (13) does not exists if $|\Omega - \lambda_3 I| = 0$. Solving the eigenvalue problem by setting $|\Omega - \lambda I| = 0$ yields all eigenvalues λ and eigenvectors x of the covariance matrix Ω. Hence, the existence of a solution for problem (11) at least requires that either (i) λ_3 is different from all eigenvalues of Ω or that (ii) the right hand side of equation (13) equals zero for a given eigenvalue/eigenvector solution.

5   Capitalisation weights

In general, the individual can choose any prior distribution for the vector of optimal portfolio weights. The moments are then given by (9) and (10). In the particular case of equity portfolio optimisation without currency risk, it can be argued that capitalisation weights b_i of a representative equity index may form a natural expectation of the prior distribution of the individual's optimal equity portfolio weights x_{i0}. This choice is discussed in the next two subsections. It can be noted that in the model application might be sensible to deviate from capitalisation weights in an international asset allocation setting.

5.1 Rationale for choosing cap weights

As a rationale for choosing capitalization weights consider the following:

- A capitalization weighted equity portfolio represents the holding of an average investor within a given stock universe. Thus selecting assets and departing from capitalisation weights means a zero sum game among active equity managers. Active equity managers as a group do not outperform market indices.[2]

- Empirical research on mutual funds did not find evidence that would allow a rejection of the efficient market hypothesis. Most individual equity managers who do outperform their benchmarks on a risk adjusted basis, do not produce stable results over longer periods of time. Hence, outperformance is mostly due to chance.

- Capital market theory suggests that the market portfolio of all risky assets offers an optimal trade off between risk and return in a market equilibrium with homogenous expectations. In practice, capitalisation weighted indices could form a market proxy and therefore offer superior diversification at low cost. This claim is empirically controversial.

5.2 Moment restricted optimisation with cap weights and quadratic tracking models

With constant capitalisation weights as expectation of the prior distribution of optimal portfolio weights, model (11.1-4) can be interpreted as an approach of managing portfolios in the context of *approximations to the market portfolio*. This concept was introduced by TREYNOR AND BLACK (1973).[3] The further development of

---

[2]   For this simple but convincing argumentation see BLACK AND SCHOLES (1974, p. 403): „*All individuals together hold exactly the market portfolio. If an individual is to make money by holding a portfolio different from the market portfolio, he must do so at the expense of another individual who holds a portfolio different from the market portfolio.*"

[3]   FISHER (1975, p. 74) interprets their model, which combines active and passive portfolio management decisions, as an application of Bayesian analysis. For a critical judgement of the practical application of their model with short sale restrictions see BREALEY (1986).

their idea lead to the occurrence of quadratic tracking models in RUDD AND ROSENBERG (1979), MARKOWITZ (1987), ROLL (1992), and SHARPE (1992). The MARKOWITZ/ROLL quadratic tracking model can be written as

$$(x - b)^T \Omega (x - b) \rightarrow \min \qquad (14.1)$$

$$\text{s.t.: } (x - b)^T \mu = E(R_E) \qquad (14.2)$$

$$x \in C. \qquad (14.3)$$

Restriction (14.2) specifies a constant expected return difference R_E, called *tracking error*. It is defined as the difference between the portfolio and the index return, $R_E \equiv R_P - R_I$. The target function (14.1) describes the variance of the tracking error, denoted by σ_E^2. RUDD/ROSENBERG and ROLL propose a quadratic tracking model with a restriction for the portfolio beta β_P. Defining the vector of asset betas $\beta = (\beta_i)_{N \times 1}$, this model is composed of (14.1-3) and

$$x^T \beta = \beta_P. \qquad (14.4)$$

In order to compare models (11.1-4), (14.1-3) and (14.1-4), note that all three are stated in the form of a variance minimisation problem. Focusing our attention on each target function and the relevant restrictions yield the following conclusions:

- Since $(x-b)^T(x-b)$ is constant in restriction (11.4), it follows that the variance of tracking error is constant as well. In particular: $\sigma_E^2 = (x-b)^T \Omega (x-b)$. Therefore, model (11.1-4) minimises variance of portfolio returns for a given variance of tracking error.

- Model (14.1-3) minimises variance of tracking error, which – since Ω is symmetric – can be written as follows: $\sigma_E^2 = x^T \Omega x - 2 x^T \Omega b + b^T \Omega b$. The variance of index returns $b^T \Omega b$ is constant, hence, variance and covariance are relevant to the choice of x in this model.

- Since $\beta_P = x^T \Omega b / b^T \Omega b$ is restricted to be constant in (14.4), model (14.1-4) implies minimising variance of portfolio returns for a given covariance between the returns of the portfolio and the index. If, in particular, the portfolio beta is constrained to a value of one, the models yields a minimum variance unit beta portfolio.

To summarise, all three portfolio selection models extend the standard Markowitz model by adding the covariance term $x^T \Omega b$ to the decision problem. This means that the individual's utility function U' is assumed to be approximable by expected portfolio returns, their variance *and* their covariance with a given portfolio. The models are based on a descriptive decision theoretic approach which violates the classical von Neumnann/Morgenstern axioms of rational behaviour. They differ in their restrictions concerning variance and covariance, therefore implying different optimal portfolio decisions.

Portfolio Selection Model:	return expectation	return variance	return covariance	tracking error variance
Standard Markowitz (2.1-3)	constant	min !	arbitrary	arbitrary
Markowitz/Roll (14.1-3)	constant	arbitrary	arbitrary	min !
Rudd/Rosenberg/Roll (14.1-4)	constant	min !	constant	min !
Moment restricted (11.1-4)	constant	min !	arbitrary	constant

Tab. 1:   Alternative portfolio selection models formulated as quadratic minimisation problems.

For a comparison of quadratic portfolio selection models in general, see table 1. In each model, an expected return restriction is imposed, where portfolio expected return is set equal to a given constant.[4] The expected return restrictions (11.2) and (14.2) are equivalent since the expected return on the equity index, $E(\mathbf{b}^T \tilde{\mathbf{r}})$, is constant and does not depend on the decision variable $\mathbf{x}$.

6   An illustration of the moment restricted optimisation framework

To illustrate the moment restricted optimisation framework with cap weights, an example is implemented with the German MDAX-index. The index represents a capitalisation weighted universe of 70 German mid-cap stocks. The risk data input is generated by point estimates drawn from a sample of daily stock returns in the period June, 1st. 1996 to May, 30th. 1997. Optimisations according to model (11.1-4) are carried out numerically by a variant of the Newton-Raphson algorithm. Two different return input assumptions are made in advance of the computations.

- (I): All expected returns are equal. The optimisation (11.1-4). is carried out without the return constraint (11.2). Restriction (11.4) allows a variation of the d-parameter. The methodology implies the selection of a moment restricted minimum variance portfolio, which typically has a beta less than one.

- (II): All returns are estimated by assuming that the CAPM for equilibrium expected returns holds (see BLACK AND LITTERMAN (1992)). In this case, the optimised portfolio's expected return (11.2) will equal the arbitrarily chosen expected return on the market if and only if the portfolio beta equals unity. Therefore, we can replace the expected return restriction (11.2) by a beta

---

[4]   Alternatively, the restriction of a constant expected portfolio return can be cancelled in each single model (i.e. the return expectation is set arbitrary in table 1). In this case, each model implies the selection of a minimum variance portfolio (see e.g. JOBSON AND KORKIE (1981) and HAUGEN AND BAKER (1991)).

restriction. This methodology implies the selection of a RUDD/ROSENBERG/ROLL constant variance unit beta portfolio.

In both cases, the calculation of optimal portfolio weights is performed without and with capitalization weight restrictions. Apart from the unrestricted solution to problem (11), four solutions with different d-parameters in (11.4) are obtained. If the value of the distance measure d is zero, the index portfolio is chosen. The results for case (I) and (II) are presented graphically in figures 1 and 2. The corresponding values for d and the portfolio beta are given in the legend as (d, β_P), where the notation „-" means that no restriction is imposed.

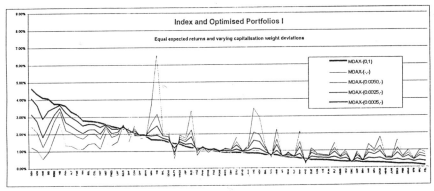

Fig. 1: Index and portfolio weights for equal expected returns and varying capitalization weight restrictions.

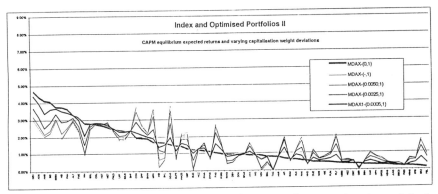

Fig. 2: Index and portfolio weights for CAPM-equilibrium expected returns and varying capitalization weight restrictions.

The cap weight restricted model obviously yields portfolios without extreme and unreasonable weightings. A tendency to equal-weight the optimised portfolio which is stronger for case (I) than for case (II) can be observed; i.e. large cap stocks are underweighted more frequently than small cap stocks and vice versa. This tendency is common to all mean-variance optimisation models. The same is true for observing a clear preference towards low volatility stocks. This tendency follows from the basic Markowitz-assumption that investors are risk averse. The tendency is stronger in case (I), caused by the implicit assumption that all stocks have identical expected returns independent of risk.

7 Conclusion

Estimation risk motivates Bayesian and various traditional approaches for practical portfolio selection problems. Apart from a given returns sample, these approaches seek to incorporate additional external information in the decision problem. The moment restricted model of portfolio selection imposes a loss function on the portfolio weights. In a national equity portfolio optimisation setting, one may chose capitalisation weights of an index as prior expectations of optimal portfolio weights. The degree of tilting towards cap weights can be varied. The model is less restrictive than the approach of imposing individual weight restrictions. It allows for a trade off between cap weight restrictions among all assets. Furthermore, it turns out that the model has common features with quadratic tracking error minimisation framework. In summary, the model presented is one of several useful and flexible methodologies for improving the practical application of Markowitz optimisation algorithms.

Acknowledgements

The author thanks H. Hubbes and other seminar participants for discussions and helpful comments. He is indebted to G. Bamberg, M. Rast and A. Szimayer.

References

Bawa, V., Brown, S., J., Klein, R. (eds.) (1979): Estimation Risk and Optimal Portfolio Choice, Studies in Bayesian Econometrics Vol. 3, North-Holland, Amsterdam, New York, Oxford

Black, F., Litterman, R. (1992): Global Portfolio Optimization, *Financial Analysts Journal*, September-October 1992, pp. 28-43

Black, F., Scholes, M. (1974): From Theory to a New Financial Product, *Journal of Finance*, Vol. 29, pp. 309-412

Blume, M., E. (1975): Betas and their Regression Tendencies, *Journal of Finance*, Vol. 30, pp. 785-796

Brealey, R., A. (1986): How to Combine Active Management with Index Funds, *Journal of Portfolio Management*, Winter 1986, pp. 4-10

Chen, S.-N., Brown, S., J. (1983): Estimation Risk and Simple Rules for Optimal Portfolio Selection, *Journal of Finance*, Vol. 30, pp. 1087-1093

Cohen, K., J., Pogue, J., A. (1967): An Empirical Evaluation of Alternative Portfolio-Selection Models, *Journal of Business*, Vol. 40, pp. 166-193

Elton, E., J., Gruber, M., J. (1973): Estimating the Dependence Structure of Share Prices – Implications for Portfolio Selection, *Journal of Finance*, Vol. 28, pp. 1203-1232

Fisher, L. (1975): Using Modern Portfolio Theory to Maintain an Efficiently Diversified Portfolio, *Financial Analysts Journal*, May-June 1975, pp.73-85

Frost, P., A., Savario, J., E. (1988): For Better Performance Constrain Portfolio Weights, *Journal of Portfolio Management*, Fall 1988, pp. 29-34

Greene, W., H. (1997): Econometric Analysis, 3rd. ed., Prentice Hall, New Jersey, London

Haugen, R., A., Baker, N., L. (1991): The Efficient Market Inefficiency of Capitalization-Weighted Stock Portfolios, *Journal of Portfolio Management*, Spring 1991, pp. 35-40

Jobson, J., D., Korkie, B. (1980): Estimation for Markowitz Efficient Portfolios, *Journal of the American Statistical Association*, Vol. 75, pp. 544-554

Jobson, J., D., Korkie, B. (1981): Putting Markowitz Theory to Work, *Journal of Portfolio Management*, Summer 1981, pp. 70-74

Markowitz, H., M. (1952): Portfolio Selection, *Journal of Finance*, Vol. 7, pp. 77-91

Markowitz, H., M. (1959): Portfolio Selection: Efficient Diversification of Investments, 2nd. ed., Blackwell, New York, 1991

Markowitz, H., M. (1987): Mean-Variance Analysis in Portfolio Choice and Capital Markets, Blackwell, New York

Michaud, R., O. (1989): The Markowitz Optimization Enigma: Is Optimized Optimal?, *Financial Analysts Journal*, January-February 1989, pp. 31-42

Roll, R. (1992): A Mean/Variance Analysis of Tracking Error, *Journal of Portfolio Management*, Summer 1992, pp. 13-22

Rosenberg, B. (1974): Extra-Market Components of Covariance in Security Returns, *Journal of Financial and Quantitative Analysis*, Vol. 9, pp. 263-274

Rudd, A., Rosenberg, B. (1979): Realistic Portfolio Optimization, in: **Elton, E., J., Gruber, M., J. (eds.)**: Portfolio Theory, 25 Years after, Studies in the Management Sciences Vol. 11, North-Holland, Amsterdam, New York, Oxford

Schoenberg, R. (1995): The Gauss Constrained Optimization Application, Aptech Systems, Maple Valley

Sharpe, W., F. (1992): Asset Allocation: Management Style and Performance Measurement, *Journal of Portfolio Management*, Winter 1992, pp. 7-19

Tobin, J. (1958): Liquidity Preference as Behavior Towards Risk, *Review of Economic Studies*, Vol. 25.26, pp.65-86

Treynor, J., L., Black, F. (1973): How to Use Security Analysis to Improve Portfolio Selection, *Journal of Business*, Vol. 46, pp. 66-86

Vasicek, O., A. (1973): A Note on Using Cross-Sectional Information in Bayesian Estimation of Security Betas, *Journal of Finance*, Vol. 28, pp. 1233-1239

Virchau, V. (1986): Portfolio Decisions and Capital Market Equilibria under Incomplete Information, in: **Bamberg, G., Spremann, K. (eds.)**: Capital Market Equilibria, Springer, Berlin, Heidelberg, et al.

ARE NEURAL NETWORK AND ECONOMETRIC FORECASTS GOOD FOR TRADING? STOCHASTIC VARIANCE MODELS AS A FILTER RULE

R. BRAMANTE, R. COLOMBO
Istituto di Statistica
Università Cattolica del Sacro Cuore, Milan, Italy
E-mail: iststat@mi.unicatt.it

G. GABBI
Istituto di Credito, Finanza e Assicurazioni
Università di Parma, Italy
Area Credito e Assicurazioni
SDA Bocconi, Milan, Italy
E-mail: giampaolo.gabbi@sda.uni-bocconi.it

A number of models exist to forecast financial time series. Forecasting results are hardly encouraging if based on statistical error indicators. However, in a trading perspective, even large statistical errors could produce good trading indications. We first present a set of structural and black-box methods that are used to model short, non-stationary time series dynamics. Then, we provide a trading model rule related to data volatility forecasts obtained by applying the ARCH methodology. Finally, out-of-sample forecast comparisons confirm that the trading rule is able to give better performance results for all the estimated models.

1. Introduction

Forecasting accuracy depends on the operating purposes of the analysts. In fact, it has already been shown that statistical error minimisation does not correspond to financial profit and wealth optimisation [Leitch and Tanner, 1991]. Moody and Wu [1996] demonstrate that trading systems yield better performance if signals are obtained via reinforcement learning to maximise profits and a measure of risk-adjusted return, such as the Sharpe ratio. Bengio [1996] proposes a financial criterion in order to substitute the usual mean squared error measure. This problem is due to the fact that the trading function is assumed to generate only position signals, and even large statistical errors could produce good trading indications. When time series are short, the risk of overfitting in the in-sample period may induce a larger discrepancy between forecasting and trading performance.

We will try to give an answer to some relevant questions:

1. Can structural and black box models be applied in forecasting financial, short, non-stationary in mean and in variance time series?

2. Are inter-market variables and technical indicator correlations useful in predicting time series dynamics?

A.-P.N. Refenes et al. (eds.), Decision Technologies for Computational Finance, 417–424.
© 1998 *Kluwer Academic Publishers. Printed in the Netherlands..*

418

3. Can the estimated models be used in trading activity and diagnostic checking based on error indicators considered as a performance measure of a trading system?

4. Does the performance of a trading system improve if decision rules are related to volatility forecasts based on ARCH models?

2. Data description

Forecasting models work with Italian stock market index futures (FIB30) time series. This contract was introduced in 1994 in order to foster efficiency in the Italian Stock Exchange. We decided to start data analysis from the end of November 1995, when the market seemed to become more efficient. All our models are estimated using daily logarithmic returns (r_t) of FIB30 time series. The empirical investigation spans the period going from November 30, 1995 to June 2, 1997, which was further divided into a training and test period, ending on March 2, 1997, and a subsequent out-of-sample period.

Figure 1: Stock Index Futures logarithmic returns 30.11.1995-2.6.1997

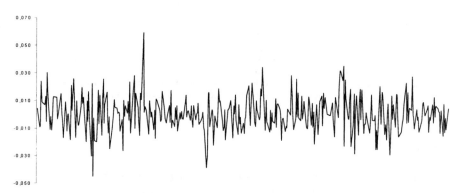

The study of some preliminary statistics of r_t allows to show our time series is:

1. mean stationary, which has been verified by the standard unit root test;

2. non stationary in variance, with evident clusters of periodic volatility; the presence of conditional heteroskedasticity has been verified with the LM test, even if the heteroskedasticity level observed in the variable is lower than the state of the art evidence;

3. non Gaussian, according to the KS test of Kiefer-Salmon;

4. slightly skewed and leptokurtic in distribution, but the values obtained are less pronounced than the ones computed on comparable financial series;

5. not to be considered a "strong" white noise, as suggested by the auto-correlograms computed on r_t and on their absolute and squared values;

6. without recursive components linked to weekly cycles; regression analysis

based on dummy daily variables denotes that the only statistically significant parameter is coupled to the Monday variable, usually explained in the efficient market literature.

In model building, we considered two types of explanatory variables, namely technical and inter-market indicators. The input variables based on technical algorithms are optimised following the search criterion within 20 past temporal periods and a 0-0.5 range for the exponential factors. All the indicators were explored at three levels of depth. The final selection was estimated using the contribution factor and cross correlation criteria. The selected indicators are: linear and exponential lagged moving average, relative and true strength index, Bollinger bands, linear regression change, slope and predict.

As regards inter-market variables, regression analysis based on non-lagged independent variables highlighted the relationships between FIB30 and the Italian Government Bonds (BTP) futures, the Standard & Poor's (S&P) Index and the spread between T-Bond futures and S&P returns.

3. Forecasting methodologies

In order to describe the behaviour of FIB30 time series we estimated different kinds of structural models and different neural network architectures. The identification of the structural component is made on the basis of alternative models, characterised by different structures, and of the selection of the most useful variables through stepwise regression. Besides the classical causal formulations, obtainable from the most general autoregressive distributed lags and state space models, three autoprojective models were estimated in order to verify possible autoregressive and/or moving average structures (ARIMA). Moreover, we compared the models' performance to extremely simple structures, such as random walk and exponential smoothing. As regards the state space model, we considered using a multivariate state space representation of an autoregressive moving average process. The form of the model was specified first by using AIC in selecting the order of the autoregressive model and then canonical correlation analysis in choosing the variables that are to be added to the state vector. The investigation is aimed at the best fitting for every model, in line with an acceptable error distribution.

With reference to r_t volatility, and in line with techniques broadly proposed in literature, we used ARCH models [Engle, 1982] which are able to model the conditional variance, according to an autoregressive scheme. More complex GARCH models were then estimated: I-GARCH, M-GARCH and E-GARCH. AIC index was then used in model selection.

Five types of neural network architectures were used in forecasting r_t. Different models were employed for each of them:
1) *Standard connections*: a) with three layers; b) with four layers; c) with five layers.
2) *Recurrent networks*: a) input layer back into input layer; b) hidden layer back

into input layer; c) output layer back into input layer.

3) *Feature detectors*: a) with two different activation functions; b) with three different activation functions; c) with two different activation functions plus jump connection.

4) *Jump connections*: a) with three layers; b) with four layers; c) with five layers.

5) *General Regression Neural Network*.

Back propagation networks utilise various activation functions, such as linear, logistic, Gaussian and tangent and were tested using several learning rates and momentum. Optimal average values are 0.1 for both parameters. General regression neural network is tested in the 20-300 range of genetic breeding pool size and with Euclidean and city block distance metric.

4. Trading system rules

Two trading systems were used to test the performance of the models. They are based on the following rules:

TRADING SYSTEM No. 1: every forecast is a signal and the trader is assumed to take a position (long, short, hold) $P_t \in \{-1; +1\}$ of constant magnitude on the futures contract. Forecast is exact if it equals the observed sign of r_t, otherwise it produces a loss.

TRADING SYSTEM No. 2: the trader builds a position $P_t \in \{-1; 0; +1\}$ if an indicator based on data volatility forecasts does not cross a threshold $k*$. Formally, if $V_{H,t}$ is the time series volatility forecast at time t, $\overline{V}_H$ its mean and $\sigma_{V,H}$ its standard deviation respectively, the threshold is defined as follows:

$$k^* = \overline{V}_H + n \cdot \sigma_{V,H} \tag{1}$$

n being a constant calculated for each model using a non-linear optimisation criterion over the sample period.

In order to compare structural and black box returns, we computed the perfect trading system, i.e. the result we could obtain by taking all the right positions in every period t. The return would be 424.63 percent on an annual basis.

5. Forecasting results

Econometric results underline that the models presented in Table 1 are generally unable to interpret and anticipate the dynamics of r_t. This is due to the value assumed by the MAE, which is high if compared with the average value of the forecasting variable and to the relative worsening observed when passing from models with non-lagged explanatory variables to those listed in Table 1.

Nevertheless, we note an improvement in the MAE and in the number of correct forecasts with causal estimations (ADL and state space) vis-à-vis the simplest autoprojective models (random walk, exponential smoothing, ARIMA). However, in out-of-sample simulations such considerations need to be reviewed, since we see an alignment of the performance results given by the different models.

In terms of prediction error characteristics, Table 1 shows how all the schemes produce uncorrelated residuals (Box-Pierce Q-test), with leptokurtic and slightly asymmetrical distribution which, at a 5 percent significance level, cannot be considered normal (KS test).

Table 1: Structural Models

Model	On sample		Out of sample		Error distribution		
	MAE	Correct Forecasts	MAE	Correct Forecasts	Excess Kurtosis	KS	Q(40)
Random-Walk	0.0100	51.50	0.0060	54.84	1.0980	22.22	39.3
Random-Walk with Drift	0.0100	50.40	0.0065	53.23	1.0820	21.58	39.5
Exponential smoothing	0.0100	49.85	0.0067	46.77	1.3980	34.11	47.8
ARIMA	0.0100	49.29	0.0060	54.84	1.0790	21.93	38.7
Autoreg. Distributed Lag	0.0094	55.77	0.0064	56.45	1.0918	20.56	18.9
State Space	0.0096	54.42	0.0066	59.68	1.1380	21.89	32.7

Unsatisfactory results are obtained by applying model outputs to daily trading (Table 2). In fact, the best solutions (state space and ADL) allow performance lower than 9% of the perfect model, while all the autoprojective methods (random walk, exponential smoothing, ARIMA) lead to negative annual performance results. Winning trades and amount winning trades show that the relative superiority underlined by the causal models can be brought back to their ability to discriminate more efficiently some periods of loss.

Table 2: Structural models out-of-sample trading simulation

Model	Trading System No. 1		Trading System No. 2	
	Annual Return	Annual Return / Perfect model	Annual Return	Annual Return / Perfect model
Random Walk	-5.24	-	15.27	3.60
Random Walk with Drift	-7.28	-	12.91	3.04
Exponential Smoothing	-5.89	-	-0.19	-
ARIMA	-7.31	-	12.88	3.03
Autoreg. Distributed Lag	18.73	4.41	42.91	10.11
State Space	35.07	8.26	51.73	12.18

These results led researchers to find new ways of treating output in a trading perspective. Episcopos and Davis [1996] use econometric volatility estimates (with an EGARCH-M model) as an input of a neural network comparing mean absolute errors. We opted for a trading application of stochastic variance estimation in order to achieve two different goals:

a) improving parameter significance of the structural function, in the presence of ARCH components;

b) obtaining excess profits by some trading strategy based on volatility forecasts.

With regards to the first goal, the application of an ARCH corrective allows to improve error distribution, with excess kurtosis and skewness levels closer to the normal distribution values (in Table 3 only ADL model results are shown; very similar evidence comes from the other models).

Table 3: ADL Structural Model with ARCH component

Model	AIC	Error Distribution		
		Skewness	Kurtosis	KS
ARCH	-2,126	0.1238	0.6106	6.42
GARCH	-2,111	0.1190	0.5947	6.07
M-GARCH	-2,112	0.1238	0.9082	13.10
E-GARCH	-2,111	-0.0102	1.4030	29.12
I-GARCH	-2,124	0.6666	0.0305	6.63

The results obtained through the application of ARCH models on r_t (Table 4), and LM test evidence, seem to exclude the presence of risk premia effects linked to high volatility periods and possible asymmetrical responses due to different reactions of operators to bad or good news.

Indices in brackets show the p and q order of ARCH(p) and GARCH(q) process. The availability of models capable of interpreting market volatility dynamics enables to improve trading system performance by using the trading rule (Table 2).

Table 4: FIB30 logarithmic returns ARCH models

Model	AIC	Equation				
ARCH	-2,231	ARCH (0)	ARCH (1)	ARCH (2)		
Parameters		0.0001	0.3580	0.2164		
t-Student		(8.46)	(2.244)	(2.52)		
GARCH	-2,228	ARCH (0)	ARCH (1)	GARCH (1)		
Parameters		0.0002	0.0984	0.7566		
t-Student		(7.49)	(2.48)	(6.78)		
M-GARCH	-2,227	ARCH (0)	ARCH (1)	ARCH (2)	GARCH (1)	Delta
Parameters		0.0001	0.052	0.213	0.108	-0.105
t-Student		(3.10)	(2.01)	(2.21)	(2.12)	(-0.04)
I-GARCH	-2,220	ARCH (0)	ARCH (1)	GARCH (1)		
Parameters		0.0001	0.154	0.846		
t-Student		(2.01)	(4.10)	-		
E-GARCH	-2,227	ARCH (0)	ARCH (1)	GARCH (1)	Theta	
Parameters		0.045	0.207	0.646	0.05	
t-Student		(2.01)	(3.08)	(8.23)	(0.22)	

Except for the exponential smoothing model, all the other simulated models show an improvement of nearly 20 basis points in terms of annual performance. By comparing the amount winning trades obtained in the two simulations (with and without volatility forecast), we verified that such correction depends, to a large extent, on the use of the new trading rule which can stop the system in high volatility periods.

Black box forecasts are extremely heterogeneous (Table 5). They reveal a wider return range than structural models. The average return, in fact, is 4.68% for structural models and 2.67% for neural networks, while the average maximum draw-down is 2.74% for econometric models and 3.53% for neural networks. Black box outputs give a lower level of winning trades (51.93% vs. 54.30%). However, the reward/risk index is better for neural nets (62.89%) than for econometric forecasts (31.90%).

Table 5- Out-of-sample neural network estimates

Models	MAE	R^2	Trading System No. 1		Trading System No. 2	
			Annual Return	Annual Return/ Perfect model	Annual Return	Annual Return/ Perfect model
Standard Connections						
A	0.00843	0.0044	22.46	5.29	14.84	3.50
B	0.00844	0.0032	21.01	4.95	22.59	5.32
C	0.00844	0.0022	30.49	7.18	16.79	3.95
Recurrent Networks						
A	0.00835	0.0011	20.01	4.71	20.47	4.82
B	0.00848	0.0000	7.45	1.75	7.94	1.87
C	0.00833	0.0037	27.98	6.59	11.69	2.75
Feature Detectors						
A	0.00855	0.0273	-29.80	-	20.01	4.71
B	0.00881	0.0003	-2.43	-	8.35	1.97
C	0.00881	0.0091	2.90	0.68	27.09	6.38
Jump Connections						
A	0.00857	0.0033	-5.49	-	9.55	2.25
B	0.00858	0.0068	-24.99	-	-6.77	-
C	0.00849	0.0048	-10.00	-	-1.75	-
GRNN	0.00881	0.0047	-24.94	-	6.19	1.46

The results of the models based on the coefficient of determination (R^2) do not offer reliable indications. According to R^2, the best network was expected to be feature detectors with two different activation functions; however, when implemented in the trading system, it shows completely divergent results. The first model in terms of R^2 becomes the last one in terms of trading system, and the first trading system ranks only seventh on the R^2 list.

Let us calculate a simple indicator of reliability (RI) as follows:

$$RI = 1 - \frac{\sum |Rank_{TS} - Rank_{R^2}|}{\max \sum |Rank_{TS} - Rank_{R^2}|} \qquad (2)$$

The index varies between 0 (minimum reliability) and 100 (maximum reliability). In this case, it was possible to show that the statistical error optimisation criterion - on which the neural net models are generally based - can produce very large errors, since the value is 7.14 percent. In order to improve our results, we applied the trading rule based on the stochastic variance estimation to neural network outputs (Table 5).

The application of ARCH volatility forecasts to the outputs produced in the generalisation set allows to reduce the number of trading systems with negative results from 6 to 2 and to increase the average annual return (12.09 percent).

6. Conclusions

1. In the forecast competition, econometric and neural network models gave very

424

similar results in terms of fitting, but very heterogeneous ones in terms of trading.
2. The FIB30 interpretative model shows that technical indices and inter-market variables are statistically significant. With regard to the latter, our statistical results are also supported by parameter signs, which are consistent with financial theory. Such significance is notably reduced if suitably appraised on the same lagged variables, in order to make them consistent with the forecasting model. Therefore, we can conclude that FIB30 reactions are completely absorbed by the evaluations expressed in the market.
3. Traditional statistical error indicators (such as MAE and R^2) are a deformed way of optimising forecasting models used in trading. This result emerges quite clearly in neural network models, where the reliability index shows a 7 percent reliability.
4. The opportunity of adding equations referred to conditional variance dynamics to the structural part of our forecasting model leads us to make the following considerations:
a)   econometric and neural network trading results improve when a volatility forecast is introduced, thus allowing a reduction in the number of negative trading systems;
b)   a final and interesting result which needs to be thoroughly investigated is the level of volatility used to stop the trading system which, if continuously tested, gives nearly the same value for all the models.

Acknowledgements

The authors thank Maria Paola Viola, Paolo De Vito and the referee for their constructive comments during the developments of the study.

References

Bengio, Y., Training a Neural Network with a Financial Criterion rather than a Prediction Criterion, in Weigend A. S.; Abu-Mostafa Y.; Refenes A.-P. N. (eds), *Decision Technologies for Financial Engineering*, NNCM '96 Proceedings, Singapore: World Scientific, 1997.
Engle, R.F., Autoregressive Conditional Heteroskedasticity with Estimates of the Variance of United Kingdom Inflation, in *Econometrica*, 1982; 50: 987-1008.
Episcopos A., Davis J., Predicting Returns on Canadian Exchange Rates with Artificial Neural Networks and Egarch-M Models, in Refenes A–P.N.; Abu-Mostafa Y.; Moody J.; Weigend A., (eds), *Neural Networks in Financial Engineering*, NNCM '95 Proceedings, Singapore: World Scientific, 1996.
Leitch G., Tanner J., Economic Forecast Evaluation: Profits versus the Conventional Error Measures, in *The American Economic Review*, 1991; 81: 580-590.
Moody J., Wu L., Optimization of Trading Systems and Portfolios, in Weigend A. S.; Abu-Mostafa Y.; Refenes A-P. N. (eds), 1997.

INCORPORATING PRIOR KNOWLEDGE ABOUT FINANCIAL MARKETS THROUGH NEURAL MULTITASK LEARNING

KAI BARTLMAE[2], STEFFEN GUTJAHR[1],
GHOLAMREZA NAKHAEIZADEH[2]

[1] *University of Karlsruhe*
Institute of Logic, Complexity and Deduction Systems
Am Fasanengarten 5, 76128 Karlsruhe, Germany
gutjahr@ira.uka.de

[2] *Daimler-Benz AG, Research and Technology FT3/KL*
P.O. Box 23 60, D-89013 Ulm, Germany
{nakhaeizadeh, bartlmae}@dbag.ulm.DaimlerBenz.com

Abstract. We present the systematic method of Multitask Learning for incorporating prior knowledge (hints) into the inductive learning system of neural networks. Multitask Learning is an inductive transfer method which uses domain information about *related tasks* as inductive bias to guide the learning process towards better solutions of the main problem. These tasks are presented to the learning system in a shared representation. This paper argues that there exist many opportunities for Multitask Learning especially in the world of financial modeling: It has been shown, that many interdependencies exist between international financial markets, different market sectors and financial products. Models with an isolated view on a single market or a single product therefore ignore this important source of information. An empirical example of Multitask Learning is presented where learning additional tasks improves the forecasting accuracy of a neural network used to forecast the changes of five major German stocks.

1 Introduction

It has been observed, that the results of inductive methods can be improved by guiding the learning process through auxiliary information about the problem. Abu-Mostafa called this information *hints* about the target function [Abu-Mostafa 1995]. Towell et al. [Towell, Shavlik 1994] showed that incorporating information about the underlying regularities of the domain into a neural network can improve its generalization performance. Especially in the case that only few input-output examples of a complex and non-linear problem are given in a noisy domain, the use of additional information in form of *knowledge-based*

A.-P.N. Refenes et al. (eds.), Decision Technologies for Computational Finance, 425–432.
© 1998 *Kluwer Academic Publishers. Printed in the Netherlands..*

domain-specific hints is essential for successful learning.

This paper presents the method of Multitask Learning which incorporates dependencies between tasks into an inductive learning system. A Multitask Learning System uses the input-output examples of related tasks in order to improve the generalization performance of at least one of these tasks. Learning related problems *at the same time* provides an inductive bias towards better representations of the domain's underlying regularities.

Multitask transfer has broad utility especially in the field of financial modeling and forecasting. Here highly complex dependencies between the ingoing and out-going variables of models are assumed. Characteristics of financial data are further extreme noisiness and non-stationarity. Because of the non-stationarity past market behavior may not longer hold in the future. Exploitable information is also reduced by the noisiness of the data.

Rather than giving direct hints about the target function like Abu-Mostafa introduced in [Abu-Mostafa 1995] we extend this idea by showing that giving indirect hints about the underlying regularities of the problem through related tasks improves the generalization performance in a financial forecasting application. These hints can be derived from a large number of theoretically supported dependencies like the integration of global financial markets, market sectors and financial products or from the observation of the correlation between markets and products.

We first introduce Multitask Learning and its realization with neural networks. Then we present an MTL application for five German stocks. Finally we summarize the methodology.

2   Multitask Learning and Hints in Neural Networks

Multitask Learning has a simple realization if used with three layer feedforward neural networks [Caruana 1996]. In the case of a three layer neural network one adds for each additional task a further output unit, which is fully connected to the hidden layer (figure1).

In this configuration a neural MTL network can be thought of as a simultaneous model for different dependent variables. But the opportunities for Multitask Learning go beyond a simple simultaneous estimation of models. MTL offers the opportunity to add additional tasks only in order to improve and stabilize the performance of the main task. The outputs of the related

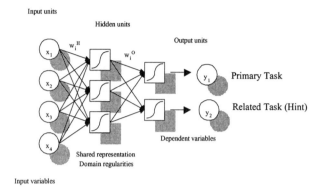

Fig. 1. A Multitask three layer backpropagation network with two related tasks.

tasks are ignored when the net is used to make predictions. Therefore it is not the major goal to find a very good model over all tasks but to find an excellent model for the main task. This order of importance over the different tasks has to be reflected in the learning algorithm, i.e. in a weighting of the different errors of each problem.

The basic idea underlying neural Multitask Learning is that the related tasks influence the hidden layer weights through the additional gradient information. This is leading to hidden layer representations, which better reflect the domain's regularities: The gradient of a hidden layer weight w_i^H is just a weighted sum of the gradient information of each single task.

Therefore the gradient points into a direction that decreases the error over all tasks. The weight itself represents after the update step a better dependency between the input variable and *all* output variables. This reflects the property of a shared domain's regularity, if a correct additional hint is given.

An improvement of generalization performance has been observed in other domain's applications [Caruana, Baluja, Mitchell 1996]. Different underlying mechanisms have been discussed in [Abu-Mostafa 1995] [Caruana 1995].

3   Application

An interesting field for Multitask Learning and the use of hints is the domain of financial forecasting. Here an application of predicting the direction of five German stocks in a one week horizon was chosen: Allianz, Daimler Benz, Deutsche Bank, Siemens and Veba. Because of its noisy and complex nature this is a well-suited problem for the use of Multitask Learning.

3.1   Hints

In this domain a variety of different dependencies exists that can be exploited as hints to improve the generalization performance of the forecasting task for a single equity.

Market Model: The first hint investigated is derived from *market model* [Steiner, Bruns 1993] applied to equities. It states that the return of stocks depends on overall environmental conditions as well on company specific developments.Therefore the market model assumes that a part of the return of a stock is highly influenced by the environmental behavior of the overall market, which can be observed through a high correlation between a stock index and the return of that stock. The behavior of the stock index DAX was therefore used as a hint for the underlying regularities of a single stock.

Time Horizons: Under the assumption that stock prices are predictable, they can be modeled by a function highly influenced by noise. But high levels of noise can be disastrous for inductive learning, since the information about the true input-output dependency of a training example can be fully blurred. Underlying dependencies can be better identified through the noise if not only the value at time step t is observed, but also the values shortly before and after time step t. Therefore we added the tasks of forecasting the return of two days and two weeks to support the forecast of the one week horizon.

Global Market Integration: In a worldwide integrated market the different national market sectors depend on each other [Gjerde, Saetten 1996]. These interdependencies can be exploited in form of related tasks. Here the Dow-Jones index was used being a leading indicator of the next day's DAX index, thus giving a hint about the return of the equities.

3.2 Results

For each stock models were estimated without hints (STL[3]) and with four hints (MTL). The additional tasks included in the MTL model were the forecasts of the DAX index, the Dow-Jones index and the two time horizons. Each model's input consisted of 20 variables representing historical information about the stocks, stock indices, exchange rates and interest rates. The number of hidden units was set to four and the learning algorithm RProp [Riedmiller, Braun 1993] was used. Each model was trained and validated on data from 1.2.1990 to 24.10.1995 and tested on data from 25.10.1995 to 25.10.1996. Training was continued until the main task reached the best performance on the validation dataset, reflecting the emphasis on the main task. The models were re-estimated 100 times with new initial weight values.

Stock	Without Hints	With Hints	Naive	Buy-and-Hold
Allianz	51,96%	$^{+}$58,70%	$^{+}$54,76%	$^{+}$53,55%
Daimler	60,06%	$^{+}$64,64%	$^{-}$45,59%	61,14%
Dt. Bank	60,83%	59,98%	$^{-}$45,23%	$^{-}$48,47%
Siemens	50,01%	$^{+}$54,95%	$^{+}$52,78%	$^{+}$56,49%
Veba	60,40%	$^{+}$62,02%	$^{-}$58,06%	$^{+}$61,84%
Average	56,65%	60,06%	51,29%	56,28%

Table 1. Classification performance without hints (STL), with four hints (MTL), the naive prediction and the buy-and-hold strategy. $\pm$ shows a statistically significantly better/worse model compared to the model without hints to level 5%

Table 1 shows that in four out of five cases the MTL models were significantly better in prediction rate compared to the models without hints and were never significantly worse. The MTL model dominated on average the buy-and-hold strategy as well as the naive forecast. The buy-and-hold strategy is the strategy that holds the equity until the end of the test interval. The naive prediction states that a change at time step t is the best predictor of the change at time step $t+1$.

In table 2 it can be seen that this is also true for the average annualized return of a simple trading strategy derived from the forecasts of the direction. In this strategy the stock was bought in case of a predicted rise and was sold otherwise. Because of the rising German stock market in 1996 the buy-and-hold

---

[3] Singletask learning

strategy represented a benchmark difficult to beat.

Stock	Without Hints	With Hints	Naive	Buy-and-Hold
Average	16,30%	21,19%	3,16%	18,21%

Table 2. Annualized return without hint (STL), with four hints (MTL), the naive prediction and the buy-and-hold strategy

In further tests with a changing number of given hints it could be observed that in most cases removing tasks from the model MTL resulted in a decrease in performance. Here two smaller Multitask models were estimated. The first model used the DAX index (MTL_{DAX}) as additional task, the second the two time horizons (MTL_{Time}). When the DAX hint was given it resulted in a performance that was better on average and in most cases compared with STL and worse compared to the models with five given tasks (Table 3). When two different time horizons were used as additional tasks, the same could be observed.

Stock	STL	MTL_{DAX}	MTL_{Time}	MTL
Allianz	51,96%	$^+$54,66%	$^+$53,24%	$^+$58,70%
Daimler	60,06%	58,94%	61,07%	$^+$64,64%
Dt. Bank	60,83%	60,35%	$^-$58,42%	59,98%
Siemens	50,01%	50,72%	$^+$52,78%	$^+$54,95%
Veba	60,40%	$^+$63,03%	$^+$62,70%	$^+$62,02%
Average	56,65%	57,54%	57,64%	60,06%

Table 3. Classification performance without hints, with one hint (DAX), with two hints (two time horizons) and with four hints. ± shows a statistically significantly better/worse model compared to the model without hints to level 5%

Theoretical considerations of good additional tasks are essential in order to gain good results, but are not always sufficient. Multitask Learning is an inductive transfer method that depends on the data of additional tasks. Therefore additional tasks can have no or even a negative influence if the quality is not good enough or if the relationship between the tasks is not present in the sample. In our experiments the MTL approach showed to be robust over many different models and resulted only in a few cases in a decrease of performance.

Two further models were estimated for the Allianz stock to investigate if the MTL effect was really based on the *domain specific* information. Each of the two models was given a different hint: The first was given a noisy hint in form of a randomly generated dataset and the second an additional task in form of the primary task. While these two models showed no impact compared to the model without hints (Table 4), the MTL_{DAX} model resulted in a statistically significant increase of the generalization performance. This shows that the usefulness of a hint clearly depends on its information value.

Equity	Random	Twice	STL	MTL_{DAX}
Allianz	52,74%	51,05%	51,96%	54,66%

Table 4. Classification rate for Allianz models: Model with a randomly generated additional task, model with twice the main task, STL model, MTL_{DAX} model

Notable is that adding further tasks resulted not only in a better performance of the main task, but also of the other additional tasks. In table 5 it can be seen, that an increase was also observed for additional tasks. The observed DAX classification rate of model MTL_{DAX} increased when further tasks were added (MTL). So not only the main task gained from the Multitask approach but also the tasks together. This shows, how the different tasks positively influence each other. It indicates that the relationship between them is successfully used to find a better model that supported more than one task.

Models	MTL	MTL_{DAX}
Allianz	62,79%	58,88%
Daimler	64,37%	52,36%
Dt. Bank	62,08%	51,84%
Siemens	62,90%	49,90%
Veba	63,33%	61,43%

Table 5. Classification rate of the additional task DAX for MTL and MTL_{DAX}

4 Conclusions

We introduced the method of neural Multitask Learning, which incorporates hints about the domain's underlying regularities in form of related learning tasks. Especially in the domain of financial modeling exists a variety of interdependencies which can be expressed as additional tasks making Multitask transfer a valuable source of domain specific information in this field.

We presented the application of MTL to forecast five major German stocks. It could be shown that a single view on one forecasting task ignores information about existing interdependencies on financial markets. Hints based on these interdependencies were successfully incorporated through Multitask Learning to improve the quality of the resulting models.

Several directions of investigation remain open: First of all, methods to identify useful additional tasks and to quantify their information value have to be found. Of further interest are weighting methods between the hints and the main problem. Here techniques like learning schedules [Abu-Mostafa 1995] or a weighting through Bayesian techniques [MacKay 1992] can be used.

References

[Abu-Mostafa 1995] Abu-Mostafa, Y.S.: *Hints*, Neural Computation, 7: 639-671, 1995

[Caruana 1995] Caruana, R.: *Learning many related tasks at the same time with backpropagation*, Advances in Neural Information Processing Systems, 7,656-664, 1995

[Caruana 1996] Caruana, R.: *Algorithms and Applications for Multitask Learning*, The 13th International Conference on Machine Learning, Bari, Italy, 87-95, 1996

[Caruana, Baluja, Mitchell 1996] Caruana, R., Baluja, S., Mitchell, T., *Using the Future to 'Sort Out' the Present: Rankprop and Multitask Learning for Medical Risk Evaluation*, Advances in Neural Information Processing Systems, 8, 1996

[Gjerde, Saetten 1996] Gjerde, O., Saetten, F.: *Linkages among European and world markets*, European Journal of Finance, 2:165-179, 1996

[MacKay 1992] MacKay, D.J.C. : *A practical Bayesian framework for backpropagation networks*, Neural Computation, 4(3): 448-472, 1992

[Riedmiller, Braun 1993] Riedmiller, M. and Braun, H.: *A direct adaptive method for faster backpropagation learning: The RPROP algorithm*, Proceedings of the IEEE International Conference on neural networks, 1993

[Steiner, Bruns 1993] Steiner, M., Bruns, C.: *Wertpapiermanagement*, Schäffer-Poeschel, 1993

[Towell, Shavlik 1994] Towell, G.G., Shavlik, J.W.: *Knowledge-Based Artificial Neural Networks*, Artificial Intelligence, 70: 119-165, 1994

PREDICTING TIME SERIES WITH A COMMITTEE OF INDEPENDENT EXPERTS BASED ON FUZZY RULES

MARTIN RAST

Math. Inst., Ludwig-Maximilians-Universität
Theresienstr. 39/334, 80333 Munich, Germany
E-mail: Martin.Rast@cd1.lrz-muenchen.de

Predicting time series is a quite important field of economic research. Neural networks provide a quite good access for analyzing nonlinear time series. Furthermore, they provide a tool for accessing problems with an unknown structure. Nevertheless it would be sometimes useful to have an access where one can put existing knowledge into the models to improve their prediction quality, and to have a more interpreterable, i.e. reliable model. Fuzzy neural networks provide such an access.

In this paper an additional improvement is discussed: setting up rules for forecasting leads in most cases to a huge set of rules. The size makes the set uneasy to be interpreted. The proposal presented here splits the set into smaller ones, which can separatly be analyzed and administered.

1 Introduction

Today the application of neural networks for forecasting of financial time series is fairly commonplace. The input data is preprocessed in a variety of ways to get reasonable results. Some years ago the combination of fuzzy logic and neural networks was explored, giving the neural network more information about the structure of the pattern set.

The approach presented below is based on the observation of proprietary trading in practice, where the traders get information from many sources, like technical analysis and economic studies, which helps them to take an appropriate position in the market. A number of *experts* are designed, each of them with a specific *knowledge* given by a rule set, which implemented in neural topology. A (standard) neural network takes these experts as input and is then trained to calculate the correct forecast from them.

2 Time Series

We now have a brief look at the task of time series prediction and how neural networks can be used to make such forecasts.

A.-P.N. Refenes et al. (eds.), Decision Technologies for Computational Finance, 433–437.
© 1998 *Kluwer Academic Publishers. Printed in the Netherlands..*

2.1 Prediction

Predicting of time series bases on the belief that there is a relationship between historical and future prices, i.e. that there is a function f with

$$P_t = f(P_{t-1}, P_{t-2}, \ldots)$$

for all t, where P_t is the price at time t. Furthermore, some additional time series can be used, which leads to a representation like

$$P_t = f(P_{t-1}, P_{t-2}, \ldots, X_{t-1}, X_{t-2}, \ldots, Y_{t-1}, Y_{t-2}, \ldots)$$

in this multivariate case.

This function can be observed for historic t. Such an approximation $\hat{f}$ of f can predict future P_t.

2.2 Classical Neural Networks

Neural networks are able to approximate every function arbitralily exact, so neural network technology can be used to provide an approximation to f.

3 Fuzzy Neural Networks

In many cases the user wants to improve classical neural networks by adding some knowlegde. Used in the traditional way neural networks only gain their approximation (and therefore predition) power from the patterns given. Sometimes there is additional knowledge available which is not very likely to be in the pattern set; this is for example in situations which are quite well analyzed but seldom happening.

Using fuzzy neural networks rules can be added to the network. Additionally the rule based network can be further optimized using the pattern set in the same way as before. This methodology bases on the possibility of representing rules in a neural topology which is only a special case of the classical neural networks; i.e. the rule based neural networks can be trained using the same optimization (learning) algorithms as in the classical case.

A rule set which is once defined can be transformed into neural topology. The procedure used here is described in (Rast 1997). So an expert defining a rule set leads to a network, i.e. the knowledge of an expert can be represented by a network.

4 Rule Sets

Before discussing the combination of different experts some types of rule sets are described is this paragraph.

4.1 Technical

Both short and long term information from technical analysis should be used. *Short term* means here the time horizon of the forecast; the experts used here are specialized on trend-following, trend-changing indicators, as well as support and resistance calculation. Data from other than the predicted time series can be used as well. Besides the *short term* also *long term* information might be useful, the same criteria applies here. Also a functionality for trend channels is often used.

4.2 Fundamental

The fundamental data is helpful, too. It provides for example information about the economic situation. Furthermore, also here some preprocessing is used; in most cases seasonal adjustment and detrending.

4.3 Other

In addition to the information mentioned above other data can be useful for forecasting, e.g.: In a day-to-day or intraday horizon the release of numbers being published by authorities or forthcoming elections can lead to major price moves. Therefore any suggestions of the above can help the neural network to be aware of sudden increases in volatility.

4.4 Combined

Certainly an expert can combine the data of different classes discussed above.

5 Combination of Experts

It is conveniant to set up the network using independent experts, better than one huge rule set. The definition of this separation is often quite straight-forward; so rule sets are often defined by interviewing several human experts, so one canonical separation is given by the human experts which provide that rules. Another separation is given by the types of the input data which is descibed in the previous section.

The predictions of the single experts are combined in a neural network. It is trained using the pattern set from history. A linear network promises an interesting insight, because irrelevant experts could be removed easily. But a nonlinear combination of experts leads to better results.

By analysis of the rule sets relevant information (i.e. input data) and rules can be determined. This analysis is an analysis of the combination layer.

6   Example

As example we try to predict the "Notionel", the long-term interest rate future for french francs. Three experts are used, all of them basing on technical indicators. Two of them are working on MAVG with different horizons, the third on the stochastics.

To estimate the quality of the proposed procedure 100 nets of both the fuzzy neural networks and the classical ones are applied to the "Notionel". The pattern set is split into training (June 3, 1996 - June 3, 1997), test (November 11, 1995 - May 31, 1996) and validation (June 4, 1997 - November 17, 1997).

The performance is as indicated in figure 1. It can be noticed that here fuzzy neural networks lead to a more stabile performance in the out-of-sample patterns.

Performance	Training	Test	oos
Fuzzy	7.953	6.668	1.802
Classical	9.863	6.023	0.353

Figure 1. Performance of fuzzy neural networks.

7   Conclusion

Experiments with the networks described above showed good results. The result of the view presented in this paper is not only the prediction quality, which is the equivalent to other fuzzy neural networks. But using this separation the analysis of the resulting network is made much more easy.

Future focus will be on the combination: It seems to be useful to give an additional rule set for the combination, which would model the trader integrating the information he gets from several sources (i.e. experts, analysts).

8 References

Ledermann J., Klein R. A., eds. *Virtual Trading.* Chicago: Probus Publishing, 1995.

London Business School. *Proceedings of the Neural Networks in the Capital Markets,* 1994.

M. Rast. Application of Fuzzy Neural Networks on Financial Problems. In *Proceedings of the NAFIPS'97,* Işik C., Cross V., eds., IEEE, 1997.

M. Rast. Forecasting Financial Time Series with Fuzzy Neural Networks. In *Proceedings of the 1997 IEEE International Conference on Intelligent Processing Systems,* IEEE, 1997.

MULTI-SCALE ANALYSIS OF TIME SERIES BASED ON A NEURO-FUZZY-CHAOS METHODOLOGY APPLIED TO FINANCIAL DATA

N. K. KASABOV, R. KOZMA

Department of Information Science
University of Otago
P.O.Box 56, Dunedin, New Zealand
E-mail: nkasabov@otago.ac.nz , rkozma@infoscience.otago.ac.nz

Integration of neuro-fuzzy and chaos tools of time series analysis is the topic of this work. In our approach, the time series is considered as a multi-level process evolving over time. Prediction is implemented as a hierarchical process when the higher-level trends are predicted first, followed by the lower level values of the time-series. This treatment may help to challenge the view that a chaotic process is not predictable in a long time, as long-term prediction could be possible for certain types of chaotic time series as a cascade of approximations with increasing accuracy. After the initial time series analysis, a corresponding hierarchical multi-modular structure is built to model the time series at different levels. A fuzzy neural network FuNN is used for the purpose of building each of the modules in the modular structure. Fuzzy rules for explaining chaotic time series at different levels of its behavior can be extracted. A case study of a stock index time series has been used through the paper to illustrate the proposed methodology and techniques.

1   Introduction

A generic methodology of a chaotic time series analysis is presented in the paper which includes:
- Developing a model of the time series through a rigorous analysis of its chaotic dynamics
- Building a connectionist-based modular hierarchical structure to model and to predict the time-series
- Extracting underlying rules to explain the chaotic process at its different levels of behaviour.

This paper treats a chaotic process as a hierarchical, compound one consisting of components with different time scales. At the highest level it is the longest trend of the process and at the lowest level is the single time moment value. A long term analysis and prediction of a time series will include first predicting the highest-level trend, then within it - the next level trend, etc, until a prediction of a single time-moment value can be attempted. This approach, which is a generic one, is illustrated on a financial data set - the SE40 index data.

The chaos study utilizes Higuchi's method for fractal and multi-fractal analysis [1,3,6,8]. Various types of networks can be used for financial applications, e.g., recurrent, time-delay neural networks and multi-layer feed-forward architectures; see, e.g, [2]. In this paper, multi-layer feed-forward networks are used which are "forced" to learn the entire data and pick all the variations and trends in it. One

A.-P.N. Refenes et al. (eds.), Decision Technologies for Computational Finance, 439–450.
© 1998 *Kluwer Academic Publishers. Printed in the Netherlands..*

danger of standard feed-forward neural networks is that while they provide an effective means of discovering potentially non-linear mappings from an input space to its corresponding output space from data, the manner in which this mapping is represented is hidden. While various techniques have been proposed for examining a network's weight matrix which represents the model's behaviour, none have been entirely successful. This *'black box'* effect severely limits the use of neural networks for knowledge discovery and hinders the verification of the model developed. Another problem with such networks is that they are entirely data driven. While the ability to learn arbitrary models from data is perhaps the greatest strength of the neural network paradigm, the exclusion of knowledge from the model building process can be seen as wasteful.

Techniques have been proposed for pre-weighting networks in such a manner as to start the network closer to a solution, but again have not been entirely successful. An alternative approach is that of using fuzzy-neural networks FuNN [5,7]. FuNN is a generic tool that provides a semantically meaningful fuzzy structure within the neural network, allowing for rule insertion, model-free training on data, and most significantly the extraction of adapted rules. If no initial knowledge can be formulated, the network can still be trained on data after random initialisation, with rules extracted from the trained structure. Such a structure synergistically combines the strengths of fuzzy expert rules and neural network learning.

In this paper a special type of fuzzy neural network FuNN is used for modeling time series. It is illustrated how to use fuzzy neural networks (FuNN) and FuNN-based hybrid systems as a powerful new approach for integrating knowledge and data into a single structure. Advanced new adaptation strategies have been developed to take full advantage of this technique. The nature of many problems in the financial domain, characterised by the employment alternative theories and the availability of large quantities of data, makes them well suited to this hybrid paradigm.

2 Multi-Modular Systems using Fuzzy Neural Networks

2.1 Description of the Fuzzy Neural Networks FuNN

The FuNN model is designed to be used in a distributed and eventually agent-based environment. It facilitates learning from data and approximate reasoning, as well as fuzzy rules extraction and insertion. It allows for the combination of both data and rules into one system, thus producing the synergistic benefits associated with the two sources. In addition, it allows for several methods of adaptation in a dynamically changing environment.

FuNN uses a multi-layer perceptron (MLP) network architecture and a modified backpropagation training algorithm. The general FuNN architecture consists of 5 layers of neurons with partial feedforward connections as shown in Fig. 1. It is an adaptable structure where the membership functions of the fuzzy predicates, as well as the fuzzy rules inserted before training or adaptation, may adapt and change according to new data. Below a brief description of the components of the FuNN architecture and the philosophy behind this architecture are given. A full mathematical presentation of the training algorithm developed for FuNN, which is a modified backpropagation algorithm, is given in [5,7].

The input layer of neurons represents the input variables as crisp values. These values are fed to the condition element layer which performs fuzzification. This is implemented in FuNN/2 using three-point triangular membership functions with centers represented as the weights into this condition element layer. The triangles are completed with the minimum and maximum points attached to adjacent centers, or shouldered in the case of the first and last membership functions. The triangular membership functions are allowed to be non-symmetrical and any input value will belong to a maximum of two membership functions with degrees differing from zero (it will always involve two, unless the input value falls exactly on a member-ship function center in which case the single membership will be activated, but this is unlikely given 16-bits floating point variables). These membership degrees for any given input will always sum up to one, ensuring that there will be rules to fire for any point in the input space.

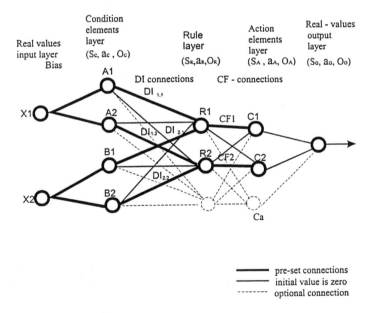

Fig. 1: A FuNN structure for two initial fuzzy rules:
R1: IF x1 is A1 (DI1,1) and x2 is B1 (DI2,1) THEN y is C1 (CF1);
R2: IF x1 is A2 (DI1,2) and x2 is B2 (DI2,2) THEN y is C2 (CF2),
where DIs are degrees of importance attached to the condition elements and CFs are confidence factors attached to the consequent parts of the rules.

Initially, the membership functions are spaced equally over the weight space and they are tuned/adapted during the training process. In order to maintain the semantic meaning of the memberships contained in this layer of connections some restrictions are placed on adaptation. In the FuNN/2 architecture, labels can be attached to weights when the network is constructed. When adaptation is taking place the centers are spatially constrained according to some rules, e.g., the membership function weight representing "low" will always have a center less than "medium", which will always be less than "high", etc.

In the rule layer, each node represents a single fuzzy rule. The layer is potentially expandable and shrinkable, i.e., nodes can be added or deleted, to represent increasing or decreasing number of rules as the network adapts. The activation function is the sigmoidal logistic function with a variable gain coefficient g (a default value of 1 is used giving the standard sigmoidal activation function). The semantic meaning of the activation of a node is the degree to which input data matches the antecedent component of an associated fuzzy rule. However, the synergistic nature of rules in a fuzzy-neural architecture must be remembered when interpreting such rules. The connection weights from the condition element layer to the rule layer represent semantically the degrees of importance of the corresponding condition elements for the activation of this node. The values of the connection weights to and from the rule layer can be limited during training to be within a certain interval, say [-1,1], thus introducing non-linearity into the synaptic weights.

In the action element layer a node represents a fuzzy label from the fuzzy quantisation space of an output variable. The activation of the node represents the degree to which this membership function is supported by the current data used for recall. The activation function for the nodes of this layer is the sigmoidal logistic function with a variable gain factor as in the previous layer. Again, this gain factor should be adjusted appropriately given the size of the weight boundary. The output layer performs a modified center of gravity defuzzification. Singletons, representing centers of gravity of membership functions are attached to the connections from the action to the output layer. Linear activation functions are used here.

There are five versions of weight updating in the FuNN according to the mode of training and adaptation [5]. These are not mutually exclusive versions but are all provided within the same environment and the versions can be interchanged and combined as needed. These methods of adaptation are: (i) a partially adaptive training, where the membership functions (MF) of the input and the output variables do not change during training; (ii) a fully adaptive training with an extended backpropagation algorithm; this version allows changes to be made to both rules and membership functions, subject to constraints necessary for retaining semantic meaning; (iii) a partially adaptive version, but a forgetting factor is introduced; (iv) a partially adaptive version with the use of a genetic algorithm for adapting the membership functions; (v) adaptive training with the use of the `Method of Training and Zeroing'.

A MS Windows version of FuNN/2, which is part of an integrated hybrid development tool called FuzzyCOPE/2 is made available free from the Web site:

http://divcom.otago.ac.nz:800/COM/INFOSCI/KEL/fuzzycop.htm

FuNN/2 allows for different training strategies to be tested before the most suitable is selected for a certain application. FuNN/2 has other interesting features in addition to the features already discussed above. Some of them are: (a) a FuNN has a symmetrical structure and it can be used to build a replicator NN; (b) FuNN can be trained with output data being the input ones and a compressed encoding can be picked up from the rule layer; (c) a FuNN structure may be used to represent all stages in a cognitive task, ie perception, data filtering, knowledge acquisition and knowledge modification, action.

2.2   Outline of the Multi-Modular System

A multi-modular architecture is proposed which consists of several FuNN modules, a rule extraction module and a module for adaptation, as given in Fig. 2. Such systems can be efficiently used for example in classification tasks when one FuNN is trained to classify examples of one particular class. This structure allows for adaptive individual tuning of each of the class FuNN units according to the performance of this class unit during the operation of the whole system. Only the FuNN units which do not operate properly need to be tuned, while the remaining ones remain unchanged. This facilitates an efficient and adaptive tuning of the system in real time.

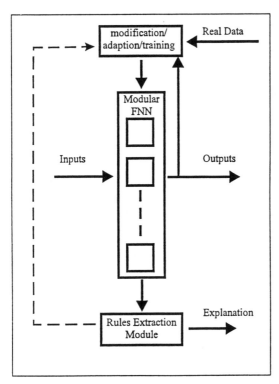

Fig. 2: Architecture of a multi-modular adaptive, intelligent FuNN-based system FuNN-based hybrid systems, which consist of several modules for adaptive training, rules extraction and explanation, on-line data manipulation and analysis, are introduced here and illustrated in the next section as a powerful methodology for building on-line adaptive intelligent systems for chaotic time-series analysis.

For example, initially, all the modules may be trained with identical data for a small number of epochs. After that, each of the units may be tuned using a specific variant of the learning and adaptation techniques. Extracting rules and explaining the behaviour of each of the units at each moment of their operation, as well as of the whole system, is accomplished by using a rule extraction module as shown in Fig. 2. The rules extracted may be used for a better adaptation in the adaptation module.

3 Tools of Chaotic Time Series Analysis

3.1 Fractal and Multi-fractal Time Series

In the present work we concentrate on signals with non-linear dynamics modeled by fuzzy neural networks FuNNs. The level of chaos determines the reliability of the short- and long-term predictions. The chaosness is related to the dimensionality of the system which has to be taken into account when designing, training, and adaptively tuning the FuNN architecture. A simple process can be modeled by considering just a few time lags at the FuNN input and a small number of nodes at the rule layer. A time series with complex chaotic dynamic may require larger number of inputs and also a lot of rule nodes.

The dynamics of the system is investigated by calculating the fractal dimension of the temporal process. The fractal dimension of self-similar time series is estimated following Higuchi's procedure elaborated in [3] and further refined in [8]. In the analysis the fractional length $L(k)$ of the graph of the time series is evaluated for a range of time steps k. If the relationship $L(k) \sim k^{(-D)}$ holds, the time series reveals fractal characteristics [16]. In the case of a fractal time series, the $\log(k)$ versus $L(k)$ curve is linear and the negative slope of the curve gives the fractal dimension value D.

In many practical situations, the signal reveals bi- or multi-fractal features; i.e., the fractal dimension value depends on the considered time scales. In a multi-fractal signal, the estimation of a set of fractal dimension values is performed by dividing the whole k-range into several segments and applying linear fitting over each sub-region. The proper choice of the sub-regions is rather complicated. Intelligent data processing methods based on artificial neural networks can be applied to this aim [2,5,7].

3.2 Implications of the Results of Chaos Analysis on FuNN Design

Usual statistical methods perform well if the analysed time series is a stationary process. In the presence of trends, seasonal patterns and cycles with not strictly periodic components, the effectiveness of traditional methods of signal analysis tends to diminish. In this section, a novel FuNN-based approach is proposed to complement or replace methods of correlation analysis.

Financial data represent very complex phenomena, therefore, even an advanced multivariate analysis technique can have only limited success in modeling these processes. Nevertheless, we demonstrate our general methodology on a simple case study, which enables us to illustrate some major ideas in a easily understandable way. The results obtained by the univariate model can be readily incorporated into a multi-modular system by using the FuNN modules described previously.

An example of the modular system is given in Fig. 3. Each individual module predicts a time series which is obtained from the original SE40 data by applying a moving average (MA) filter of a given order. MA-based forecasting techniques are widely used in financial data analysis [2]. The modules indicated in Fig. 3 predict MA values of order 1, 10, 30, and 60, respectively. The proper choice of the MA scales is a difficult problem and chaos-based techniques can be used to this end.

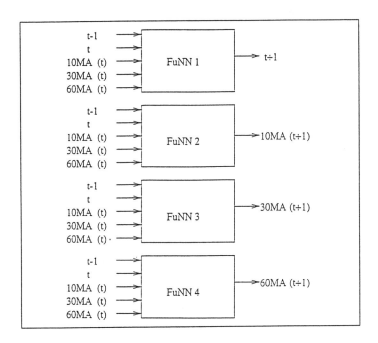

Fig. 3: Modular system for multi-scale time-series prediction

A multi-modular FuNN system has been designed to model different time scales of the data. In the following discussions, the design of a single FuNN module will be described. The size and structure of the input layer depends on the embedding dimension d (see [1] for explanation of the term embedding dimension). If d is small, a few input nodes representing previous time steps are sufficient to describe the dynamics of the system. It is important to note that an excessive use of input nodes makes the modeling not just more complicated but less accurate as well. Indeed, information supplied by the extra time lags is not used in generating the desired mapping, rather it acts as a noise component and makes the identification more difficult [9,10]. Therefore, the optimum design of the structure of each FuNN module is a crucial issue.

4   The Case Study of NZSE40 Modeling and Prediction

4.1   NZSE40 Time Series Data Characteristics

The NZSE40 data set contains the stock exchange index collected daily [5]. The results of time series analysis are summarised in Fig. 4. The power spectrum of the SE40 index is given in Fig. 4a. The behaviour of the power spectrum is close to a 1/f power law, although, large statistical fluctuations make it difficult to determine the exact shape of the spectrum, especially at high frequencies.

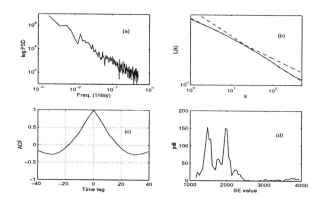

Fig. 4: Characterisation of the SE40 data; (a) power spectral density; (b) fractional length of the graph of the time series; (c) auto correlation function; (d) probability density (histogram).

Figure 4b illustrates the fractal properties of the time series. Two major ranges can be distinguished in the wave number space. Namely, the L(k) versus k curve is less steep at low k values compared to the high k region. This is a typical bi-fractal behaviour with a breaking point at k approx. 20. The value of the fractal dimension D has been determined based on the least-square fit of the corresponding segments of the curve.

The least-square fits to the fractal curve are shown shown as dashed lines in Fig. 4b. The obtained fractal dimension values are 1.35+/-0.02 and 1.70+/-0.03 over k-ranges [1 - 22] and [53 - 362], respectively, which suggests that at least two scales of modeling and prediction would be appropriate to apply.

Figures 4c-d contain additional information about the statistics of the data. The cross correlation function in Fig. 1c indicates a memory effect of up to 10 days. The probability density function (histogram) in Fig.1d is far from having a Gaussian behaviour and its two distinct peaks are caused by an apparent bimodality of the SE40 values.

MA-based forecasting techniques are widely used in financial data analysis and the method of integrating multi-scale chaos analysis with neuro-fuzzy modeling can be viewed as a generalisation of the MA approach. Consider the results obtained in the previous section when analysing the multi-fractalness of the NZSE40 index. It has been shown that there are two distinct time-scales in the data, i.e, the ones below about 20 time lags and another one above 20 to about 1 year.

Time scales longer than 1 year has not been analysed because the limited amount of data. It has been found that the dimensionality of the system is lower for small wave numbers k than for large k values, therefore different modeling methods are required to predict the time series for small and large k values. The times scales identified in this way may not correspond exactly to the ones applied in MA analysis, although there is a connection between these quantities. Research is going on to identify the relationship between MA indices and fractal properties.

4.2   Modeling NZSE40 index by FuNN

In the initial FuNN model, 10 previous time steps have been used to model the change of the NZSE40 value from between two consecutive time recordings. Three triangular fuzzy membership functions have been used at each input node as well as at the output. Accordingly, there were 30 nodes in the condition layer and 3 nodes in the action layer. The number of rule nodes has been 20 and fully-connected weight matrices were used between the condition/rule, and the rule/action layers.

Experiments have been performed with structural learning with forgetting. The choice of the forgetting rate is crucial, therefore, extensive parameter studies have been conducted to find an optimum value of forgetting. In the experiments shown in this paper, a forgetting rate of 0.0005 is used. This value allowed a proper convergence of the training and also an efficient pruning within several thousands iterations.

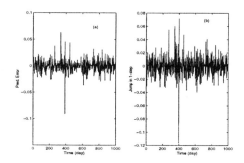

Fig. 5: Predicting the SE40 index by FuNN;
(a)   prediction error by FuNN, (b) daily change of SE40.

In Figure 5a, results of training of the 10-30-20-3-1 FuNN are introduced, while Fig. 5b shows the actual value of the day-by-day change of SE40. The variance of the prediction error is 0.0118, while the variance of a random step-by-step walk would result in 0.0123.

The performance of the forecasting system can be improved further by implementing the multi-modular scheme which is the topic of future research.

4.3 Rule Extraction from the FuNN Structure

Finally, rule and knowledge extraction is performed based on the skeleton structure of the fuzzy neural network trained by structural learning with forgetting. Figures 6a-b illustrate the structure of the initial (fully-connected) and final (skeleton) structure of the hidden layers of FuNN. In this experiment, the actual SE40 index values are used at both the input and output layers which allows to extract some rules from the network. The input and output layers are not shown as they are not tuned during this set of experiments.

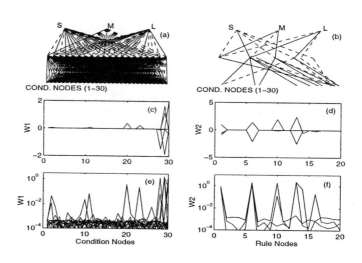

Fig. 6: Memory effects in the FuNN trained by learning-with-forgetting;
(a) fully connected FuNN structure 10-30-20-3-1, (b) skeleton FuNN structure 4-12-6-3-1
(c) weights between condition and rule layers, (d) weights between rule and action layer,
(e) log(abs(W1)), (f) log(abs(W2))

It is clear that only 6 rules remain active from the initial 20 rules after structural learning has been completed; see Fig. 6d. These 6 rules are still quite complicated but a few interesting observations can be made. Nodes #14 and #16 represent rules which can be formulated as ``large stays large" and ``small stays small", respectively. These rules support a 'do not change' strategy. Some other rules, however, yield an effect which slightly deviates from the random walk. Exactly these are the rules which account for the increased prediction accuracy. For example, rule node #10 supports an implication relation concerning the "Medium (M)" future values and it writes:

IF   [Y(t-7) is M (0.07)] and [Y(t-2) is M (0.06)]
and   [Y(t-1) is M (1.66)] and [Y(t-1) is not-L (0.22)]
THEN [Y(t) is M (1.95)]

Interesting effects are seen in the condition layer as well. A clear memory effect takes place, i.e., the 3 membership functions belonging to the most recent time instant have far the highest contribution due to the large weight magnitudes at time t-1, as it is shown in Fig.6c. In addition to the dominance of time t-1, certain secondary effects are also obvious, which influence the nodes belonging to time points t-4, t-7, and t-10. To emphasize this effect, the magnitudes of the weights W1 and W2 are depicted in Fig.6e-f in logarithmic coordinates.

5   Conclusions and Directions for Future Research

* The paper presents, and illustrates on financial data, a neuro-fuzzy-chaos methodology for time series analysis which includes: multi-scale analysis, modeling, prediction, and knowledge acquisition.
* In the first part, chaos and fractal analysis methods are introduced to analyse the chaosness of the data, to discover the time scales in which modeling and prediction would be possible, and to find out the dimensionality of the processes at the different time scales.
* Based on the chaos and fractal analysis and on the multi-scale representation, a multi-modular system is built to model and predict the time series and to extract knowledge about its behaviour.
* A general methodology for building on-line adaptive systems for time-series data analysis and prediction is given. In the modeling, fuzzy neural networks (FuNNs) were used which have been trained by a structural learning algorithm.
* Rules have been extracted from the skeleton structure of the trained FuNN module. In addition to the prediction made by the FuNN.
* In addition to time series prediction and rule extraction, the trained fuzzy neural network has been used also for estimating the extent of the memory of the process. This new, FuNN-based methodology of estimating the parameters of the chaotic process, in combination with evaluating the fractal dimension directly from the time series, can be used for iteratively refining our model and for improving the accuracy of the predictions made by the model.
* There is a close connection between moving average prediction techniques and the time scales identified by multi-fractal analysis introduced in this paper. Future research should reveal the details of this relationship. Results of this study can be utilised in the implementation of the adaptive, multi-modular forecasting technique.

6   Acknowledgement

This work has been completed as part of the Connectionist Based Information System (CBIS) project # UOO 606 funded by the Public Good Science Fund of the Foundation of Research Science & Technology (FRST) in New Zealand.

450

7 References

1. Bai-Lin, H., Chaos II, World Scientific (1990)
2. Deboeck, G.J. (ed.) Trading on the Edge, Neural, Genetic, and Fuzzy Systems for Chaotic Financial Markets, John Wiley & Sons, N.Y.(1994)
3. Higuchi, T., "Approach to an Irregular Time Series on the Basis of the Fractal Theory," Physica D, Vol.31, pp. 277-283 (1988)
4. Ishikawa, M., "Learning of Modular Structured Networks", Artificial Intelligence, 75, 51-62 (1995)
5. Kasabov, N., Foundations of Neural Networks, Fuzzy Systems and Knowledge Engineering, The MIT Press, CA, MA (1996)
6. Kozma, R., M. Sakuma, Y. Yokoyama, M. Kitamura, "On the Accuracy of Mapping by Neural Networks Trained by Backpropagation with Forgetting", Neurocomputing, 13, 2-4 (1996)
7. Kozma, R. and Kasabov, N. Neuro-embedding of chaotic time series, In Brain-like computing and intelligent information systems. S. Amari and N. Kasabov eds. Singapore, Springer Verlag, 213-237 (1997)
8. Sakuma, M., R. Kozma, M. Kitamura, ``Characterisation of Anomalies by Applying Methods of Fractal Analysis," Nucl. Technol. 113, 86-99 (1996)
9. Smith, L.A., ``Local Optimal Prediction: Exploiting Strangeness and the Variation of Sensitivity to Initial Conditions," Phil. Trans. R. Soc. London A 446, 1-11 (1994)
10. Sugihara, G., R.M. May, ``Non-linear Forecasting as a Way of Distinguishing Chaos from Measurement Error in Time Series," Nature, 344, 734-741 (1990)

ON THE MARKET TIMING ABILITY OF NEURAL NETWORKS:
AN EMPIRICAL STUDY TESTING THE FORECASTING PERFORMANCE

TAE HORN HANN
Institute for Statistics and Mathematical Economics
University of Karlsruhe
Rechenzentrum, Zirkel 2
76128 Karlsruhe, Germany

JÖRN HOFMEISTER
University of Ulm
present address: Rosenweg 17, 71706 Markgröningen, Germany

The evaluation of the forecasting performance of a neural network is essential especially for practitioners. Measures such as mean square error (MSE in the following), mean error (ME) or mean absolute error(MAE) are widely used in applied econometrics. However, these measures are not very meaningful in forecasting, as we usually are interested in sign prediction only. On the other hand, economic performance measures (annualized return, Sharpe ratio, etc.) which are used to evaluate trading models, are sensitive to market behavior (trends, volatility) and have to be compared to benchmarks. In this paper we test for significant market timing ability in order to assess the performance of trading models based on neural nets. We use three modeling approaches and show that they have a significant influence on market timing ability.

1   Introduction

Recently several methods have been proposed to design trading models with neural networks. Moody and Wu (1997), Kang et al. (1997) or Bengio (1997) for example propose to optimise the financial criterion of interest and report superior results relative to the standard approach of minimising the MSE. However, the results of these case studies cannot be compared as they are dependent on the time series to be predicted and on the time period chosen. In this paper the influence of three neural network models on market timing ability is tested. This test was proposed by Hendriksson and Merton (1981) and tests for independence between the forecasts and the realized return based on sign prediction.

A.-P.N. Refenes et al. (eds.), Decision Technologies for Computational Finance, 451–460.
© 1998 *Kluwer Academic Publishers. Printed in the Netherlands..*

2 Forecasting the Bund-Future using Technical Indicators

2.1 The Bund-Future

The Bund-Future is a future contract on a generic German long term bond. Months of maturity are March, June, September, and December, and a contract is valid for 9 months. When a trading model of a future-contract is modeled, problems such as the roll-over-effect, cheapest -to-deliver-bond and the cost-of-carry have to be considered.[1]

The Bund-Future market is considered to be a highly technical market. As the markets are centralized we have access to all information necessary for technical indicators such as high, low, open, and close prices as well as open interest. Recently there has been an increased academic interest in technical trading rules. Studies such as Levich and Thomas (1993), Sweeney (1986) or Allen and Taylor (1990) report that technical indicators are widely used, especially in short term forecasting, and that they proved to be profitable.

As there is no sound theoretical base for the choice of parameters[2] we optimized them with respect to their parameters on the training sample. This procedure leads to more significant indicators and avoids an arbitrary choice of parameters. We chose technical indicators from Reuters (1994). In addition to these indicators we used the Bund-Future with lag 1, 2, and 3 as well as a moving average of five trading days.

2.2 The Complexity of the Neural Network

The specification of neural nets is of major interest in time series application. To avoid overparameterized models which lead to overfitting and thus to inferior generalization results, methods such as pruning, penalty terms and recently testing are widely used. However, during the training process we observed the following:

- The number of hidden units (we used 2, ,4, 6, and 8 hidden units) did not lead to the well known overfitting effect which is most visible when the error curve of the training set gets close to zero, whereas concurrently the error on the validation set increases.
- In addition, when the error of the early stopping point is compared with later stopping points, the increase is minimal.

---

[1] for more detailed information see Azoff (1994)

[2] see Menkhoff and Schlumberger (1995)

These observations as well as the results obtained (see section 5), indicate that optimal specification has only a minor influence on performance. The models found give no indication of an optimal number of hidden units. Given these observations we trained each model (standard, nonlinear transformation and the model with interaction layer) with 2, 4, 6, and 8 hidden units 10 times. We report the best three results based on early stopping. Only the economically important results are stated, as the MSE is different for all models and the variation within each model is minor.

3.   The appropriate Choice of the Neural Network Model

During the training process it can be observed that the minimised MSE does not necessarily lead to optimal economic performance measures such as annualised return or Sharpe Ratio. Recently this problem has been addressed among others by Moody and Wu (1997), Kang et al. (1997) or Bengio (1997). They propose to optimise the financial criterion of interest and report superior results relative to the standard approach of minimising the MSE.

In this paper instead of optimising a financial criterion we use techniques which are supposed to lead to a better classification between down- and upward movements of a time series. It is well known that point prediction has proved to be extremely difficult. Thus it is common place to interpret results as sign predictions. Based on these sign predictions the economic significance is demonstrated. Two different approaches which are supposed to increase the performance with respect to financial performance measures are tested and compared with the standard approach of minimising the MSE:

The Interaction Layer

In this approach - which was proposed by Zimmermann and Weigend (1997) - the standard output layer consists of several units such as y_t, y_{t+1}, y_{t+2}. This layer is called point-prediction layer. On top of this layer an additional layer is specified to depict the relation between these point predictions. This Interaction layer may have the following form:

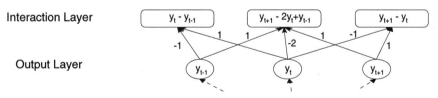

Figure 1: An example of the Interaction Layer

The targets in the interaction layer contain additional information about the time series to be predicted, as these nodes represent discrete forms of the first and second derivative. The relationship between these layers are known, the weights between those layers are fixed and thus do not increase the number of parameters to be estimated. As the error signals of all nodes in the interaction layer and the output layer are summed up, the advantage is the extra number of output units which propagate back the error. The neural network is trained to fit the dynamics of a time series rather than a single point. Using the interaction layer not only the distance between output and target is considered but the slope of adjacent points. If the dynamic can be depicted as proposed, this structure helps to avoid overfitting.

Non-linear Transformation of the target

In most applications of neural nets in financial engineering stationary variables are used to avoid spurious regression. Thus the (relative) change of a price is to be predicted. One shortcoming of point prediction is its indifference with regard to the correct sign (when the error function is the MSE). However, we are usually interested in directional forecasts only. Instead of a binary coding - which would lead to a loss in information- we use the third root of the target $f(y) = \sqrt[3]{y}$.

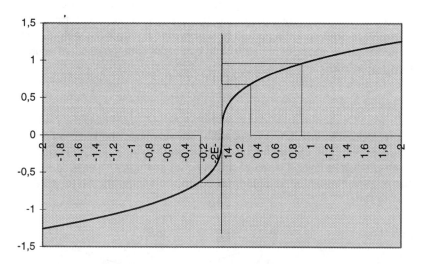

Figure 2: The transformed target; the target equals the first difference of a time series (Δx)

As shown in the figure above the error increases when the sign is not predicted correctly due to the non-linear transformation. On the other hand the error gets smaller if the output and the target have the same sign. The hypothesis to be tested is whether these approaches really do produce superior results which are economically significant. This approach leads to two main clusters in the distribution of the transformed target.

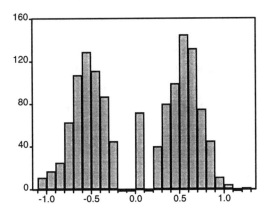

Figure 3: Distribution of the third root of the target and of the target

4   Testing for market timing ability (MTA)

To evaluate the forecasting performance of the models described in the foregoing chapter, we test for the market timing ability and thus for their economic value. This test allows for probability statements about the magnitudes of the trading strategy using the sign prediction only. In the following we briefly describe the test statistic which was proposed by Hendrikson and Merton (1981). Define the trading signal γ(t) given at t-1 for the time period t by

$$\gamma(t) = \begin{cases} 1 & \text{if the forecast is } r(t) > 0 \\ 0 & \text{if the forecast is } r(t) \le 0 \end{cases}, \quad r(t): \text{the realized return in t} \qquad (1)$$

Conditional probability for γ(t) is given by

$$p_1(t) \equiv \text{prob}\big[\gamma(t) = 0 \mid r(t) \le 0\big]$$
$$p_2(t) \equiv \text{prob}\big[\gamma(t) = 1 \mid r(t) > 0\big] \qquad (2)$$

where $p_1(t)$ is the conditional probability of a correct forecast given that r(t) ≤ 0. Analogously (1 - $p_2(t)$) is defined as the conditional probability of an incorrect forecast given that r(t) > 0. Merton (1981) has shown that $p_1(t) + p_2(t)$ is a sufficient statistic for the evaluation of forecasting ability. He also showed that a sufficient condition for an economically valuable forecast the conditional probability is required to be greater than one ($p_1(t) + p_2(t) > 1$). Thus the null hypothesis to be tested is H_0: $p_1(t) + p_2(t) = 1$.

In order to obtain estimates of these probabilities we have to define the following variables: let N be the out-of-sample size, and N_1 the number of forecasts where $r(t) \leq 0$. $N_2 = N - N_1$ is thus the number of observation where $r(t) > 0$. n_1 is the number of successful predictions, given $r(t) \leq 0$; n_2 is the number of unsuccessful predictions , given $r(t) > 0$. $n = n_1 + n_2$ is the number of times forecast that $r(t) \leq 0$. Thus p_1 can be estimated by $E(n_1/N_1)$ and $(1 - p_2)$ by $E(n_2/N_2)$. The null hypothesis can be rewritten as

$$E(n_1/N_1) = p_1 = 1 - p_2 = E(n_2/N_2)$$
$$H_0$$
$$(3)$$

Using simple transformations we obtain

$$E\left[(n_1 + n_2)/(N_1 + N_2)\right] = E(n/N) \underset{H_0}{=} p_1 \equiv p \tag{4}$$

n_1 and n_2 are sums of i.i.d. random variables with binomial distributions. Thus the probabilities that $n_i = x$ can be computed as

$$\text{prob}(n_i = x | N_i, p) = \binom{N_i}{x} p^x (1-p)^{N_i - x}; \quad i = 1, 2 \tag{5}$$

Given that n_1 and n_2 are sums of i.i.d. random variables with binomial distributions and Bayes' Theorem, Hendrikson and Merton (1981) show that under the null the probability distribution for the number of correct forecasts for $r \leq 0$ is

$$P(n_1 = x | N_1, N_2, n) = \frac{\binom{N_1}{x}\binom{N_2}{n-x} p^x (1-p)^{N_1-x} p^{n-x}(1-p)^{N_2-n+x}}{\binom{N}{m} p^n (1-p)^{N_1-n}}$$

$$= \frac{\binom{N_1}{x}\binom{N_2}{n-x}}{\binom{N}{n}}$$

(6)

Note that the probability distribution is hypergeometric and independent of the conditional probabilities p_1 and p_2. As we are interested in the right-hand tale of the distribution the following equation has to be solved for a one-tail test with a confidence level of α:

$$\sum_{x=x^*}^{\bar{n}_1} \binom{N_1}{x}\binom{N_2}{n-x} \Big/ \binom{N}{n} = 1 - c$$

(7)

The upper bound is given by $\bar{n}_1 \equiv \min(N_1, n)$.

5   Data and Results

In the empirical investigation we use the Bund-Future from September 2nd, 1992 through November 17th, 1995. Table 1 below shows how the data is split.

Set	Date	Number of days
Training	02.09.92 - 09.09.94	528
Validation	12.09.94 - 27.01.95	100
Test	30.01.95 - 17.11.95	210

Table 1: Training-, validation- and test set

We use 10 technical indicators as well as some lagged values of the Bund-Future as inputs. As the choice of parameter is somewhat arbitrary, we optimized the indicators with respect to the annualized return on the training set. The optimal settings with respect to the training set can be seen in table 2.

technical Indicators	optimal Parameter
Commodity Channel Index	29
Directional Movement Index	18
MACD	14\07\05
Money Flow Index	4
Open-High-Low-Close-Volatility	10
Oscillator	28\07
Percent R	6
Relative Strength Index	5
Fast and Slow Stochastics	05\2\2
Volume Price Trend	-

Table2: Technical Indicators and parameters chosen

The tables below show the results achieved out-of-sample using different models and network complexity.[3] All performance measures are given in [%]. Realized potential gives a percentage of the optimal trading strategy. The high returns have to be compared with the linear regression (8,9%) and buy & hold (8%). As can be seen from the tables all neural nets outperformed the linear regression. Surprisingly, there is no indication for an optimal network topology. The number of hidden units does not have a significant influence on the performance.

The choice of the model has a significant influence on the tested market timing ability: The standard approach was clearly inferior to the other methodologies. The null hypothesis of no market timing ability was never rejected. The model with the interaction layer was the superior approach. In all but two simulations the null hypothesis of no MTA was rejected: In three simulations on the sign. 10% level and in seven simulations on the 5% significance level. It is shown that a simple nonlinear transformation improves the MTA, although not to the same extent as the interaction layer does.

Standard, 8 hidden units

return p.a.	real. pot.	hit rate	p-value
14,29	17,8	49,3	0,626
15,92	19,8	50,72	0,420
16,30	20,3	51,67	0,3413

4 hidden units

return p.a.	real. pot.	hit rate	p-value
12,08	15,05	50,24	0,418
14,05	17,51	50,71	0,4964
13,29	16,56	48,80	0,6785

6 hidden units

return p.a.	real. pot.	hit rate	p-value
12,80	15,95	49,76	0,576
13,02	16,22	47,85	0,847
12,97	16,16	54,07	0,053

2 hidden units

return p.a.	real. pot.	hit rate	p-value
10,21	12,73	48,33	0,755
10,52	13,11	49,76	0,486
13,60	16,95	49,76	0,586

---

[3] The MSE is not reported as they are dependent on the modeling approach.

Interaction layer, 8 hidden units

return p.a.	real. pot.	hit rate	p-value
16,02	19,89	55,07	0,0149**
18,29	22,70	56,04	0,0094**
18,91	23,48	52,66	0,1044

6 hidden units

return p.a.	real. pot.	hit rate	p-value
19,16	23,79	53,62	0,0648*
17,76	22,05	52,66	0,0315**
16,51	20,49	52,17	0,0926*

4 hidden units

return p.a.	real. pot.	hit rate	p-value
16,12	20,02	55,07	0,0204**
17,94	22,27	52,17	0,1664
22,92	28,46	54,59	0,0024**

2 hidden units

return p.a.	real. pot.	hit rate	p-value
18,11	22,49	54,11	0,0062**
18,95	23,53	56,04	0,0128**
19,26	23,92	56,04	0,0128**

Nonlinear Transformation, 8 hidden units

return p.a.	real. pot.	hit rate	p-value
17,19	14,52	52,86	0,0293**
15,58	13,16	51,90	0,190
21,36	18,04	53,33	0,041**

6 hidden units

return p.a.	real. pot.	hit rate	p-value
16,33	13,79	51,90	0,197
19,20	16,22	52,86	0,041**
13,23	11,17	50,48	0,352

4 hidden units

return p.a.	real. pot.	hit rate	p-value
19,35	16,34	53,33	0,082*
8,79	7,43	48,57	0,636
18,26	15,44	52,38	0,147

2 hidden units

return p.a.	real. pot.	hit rate	p-value
15,29	12,92	50,48	0,420
19,77	16,70	53,33	0,089*
18,73	15,82	52,86	0,102

Table 3: performance measures

6 Conclusion

In this paper we compare the performance of three different approaches to neural network modeling. Our empirical results show that the choice of neural network model is most crucial when a trading model is designed. Though all models give positive returns the test statistic indicates that the forecasting ability of the standard approach is questionable. This work can be seen as a complement to Kuan and Liu (1995) who used a standard univariate approach to forecasting. We believe that the test proposed by Hendrikson and Merton is a useful additional criterion to assess the performance of a trading model.

7 References

Azoff, M.E. Neural Network Time Series Forecasting of Financial Markets, John Wiley, New York, 1994

Bengio, Y. "Training a Neural Network with a Financial Criterion Criterion Rather than a Prediction Criterion", in: Weigend et al., Decision Technologies for Financial Engineering, Progress in Neural Processing 7,World Scientific, 1997

Choey, M., Weigend, A. "Nonlinear Trading ModelsThrough Sharpe Ratio Maximization", in: Weigend et al., Decision Technologies for Financial Engineering, Progress in Neural Processing 7,World Scientific, 1997

Bishop, C.M. Neural Networks for Pattern Recognition, Clarendon Press, Oxford, 1995

Hendriksson, R.D. and Merton, R.C. On Market Timing and Investment Performance. II Statistical Procedures for Evaluating Forecasting Skills, Journal of Business, 1981, vol. 54, no.4

Hofmeister, J. Kurzfristige Prognose des Bund-Futures mit neuronalen Netzen, Master Thesis, University of Ulm, May 1997

Menkhoff, L. and Schlumberger, M. Persistent Profitability of Technical Analysis on Foreign Exchange Markets?, Banca Nazionale del Lavoro Quaterly Review, vol. 48, no. 193, 189 - 216, 1995

Moody, J. and Wu, L.Z. " Optimization of Trading Systems and Portfolios", in: Weigend et al., Decision Technologies for Financial Engineering, Progress in Neural Processing 7,World Scientific, 1997

Reuters Technical Analysis for Unix, User Guide, London, 1994

Zimmermann, H.G., and Weigend, A.S. " Representing Dynamical Systems in Feed-Forward Networks: A Six Layer Architecture", in: Weigend et al., Decision Technologies for Financial Engineering, Progress in Neural Processing 7,World Scientific, 1997

CURRENCY FORECASTING
USING RECURRENT RBF NETWORKS OPTIMIZED
BY GENETIC ALGORITHMS

A. ADAMOPOULOS, A. ANDREOU , E. GEORGOPOULOS , N. IOANNOU
AND S. LIKOTHANASSIS

Department of Computer Engineering & Informatics,
School of Engineering,
University of Patras,
Patras 26500, Greece, tel.: +61 997755, fax: +61 997706.

In recent years, there has been an increasing number of papers in the literature that use neural networks for financial time-series prediction. This paper focuses on the Greek Foreign Exchange Rate Currency Market. Using four major currencies, namely the U.S. Dollar (USD), the Deutsche Mark (DM), the French Franc (FF) and the British Pound (BP), against the Greek Drachma, on a daily basis for a period of 11 years, we try to forecast the above time-series, using two different approaches. The first one involves RBF training using a Kalman filter, while the second one uses genetic algorithms in order to optimize the RBF network parameters. The goal of this effort, is, first, to predict, as accurately as possible, currencies future behaviour, in a daily predicting horizon and second, to have a comparison between the two methods.

1.   Introduction

The areas of Economics and Finance with special reference to predictability issues related to stock and foreign exchange markets seem to attract increasing interest during the last few years. The foreign-exchange market, in particular, often ample room for macro-policy considerations, since the exchange-rate is often selected as a major policy instrument for attaining important targets, like price stability or balance-of-payment equilibrium. But even in cases where the exchange-rate is allowed to fluctuate in the international markets within margins that differ considerably between currencies, the fact remains that central banks retain the power to interfere with the market prices, manipulating the exchange-rate of their respective currencies whenever the authorities consider it necessary. Such manipulations can take place either directly, as in cases in which the exchange-rate has been designed to attain a specific target value in year-end terms, or indirectly via interest rate policy. Whatever the economic impact of such strategies may be, the

A.-P.N. Refenes et al. (eds.), Decision Technologies for Computational Finance, 461–470.
© 1998 *Kluwer Academic Publishers. Printed in the Netherlands..*

fact remains that such methods of interference tend to increase the noise level which characterizes the behavior of the time series under study, an issue which introduces a considerable degree of difficulty when it comes to forecasting. The relevant literature, in fact, is full of cases in which forecasting the exchange-rate of various currencies yields results which either poor [6,8,10], or difficult to interpret [4,5]. Some authors even conclude that there is no such thing as the best forecasting technique and the method chosen must depend on the time horizon selected or the objectives of the policy-maker [9].

There are, in addition, cases in which high persistence but no long-range cycle has been reported [1], something that leads to the conclusion that currencies are true Hurst processes with infinite memory. On the other hand, long term dependence, supporting that cycles do exist in exchange rates, has been found by other researchers [2,3]. Despite various attempts to settle such controversies [7] it is not clear whether the source of the dispute is, (i) the nature of the different data sets employed (i.e. sample size, noise level, pre-filtering processes etc.), (ii) the different tests that have been used, or (iii) combination of these factors.

In a former work [15] we considered the above issues in the analysis of the behavior of the exchange rate of the four currencies, namely the U.S. Dollar (USD), the Deutsche Mark (DM), the French Franc (FF) and the British Pound (BP), against the Greek Drachma. Our primary goal was to reveal whether the time series involved exhibit chaotic behavior or not, a prerequisite for applying the well-known Farmer's algorithm for prediction and secondly to test the level of predictability using the emerging technology of artificial neural networks. In the current work, taking in mind the results of this previous analysis, we use RBF neural networks in order to predict, as accurately as possible, currencies future behaviour, in a daily predicting horizon. For this purpose, two different approaches are implemented: The first one involves RBF networks trained using a Kalman training algorithm [12], while the second one uses a RBF network optimized by a modified genetic algorithm.

1.1   Data

Our time series data consist of daily exchange rates of the four currencies mentioned against the Greek drachma. The rates are those determined during the daily "fixing" sessions in the Bank of Greece. The data cover an 11-year period, from the 1st of January 1985 to the 31st of December 1995, consisting of 2660 daily observations. This amount of data is relatively small compared to the time series used in Natural Sciences, but large enough compared to other studies in Economics and Finance, in most of which the data length merely reach 2000 observations.

The paper is organized as follows: Section 2 is a description of the methodology used; in Section 3 the results of the numerical experiments are shown; finally in Section 4 discussion and economic interpretation of the results are given.

2.   Methodology

Radial Basis Function (RBF) Neural Networks are a class of multilayer feedforward neural networks that use radial basis functions as activation function. Since, RBF networks are a very well known class of neural networks, we do not think that there is any need to state more about them.

As stated above, this paper implements two different approaches: The first one, involves RBF networks trained using a Kalman filter training algorithm [12], while the second one uses genetic algorithms in order to optimize the RBF network parameters. In both approaches the number of inputs of the network (input nodes) is assumed to be known. In the case of RBF networks trained with Kalman filter algorithm the structure of the network is assumed predetermined, and the algorithm is used to optimize the centres and weights. On the contrary, in the case of Genetically trained RBF networks the minimization of the objective function will determine both the network structure and the network parameters (weights and centres) simultaneously.

For the implementation of the Radial Basis Function trained with Kalman filtering the algorithm developed by Birgmeir [12] was used. The novelty in this paper is the training of the RBF networks using Genetic Algorithms, so in the subsequent section, we focus primarily in the description of the modified genetic algorithm and the genetic operators that were implemented for the needs of this work.

2.1   The Genetically Trained RBF Network

Genetic Algorithms [13] are a class of optimization techniques that are most appropriate at exploring a large and complex space of a given problem in an intelligent way, in order to find solutions close to the global optimum. In the present work we have implemented a modified Genetic Algorithm [13] that works as follows:

It maintains a population of individuals, $P(t)=\{i_1^t, \ldots ,i_n^t\}$ for iteration (generation) t. In our problem each individual is an RBF network with its own number of hidden nodes, centres and weights values. Each individual represents a potential solution to the problem at hand, and is implemented as a linked list. Every solution, (individual) i_j^t, is evaluated to give a measure of its fitness. As such fitness function it is used the inverse Mean Square Error of the network. A new population, (iteration t+1), is created by selecting the more fit individuals according to their fitness, using the elitism roulette wheel selection (select step). Some members of the population undergo transformations (alter step) by means of "genetic" operators to form the new solutions (individuals). There are unary transformations m_i (mutation type), which create new individuals by a small change in a single individual, (add or delete a random number of hidden nodes to or from the hidden layer, change the values of a random number of weights or centres of the network, e.t.c.), and higher order transformations c_j (crossover type), which create new individuals by combining parts from two or more individuals (take a random number n_1 of hidden nodes from a RBF network and a number n_2 from another RBF, and create a new RBF with n_1+n_2 hidden nodes). That way we can train the RBF networks and simultaneously change their structure. After some number of iterations (generations) the program converges. At this point it is expected that the best individual represents a near-optimum (reasonable) solution.

At this point, it would be quite interesting to produce a short implementation of the model of the RBF network that is processed by the modified genetic algorithm. In the approach of [11], the researchers code the RBF network as a string, use the genetic algorithm to manipulate this string, and then they decode it back to a network in order to measure its performance. In our approach the basic philosophy is that we do not make use of some coding function in order to "go" from a neural network, to a floating point or binary, string that represents the network, and then having a genetic algorithm manipulating this binary string. On the contrary, a modified genetic algorithm is used that handles directly the neural networks and not some strings. The drawback of this approach is that we have to deal with neural networks, structures much more complicated than strings, that costs in computer memory and computation time. This disadvantage was overcome by the great flexibility that gives; we can manipulate networks with different number neurons (nodes) in the hidden region, add or delete hidden neurons (nodes) e.t.c. This approach was first introduced for the case of MLP networks in a previous work [14].

3.   Numerical Experiments

As stated above four major foreign currencies, namely the U.S. Dollar (USD), the British Pound (BP), the Deutsche Mark (DM) and the French Franc (FF), against the Greek Drachma, are the available sets of data used. The data consist of daily observations and cover a period of 11-years, starting from the 1st of January 1985 and ending at the 31st of December 1995. The two models (RBF with Kalman and RBF with Genetic Algorithms) have been tested and evaluated using the first differences of the natural logarithms of the raw data.

The results we have, seem to confirm our initial intuition about the data, so:

1. Performance of the two models is improved for DM and FF, which participate with the ERM (Exchange Rate Mechanism), when using those subsets of data corresponding to the period after which the ERM bands were widen. BP even not in the ERM gives a good success level. USD performance, on the other hand, remains at a rather low success level.

2. The genetically optimized RBF network seems to exhibit a better prediction performance compared to the RBF network trained with the extended Kalman filter. This is more than obvious in the subsequent figures.

The following figures present graphically the performance of the two different approaches. The first four show the performance of the genetically trained RBF network using 5 inputs (values) and one output - this means that 5 values were used in order to predict the next one (weekly predictions). The next four figures show the performance of the Kalman filter trained RBF network with the same number of inputs and outputs. Finally the last four figures depict the performance of the Kalman trained RBF, using 20 inputs and 1 output (monthly predictions).

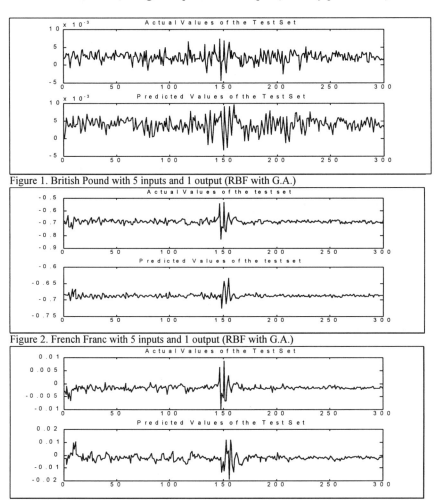

Figure 1. British Pound with 5 inputs and 1 output (RBF with G.A.)

Figure 2. French Franc with 5 inputs and 1 output (RBF with G.A.)

Figure 3. Deutsche Mark with 5 inputs and 1 output (RBF with G.A.)

466

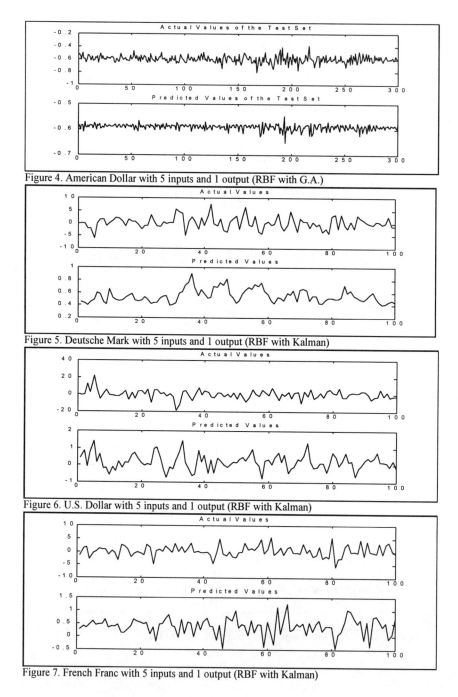

Figure 4. American Dollar with 5 inputs and 1 output (RBF with G.A.)

Figure 5. Deutsche Mark with 5 inputs and 1 output (RBF with Kalman)

Figure 6. U.S. Dollar with 5 inputs and 1 output (RBF with Kalman)

Figure 7. French Franc with 5 inputs and 1 output (RBF with Kalman)

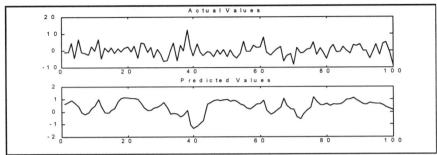

Figure 8. British Pound with 5 inputs and 1 output (RBF with Kalman)

4. Economic interpretation of results - Conclusions

Before we move on examining the reasoning of the results, it is important to underline the peculiarities involved in working with drachma exchange rates. The exchange rate is considered an important policy measure by the authorities and its role has been a very particular one during the period under consideration. The policy has been exercised by setting a target depreciation rate at the beginning of the planning period in year-end terms versus the ECU. For the time period under review, this policy has provided for a devaluation in 1985 which resulted to the drachma depreciating by 16.3% in 1985, and 23.1% in 1986, mainly aiming at promoting export activity in the economy by restoring or even improving price competitiveness in the international markets. The depreciation rates, however, decrease dramatically since then, after the authorities realised the extent of the failure of this accommodating exchange rate policy, since both the 1985 devaluation and the one preceded it in 1983, let to results that leave a lot to be desired as regards export promotion. The failure, which is, mainly, due to the increased import penetration of the Greek economy, because of the inability to resort to structural changes in its production structure, is a supply-side problem, touching upon issues like the application of the Marshall-Lerner condition [16] and its examination is beyond the scope of the present analysis. The fact remains that the exchange rate policy is still conducted in terms of the exchange rate vis-à-vis the ECU, the only difference now being that the depreciation rate has declined to 4.1% for 1995 and 0.6% in 1996, acting as an anti-inflationary policy instrument [17] in anticipation of the drachma participation with the ERM [18]. The policy undoubtedly provides for increased degree of discipline for the drachma fluctuations versus all ECU participant currencies, which include all currencies involved in the analysis except the USD. This leads to expecting the predictability of the rate of the drachma versus the USD to be reduced compared to that of the drachma rates vis-à-vis the rest three currencies, due to the absence of any discipline framework in this case.

Irrespective of the prediction performance, regarding the drachma rates versus the various currencies involved in this paper, one must point out that all four time series are expected to be noise-polluted due to exogenous disturbances of two categories: Those resulting form corrective measures taken by the authorities in order to offset possible undesired exchange rate developments and those resulting from certain irregular factors, not necessarily of economic nature. Typical cases of the latter include the 1987 stock market collapse, the German political and economic reunification in 1990 and the ERM wider bands in 1993. Similar factors introducing noise on the drachma side may be taken to be the 1985 devaluation, the prolonged pre-election period between 1989 and 1990 and the complete capital movement liberalisation in 1994.

It becomes obvious, therefore, that data series like exchange rates derived in the fixing sessions of the Bank of Greece are very difficult to manipulate and that minimising the presence of noise in such cases is a tedious task. The main problem arises because, as earlier stated, these rates are to a significant extend affected by authorities interference in the framework of a predetermined exchange-rate policy. An additional complication is introduced due to the choice of the particular sample period, during which both the logic and the extent of the government intervention have not been constant. Thus, the beginning of the period under consideration is characterised by generous depreciation rates, including drachma devaluation, while the end of this period involves very low depreciation rates in the context of a different policy approach from the part of the government.

These complications suggest that future research should be undertaking focusing on the rates of the major currencies as these are determined in the international markets and in the case of which the presence of noise is expected to be weaker. Once a successful forecast for such rates has been realised, these rates may be used to derive drachma cross-rates, on the basis of a pre-announced government policy. This tactical move is expected to avoid a considerable degree of noise and yield more reliable results.

The conclusion, therefore, is that the results obtained have been as expected and the explanation lies with the degree of discipline of behaviour that characterises the fluctuations of each of the currencies involved with respect to the drachma. In three out of four cases, with the exception of the dollar case, the drachma factor introduces a considerable degree of consistency in its behaviour thanks to its exchange rate versus the ECU, which is a policy guideline. The increased predictability in the cases of DM and FF comes as a result of their ERM membership, which, unlike the case of the Pound, provides for fluctuation bands and consequently for increased predictability. The above justify as well the results of the chaotic analysis which revealed a deterministic part in the DM and FF data series and an almost random character for the USD and BP series.

In the present paper, we investigated the application of neural network methodology in cases of currency forecasting models. The results of both methods, i.e., the RBF networks with Kalman filtering, as well as RBF networks evolution with Genetic Algorithms, have been positive and encouraging. Remarkable success has been achieved in training the networks to learn the FF and DM currencies and thereby to make accurate predictions. Our results show that the evolutionary trained neural network approach leads to better predictions than the Farmer's algorithm or the conventional networks with Back Propagation training. We obtained a very close fit during the training phase and the network we developed consistently outperformed these methods. We are currently exploring more refined neural networks as well as evolutionary techniques and we expect that they can further improve the performance in the task of financial time series prediction.

5.   Acknowledgements

The authors would like to thank G. A. Zombanakis, Research Department, Bank of Greece, for providing the data series used in this paper and for his contribution in the economic interpretation of the results.

6.   References

[1] Peters E., "Fractal Market Analysis - Applying Chaos Theory to Investment and Economics, (Wiley Finance Edition, 1994)

[2] Booth, G. G., Kaen, F. R. and Koveos, P. E. "R/S analysis of foreign exchange rates under two international monetary regimes", Journal of Monetary Economics, vol.10, 407-415, 1982.

[3] Cheung Y. W., "Long Memory in Foreign-Exchange Rates", Journal of Business & Economic Statistics, Vol. 11 no 1, 1993.

[4] J. C. B. Kim and S. Mo, "Cointegration and the long-run forecast of exchange rates", Economic Letters, 48, pp. 353-359, 1995.

[5] K. K. Lewis, "Can learning affect exchange-rate behavior? The case of the Dollar in the early 1980's", Journal of Monetary Economics, 23, pp.79-100, 1989.

[6] I. W. Marsh and D. M. Power, "A note on the performance of foreign exchange forecasters in a portfolio framework", Journal of Banking & Finance, 20, pp.605-613, 1996.

[7] H. M. Pesaran and S. M. Potter, "Nonlinear dynamics and econometrics: An introduction", Journal of Applied Econometrics, Vol. 7, pp. s1-s7, 1992.

[8] A. C. Pollock and M. E. Wilkie, "The quality of bank forecasts: The dollar-pound exchange rate 1990-1993", European Journal of Operational Research, 91, pp.306-314, 1996.

[9] M. Verrier, "Selection & Application of Currency Forecasts, in C. Dunis & M., Feeny (eds.), Exchange-Rate Forecasting", Probus, Chicago, USA, pp. 303-343, 1989.

[10] K. D. West and D. Cho, "The predictive ability of several models of exchange rate volatility", Journal of Econometrics, 69, pp. 367-391, 1995.

[11] Billings, S. A. and Zheng, G. L., "Radial basis function network configuration using genetic algorithms", Neural Networks, vol. 8, no 6, pp. 877-890, 1995.

[12] Birgmeier M. "A Fully Kalman-Trained Radial Basis Function Network for Nonlinear Speech Modeling ", ICNN '95, pp. 259-264, 1995.

[13] Michalewicz, Z., Genetic Algorithms + Data Structures = Evolution Programs, Second Ext. Edition, Springer Verlag, 1994.

[14] Likothanassis, S. D., Georgopoulos, E. and Fotakis, D., Optimizing the Structure of Neural Networks using Evolution Techniques, 5th Int. Conf. on HPC in Engineering, Spain, 4-7 July, 1997.

[15] Andreou, A., Georgopoulos E., and Likothanassis, S., and Polidoropoulos, P., "Is the Greek foreign exchange-rate market predictable? A comparative study using chaotic dynamics and neural networks", Proceedings of the *Fourth International Conference on Forecasting Financial Markets*, Banque Nationale de Paris and Imperial College, London, 1997a.

[16] P. Karadeloglou, "On the existence of an inverse j-curve", Greek Economic review, 12, pp. 285-305, 1990.

[17] P. Karadeloglou, C. Papazoglou and G. A. Zombanakis, "Is the exchange rate an effective anti-inflationary policy instrument?", L[th] International Conference of Applied Econometrics Association, Paris 1996.

[18] Bank of Greece, "Report of the governor", Athens, 1995.

EXCHANGE RATE TRADING USING A FAST RETRAINING PROCEDURE FOR GENERALISED RADIAL BASIS FUNCTION NETWORKS

D. R. DERSCH, B. G. FLOWER AND S. J. PICKARD

Crux Cybernetics Pty. Ltd.
Level 7 Carrington House. 50 Carrington St. NSW, 2000, Australia
http://www.cybernetics.com.au, email: crux@cybernetics.com.au

The authors propose to train a network in two optimisation steps. In the first step the input weights are obtained by an unsupervised Vector Quantisation (VQ) procedure. In the second step the output weights are calculated by minimising the quadratic error of the network for an input data vector. For the special case of a Gaussian activation a Radial Basis Function Network is described, as the hidden nodes show a radial symmetric response with respect to the centre. It has been shown that the simultaneous optimisation of the centres and the widths of the hidden neurons is prone to result in sub-optimal solutions as they can be unstable. We therefore follow in our approach the general concept of a two step incremental optimisation process. The technique is applied to the forecasting of the US Dollar Deutsche Mark and US Dollar Japanese Yen Exchange rates and the results evaluated using a trade simulation environment.

1. Introduction

Multi Layer Perceptrons (MLP) are well established function approximators covering applications in the fields of pattern recognition and classification. Such a network defines a mapping of $\mathbf{R}^n \to \mathbf{R}^m$. A number of training procedures have been proposed to calculate the network parameters for a given training set with known class membership $c(\mathbf{x}_r) \in \{[1, \ldots, m] \mid r = 1, \ldots, k_T\}$.

A commonly used training algorithm for MLP is the Backpropagation algorithm (Rumelhart and McClelland, 1986), which performs a gradient descent on the quadratic classification error. The backpropagation algorithm has been demonstrated to yield satisfying results in a wide range of applications. However, a network trained by backpropagation is a "black box", as the internal structure is hard to interpret. The lack of biological interpretation and the problem of local minima and thus the strong dependency on the initial conditions are major drawbacks of such a gradient descent method. Moody and Darken (1989) suggested a promising alternative training procedure for a three layer network.

The authors propose to train a network in two optimization steps. In the first step the input weights $w_r \in W \equiv \{w_r \in \mathbf{R}^n \mid r = 1, \ldots, N\}$ of the N-hidden neurons are obtained by an unsupervised Vector Quantisation (VQ) procedure. In the second step the output weights $m_j \in M \equiv \{m_j \in \mathbf{R}^m \mid j = 1, \ldots, N\}$ are then calculated by minimizing the quadratic error

A.-P.N. Refenes et al. (eds.), Decision Technologies for Computational Finance, 471–478.
© 1998 *Kluwer Academic Publishers. Printed in the Netherlands..*

472

$$E = \left\langle \left\| \mathbf{y}(\mathbf{x}) - M\mathbf{A}(x) \right\|^2 \right\rangle_x \tag{1}$$

where $\mathbf{y}(\mathbf{x}) \in \Re^m$ is the desired output vector of the network for a data vector *x*. *M* is the $(m \times N)$ matrix of the output weights m_{jr} and $\mathbf{A}(\mathbf{x})$ is the *N*-dimensional vector of the hidden layer activity, and $\langle ... \rangle_x$ denotes the average over the training data set. For the special case of a Gaussian activation function

$$\mathbf{A}(\mathbf{x}; a_o, \mathbf{w}_r, \rho) = a_o e^{-\left(\frac{\left\| w_r - x \right\|^2}{2\rho^2} \right)} \tag{2}$$

Eq. (1) describes a *Radial Basis Function Network*, as the hidden nodes show a radial symmetric response with respect to the centre w_r. In our approach we follow the general concept of a two step optimization process but we make a number of significant changes which will be presented in the next section. In Section 3 we apply the method to the trading of currencies, e.g., the US Dollar Deutsch Mark and the US Dollar Japanese Yen exchange rates. A summary and discussion concludes the paper.

2.   Incremental Training in Generalised Radial Basis Function Networks

The performance of a classification system, which is trained according to the two step process, as described above depends on the quality of the results in each optimization step.

2.1.   Vector Quantisation

The quality of the codebook obtained in the first optimization step, e.g. the quality of the representation of a data space $X \subset \Re^n$ by the set of N codebook vectors $w_r \in W$ is of central importance. In the approach suggested by Moody and Darken the Max-Lloyd algorithm (Max, 1960 and Lloyd, 1982) is applied. However, the slow convergence and the strong dependency on the initial conditions are major drawbacks of this algorithm. This drawback becomes even more critical for an on-line system. As a new data vector is obtained in each time step, we might also gradually change the training set by adding new data vectors and removing the oldest data vectors. Retraining may be necessary if new data vectors are poorly represented by the codebook. Due to the strong dependency on the initial conditions and the slow convergence the Max-Lloyd algorithm might be inadequate to find good solutions.

A fuzzy VQ scheme derived from a minimal free energy criterion (Rose et al., 1990) has been shown to out perform the classical Max-Lloyd algorithm (Dersch,

1996). This algorithm belongs to a class of neural motivated VQ procedures together with the Kohonen algorithm (Kohonen, 1982) and the "Neural-gas" algorithm (Martinetz and Schulten, 1991). These soft competing VQ procedures are characterized by *cooperative competitive* learning rules. The batch version of these learning rules is of the form;

$$w_r = \frac{\langle a_r \mathbf{x} \rangle_x}{\langle a_r \rangle_x} \tag{3}$$

Here, $a_r(x; W, \rho)$, the cooperativity function, is a function of the data vector **x** and depends parametrically on the state of the codebook W and the value ρ of a *cooperativity parameter* $(\rho \geq 0)$. $\langle ... \rangle_x$ denotes the average over the data set. For the fuzzy VQ scheme the cooperativity function

$$a_r(\mathbf{x}; W, \rho) = \frac{e^{-\left(\|w_r - x\|^2 / 2\rho^2\right)}}{A} \tag{4}$$

is given by globally normalized Gaussians. $A = \sum_r e^{-\left(\|w_r - x\|^2 / 2\rho^2\right)}$ is the normalisation factor and the width ρ is the cooperativity parameter of this model. The cooperativity parameter defines a length scale in the data space. For a given data set X, an initial choice of W and the fuzzy range ρ, the update rule from Eq. (3) is applied until a stationary codebook W is obtained. In a simulated annealing process ρ is gradually reduced. For $\rho \to 0$ the update rule from Eq. (3) is then the centroid condition of the Max-Lloyd training algorithm. The fuzzy VQ scheme has been thoroughly studied (Rose et al., 1990, Dersch, 1996 and Dersch and Tavan, 1994). By adding noise to the Learning rule from Eq. (3) and a_r given by Eq. (4), Eq. (3) describes a stochastic gradient descent on a error function which is *the free energy* in a mean-field approximation. It has been shown that codebooks obtained by this scheme are characterized by well defined properties (Dersch and Tavan, 1994). These properties can be exploited to control the learning process and enhance the quality of the resulting codebooks. In an on-line system with a gradually changing data set these properties enable fast retraining of an existing codebook.

2.2. Calculation of output weights

The output weights are calculated according to Eq. (1) but we globally normalise the activity function of the hidden nodes according to Eq. (4). Here, we follow a scheme proposed by Girosi and Poggio (1989), rather than using unnormalised Gaussians. As the hidden nodes no longer show a radial response centred at w_r we call the network a Generalised Radial Basis Function Network (GRBFN). The normalised activation function allows better modeling of the decision boundaries between codebook vectors.

3. APPLICATION TO CURRENCY EXCHANGE RATES

3.1. Data set and preprocessing

The GRBFN system was used to predict a trading signal for the daily closing price for two currency exchange rates, the US Dollar Deutsch Mark (USDM) and the US Dollar Japanese Yen (USJY). The USDM covers the range 1/3/1990 to 1/2/1997 (1835 data points) and the USJY covers the range 10/2/1986 to 11/2/1997 (2873 data points). Each time step $x(t)$ is labelled according to a *buy*, *hold* or *sell* trading signal using a procedure that considers the current volatility and the risk-reward ratio of a trade executed at that data point. To ensure that there is no offset effect we ignored the first 20 data vectors. The label transition matrices and the total number of labels for each label type, for the two time series are shown in Table 1.

Table 1 USDM and USJY Label Transition Matrix

From / To	USDM				USJY			
	Buy	Hold	Sell	Sum	Buy	Hold	Sell	Sum
Buy	194	107	1	302	260	207	0	467
Hold	106	947	129	1182	206	1467	198	1871
Sell	2	129	220	351	1	197	337	535

The labeling of the two time series show transitions with a very high frequency of *hold* states and a large likelihood that the states in consecutive time steps are identical. Interestingly, a transition from *buy* to *sell* and vice versa is very rare.

3.2. Classification experiments

A GRBFN is trained to predict the trading signal $L(t+1)$ for each of the two time series, where $L(t)$ is the label of the time series at time t, from a sequence of 8 retrospective differential values $x = \{\Delta x(t-7), ..., \Delta x(t)\}$. For both time series we train a GRBFN with 60 hidden nodes. The training and testing is performed as follows: The network is trained on the first 900 data vectors and tested on an out of sample set of 45 data vectors. A new data set is obtained by adding these test vectors and deleting the 45 oldest data vectors. The old codebook is then retrained in an annealing process according to Eq. (3). The start and stop values for ρ are automatically selected from the new data set. The output weights are then calculated by solving Eq. (1). Again, the network is tested on the following out of sample set of

45 data vectors. This process is repeated until the end of the data set is reached. Table 2 summarises the classification results on the test sets. It shows the confusion matrix c_{ij}, the sensitivity $\mathbf{sen}(j) = c_{ii}/\sum_j c_{ij}$ (column 4) and specificity $\mathbf{spe}(j) = c_{jj}/\sum_i c_{ij}$ (row 4) of each label and the overall accuracy of the classifier (column 4, row 4) for both experiments.

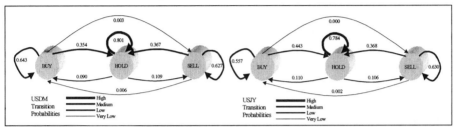

Figure 1 Transition Diagram of BUY, and SELL states for the USDM and USJY training data.

Table 2 USDM Classification Results

Output	USDM				USJY			
True	buy	hold	sell	sen(i)	buy	hold	sell	sen(i)
buy	49	95	0	0.34	84	217	5	0.275
hold	6	565	20	0.956	37	1159	70	0.915
sell	0	96	69	0.418	0	192	171	0.471
spe(j)	0.891	0.747	0.775	0.759	0.694	0.739	0.695	0.731

4.   DISCUSSION

For the USDM and the USJY we obtained an over all classification accuracy of 75.9% and 73.1% respectively. In both cases we obtain a high specificity for all three states, a very high sensitivity for *hold* states and low sensitivities for the *buy* and *sell* states. Table 3 shows the probabilities for false trading recommendations.

Table 3 Probabilities of False Recommendations

Commodity	False buy for sell	False sell for buy	False buy for hold	False sell for hold	False hold for buy or sell
USDM	0	0	0.010	0.034	0.253
USJY	0	0.029	0.028	0.054	0.261

The probability of recommending a *buy* or *sell* when the opposite should have been recommended is less than 3% for both data sets. The combined probability of confusing a *buy* or *sell* as a *hold* is less than 27% for both data sets. However, this will not translate to a trading loss as no trade action is taken and merely represents lost opportunity. The combined probability of confusing a *hold* as a *buy* or *sell* is less than 9% for both data sets. This represents possible losing trades but it is likely that the number of losing and wining trades from this segment will be equal, thus the P&Ls will cancel resulting in a small loss due to slippage and brokerage.

Table 4 Trading Simulation Results

Strategy	USDM				USJY			
	P&L ($US)	Win/Loss Ratio (%)	Sharpe Index	# of Trades	P&L ($US)	Win/Loss Ratio (%)	Sharpe Index	# of Trades
3 day Expiry	7980	55.32	2.59	48	-8090	50.57	-9.42	87
4 day Expiry	11030	48.94	4.21	48	-780	56.32	-3.93	87
5 day Expiry	12860	54.17	4.43	48	6730	50.57	0.60	87
6 day Expiry	12080	58.33	3.83	48	8900	51.16	1.67	87
7 day Expiry	6490	47.92	0.62	48	7650	50.00	0.94	87
3 day Expiry+M	10010	55.32	4.94	48	1740	50.57	-4.88	87
4 day Expiry+M	13000	48.94	5.89	48	20490	56.323	11.80	87
5 day Expiry+M	16720	54.17	7.10	48	22560	50.57	11.44	87
6 day Expiry+M	18600	58.33	-0.69	48	25890	51.16	10.84	87
7 day Expiry+M	14900	47.92	5.86	48	32160	50.00	14.00	87

1 - trade is novated after X days

2 - trade expires after X days, or if the trade exceeds a loss of greater US$1000 for the USDM, and US$2000 for the USJY

Trading results were simulated using the REMM[1] trade simulation environment for each of the data sets with and without trade management strategies. The period of trade simulation is between 20/7/95 and 12/11/96 (16 months) for USDM and between 12/7/95 and 16/12/96 (17 months) for USJY. The trading simulation used a notional fund of $US100,000 with a risk limit per trade of 1% (i.e., $US1000). The results are shown in Table 4 where *X day Expiry* means the trade is novated after X days and *X day Expiry+M* means that the trade expires after X days or if the trade exceeds a loss of greater $US1000. The trade management reduces the maximum drawdown that occurs.

The Sharp Index is based on a risk free rate of 4% pa with the best USDM performance exceeding 7, and for the USJY equal to 14. Without trade management the 5 and 6 day expiry performs the best for both of the data sets and with trade management this performance is significantly improved for both the total P&L and the Sharpe Index.

The performance of the GRBFN system is similar to that of other neural network based forecasting systems including that described by Flower (Flower et al. 1995) which showed win/loss ratios in the high 50s and low 60s (in percentage), and Sharpe Indexes of greater than 3. As the REMM trading environment has been validated against actual trading results using a real $A250,000 fund over 2½ years,

---

[1] REMM is a proprietary trading environment developed by Crux Cybernetics. It provides a realistic simulated trading environment for any commodity or financial instrument. REMM facilitates the testing of a trade entry strategy by accurately modeling the market dynamics using historical data. Accurate and realistic risk management strategies can be selected which take into account slippage, intra-tick volatility stops, tick to tick volatility stops, money stops, trailing stops and other user definable exit strategies.

the trading results for the GRBFN are expected to be realised in actual trading within 20% of the predicted P&L and Sharpe Index. The P&L trajectories are shown in Figure 2 and Figure 3 respectively.

The system will be live tested using paper trading and a real fund of $A250,000 over the next 6 months to verify that the simulated results.

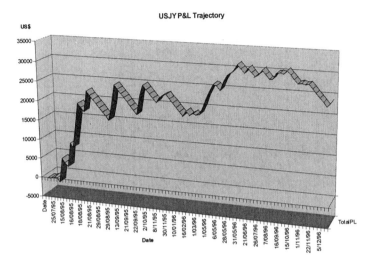

Figure 2 P&L Trajectory for USJY Forecasts

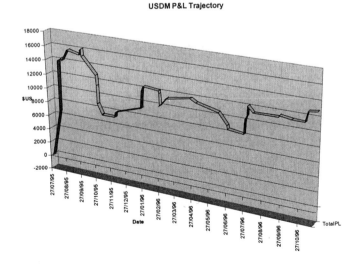

Figure 3 P&L Trajectory for USDM Forecasts

5.   Conclusions

In this paper we presented a fast retraining procedure for Generalised Radial Basis Function Networks and its application to time series prediction. For the US Dollar Deutsch Mark and the US Dollar Japanese Yen exchange rates we obtained an overall labeling classification accuracy of 75.9% and 73.1%. In both cases we obtain a high specificity for all three states, a very high sensitivity for the *hold* states and a low sensitivity for the *buy* and *sell* states. This translated to substantial simulated P&Ls and Sharpe Indexes for the two currency exchange rates. The best performance was P&Ls over 16 and 17 months of $US16,720 and $US32,160 with Sharpe Indexes of 7.1 and 14 for the USDM and USJY exchange rates respectively. These results are consistent with those achieved by other neural network based forecasting techniques.

6.   REFERENCES

Dersch D.R. and Tavan P., "Control Of Annealing In Minimal Free Energy Vector Quantization", Proceedings of the IEEE International Conference on Neural Networks ICNN 94, 698-703, 1994.

Dersch D. R., () "Eigenschaften neuronaler Vektorquantisierer und ihre Anwendung in der Sprachverarbeitung," Harri Deutsch, Frankfurt am Main, 1996.

Flower B.G., Cripps T., Jabri M. And White A., "An Artificial Neural Network Based Trade Forecasting System For Capital Markets", *Proceedings of Neural Networks in the Capital Markets* 1995.

Girosi F. and Poggio T., "Networks And The Best Approximation Property", A. I. Memo 1164, Massachusetts Institute of Technology 10, 1989.

Kohonen T., "Self-Organized Formation Of Topologically Correct Feature Maps", *Biol. Cybern*, 43:59-69, 1982.

Lloyd S. P., "Least Squares Quantization In PCM", *IEEE Trans. Inform. Theory*, 28:129-137, 1982.

Marr D., "A Theory Of Cerebellar Cortex", *J. Physiol* 202:437-470, 1969.

Martinetz T. M. and Schulten K. J., "A `Neural Gas' Network Learns Topologies", *Proceedings of the International Conference on Artificial Neural Networks*, ICANN 91, 397--402, Elsevier Science Publishers, Amsterdam, 1991.

Max J., "Quantizing For Minimum Distortion", *IRE Trans. Inform. Theory*, 3:7-12, 1960.

Moody J. and Darken C., "Fast Learning In Networks Of Locally-Tuned Processing Units", *Neural Computation*, 1:281-294, 1989.

Poggio T., "A Theory Of How The Brain Might Work", Cold Spring Harbor Laboratory Press, 899—910, 1990.

Rose K., Gurewitz E., and Fox G., "Statistical Mechanics And Phase Transitions In Clustering", *Phys. Rev. Lett.*, 65:945-948, 1990.

Rosenblatt F., "The Perceptron: The Probabilistic Model For Information Storage And Organization In The Brain", *Psychological Review*, 65:386—408, 1958.

Advances in Computational Management Sciences

1. J.-M. Aurifeille and C. Deissenberg (eds.): *Bio-Mimetic Approaches in Management Science*. 1998   ISBN 0-7923-4993-8

2. A.-P.N. Refenes, A.N. Burgess and J.E. Moody (eds.): *Decision Technologies for Computational Finance*. Proceedings of the fifth International Conference Computational Finance. 1998   ISBN 0-7923-8308-7 (HB); ISBN 0-7923-8309-5 (PB)

KLUWER ACADEMIC PUBLISHERS – BOSTON / DORDRECHT / LONDON